CONTEMPORARY LINGUISTICS

AN INTRODUCTION

CONTEMPORARY LINGUISTICS

AN INTRODUCTION

Fifth Edition

Edited by

William O'Grady
University of Hawaii at Manoa
and
John Archibald
University of Calgary

U.S. edition prepared by

Mark Aronoff
State University of New York at Stony Brook
and
Janie Rees-Miller
Marietta College

Bedford/St. Martin's
Boston ♦ New York

For Bedford/St. Martin's

Developmental Editor: Joelle Hann
Senior Production Editor: Harold Chester
Production Supervisor: Yexenia (Jessie) Markland
Marketing Manager: Jenna Bookin Barry
Art Direction and Cover Design: Lucy Krikorian
Cover Art: Uta Uta Tjangala, "Emu Dreaming." Acrylic on canvas. Aboriginal art, 20th century. *Photo:* Jennifer Steele/Art Resource, NY.
Text Design: Kyle Gell
Composition: the dotted i
Printing and Binding: R.R. Donnelley & Sons Company

President: Joan E. Feinberg
Editorial Director: Denise B. Wydra
Editor in Chief: Nancy Perry
Director of Marketing: Karen Melton Soeltz
Director of Editing, Design, and Production: Marcia Cohen
Managing Editor: Erica T. Appel

Library of Congress Control Number: 2004108139

Manufactured in the United States of America.

0 9 8 7 6
f e d

For information, write: Bedford/St. Martin's, 75 Arlington Street, Boston, MA 02116 (617-399-4000)

ISBN: 0-312-41936-8

EAN: 978-0-312-41936-3

Acknowledgments

Acknowledgments and copyrights appear at the back of the book on pages 659–64, which constitutes an extension of the copyright page.

To the memory of
our friend and colleague
Ewa Iwanicka
1950–1986

Convinced at once that, in order to break loose from the beaten paths of opinions and systems, it was necessary to proceed in my study of man and society by scientific methods, and in a rigorous manner, I devoted one year to philology and grammar; linguistics, or the natural history of speech, being, of all the sciences, that which best suited the researches which I was about to commence.

–PIERRE-JOSEPH PROUDHON, *What Is Property?* (1840)

PREFACE

It has been our goal since *Contemporary Linguistics* was first published in 1989 to provide a comprehensive introductory linguistics textbook that conveys the fascinating aspects of language study to students in a way that is accessible and enlightening. By including up-to-date coverage of all the important areas of linguistics—from phonology, morphology, syntax, and semantics to cross-curricular topics such as sociolinguistics and psycholinguistics—we aim to prepare students for further work in the subject. At the same time, we strive for a clear, direct presentation of the material so that students at differing levels, and with differing goals for taking the course, can come to understand and appreciate how language works. To our gratification, feedback from users of previous editions indicates that *Contemporary Linguistics* has succeeded at both tasks.

In updating both presentation and content of the material in the text, we have retained those features that have proved themselves over time in a variety of classroom settings, providing:

The most comprehensive introductory text available. *Contemporary Linguistics* provides the best coverage of core concepts of any introductory text—phonology, morphology, syntax, and semantics—while exploring cross-curricular issues as diverse as sociolinguistics, sign language, and computational linguistics.

A flexible organization to match instructors' teaching needs. The subject of linguistics is treated as a cohesive whole, yet each chapter can also stand alone—a feature that enables instructors to teach the topics in the order they prefer.

The knowledge of working experts in the field. Each chapter is written by an expert or a team of experts on a particular topic in linguistics, providing the most current and in-depth information available.

Language students understand. The direct writing style makes complex concepts accessible to students at different levels of learning.

Extensive support for students. To help students master concepts, each chapter begins with a list of bulleted objectives and concludes with a summary, a list of key terms and ideas, recommended readings, and exercises that test and reinforce material presented in the chapter. Each chapter is broken down into carefully numbered subsections for students'—and instructors'—ease of reference.

"For the Student Linguist" boxes. Written by actual students, these boxes highlight linguistic problems and help other students gain a richer perspective on each subject.

New to This Edition

One of the joys of working on *Contemporary Linguistics* through its various editions has been charting new developments in the field and adding material that reflects the expanding research in its various subdisciplines. As linguistics has expanded, so too has the size of this textbook, and with each expanded edition has come the risk that the book would grow into an unmanageable tome. For the fifth edition, the Canadian editors of *Contemporary Linguistic Analysis*, the book on which *Contemporary Linguistics* has always been based, have taken the bold step of moving more advanced and detailed information and exercises online, an innovation that we have embraced in the U.S. version. In this way, we can take advantage of the exciting possibilities of multimedia technology while controlling the physical size of the book. In fact, the Web site will extend the book's offerings not only with advanced material online but also with audio and video interactivity, bringing this introductory linguistics textbook into the twenty-first century.

In addition, all chapters in *Contemporary Linguistics* have been revised to reflect recent research, to include or expand material of current interest to instructors, and to streamline the presentation. Highlights include:

Core chapters updated to reflect current scholarship. All chapters that introduce the fundamental concepts of linguistics (Chapters 1–6) have been thoroughly updated—particularly the chapters on phonetics and syntax. The syntax chapter has moved to X' structure (with a simplified structure available in the Appendix of Chapter 5 for those instructors for whom that is more appropriate).

A new chapter on sign language. In response to instructors' requests, we are pleased to include a new chapter on sign language, authored by Wendy Sandler and Diane Lillo-Martin, who are in the forefront of linguistic research in this field.

An updated computational linguistics chapter. Thoroughly revised by Amanda Stent, a specialist in computational linguistics, the chapter reflects advances in speech recognition, parsing, and natural language generation.

***Expanded Web Features at* bedfordstmartins.com/linguistics/**

- ***Advanced material available.*** Students who have progressed beyond the introductory level will find all advanced lessons and exercises on the companion Web site.
- ***Audio added to Web features.*** Students will be able to listen to actual audio related to chapters that deal directly with sound—phonetics, phonology, sign language.
- ***Streaming video for sign language.*** Students will find streaming media that demonstrate signing and other issues in the field of sign language.

Ancillaries

The Study Guide, updated for the fifth edition, offers summaries of the most important concepts from *Contemporary Linguistics'* core chapters, as well as a range of supplemental exercises with an answer key. ***The Instructor's Resource Manual*** provides teaching advice and includes answers to the exercises at the ends of chapters, while the ***Transparency Masters*** provide more than 100 key charts, images, and other teaching aids from the main text for use in the classroom.

Acknowledgments

A book such as this one, with four editors and eighteen contributors, is clearly a team effort. However, the success of such a team effort rests on how well the book fulfills its purpose for the instructors and students who use it. We are indeed fortunate that our colleagues have been generous in providing us with valuable feedback and suggestions based on their experiences using the text in a wide variety of settings, and we express our heartfelt thanks to them.

Many individuals contributed comments and suggestions to the first four editions of the book, and their assistance continues to be reflected in this edition:

Howard Aronson, Peter Avery, Derek Bickerton, Robert Blust, Patrick Bruke, Vit Bubenik, Gary Byma, Lyle Campbell, Steven Carey, Andrew Carnie, Jack Chambers, Shuji Chiba, Vanna Condax, Eung-Do Cook, Lynda Costello, John Davison, John DeFrancis, Nicole Domingue, Elan Dresher, Matthew Dryer, Sheila Embleton, Robert Fisher, Michael Forman, Donald Frantz, Donna Gerdts, John Haiman, John Hewson, Joyce Hildebrand, Robert Hsu, David Ingram, Ricky Jacobs, Kazue Kanno, Brian King, Uptal Lahiri, Margaret Larock, Gary Libben, Anatole Lyovin, Joyce McDonough, Barry Meislin, Marianne Mithun, Yves-Charles Morin, Woody Mott, Robert Murray, Michael O'Grady, Douglas Parks, George Patterson, Mary Pepper, Marilyn Phillips, Thomas Purnell, R. Radhakrishnan, Laurence Reid, Lori Repetti, Keren Rice, Lorna Rowsell, Lynn Santelmann, Yataka Sato, Coral Sayce, Albert Schütz, Peter Seyffert, Patricia Shaw, Ronald Southerland, Stanley Starosta, the students in Terry Pratt's linguistics course at the University of Prince Edward Island, Allison Teasdale, Charles Ulrich, Tim Vance, Theo Venneman, Douglas Walker, Lydia White, Norio Yamada, Mehmet Yavaş, and Nava Zaig.

For this fifth edition, we are especially grateful for the meticulous reading and detailed comments provided by our reviewers: Barbara Abbott (Michigan State University), Andrew Carnie (University of Arizona), Janet Cowal (Portland State University), Suzanne Flynn (Massachusetts Institute of Technology), Glenn Gilbert (Southern Illinois University), Lynn Guinden (University of Kentucky), Sharon Hargus (University of Washington), Darya Kavitskay (Yale University), Saundra Wright (California State University, Chico), and Doug Wulf (George Mason University).

Taking the cue from our reviewers' requests, we added a new chapter on sign language to *Contemporary Linguistics,* Fifth Edition. We were fortunate to have Wendy Sandler revise and update the excellent chapter she coauthored with Diane Lillo-Martin on this topic from Blackwell Publishing's *Handbook of Linguistics* (2002).

We are delighted to have worked once again with Bedford/St. Martin's. Nancy Perry, now editor in chief, was instrumental in getting the first edition off the ground and has given unflagging support throughout the history of the book. President Joan Feinberg and editorial director Denise Wydra also lent their support to this edition. We are grateful to Erica Appel, managing editor, for her patience and knowledge as the book went through production. Lucy Krikorian, art director, helped design the book's bold new cover. We are particularly delighted to have Harold Chester, senior project editor, working with us again; Harold distinguished himself on the fourth edition with his meticulous attention to detail. His eagle eye has not dimmed.

Perhaps our greatest debt at Bedford/St. Martin's is to Joelle Hann, the developmental editor for the fifth edition. Joelle joined Bedford/St. Martin's at about the time we began work on the fifth edition; she has taken the reins with professionalism and good cheer and guided us and the book through all stages from the beginning to the finished product. We gratefully acknowledge her efforts and thank her most sincerely.

Finally, we acknowledge our students, without whom this endeavor would be meaningless. In their questions and in their joy in discovering the elegance and beauty of language, they remind us why we have become linguists and why we are teachers.

Mark Aronoff
Janie Rees-Miller

PREFACE TO THE FIRST EDITION

Thanks to the application of rigorous analysis to familiar subject matter, linguistics provides students with an ideal introduction to the kind of thinking we call "scientific." Such thinking proceeds from an appreciation of problems arising from bodies of data, to hypotheses that attempt to account for those problems, to the careful testing and extension of the hypotheses. But science is more than a formal activity. One of the great pleasures offered introductory students of linguistics is the discovery of the impressive body of subconscious knowledge that underlies language use. This book attempts to emphasize the extent of this knowledge as well as to introduce the scientific methodology used in linguistic analysis.

Although this is the first linguistics textbook designed primarily for a Canadian readership, we have tried to do much more than simply provide coverage of linguistic phenomena peculiar to Canada. As the title suggests, we have attempted an introduction to linguistic analysis as it is practiced at this stage in the development of our discipline. While we do not ignore or reject other fruitful approaches to linguistics, we have taken the generative paradigm as basic for two reasons. First, generative linguistics provides a relatively coherent and integrated approach to basic linguistic phenomena. Phonetics, phonology, morphology, syntax, and semantics are viewed within this framework as perhaps in no other as fully integrated and interrelated. Secondly, the generative approach has been widely influential in its application to a broad range of other linguistic phenomena over the past twenty years.

The extent of our "contemporariness" has been limited by the inevitable compromise between the need to present basic concepts and the demands of sophisticated and competing recent approaches. In many cases, early versions of our chapters were judged "too contemporary" by instructors who were not specialists in the subfields in question. This led to substantial revisions and a somewhat more traditional approach to certain issues than was originally intended. Where possible, however, later sections of the chapters are used to present more contemporary material. In this way, we have attempted to provide what is promised by the title—an introductory text that provides a solid grounding in basic linguistic concepts, but one that also prepares the student to go on to current work in the discipline. For this reason, the student is introduced to multilevelled phonology (in preparation for further tiered analysis), allophonic/morphophonemic distinctions (in preparation for lexical phonology), interaction among components of the grammar (in preparation for a more extended modular approach), word-formation rules in morphology, and examples of parametric variation in syntax.

To the extent possible, we have attempted to integrate the basic mechanisms outlined in the first five chapters of the book into our discussion of phenomena in later chapters. Thus, our discussion of semantics, historical linguistics, first and second language acquisition, and neurolinguistics draws to some degree on the notions presented in our introduction to generative grammar.

No textbook can be all things to all users. We hope that this book will provide students not only with a springboard to the realm of scientific linguistic analysis, but with a greater appreciation for the wonder of human language, the variety and complexity of its structure, and the subtlety of its use.

We gratefully acknowledge the assistance of Jack Chambers and Sheila Embleton, both of whom read the manuscript in its entirety and provided invaluable comments. Thanks are also due to those who have read and commented upon individual chapters and sections, including Steven Carey, Matthew Dryer, David Ingram, Gary Byma, Gary Libben, Robert Murray, R. Radhakrishnan, Ronald Southerland, Mary Pepper, Derek Bickerton, Robert Blust, Ricky Jacobs, Don Frantz, John Haiman, John Hewson, Nicole Domingue, Lydia White, George Patterson, Donna Gerdts, Elan Dresher, Keren Rice, Robert Fisher, Marilyn Philips, Lorna Rowsell, and Joyce Hildebrand. For assistance in the planning, editing, and production of the manuscript, we are grateful to Coral Sayce, Lynda Costello, Joyce Hildebrand, Brian Henderson, Patrick Burke, Les Petriw, and our project editor at Copp Clark, Margaret Larock.

CONTENTS

ten

Natural sign languages 343

eleven

First language acquisition 361

fourteen

BRAIN AND LANGUAGE 463

fifteen

LANGUAGE IN SOCIAL CONTEXTS 485

LIST OF TECHNICAL ABBREVIATIONS

*	(in historical linguistics) protoform
*	(in syntactic rules) one or more
*	(in front of words or sentences) unacceptable
#	word boundary
1	first person
1	primary stress
2	second person
2	secondary stress
3	third person
A	adjective
AAVE	African American Vernacular English
ABL	ablative case
ABS	absolutive case
ACC	accusative case
Adv	adverb
AdvP	adverb phrase
Af	affix
ag	agent
AP	adjective phrase
ASL	American Sign Language
Aux	auxiliary verb
C	complementizer
C	consonant
caus	cause
CG	constricted glottis
cmpl	completed action
C_o	any number of consonants
Co	coda
COM	comitative case
Con	conjunction
CP	complementizer phrase
CT	computerized axial tomography
DA	derivational affix
DAT	dative case
Deg	degree word
Det	determiner
DR	delayed release
ERG	ergative case
ERP	event-related potential
ESL	English as a second language
fMRI	functional magnetic resonance imaging
Fut	future tense
GEN	genitive case
go	goal
H	high tone
HAB	habitual aspect
IA	inflexional affix
IL	interlanguage
INDIC	indicative
IP	inflectional phrase
IPA	International Phonetic Alphabet
ISL	Israeli Sign Language
L	low tone
L1	first language
L2	second language
LN	last name
Loc	location
LOC	locative case
M	mid tone
MEG	magnetoencephalography
MRD	machine readable dictionary
N	(first) name
N	noun
N	nucleus
NEG	negative
NOM	nominative case
NP	noun phrase
O	(direct) object
O	onset
Obl	oblique
OE	Old English
P	preposition, postposition
PASS	passive
PET	positron emission tomography
PIE	Proto-Indo-European
PL	plural
PP	prepositional phrase
PR	phonetic representation
PRES	present tense
PROG	progressive aspect
Pst	past tense
QUES	question marker
R	rhyme
R	rounded
rc	relative clause
REA	right ear advantage
recip	recipient
S	subject
σ	syllable
SG	spread glottis
SG	singular
SLA	second language acquisition
T	title alone
th	theme
TLN	title + last name

t	topicalization
TOP	topic
UG	Universal Grammar
UR	underlying representation
UR	unrounded
V	verb
V	vowel
VP	verb phrase
Wd	word

CONTEMPORARY LINGUISTICS

AN INTRODUCTION

one

Language: A Preview

William O'Grady

The gift of language is the single human trait that marks us all genetically, setting us apart from the rest of life.

– Lewis Thomas, *The Lives of a Cell*

Objectives

In this chapter, you will learn:

- that human beings are specialized for language
- that all human languages are creative, have a grammar, and change over time
- that all grammars are alike in basic ways
- that grammatical knowledge is subconscious in all native speakers of a language

Language is many things—a system of communication, a tool for thought, a medium for self-expression, a social institution, a source of ethnic pride and political controversy. All normal human beings have at least one language, and it is difficult to imagine much significant social, intellectual, or artistic activity taking place in the absence of language.

The centrality of language to virtually every aspect of human life gives each of us a reason to want to be curious about its nature and use. This book takes a first step in that direction by providing a basic introduction to **linguistics**, the study of how language works.

1 Specialization for Language

Modern *Homo sapiens* (our species) made their appearance 100,000 to 200,000 years ago, by many estimates. Early humans were anatomically just like us—they had large brains and vocal tracts capable of producing speech. Archaeological evidence (such as tools, carvings, and cave paintings) suggests that they also had the type of intellect that could support language.

Hundreds of thousands of years of evolution created a special capacity for language in humans not found in any other species. The evidence is literally inside us. For example, our speech organs (the lungs, larynx, tongue, teeth, lips, soft palate, and nasal passages) were—and still are—directly concerned with breathing and eating. However, they have also all become highly specialized for use in language (Table 1.1). Their structure and shape is unique to our species, as is the highly developed network of neural pathways that exercises control over them during speech production.

Table 1.1 Dual functions of the speech organs

Organ	*Survival function*	*Speech function*
Lungs	to exchange CO_2 and oxygen	to supply air for speech
Vocal cords	to create seal over passage to lungs	to produce vibrations for speech sounds
Tongue	to move food to teeth and back into throat	to articulate vowels and consonants
Teeth	to break up food	to provide place of articulation for consonants
Lips	to seal oral cavity	to articulate vowels and consonants
Nose	to assist in breathing	to provide nasal resonance during speech

Breathing during speech is associated with higher lung pressure and a longer exhalation time than ordinary respiration, and abdominal muscles that are not normally employed for respiration are brought into play in order to regulate the air pressure needed for speech.

Human beings are also especially equipped for the perception of speech. Newborns respond differently to human voices than to other types of sounds, and six-month-old infants are able to perceive subtle differences among sounds in languages that they have never heard before (this is discussed in more detail in Chapter 11).

Even the ability to deal with nonvocal, cognitive aspects of language—such as word formation, sentence building, the interpretation of meaning—seems to be the product of neurological specialization. Particular parts of the brain tend to be associated with specific types of linguistic phenomena (see Chapter 14 for discussion), and species with different types of brains appear to be unable to acquire or use human language (see Chapter 17).

2 A Creative System

Knowing that human beings are especially suited for language only increases the mystery that surrounds this phenomenon. What, precisely, is language? What does it mean to know a language? To answer these questions, it is first necessary to understand the resources that a language makes available to its **native speakers**, those who have acquired it as children in a natural setting (say, a home rather than a classroom).

The breadth and diversity of human thought and experience place great demands on language. Because communication is not restricted to a fixed set of topics, language must do something more than provide a package of ready-made messages. It must enable us to produce and understand new words and sentences as the need arises. In short, human language must be creative, allowing novelty and innovation in response to new thoughts, experiences, and situations.

The **creativity** of language goes hand in hand with a second defining characteristic—the presence of systematic constraints that establish the boundaries within which innovation can occur. As a preliminary illustration of this, let us consider the process that creates verbs from nouns in English as shown in Table 1.2. (For now, you can think of verbs as words that name actions and nouns as words that name things.)

Table 1.2 Nouns used as verbs

Noun use	*Verb use*
pull the boat onto the *beach*	*beach* the boat
keep the airplane on the *ground*	*ground* the airplane
tie a *knot* in the string	*knot* the string
put the wine in *bottles*	*bottle* the wine
catch the fish with a *spear*	*spear* the fish
clean the floor with a *mop*	*mop* the floor

As the sentences in *1* show, there is a great deal of freedom to innovate in the formation of such verbs.

1)

a. I *wristed* the ball over the net.
b. He would try to *stiff-upper-lip* it through.
c. She *Houdini'd* her way out of the locked closet.

However, there are also limits on this freedom. For instance, a new verb is rarely coined if a word with the intended meaning already exists. Although we say *jail the robber* to mean 'put the robber in jail', we do not say *prison the robber* to mean 'put the robber in prison'. This is because the well-established verb *imprison* already has the meaning that the new form would have.

There are also special constraints on the meaning and use of particular subclasses of these verbs. One such constraint involves verbs that are created from time expressions such as *summer, vacation,* and so on.

2)

a. Julia *summered* in Paris.
b. Harry *wintered* in Mexico.
c. Bob *vacationed* in France.
d. Harry and Julia *honeymooned* in Hawaii.

Although the sentences in *2* are all natural-sounding, not all time expressions can be used in this way. (Throughout this book an asterisk is used to indicate that an utterance is unacceptable.)

3)

a. *Jerome *midnighted* in the streets.
b. *Andrea *nooned* at the restaurant.
c. *Philip *one o'clocked* at the airport.

These examples show that when a verb is created from a time expression, it must be given a very specific interpretation—roughly paraphrasable as 'to be somewhere for the period of time X'. Thus, *to summer in Paris* is 'to be in Paris for the summer', *to vacation in France* is 'to be in France for a vacation', and so on. Since *noon* and *midnight* express *points* in time rather than extended *periods* of time, they cannot be used to create new verbs of this type.

Systematic constraints are essential to the viability of the creative process. If well-established words were constantly being replaced by new creations, a language's vocabulary would be so unstable that communication could be jeopardized. A similar danger would arise if there were no constraints on the meaning of words newly derived from other words. If *They winter in Hawaii* could mean 'They make it snow in Hawaii' or 'They wish it were winter in Hawaii' or any other arbitrary thing, the production and interpretation of new forms would be chaotic and unsystematic, undermining the usefulness of language for communication.

Some Other Examples

Systematic creativity is the hallmark of all aspects of language. For instance, consider the way in which sounds are combined to form words. Certain patterns of sounds, like the novel forms in *4,* have the look of English words—we recognize that they could become part of the language and be used as names for new products or processes, for example.

4)

a. prasp
b. flib
c. traf

In contrast, the forms in *5* contain combinations of sounds that English does not permit. As a result, they simply do not have the shape of English words.

5)

a. *psapr
b. *bfli
c. *ftra

Still other constraints determine how new words can be created from already existing forms with the help of special endings. Imagine, for example, that the word *soleme* entered the English language (used perhaps for a newly discovered atomic particle). As a speaker of English, you would then automatically know that something with the properties of a soleme could be called *solemic*. You would also know that to make something solemic is to *solemicize* it, and you would call this process *solemicization*. Further, you would know that the *c* is pronounced as *s* in *solemicize* but as *k* in *solemic*. Without hesitation, you would also recognize that *solemicize* is pronounced with the stress on the second syllable. (You would say *soLEmicize,* not *SOlemicize* or *solemiCIZE*.)

Nowhere is the ability to deal with novel utterances more obvious than in the production and comprehension of sentences. Apart from a few fixed expressions and greetings, much of what you say, hear, and read in the course of a day consists of sentences that are new to you. In conversations, lectures, newscasts, and textbooks, you are regularly exposed to novel combinations of words, unfamiliar ideas, and new information. Consider, for instance, the paragraph that you are currently reading. While each sentence is no doubt perfectly comprehensible to you, it is extremely unlikely that you have ever seen any of them before.

Not all new sentences are acceptable, however. For example, the words in *6* are all familiar, but they are simply not arranged in the right way to make a sentence of English.

6)

*Frightened dog this the cat that chased mouse a.
(cf. This dog frightened the cat that chased a mouse.)

As with other aspects of language, the ability to form and interpret sentences is subject to systematic limitations. One of the principal goals of contemporary linguistic analysis is to identify and understand these limitations.

3 Grammar and Linguistic Competence

As we have just seen, speakers of a language are able to produce and understand an unlimited number of utterances, including many that are novel and unfamiliar. At the same time, they are able to recognize that certain utterances are not acceptable and simply do not belong in their language. This ability, which is often called **linguistic competence**, constitutes the central subject matter of linguistics and of this book.

In investigating linguistic competence, linguists focus on the mental system that allows human beings to form and interpret the sounds, words, and sentences of their language. Linguists call this system a **grammar** and often break it down into the components in Table 1.3.

Table 1.3 The components of a grammar

Component	*Domain*
Phonetics	the articulation and perception of speech sounds
Phonology	the patterning of speech sounds
Morphology	word formation
Syntax	sentence formation
Semantics	the interpretation of words and sentences

As you can see, the term *grammar* is used in a special way within linguistics. A linguist's grammar is not a book and it is not concerned with just the form of words and sentences. Rather, it is an intricate system of knowledge that encompasses sound and meaning as well as form and structure.

The study of grammar lies at the core of our attempts to understand what language is and what it means to know a language. Five simple points should help clarify why the investigation of grammatical systems is so important to contemporary linguistic analysis.

3.1 Generality: All Languages Have a Grammar

One of the most fundamental claims of modern linguistic analysis is that all languages have a grammar. It could not be any other way. If a language is spoken, it must have a phonetic and phonological system; since it has words and sentences, it must also have a morphology and a syntax; and since these words and sentences have systematic meanings, there must obviously be semantic principles as well. In other words, each spoken language must have an intricate system of knowledge that encompasses sound and meaning as well as form and structure.

It is not unusual to hear the remark that some language—say, Puerto Rican Spanish, American Sign Language, or Swahili—has no grammar. (This is especially common in the case of languages that are not written or are not taught in schools and universities.) Unfamiliar languages sometimes appear to an untrained observer to have no grammar simply because their grammatical systems are different from those of better-known languages. In Walbiri (an indigenous language of Australia), for example, the relative ordering of words is so free that the English sentence *The two dogs now see several kangaroos* could be translated by the equivalent of any of the following sentences.

7)

- *a.* Dogs two now see kangaroos several.
- *b.* See now dogs two kangaroos several.
- *c.* See now kangaroos several dogs two.
- *d.* Kangaroos several now dogs two see.
- *e.* Kangaroos several now see dogs two.

Although Walbiri may not restrict the order of words in the way English does, its grammar imposes other types of requirements. For example, in the sentence types we are considering, Walbiri speakers must place the ending *lu* on the word for 'dogs' to indicate that it names the animals that do the seeing rather than the animals that are seen. In English, by contrast, this information is conveyed by placing *two dogs* in front of the verb and *several kangaroos* after it.

Rather than showing that Walbiri has no grammar, such differences simply demonstrate that it has a grammar that is unlike the grammar of English in certain respects. This point holds across the board: although no two languages have exactly the same grammar, there are no languages without a grammar.

A similar point can be made about different varieties of the same language. Appalachian English, Jamaican English, and Hawaiian English each have pronunciations, vocabulary items, and sentence patterns that may appear unusual to outsiders. But this does not mean that they have no grammar; it just means that their grammars differ from those of more familiar varieties of English in particular ways.

3.2 Parity: All Grammars Are Equal

Contrary to popular belief, there is no such thing as a primitive language, even in places untouched by modern science and technology. Indeed, some of the most complex linguistic phenomena we know about are found in societies that have neither writing nor electricity.

Moreover, there is no such thing as a good grammar or a bad grammar. In fact, all grammars do essentially the same thing: they tell speakers how to form and interpret the words and sentences of their language. The form and meaning of those words and sentences vary from language to language and even from community to community, of course, but there is no such thing as a language that doesn't work for its speakers.

Linguists sometimes clash over this point with people who are upset about the use of nonstandard varieties of English that permit sentences such as *I seen that, They was there, He didn't do nothing, He ain't here,* and so forth. Depending on where you live and who you talk to, speaking in this way can have negative consequences: it may be harder to win a scholarship, to get a job, to be accepted in certain social circles, and so forth. This is an undeniable fact about the social side of language and we'll return to it in Chapter 15. From a purely linguistic point of view, however, there is absolutely nothing wrong with grammars that permit such structures. They work for their speakers, and they deserve to be studied in the same objective fashion as the varieties of English spoken by the rich and educated.

The bottom line for linguistics is that the analysis of language must reflect the way it is actually used, not someone's idealized vision of how it should be used. The linguist Steven Pinker offers the following illustration to make the same point.

> Imagine that you are watching a nature documentary. The video shows the usual gorgeous footage of animals in their natural habitats. But the voiceover reports some troubling facts. Dolphins do not execute their swimming strokes properly. White-crowned sparrows carelessly debase their calls. Chickadees' nests are incorrectly constructed, pandas hold bamboo in the wrong paw, the song of the humpback whale contains several well-known errors, and the monkey's cries have been in a state of chaos and degeneration for hundreds of years. Your reaction would probably be, What on earth could it mean for the song of the humpback whale to contain an "error"? Isn't the song of the humpback whale whatever the humpback whale decides to sing? . . .

As Pinker goes on to observe, language is like the song of the humpback whale. The way to determine whether a particular sentence is permissible is to find people who speak the language and observe how they use it.

In sum, linguists don't even think of trying to rate languages as good or bad, simple or complex. Rather, they investigate language in much the same way that other scientists study snails or stars—with a view to simply figuring out how it works. This same point is sometimes made by noting that linguistics is **descriptive**, not

prescriptive. Its goal is to describe and explain the facts of languages, not to change them.

3.3 Universality: Grammars Are Alike in Basic Ways

In considering how grammars can differ from each other, it is easy to lose sight of something even more intriguing and important—the existence of principles and properties shared by all human languages.

For example, all languages use a small set of contrastive sounds that help distinguish words from each other (like the *t* and *d* sounds that allow us to recognize *to* and *do* as different words). There are differences in precisely which sounds particular languages use, but there are also fundamental similarities. For instance, all languages have more consonant sounds (*p, t, d,* etc.) than vowel sounds (*a, e, i*); any language that has an *f* sound also has an *s* sound; and all languages have a vowel that sounds like the 'ah' in *father.* (For more on this, see Chapter 8.)

There are also universal constraints on how words can be put together to form sentences. For example, no language can use the second of the sentences in *8* for a situation in which *he* refers to *Ned.*

8)

a. Ned lost his wallet.
b. He lost Ned's wallet.

Moreover, even when languages do differ from each other, there are often constraints on how much variation is possible. For example, some languages (like English) place question words at the beginning of the sentence.

9)

What did Mary donate to the library?

Other languages, like Mandarin, make no such changes.

10)

Mali juan shenme gei tushuguan?
Mary donate what to library

But no language uniformly places question words at the end of the sentence.

In other cases, variation is constrained by strong tendencies rather than absolute prohibitions. Take three-word sentences such as *Canadians like hockey,* for instance. There are six logically possible orders for such sentences.

11)

a. Canadians like hockey.
b. Canadians hockey like.
c. Like Canadians hockey.
d. Like hockey Canadians.
e. Hockey like Canadians.
f. Hockey Canadians like.

All other things being equal, we would expect to find each order employed in about one-sixth of the world's languages. In fact, though, more than 95 percent of the world's languages adopt one of the first three orders for basic statements (and the vast majority of those use one or the other of the first two orders). Only a handful of languages use any of the last three orders as basic.

These are not isolated examples. As later chapters will show, languages—like the people who use them—are fundamentally alike in important ways.

3.4 Mutability: Grammars Change over Time

The features of language that are not universal and fixed are subject to change over time. Indeed, within these limits, the grammars of all languages are constantly changing. Some of these changes are relatively minor and occur very quickly (for example, the addition of new words such as *blog, morphing, Internet, e-business,* and *cyberspace* to the vocabulary of English). Other changes have a more dramatic effect on the overall form of the language and typically take place over a long period of time. One such change involves the manner in which we negate sentences in English. Prior to 1200, English formed negative constructions by placing *ne* before the verb and a variant of *not* after it.

12)

a. Ic *ne* seye *not.* ('I don't say.')
b. He *ne* speketh *nawt.* ('He does not speak.')

By 1400 or thereabouts, *ne* was used infrequently and *not* (or *nawt*) typically occurred by itself after the verb.

13)

a. I seye *not* the wordes.
b. We saw *nawt* the knyghtes.

It was not until several centuries later that English adopted its current practice of allowing *not* to occur after only certain types of verbs (such as *do, have, will,* and so on).

14)

a. I will *not* say the words. (versus *I will say not the words.)
b. He did *not* see the knights. (versus *He saw not the knights.)

These changes illustrate the extent to which grammars can be modified over time. The structures exemplified in *13* are archaic by today's standards and those in *12* sound completely foreign to most speakers of modern English.

Through the centuries, those who believe that certain varieties of language are better than others have frequently expressed concern over what they perceive to be the deterioration of English. In 1710, for example, the writer Jonathan Swift (author of *Gulliver's Travels*) lamented "the continual Corruption of our English Tongue." Among the corruptions to which he objected were contractions such as *he's* for *he is,* although he had no objection to *'Tis* for *It is.*

In the nineteenth century, Edward S. Gould, a columnist for the New York *Evening Post,* published a book entitled *Good English; or, Popular Errors in Language,* in which he accused newspaper writers and authors of "sensation novels" of ruining the language by introducing "spurious words" like *jeopardize, leniency,* and *underhanded.* The tradition of prescriptive concern about the use of certain words continues to this day in the work of such popular writers as Edwin Newman and John Simon, who form a kind of self-appointed language police.

Linguists reject the view that languages attain a state of perfection at some point in their history and that subsequent changes lead to deterioration and corruption. As noted above, there are simply no grounds for claiming that one language or variety of language is somehow superior to another.

3.5 Inaccessibility: Grammatical Knowledge Is Subconscious

Knowledge of a grammar differs in important ways from knowledge of arithmetic, traffic rules, and other subjects that are taught at home or in school: it is largely subconscious and not accessible to introspection (that is, you can't figure out how it works just by thinking about it). As an example of this, consider your pronunciation of the past tense ending written as *ed* in the following words.

15)

a. hunted
b. slipped
c. buzzed

You probably didn't notice it before, but the *ed* ending has a different pronunciation in each of these words. Whereas you say *id* in *hunted,* you say *t* in *slipped* and *d* in *buzzed.* Moreover, if you heard the new verb *flib,* you would form the past tense as *flibbed* and pronounce the ending as *d.* If you are a native speaker of English, you acquired the grammatical subsystem regulating this aspect of speech when you were a child and it now exists subconsciously in your mind, allowing you to automatically make the relevant contrasts.

The same is true for virtually everything else about language. Once we go beyond the most obvious things (such as whether words like *the* and *a* come before or after a noun), there is not much that the average person can say about how language works. For example, try explaining to someone who is not a native speaker of English why we can say *I went to school* but not **I went to movie.* Or try to figure out for yourself how the word *too* works. Notice that it sounds perfectly natural in sentences such as the following.

16)

a. Mary ate a cookie, and then Johnnie ate a cookie too.
b. Mary ate a cookie, and then she ate some cake too.

For some reason, though, it doesn't sound so natural in the following sentence.

17)

*Mary ate a cookie, and then Johnnie ate some cake too.

You might think that that is because Mary and Johnnie didn't eat the same thing. But, if that's so, then why does *too* sound natural in the next sentence, even though Johnnie didn't have a cookie for his snack?

18)

Mary ate a cookie, and then Johnnie had a snack too.

Speakers of a language know what sounds right and what doesn't sound right, but they are not sure how they know.

Because most of what we know about our language is subconscious, the analysis of human linguistic systems requires considerable effort and ingenuity. As is the case in all science, information about facts that can be observed (the pronunciation of words, the interpretation of sentences, and so on) must be used to draw inferences about the sometimes invisible mechanisms (atoms, cells, or grammars, as the case may be) that are ultimately responsible for these phenomena. A good deal of this book is concerned with the findings of this research and with what they tell us about the nature and use of human language and how it is represented in the mind.

Summing Up

Human language is characterized by **creativity**. Speakers of a language have access to a **grammar**, a mental system that allows them to form and interpret both familiar and novel utterances. The grammar governs the articulation, perception, and patterning of speech sounds; the formation of words and sentences; and the interpretation of utterances. All languages have grammars that are equal in their expressive capacity, and all speakers of a language have (subconscious) knowledge of its grammar. The existence of such linguistic systems in humans is the product of unique anatomical and cognitive specialization not found in other species.

Key Terms

creativity
descriptive (grammar)
grammar
linguistic competence
linguistics
native speakers
prescriptive (grammar)

For information on the sources used in this chapter, go to **bedfordstmartins.com/linguistics/language** and click on **Sources**.

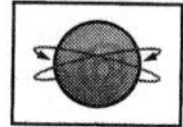

Recommended Reading

Bickerton, Derek. 1990. *Language and Species*. Chicago: University of Chicago Press.

Crystal, David. 2003. *The Cambridge Encyclopedia of the English Language*. 2nd ed. New York: Cambridge University Press.

Pinker, Steven. 1994. *The Language Instinct: How the Human Mind Creates Language.* New York: Morrow.

Exercises

1. The following sentences contain verbs created from nouns in accordance with the process described in Section 2 of this chapter. Describe the meaning of each of these new verbs.
   a) We punk-rocked the night away.
   b) She dog-teamed her way across the Arctic.
   c) We MG'd to Oregon.
   d) You should Band-Aid that cut.
   e) He Gretzky'd his way to the net.
   f) We Greyhounded to Columbus.
   g) We'll have to Ajax the sink.
   h) He Windexed the windows.
   i) You should Clairol your hair.
   j) Let's carton the eggs.

2. Using the examples in the preceding exercise as a model, create five new verbs from nouns. Build a sentence around each of these new verbs to show its meaning.

3. Which of the following forms are possible words of English? Solicit the help of an acquaintance and see if you agree on your judgments.

a) mbood	e) sproke
b) frall	f) flube
c) coofp	g) wordms
d) ktleem	h) bsarn

4. Imagine that you are an advertising executive and that your job involves inventing new names for products. Create four new forms that are possible words of English and four that are not.

5. Part of linguistic competence involves the ability to recognize whether novel utterances are acceptable. Consider the following sentences and determine which are possible sentences in English. For each unacceptable sentence, change the sentence to make it acceptable, and compare the two.
   a) Jason's mother left himself with nothing to eat.
   b) Miriam is eager to talk to.
   c) This is the man who I took a picture of.
   d) Colin made Jane a sandwich.
   e) Is the dog sleeping the bone again?
   f) Wayne prepared Zena a cake.
   g) Max cleaned the garden up.
   h) Max cleaned up the garden.
   i) Max cleaned up it.
   j) I desire you to leave.
   k) That you likes liver surprises me.

6. Consider the following sentences, each of which is acceptable to some speakers of English. Try to identify the prescriptive rules that are violated in each case.
   a) He don't know about the race.
   b) You was out when I called.
   c) There's twenty horses registered in the show.
   d) That window's broke, so be careful.
   e) Jim and me are gonna go campin' this weekend.
   f) Who did you come with?
   g) I seen the parade last week.
   h) He been lost in the woods for ten days.
   i) My car needs cleaned 'cause of all the rain.
   j) Julie ain't got none.
   k) Somebody left their book on the train.
   l) Murray hurt hisself in the game.

   What is the reaction of linguists to the claim that sentences of this sort are wrong?

two

Phonetics: The Sounds of Language

Michael Dobrovolsky

Heavenly labials in a world of gutturals

– WALLACE STEVENS

OBJECTIVES

In this chapter, you will learn:

- how we use special symbols to represent all the different sounds in human languages, beginning with English
- how to write down your own speech using these symbols
- how we use articulators in the vocal tract to produce specific sounds
- how we can group language sounds into classes
- how human languages use tone, intonation, and sound length to create meaning
- how language sounds in context can be modified by neighboring sounds

We do not need to speak in order to use language. Language can be written, manually signed, mechanically reproduced, and even synthesized by computers with considerable success. Nevertheless, speech remains the primary way humans express themselves through language. Our species spoke long before we began to write, and, as we saw in the first chapter of this book, this long history of spoken language is reflected in our anatomical specialization for it. Humans also appear to have specialized neural mechanisms for the perception of speech sounds. Because language and speech are so closely linked, we begin our study of language by examining the inventory and structure of the sounds of speech. This branch of linguistics is called **phonetics**.

Human languages display a wide variety of sounds, called **phones** (from Greek *phōnē* 'sound, voice') or **speech sounds**. There are a great many speech sounds, but not an infinite number of them. The class of possible speech sounds is finite, and a portion of the total set will be found in the inventory of any human language. Humans can also make sounds with the vocal tract that do not occur in speech, such as the sound made by inhaling through one corner of the mouth, or the "raspberry" produced by sticking out the tongue and blowing hard across it. Nonetheless, a very wide range of sounds is found in human language (600 consonants and 200 vowels, according to one estimate), including such sounds as the click made by drawing the tongue hard away from the upper molars on one side of the mouth, or the sound made by constricting the upper part of the throat as we breathe out. Any human, child or adult, can learn to produce any human speech sound.

There are two ways of approaching phonetics. One approach studies the physiological mechanisms of speech production. This is known as **articulatory phonetics**. The other, known as **acoustic phonetics**, is concerned with measuring and analyzing the physical properties of the sound waves we produce when we speak. Both approaches are indispensable to an understanding of speech. This chapter focuses on articulatory phonetics, but also makes some reference to the acoustic properties of sounds and to acoustic analysis.

1 Phonetic Transcription

Since the sixteenth century, efforts have been made to devise a universal system for transcribing the sounds of speech. The best-known system, the **International Phonetic Alphabet (IPA)**, has been evolving since 1888. This system of transcription attempts to represent each sound of human speech with a single symbol. These symbols are enclosed in brackets [ ] to indicate that the transcription is phonetic and does not represent the spelling system of a particular language. For example, the sound spelled *th* in English *this* is transcribed as [ð] (pronounced *eth,* as in *weather*). The IPA uses this symbol to represent the sound in whichever language it is heard, whether it is English, Spanish, or Turkmen (a Turkic language spoken in Central Asia and written with the Cyrillic alphabet), as shown in Table 2.1.

Table 2.1 Use of [ð] in the International Phonetic Alphabet

Language	*Spelling*	*IPA*	*Meaning*
English	this	[ðɪs]	'this'
Spanish	boda	[boða]	'wedding'
Turkmen	адак	[aðak]	'foot'

The use of a standardized phonetic alphabet enables linguists to transcribe languages consistently and accurately. In North American (NA) usage, though, some phonetic symbols differ from those employed by IPA transcription. For a comparison of North American (NA) symbols with IPA symbols, go to **bedfordstmartins.com/linguistics/phonetics** and click on **NA symbols**. This book employs IPA transcription.

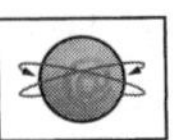

If you wish to start practicing the phonetic transcription of English, turn to Tables 2.16 and 2.17, pages 36–37, for examples.

1.1 Units of Representation

Anyone who hears a language spoken for the first time finds it hard to break up the flow of speech into individual units. Even when hearing our own language spoken, we do not focus attention on individual sounds as much as we do on the meanings of words, phrases, and sentences. Many alphabets, including the IPA, represent speech in the form of **segments**—individual phones like [p], [s], or [m]. (Using segments, however, is only one way to represent speech. The **syllable**, presented in Chapter 3, is also represented in some writing systems [see Chapter 16, Sections 1.2, 3.2, and 4.2]. In one type of Japanese writing, for example, signs such as か [ka], と [to], and み [mi] represent syllables without recourse to segmental transcription.)

Segments are produced by coordinating a number of individual articulatory gestures including jaw movement, lip shape, and tongue placement. Many of these individual activities are represented as smaller subunits called **features**, which segments are made up of. Even though features are almost never represented in writing systems, they are important elements of linguistic representation. Features reflect individual aspects of articulatory control or acoustic effects produced by articulation. This chapter presents segmental transcription, since it is the most widely used way of representing speech. Features and syllables are introduced in the following chapter.

1.2 Segments

We have defined the segment as an individual speech sound (phone). There are several kinds of evidence that suggest that speakers have the linguistic knowledge that makes it possible to break down a stream of speech into sound segments.

Errors in speech production provide one kind of evidence for the existence of segments. Slips of the tongue such as *Kolacodor* for *Kodacolor* and *melcome wat* for *welcome mat* show segments shifting and reversing position within and across words. This suggests that segments are individual units of linguistic structure and can be represented individually in a system of transcription.

The relative invariance of speech sounds in human language also suggests that segmental phonetic transcription is a well-motivated way of transcribing speech. It is impossible to represent all variants of human speech sounds, since no one says the same sound in exactly the same way twice. Nonetheless, the sounds of speech remain invariant enough from language to language for us to transcribe them consistently. A *p* sound is much the same in English, Russian, or Uzbek. The fact that when producing a *p* sound, English speakers press their lips together but Russian speakers draw theirs slightly inward does not make the sounds different enough to warrant separate symbols. But the sounds *p* and *t* are distinct enough from each other in languages the world over to be consistently transcribed with separate symbols.

When we use the same symbol to represent two sounds that are not exactly the same phonetically, we are making a **broad transcription**. A broad transcription uses a relatively simple set of symbols to represent contrasting segments but does not show all phonetic detail. If we wish to show more phonetic detail, we can use a more elaborate set of symbols and **diacritics**. In this case, we are making a **narrow transcription**. The terms *broad* and *narrow* are relative, not absolute: the less phonetic detail we show, the broader the transcription; the more phonetic detail, the narrower the transcription.

2 The Sound-Producing System

Sound is produced when air is set in motion. Think of the speech production mechanism as consisting of an air supply, a sound source that sets the air in motion in ways specifically relevant to speech production, and a set of filters that modifies the sound in various ways (see Figure 2.1). The air supply is provided by the lungs. The sound source is in the **larynx** (commonly known as the voice box or Adam's apple), where a set of muscles called the **vocal folds** (or **vocal cords**) are located. The filters are the organs above the larynx: the tube of the throat between the larynx and the oral cavity, which is called the **pharynx**; the oral cavity; and the nasal cavity. These passages are collectively known as the **vocal tract**.

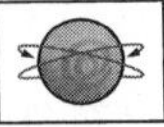

For more information on the lungs and the larynx, go to **bedfordstmartins.com/linguistics/phonetics** and click on **lungs and larynx**.

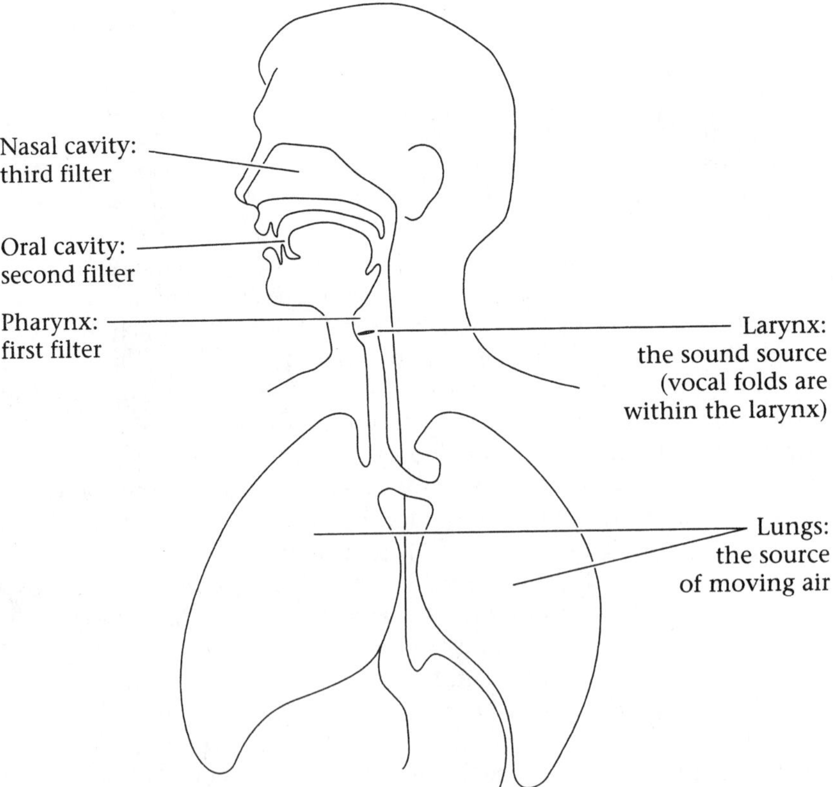

Figure 2.1 The sound-producing system

2.1 Glottal States

The space between the vocal folds is called the **glottis**. The vocal folds may be positioned in a number of ways to produce different glottal states. The first two glottal states presented in Figure 2.2 are commonly encountered in most of the world's languages. The third glottal state in Figure 2.2 underlies a common speech phenomenon, and the fourth illustrates one of a number of glottal states not encountered in English.

Voicelessness

When the vocal folds are pulled apart as illustrated in Figure 2.2, air passes directly through the glottis. Any sound made with the vocal folds in this position is said to be **voiceless**. You can confirm a sound's voicelessness by touching your fingers to the larynx as you produce it. You will not feel any vibration from the vocal folds being transmitted to your fingertips. The initial sounds of *fish, sing,* and *house* are all voiceless. Voicelessness is a true speech state distinct from breathing; the vocal folds are not as far apart during speech voicelessness as they are in silent breathing.

Voicing

When the vocal folds are brought close together, but not tightly closed, air passing between them causes them to vibrate, producing sounds that are said to be **voiced**. (See Figure 2.2, where the movement of the vocal folds during voicing is indicated by the wavy lines.) You can determine whether a sound is voiced in the same way you determined voicelessness. By lightly touching the fingers to the larynx as you produce an extended version of the initial sounds of the words *zip* or *vow,* or any vowel, you can sense the vibration of the vocal folds within the larynx.

Whisper

Another glottal state produces a **whisper**. Whispering is voiceless, but, as shown in Figure 2.2, the vocal folds are adjusted so that the anterior (front) portions are pulled close together while the posterior (back) portions are apart.

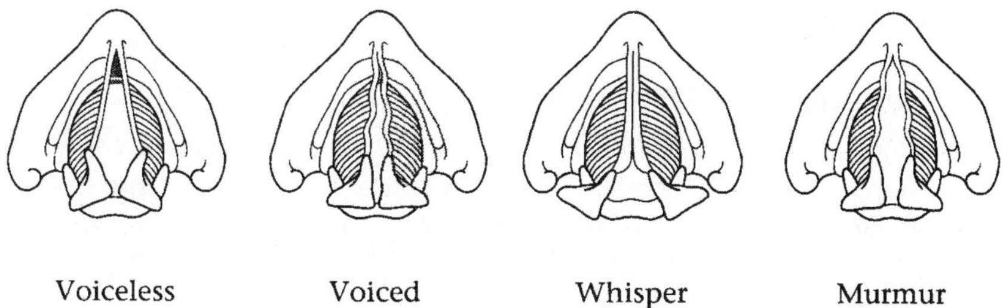

Figure 2.2 Four glottal states: the stylized drawings represent the vocal folds and glottis from above; the anterior portion at the larynx is toward the top. The small triangles represent the arytenoid cartilages, which help spread or close the vocal folds.

Murmur

Yet another glottal state produces a **murmur**, also known as **breathy voice**. Sounds produced with this glottal configuration are voiced, but the vocal folds are relaxed to allow enough air to escape to produce a simultaneous breathy effect.

These four glottal states represent only some of the possibilities of sound production at the glottis. The total number of glottal states is still undecided, but there are more than a dozen. Combined with various articulations made above the larynx, they produce a wide range of phones. Before examining phones in more detail, we will first consider the three major classes of speech sound.

3 Sound Classes

The sounds of language can be grouped into **sound classes** based on the phonetic properties that they share. You have already seen what some of these properties can be. All voiced sounds, for example, form a class, as do all voiceless sounds. The most basic division among sounds is into two major classes, **vowels** and **consonants**. Another class of sounds, the **glides**, shares properties of both vowels and consonants. Each class of sounds has a number of distinguishing features.

3.1 Vowels, Consonants, and Glides (Syllabic and Nonsyllabic Elements)

Vowels, consonants, and glides can be distinguished on the basis of differences in articulation, or by their acoustic properties. We can also distinguish among these elements with respect to whether they function as **syllabic** or **nonsyllabic** elements.

The Articulatory Difference

Consonantal sounds, which may be voiced or voiceless, are made with either a complete closure or a narrowing of the vocal tract. The airflow is either blocked momentarily or restricted so much that noise is produced as air flows past the constriction. In contrast, vowels are produced with little obstruction in the vocal tract and are usually voiced.

The Acoustic Difference

As a result of the difference in articulation, consonants and vowels differ in the way they sound. Vowels are more **sonorous** (acoustically powerful) than consonants, and so we perceive them as louder and longer lasting.

Syllabic and Nonsyllabic Sounds

The greater sonority of vowels allows them to form the basis of syllables. A syllable can be defined as a peak of sonority surrounded by less sonorous segments. For example, the words *a* and *go* each contain one syllable, the word *laughing* two syllables, and the word *telephone* three syllables. In counting the syllables in these words, we are in effect counting the vowels. A vowel is thus said to form the **nucleus** of a syllable. In Section 5.7, we will see that certain types of consonants can form syllabic nuclei as well. It is a good idea, therefore, to think of vowels and consonants not simply as types of articulations but as elements that may or may not be syllabic. In *1,* the initial sounds of the words in the left column are all consonants; those on the right are all vowels.

1)

take	above
cart	at
feel	eel
jump	it
think	ugly
bell	open

Table 2.2 sums up the differences between consonants and vowels.

Table 2.2 Major differences between syllabic and nonsyllabic elements

Vowels (and other syllabic elements)	Consonants (nonsyllabic elements)
• are produced with relatively little obstruction in the vocal tract	• are produced with a complete closure or narrowing of the vocal tract
• are more sonorous	• are less sonorous

Glides

A type of sound that shows properties of both consonants and vowels is called a glide. Glides may be thought of as rapidly articulated vowels—this is the auditory impression they produce. Glides are produced with an articulation like that of a vowel. However, they move quickly to another articulation, as do the initial glides in *yet* or *wet,* or quickly terminate, as do the word-final glides in *boy* and *now.*

Even though they are vowel-like in articulation, glides pattern as consonants. For example, glides can never form the nucleus of a syllable. Since glides show properties of both consonants and vowels, the terms *semivowel* and *semiconsonant* may be used interchangeably with the term *glide.*

4 Consonant Articulation

Airflow is modified in the vocal tract by the placement of the tongue and the positioning of the lips. These modifications occur at specific **places** or **points of articulation**. The major places of articulation used in speech production are outlined in this section. Figure 2.3 provides a midsagittal section, or cutaway view, of the vocal tract on which each place of articulation has been indicated.

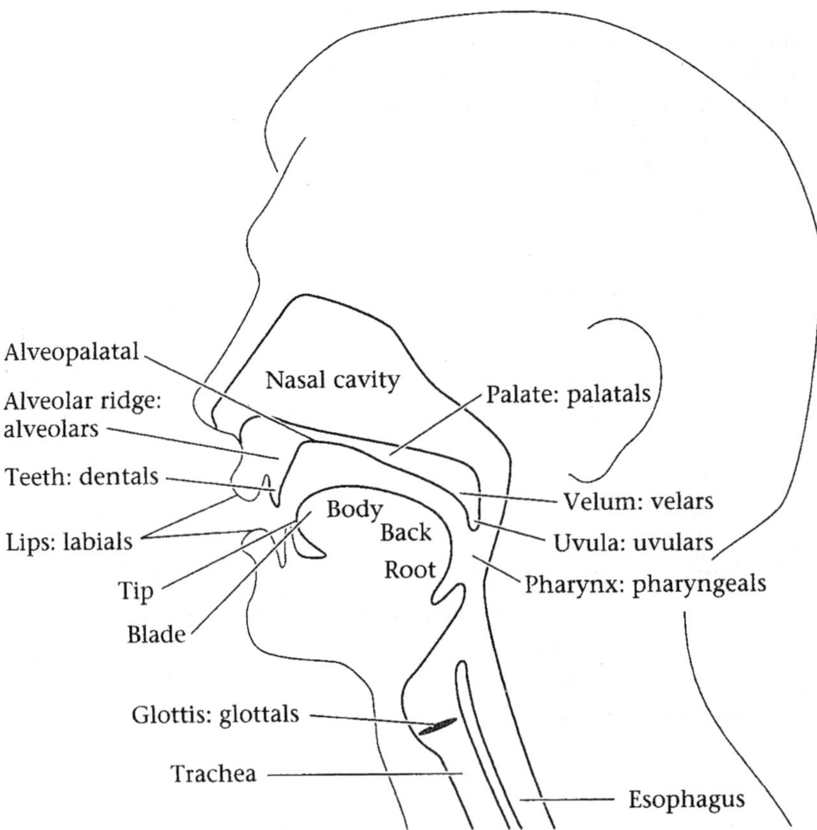

Figure 2.3 The vocal tract

4.1 The Tongue

The primary articulating organ is the tongue. It can be raised, lowered, thrust forward or retracted, and even rolled back. The sides of the tongue can also be raised or lowered.

Phonetic description refers to five areas of the tongue. The **tip** is the narrow area at the front. Just behind the tip lies the **blade**. The main mass of the tongue is called the **body**, and the hindmost part of the tongue that lies in the mouth is called the **back**. The body and back of the tongue can also be referred to jointly as the **dorsum**. The **root** of the tongue is contained in the upper part of the throat (pharynx).

4.2 Places of Articulation

Each point at which the airstream can be modified to produce a different sound is called a place of articulation. Places of articulation are found at the lips, within the oral cavity, in the pharynx, and at the glottis.

Labial

Any sound made with closure or near-closure of the lips is said to be **labial**. Sounds involving both lips are termed **bilabial**; sounds involving the lower lip and upper teeth are called **labiodentals**. English includes the bilabials heard word-initially in *peer, bin,* and *month,* and the labiodentals heard initially in *fire* and *vow.*

Dental and Interdental

Some phones are produced with the tongue placed against or near the teeth. Sounds made in this way are called **dentals**. European French has dental sounds at the beginning of the words *temps, dire, sept,* and *zizi.* (Some English speakers produce *s* and *z* as dentals; see Section 5.3 for more details.)

If the tongue is placed between the teeth, the sound is said to be **interdental**. Interdentals in English include the initial consonants of the words *this* and *thing.*

Alveolar

Within the oral cavity, a small ridge protrudes from just behind the upper front teeth. This is called the **alveolar ridge**. The tongue may touch or be brought near this ridge. Alveolar sounds are heard at the beginning of the English words *top, deer, soap, zip, lip,* and *neck.* Some languages, such as Spanish, have an *r* that is made by touching the tongue to the alveolar ridge.

Alveopalatal and Palatal

Just behind the alveolar ridge, the roof of the mouth rises sharply. This area is known as the **alveopalatal** area (**palatoalveolar** in some books). Alveopalatal consonants are heard in the English words *show, measure, chip,* and *judge.*

The highest part of the roof of the mouth is called the **palate**, and sounds produced with the tongue on or near this area are called **palatals**. The word-initial phone in *yes* is a palatal glide.

Velar

The soft area toward the rear of the roof of the mouth is called the **velum**. Sounds made with the tongue touching or near this position are called **velars**. Velars are heard in English at the beginning of the words *call* and *guy,* and at the end of the word *hang.* The glide heard word-initially in *wet* is called a **labiovelar**, since the tongue is raised near the velum and the lips are rounded at the same time.

Uvular

The small fleshy flap of tissue known as the **uvula** hangs down from the velum. Sounds made with the tongue near or touching this area are called **uvulars**. English has no uvulars, but the *r* sound of standard European French is uvular.

Pharyngeal

The area of the throat between the uvula and the larynx is known as the pharynx. Sounds made through the modification of airflow in this region by retracting the tongue or constricting the pharynx are called **pharyngeals**. Pharyngeals can be found in many dialects of Arabic, but not in English.

Glottal

Sounds produced using the vocal folds as primary articulators are called **glottals**. The sound at the beginning of the English words *heave* and *hog* is made at the glottis.

5 Manners of Articulation

The lips, tongue, velum, and glottis can be positioned in different ways to produce different sound types. These various configurations are called the **manners of articulation**.

5.1 Oral versus Nasal Phones

A basic distinction in manner of articulation is between **oral** and **nasal phones**. When the velum is raised, cutting off the airflow through the nasal passages, oral sounds are produced. The velum can also be lowered to allow air to pass through the nasal passages, producing a sound that is nasal. Both consonants and vowels can be nasal, in which case they are generally voiced. (Unless otherwise noted, all nasals represented in this chapter are voiced.) The consonants at the end of the English words *sun, sum,* and *sung* are nasal. For many speakers of English, the vowels of words such as *bank* and *wink* are also slightly nasal.

5.2 Stops

Stops are made with a complete closure either in the oral cavity or at the glottis. In the world's languages, stops are found at bilabial, dental, alveolar, palatal, velar, uvular, and glottal points of articulation.

Oral Stops

Oral stops are articulated by a complete closure of articulators in the oral cavity, and the air flow is stopped completely. In English, bilabial, alveolar, and velar oral stops occur in the words shown in Table 2.3.

The Glottal Stop

The glottal stop is commonly heard in English in the expression *uh-oh* [ʔʌʔow]. The two vowels in this expression are preceded by a momentary closing of the airstream at the glottis. In some British dialects, the glottal stop is commonly heard in place of the [t] in a word like *bottle.* This glottal stop is often spelled with an apostrophe <bo'l>.

Nasal Stops

Nasal stops are articulated with a complete closure in the oral cavity. However, the air flow is not stopped but continues through the nasal passages, making nasal con-

Table 2.3 English stops and their transcription

Place of articulation			*Transcription*
Bilabial			
Oral	Voiceless	span	[p]
	Voiced	ban	[b]
Nasal	(Voiced)	man	[m]
Alveolar			
Oral	Voiceless	stun	[t]
	Voiced	done	[d]
Nasal	(Voiced)	none	[n]
Velar			
Oral	Voiceless	scold	[k]
	Voiced	gold	[g]
Nasal	(Voiced)	long	[ŋ]
Glottal			
	Voiceless	uh-oh	[ʔ]

sonants sonorous. Because they are sonorous, in contrast with other stops, nasal consonants are usually treated separately from other stops. (This will be explained in more detail in Chapter 3, Section 4.)

The nasal stops in English are articulated with a closure of articulators at the bilabial, alveolar, and velar points of articulation, as shown in the words in Table 2.3. Note that [ŋ] does not occur word-initially in English.

A Grid for Stops

Table 2.4 presents a grid on which the stop consonants of English are arranged according to point of articulation. As you can see, each nonnasal stop, with one exception, has voiced and voiceless counterparts. The glottal stop is always voiceless. It is produced with the vocal folds drawn firmly together; since no air can pass through the glottis, the vocal folds cannot be set in motion. The nasal stops, on the other hand, are all voiced in English.

Table 2.4 English stop consonants

		Bilabial	*Alveolar*	*Velar*	*Glottal*
Nonnasal	Voiceless	[p]	[t]	[k]	[ʔ]
	Voiced	[b]	[d]	[g]	
Nasal	(Voiced)	[m]	[n]	[ŋ]	

5.3 Fricatives

Fricatives are consonants produced with a continuous airflow through the mouth. They belong to a large class of sounds called **continuants** (a class that also includes vowels and glides), all of which share this property. The fricatives form a special class of continuants; during their production, they are accompanied by a continuous audible noise because the air used in their production passes through a very narrow opening either at the glottis or in the vocal tract.

English Fricatives

English has voiceless and voiced labiodental fricatives at the beginning of the words *fat* and *vat,* voiceless and voiced interdental fricatives word-initially in the words *thin* and *those,* alveolar fricatives word-initially in *sing* and *zip,* and a voiceless alveopalatal fricative word-initially in *ship.* The voiced alveopalatal fricative is rare in English. It is the first consonant in the word *azure* and is also heard in the words *pleasure* and *rouge.* The voiceless glottal fricative of English is heard in *hotel* and *hat.* See the transcription of English fricatives in Table 2.5.

Special note must be taken of the alveolar fricatives [s] and [z]. There are two ways that English speakers commonly produce these sounds. Some speakers raise the tongue tip to the alveolar ridge (or to just behind the upper front teeth) and allow the air to pass through a grooved channel in the tongue. Other speakers form this same channel using the blade of the tongue; the tip is placed behind the lower front teeth.

Table 2.5 The transcription of English fricatives

Glottal state	*Point of articulation*	*Transcription*
	Labiodental	
Voiceless	fan	[f]
Voiced	van	[v]
	Interdental	
Voiceless	thin	[θ]
Voiced	then	[ð]
	Alveolar	
Voiceless	sun	[s]
Voiced	zip	[z]
	Alveopalatal	
Voiceless	ship	[ʃ]
Voiced	azure	[ʒ]
	Glottal	
Voiceless	hat	[h]

A Grid for Fricatives

Table 2.6 presents a grid on which the fricative consonants of English are arranged according to point of articulation. As in Table 2.5, dentals are not distinguished from alveolars, since most languages have sounds with either one or the other point of articulation, but not both.

Table 2.6 English fricatives

	Labiodental	*Interdental*	*Alveolar*	*Alveopalatal*	*Glottal*
Voiceless	[f]	[θ]	[s]	[ʃ]	[h]
Voiced	[v]	[ð]	[z]	[ʒ]	

5.4 Affricates

When a stop articulation is released, the tongue moves rapidly away from the point of articulation. However, some noncontinuant consonants show a slow release of the closure; these sounds are called **affricates**. English has only two affricates, both of which are alveopalatal. They are heard word-initially in *church* and *jump,* and are transcribed as [tʃ] and [dʒ], respectively.

A Grid for Affricates

Table 2.7 presents a grid showing the two English affricates.

Table 2.7 English affricates

	Alveopalatal (= IPA Palatoalveolar)
Voiceless	[tʃ]
Voiced	[dʒ]

Stridents and Sibilants

At the beginning of this chapter, it was noted that acoustic as well as articulatory criteria are sometimes used in describing speech sounds. An acoustic criterion comes into play to describe fricatives and affricates, which are subdivided into two types based on their relative loudness. The noisier fricatives and affricates are called **stridents** (see Table 2.8). Their quieter counterparts, such as [θ] or [ð], which have the same or nearly the same place of articulation, are considered **nonstrident**. Stridents are also known as **sibilants**.

Table 2.8 Strident fricatives and affricates in English

Place of articulation	*Strident*	
	Voiceless	*Voiced*
Alveolar	[s]	[z]
Alveopalatal	[ʃ]	[ʒ]
	[tʃ]	[dʒ]

5.5 Voice Lag and Aspiration

After the release of certain voiceless stops in English, you can hear a lag or brief delay before the voicing of a following vowel. Since the lag in the onset of vocalic voicing is accompanied by the release of air, the traditional term for this phenomenon is **aspiration**. It is transcribed with a small raised [ʰ] after the aspirated consonant (a narrower transcription of English will show aspiration). Table 2.9 provides some examples of aspirated and unaspirated consonants in English (some vowel symbols are introduced here as well). Notice that the sounds that have both aspirated and unaspirated varieties are all voiceless stops. In other languages, voiceless fricatives and affricates may also be aspirated or unaspirated.

Table 2.9 Aspirated and unaspirated consonants in English

Aspirated		*Unaspirated*	
[pʰæt]	pat	[spæt]	spat
[tʰʌb]	tub	[stʌb]	stub
[kʰowp]	cope	[skowp]	scope

Figure 2.4 shows how aspiration of a voiceless consonant takes place, using the aspirated consonant [pʰ] as an example. Though the sequence of articulations takes place continuously, the figure illustrates only certain moments.

Figures 2.5 and 2.6 show the relation between articulation and voicing for unaspirated and voiced consonants. The unaspirated consonant, such as the [p] of English *spill,* shows voicing of the vowel starting very soon after release of the consonant articulation. The voiced initial [b] of English *bill* shows voicing starting just before the release of the bilabial articulation. In Figure 2.6, note how voicing precedes the release of the labial articulators.

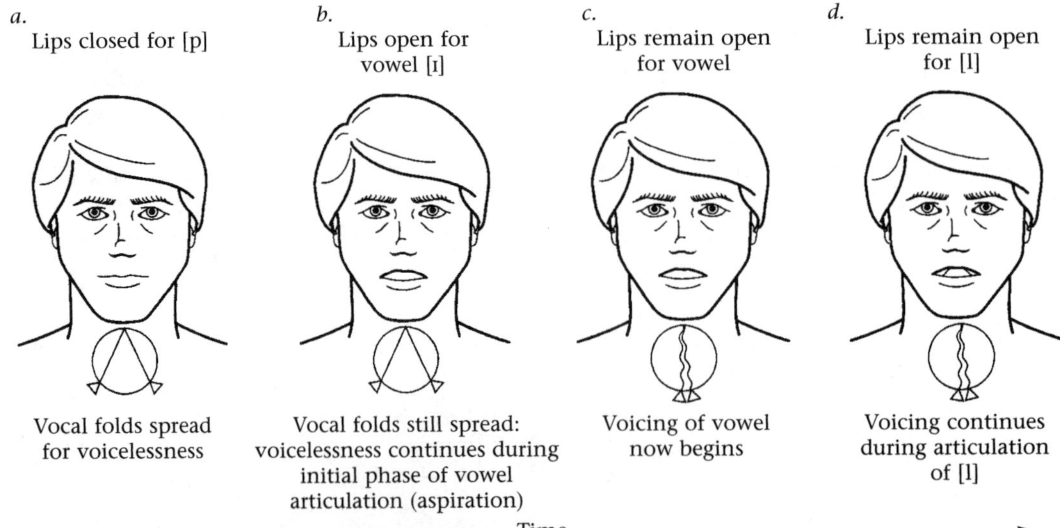

Figure 2.4 Aspirated consonant production (English *pill*)

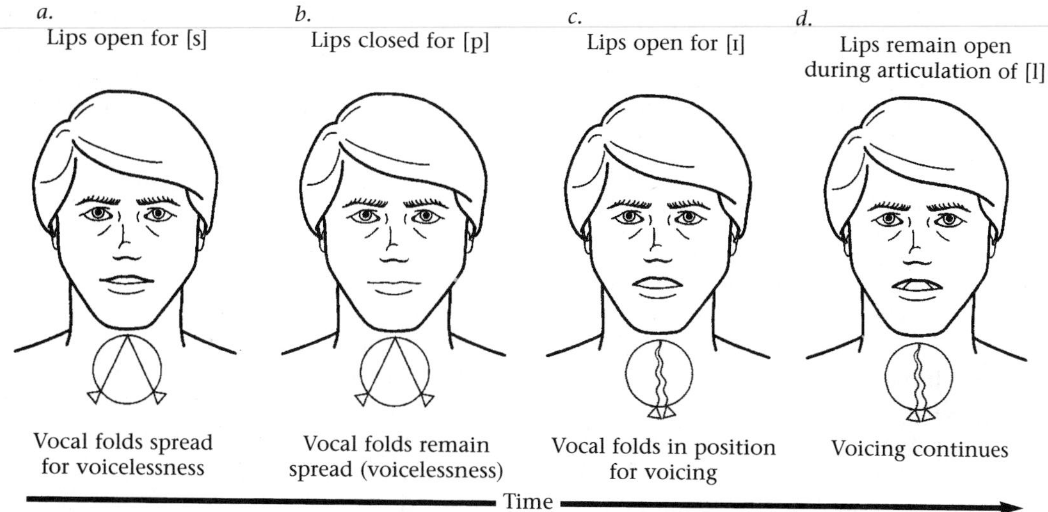

Figure 2.5 Unaspirated consonant production (English *spill*)

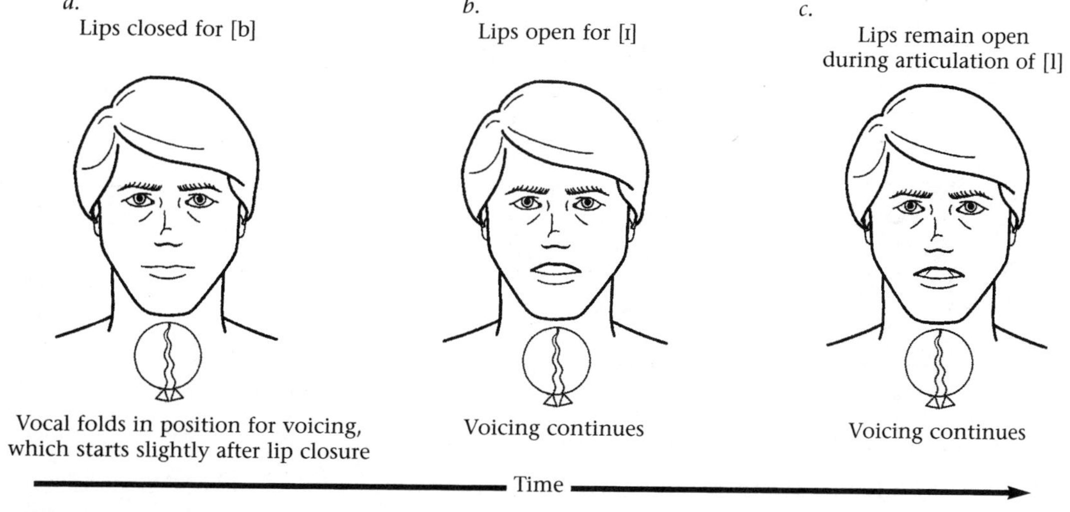

Figure 2.6 Voiced consonant release (English *bill*)

5.6 Liquids

Among the sounds commonly found in the world's languages are *l* and *r* and their numerous variants. They form a special class of consonants known as **liquids**.

Laterals

Varieties of *l* are called **laterals**. As laterals are articulated, air escapes through the mouth along the lowered sides of the tongue. When the tongue tip is raised to the dental or alveolar position, the dental or alveolar laterals are produced. Both may be transcribed as [l].

Because laterals are generally voiced, the term *lateral* used alone usually means 'voiced lateral'. Still, there are instances of voiceless laterals in speech. The voiceless dental or alveolar lateral is written with an additional phonetic symbol, called a *diacritic*. In this case, the diacritic is a circle beneath the symbol: [l̥]. Voiceless laterals can be heard in the pronunciation of the English words *please* and *clear.*

English *r'*s

Numerous varieties of *r* are also heard in the world's languages. This section describes the types found in English.

The *r* of English as it is spoken in the United States and Canada is made either by curling the tongue tip back into the mouth or by bunching the tongue upward and back in the mouth. This *r,* which is known as a **retroflex** *r,* is heard in *ride* and *car.* In a broad transcription, the symbol [r] can be used for the English *r* as well as *r*'s in other languages. However, in narrower IPA transcription, [r] is reserved for a trilled *r,* as in Spanish *perro* 'dog'. The IPA transcription for the retroflex *r* is [ɹ], and that is the symbol we will use in this book for the English *r.*

Another sound commonly identified with *r* is the **flap**. The flap is produced when the tongue tip strikes the alveolar ridge as it passes across it. It is heard in the North American English pronunciation of *bitter* and *butter,* and in some British pronunciations of *very.* It is commonly transcribed as [ɾ] and is generally voiced. Table 2.10 presents the liquids *r, l,* and the flap of American English.

Table 2.10 English liquids

		Alveolar	
Laterals		voiced	[l]
		voiceless	[l̥]
*r'*s	retroflex	voiced	[ɹ]
		voiceless	[ɹ̥]
	flap		[ɾ]

5.7 Syllabic Liquids and Nasals

Liquids and nasals are more sonorous than other consonants and in this respect are more like vowels than are the other consonants. In fact, they are so sonorous that they may function as syllabic nuclei. When they do so, they are called **syllabic liquids** and **syllabic nasals** (see Table 2.11). Syllabic liquids and nasals are found in many of the world's languages, including English. In transcription, they are usually marked with a short diacritic line underneath. Unfortunately for beginning linguistics students, linguists are not always consistent here, and there is some dialectal variation as well. A broad transcription simply uses schwa plus the liquid or nasal. In this book, we will transcribe a nasal as syllabic in English when it occurs in an unstressed syllable at the end of a word after a stop, affricate, or fricative. We will transcribe a liquid as syllabic in English when it occurs in an unstressed syllable at the end of a word after any consonant. We will also use the syllabic *r* [ɹ̩] in words like *bird, earth,* and *girl.*

Table 2.11 Syllabic liquids and nasals in English

	Syllabic		*Nonsyllabic*
bottle	[bɑɾl̩]	lift	[lɪft]
funnel	[fʌnl̩]	pill	[pʰɪl]
bird	[bɹ̩d]	rat	[ɹæt]
her	[hɹ̩]	car	[kʰɑɹ]
button	[bʌtn̩]	now	[naw]
'm-m'	[ʔm̩ʔm̩] (meaning 'no')	mat	[mæt]

For other ways of transcribing these sounds and others, go to **bedfordstmartins .com/linguistics/phonetics** and click on **transcription**.

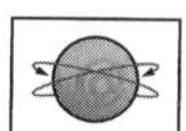

5.8 Glides

Recall that a glide is a very rapidly articulated nonsyllabic segment. The two glides of American English are the jod [jɑd] [j] of *y̲es* and *boy̲*, and the w-glide [w] of *w̲et* and *now̲*.

The [j] is a palatal glide whose articulation is virtually identical to that of the vowel [i] of *se̲e̲*. You can verify this by pronouncing a [j] in an extended manner; it will sound very close to an [i].

The glide [w] is made with the tongue raised and pulled back near the velum and with the lips protruding, or rounded. For this reason, it is sometimes called a labio-velar. The [w] corresponds closely in articulation to the vowel [u] of *who̲*. This can be verified by extending the pronunciation of a [w]. We will consider [w] a rounded velar glide for purposes of description. Some speakers of English also have a voiceless (labio)-velar glide, transcribed [ʍ], in the words *wh̲en*, *wh̲ere*, and *wh̲ich* (but not in *witch*).

Table 2.12 provides a summary of the places and manners of articulation of English consonants.

Table 2.12 English consonants: places and manners of articulation

		Place of articulation							
Manner of articulation		*Labial*	*Labiodental*	*Interdental*	*Alveolar*	*Alveopalatal*	*Palatal*	*Velar*	*Glottal*
Stop	voiceless	p			t			k	ʔ
	voiced	b			d			g	
Fricative	voiceless		f	θ	s	ʃ			h
	voiced		v	ð	z	ʒ			
Affricate	voiceless					tʃ			
	voiced					dʒ			
Nasal	voiced	m			n			ŋ	
Liquid	voiced lateral				l				
	voiced retroflex				ɹ				
Glide	voiced	w					j	w	
	voiceless	ʍ						ʍ	

6 Vowels

Vowels are sonorous, syllabic sounds made with the vocal tract more open than it is for consonant and glide articulations. Different vowel sounds (also called **vowel qualities**) are produced by varying the placement of the body of the tongue and shaping the lips. The shape of the vocal tract can be further altered by protruding the lips to produce rounded vowels, or by lowering the velum to produce a nasal vowel. Finally, vowels may be tense or lax, depending on the degree of vocal tract constriction during their articulation.

The following section on vowels introduces most of the basic vowels of English. Some phonetic detail is omitted that will be introduced in the following chapter.

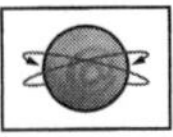

Note that vowels are particularly subject to dialectal variation. For examples of how American dialects vary, go to **bedfordstmartins.com/linguistics/phonetics** and click on **American dialects**.

6.1 Simple Vowels and Diphthongs

English vowels are divided into two major types, **simple vowels** and **diphthongs**. Simple vowels do not show a noticeable change in quality during their articulation. The vowels of *pit, set, cat, dog, but, put,* and the first vowel of *suppose* are all simple vowels.

Diphthongs are vowels that exhibit a change in quality within a single syllable. English diphthongs show changes in quality that are due to tongue movement away from the initial vowel articulation toward a glide position. This change in vowel quality is clearly perceptible in words such as *say, buy, cow, ice, lout, go,* and *boy*. (For some English speakers, there is also a change in vowel quality in the vowels of words like *heed* and *lose*, but this change is less easy to hear. Because the glides on these vowels are quite weak and are not produced by all speakers, we do not show the vowels in *heed* and *lose* as diphthongs.) Table 2.13 presents the simple vowels and diphthongs of English. The diphthongs are transcribed as vowel-glide sequences.

Table 2.13 Some simple vowels and diphthongs of American English

Simple vowel		*Diphthong*	
pit	[ɪ]		
set	[ɛ]	say	[ej]
put	[ʊ]		
bought	[ɔ]	grow	[ow]
cut	[ʌ]		
mat	[æ]	my	[aj]
pot	[ɑ]	now	[aw]

In all cases, the diphthongs are somewhat longer than the simple vowels. Notice that the diphthongs [aj] and [aw] are transcribed with a low back unrounded vowel symbol [a] that is different from the one used to transcribe the vowel of, say, *ah:* [ɑ]. The symbol [a] represents a vowel that is made further forward in the mouth than [ɑ].

Try to pronounce the vowel [ɑ] in place of the [a] in these diphthongs; you will hear why a different vowel symbol is needed.

6.2 Basic Parameters for Describing Vowels

Vowel articulations are not as easy to feel at first as consonant articulations, since the vocal tract is not narrowed as much. To become acquainted with vowel articulation, alternately pronounce the vowels of *he* and *ah*. You will feel the tongue move from a **high** front to a **low** back position. Once you feel this tongue movement, alternate between the vowels of *ah* and *at*. You will feel the tongue moving from the low **back** to low **front** position. Finally, alternate between the vowels of *he* and *who*. You will notice that in addition to a tongue movement between the high front and high back position, you are also **rounding** your lips for the [u]. Figure 2.7 shows a midsagittal view of the tongue position for the vowels [i], [ɑ], and [u] based on X-ray studies of speech.

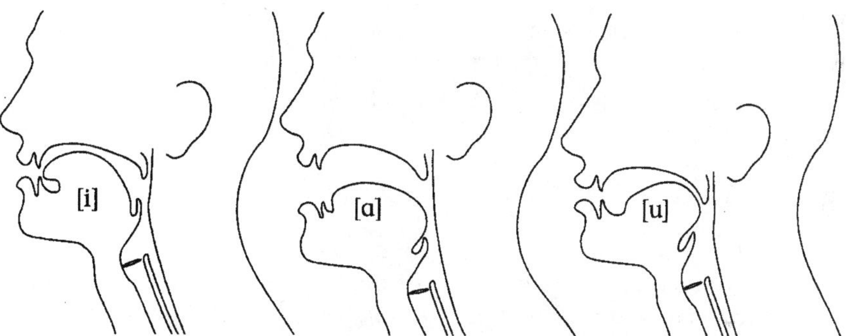

Figure 2.7 Tongue position and transcription for three English vowels

Vowels for which the tongue is neither raised nor lowered are called **mid vowels**. The front vowel of English *made* or *fame* is mid, front, and unrounded. The vowel of *code* and *soak* is mid, back, and rounded. In the case of diphthongs, the articulatory descriptions refer to the tongue position of the vowel nucleus. The vowels presented so far in this section are summed up in Table 2.14. Note that in describing the vowels, the articulatory parameters are presented in the order *height, backness, rounding*.

Table 2.14 Basic phonetic parameters for describing American English vowels

heat	[i]	high front unrounded
fate	[ej]	mid front unrounded
mad	[æ]	low front unrounded
Sue	[u]	high back rounded
boat	[ow]	mid back rounded
caught	[ɔ]	mid back rounded
sun	[ʌ]	mid back unrounded
cot	[ɑ]	low back unrounded

As Table 2.14 shows, the vowel of *caught* (and certain other words such as *law*) is the mid back rounded lax vowel [ɔ] in many dialects of English, both in the United States and worldwide. However, in some dialects of North American English, the vowel [ɔ] has merged with the vowel [ɑ], and there is, therefore, no difference between *cot* and *caught;* the vowel in both words is [ɑ].

Tongue positions for these vowels are illustrated in Figure 2.8. The trapezoid corresponds roughly to the space within which the tongue moves, which is wider at the top of the oral cavity and more restricted at the bottom. Nonfront vowels are traditionally divided into central and back vowels (see Figures 2.8 and 2.9); often the term *back* alone is used for all nonfront vowels.

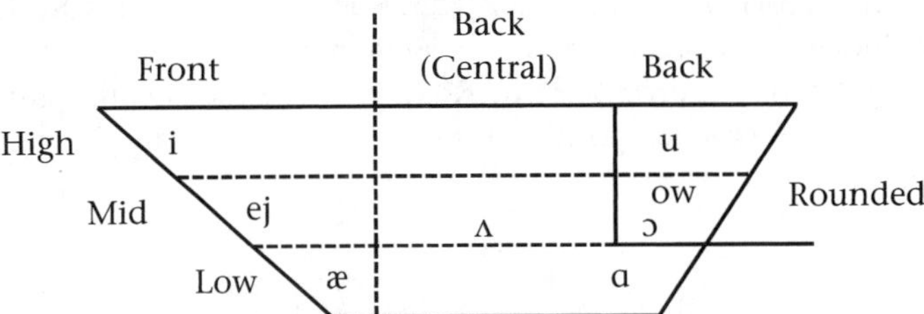

Figure 2.8 Basic tongue positions for English vowels

6.3 Tense and Lax Vowels

All the vowels illustrated in Figure 2.8 except [æ], [ʌ], and [ɔ] are **tense vowels**; they are produced with a placement of the tongue that results in greater vocal tract constriction than that of nontense vowels; as well, tense vowels are longer than nontense vowels. Some vowels of English are made with roughly the same tongue position as the tense vowels, but with a less constricted articulation; they are called **lax vowels**. The representation of vowels and their articulatory positions (Figure 2.8) is expanded in Figure 2.9 to include both tense and lax vowels.

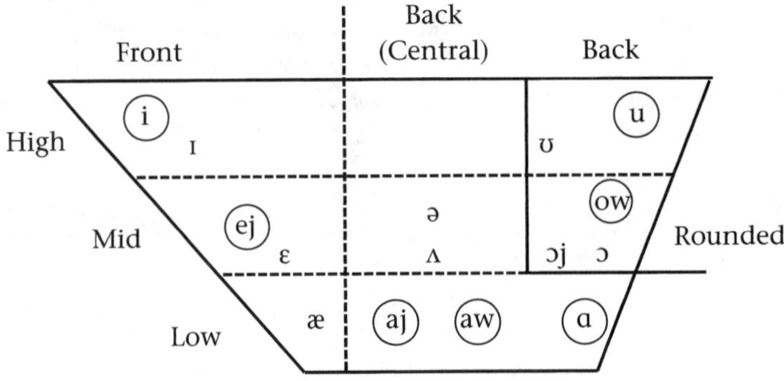

Figure 2.9 American English vowels (tense vowels are circled)

Table 2.15 provides examples from English comparing tense and lax vowels. Note that not all the vowels come in tense/lax pairs.

Table 2.15 Tense and lax vowels in American English

Tense		*Lax*	
heat	[i]	hit	[ɪ]
mate	[ej]	met	[ɛ]
—	—	mat	[æ]
shoot	[u]	should	[ʊ]
coat	[ow]	caught	[ɔ] (in some dialects)
		boy	[ɔj] (in some dialects)
—	—	cut	[ʌ]
—	—	Canada	[ə]
lock	[ɑ]	—	—
lies	[aj]		
loud	[aw]		

The difference between two of the vowels illustrated in Table 2.15 is often not easy to hear at first. Both the vowel [ʌ] in *cut, dud, pluck,* and *Hun,* and the vowel [ə] of *Canada, about, tomahawk,* and *sofa* are mid, back, unrounded, and lax. The vowel of the second set of examples, called **schwa**, is referred to as a **reduced vowel**. In addition to being lax, it has a very brief duration (briefer than that of any of the other vowels).

There is a simple test that helps determine whether vowels are tense or lax. In English, monosyllabic words spoken in isolation do not end in lax vowels (except for [ɔ]). We find *see* [si], *say* [sej], *Sue* [su], *so* [sow], and *spa* [spɑ] in English, but not *s[ɪ], *s[ɛ], *s[æ], *s[ʊ], or *s[ʌ]. Schwa, however, frequently appears in unstressed positions in polysyllabic words like *sof*[ə] and *Can*[ə]*d*[ə]. It should be pointed out—especially for those who think their ears are deceiving them—that some speakers produce the final vowel in the last two examples as [ʌ] and not as [ə].

This rather formidable crowd of vowels should not intimidate you. If you are a native speaker of English, you have been using these vowels (and others, some of which you will be introduced to in the next chapter) most of your life. Learning to hear them consciously and transcribe them is not a difficult task. The next section provides more examples of the transcription of English consonants and vowels.

7 Phonetic Transcription of American English Consonants and Vowels

Tables 2.16 and 2.17 present the phonetic symbols for consonants and vowels commonly used to transcribe American English. To illustrate how each symbol is used, one word is transcribed completely, and then some other words in which the same sound is found are given. You will notice that in the example words, the spelling of the sound may vary. Be careful of this when you transcribe words phonetically—the sound of a word, not its spelling, is what is transcribed!

Table 2.16 Transcribing English consonants

	Symbol	*Word*	*Transcription*	*More examples*
Stops	[p]	spit	[spɪt]	spar, crispy, upper, culprit, bumper
	[b]	bib	[bɪb]	boat, liberate, rob, blast
	[t]	stuck	[stʌk]	stem, hunter, nasty, mostly
	[d]	dip	[dɪp]	dust, sled, draft
	[k]	skip	[skɪp]	scatter, uncle, blacklist, likely
	[g]	get	[gɛt]	gape, mugger, twig, gleam
Aspirated Stops	[pʰ]	pit	[pʰɪt]	pain, upon, apart
	[tʰ]	tick	[tʰɪk]	tell, attire, terror, tutu
	[kʰ]	keep	[kʰip]	cow, kernel, recur
Affricates	[tʃ]	chip	[tʃɪp]	lunch, lecher, ditch, belch
	[dʒ]	judge	[dʒʌdʒ]	germ, journal, budge, wedge
Fricatives	[f]	fit	[fɪt]	flash, coughing, proof, phlegmatic, gopher
	[v]	vat	[væt]	vote, oven, prove
	[θ]	thick	[θɪk]	thought, ether, teeth, three, bathroom
	[ð]	though	[ðow]	then, bother, teethe, bathe
	[s]	sip	[sɪp]	psychology, fasten, lunacy, bass, curse, science
	[z]	zap	[zæp]	Xerox, scissors, desire, zipper, fuzzy
	[ʃ]	ship	[ʃɪp]	shock, nation, mission, glacier, wish
	[ʒ]	rouge	[ruʒ]	measure, azure, visual, garage (for some speakers)
	[h]	hat	[hæt]	who, ahoy, forehead, behind
Nasals	[m]	moat	[mowt]	mind, humor, shimmer, sum, thumb
	[n]	note	[nowt]	now, winner, angel, sign, wind
	[ŋ]	sang	[sæŋ]	singer, longer, bank, twinkle, speaking
Syllabic Nasals	[m̩]	m-m	[ʔm̩ʔm̩]	bottom, prism
	[n̩]	button	[bʌtn̩]	Jordan, fatten
Liquids	[l]	leaf	[lif]	loose, lock, alive, hail
	[ɹ]	reef	[ɹif]	rod, arrive, tear
Flap	[ɾ]	hitting	[hɪɾɪŋ]	butter, madder, writer, rider, pretty, amity
Syllabic Liquids	[l̩]	huddle	[hʌdl̩]	bottle, needle (for many speakers)
	[ɹ̩]	bird	[bɹ̩d]	early, hurt, stir, purr, doctor, leader
Glides	[j]	yet	[jɛt]	_use, c_ute, yes
	[w]	witch	[wɪtʃ]	wait, weird, queen, now
	[ʍ]	which	[ʍɪtʃ]	what, where, when (only for some speakers)

Table 2.17 Transcribing English vowels

Symbol	*Word*	*Transcription*	*More examples*
[i]	fee	[fi]	she, cream, believe, receive, serene, amoeba, highly
[ɪ]	fit	[fɪt]	hit, income, definition, been (for some speakers)
[ej]	fate	[fejt]	they, clay, grain, gauge, engage, great, sleigh
[ɛ]	let	[lɛt]	led, head, says, said, sever, guest
[æ]	bat	[bæt]	panic, racket, laugh, Nantucket
[u]	boot	[but]	do, two, loose, brew, Louise, Lucy, through
[ʊ]	book	[bʊk]	should, put, hood
[ow]	note	[nowt]	no, throat, though, slow, toe, oaf, O'Conner
[ɔ]	fought	[fɔt]	caught, normal, all
[ɔj]	boy	[bɔj]	voice, boil, toy
[ɑ]	rob	[ɹɑb]	cot, father, body
[ʌ]	shut	[ʃʌt]	other, udder, tough, lucky, what, flood
[ə]	suppose	[səpʰowz]	collide, hinted, telegraph, about
[aw]	crowd	[kɹawd]	(to) house, plow, bough
[aj]	lies	[lajz]	my, tide, thigh, buy

8 Suprasegmentals

All phones have certain inherent **suprasegmental** or **prosodic properties** that form part of their makeup no matter what their place or manner of articulation. These properties are **pitch**, **loudness**, and **length**.

All sounds give us a subjective impression of being relatively higher or lower in pitch. Pitch is the auditory property of a sound that enables us to place it on a scale that ranges from low to high. Pitch is especially noticeable in sonorous sounds like vowels, glides, liquids, and nasals. Even stop and fricative consonants convey different pitches. This is particularly noticeable among the fricatives, as you can hear by extending the pronunciation of [s] and then of [ʃ]; the [s] is clearly higher pitched. All sounds have some degree of intrinsic loudness as well or they could not be heard. Moreover, all sounds occupy a certain stretch of time—they give the subjective impression of length.

8.1 Pitch: Tone and Intonation

Speakers of any language have the ability to control the level of pitch in their speech. This is accomplished by controlling the tension of the vocal folds and the amount of air that passes through the glottis. The combination of tensed vocal folds and greater air pressure results in higher pitch on vowels and sonorant consonants, while less tense vocal folds and lower air pressure result in lower pitch. Two kinds of controlled pitch movement found in human language are called **tone** and **intonation**.

Tone

A language is said to have tone or be a **tone language** when differences in word meaning are signaled by differences in pitch. Pitch on forms in tone languages functions very differently from the movement of pitch in a nontone language. When a speaker of English says *a car?* with a rising pitch, the word *car* does not mean anything different from the same form pronounced on a different pitch level or with a different pitch contour. In contrast, when a speaker of a tone language such as Mandarin pronounces the form *ma* [mà] with a falling pitch, it means 'scold', but when the same form (*ma*) is pronounced with a rising pitch, as [má], the meaning is 'hemp' (see Figure 2.12). There is no parallel to anything like this in nontone languages such as English and French.

Unlike the preceding Mandarin falling or rising tone examples, some languages show only what are known as level tones. Sarcee, an Athabaskan language spoken in Alberta, Canada, has high, mid, and low pitch level tones. In Figure 2.10, the uppercase letters H, M, and L stand for high, mid, and low tones, respectively. An **association line** drawn from the letters to the vowel links the segments with their respective tones. This is an example of **autosegmental notation**.

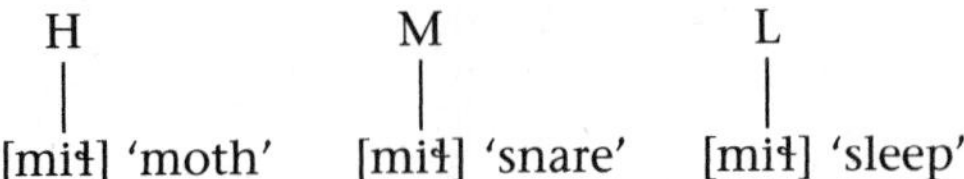

Figure 2.10 Sarcee level tones ([ɬ] is a voiceless lateral fricative)

Level tones that signal meaning differences are called **register tones**: two or three register tones are the norm in most of the world's register tone languages, though four have been reported for Mazatec, a language spoken in Mexico.

A single tone may be associated with more than one syllabic element. In Mende, spoken in West Africa, certain polysyllabic forms show the same tone on each syllable (in Table 2.18, the diacritic [´] indicates a high tone and the diacritic [`] indicates a low tone).

Table 2.18 High-tone and low-tone words in Mende

pɛ́lɛ́	'banana'
háwámá	'waistline'
kpàkàlì	'tripod chair'

Autosegmental notation and association lines allow us to represent the tone as characteristic of an entire form. The single underlying tone unit is associated with all vowels.

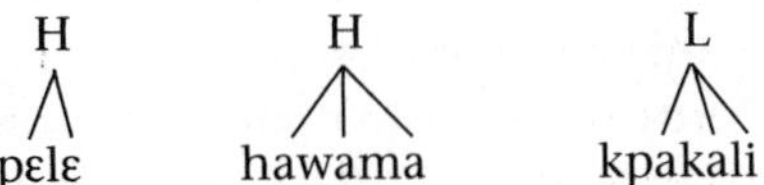

Figure 2.11 Tone as a word feature

In some languages, tones can change pitch within a single syllabic element. Moving pitches that signal meaning differences are called **contour tones**. In Mandarin, both register and contour tones are heard. Contour tones are shown by pitch level notation lines that converge above the vowel, as shown in Figure 2.12.

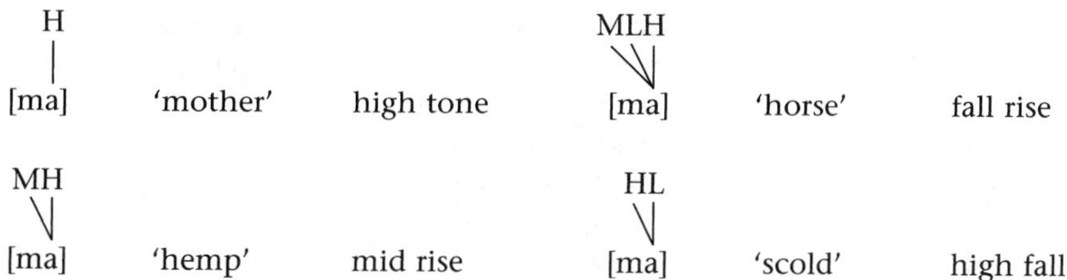

Figure 2.12 Register and contour tones in Mandarin

In Figure 2.12, there is one (high) register tone. The other tones are all contour tones.

In other languages, tone can have a grammatical function. In Bini, a language spoken in Nigeria, tone can signal differences in the tense of a verb (such as past versus present), as Figure 2.13 shows.

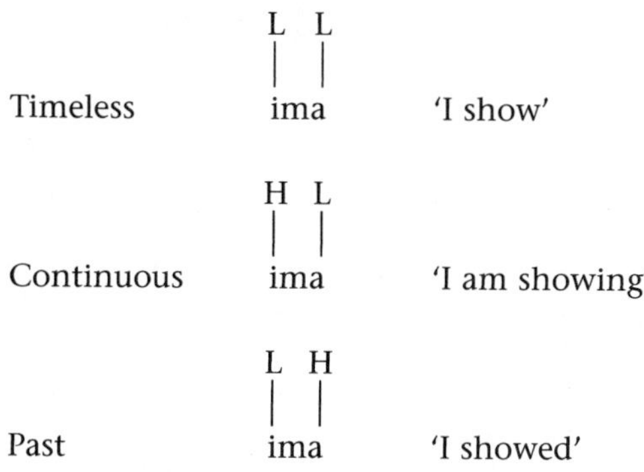

Figure 2.13 Tense and tone in Bini

Although tones may seem exotic to native speakers of Western European languages, they are very widespread. Tone languages are found throughout North and South America, sub-Saharan Africa, and the Far East.

Intonation

Pitch movement in spoken utterances that is not related to differences in word meaning is called intonation. It makes no difference to the meaning of the word *seven*, for example, whether it is pronounced with a rising pitch or a falling pitch.

Intonation often does serve to convey information of a broadly meaningful nature, however. For example, the falling pitch we hear at the end of a statement in English such as *Fred parked the car* signals that the utterance is complete. For this reason, falling intonation at the end of an utterance is called a **terminal (intonation) contour**. Conversely, a rising or level intonation, called a **nonterminal (intona-**

tion) contour, often signals incompleteness. Nonterminal contours are often heard in the nonfinal forms found in lists and telephone numbers.

In questions, final rising intonations also signal a kind of incompleteness in that they indicate that a conversational exchange is not finished. However, English sentences that contain question words like *who, what, when,* and *how* (for example, *What did you buy?*) ordinarily do not have rising intonation. It is as if the question word itself is enough to indicate that an answer is expected.

Although intonation can be represented graphically as in Figures 2.14 and 2.15, a more formal way of representing intonation is shown in Figure 2.16. Here, as in tonal representation, L and H are relative terms for differences in pitch. The letters HL are placed above the syllabic elements on which the pitch change occurs. The dotted lines indicate that the lowering pitch spreads across the remaining pitch-bearing elements.

Sally Fred Helen and Joe

two eight four two five one three

Figure 2.14 Rising nonterminal intonations in a list and a telephone number

Did you have a nice time

Figure 2.15 Nonterminal intonation in a question

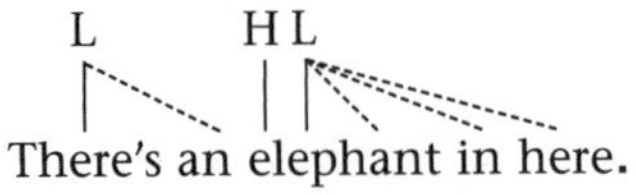

L HL

There's an elephant in here.

Figure 2.16 A terminal contour

Rising intonation on names or requests is commonly heard in addressing people. Its use indicates that the speaker is opening a conversation or that some further action is expected from the addressee, as shown in Figure 2.17.

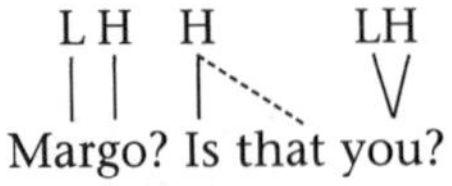

LH H LH

Margo? Is that you?

Figure 2.17 Two nonterminal contours

The complex use of intonation has just been touched on here. For example, rising intonation is often used to express politeness, as in *Please sit down.* Some linguists think that this is an extension of the open-ended mode of intonation, and that since a rising intonation indicates that further response is expected (but not demanded) of the addressee, a sentence uttered with a rising intonation sounds less like an order and so is more polite.

Intonation and Tone

Tone and intonation are not mutually exclusive. Tone languages show intonation of all types. This is possible since tones are not absolute but relative pitches. For example, a tone is perceived as high if it is high relative to the pitches around it. As long as this relative difference is maintained, the pitch distinctions will also be maintained. This is shown graphically in Figure 2.18, which represents the overall pitch of a declarative sentence in Igbo, a West African language with register tones. Note how an Igbo speaker clearly maintains the distinction among the pitch registers even as the overall pitch of the utterance falls. Each high tone is always lower than the preceding high tone, but higher than the low tone that immediately precedes it. This phenomenon is known as **downdrift**.

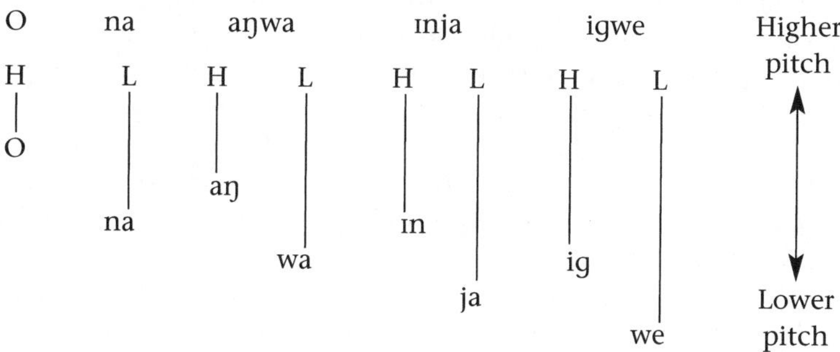

Figure 2.18 Tone and intonation: downdrift in Igbo

8.2 Length

In many languages, there are both vowels and consonants whose articulation takes longer relative to that of other vowels and consonants. This phenomenon, known as length, is widespread in the world's languages. Length is indicated in phonetic transcription by the use of an IPA style colon [ː] placed after the segment in question.

Hungarian, German, Cree, and Finnish are a few of the many languages that have long and short vowels. Yapese, a language spoken on the island of Yap in the Western Pacific, shows short and long vowels in pairs of words such as in Table 2.19.

Table 2.19 Short and long vowels in Yapese

[θis]	'to topple'	[θiːs]	'(a) post'
[pul]	'to gather'	[puːl]	'moon'
[ʔer]	'near you'	[ʔeːr]	'part of a lagoon'

Italian has short and long consonants in pairs of words such as those shown in Table 2.20. Long and short consonants are also found in many other languages, including Finnish, Turkish, and Hungarian.

Table 2.20 Short and long consonants in Italian

fato	[fatɔ]	'fate'	fatto	[fatːɔ]	'fact'
fano	[fanɔ]	'grove'	fanno	[fanːɔ]	'they do'
casa	[kasa]	'house'	cassa	[kasːa]	'box'

8.3 Stress

In any utterance, some vowels are perceived as more prominent than others. In a word such as *telegraphic* [tʰɛ̀ləɡɹǽfɪk], the two vowel nuclei that are more prominent than the others are [ɛ] and [æ]. Syllabic segments perceived as relatively more prominent are stressed. **Stress** is a cover term for the combined effects of pitch, loudness, and length—the result of which is perceived prominence. In each language, the effect of these prosodic features varies. In general, English stressed vowels are higher in pitch, longer, and louder than unstressed ones. But this is not always the case. The example word *telegraphic* could just as well be pronounced with the stressed syllables lower in pitch than the unstressed ones. The important thing is that they be prominent with respect to the syllables around them, and this is usually accomplished by a relatively large shift in one, two, or all three of the parameters of pitch, loudness, and length.

In some languages, the impression of vowel prominence results from an interaction of the prosodic parameters that is different from that found in English. In Modern Greek, for example, syllables tend to be of equal length. Stress, therefore, is manifested by a change only in pitch and loudness and not in syllable length. Tone languages do not change the pitch level or contour of tones to mark stress. In many of these languages, relative prominence is marked by exaggerating the vowel length or pitch contour.

There are various ways to mark stress in phonetic transcription. We will use an acute accent [´] placed over the vowel nucleus in question to mark the most prominent or **primary stress**, and a grave accent [`] to mark the second most prominent or **secondary stress** or stresses. (This should not be confused with the use of the same diacritics to mark tone in tone languages.) Stress can also be marked by placing numbers above the stressed vowels, usually ¹ for a primary stress and ² for a secondary stress. The word *telegraphic* can therefore be transcribed in either of the following ways:

2)

[tʰɛ̀ləɡɹǽfɪk] or [tʰɛ²ləɡɹæ¹fɪk]

The examples in Table 2.21 show some differences in English stress placement.

Table 2.21 Differing stress placement in English

(an) éxport	[ɛ́kspɔɹt]	(to) expórt	[ɛkspɔ́ɹt]
(a) présent	[pɹɛ́zn̩t]	(to) presént	[pɹəzɛ́nt]
télegràph	[tʰɛ́ləɡɹæ̀f]		
telégraphy	[tʰəlɛ́ɡɹəfì]		
tèlegráphic	[tʰɛ̀ləɡɹǽfɪk]		

To hear audio versions of differing stress placement in English words, go to **bedfordstmartins.com/linguistics/phonetics** and click on **stress placement**.

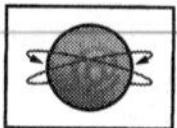

In the last four examples, you can also see that the quality of certain vowels varies depending on whether they are stressed or unstressed. This phenomenon is common in English, Russian, Palauan, and many other languages, but is not universal.

9 Speech Production

Up to this point, we have for the most part been describing phonetic segments as if they existed in isolation and did not affect one another. However, speech production is not a series of isolated events. The phenomenon is a complex one, as the articulatory organs are operating independently of each other (as we saw in Section 5.5) and many fine adjustments are carried out very rapidly as we speak. As a consequence, speech production often results in the articulation of one sound affecting that of another sound.

9.1 Coarticulation

In order to articulate a sequence of phonetic segments, we have to plan a complex series of muscular movements. Due to the rapidity of speech (we can produce many segments in a second) and the design of the vocal tract, if our goal is to produce a [pl] sequence, we cannot first make the [p] and then make the [l]. Indeed, early speech synthesizers that produced speech in this way were practically unintelligible. Rather, as the sequence [pl] is produced, the tongue tip will start to move toward the alveolar ridge *before* the lips separate. The term **coarticulation** is used for situations such as this in which more than one articulator (here the lips and the tongue tip) is active. For more detailed information on this phenomenon, please see the Web site at **bedfordstmartins.com/linguistics/phonetics** and click on **coarticulation**.

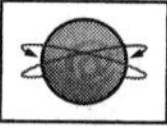

9.2 Articulatory Processes

Articulatory adjustments that occur during the production of connected speech are called **articulatory processes**. Processes change the nature of the individual segment. Their cumulative effect often results in making words easier to articulate, and in this sense they are said to make speech more efficient. For example, when speakers of English say the vowel in the word *bank,* they do not delay lowering the velum until the exact moment the nasal consonant articulation is reached. Instead, most English speakers begin lowering the velum for a nasal consonant almost as soon as they articulate the vowel that precedes it. As a result, the vowel is nasalized.

In a parallel manner, speakers pronounce [k] as more palatal (represented as [k̟]) before a high front vowel in words such as *key.* They are speaking more efficiently from the point of view of articulation since they are making a less drastic adjustment in moving from the articulation of a more palatal [k̟] to that of a high front vowel than they would make in moving from a velar [k] to a high front vowel. Even more drastically, a speaker of English who says [pɹ̥ejd] for *parade* is making a major adjustment that results in a more efficient articulation: the two syllables of a careful pronunciation of *parade* are reduced to one by dropping the unstressed vowel of the first syllable; the tongue position for [ɹ] can be anticipated during pronunciation of the [p]; and the voicelessness of the initial stop is carried on through the [ɹ̥].

Some processes appear to make articulation less, not more, efficient. For example, English speakers often lengthen consonants and vowels when they are asked to repeat a word that someone has not heard clearly. The following kind of exchange is typical.

3)

"It's Fred."
"Did you say, 'It's red'?"
"No, I said, 'Fffreeed!'"

Lengthening segments results in a greater articulatory effort, but the process results in a more distinct form that is easier to perceive.

Another process that results in more easily perceivable speech adds a segment under certain conditions. When speaking slowly and carefully in a noisy environment, for example, English speakers often insert a vowel inside a group of consonants. This breaks up the sequence of consonants into separate syllables. To judge from the use people often make of this process when they wish to be clearly understood, it may well make words easier to perceive.

4)

"Stop screaming!"
"What? Stop dreaming?"
"I said, 'Stop sc[ə]reaming!'"

These examples show that there are two basic reasons for the existence of articulatory processes. Some processes result in a *more efficient articulation* of a series of sounds in that the precise timing and coordination of speech is relaxed to various degrees. Other processes result in a *more distinct output,* which is easier to perceive than fluent or rapid everyday speech. Although these two types of processes might at first appear to be contradictory, each serves a particular end in speech production.

9.3 Some Common Articulatory Processes

Only a finite number of processes operate in language, though their end result is a great deal of linguistic variability. In this section, we survey some of the most common of these processes.

Assimilation

A number of different processes, collectively known as **assimilation**, result from the influence of one segment on another. Assimilation always results from a sound becoming more like another nearby sound in terms of one or more of its phonetic characteristics.

Nasalization of a vowel before a nasal consonant is caused by speakers anticipating the lowering of the velum in advance of a nasal segment. The result is that the preceding segment takes on the nasality of the following consonant as in [kʰæ̃nt] *can't.* This type of assimilation is known as **regressive assimilation**, since the nasalization is, in effect, moving *backward* to a preceding segment.

The nasalization of vowels following nasal consonants in Scots Gaelic is an example of **progressive assimilation**, since the nasality moves *forward* from the nasal consonant onto the vowel. It results from not immediately raising the velum after the production of a nasal stop.

Table 2.22 Progressive nasalization of vowels in Scots Gaelic

[mõːr]	'big'
[nĩ]	'cattle'
[mũ]	'about'
[nẽːl]	'cloud'

Voicing assimilation is also widespread. For many speakers of English, voiceless liquids and glides occur after voiceless stops in words such as *please* [pl̥iz], *proud* [pɹ̥awd], and *pure* [pj̊uɹ]. These sounds are said to be devoiced in this environment. **Devoicing** is a kind of assimilation since the vocal folds are not set in motion immediately after the release of the voiceless consonant closure. The opposite of devoicing is voicing. In Dutch, voiceless fricatives assimilate to the voicing of the stops that follow them, in anticipation of the voiced consonant. For example, the word *af* [ɑf] 'off, over' is pronounced with a [v] in the words *afbellen* 'to cancel' and *afdekken* 'to cover'.

Assimilation for place of articulation is also widespread in the world's languages. Nasal consonants are very likely to undergo this type of assimilation, as shown in Table 2.23. The negative form of each of these words is made with either *im* or *in.* In both cases, the form shows a nasal consonant that has the same place of articulation as the stop consonant that follows it: labial in the case of *possible* and *potent,* and alveolar in the case of *tolerable* and *tangible.* In informal speech, many English speakers pronounce words like *inconsequential* and *inconsiderate* with an [ŋ] where the spelling shows *n.* Assimilation can also be heard in pronunciations such as *A*[ŋ]*chorage* and *sy*[ɱ]*phony* (the symbol [ɱ] represents a labiodental nasal). Assimilation may even cross the boundary between words. In rapid speech, it is not uncommon to hear people pronounce phrases such as *in code* as [ɪŋkʰowd].

Table 2.23 Assimilation for place of articulation in English

possible	i<u>mp</u>ossible
potent	i<u>mp</u>otent
tolerable	i<u>nt</u>olerable
tangible	i<u>nt</u>angible

The preceding English example shows regressive assimilation for place of articulation. The following example, taken from German, shows progressive assimilation that again affects nasal consonants. In careful speech, certain German verb forms are pronounced with a final [ən], as in *laden* 'to invite', *loben* 'to praise', and *backen* 'to bake'. In informal speech, the final [ən] is reduced to a syllabic nasal, which takes on the point of articulation of the preceding consonant. (Recall that the diacritic line under the phonetically transcribed nasals indicates that they are syllabic.)

Table 2.24 Progressive assimilation in German

Careful speech		*Informal speech*	
laden	[laːdən]	[laːdn̩]	'to invite'
loben	[loːbən]	[loːbm̩]	'to praise'
backen	[bakən]	[bakŋ̍]	'to bake'

Flapping is a process in which a dental or alveolar stop articulation changes to a flap [ɾ] articulation. In American English, this process applies to both [t] and [d] that occur between vowels, the first of which is generally stressed. Flaps are heard in the casual speech pronunciation of words such as *butter, writer, fatter, wader,* and *waiter,* and even in phrases such as *I bought it* [ajbɔ́ɾɪt]. The alveolar flap is always voiced. Flapping is considered a type of assimilation because it changes a noncontinuant segment (a stop) to a continuant segment (flaps are classified as continuants) in the environment of other continuants (vowels). In addition, note that voicing assimilation also occurs in the change of the voiceless [t] to the voiced [ɾ].

Dissimilation

Dissimilation, the opposite of assimilation, results in two sounds becoming less alike in articulatory or acoustic terms. The resulting sequence of sounds is easier to articulate and distinguish. It is a much rarer process than assimilation. One commonly heard example of dissimilation in English occurs in words ending with three consecutive fricatives, such as *fifths.* Many speakers dissimilate the final [fθs] sequence to [fts], apparently to break up the sequence of three fricatives with a stop.

Deletion

Deletion is a process that removes a segment from certain phonetic contexts. Deletion occurs in everyday rapid speech in many languages. In English, a schwa [ə] is often deleted when the next vowel in the word is stressed, as shown in Table 2.25.

Table 2.25 Deletion of [ə] in English

Slow speech	*Rapid speech*	
[pʰəɹéjd]	[pɹ̥éjd]	parade
[kʰəɹówd]	[kɹ̥ówd]	corrode
[səpʰówz]	[spówz]	suppose

Deletion also occurs as an alternative to dissimilation in words such as *fifths.* Many speakers delete the [θ] of the final consonant cluster and say [fɪfs]. In very rapid speech, both the second [f] and [θ] are sometimes deleted, resulting in [fɪs].

Epenthesis

Epenthesis is a process that inserts a syllabic or nonsyllabic segment within an existing string of segments. For example, in careful speech, the words *warmth* and *something* are pronounced [wɔɹmθ] and [sʌ̃mθĩŋ] (see Table 2.26). It is common in casual speech for speakers to insert a [p] between the *m* and the *th* and pronounce the words [wɔɹmpθ] and [sʌ̃mpθĩŋ]. Consonant epenthesis of this type is another example of a coarticulation phenomenon. In English, the articulatory transition from a sonorant consonant to a nonsonorant appears to be eased by the insertion of a consonant that shares properties of both segments. Notice that the epenthesized consonants are all nonsonorant, have the same place of articulation as the sonorant consonant before them, and have the same voicing as the nonsonorant consonant after them.

Table 2.26 Some examples of English consonant epenthesis

Word	*Nonepenthesized pronunciation*	*Epenthesized pronunciation*
something	[sʌ̃mθĩŋ]	[sʌ̃mpθĩŋ]
warmth	[wɔɹmθ]	[wɔɹmpθ]
length	[lɛ̃ŋθ]	[lɛ̃ŋkθ]
prince	[pɹ̥ĩns]	[pɹ̥ĩnts]
tenth	[tɛ̃nθ]	[tɛ̃ntθ]

Vowels may also be epenthesized. In Turkish, a word may not begin with two consonants. When words are borrowed into Turkish, an epenthetic vowel is inserted between certain sequences of two initial consonants, creating a new and permissible sequence (see Table 2.27). (The reason for the differences among the vowels need not concern us here; note, though, that the vowel is always high.

Table 2.27 Vowel epenthesis in Turkish

[y] is a high front rounded tense vowel; [ʏ] is a high front rounded lax vowel; [ɯ] is a high back unrounded tense vowel

Source word	*Turkish form*
train	[ti̲ɾen]
club	[ky̲lʏp]
sport	[sɯ̲poɾ]

Metathesis

Metathesis is a process that reorders a sequence of segments. This often results in a sequence of phones that is easier to articulate. It is common to hear metathesis in the speech of children, who often cannot pronounce all the consonant sequences that adults can. For example, some English-speaking children pronounce *spaghetti* as *pesghetti* [pəskɛɾi]. In this form, the initial sequence [spə], which is often difficult for children to pronounce, is metathesized to [pəs].

The pronunciations of *prescribe* and *prescription* as *perscribe* and *perscription* are often-cited examples of metathesis in adult speech. In these cases, metathesis appears to facilitate the pronunciation of two successive consonant-*r* sequences in each word.

Vowel Reduction

In many languages, the articulation of vowels may move to a more central position when the vowels are unstressed. This process is known as **(vowel) reduction**. Typically, the outcome of vowel reduction is a schwa [ə]; this can be observed in pairs of related words that show different stress placement such as *Canada* [kʰǽnədə] versus *Canadian* [kʰənéjdiən]. Note that the first vowel of the word *Canada* is [æ] when stressed but schwa when unstressed, whereas the second vowel of the word *Canadian* is [ej] when stressed but a schwa when unstressed. Since we cannot predict what vowel a schwa may turn into when it is stressed, we assume that [æ] and [ej] are basic to the words in question and are reduced in unstressed position.

10 Other Vowels and Consonants

So far, this chapter has described only the vowels and consonants of English. Many, but not all, of these sounds are found in other languages. Moreover, many of the sounds found in other languages do not occur in English. Tables 2.28 and 2.29 introduce a number of other vowels and consonants that are relevant to the discussion and problems throughout this book. Once the basic articulatory parameters have been understood, it's not a big jump to describe and to pronounce new and unfamiliar sounds.

Table 2.28 Modified IPA chart for vowels, including the vowels of English (shaded) and many of those found in other languages. Where symbols appear in pairs, the phone on the left is unrounded, and the one on the right is rounded.

	Front	(Central)	Back
High	i y ɪ ʏ	ɨ ʉ	ɯ u ʊ
Mid	e ø ɛ œ	ə ʌ	ɤ o ɔ
Low	æ	a	ɑ ɒ

Remember that phonetic descriptions are universal—they apply to the sounds of any human language. If you encounter the description "voiced velar fricative," you know that the sound to be made is a voiced continuant consonant made (as is the stop [g]) at the velum. If you want to make this sound, the articulatory description

Table 2.29 Modified IPA chart for consonants, including the sounds of English (shaded) and many of those found in other languages. Where symbols appear in pairs, the phone on the left is voiceless, and the one on the right is voiced. The term *approximant* is used by the IPA to include glides and some liquids, in which there is a relatively free flow of air with no friction.

	Bilabial	*Labiodental*	*Interdental*	*Alveolar*	*Alveopalatal*	*Retroflex*	*Palatal*	*Velar*	*Uvular*	*Pharyngeal*	*Glottal*
Stop	p b			t d		ʈ ɖ	c ɟ	k g	q ɢ		ʔ
Fricative	ɸ β	f v	θ ð	s z	ʃ ʒ	ʂ ʐ	ç ʝ	x ɣ	χ ʁ	ħ ʕ	h ɦ
Nasal	m	ɱ		n		ɳ	ɲ	ŋ	ɴ		
Trill				r					ʀ		
Flap				ɾ							
Approximant	ʍ w ɥ			ɹ		ɻ	j ɥ	ʍ w			
Lateral Approximant				l̥ l			ʎ̥ ʎ				
Lateral Fricative				ɬ ɮ							

can guide you: make a near closure at the velum and allow airflow to pass though. If you come across the description "high front rounded vowel" and want to produce this sound, make the high front unrounded vowel [i] and then round the lips to produce the high front rounded vowel [y].

For detailed descriptions and examples of the sounds presented in Tables 2.28 and 2.29, go to the Web site at **bedfordstmartins.com/linguistics/phonetics** and click on **IPA vowels and consonants**.

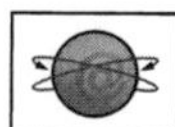

Summing Up

The study of the sounds of human language is called *phonetics*. These sounds are widely transcribed by means of the **International Phonetic Alphabet**.

The sounds of language are commonly described in **articulatory** and **acoustic** terms, and fall into two major types: syllabic sounds (**vowels**, **syllabic liquids**, and **syllabic nasals**) and nonsyllabic sounds (**consonants** and **glides**). Sounds may be **voiced** or **voiceless**, and **oral** or **nasal**. Consonants are produced at various **places of articulation**: labial, dental, alveolar, alveopalatal, palatal, velar, uvular, glottal, and pharyngeal. At the places of articulation, the airstream is modified by different **manners of articulation** and the resulting sounds are **stops**,

fricatives, or **affricates**. Vowels are produced with less drastic closure and are described with reference to tongue position (**high**, **low**, **back**, and **front**), tension (**tense** or **lax**), and lip rounding (**rounded** or **unrounded**). Language also exhibits **suprasegmental** phenomena such as **tone**, **intonation**, and **stress**.

Key Terms

General terms

acoustic phonetics
articulatory phonetics
broad transcription
diacritics
features
International Phonetic Alphabet (IPA)
narrow transcription
phones
phonetics
segments
speech sounds
syllable

Parts of the vocal tract below the mouth

glottis
larynx
pharynx
vocal folds (vocal cords)
vocal tract

Terms concerning glottal states

breathy voice
murmur
voiced (sounds)
voiceless (sounds)
whisper

Terms concerning sound classes

consonants
glides
nonsyllabic
nucleus
sonorous (sounds)
sound classes
syllabic
vowels

Terms concerning the mouth

alveolar ridge
dorsum
palate
tongue back
tongue blade
tongue body
tongue root
tongue tip
uvula
velum

Types of sounds based on places (points) of articulation

alveopalatal (palatoalveolar)
bilabial (sounds)
dentals
glottals
interdental (sounds)
labial (sounds)
labiodentals
labiovelar (sounds)
palatals
pharyngeals
places (points) of articulation
uvulars
velars

General terms concerning manners of articulation

manners of articulation
nasal phones
oral phones

Terms for consonant sounds based on manner of articulation

affricates
aspiration
continuants
flap
fricatives
laterals
liquids
nonstrident
retroflex
sibilants
stops
stridents
syllabic liquids
syllabic nasals

Terms used for vowel sounds

back
diphthongs
front
high
lax vowels
low
mid vowels
reduced vowel
rounding
schwa
simple vowels
tense vowels
vowel qualities

Terms concerning suprasegmental properties

association line
autosegmental notation
contour tones
downdrift
intonation
length
loudness
nonterminal (intonation) contour
pitch
primary stress
prosodic properties
register tones
secondary stress
stress
suprasegmental properties
terminal (intonation) contour
tone
tone language

Terms concerning sounds in context

articulatory processes
assimilation
coarticulation
deletion
devoicing
dissimilation
epenthesis
flapping
metathesis
nasalization
progressive assimilation
regressive assimilation
voicing assimilation
(vowel) reduction

For information on the sources used in this chapter, go to **bedfordstmartins.com /linguistics/phonetics** and click on **Sources**.

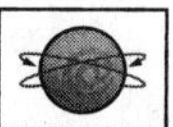

Recommended Reading

Catford, J.C. 2001. *A Practical Introduction to Phonetics*. 2nd ed. New York, NY: Oxford University Press.

Kent, R.D., and C. Read. 1993. *The Acoustic Analysis of Speech*. San Diego, CA: Singular Publishing Group.

Ladefoged, P. 2001. *A Course in Phonetics*. 4th ed. Toronto: Harcourt College Publishers.

Ladefoged, P., and I. Maddieson. 1995. *The Sounds of the World's Languages*. Cambridge, MA: Blackwell.

Pullum, G.K., and W.A. Ladusaw. 1986. *Phonetic Symbol Guide*. Chicago: University of Chicago Press.

Rogers, H. 1991. *Theoretical and Practical Phonetics*. Toronto: Copp Clark Pitman.

Shearer, William M. 1968. *Illustrated Speech Anatomy*. Springfield, IL: Charles C. Thomas.

Exercises

1. In order to become more aware of the differences between spelling and pronunciation, answer the following questions about English spelling.
   a) Find four words that show four alternative spellings of the sound [f].
   b) Find six words that have the letter <a> pronounced differently.
   c) Find four words in which different groups of letters represent only one sound.
   d) Find two words in which two different sounds are pronounced but not spelled out.

2. How many segments are there in the following words?

a) at	e) psychology
b) math	f) knowledge
c) cure	g) mailbox
d) hopping	h) awesome

3. Is the first sound in each of the following words voiced or voiceless?

a) though	e) zoom	i) huge	m) when (*may vary*)
b) thought	f) silk	j) choose	n) ghetto
c) form	g) pan	k) judge	o) pneumatic
d) view	h) boat	l) buns	p) winced

4. Using the words presented in question 3, state whether the last sound of each word is voiced or voiceless.

5. For each of the following pairs of sounds, state whether the place of articulation is the same or different. Then identify the place of articulation for each sound.

a) [s] : [l]	e) [m] : [n]	i) [b] : [f]
b) [k] : [ŋ]	f) [dʒ] : [ʃ]	j) [tʃ] : [dʒ]
c) [p] : [g]	g) [f] : [h]	k) [s] : [v]
d) [l] : [ɹ]	h) [w] : [j]	l) [θ] : [t]

6. For each of the following pairs of sounds, state whether the manner of articulation is the same or different. Then identify the manner of articulation for each sound.

a) [s] : [θ]	e) [l] : [t]	i) [ɹ] : [w]
b) [k] : [g]	f) [ð] : [v]	j) [tʃ] : [dʒ]
c) [w] : [j]	g) [tʃ] : [s]	k) [h] : [ʔ]
d) [f] : [ʃ]	h) [m] : [ŋ]	l) [z] : [dʒ]

7. After each of the following articulatory descriptions, write the sound described in phonetic brackets.

a) voiceless velar stop	e) voiced velar nasal
b) voiced labiodental fricative	f) voiceless interdental fricative
c) voiced alveopalatal affricate	g) high back rounded lax vowel
d) voiced palatal glide	h) low front unrounded vowel

8. Which of the following pairs of words show the same vowel sound in your dialect? Mark each pair as *same* or *different*. Then transcribe the vowels of each word.

a)	back	sat	h) hide	height
b)	cot	caught	i) least	heed
c)	bid	key	j) drug	cook
d)	luck	flick	k) sink	fit
e)	ooze	deuce	l) oak	own
f)	cot	court	m) pour	port
g)	fell	fail	n) mouse	cow

9. Using descriptive terms like *strident, fricative,* and so on, provide a single phonetic characteristic that all the segments in each group share. Try to avoid over-obvious answers such as "consonant" or "vowel."
Example: [b d g u m j] are all voiced.

a) [p t k g ʔ]	e) [ʌ ə ʊ a]	i) [l ɹ m n ŋ j w]
b) [i e ɛ æ]	f) [h ʔ]	j) [t d l ɹ n s z]
c) [tʃ ʒ ʃ dʒ]	g) [u o]	
d) [p b m f v]	h) [s z tʃ dʒ ʃ ʒ]	

10. Transcribe the following sets of words. You may use these words to practice transcribing aspiration.

a) tog	i) peel	q) spell
b) kid	j) stun	r) cord
c) attain	k) Oscar	s) accord
d) despise	l) cooler	t) astound
e) elbow	m) sigh	u) pure
f) haul	n) hulk	v) wheeze
g) juice	o) explode	w) remove
h) thimble	p) tube	x) clinical

11. Using H, L, and association lines, transcribe the intonation of the following English phrases. Compare your results with the transcriptions of several class-

mates. Are they the same? If they aren't, discuss what aspects of intonation (such as emotion or speech context) might account for the differences in transcription.
a) "Hi, Alice."
b) "Three people got off the bus at the last stop."
c) "My uncle likes to mountain-climb."

12. Mark primary and (where present) secondary stresses on the following words. It is not necessary to transcribe them.

a) sunny	f) arrive	k) secret
b) banana	g) defy	l) exceed
c) blackboard	h) summary	m) summery
d) Canada	i) Canadian	n) Canadianize
e) (to) reject	j) (a) reject	o) difficult

13. Find a fluent speaker of a language other than English and transcribe phonetically ten words of that language. If you encounter any sounds for which symbols are not found in this chapter, attempt to describe them in phonetic terms and then invent diacritics to help you transcribe them.

14. Name the articulatory process responsible for the change from standard Spanish to the dialectal variant in each item below.
a) [poβɾe] → [pɾoβe] (US southwestern Spanish) 'poor'
b) [grasjas] → [grasja] (Caribbean Spanish) 'thank you'
c) [gatito] → [gatiko] (Costa Rican Spanish) 'kitty'
d) [kaɾne] → [kanne] (Cuban Spanish) 'meat'
e) [pesos] → [peso̥s] (Mexican Spanish) 'pesos'
f) [estomaɣo] → [estoɣamo] (US southwestern Spanish) 'stomach'
g) [alβɾisjas] → [aβɾisjas] (US southwestern Spanish) 'gift, reward'

15. Compare the careful speech and rapid speech pronunciations of the following English words and phrases. Then, name the process or processes that make the rapid speech pronunciation different from the careful speech pronunciation. (Stress is omitted here.)

	Careful speech	*Rapid speech*
a) in my room	[ɪn maj ɹum]	[ɪm maj ɹum]
b) I see them	[aj si ðɛm]	[aj siəm]
c) I see him	[aj si hɪm]	[aj siəm]
d) within	[wɪθɪn]	[wɪðɪn]
e) balloons	[bəlunz]	[blunz]
f) careful	[kʰɛɹfʊl]	[kʰɛɹfl̩]
g) sit down	[sɪt dawn]	[sɪɾawn]
h) my advice	[maj ədvajs]	[maj əvajs]
i) Scotch tape	[skɑtʃ tʰejp]	[kʰɑtʃstejp]
j) protection	[pɹ̥owtʰɛkʃn̩]	[pɹ̩tʰɛkʃn̩]
k) hand me that	[hænd mi ðæt]	[hæ̃miðæt]
l) Pam will miss you	[pæm wɪl mɪs juw]	[pæml̩mɪʃjə]

For the Student Linguist

DON'T WORRY ABOUT SPELLING

What if you had to choose: either nobody would read and write ever again, or nobody would speak or hear language? This is a total nonchoice for me—I'd pitch out liner notes and lyric sheets in a second, but would be really upset about losing all my Ella Fitzgerald CDs. Not that it would be easy to function without reading and writing. Road signs, for example, are pretty important, and even linguistics textbooks have their uses. But the point is, I think spoken language is more fundamental than reading or writing. Let's assume it is, but let's also assume that writing is pretty important to modern society. The question, then, is how closely writing should resemble speaking.

Current spelling is much closer to the way English *used* to be spoken than the way it's spoken today, and for years various folks have been proposing spelling reforms. Would learning to read be easier if you didn't have to deal with spelling nightmares like *night, though, tough, cough, two, due, who, threw, shoe, through,* or *answer?* Some of these words are already being changed informally in advertising, pop music, and casual writing. For example, when my best friend sends me emails, she always writes *nite, tho, tuff, cough, 2, due, who, threw, shoe, thru,* and *anser.* Are these spellings any better? For someone who's learning to read English, it could be hard to figure out that *tho* and *who* aren't supposed to rhyme but *2, due, who, threw, shoe,* and *thru* are supposed to rhyme, although there's now a difference in spelling for the nonrhyming *tho* and *tuff.*

Phonetic transcription—using the IPA—is unambiguous about what rhymes with what. For every sound there's exactly one symbol (except for a couple of substitutions for different keyboards), and for every symbol there's exactly one sound. Thus the word list becomes: najt, ðow, t^{h}ʌf, k^{h}ɔf, t^{h}u, du, hu, θɹu, ʃu, θɹu, and ænsɹ̩. Making the changeover from standard spelling to IPA would be a nightmare, though. We'd have to reconfigure our keyboards, for starters. Instead of five vowel symbols (and many combinations of them) and twenty-one consonants, we'd have about eighteen vowels and twenty-five consonants.

Imagine all the changeover details could be taken care of (including instantly teaching everyone the IPA). Think about how much richer writing could be if it included all the information you get from hearing someone speak. You'd have information about the writer's regional background and class, plus information about the level of formality of the piece you were reading. Depending on how detailed the writing system was, you would be able to read all sorts of nuances of stress and intonation.

I've transcribed the same piece of dialogue in several different systems below. The first system is probably the hardest to read, and the following systems get progressively easier. Try to figure out the dialogue from the first system, checking the later ones for clarification if you get stuck. Also try to figure out the stylistic differences among the different versions of the dialogue.

1. ʃiləˀejtʰejlaɹdʒpʰʌmpkʰɪnpʰaj ˀəwɛɹðæt ˀælənwəzwɑtʃɪŋ o̥ːw̥ ˀæ̥l̥ə̥n̥ ʃisɛdbɹɛθɪli pʰæ̥sm̥i̥ ð̥i̥ w̥ɪ̥ptʰ kʰɹ̥i̥m̥ ʃilə hiwajnd ˀajmtʃɹajɪŋ tʰufɪnɪʃgɹajndɪŋðikʰɔfi
2. ʃiləˀejɾəlɑːdʒpʰʌmpkʰɪnpʰaj ˀəwɛɹðæˀæln̩wəzwɑtʃn̩ oːw ˀæln̩ ʃisɛˀbɹɛθli pʰæsmiðəwɪpkʰɹim ʃilə hiwajnd ˀajmtʃɹajn̩tʰəfɪnɪʃgɹajndn̩ðəkʰɔfi
3. ʃíləˀejɾəlɑːdʒpʰʌmpkʰɪnpʰáj ˀəwɛɹðæˀæln̩wəzwɑ́tʃn̩ oːw ˀǽln̩ ʃisɛˀbɹɛθli pʰæsmiðəwɪpkʰɹím ʃílə hiwájnd ˀajmtʃɹájn̩tʰəfɪnɪʃgɹájndn̩ðəkʰɔ́fi
4. ʃilə ejt ej laɹdʒpʰʌmpkʰɪn pʰaj ˀəwɛɹ ðæt ˀælən wəz wɑtʃɪŋ oːw ˀælən ʃi sɛd bɹɛθɪli pʰæs mi ði wɪptʰ kʰɹim ʃilə hi wajnd ˀajm tʃɹajɪŋ tʰu fɪnɪʃ gɹajndɪŋ ði kʰɔfi
5. ʃilə ejt ej laɹdʒ pʰʌmpkʰɪn pʰaj, ˀəwɛɹ ðæt ˀælən wəẓ wɑtʃɪŋ. "oːw ˀælən," ʃi sɛd bɹɛθɪli, "pʰæs mi ði wɪptʰ kʰɹim." "ʃilə," hi wajnd, "ˀajm tʃɹajɪŋ tʰu fɪnɪʃ grajndɪŋ ði kʰɔfi."

The downside of this type of writing is that there'd be so much variability. For instance, you might care about the accent or tone of a character in a novel, but do you really need to know where the journalist who wrote this morning's article on the economy was raised? And what if his or her editor were from someplace else? Whose accent would get printed? Not to mention the difficulties of something like a GRE exam or SAT test written in someone else's dialect.

Of course, the degree of variability depends on how extreme the system is. There's a wide gap between standard spelling and the fairly narrow (detailed) transcription system used in examples *1* through *3.* Writing could be more phonetic than it is now, but we don't have to force people to include every minor variation in pronunciation. We could forget about stress marks and anything to show intonation—except for a few simple things like question marks and exclamation points. We could also leave off fairly predictable things like aspiration (you'll discover how predictable aspiration is in the next chapter). Examples *4* and *5* are probably a lot easier to understand than *1* through *3,* since *4* and *5* are not as detailed (broad transcription) and, most importantly, because they have spaces between the words. Putting in spaces makes the writing less like the actual pronunciation, but it also takes away the ambiguity of figuring out whether something like [ʃilə] is supposed to be *she lo*... (as in *she locked the door*...) or *Sheila.*

In fact, the new writing system could keep punctuation, keep word spaces, and have nothing but the bare minimum to distinguish the way one word sounds from the way other words sound. The trick, then, is to figure out what the bare minimum is. It's a pretty difficult question, and before you can answer it, you'll need to read about phonology and morphology. You'll also need to figure out what exactly a word *is,* anyway. So, read the next two chapters and then come back to this section and read it again. Then devise the perfect writing system, use it for your senior thesis, patent it, market it, make a fortune off of it, and retire to a lovely little tropical island (with good food) where they don't speak English.

three

Phonology: The Function and Patterning of Sounds

Ewa Czaykowska-Higgins
Michael Dobrovolsky

A person's tongue is a twisty thing, there are plenty of words there of every kind, and the range of words is wide, and their variation.
– HOMER, *The Iliad*

OBJECTIVES

In this chaper, you will learn:

- how we know which language sounds are distinctive in a particular language
- how distinctive sounds in a particular language can vary systematically according to the context in which they occur
- how we use transcription to represent distinctive sounds and systematic variations of these sounds
- how individual sounds can be broken down further, according to specific features
- how syllables are constructed and the influence of language-specific syllable structure
- how we can construct rules to explain systematic variations in the production of sounds

We saw in Chapter 2 that human beings can produce and perceive a large number of speech sounds. No human language exploits all of these phonetic possibilities. Instead, every language makes its own particular selection from the range of all possible speech sounds and organizes them into a more or less regular system. The component of grammar that determines the selection of speech sounds and that governs both the sound patterns and the systematic phonetic variation found in language is known as **phonology**.

Speakers have (at least) some subconscious knowledge of the phonetic patterns that make up phonological systems. For example, as we saw in Chapter 1, speakers of English recognize without being taught that certain combinations of consonants are acceptable in English, even if those combinations occur in forms that are not real words, while other combinations are not acceptable; thus, *slish* and *screnk* are acceptable to English speakers, while *srish* and *screpk* are not. In fact, speakers can do more than recognize that certain forms are unnatural in their system; they can even correct unnatural forms to make them conform to the patterns that are acceptable in their own language. Without knowing exactly why, most English speakers would pronounce a form like *srish* as [səɹɪʃ], breaking up the unacceptable consonant combination with a vowel rather than, say, deleting one of the consonants to form [sɪʃ] or [ɹɪʃ]. The task of phonologists, then, is (1) to discover and describe the systematic phonetic patterns found in individual languages and (2) to discover the general principles that underlie the patterning of sounds across all human languages. In doing this, phonologists hope to uncover the largely subconscious knowledge that speakers have of sound patterns.

The existence of phonological patterns in language is a result of the organization of certain basic elements or units that combine to make up these patterns. In our discussion of phonology we will examine three major phonological units: the **feature**, the **segment**, and the **syllable**.

We are already acquainted with the idea that the flow of speech can be divided into segments and that segments are characterized by specific phonetic properties. In this chapter we will investigate the types of patterned phonetic variation that segments exhibit in individual languages and cross-linguistically. We will also learn that segments are composed of features. Features correspond to articulatory or acoustic categories such as [voice] or [strident]. They are the smallest building blocks of phonological structure, and as we will see, the types of phonological patterns found in language are directly related to the properties of the features that make up segments. Finally, we will learn about the ways in which segments combine to form syllables. Syllables consist of a syllabic element—usually a vowel—and any preceding or following segments that are associated with it. As the representation of the word *segment* in Figure 3.1 illustrates, features, segments, and syllables are organized into hierarchical levels, where each level is composed of units from the level beneath it. In Figure 3.1, *segment* is a word-level unit represented by the abbreviation *Wd*. This word in turn consists of two syllables, each of which is represented by the Greek letter σ (sigma). Each syllable itself consists of several segments. Finally, each segment is composed of features. (For purposes of illustration, only a few features are pro-

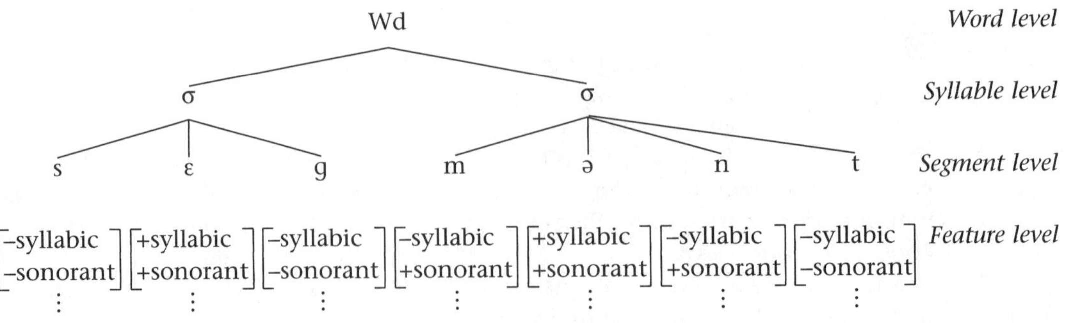

Figure 3.1 Partial phonological representation of *segment*

vided for each segment. The internal hierarchical structure of syllables and segments is not represented; these are treated later, in Sections 4.2 and 5.)

As units of phonological structure, syllables, segments, and features play major roles in the processes we investigated in the previous chapter and, in combination with certain general principles of phonology, produce the sound patterns of language. In the next sections we examine these sound patterns and the phonological knowledge that enables speakers to distinguish among forms and to deal with the systematic phonetic variation found in the pronunciation of speech sounds.

1 Segments in Contrast

All speakers know which segments of their language **contrast** and which do not. Segments are said to contrast (or to be *distinctive* or be in *opposition*) in a particular language when their presence alone may distinguish forms with different meanings from each other. For instance, the phonetically distinct segments [s] and [z] contrast in the English words *sip* and *zip,* as do the vowels in the words *hit, hate,* and *hot.*

In this section we will consider how to determine which segments contrast in a language. In Section 2 we will consider the systematic patterns associated with phonetically similar segments when they do not contrast.

1.1 Minimal Pairs

Since knowledge of segmental contrasts is fundamental to knowing any language, the first step in an analysis of the phonology of a language is to establish which sounds in that language are in contrast with each other. In order to establish contrasts, it is necessary to examine the distribution of sounds in words and to compare word meanings. The most straightforward way to accomplish this examination is by way of the **minimal pair** test.

A minimal pair consists of two forms with distinct meanings that differ by only one segment found in the same position in each form. Thus, the examples [sɪp] *sip* and [zɪp] *zip* form a minimal pair, which shows that the sounds [s] and [z] contrast in English.

A number of minimal pairs that demonstrate consonant contrasts for English are given in Table 3.1. It is important to remember that it is on the basis of *sound* and not spelling that minimal pairs are established. For purposes of analysis, contrasting words are often placed along the horizontal axis with respect to their place of articulation, reading from left to right (labial, alveolar, and so on), and vertically with respect to manner of articulation, in order to show which places and manners of articulation are exploited by the language in question.

The phonetic context in which a sound occurs is called its **environment**. Pairs of words that have segments in nearly identical environments, such as *assure* [əʃʊ́ɹ]/ *azure* [ǽʒɹ̩], which contrast [ʃ] and [ʒ], or *author* [ɔ́θɹ̩]/*either* [íðɹ̩], which contrast [θ] and [ð], are called **near-minimal pairs**. They can be used to establish contrasts if no minimal pairs for a particular set of segments can be found.

Table 3.1 Contrasts among consonants in English

Labial	*Interdental*	*Alveolar*	*Alveopalatal*	*Velar*	*Glottal*
Stops and affricates (noncontinuants)					
tap [p]		pat [t]	match [tʃ]	pick [k]	
tab [b]		pad [d]	Madge [dʒ]	pig [g]	
Continuants					
leaf [f]	thigh [θ]	sip [s]	mesher [ʃ]		hip [h]
leave [v]	thy [ð]	zip [z]	measure [ʒ]		
Nasals					
sum [m]		sun [n]		sung [ŋ]	
Liquids and glides					
			yet [j]	wet [w]	
		leer [l]	(palatal)		
		rear [ɹ]			

Once you have established the existence of a minimal or a near-minimal pair for a set of two segments, you may assume that those two segments contrast or are distinctive. Segments that contrast with each other in a particular language are said to belong to separate **phonemes** of that language. Phonemes in a particular language are heard by native speakers of that language as different and distinctive sounds. Phonemes then are contrastive phonological units. Thus, all the consonants in Table 3.1 belong to separate phonemes in English, since all of them are contrastive in the language.

When looking for the contrastive sounds of a language, it is rare to find minimal pairs for all possible pairs of sounds, since some sounds are used more frequently than others, and some do not occur in particular environments. For example, you will find no minimal pairs involving [h] and [ŋ] in word-initial or word-final position in English, because there are no words that begin with [ŋ] or end in [h]. It is also difficult to find minimal pairs in English that have the phone [ʒ], which occurs for the most part in words borrowed from French such as *azure* and *mirage.*

Vowel Contrasts in English

Vowel contrasts in English can be established with a few sets of examples. We assume in Table 3.2 that English vowel-glide sequences like [ej] and [ow] are single vowels. From this perspective, we can say that the vowels [ej] and [ɛ] or [aw] and [aj] contrast.

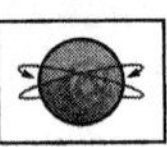

For dialectal differences in vowel contrasts in North American English, go to **bedfordstmartins.com/linguistics/phonology** and click on **American dialects.**

Table 3.2 Vowel contrasts in American English

beet	[bit]	[i]
bit	[bɪt]	[ɪ]
bait	[bejt]	[ej]
bet	[bɛt]	[ɛ]
bat	[bæt]	[æ]
cooed	[kʰud]	[u]
could	[kʰʊd]	[ʊ]
code	[kʰowd]	[ow]
cawed	[kʰɔd]	[ɔ] (for some dialects)
cod	[kʰɑd]	[ɑ]
cud	[kʰʌd]	[ʌ]
lewd	[lud]	[u]
loud	[lawd]	[aw]
lied	[lajd]	[aj]
Lloyd	[lɔjd]	[ɔj]

1.2 Language-Specific Contrasts

Whether segments contrast with each other is determined on a language-particular basis. In other words, two sounds can be phonetically distinct without necessarily being phonologically distinct or contrastive. Moreover, sounds that are contrastive in one language may not necessarily be contrastive in another. For example, the difference between the vowels [ɛ] and [æ] is crucial to English, as we can see from minimal pairs like *Ben* [bɛn] and *ban* [bæn] (see Table 3.3). But in Turkish, this difference in pronunciation is not distinctive. A Turkish speaker may pronounce the word for 'I' as [bɛn] or [bæn], and it will make no difference to the meaning.

Table 3.3 Language-specific vowel contrasts: English versus Turkish

English		*Turkish*	
[bɛn]	Ben	[bɛn]	'I'
[bæn]	ban	[bæn]	'I'

Conversely, sounds that do not contrast in English, such as long and short vowels, may be distinctive in another language. There are no minimal pairs of the type [hæt]/[hæːt] or [lus]/[luːs] in English. But in Japanese and Finnish, short and long vowels contrast, as the examples in Table 3.4 show.

Establishing the contrasting segments in a language is a first step in phonological analysis. However, in any language, there are also many sounds that never contrast. The following section deals with this aspect of phonology.

Table 3.4 Short/long vowel contrasts in Japanese and Finnish

Japanese (The symbol [ɽ] is a postalveolar flap.)			
[toɽi]	'bird'	[toɽiː]	'shrine gate'
[kibo]	'scale'	[kiboː]	'hope'
Finnish			
[tuli]	'fire'	[tuːli]	'wind'
[hætæ]	'distress'	[hæːtæː]	'to evict'

2 Phonetically Conditioned Variation: Phonemes and Allophones

Everyday speech contains a great deal of phonetic variation that speakers pay little or no attention to. Some of this variation arises from nonlinguistic factors such as fatigue, excitement, orthodontic work, gum chewing, and the like. This kind of variation is not part of the domain of phonology. But much phonetic variation is systematic. It occurs most often among phonetically similar segments and is conditioned by the phonetic context or environment in which the segments are found. This variation occurs because segments are affected and altered by the phonetic characteristics of neighboring elements or by the larger phonological context in which they occur. Speakers and listeners of any language tend to filter out this type of variation in order to focus on the contrasts that affect meaning, which is why you may never have noticed it. In this section we will consider the patterns of variation exhibited by noncontrastive sounds, how to analyze these patterns, and the conclusions that can be drawn from them.

2.1 Complementary Distribution

When first learning phonetic transcription, English speakers are often surprised that all *l*s are not identical. In Table 3.5, the *l*s in column A are voiced, while those in column B are voiceless (indicated here by the subscript ̥). Many speakers of English are unaware that they routinely produce this difference, which can be heard clearly when the words in column B are pronounced slowly.

Table 3.5 Voiced and voiceless *l* in English

A		*B*	
blue	[blu]	plow	[pl̥aw]
gleam	[glim]	clap	[kl̥æp]
slip	[slɪp]	clear	[kl̥iɹ]
flog	[flɔg]	play	[pl̥ej]
leaf	[lif]		

In fact, as it turns out, the two *l*s never contrast in English: there are no minimal pairs like [plej] and [pl̥ej] in which the phonetic difference between [l] and [l̥] functions to indicate a difference in meaning.

Moreover, when one examines the distribution of the two *l*s in English, it becomes apparent that voiced and voiceless *l*s vary systematically: all of the voiceless [l̥]s occur after the class of voiceless stops, while the voiced [l]s never occur after voiceless stops. The voicelessness of the *l*s in column B is thus a consequence of their phonetic environment. It is also a predictable property of the phonology of English in the sense that in English, only voiceless [l̥]s occur after voiceless stops.

Since no voiced [l] ever occurs in the same phonetic environment as a voiceless one (and vice versa), we say that the two variants of *l* are in **complementary distribution**. Complementary distribution means that the two sounds never occur in the same place (like Clark Kent and Superman).

In the data in Table 3.5, voiced [l] occurs in a greater number of phonetic environments (after voiced stops, voiceless fricatives, and in word-initial position) than does voiceless [l̥]. Moreover, the various environments in which voiced [l] occurs cannot be easily described, as they do not naturally fall together as a class. Therefore, when two (or more) segments are in complementary distribution, the term *elsewhere* is used, as in Table 3.6, to indicate the kind of wider distribution exhibited by [l] in Table 3.5. Specifically, we find [l̥] after voiceless stops and [l] elsewhere.

Table 3.6 Complementary distribution of [l] and [l̥] in English

	[l]	[l̥]
After voiceless stops	no	yes
Elsewhere	yes	no

In spite of these differences in phonetic environment, native speakers of English consider the two *l*s to be instances of the same segment, since they are not contrastive and are similar phonetically (they are both types of *l*s). The differences between them are systematic and predictable. We can sum up the relationship that the two *l*s bear to each other by stating that the two *l*s are *phonetically* distinct but that because of their phonetic similarity, predictable distribution, and noncontrastiveness, they are *phonologically* the same in the sound system of English.

2.2 Phonemes and Allophones

When two (or more) segments are phonetically distinct but phonologically the same, they are referred to as **allophones** (predictable variants) of one phoneme (contrastive phonological unit). The ability to group phonetically distinct sounds into phonemes is shared by all speakers of all languages. Phonologists represent this phonological knowledge formally by distinguishing two levels of representation: the **phonetic representation** that consists of predictable variants or allophones, and the **phonemic** (or phonological) **representation** that consists of the phonemes to which the allophones belong. A representation of the relationship between phonemes and their allophones is given in Figure 3.2.

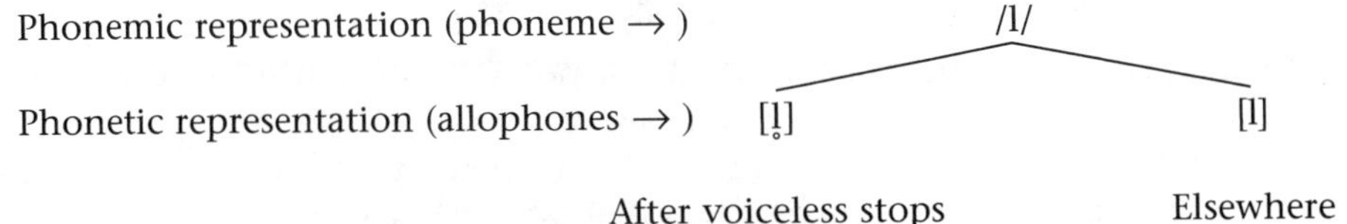

Figure 3.2 The phoneme /l/ and its allophones [l̥] and [l] in English

In Figure 3.2 the symbols for allophones are enclosed in square brackets, while the symbol for the phoneme is placed between slashes. Notice that the phoneme /l/ in Figure 3.2 is the same as its voiced allophone [l]. In most cases, the elsewhere variant or allophone of a phoneme can be chosen to represent the phoneme itself. In thinking of the difference between phonemic and phonetic representations, remember the following: Phonemes are mental representations; they represent the way in which sounds are stored in the mind. When you memorize a word, you need to remember the phonemes because they make a difference when it comes to the meaning of a word. Allophones, on the other hand, are not part of what you remember when you store a word in your mind. We have a phonological system that automatically produces the appropriate variant of a particular phoneme when you pronounce a word. Phonemes (like /l/) are in your head, but allophones (like [l] and [l̥]) come out of your mouth.

As we have seen, segments that can be considered allophones of one phoneme are phonetically similar and occur in phonetically predictable environments. In fact, it is frequently the case that allophones of one phoneme are in complementary distribution with each other. (That is, they never occur in the same environment.) Consequently, we can use the fact that allophones occur in complementary distribution as a way of testing whether or not two (or more) segments should be considered to be allophones of one phoneme.

Allophonic variation is found throughout language. In fact, every speech sound we utter is an allophone of some phoneme. An important part of phonological analysis thus deals with discovering inventories of the phonemes of languages and accounting for allophonic variation.

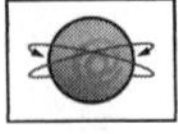

For information about some problematic distributions, go to **bedfordstmartins .com/linguistics/phonology** and click on **problematic distributions**.

2.3 Classes and Generalization in Phonology

Phonological analysis permits us to account for the great amount of phonetic variation in everyday speech. This variation, which is usually systematic, is found throughout language. Evidence of its systematic nature comes from the fact that allophones in languages pattern according to their membership in phonetic classes. This point is illustrated in Table 3.7 by comparing the patterns of distribution of *r*s and glides in English to the patterning of *l*s that was illustrated earlier in Table 3.5.

The data in Table 3.7 show that in English, voiceless [ɹ̥] occurs after voiceless stops, while voiced [ɹ] occurs elsewhere. Based on this information, we can conclude that there is an /ɹ/ phoneme in English with (at least) two allophones—one voiced, the other voiceless—and that the allophones of English /ɹ/ thus pattern like those of /l/.

Table 3.7 Voiced and voiceless allophones of English /r/

A		*B*	
brew	[bɹu]	prow	[pɹ̥aw]
green	[gɹin]	trip	[tɹ̥ɪp]
drip	[dɹɪp]	creep	[kɹ̥ip]
frog	[fɹɔg]	pray	[pɹ̥ej]
shrimp	[ʃɹɪmp]		

But if we were to stop there, we would overlook an important point. The phonemes /ɹ/ and /l/ belong to the same class of sounds: both are *liquids*. By taking this information into account, we can state a general fact about English.

1)

In English, liquids have voiceless allophones after voiceless stops, and voiced allophones elsewhere.

Now examine the data in Table 3.8.

Table 3.8 Voiced and voiceless allophones of English glides

A		*B*	
beauty	[bjuɾi]	putrid	[pj̥utɹ̥ɪd]
Duane	[dwejn]	twin	[tw̥ɪn]
Gwen	[gwɛn]	quick	[kw̥ɪk]
view	[vju]	cute	[kj̥ut]
swim	[swɪm]		
thwack	[θwæk]		

These forms demonstrate that the contrasting glides /j/ and /w/ pattern like the liquids. We can now extend our general statement even further.

2)

In English, liquids and glides have voiceless allophones after voiceless stops, and voiced allophones elsewhere.

When we consider the fact that liquids and glides all belong to the same phonetic class, namely, the class of nonnasal sonorant consonants, we can understand why the allophones of liquids and glides pattern similarly. One of the major goals of phonological description is the discovery of such broad patterns of variation, and the formulation of the most general statements possible to describe them.

2.4 Canadian Raising

Another example of allophonic variation comes from English. In most Canadian and some American dialects, pronunciations like those illustrated in Table 3.9 are common.

Table 3.9 Low and midcentral vowel allophones in raising dialects

[ajz]	eyes	[ʌjs]	ice
[lajz]	lies	[lʌjs]	lice
[tɹ̥ajd]	tried	[tɹ̥ʌjt]	trite
[tɹ̥ajb]	tribe	[tɹ̥ʌjp]	tripe
[hawz]	(to) house (verb)	[hʌws]	house (noun)
[lawd]	loud	[lʌwt]	lout
[kaw]	cow	[skʌwt]	scout
[flaj]	fly	[flʌjt]	flight

In Table 3.9, the vowels [aj] and [ʌj] are in complementary distribution. The [aj] occurs before the class of voiced consonants or in word-final position, and the [ʌj] occurs before the class of voiceless consonants. The two are allophones of a single phoneme /aj/. The same relationship holds between the vowels [aw] and [ʌw], which are allophones of /aw/ (see Figure 3.3).

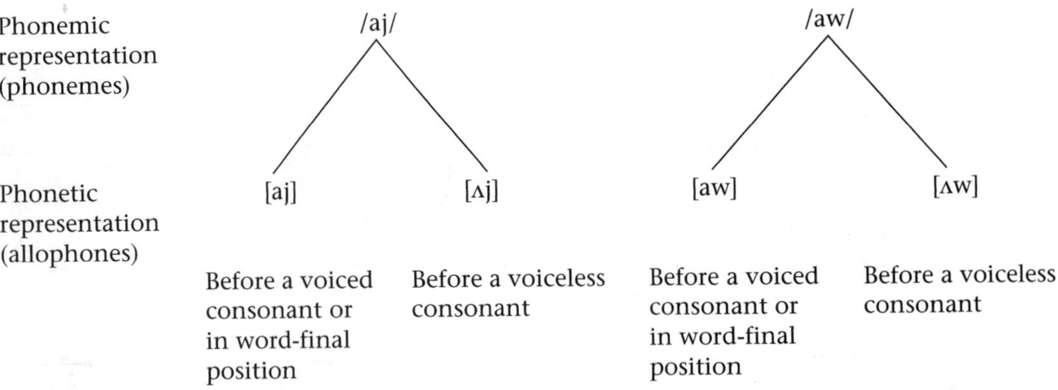

Figure 3.3 Allophones of /aj/ and /aw/ in raising dialects

Again, we see this phonological fact reflected in everyday language use. Most speakers of Canadian English, for example, find it difficult to distinguish between these allophones, even when the difference is pointed out to them. This is because the difference is not contrastive. On the other hand, many people who speak varieties of English that do not have the [ʌj] or [ʌw] allophones are very much aware of their presence in Canadian English. To them, a Canadian speaker sounds markedly different, even though they may be confused about what causes the difference.

> *I don't agree he was an American. . . . Where all other English-speaking people pronounce OU as a diphthong, the Canadian . . . makes a separate sound for each letter. The word* about, *for instance, he pronounces as* ab-oh-oot.
>
> Philip MacDonald, *The List of Adrian Messenger*

This phenomenon is sometimes referred to as Canadian Raising, since the allophones [ʌj] and [ʌw] have higher vowel components than the elsewhere variants [aj] and [aw].

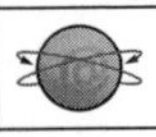

For audio examples of Canadian Raising, go to **bedfordstmartins.com/linguistics/phonology** and click on **Canadian Raising**.

2.5 English Mid Vowels and Glides

The vowels that exhibit the Canadian Raising alternation are all and only the central (unreduced) vowels of raising dialects; the two mid allophones [ʌj] and [ʌw] both occur before voiceless consonants, while the two low allophones [aj] and [aw] both occur elsewhere. Just as in the case of the liquid and glide patterns seen in Section 2.3, the allophones that participate in the Canadian Raising pattern are distributed according to their membership in phonetic classes. A final example of predictable variation that refers to classes of segments but that differs crucially from examples seen so far also comes from English.

Table 3.2 showed contrasts among English vowels. In most dialects of English, the mid tense vowels [ej] and [ow] are always diphthongized and thus end in the glide [j] or [w]. Significantly, the nonback (i.e., front) vowel [e] is always followed by the palatal glide [j], which is a nonback unrounded segment, while the back rounded vowel [o] is always followed by the labiovelar glide [w], which is a back rounded segment. These facts are summed up in Table 3.10.

Table 3.10 Tense vowel-glide combinations in English

Vowel	*Glide*			*Vowel*	*Glide*		
(both nonback and unrounded)				*(both back and rounded)*			
e	j	[fejt]	fate	o	w	[bowt]	boat
		[kejn]	cane			[kown]	cone

In other words, the occurrence of the glides following the mid tense vowels is predictable. The following generalization states the distribution of the two glides.

3)

The mid tense vowels of English are predictably followed by a glide that has the same backness and roundness as the vowel.

The data in Table 3.10 show parallels with the **allophonic distribution** we have considered so far in the sense that certain elements in it are predictable under certain systematically statable phonetic conditions. However, there is a difference between allophonic distribution and the kind of distribution exhibited by the glides. Specifically, in Table 3.10, instead of a number of variants of one phoneme, we have two segments, [ej] and [ow], that share a predictable phonetic characteristic: these mid tense vowels of English are always followed by glides of the same backness and roundness. We have seen that when certain sounds are found predictably in a given environment, they are not included in phonemic representations. Thus, although the phonetic representations of English mid vowels include the glides, the corresponding phonemic representations do not (see Figure 3.4). In other words, the phonemes in English are the simple vowels /e/ and /o/, but they are produced phonetically as the diphthongs [ej] and [ow].

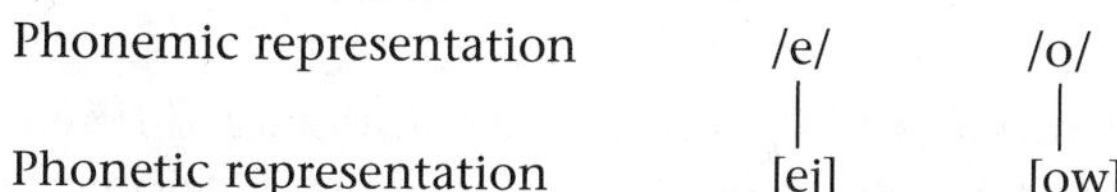

Figure 3.4 Two representations of mid vowels in English

2.6 Language-Specific Patterns

The phenomenon of allophonic variation is universal. However, just as the phonemic contrasts found in each language are specific to that language, the actual patterning of phonemes and allophones is also language-specific. Thus, whatever distribution we discover for one language may not hold true for another.

Language-Specific Variation in Allophonic Nasalization

Some languages have nasal as well as oral vowels and glides. It is usual in such languages for nasal vowel (and nasal glide) allophones to occur near nasal consonants, but as Tables 3.11 and 3.12 illustrate, the details of the patterning may vary from language to language.

In Scots Gaelic, for instance, whenever a nasal consonant occurs in a word, the vowel adjacent to it is nasalized. Glides do not get nasalized, however.

Table 3.11 Nasal and oral vowels in Scots Gaelic

[mõːɾ]	'big'
[nĩ]	'cattle'
[nẽːl]	'cloud'
[mũ]	'about'
[ɾũːn]	'secret'
[ʃalak]	'hunting'

The generalization governing the distribution of nasal vowels in Scots Gaelic is stated as follows.

4)

Vowels are nasal in Scots Gaelic when preceded or followed by a nasal consonant.

Malay, a language spoken in Malaysia and Singapore, has both nasalized vowels and glides. In Malay, all vowels and glides following a nasal are predictably nasalized until an obstruent (stop or fricative), liquid, or glottal ([h], [ʔ]) is reached.

Table 3.12 Nasalization in Malay

[mẽw̃ãh]	'luxurious'
[mãj̃ãn]	'stalk'
[mãrah]	'scold'
[nãẽʔ]	'ascend'
[mə̃laraŋ]	'forbid'
[mãkan]	'eat'
[rumãh]	'house'
[kəreta]	'car'

For Malay, then, the generalization governing nasalization is different from the Scots Gaelic case both in the direction and the targets of nasalization.

5)
In Malay, all vowels and glides following a nasal consonant and not separated from it by a nonnasal consonant are nasalized.

Language-Specific Variation in Allophonic Distribution

In Section 1.2 we saw that a phonemic contrast in one language may not prove to be a phonemic contrast in another. This means that the relationship of phonemes to allophones may vary. A comparison of the contrasts among stops in English and Khmer (Cambodian) in Table 3.13 illustrates this point. In both languages, aspirated and unaspirated phones can be heard.

Table 3.13 Stop phones in English and Khmer

English		*Khmer*	
[p]	[pʰ]	[p]	[pʰ]
[t]	[tʰ]	[t]	[tʰ]
[k]	[kʰ]	[k]	[kʰ]

In English, aspirated and unaspirated stops are allophones of their respective phonemes (the distribution is explained in Section 5.5 of this chapter); there are no contrasting forms like [pɪk] and [pʰɪk]. In Khmer, though, unaspirated and aspirated voiceless stops contrast (see Table 3.14).

Table 3.14 Khmer contrastive voiceless stops

[pɔːŋ]	'to wish'	[pʰɔːŋ]	'also'
[tɔp]	'to support'	[tʰɔp]	'be suffocated'
[kat]	'to cut'	[kʰat]	'to polish'

The phonological contrasts of the two languages are different, even though the phones are not (see Figure 3.5). These distributions are the same for the other voiceless stops in both languages.

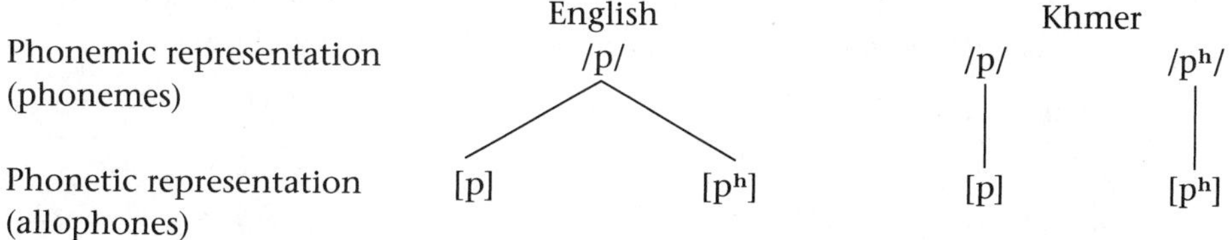

Figure 3.5 English and Khmer voiceless bilabial stop phonemes and allophones

3 Phonetic and Phonemic Transcription

We have seen so far that each language has a set of contrastive phonemes (which can be established largely by means of the minimal pair test) and that phonemes themselves can have predictable variants or allophones (which are usually in complementary distribution with each other). We have also seen that there are two distinct levels of representation: the phonemic (or phonological) and the phonetic. We can now illustrate more clearly the types of transcription used at each level of representation.

The phonetic level of representation includes both predictable and unpredictable phonetic information. In contrast, the phonemic level includes all and only those aspects of a representation that are unpredictable; all predictable information is excluded. The examples in Table 3.15 show this difference for the classes of sounds in English that we have examined so far.

Table 3.15 Phonetic and phonemic transcription of English

Phonetic transcription	*Phonemic transcription*	*Word*	*Predictable property(s) not represented in phonemic transcription*
[pl̥aw]	/plaw/	plow	voicelessness of liquid
[kɹ̥ip]	/kɹip/	creep	voicelessness of liquid
[kw̥ɪk]	/kwɪk/	quick	voicelessness of glide
[lejt]	/let/	late	glide after mid tense vowel
[lɛt]	/lɛt/	let	—
[tʰajd]	/tajd/	tied	aspiration
[tʰʌjt]	/tajt/	tight	aspiration; Canadian Raising

In the **phonemic transcriptions** in Table 3.15, the words are transcribed using only phonemes; in the phonetic transcriptions, however, the allophones of each phoneme are transcribed (in the environments in which they predictably occur). There is thus more phonetic information in the phonetic transcriptions than in the phonemic ones. If one compares the two transcriptions of *tight,* for instance, one sees that the phonetic transcription indicates the aspiration of the initial *t* and the raised pronunciation of the vowel. In the corresponding phonemic transcription, the aspiration is left out, because its occurrence is predictable, and the [ʌj] allophone of /aj/ is replaced by its phoneme.

The contrast between phonetic and phonemic representation is even more striking for the Malay forms given earlier, as shown in Table 3.16.

Table 3.16 Phonetic and phonemic transcription of Malay nasal vowels

Phonetic transcription	*Phonemic transcription*	*Word*	*Predictable property(s) not represented in phonemic transcription*
[mẽw̃ãh]	/mewah/	'luxurious'	nasalization
[mãj̃ãn]	/majan/	'stalk'	nasalization
[nãɛ̃ʔ]	/naɛʔ/	'ascend'	nasalization

Here, nasalization on all vowel and glide segments is predictable and is therefore omitted from the phonemic representation.

3.1 Phonetic and Phonemic Inventories

All languages have both a phonetic level of representation and a phonemic one. The phonetic level represents the allophones of a language. The phonemic level represents the language's phonemes. What this means is that each language has two inventories of sounds: one inventory, which includes the allophones of the language, is used in phonetic transcription; the other inventory, which includes only the phonemes of the language, is used in phonemic transcription. Since every language has more allophones of phonemes than it has phonemes, phonetic inventories of sounds are always larger than phonemic ones. Table 3.17 illustrates a partial phonetic inventory and the phonemic inventory for the vowels of English. Only those allophones that we have discussed so far in this chapter are listed (the phonetic inventory is thus obviously incomplete).

Table 3.17 Phonetic and phonemic inventories of the vowels of English

Partial phonetic inventory				*Phonemic inventory*			
Front	*Central*		*Back*	*Front*			*Back*
i			u	i			u
ɪ			ʊ	ɪ			ʊ
ej	ə		ow	e	ə		o
ɛ	ʌ	ʌj	ɔj	ɛ	ʌ		ɔj
		ʌw	ɔ				ɔ
æ	aj	aw	ɑ	æ	aj	aw	ɑ

Table 3.18 illustrates a partial phonetic inventory (again based on allophones discussed so far) and the phonemic inventory of English consonants.

Table 3.18 Phonetic and phonemic inventories of the consonants of English

Partial phonetic inventory						*Phonemic inventory*					
p		t		k		p		t		k	
p^h		t^h		k^h							
b		d		g		b		d		g	
			tʃ						tʃ		
			dʒ						dʒ		
	f θ	s	ʃ		h		f θ	s	ʃ		h
	v ð	z	ʒ				v ð	z	ʒ		
m		n		ŋ		m		n		ŋ	
		l	j	w				l	j	w	
		l̥	j̥	w̥							
		ɹ						ɹ			
		ɹ̥									

Since there are two levels of representation—the phonetic and the phonemic—one obvious question to ask is how they are related to each other. In Section 6 we consider in detail the nature of the relationship between phonetic and phonemic levels and inventories and discuss how this relationship can be represented formally.

4 Features

In this section we will discover that segments themselves are composed of even smaller, subsegmental, phonological units known as **features**. In fact, features are like atoms: they are the smallest units of phonology and as such are the basic building blocks of human speech sounds.

4.1 Why We Use Features

There are a number of reasons why linguists consider features to be the most basic units of phonology.

Features as Independent and Coordinated Phonetic Elements

We have already seen in Chapter 2 that speech is produced by a number of independent but coordinated articulatory activities such as voicing, tongue position, lip rounding, and so on. For example, when we produce the voiceless bilabial stop [p], the vocal cords in the larynx are open and not vibrating (hence the sound is voiceless), and the lips are pressed together to form a complete constriction (hence the sound is a labial stop). Each sound is thus the result of the coordinated articulatory activity of the larynx and the various articulators, such as the tongue body, the tongue blade, the lips, and the velum, found in the oral and nasal cavities of the vocal tract. By assuming that segments are composed of features, we are able to model this phonetic reality.

Features reflect the articulatory basis of speech in the sense that each feature encodes one of the independently controllable aspects of speech production. For example, in the case of [p], the feature [–voice] reflects laryngeal activity; the feature [LABIAL] reflects the activity of the lips; and the feature [–continuant] reflects the stop manner of articulation (note that features are written in square brackets; the use of '+' and '–' signs and upper- versus lowercase letters is explained below). As a further example, consider the sound [ɑ]. This sound is produced with a low, back, and tense tongue body (dorsal) position, with no rounding of the lips (therefore no labial activity) and little constriction. It is a vowel, and therefore is voiced and sonorant as well. All these phonetic properties are represented in terms of separate features in Figure 3.6. An 'o' before a feature indicates place of articulation.

In this representation, the features of the segment are listed in an array called a **matrix**. This is a common way of presenting sets of features.

Features and Natural Classes

A second reason for viewing segments as composed of features is that doing so gives us an economical way of characterizing natural classes. **Natural classes** are classes of sounds that share a feature or features and that pattern together in sound systems.

[ɑ]

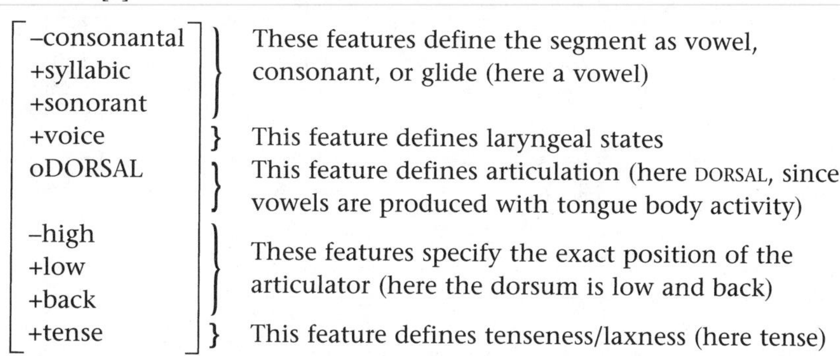

Figure 3.6 Feature representation for the English vowel /ɑ/

To see what is meant by this, consider the set of English sounds /p/, /t/, /k/, /f/, /s/, /ʃ/, and /b/, /d/, /g/, /v/, /z/, /ʒ/ given in Figure 3.7. All these sounds belong to the class of **obstruents** (/tʃ/, /dʒ/, /θ/, and /ð/ are also obstruents, but we will ignore them for now). Because obstruents obstruct the flow of air through the vocal tract, they are not singable, or **sonorant**. In order to capture this fact, we can say that obstruents are all [–sonorant] (the '–' means 'not' in this context; definitions of the features are given in Section 4.2). In addition, a subset of the members of this [–sonorant] class, namely /p/, /t/, /k/, /f/, /s/, /ʃ/, all of which differ in place and (in part) in manner of articulation, can be readily distinguished from the subset /b/, /d/, /g/, /v/, /z/, /ʒ/ by the single feature [voice] alone. Finally, a third feature, [continuant] (which refers to whether or not a sound is produced with continuous, free airflow), can distinguish all the (noncontinuous) stops in the obstruent class, /p/, /t/, /k/, /b/, /d/, /g/, from all the (continuous) fricatives, /f/, /s/, /ʃ/, /v/, /z/, /ʒ/. Thus, by using these three features we are able to capture nine different natural classes of sounds; these are given in Table 3.19.

[–sonorant]		
[–voice]	[+voice]	
p t k	b d g	[–continuant]
f s ʃ	v z ʒ	[+continuant]

Figure 3.7 Natural classes: obstruents in English

Any natural class requires fewer features to define it than to define any one of its members. Thus, in Table 3.19 the largest class, that of the obstruents, is defined by only one feature, while the four classes containing three segments each are defined by three features each.

Table 3.19 Nine natural classes: obstruents in English

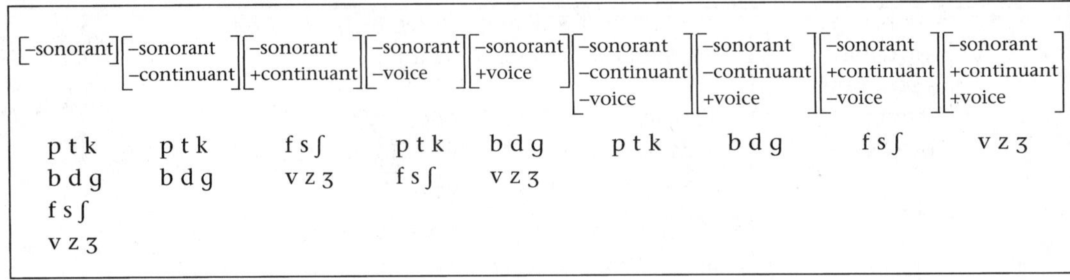

[–sonorant]	[–sonorant, –continuant]	[–sonorant, +continuant]	[–sonorant, –voice]	[–sonorant, +voice]	[–sonorant, –continuant, –voice]	[–sonorant, –continuant, +voice]	[–sonorant, +continuant, –voice]	[–sonorant, +continuant, +voice]
p t k	p t k	f s ʃ	p t k	b d g	p t k	b d g	f s ʃ	v z ʒ
b d g	b d g	v z ʒ	f s ʃ	v z ʒ				
f s ʃ								
v z ʒ								

Every set of sounds that constitutes a natural class has the potential to pattern together in some way in the phonology of a language. For instance, we saw in Chapter 2, Section 5.5, that aspiration in English affects /p/, /t/, and /k/, the [–sonorant, –continuant, –voice] sounds of the language. All and only these sounds are affected by the aspiration process. An interesting point about features is that their use allows us to exclude sounds from (as well as to include them in) natural classes. Thus, because /b/ is [+voice], it does not belong to the same class in English as /p/, /t/, and /k/. As a result, /b/ is not affected by aspiration.

Table 3.20 provides an additional illustration of the use of features to distinguish natural classes—in this case, the class of front and back vowels in English. Again we see that fewer features are needed to define the larger class of English front vowels than to capture the vowel /æ/ alone.

Table 3.20 Two natural classes: front and back vowels in English

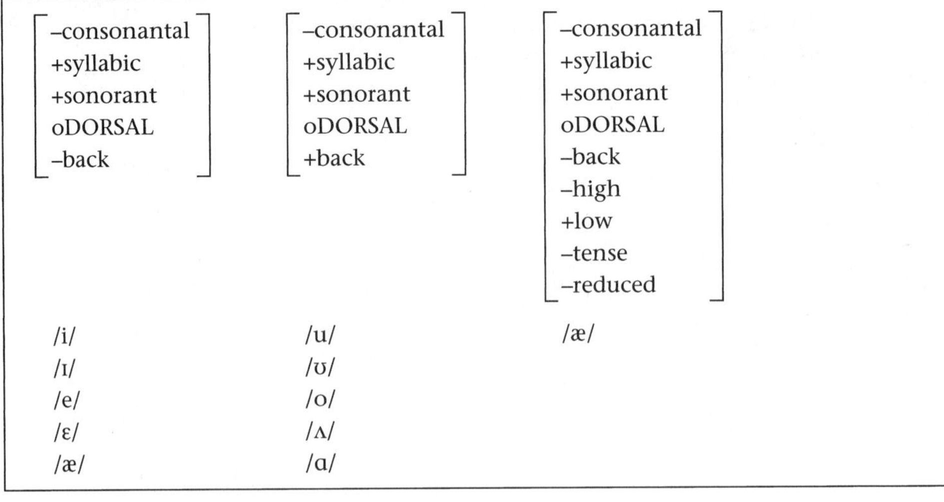

[–consonantal, +syllabic, +sonorant, oDORSAL, –back]	[–consonantal, +syllabic, +sonorant, oDORSAL, +back]	[–consonantal, +syllabic, +sonorant, oDORSAL, –back, –high, +low, –tense, –reduced]
/i/	/u/	/æ/
/ɪ/	/ʊ/	
/e/	/o/	
/ɛ/	/ʌ/	
/æ/	/ɑ/	

In preceding sections we listed those segments of English that contrast, and that therefore make up the phonemes of English. Because features define natural classes, it is not just individual phonemes such as /p/, /b/, /k/, and /g/ that contrast in English; in fact, the entire class of voiced stops contrasts with the class of voiceless stops. All the contrasts found in the English sound system (and in the sound system of any language) can be defined in terms of the features that make up those phonemes. Thus, the distinctions between /p/ and /b/, /t/ and /d/, and /k/ and /g/ all reside in the feature [voice]. In addition, words like *pit* and *bit,* which constitute a minimal pair, contrast in the segments /p/ and /b/, and /p/ and /b/ themselves contrast in the feature [voice]. What these examples show us, then, is that features as well as segments can be contrastive. When a feature is the source of phonemic contrasts in a language, we say that it is a **distinctive feature** in the language. Thus, [voice] is a distinctive feature in English.

Other features provide for other contrasts. For example, we can capture the contrast between /t/ and /s/ in English with the feature [continuant]. Both /t/ and /s/ are voiceless and have an alveolar point of articulation. By viewing the relevant distinctive feature as [continuant], we can use the same feature to distinguish between /p/ and /f/, /b/ and /v/, and /d/ and /z/ (see Table 3.21).

Table 3.21 Stop-fricative contrasts as a feature

[–continuant]	[+continuant]
p	f
b	v
t	s
d	z

By systematically examining the phonemic contrasts of a language, we can extract the distinctive features and use these irreducible linguistic elements to describe the phonemic inventory.

Features, Processes, and Allophonic Variation

A third reason for using features is that reference to features enables us to understand the nature of allophonic variation more exactly. Viewed from the perspective of features, allophonic variation is seen to be not simply the substitution of one allophone for another, but rather the environmentally conditioned change or specification of a feature or features. The liquid-glide devoicing that occurs in English words like *tree* and *twinkle,* for example, is a change in the value of the feature [voice] from [+voice] to [–voice] after voiceless (i.e., [–voice]) stop consonants. Similarly, the vowel and glide nasalization that occurs in Malay forms like /mewah/ [mẽw̃ãh] 'luxurious' is a change in the value of the feature [nasal] from [–nasal] to [+nasal] following a nasal (i.e., [+nasal]) consonant (see *5* in Section 2.6).

We saw above that features reflect the fact that speech is produced by a number of independent but coordinated articulatory activities. Certain features, however, reflect classes of sounds that are not always recognized in the traditional descriptive terminology of phonetics that was introduced in Chapter 2 but that are nevertheless relevant to phonological patterning. For example, the feature [CORONAL] (the use of uppercase as opposed to lowercase letters here reflects a difference in feature type that will be clarified below) refers to the class of sounds made with the tongue tip or blade raised: this class includes sounds made with interdental, alveolar, and alveopalatal places of articulation. It turns out that just this feature is necessary to explain various constraints and processes in world languages. For example, in Lebanese

Arabic, the definite article *the* is /il/, as in [ilkʊrsi] 'the chair', [ilba:b] 'the door', and [ilfɪnʒa:n] 'the cup'. However, when the definite article occurs before a word starting with a coronal, the [l] of the definite article assimilates completely, for example: [iʃʃanta] 'the suitcase', [iddaftar] 'the notebook', [irraʔi:s] 'the headman', [inna:s] 'the people'. Although the feature [CORONAL] does not reflect a traditional phonetic term, it plays a very important role in the phonologies of many languages. This fact shows us that features reflect articulatory reality in a way that involves more than just presenting traditional phonetic descriptions in a different guise.

4.2 Feature Representations

We have seen that segments are composed of subsegmental units or features and that features reflect phonetic reality. Since features are considered to be the basic building blocks of speech sounds, and thus of phonology, linguists have attempted to state all possible phonological facts about language with the fewest number of features possible. Only a limited number of features—currently around twenty-four—have been proposed. Features thus constitute an important part of a theory of what is possible (and what is not possible) in the phonological behavior of human beings. In this section we present and define features that are needed to characterize the sounds of English, as well as of many other languages.

Defining the Features of English

Most features have labels that reflect traditional articulatory terms such as [voice], [consonantal], and [nasal]. These features require little further description. A few features have less familiar labels, such as [CORONAL] and [anterior]. From this point on, features will be used to describe classes of sounds. At the same time, we will continue throughout the book to use terms such as *consonant, glide,* and *obstruent* (a fricative, affricate, or nonnasal stop) in phonetic description. This traditional terminology will be maintained because it is still widely used in phonetic description.

Features are organized into groups that reflect natural classes. The following headings indicate what these classes are and how the features represent them. Most of the features given below are written in lowercase and are **binary features**; in other words, they can have one of two values, '+' or '–', each of which defines a particular class of sounds. For example, [+voice] sounds involve vibration or voicing in the larynx, while [–voice] sounds involve an open glottis and therefore no vibration or voicing. Three of the features ([LABIAL], [CORONAL], and [DORSAL]) are written in uppercase and have only one value. These features classify the places of articulation in the mouth in terms of the articulators that are used to produce them. Thus [LABIAL] represents sounds made using the lips, [CORONAL] represents sounds made with the tongue tip or tongue blade, and [DORSAL] represents sounds made with the tongue body/back.

- **Major class features:** *features that represent the classes consonant, obstruent, and sonorant (nasal, liquid, glide, vowel)*

  [±consonantal] Sounds that are [+consonantal] are produced with a major obstruction in the vocal tract. All nonsonorant consonants (except the glottals

[h] and [ʔ]) as well as liquids and nasals are [+consonantal]. Glides and vowels are [–consonantal].

[±syllabic] Sounds that can act as syllable peaks are [+syllabic]; this includes vowels, and syllabic liquids or syllabic nasals. All other sounds are [–syllabic].

[±sonorant] All and only those sounds that are singable are [+sonorant]; this includes vowels, glides, liquids, and nasals (even if the [+sonorant] sounds are voiceless). All nonsingable sounds (obstruents) are [–sonorant].

Table 3.22 illustrates how the major class features are used to divide sounds into classes. Note that nasals and liquids have the same values for the three major class features; to distinguish these two classes from each other, additional (manner) features are therefore needed.

Table 3.22 Use of major class features

	Obstruents	*Nasals*	*Liquids*	*Glides*	*Vowels*
[±consonantal]	+	+	+	–	–
[±syllabic]	–	–/+	–/+	–	+
[±sonorant]	–	+	+	+	+
Examples:	p d v tʃ	m n	l ɹ	j w	i a

The manner features given next represent manners of articulation. Their use is particularly important in distinguishing the following classes: stops/affricates as opposed to fricatives ([±continuant]); affricates as opposed to stops ([±delayed release]); nasals from nonnasals ([±nasal]); and laterals from nonlaterals ([±lateral]).

- **Manner features:** *features that represent manner of articulation*

[±continuant] Sounds produced with free or nearly free airflow through the oral cavity are [+continuant]; these include vowels, glides, liquids, and fricatives. All other sounds are [–continuant]; these include nasal and oral stops.

[±delayed release] ([±DR]) In the stop portion [t] of an affricate sound such as [tʃ], the tongue is slower in leaving the roof of the mouth than when a stop like [t] is produced on its own. Hence affricates are said to be produced with "delayed release." All and only affricates, such as [tʃ] and [dʒ], are [+delayed release]. All other sounds are [–delayed release].

[±nasal] Sounds produced with a lowered velum are [+nasal]; this includes nasal stops and all nasalized sounds. Sounds that are oral, and thus produced with a raised velum, are [–nasal].

[±lateral] All and only varieties of *l* are [+lateral]. All other sounds are [–lateral].

Voicing, aspiration, and glottal constriction are all the result of laryngeal activity. To represent different laryngeal states, we use the features [±voice], [±spread glottis], and [±constricted glottis].

- **Laryngeal features:** *features that represent laryngeal activity*

  [±voice] All voiced sounds are [+voice]; all voiceless sounds are [–voice].

  [±spread glottis] ([±SG]) All aspirated consonants are [+SG]; all others are [–SG].

  [±constricted glottis] ([±CG]) All sounds made with a closed glottis are [+CG]; all others are [–CG]. In English, only the glottal stop [ʔ] is [+CG].

The last set of features is used to represent supralaryngeal (above the larynx) articulatory activity, which determines place of articulation. So far, all the features that we have discussed have been binary, and have therefore had either '+' or '–' values. Articulatory features, however, are of two types.

The first type includes the features [LABIAL], [CORONAL], and [DORSAL] that, as noted above, are used specifically to represent and to distinguish the *articulators* that are active at particular places of articulation. For instance, the sound [k] is produced when the dorsum or body of the tongue touches the velum (soft palate) to form a constriction. Thus [k] has a *velar* place of articulation that is executed (produced) by moving the DORSAL (tongue body) articulator. The sound [k] therefore has the feature [DORSAL] in its feature representation.

In addition, when [k] is pronounced, the tongue body is always positioned high and back in the oral cavity. In this respect, [k] is different from [j]. Like [k], [j] is [DORSAL]. However, unlike [k], [j] is pronounced with the tongue body positioned high and front. In order to indicate that the LABIAL, CORONAL, and DORSAL articulators can occur in different positions, we use binary features such as [±high], [±back], [±round], etc., in addition to the articulator features. For instance, since [k] is pronounced with a high, back tongue body position, it is represented as being [+high] and [+back] as well as being [DORSAL]; in contrast, [j] is [+high] and [–back] in addition to being [DORSAL].

- **Place of articulation features:** *features that represent supralaryngeal activity*

  [LABIAL] This feature represents the LABIAL articulator: any sound that is produced with involvement of one or both of the lips is [LABIAL].

    [±round] A sound produced with the LABIAL articulator may be produced by protruding the lips; such sounds are [+round]. Labial sounds made with no lip protrusion are [–round]. [+round] labial sounds are rounded vowels and the rounded labiovelar glide [w]. [–round] labial sounds include [p, b, f, v].

  [CORONAL] This feature represents the CORONAL articulator: any sound that is produced with involvement of the tongue tip or blade raised is [CORONAL].

    [±anterior] All coronal sounds articulated in front of the alveopalatal region (interdentals and alveolars) are [+anterior]; coronal sounds articulated at or behind the alveopalatal region (alveopalatals) are [–anterior].

    [±strident] All "noisy" coronal fricatives and affricates ([s, z, ʃ, ʒ, tʃ, dʒ]) are [+strident]; all other coronal fricatives and affricates ([θ, ð]) are [–strident].

[DORSAL] This feature represents the DORSAL articulator: any sound that is produced with involvement of the body of the tongue is [DORSAL].

[±high] Dorsal consonants (velars or palatals) or vowels produced with the tongue body raised from a central position in the oral cavity are [+high]. Sounds produced with a neutral or lowered tongue body are [–high].

[±low] Vowels produced with the tongue body lowered from a central position in the oral cavity are [+low]. All other vowels are [–low]. [low] is not needed for consonants in English, although it may be used in languages that have uvular or pharyngeal consonants.

[±back] Dorsal consonants or vowels produced with the tongue body behind the palatal region (hard palate) in the oral cavity are [+back]. Sounds produced with the tongue body at the palatal region are [–back].

[±tense] Vowels that are tense are [+tense]; vowels that are lax are [–tense].

[±reduced] The vowel schwa ([ə]) is a lax and exceptionally brief vowel and is therefore [+reduced]; all other vowels are [–reduced].

To set the articulator features apart from other features, they are written with capitals. They do not have '+' and '–' values associated with them because if they are not being used to execute an articulation, they are simply inactive and are therefore absent from a representation. In other words, if a sound is a velar [k], it is produced with the tongue body, and neither the lips nor the tongue blade/tip are actively involved in the production of the sound. Consequently, the feature representation for [k] does not include the articulator features [LABIAL] and [CORONAL]; it only includes the feature [DORSAL].

It is important to remember that the binary articulatory features like [±round], [±anterior], or [±high] are specific to individual articulators. In other words, only the tongue body DORSAL articulator can be in [±high] or [±back] positions. The LABIAL articulator, the lips, can be rounded or unrounded, namely, [±round], but lips do not have high or back positions, and therefore DORSAL features like [±high] and [±back] are irrelevant to sounds made exclusively with the lips. Conversely, the tongue body never manifests roundness. Therefore, the feature [±round] is relevant only to the LABIAL articulator. Thus, the binary articulatory features are used only to distinguish sounds produced by specific articulators. For instance, only sounds like [k] that are [DORSAL] and produced with the tongue body may be [±high], [±low], or [±back]. Sounds made with other articulators are *not* represented with values for these features.

To see exactly how the articulator features are used to represent the various places of articulation of the consonants found in English, let us look at Table 3.23. In the feature representations, "o" indicates that the relevant articulator is active in the production of a sound. Where no "o" is present, the articulator is inactive.

The feature representations in Table 3.23 can be understood as follows:

- [p] is produced with the lips and is therefore [LABIAL]. Because the lips are unrounded, it is [–round]. The tongue blade and the tongue body are not used in the production of [p], and therefore it has no feature specifications for CORONAL and DORSAL articulators or for [CORONAL] or [DORSAL] features.

Table 3.23 Use of place of articulation features in representing some English consonants

	Labials		*Interdentals*	*Alveolars*	*Alveopalatals*	*Palatals*	*Velars*
	p	w	θ	s	ʃ	j	k
LABIAL	o	o					
[±round]	–	+					
CORONAL			o	o	o		
[±anterior]			+	+	–		
[±strident]			–	+	+		
DORSAL		o				o	o
[±high]		+				+	+
[±back]		+				–	+

- [θ s ʃ] are all [CORONAL] because they are produced with the tongue blade. [θ s] are produced with the tongue blade before or at the alveolar ridge and are therefore [+anterior], while [ʃ] is produced with the tongue blade behind the alveolar ridge and is therefore [–anterior]. [θ] is produced with a quiet airflow and so is [–strident], while [s ʃ] are produced with noisy airflow and so are [+strident]. Since neither the lips nor the tongue body are used to produce these sounds, they have no specifications for the LABIAL and DORSAL articulators or for [LABIAL] or [DORSAL] features.

- [j k] are both produced with the tongue body and are therefore [DORSAL]. Both have a raised tongue body and so are [+high], but [j] is pronounced with the tongue body at the hard palate, so is [–back]. In contrast, [k] is pronounced with the tongue body behind the hard palate, so is [+back]. Finally, since neither the lips nor the tongue blade are used to produce these sounds, they have no specifications for the LABIAL and CORONAL articulators or for [LABIAL] or [CORONAL] features.

- [w] is a labiovelar sound and is thus coarticulated: it is produced with both a tongue body that is raised and behind the hard palate, *and* with lip rounding. This means that both the dorsum and the lips are used to produce [w], so it is executed with two articulators acting simultaneously. It is therefore both [LABIAL] and [DORSAL]; as a [LABIAL] it is [+round], and as a [DORSAL] it is [+high, +back]. Since the tongue blade is not used to produce this sound, it has no specifications for the [CORONAL] articulator or for CORONAL features.

Table 3.24 exemplifies how the place of articulation features are used to represent vowels in English. All the vowels in the table are produced with an active tongue body and therefore are [DORSAL]; this is true of all vowels, in English and in all other languages. Vowels that involve lip rounding are also produced with the [LABIAL] articulator. [CORONAL] is never used in the feature representations of vowels. All vowels except schwa are unreduced and therefore specified as [–reduced].

Table 3.24 Use of place of articulation features in representing some English vowels

	ɛ	ə	u	ɑ
LABIAL			o	
[±round]			+	
DORSAL	o	o	o	o
[±high]	–	–	+	–
[±low]	–	–	–	+
[±back]	–	+	+	+
[±tense]	–	–	+	+
[±reduced]	–	+	–	–

- [ɛ] is a mid, front (nonback), lax, unrounded vowel. Since it is unrounded, it does not use the LABIAL articulator. As a mid vowel, it has neither a raised nor a lowered tongue body, so it is [DORSAL] and specified as both [–high] and [–low]. As a front vowel, it is [–back], and as a lax vowel, it is [–tense].

- [ə] is a mid, central, unrounded, lax, and reduced vowel. As a mid vowel, it is [DORSAL, –high] and [–low]. As a central and therefore nonfront vowel, it is [+back] (all central vowels are always [+back] in feature representations). Being unrounded, it does not involve the LABIAL articulator. Because it is a lax reduced vowel, it is [–tense] and [+reduced].

- [u] is a high, back, tense vowel, and is therefore specified as [+high], [+back], and [+tense]. Since it is round, it is [LABIAL, +round] in addition to being [DORSAL]. Since it is [+high], it is also [–low] (since the tongue body cannot be both raised and lowered at the same time, all [+high] vowels are also [–low]).

- [ɑ] is a low, back, unrounded, tense vowel. Since it is produced with a lowered tongue body, it is [DORSAL, +low]; because a lowered tongue body cannot be simultaneously raised, it is also [–high]. Since it is back, it is [+back]. Being tense, it is [+tense], and being unrounded, it has no LABIAL specifications.

Feature notation does not provide a convenient way to distinguish diphthongs such as [aj], [aw], and [ɔj] from the other vowels. These diphthongs may be treated as vowel-glide sequences when using features.

For more advanced information on determining feature representations, go to **bedfordstmartins.com/linguistics/phonology** and click on **feature representations**.

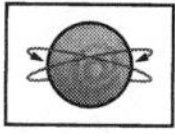

Tables 3.25 and 3.26 provide the feature representations for all the consonants and vowels of English. As you go through these tables, notice that for every sound, features are listed in the following order: major class features, manner features, laryngeal features, and place of articulation features. To remind yourselves of what a feature matrix for a segment looks like, go back to Figure 3.6, which illustrates the matrix for the segment [ɑ].

For further discussion of how to determine feature representations, go to **bedfordstmartins.com/linguistics/phonology** and click on **representations**.

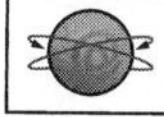

Table 3.25 Feature matrix for English consonants

		Stops						*Fricatives*								*Affricates*		*Nasals*			*Liquids*		*Glides*			*Glottals*	
		p	b	t	d	k	g	f	v	θ	ð	s	z	ʃ	ʒ	tʃ	dʒ	m	n	ŋ	l	ɹ	j	w	ʍ	h	ʔ
Major class features	[consonantal]	+	+	+	+	+	+	+	+	+	+	+	+	+	+	+	+	+	+	+	+	+	–	–	–	–	–
	[sonorant]	–	–	–	–	–	–	–	–	–	–	–	–	–	–	–	–	+	+	+	+	+	+	+	+	–	–
	[syllabic]	–	–	–	–	–	–	–	–	–	–	–	–	–	–	–	–	–	–	–	–	–	–	–	–	–	–
Manner features	[nasal]	–	–	–	–	–	–	–	–	–	–	–	–	–	–	–	–	+	+	+	–	–	–	–	–	–	–
	[continuant]	–	–	–	–	–	–	+	+	+	+	+	+	+	+	–	–	–	–	–	+	+	+	+	+	+	–
	[lateral]	–	–	–	–	–	–	–	–	–	–	–	–	–	–	–	–	–	–	–	+	–	–	–	–	–	–
	[delayed release]	–	–	–	–	–	–	–	–	–	–	–	–	–	–	+	+	–	–	–	–	–	–	–	–	–	–
Laryngeal features	[voice]	–	+	–	+	–	+	–	+	–	+	–	+	–	+	–	+	+	+	+	+	+	+	+	–	–	–
	[CG]	–	–	–	–	–	–	–	–	–	–	–	–	–	–	–	–	–	–	–	–	–	–	–	–	–	+
	[SG]	–	–	–	–	–	–	–	–	–	–	–	–	–	–	–	–	–	–	–	–	–	–	–	–	+	–
Place of articulation features	LABIAL	o	o					o	o									o						o	o		
	[round]	–	–					–	–									–						+	+		
	CORONAL			o	o					o	o	o	o	o	o	o	o		o		o	o					
	[anterior]			+	+					+	+	+	+	–	–	–	–		+		+	+					
	[strident]			–	–					–	–	+	+	+	+	+	+		–		–	–					
	DORSAL					o	o													o			o	o	o		
	[high]					+	+													+			+	+	+		
	[back]					+	+													+			–	+	+		

Note: [low], [tense], and [reduced] are not used for English consonants.
Aspirated stops [p^h, t^h, k^h] will have the feature [+SG].
Syllabic liquids and nasals will have the feature [+syllabic].

Table 3.26 Feature matrix for English vowels

		i	ɪ	e	ɛ	æ	ə	ʌ	u	ʊ	o	ɔ	ɑ/a
Major class features	[consonantal]	−	−	−	−	−	−	−	−	−	−	−	−
	[sonorant]	+	+	+	+	+	+	+	+	+	+	+	+
	[syllabic]	+	+	+	+	+	+	+	+	+	+	+	+
Manner feature	[continuant]	+	+	+	+	+	+	+	+	+	+	+	+
Laryngeal feature	[voice]	+	+	+	+	+	+	+	+	+	+	+	+
Place of articulation features	LABIAL								o	o	o	o	
	[round]								+	+	+	+	
	DORSAL	o	o	o	o	o	o	o	o	o	o	o	o
	[high]	+	+	−	−	−	−	−	+	+	−	−	−
	[low]	−	−	−	−	+	−	−	−	−	−	−	+
	[back]	−	−	−	−	−	+	+	+	+	+	+	+
	[tense]	+	−	+	−	−	−	−	+	−	+	−	+
	[reduced]	−	−	−	−	−	+	−	−	−	−	−	−

For more advanced discussion of the feature hierarchy, go to **bedfordstmartins .com/linguistics/phonology** and click on **feature hierarchy**.

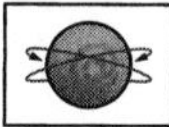

5 Above the Segment: Syllables

So far we have been discussing the distributional properties of segments, and have established the existence of the segmental units of phonological analysis known as phonemes and their allophones. We have also seen that allophonic variation may be conditioned by neighboring segments. We turn now to a different unit of phonological representation, namely, the **syllable**. We will see that syllables are composed of segments, and thus impose an organization on segments; in this sense, syllables are **suprasegmental** (above the segment) units. We will also see that the shapes of syllables are governed by both universal and language-specific constraints. Finally, we will examine examples of allophonic variation that is conditioned by syllable structure rather than by neighboring segments.

5.1 Defining the Syllable

As we saw in Chapter 2, vowels, glides, liquids, and nasals are sonorant (singable) sounds, while obstruents are not; of the sonorant sounds, vowels are most sonorous, and glides, liquids, and nasals are correspondingly less sonorous. A syllable consists of a sonorous element and its associated nonsyllabic (less sonorous) segments. Since vowels are the most sonorous sounds, syllables usually have a vowel nucleus at their core. Less sonorous sounds may appear on either side of a nucleus. Thus, the word *telegraph* has three syllables because it has three vowels that serve as syllable nuclei.

Native speakers of a language demonstrate their awareness of the sonority values of segments and of the syllable as a unit of phonological structure whenever they count syllables in a word. No English speaker would hesitate to say that the words *telegraph* and *accident* have three syllables, and most speakers would feel confident that the words could be broken up into the syllables [tɛ.lə.gɹæf] and [æk.sə.dənt] (the "." marks syllable divisions informally).

Speakers also know that syllables have internal subsyllabic structure as well. This internal organization of the syllable unit is shown in Figure 3.8 for the monosyllabic English word *sprint*. As you can see, syllables consist of an **onset** and a **rhyme**; the rhyme, in turn, consists of the **nucleus**, or syllable core, and a **coda**.

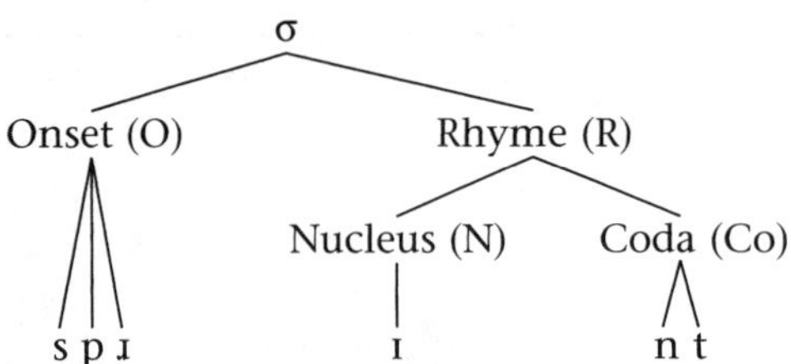

Figure 3.8 Internal structure of a syllable

We will see later on in this chapter that some allophonic variation makes reference to internal subsyllabic structure such as the coda.

There are other kinds of evidence that subsyllabic structure is part of speakers' knowledge. In English rhyming verses, for instance, it is always the rhymes of syllables that match each other (in other words, that rhyme), while onsets may vary: thus *sprite* and *fright* rhyme by virtue of having identical rhyme (nucleus and coda) constituents, but the onsets of each are different. In addition, one version of the English language game known as Pig Latin is played by displacing the onset of the first syllable of a word to the end of the word and then tacking on the rhyme *ay* [ej]: thus *strong* becomes *ong-str-ay,* and *swivel* becomes *ivel-sw-ay.*

Furthermore, when speakers are asked to syllabify words, they are able to do so in ways that are neither random nor variable. The word *extreme* /ɛkstɹim/ would never be syllabified as /ɛ.kstɹim/, for example. Instead, syllables comply with certain constraints that prohibit them from beginning with a sequence like *kstr* and thus result in the actual syllabification /ɛk.stɹim/. The examples in Table 3.27 are all from English, but similar kinds of evidence for the existence of subsyllabic constituents can be found in many other languages as well.

Table 3.27 Some examples of English syllables

/ə.plɔd/	applaud
/di.klajn/	decline
/ɛk.splen/	explain
/ɪm.pɹə.vajz/	improvise

All languages have syllables. The shapes of these syllables are governed by various kinds of constraints, but certain universal tendencies are observable: (1) syllable nuclei usually consist of one vowel (V); (2) syllables usually begin with onsets; (3) syllables often end with codas; (4) onsets and codas usually consist of one consonant (C). Putting these tendencies together, we find that the most common types of syllables found in languages throughout the world take the shapes CV and CVC. These are general tendencies, not absolute laws, and languages may, and often do, violate them. But even when a language violates the universal tendencies, the types of syllables that do occur are governed by other constraints on the shapes of the subsyllabic units O, N, and Co. To illustrate this, we turn to the constraints that govern the phonological shape of consonant sequences in onsets in English.

5.2 Onset Constraints and Phonotactics

Native speakers of any language intuitively know that certain words from other languages sound unusual, and they often adjust the segment sequences of these words to conform with the pronunciation requirements of their own language. These intuitions are based on a tacit knowledge of the permissible syllable structures of the speaker's own language. For example, English-speaking students learning Russian have difficulty pronouncing a word like *vprok* /fprɔk/ 'for future use', since the sequence /fpr/ is never found in English onsets. Since speakers typically adjust an impermissible sequence by altering it to a permissible one, many English speakers would pronounce the Russian word [fprɔk] as [fəprɔk] or even delete the initial /f/ and say [prɔk] in order to adjust the impermissible sequence /fpr/ to a permissible English onset. **Phonotactics**, the set of constraints on how sequences of segments pattern, forms part of a speaker's knowledge of the phonology of his or her language.

Some English Onsets

English is a language that allows onsets to contain more than one consonant; in this sense, English permits syllables that are more complex than those found in many languages. Nevertheless, there are very strict phonotactic constraints on the shapes of English onsets. Table 3.28 contains examples of the possible syllable-initial consonant sequences of English that contain a voiceless stop consonant. These sequences are all illustrated in word-initial position to make them easier to pick out. (Stress

Table 3.28 Initial consonant clusters in English containing a voiceless stop

Labial + sonorant		*Coronal + sonorant*		*Velar + sonorant*	
[pl]	please	[tl]	—	[kl]	clean
[pɹ]	proud	[tɹ]	trade	[kɹ]	cream
[pw]	—	[tw]	twin	[kw]	queen
[pj]	pure	[tj]	tune (British)	[kj]	cute
[spl]	splat	[stl]	—	[skl]	sclerosis
[spɹ]	spring	[stɹ]	strip	[skɹ]	scrap
[spw]	—	[stw]	—	[skw]	squeak
[spj]	spew	[stj]	stew (British)	[skj]	skewer

marking and phonetic details such as liquid-glide devoicing that are not relevant to the present discussion are omitted here.)

The examples in Table 3.28 show that the first segment of a word-initial three-consonant cluster in English is always *s*; the second consonant in the series is always a voiceless stop, and the third is either a liquid or a glide. These sound patterns can be formally represented as follows:

$$\sigma \; [\text{s} \quad \begin{Bmatrix} \text{p} \\ \text{t} \\ \text{k} \end{Bmatrix} \quad \begin{Bmatrix} \text{(l)} \\ \text{ɹ} \\ \text{(w)} \\ \text{j} \end{Bmatrix}$$

In this formalization, σ indicates the boundary of a syllable and the curly braces designate 'either/or'. The sounds in parentheses are not found in all combinations. An important observation about the types of onsets that are allowed in English is that the consonant combinations are not random; in fact, (1) the consonant combinations are dependent primarily on the manners of articulation of the consonants, and (2) sonorant consonants (here liquids and glides) are closer to the nucleus than are stops and fricatives. Both these phonotactic constraints reflect universal restrictions on consonant combinations and are found in other languages that allow complex onsets. For more information about sequences that are not found, go to **bedfordstmartins.com/linguistics/phonology** and click on **gaps**.

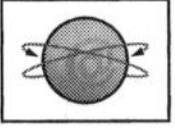

5.3 Language-Specific Phonotactics

It is important to emphasize again that certain aspects of the particular constraints discussed in the previous section are universal whereas others are language-specific. An onset like *pl* is found in many languages besides English (for example, in Russian, Thai, and French), while an onset sequence like *lp* is never found. We may therefore say that no restrictions against an onset like *pl* appear to exist as part of universal linguistic knowledge, whereas the nonexistence of onsets like **lp* suggest that something in their phonetic makeup disqualifies them from occurring in language. Language-specific constraints, on the other hand, hold true for individual languages such as English, but they may or may not be found in other languages. Each language has its own set of restrictions on the phonological shapes of its syllable constituents. Speakers of Russian, for example, are quite accustomed to pronouncing onset sequences such as *fsl-* and *mgl-*, which are not found in English (see Table 3.29).

Table 3.29 Some onset sequences in Russian

[fslux]	'aloud'
[mgla]	'fog'

Phonotactic constraints of the kind that we have seen for English represent one kind of phonological knowledge. You might, however, wonder what prevents English words like *extreme, applaud, decline, explain,* and *improvise* from being syllabified as the incorrect */ɛks.tɹim/, */əp.lɔd/, */dik.lajn/, */ɛks.plen/, and */ɪmp.ɹəv.ajz/ instead of the correct /ɛk.stɹim/, /ə.plɔd/, /di.klajn/, /ɛk.splen/, and /ɪm.pɹə.vajz/. In the incorrect syllabifications, the syllable divisions do not violate any phonotactic constraints, raising the question of why the syllabifications are nevertheless incorrect. The answer is that such syllabifications are prevented by a universal constraint on general syllable shapes, rather than by a phonotactic constraint on segment sequences. As mentioned in Section 5.1, there is a universal syllable-shape constraint that encourages languages to make syllables with onsets; as a result, onsets in languages tend to be as large as possible. The next section illustrates how this universal constraint works by providing a procedure for establishing the association of consonants and vowels within syllables.

5.4 Setting Up Syllables

Each language defines its own syllable structure through the interaction of universal and language-specific constraints. The process for setting up syllables in a given language involves three steps: nucleus formation, onset formation, and coda formation; a fourth step, word-level construction, ensures that syllables are incorporated into word-level units. The first step reflects the universal tendency for syllables to have a sonorant core, the second step reflects the tendency for syllables to have onsets, and the third step reflects the tendency for syllables to have codas. Ordering onset-formation before coda-formation reflects a cross-linguistic constraint—*Onsets before codas* (in a sequence of VCV, the consonant C will always be syllabified as an onset rather than a coda)—and ensures that onsets gather up as many consonants as possible before any codas are formed.

- **Step a** *Nucleus formation:* Since the syllable nucleus is the only obligatory constituent of a syllable, it is constructed first. Each vowel segment in a word makes up a syllabic nucleus. To represent this, link a vowel to an N symbol above it by drawing an **association line**. Above each nucleus symbol, place an R symbol (for rhyme—in Section 5.1 we saw that the rhyme consists of the nucleus plus the coda), which is filled out in step c below. Above each R, place a σ symbol; link all with association lines (see Figure 3.9).

Figure 3.9

- **Step b** *Onset formation:* The longest sequence of consonants to the left of each nucleus that does not violate the phonotactic constraints of the language in question is the onset of the syllable. Link these consonants to an O symbol and join it to the same syllable as the vowel to the right (see Figure 3.10). Note that there is no onset in the first syllable of *extreme.*

Figure 3.10

- **Step c** *Coda formation:* Any remaining unassociated consonants to the right of each nucleus form the coda and are linked to a Co symbol above them. This Co is associated with the syllable nucleus to its left in the rhyme (see Figure 3.11). A syllable with a coda is called a **closed syllable**; a syllable without a coda is called an **open syllable**.

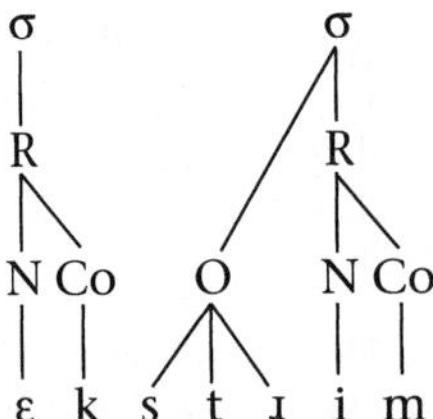

Figure 3.11

- **Step d** *Word-level construction:* Syllables that make up a single form (usually a word) branch out from the representation *Wd* as in Figure 3.12 (this step is frequently omitted from phonological representations to save space; the complete representation is understood even when *Wd* is not written out).

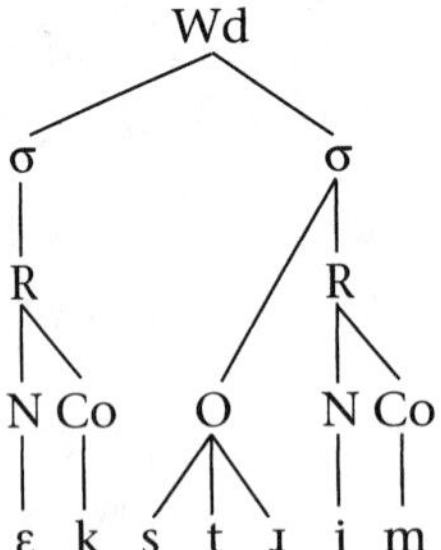

Figure 3.12

The steps in the procedure just outlined reflect universal constraints on syllable shapes. These interact with universal and language-specific phonotactic constraints. Given the procedure and the phonotactic constraints, we can now explain why words such as *applaud* and *explain* are syllabified as /ə.plɔd/ and /ɛk.splen/ (see Figure 3.13). In accordance with step b, onset formation, all the consonants in the clusters

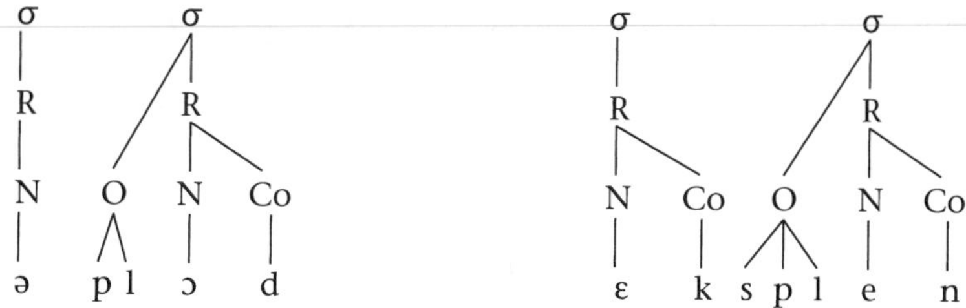

Figure 3.13 Syllabification: onsets before codas and phonotactic constraints

between the two vowel nuclei in each word (*pl* and *kspl,* respectively) could be syllabified as onsets of the second syllable. Thus *pl* is a possible candidate for an onset. According to the phonotactic constraints that are active in English, it is also a permissible onset, so both consonants are syllabified as part of the second syllable onset. In contrast, *kspl* is not a permissible onset in English; *spl* is a permissible onset, however, so the last three consonants of *kspl* are syllabified as part of the second syllable onset, and the first consonant *k* is left to be syllabified as a coda to the preceding syllable.

For a more advanced discussion of these issues, go to **bedfordstmartins.com /linguistics/phonology** and click on **syllabification**.

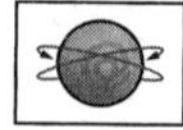

5.5 Syllabic Phonology

One reason that syllables are treated as units of phonological structure is that they are relevant to stating generalizations about the distribution of allophonic features. The next sections provide examples of the role of syllables and subsyllabic constituents in phonological patterns. The fact that syllables and their internal constituents have such a role is thus evidence that they are part of the knowledge that speakers have of the phonology of their language.

Aspiration in English

As Table 3.30 shows, the voiceless stops of English each have an aspirated and an unaspirated allophone.

The distribution of aspiration can be stated generally by referring to syllable structure and, in the case of the distribution of unaspirated stops, by referring to the subsyllabic onset and coda units (see Table 3.31).

The phonemic representations of the three English stops are unaspirated, since aspiration is predictable. The environments where aspiration occurs can be stated very generally by referring to syllable structure.

6)

English voiceless stops are aspirated syllable-initially.

This statement accounts for all the data in column A of Table 3.30, where voiceless stops appear syllable-initially. No aspiration is found in the forms in columns B

Table 3.30 English aspiration

A		*B*		*C*	
[pʰǽn]	pan	[spǽn]	span	[slǽp]	slap
[pʰéjn]	pain	[spéjn]	Spain	[slát]	slot
[pʰówk]	poke	[spówk]	spoke	[blák]	block
[tʰówn]	tone	[stówn]	stone		
[kʰín]	kin	[skín]	skin		
[pʰɹ̩spájɹ]	perspire	[splǽt]	splat		
[tʰəméjɾow]	tomato	[ʌpsɛ́t]	upset		
[kʰənú]	canoe				
[əpʰɔ́n]	upon				
[ətʰǽk]	attack				
[tʰəkʰílə]	tequila				

Table 3.31 Distribution of aspirated stops in English

Aspirated stops	*Unaspirated stops*
• syllable-initially	Elsewhere • in a syllable onset preceded by *s* (whether another C follows or not) • in a coda

and C since the voiceless stops appear either as the second member of the syllable onset (in *span, Spain, spoke, stone, skin,* and *splat*) or in a coda, as in *upset.*[1]

Phonetic Length in English Vowels

English offers a second example of the phonological relevance of syllables. Phonetic length is predictable in English vowels, as the examples in Table 3.32 show.

English vowels, whether or not they are diphthongs, are shorter before voiceless consonants, before sonorant consonants, and in word-final position; they are longer before voiced nonsonorant consonants provided these nonsonorant consonants are in coda position in the same syllable. As the next examples show, if vowels are fol-

[1] Some English words, such as *upper, happy,* and *walking,* do not show aspiration where it is expected, given that the syllabification procedure results in the following: /ʌ.pɹ̩/, /hæ.pi/, and /wɔ.kɪŋ/. This fact is accounted for by assuming that the voiceless stops in these forms are simultaneously in both syllables, a phenomenon that is known as **ambisyllabicity**:

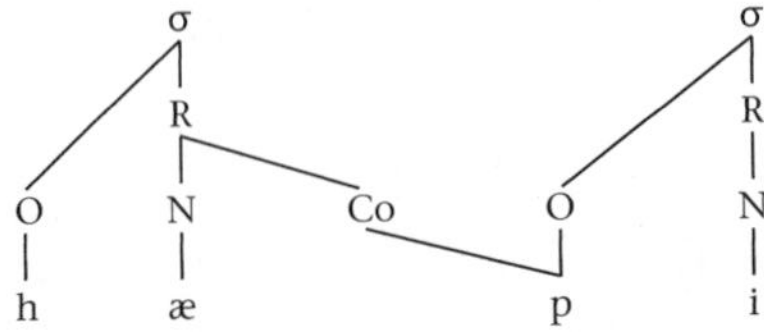

We will not address the details and motivations of ambisyllabicity here.

Table 3.32 Phonetic length in English: long vowels before voiced coda consonants

A		*B*	
bad	[bæːd]	bat	[bæt]
Abe	[eːjb]	ape	[ejp]
phase	[feːjz]	face	[fejs]
leave	[liːv]	leaf	[lif]
tag	[tʰæːg]	tack	[tʰæk]
brogue	[bɹoːwg]	broke	[bɹowk]
		tame	[tʰẽjm]
		meal	[mil]
		soar	[sɔɹ]
		show	[ʃow]

lowed by nonsonorant consonants that are onsets of the following syllable, the vowels are short. Thus, in Table 3.33, the vowels in the first syllable all precede a voiced, nonsonorant consonant, but they are short since the voiced consonant is in the following syllable.

Table 3.33 Short vowels before voiced onset consonants in English

obey	[ow.bej]	/obe/
redo	[ɹi.du]	/ɹidu/
regard	[ɹi.gɑɹd]	/ɹigɑɹd/

In order for an English vowel to be long, it must be followed by a voiced obstruent in the same syllable. The following generalization can now be made.

7)

English vowels are long when followed by a voiced obstruent in the coda position of the same syllable.

As the analyses of the distribution of aspiration and vowel length in English have shown, using syllabic representations in phonology permits us to make more general statements about certain allophonic patterns in language than using only statements that do not make reference to syllable structure.

For more discussion of syllables and stress in English, go to **bedfordstmartins .com/linguistics/phonology** and click on **syllables and stress**.

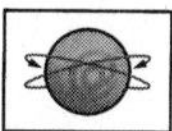

6 Derivations and Rules

To this point we have established the existence of related levels of phonological structure. In this model, phonological units from a lower level of structure are organized and grouped into higher-level structural units. Thus, features are grouped into segments, which in turn are organized into syllables. We have established that segments can be contrastive and hence belong to separate phonemes, or noncontrastive and hence function as predictable allophonic variants of phonemes. We have also seen that general statements referring to natural classes and to syllable structure can account for the patterning of noncontrastive elements. Finally, we have seen that there are two levels of representation associated with the difference between contrastive and noncontrastive segments: the phonemic level represents unpredictable, phonemic properties and units of a language, while the phonetic level represents predictable, allophonic properties and units. In this section we will explore the relationship between the phonemic and phonetic levels of representation and illustrate how this relationship is formalized.

Phonologists assume that phonemic representations are equivalent to the mental representations that speakers have of the words in their language, while phonetic representations are equivalent to the actual phonetic outputs that are produced in the course of speech. In this sense, phonemic representations are understood to be the basic representations of units such as the word. The unpredictable phonological information represented in a phonemic representation thus underlies all actual phonetic forms; for this reason, phonemic representations are also called **underlying representations** (or forms) while phonetic representations are also called **surface representations** (or forms).

Phonemic representations become phonetic representations as a result of being acted upon by **phonological processes** such as the devoicing of liquids and glides that follow voiceless stops in English, the aspiration of voiceless stops at the beginning of syllables in English, the lengthening of English vowels preceding voiced coda obstruents, and so on. Thus we say that phonetic or surface forms are derived from phonemic or underlying forms by means of phonological processes. These phonological processes are formalized as **phonological rules** (formalized statements of phonological processes). In this section, we focus on understanding how rules act in **derivations** and how they should be formalized.

6.1 The Form and Notation of Rules

General statements about allophonic distribution are formalized as rules, which are written so as to reflect the dynamic nature of articulatory processes (see Chapter 2, Section 9).

Rules

Rules take the following form.

8)

A→B / X __ Y

In this notation, *A* stands for an element in the underlying representation, *B* for the change it undergoes or for the output of the rule, and *X* and *Y* for the conditioning environment. Either *X* or *Y* may be absent (null) if the conditioning environment is found only on one side of the allophone. The __ (focus bar) indicates the position of the segment undergoing the rule. The slash separates the statement of the change from the statement of the conditioning environment, and can be thought of as meaning 'in the environment of'. This rule is therefore read as *A becomes B in the environment between X and Y.*

As an example of rule writing, we return to the distribution of liquid-glide devoicing in English (Section 2.3): liquids and glides have voiceless allophones after syllable-initial voiceless stops (and voiced allophones elsewhere). The rule statement treats the voiced allophones of liquids and glides as basic (underlying) and changes the feature [+voice] to [–voice] in the appropriate environment (see Figure 3.14).

$$\begin{bmatrix} \text{–syllabic} \\ \text{+sonorant} \\ \text{+voice} \\ \text{–nasal} \end{bmatrix} \rightarrow \text{[–voice]} \; / \; \sigma \begin{bmatrix} \text{–syllabic} \\ \text{+consonantal} \\ \text{–sonorant} \\ \text{–continuant} \\ \text{–voice} \\ \text{–delayed release} \end{bmatrix} \underline{\qquad}$$

Figure 3.14 Liquid-glide devoicing in English expressed as a rule

The rule in Figure 3.14 is shorthand for the prose statement given in *9.*

9)

Liquids and glides become voiceless after syllable-initial voiceless stops.

The use of features in Figure 3.14 expresses the fact that liquids and glides form a natural class of sounds: specifically, they are the nonnasal sonorant consonants of English. It also formally represents the fact that the process is phonetically based. For example, the devoicing of liquids and glides in English is a typical process of assimilation. The rule notation in Figure 3.14 explicitly shows this by indicating that the [+voice] feature of sonorant consonants changes to [–voice] following the class of voiceless stops, sounds that are themselves [–voice].

Deletion and Epenthesis as Rules

English speakers (optionally) drop a schwa [ə] in an open syllable when it is followed by a stressed syllable, as in *police* [pl̥ís] and *parade* [pr̥éjd]. (Schwa deletion would not apply in cases where the result would be an impermissible sequence of consonants.) The rule can be formalized as in Figure 3.15. Here, C_0 is an abbreviation for any number of successive consonants from zero on up and the σ represents a syllable boundary.

$$\text{[ə]} \rightarrow ø \; / \; C_0 \underline{\quad} \sigma \; C_0 \quad \begin{matrix} \text{V} \\ \text{[+stress]} \end{matrix}$$

Figure 3.15 Schwa deletion in English

The null sign ø in Figure 3.15 is used in writing both deletion and epenthesis rules. **Deletion** gets rid of something that was present in the underlying form; conversely, **epenthesis** adds something that was not present in the underlying form, as shown schematically in *10:*

10)

	Underlying form →	Surface form	/ (Environment)
Rule form:	A	→ B	/ . . .
Deletion:	A	→ Ø	/ . . .
Epenthesis:	Ø	→ B	/ . . .

An example of epenthesis in English involves vowel insertion that is frequently triggered when an impermissible phonotactic structure is encountered in a borrowed word, as in the English pronunciation of the name *Dmitri*. It is also the case that in some dialects of English, a coda consisting of *l* and another consonant is not permitted. In these dialects, *milk* is pronounced [mɪlək] and *film* [fɪləm]. This latter change can be represented in rule format as in Figure 3.16.

$$\text{Ø} \rightarrow [\text{ə}] \ / \ [\text{+lateral}] \ \_\_\_\_ \begin{bmatrix} \text{–syllabic} \\ \text{+consonantal} \end{bmatrix} \ \sigma$$

Figure 3.16 Schwa epenthesis in English as a rule

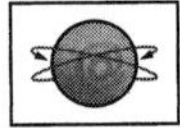

For more on the rules of epenthesis, go to **bedfordstmartins.com/linguistics/phonology** and click on **epenthesis: alpha notation**.

Rules that Refer to Syllable Structure

The epenthesis rule in Figure 3.16 refers to syllable structure. Notice that there is a syllable boundary marker [σ] at the end of the rule statement; this marker is used to indicate that the schwa is inserted between a lateral and another consonant at the end of a syllable. Although the rule formulated in Figure 3.16 does not explicitly state this, the insertion of the schwa actually changes the syllable structure of the input word. In other words, a word such as *film*, which constitutes one syllable initially, becomes two syllables after epenthesis. This change in syllable structure is illustrated in Figure 3.17.

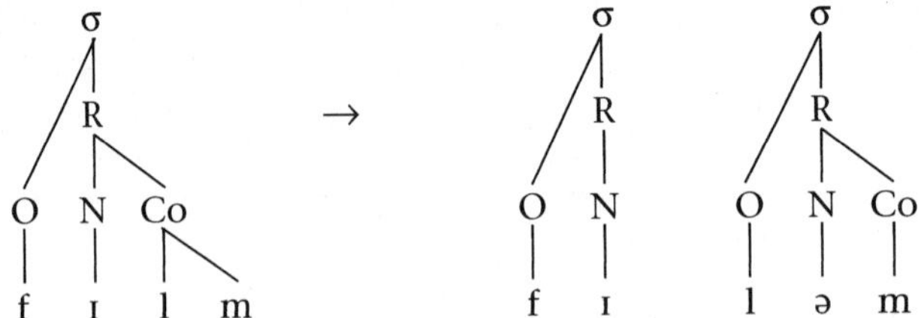

Figure 3.17 Syllabic representations of schwa epenthesis in English

Many other rules in English and in other languages make reference to syllable structure. One of these is the rule of vowel lengthening in English. The data from Table 3.32 showing the differences in vowel length in words such as *phase* versus *face* can be generalized as in *11:*

11)

English vowels are long when followed by a voiced obstruent in the same syllable.

The corresponding rule (in Figure 3.18) states that an underlying short vowel is lengthened in the appropriate context. As in the case of the epenthesis rule, the boundary of the syllable is represented by a syllable marker σ. Notice that the onset of the syllable is irrelevant to the statement of the rule and so is not included in the formalization.

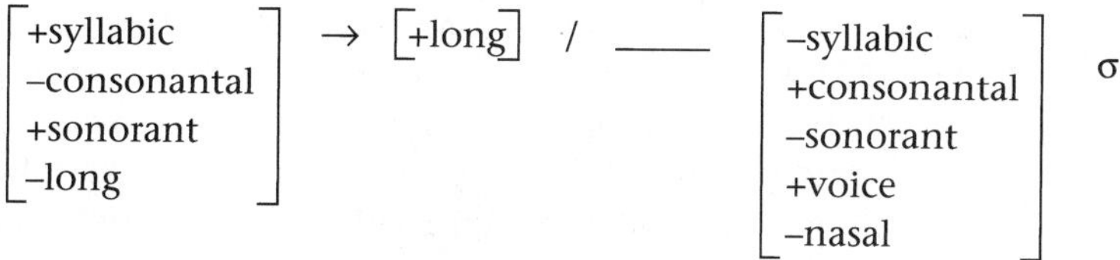

Figure 3.18 Vowel lengthening in English

For an advanced discussion of the nature and structure of phonological representations, go to **bedfordstmartins.com/linguistics/phonology** and click on **representations**.

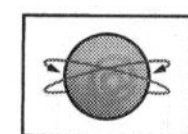

6.2 Derivations

Underlying representations are composed of phonemes (which are composed of distinctive features). Phonetic forms are derived by allowing phonological processes—formalized as rules—to operate on underlying representations in those contexts where the processes are relevant.

The derivation of three phonetic representations (PRs) from underlying representations (URs) is illustrated in Figure 3.19. Here, the underlying representation is on the top line (the crosshatch # symbolizes a word boundary); reading downward, each rule applies in sequence, and the underlying representation is adjusted as required. Where a rule fails to apply, the form remains unchanged; this information is conveyed by dashes. The resulting output then serves as the input to the following rule. Finally, when all rules relevant to the derivation in question have applied, a phonetic representation is formed. The two rules presented in the following example are aspiration and vowel lengthening (see Section 5.5).

UR	#slæp# slap	#tæp# tap	#pæd# pad
Aspiration	—	#tʰæp#	#pʰæd#
V-length	—	—	#pʰæːd#
PR	[slæp]	[tʰæp]	[pʰæːd]

Figure 3.19 The phonological derivation of three English words

In this example, two rules have applied. (Since the words being derived are all monosyllabic, the syllable boundaries are equivalent to word boundaries and so are not indicated here.) The first accounts for aspiration. Since the initial consonant of the URs #tæp# and #pæd# are voiceless stops found in onset position, they fulfill the conditions under which English stops become aspirated. We therefore indicate that aspiration occurs by providing an intermediate form on a new line.

We have also seen that in English, vowels are predictably long when they occur before a voiced stop in the same syllable. In Figure 3.19, the /æ/s of *slap* and *tap* occur before voiceless stops and so are not lengthened. The vowel of *pad,* however, occurs in just the environment associated with long vowels and so is predictably lengthened.

The use of such derivations underscores the fact that allophonic variation is the result of processes that apply in the course of language use. Underlying representations capture the knowledge that speakers have about the nature of their phonological system, rules reflect the application of allophonic processes, and the phonetic representation reflects the speech output. The relationship between phonemic or underlying representations and phonetic or surface representations is the result of the action of phonological processes.

6.3 Rule Application

We have seen that more than one rule may be employed in a derivation. Consequently, we must now ask how several rules are applied to a given underlying form when these rules interact.

Rule Ordering

In Figure 3.19 we examined the application of the rules of English aspiration and vowel lengthening, which apply to voiceless stops and vowels, respectively. Note that the environments in which each of these rules apply (onset and precoda position, respectively) are entirely different. Therefore, these rules do not interact or affect each other in any way; the order in which they are applied makes no difference to the outcome of the derivation. As Figure 3.20 shows, there is no difference in the outcome when the same rules are applied in reverse order.

UR	#slæp#	slap	#tæp#	tap	#pæd#	pad
V-length	—		—		#pæːd#	
Aspiration	—		#tʰæp#		#pʰæːd#	
PR	[slæp]		[tʰæp]		[pʰæːd]	

Figure 3.20 Unordered rule application

We therefore say that the rules of aspiration and vowel lengthening are **unordered** with respect to each other. There are cases, however, in which two rules have to be **ordered** with respect to each other. For example, in some instances, the application of one rule creates an environment that makes possible the application of another rule. A case of ordered rules is illustrated in Figure 3.21. In casual speech, the word *parade* in English is pronounced [pɹ̥éːjd]: there is initially a schwa between *p* and *r* which gets deleted by means of a rule of schwa deletion because it is unstressed. After the schwa is deleted, the liquid *r* that follows the schwa in the underlying representation gets positioned directly after a voiceless stop. As a result,

UR	#pəɹed#	parade
Stress	#pəɹéd#	
Schwa deletion	#pɹéd#	
→ Liquid-glide devoicing	#pɹ̥éd#	
Diphthongization	#pɹ̥éjd#	
Vowel lengthening	#pɹ̥éːjd#	
PR	[pɹ̥éːjd]	

Figure 3.21 Rule order in a derivation

the *r* becomes subject to the rule of liquid-glide devoicing (given in example *2* in Section 2.3), and is therefore devoiced.

In Figure 3.21 the arrow, which is not normally written in derivations, indicates that the schwa-deletion rule must apply before liquid-glide devoicing. Notice also that a rule that assigns stress to the final vowel applies before schwa deletion. In addition, notice that if liquid-glide devoicing applied before schwa deletion, the devoicing of *r* would not be able to take place because *r* would not be positioned right after the voiceless *p* and therefore would not get devoiced. What is clear, then, is that to get the correct surface form [pɹ̥éːjd], schwa deletion must be ordered before liquid-glide devoicing.

6.4 Processes and Rules: A Last Word

The combined use of features and processes in phonological description reflects the dynamic nature of linguistic behavior. First, the use of features reflects a basic level of phonological activity—contrasts take place on the feature level, not on the level where segments are represented. Second, the use of process notation and formalization with rules reflects the realities of linguistic production, in which sounds are affected by the context in which they are pronounced as we speak. Overall, the patterning of phonological units follows from the interaction of a universal set of features, universal and language-specific phonotactic constraints and syllabification procedures, and the use of rules. This current theory of phonology is based on principles that are applicable to the study of any human language.

Summing Up

Phonology deals with the sequential and phonetically conditioned patterning of sounds in language. To account for this patterning, three units of phonological representation have been established: the **feature**, the **phoneme**, and the **syllable**. Phonemes are contrastive segmental units composed of distinctive features. Phonetically conditioned variants of phonemes are called **allophones**.

Phonology makes use of **underlying forms**, **derivations**, and **phonological rules** in its formal notation. Some rules are ordered with respect to each other.

Key Terms

General terms

environment
feature
phonology
segment
syllable

Distinctive sounds and their variations

allophones
allophonic distribution
complementary distribution
contrast
minimal pair
near-minimal pairs
phonemes
phonemic representation
phonemic transcriptions
phonetic representation

General terms concerning classes of sounds and features

binary features
consonantal
distinctive feature
features
matrix
natural classes
obstruents
sonorant
syllabic

Manner features

continuant
delayed release (DR)
lateral
nasal

Laryngeal features

constricted glottis (CG)
spread glottis (SG)
voice

Place features

anterior
back
CORONAL
DORSAL
high
LABIAL
low
reduced
round
strident
tense

Terms concerning syllable structure

ambisyllabicity
association line
closed syllable
coda
nucleus
onset
open syllable
phonotactics
rhyme
suprasegmental
syllable

Terms concerning rules, representations, and processes

deletion
derivations

epenthesis
ordered (rule application)
phonemic representations
phonological processes
phonological rules
surface representations (forms)
underlying representations (forms)
unordered (rule application)

For more information on the sources used in this chapter, go to **bedfordstmartins.com/linguistics/phonology** and click on **Sources**.

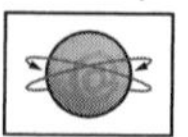

Recommended Reading

Anderson, Stephen R. 1985. *Phonology in the Twentieth Century.* Chicago: University of Chicago Press.

Carr, Philip. 1993. *Phonology.* London: Macmillan.

Clements, George N., and Samuel Jay Keyser. 1983. *CV Phonology.* Cambridge, MA: MIT Press.

Goldsmith, John. 1990. *Autosegmental and Metrical Phonology.* Cambridge, MA: Blackwell.

Goldsmith, John, ed. 1995. *The Handbook of Phonological Theory.* Cambridge, MA: Blackwell.

Gussman, Edmund; S. R. Anderson; J. Bresnan; B. Comrie; W. Dressler; and C. J. Ewen. 2002. *Phonology: Analysis and Theory.* Cambridge: Cambridge University Press.

Hyman, Larry M. 1975. *Phonology: Theory and Analysis.* New York: Holt, Rinehart and Winston.

Keating, Patricia. 1988. "The Phonology-Phonetics Interface." In *Linguistics: The Cambridge Survey.* Vol. 1. Edited by F. Newmeyer, 281–302. London: Cambridge University Press.

Kenstowicz, Michael. 1994. *Phonology in Generative Grammar.* Cambridge, MA: Blackwell.

Stampe, David. 1980. *A Dissertation on Natural Phonology.* New York: Garland.

Appendix: Hints for Solving Phonology Problems

The task of solving a phonology problem is made easier if certain facts presented in this chapter and summarized here are kept in mind. The data that we consider below are taken from Tagalog (Filipino), a language spoken in the Philippines.

1. In the following data, consider the phones [h] and [ʔ] and determine whether they contrast or whether they are allophones of one phoneme.

a) kahon	'box'	d) ʔaɾi	'property'
b) haɾiʔ	'king'	e) kaʔon	'to fetch'
c) ʔumagos	'to flow'	f) humagos	'to paint'

In order to determine whether the phones contrast, we begin by looking for minimal pairs. These establish which segments are contrastive. For example, in the data in a) through f), minimal pairs occur in items a/e and c/f; b/d is a near-minimal pair. The existence of minimal and near-minimal pairs of words indicates that [h] and [ʔ] contrast. Therefore we can conclude that /h/ and /ʔ/ are separate phonemes.

2. Now consider the following data, and determine whether the two sounds [d] and [ɾ] contrast or whether they are allophones of one phoneme.

a) datiŋ	'to arrive'	f) daɾaʔiŋ	'will complain'
b) dami	'amount'	g) maɾumi	'dirty'
c) dumi	'dirt'	h) maɾami	'many'
d) daɾatiŋ	'will arrive'	i) daʔiŋ	'to complain'
e) manduɾukot	'pickpocket'	j) mandukot	'to go pickpocketing'

Since there are no minimal pairs in the data that contrast [d] and [ɾ], we proceed to check whether the two sounds are in complementary distribution. Normally, when two sounds are in complementary distribution and therefore allophones of one phoneme, they must be phonetically similar. In Tagalog, [d] and [ɾ] are both voiced alveolar segments; thus they are sufficiently similar phonetically to be viewed as potential allophones of one phoneme.

To check whether two (or more) sounds are in complementary distribution, the best thing to do is to list the environments in which the sounds occur:

[d] occurs:	[ɾ] occurs:
–word-initially (e.g., *dami*)	–between two vowels (e.g., *maɾami*)
–following a nasal (e.g., *mandukot*)	

[d] never occurs between two vowels, and [ɾ] never occurs word-initially or following a nasal. Since the two sounds never occur in identical environments, they are in complementary distribution and their distributions are predictable.

3. If two potential allophones of one phoneme are in complementary distribution, we can be reasonably sure that they are allophones of one phoneme. We can therefore make a general statement about their distribution, in terms of some natural phonological class. For example: Tagalog [d] and [ɾ] are in complementary distribution and are allophones of one phoneme. The allophone [ɾ] occurs between vowels; [d] occurs elsewhere—here, word-initially, as in items a), b), c), f), and so on, and after nasal consonants, as in items e) and j).

4. Once we have determined that two sounds are allophones of one phoneme, we need to determine which phoneme they are both derived from. Usually this can be done by selecting one of the allophones as basic. In most cases, the allophone chosen to represent the phoneme is the one with the widest distribution (the elsewhere variant). In the Tagalog case, the elsewhere variant is [d], so we posit the phoneme /d/, which has two allophones, [d] and [ɾ]. It may be helpful to set up a traditional phoneme-allophone diagram to illustrate this (see Figure 3.2).

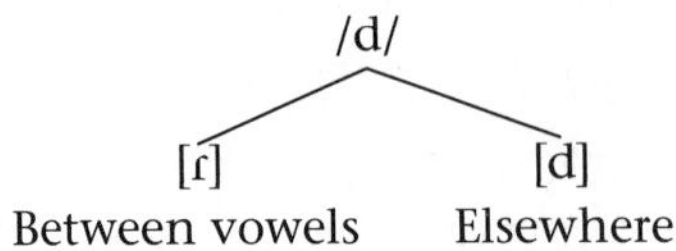

5. Now that we know that [d] and [ɾ] are allophones of the phoneme /d/, we need to determine the phonological rule that accounts for the predictable features of the other allophones. Our rule is probably correct if it describes a common linguistic process (such as assimilation) in terms of natural classes of sounds interacting with neighboring segments and/or syllable structure.

   For example, for the above: d→ɾ / V___V

   The process at work here is a form of assimilation, in that an underlying voiced stop consonant becomes a continuant when found between two continuants (vowels).

6. We can assume that segments are phonemic if there are no minimal pairs for them but they cannot be shown to be allophones of one phoneme. In such a case, we can conclude that the data simply did not provide minimal pairs.

Exercises

Assume phonetic transcription of the data in all exercises.

1. *Inuktitut* (Eastern) (Native Canadian)

   The data here are in a relatively broad transcription.

a)	iglumut	'to a house'	h)	pinna	'that one up there'
b)	ukiaq	'late fall'	i)	ani	'female's brother'
c)	aiviq	'walrus'	j)	iglu	'(snow)house'
d)	aniguvit	'if you leave'	k)	panna	'that place up there'
e)	aglu	'seal's breathing hole'	l)	aivuq	'she goes home'
f)	iglumit	'from a house'	m)	ini	'place, spot'
g)	anigavit	'because you leave'	n)	ukiuq	'winter'

   i) List all the minimal pairs in this data. Based on the minimal pairs you have found, list all the contrastive pairs of vowels.

   ii) Using the vowel charts in Figures 2.8 and 2.9 as your models, make a chart of Inuktitut vowel phonemes.

   iii) Now consider the data again; here it is transcribed in more phonetic detail. In it, there are phonetically similar segments that are in complementary distribution. Look for them and then answer the question that follows the data.

aa)	iglumut	'to a house'	hh)	pinna	'that one up there'
bb)	ukiaq	'late fall'	ii)	anɪ	'female's brother'
cc)	aivɪq	'walrus'	jj)	iglʊ	'(snow)house'
dd)	aniguvit	'if you leave'	kk)	panna	'that place up there'
ee)	aglʊ	'seal's breathing hole'	ll)	aivʊq	'she goes home'
ff)	iglumit	'from a house'	mm)	inɪ	'place, spot'
gg)	anigavit	'because you leave'	nn)	ukiʊq	'winter'

   iv) List the phonetically similar segments that are in complementary distribution. State their distribution in words.

2. *Hindi* (Hindi is a language of the Indo-European family spoken in India)
   Consider the segments [b] and [b̤] in the data below and answer the questions that follow. The segment transcribed [b̤] is a murmured voiced stop (which is all you need to know to solve the problem).

   a) [bara] 'large'
   b) [b̤ari] 'heavy'
   c) [bina] 'without'
   d) [b̤ir] 'crowd'
   e) [bori] 'sackcloth'
   f) [b̤ɛd] 'disagreement'
   g) [bais] 'twenty-two'
   h) [b̤əs] 'buffalo'
   i) [bap] 'father'
   j) [b̤ag] 'part'

   i) Are the segments [b] and [b̤] allophones of the same phoneme or do they belong to separate phonemes? If you believe they belong to separate phonemes, give evidence from the data to support your analysis. If you believe they are allophones of the same phoneme, list the conditioning environments.

3. *Mokilese* (Mokilese is an Austronesian language of the South Pacific)
   Examine the following data from Mokilese carefully, taking note of where voiceless vowels occur.

   a) pi̥san 'full of leaves'
   b) tu̥pu̥kta 'bought'
   c) pu̥ko 'basket'
   d) ki̥sa 'we two'
   e) su̥pwo 'firewood'
   f) kamwɔki̥ti 'to move'
   g) uduk 'flesh'
   h) kaskas 'to throw'
   i) poki 'to strike something'
   j) pil 'water'
   k) apid 'outrigger support'
   l) ludʒuk 'to tackle'

   i) The vowel phonemes of Mokilese are /i e ɛ u o ɔ a/. In Mokilese, [i̥] is an allophone of /i/, and [u̥] is an allophone of /u/. No other vowels have voiceless allophones. State in words the conditioning factors that account for this. Be as general as possible in referring to classes of sounds.

   ii) If you have completed the section on rule formalization, write a rule (using features) that accounts for the derived allophones.

4. *Gascon* (Gascon is spoken in southwest France)
   The phones [b], [β], [d], [ð], [g], and [ɣ] are all found in Gascon, as the following examples show. The phone [β] is a voiced bilabial fricative; [ɣ] is a voiced velar fricative. The phone [y] is a tense high front rounded vowel.

   a) brẽn 'endanger'
   b) bako 'cow'
   c) ũmbro 'shadow'
   d) krãmbo 'room'
   e) dilys 'Monday'
   f) dũŋko 'until'
   g) duso 'sweet'
   h) taldepãn 'leftover bread'
   i) pũnde 'to lay eggs'
   j) dudze 'twelve'
   k) guteʒa 'flow'
   l) ẽŋgwãn 'this year'
   m) puðe 'to be able'
   n) gat 'cat'
   o) lũŋg 'long'
   p) saliβo 'saliva'
   q) noβi 'husband'
   r) aβe 'to have'
   s) ʃiβaw 'horse'
   t) byðɛt 'gut'
   u) eʃaðo 'hoe'
   v) biɣar 'mosquito'
   w) riɣut 'he laughed'
   x) agro 'sour'
   y) ʒuɣɛt 'he played'

i) Group the six phones [b], [β], [d], [ð], [g], and [ɣ] into three pairs. The two phones in each pair should be phonetically similar. For each pair, state the phonetic similarities shared by the members of the pair.

ii) List the environments in which the phones [b], [β], [d], [ð], [g], and [ɣ] are found. You may ignore word-final position in your consideration.

iii) Is there any evidence for grouping these pairs of sounds into phonemes? State the evidence for each pair.

iv) Make a general statement about the patterning of the phonemes you have established.

v) Following your analysis, write the following forms in phonemic transcription.

a) [puɣo] b) [deðat] c) [ʃiβaw] d) [krãmbo]

5. *Swampy Cree* (Swampy Cree is a Native Canadian language of the Algonquian family)

The following data from Swampy Cree shows a number of different voiced and voiceless consonantal segments.

a)	niska	'goose'	l)	nisto	'three'
b)	kodak	'another'	m)	tʃiːgahigan	'axe'
c)	asabaːp	'thread'	n)	adim	'dog'
d)	waskoːw	'cloud'	o)	miːbit	'tooth'
e)	paskwaːw	'prairie'	p)	pimiː	'lard'
f)	niːgi	'my house'	q)	mide	'heart'
g)	koːgoːs	'pig'	r)	oːgik	'these'
h)	tahki	'often'	s)	tʃiːmaːn	'canoe'
i)	namwaːtʃ	'not at all'	t)	waːbos	'rabbit'
j)	ospwaːgan	'pipe'	u)	naːbeːw	'man'
k)	midʒihtʃij	'hand'	v)	miːdʒiwin	'food'

i) Do [p] and [b] belong to separate phonemes, or are they allophones of one phoneme? If you think they belong to separate phonemes, list data to support your case. If you think they are allophones, first state the conditioning factors in words, and then, using features, write a rule that accounts for their distribution.

ii) Do the same for [t] and [d], [k] and [g], and [tʃ] and [dʒ].

iii) Make a general statement about the relationship among all the consonantal pairs whose distribution you have examined.

iv) Using Figure 3.19 as your model, provide complete derivations of the forms for k) *hand,* m) *axe,* and o) *tooth.*

6. There are a number of natural classes in the vowel and consonant data below. Circle three natural classes in each set of data. Indicate which feature or features define the class, as in the example. The phone [x] is a voiceless velar fricative.

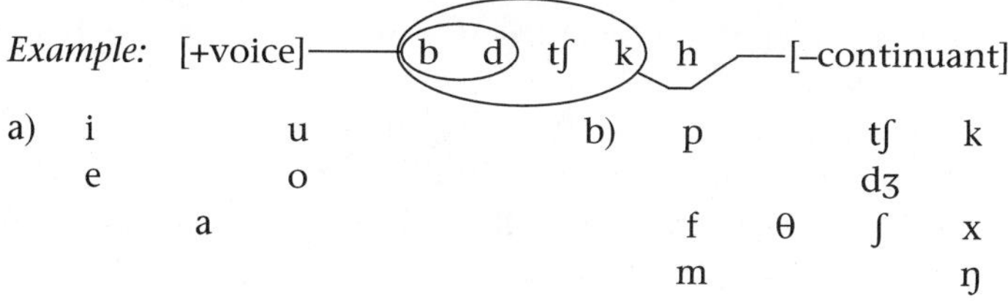

7. Name the single feature that distinguishes the following pairs of sounds.

a) [θ]	:	[ð]	e) [b]	:	[m]	i) [ʌ]	:	[ə]
b) [p]	:	[f]	f) [s]	:	[ʃ]	j) [s]	:	[θ]
c) [u]	:	[ʊ]	g) [i]	:	[ɪ]	k) [e]	:	[ɛ]
d) [i]	:	[e]	h) [k]	:	[g]	l) [u]	:	[o]

8. Complete the feature matrix for each of the sounds indicated. The V abbreviates the features [+syllabic, –consonantal], and the C abbreviates the features [–syllabic, +consonantal].

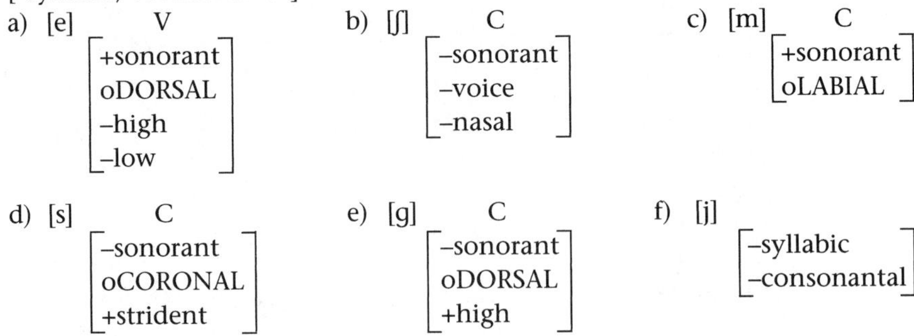

9. *English/Korean*

As we have seen, phonological adaptation of loan words may reflect facts about syllable structure. The Korean automobile name *Hyundai* has been adapted into English in various ways, one of which follows. Given the Korean form and the English adaptation provided, state two reasons based on syllable structure conditions that explain why the English form is pronounced the way it is.

Korean form		*English form*
/hjʌndæ/	→	/hʌnde/ [hʌndej]

10. *English*

Many speakers of English have two variants of [l]. One, called *clear l,* is transcribed as [l] in the following data. The other, called *dark l,* is transcribed as [ɫ]. Examine the data, and answer the questions that follow.

a)	[lajf]	'life'	g)	[pʰɪɫ]	'pill'
b)	[lip]	'leap'	h)	[fiɫ]	'feel'
c)	[luːz]	'lose'	i)	[hɛɫp]	'help'
d)	[ilowp]	'elope'	j)	[bʌɫk]	'bulk'
e)	[dilajt]	'delight'	k)	[sowɫd]	'sold'
f)	[slip]	'sleep'	l)	[fʊɫ]	'full'

Do [l] and [ɫ] belong to separate phonemes or are they allophones of the same phoneme? If you think they belong to separate phonemes, answer question *i.* If you think they are allophones of the same phoneme, answer questions *ii–iv.*

i) List the evidence that makes your case for considering [l] and [ɫ] as separate phonemes.

ii) State the distribution of [l] and [ɫ] in words.

iii) Which variant makes the best underlying form? Why?

iv) Can you make reference to syllable structure in your distribution statement? If you can, do so in rule form.

11. *Canadian French*

For the purposes of this problem, you may assume that syllables in Canadian French have the following structure:

- Maximum number of consonants in an onset: 2. Where there are two onset consonants, the first must be an obstruent, the second a sonorant or a fricative.
- Each vowel forms a syllable nucleus.
- Maximum number of consonants in a coda: 2.

i) With these stipulations in mind, syllabify the following forms:

a) bukan	'smoke'	c) pudrəri	'snowstorm'
b) erite	'to inherit'	d) plie	'to fold'

In the following data from Canadian French, each pair of phones is in complementary distribution.

[i] and [ɪ]	are allophones of one phoneme
[y] and [ʏ]	are allophones of a second phoneme
[u] and [ʊ]	are allophones of a third phoneme

It is possible to make a general statement about the distribution of the vowel allophones that accounts for all three phonemes. [y] is a high, front, rounded, tense vowel, while [ʏ] is a high, front, rounded, lax vowel.

Examine the data and answer the questions that follow.

a)	pilʏl	'pill'	o)	fini	'finished'
b)	griʃe	'to crunch'	p)	fɪj	'girl'
c)	grɪʃ	'it crunches'	q)	dzʏr	'hard'
d)	pətsi	'little' (masc.)	r)	tryke	'to fake'
e)	pətsɪt	'little' (fem.)	s)	fʊl	'(a) crowd'
f)	vitamɪn	'vitamin'	t)	plʏs	'more'
g)	saly	'hi'	u)	ru	'wheel'
h)	ʒʏp	'skirt'	v)	rʊt	'road'
i)	fyme	'smoke'	w)	suvã	'often'
j)	lynɛt	'glasses'	x)	trupo	'herd'
k)	tɔrdzy	'twisted'	y)	sʊp	'flexible'
l)	lʏn	'moon'	z)	tʊʃ	'touch'
m)	pɪp	'pipe'	aa)	fu	'crazy' (masc.)
n)	grimas	'grimace'	bb)	trʏk	'(a) trick'

ii) Provide a statement of the distribution of [i] and [ɪ], [y] and [ʏ], and [u] and [ʊ] in words. Make your statement as general as possible, but be precise.

iii) If you have completed the section on rule formalization, write a single rule that derives the allophones of each phoneme from the underlying form. Use features. Be sure to give your rule a name; use this name in the answer to question *iv*.

iv) Provide derivations for the following underlying forms.

UR	# # 'vitamin'	# # 'glasses'
PR	[vitamɪn]	[lynɛt]

12. *English*

The following data contain both careful speech and fast speech forms. Note the differences and answer the questions that follow. Some phonetic detail irrelevant to the question has been omitted from the transcription. Remember that an asterisk before a form indicates that it is not acceptable to (most) native speakers.

	Careful speech	*Fast speech*	*Spelled form*
a)	[ǽspəɹən]	[ǽspɹən]	aspirin
b)	[pɔ́ɹsələn]	[pɔ́ɹslən]	porcelain
c)	[nǽʃənəlàjz]	[nǽʃnəlàjz]	nationalize
d)	[ɹízənəbl̩]	[ɹíznəbl̩]	reasonable
e)	[ɪmǽdʒənətɪv]	[ɪmǽdʒnətɪv]	imaginative
f)	[sɛ̀pəɹəbílɪɾi]	[sɛ̀pɹəbílɪɾi]	separability
g)	[mɛ́θəd]	[mɛ́θəd] *[mɛ́θd]	method
h)	[féjməs]	[féjməs] *[féjms]	famous
i)	[mɛ́məɹàjz]	[mɛ́məɹàjz] *[mɛ́mɹàjz]	memorize
j)	[kʰənsìdəɹéjʃn̩]	[kʰənsìdəɹéjʃn̩] *[kʰənsìdɹéjʃn̩]	consideration

i) The schwa deletion between the careful speech forms and the rapid speech forms in items a–f is systematic. State in words the phonetic conditions that account for the deletion.

ii) The same pattern that occurs between the careful speech forms and the rapid speech forms in items a–f does not occur in items g–j. State in words the phonetic difference between these sets of forms that accounts for the lack of schwa deletion.

iii) Now that you have taken items g–j into account, will you have to change your original statement about the phonetic conditions governing schwa deletion in the fast speech forms? If so, do this in words.

iv) If you have completed the section on rule formalization, convert your statement in *iii* into formal notation.

13. Change the following statements into rule notation. Be sure to name the process in question for each case.
    a) Voiceless stops become corresponding fricatives between vowels.
    b) A schwa is inserted between a voiced stop and a word-final voiced fricative.
    c) Low unrounded vowels become rounded before *m*.

14. State each of the following rules in English, making reference to natural classes and common linguistic processes.

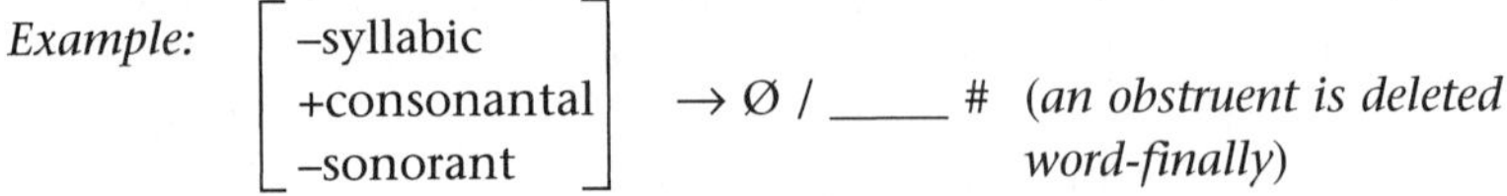

Example: $\begin{bmatrix} \text{-syllabic} \\ \text{+consonantal} \\ \text{-sonorant} \end{bmatrix} \rightarrow \emptyset \; / \; \_\_\_\_ \; \#$ (*an obstruent is deleted word-finally*)

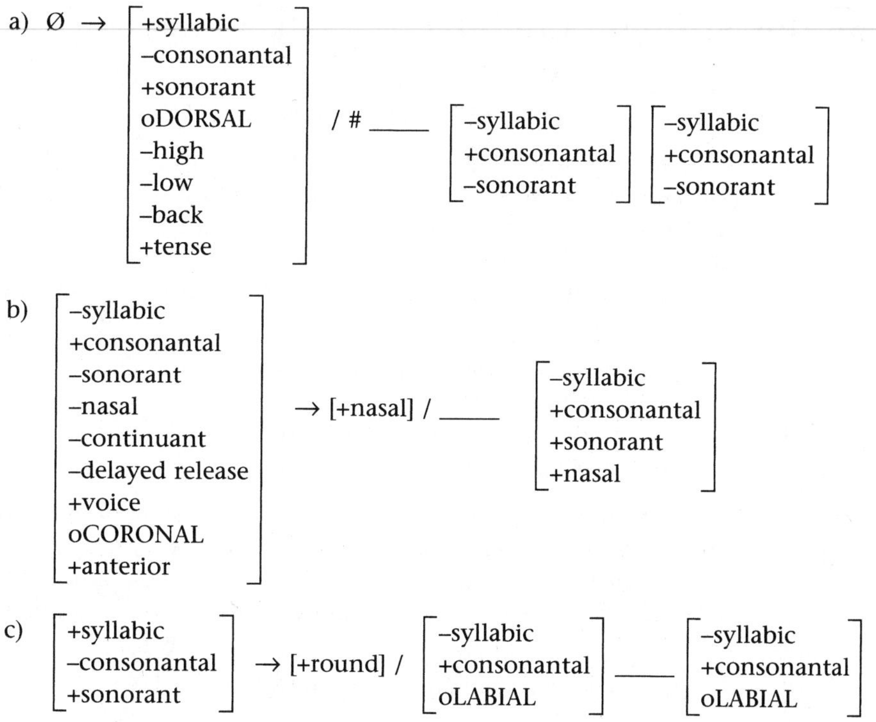

15. *Tamil* (Tamil is a Dravidian language spoken in South India and Sri Lanka) In the following Tamil data, some words begin with glides while others do not. The symbol [ɖ] represents a voiced retroflex stop, and the diacritic [̪] indicates dentals.

	Initial j-glide			*Initial w-glide*			*No initial glide*	
a)	jeli	'rat'	f)	woɖi	'break'	k)	arivu	'knowledge'
b)	jiː	'fly'	g)	woːlaj	'palm leaf'	l)	ain̪t̪u	'five'
c)	jilaj	'leaf'	h)	wuːsi	'needle'	m)	aːsaj	'desire'
d)	jeŋgeː	'where'	i)	wujir	'life'	n)	aːru	'river'
e)	jiɖuppu	'waist'	j)	woːram	'edge'	o)	aːdi	'origin'

i) The occurrence of these glides is predictable. Using your knowledge of natural classes, make a general statement about the distribution of the glides.

ii) Assuming the glides are not present in the underlying representations, name the process that accounts for their presence in the phonetic forms.

For the Student Linguist

THE FEATURE PRESENTATION

You've already read that features are the fundamental building blocks of phonemes. By writing rules with features, you can describe simply a change that happens to an entire class of sounds. You also make a stronger statement when you use features in a rule. For example, rule *1* says something about all the stops in a language, but rule *2* only says something about a list of sounds.

1) [–continuant] → [–voice] / ___ #
(stops become voiceless at the end of a word)

2) {p,t,k,b,d,g} → {p,t,k,p,t,k} / ___ #
(p "becomes" p at the end of a word;
b becomes p at the end of a word; etc.)

If you're just listing sounds, nothing requires them to have anything in common with each other. The sounds in the list could be a totally random selection of sounds turning into another totally random selection of sounds, as in rule *3,* and you'd have no way of predicting that *3* should be less common than *2.*

3) {e,t,w,b,n,h} → {ʃ,p,tʃ,g,a,m} / ___ #
(e becomes ʃ at the end of a word; etc.)

If you use features, you can predict that the set of changes described by rule *2* should be common (because once the rule is translated to features, it's merely rule *1,* a delightfully simple rule), but the set of changes described by rule *3* should be weird and unlikely. To describe rule *3* with features, you'd have to write six different rules, and each rule would be ugly and complicated. (I'm assuming that the more features you have to include in a rule, the more complicated it is.) For example, the first rule, changing [e] to [ʃ], would be:

4)
$$\left[\begin{array}{l}-\text{consonantal}\\+\text{voice}\\-\text{high}\\-\text{low}\\-\text{back}\\+\text{tense}\end{array}\right] \rightarrow \left[\begin{array}{l}+\text{consonantal}\\-\text{voice}\\\text{oCORONAL}\\+\text{continuant}\\+\text{strident}\\-\text{anterior}\\-\text{delayed release}\end{array}\right] \;/\; \_\_\_\ \#$$

However, you can accept the brilliance of features without buying the idea of using a matrix of binary features (like you've done so far) or a hierarchy of binary features. Features could have only one value (these are called "monovalent" or "privative" features). So instead of, say, [–nasal] and [+nasal], there'd only be [nasal]. Sounds that had [nasal] in the matrix/representation would be nasal; everything else would be oral. How is that any different from using a binary feature? The difference is that with a binary feature, you can write rules about things that are [–nasal]. You could write a rule like this:

5) $\begin{bmatrix}\text{–continuant}\\ \text{–nasal}\end{bmatrix}$ → [–voice] / ___ #
(oral stops become voiceless at the end of a word)

But if [–nasal] didn't exist, the only rule you could write would be:

6) [–continuant] → [–voice] / ___ #
(all stops, including nasal stops, become voiceless at the end of a word)

If [–nasal] did exist, you could write rule *5 or* rule *6*. Monovalent features, then, give you fewer possible rules. That's great if you can still write all the rules you need for every language, but awful if you can't write every rule you need.

Having fewer possible rules isn't important just because it would make this unit of linguistics easier. It's also important because, theoretically, if there are fewer possible rules in a language, it's easier for a child trying to learn the language to figure out how the sound system in that language works. He or she has fewer options to consider.

What if features could have three values? Or four? Or an infinite number of values? For example, there could be four features for the different laryngeal states: [A laryngeal], for glottal stops; [B laryngeal], for voiced sounds; [C laryngeal], for voiceless unaspirated sounds; and [D laryngeal], for voiceless aspirated sounds. Just like nothing can be both [+voice] and [–voice] at the same time, nothing could be [A laryngeal] and [B laryngeal] at the same time (or [A laryngeal] and [C laryngeal], etc.). Place of articulation could be handled the same way: [A place] for labials, [B place] for dentals, [C place] for alveolars, etc.

With this type of multivalued system, none of the subgroups (like dentals and alveolars) could be lumped together in a rule. Thus, for the place system I described, you couldn't talk about all of the coronals at once—you could only talk about the dentals or the alveolars or the alveopalatals and so forth. Once again, whether this is good or bad depends on how well it describes actual languages. (You might want to try out a multivalued feature system for place on some of the phonology problems you've already solved for homework or in class discussions, and see if they're harder or easier to do this way than with a binary feature system.)

These are just a couple of the possible variations on feature systems. I haven't even begun to question the merit of these *features*—that is, do we *really* need [voice]? Or [strident]? Or [delayed release]? Think about this as you work on a few phonology problems, and see if you can come up with a better feature system. There's a lot of room for change here.

four

Morphology: The Analysis of Word Structure

William O'Grady
Videa de Guzman

Carve every word before you let it fall.

– Oliver Wendell Holmes Sr.

Objectives

In this chapter, you will learn:

- how we analyze the structure of words
- how we form words by adding prefixes, suffixes, and infixes
- how we form words by putting two or more existing words together
- how we mark words to show grammatical concepts such as number, case, agreement, and tense
- how we form words by less common means
- how the processes of word formation interact with phonology

Nothing is more important to language than words. Unlike phonemes and syllables, which are simply elements of sound, words carry meaning in addition to their phonological form. And unlike sentences, which are made up as needed and then discarded, words are permanently stored in a speaker's mental dictionary or **lexicon**. They are arguably the fundamental building blocks of communication.

The average high school student knows about 60,000 basic words—items such as *read, language, on, cold,* and *if,* whose form and meaning cannot be predicted from anything else. Countless other words can be constructed and comprehended by the application of general rules to these and other elements. For example, any speaker of English who knows the verb *fax* recognizes *faxed* as its past tense form and can construct and interpret words such as *faxable* (for things that can be faxed) and *fax machine* (for the device that sends and receives faxes).

Linguists use the term **morphology** to refer to the part of the grammar that is concerned with words and word formation. As we will see, the study of morphology offers important insights into how language works, revealing the need for different categories of words, the presence of word-internal structure, and the existence of operations that create and modify words in various ways.

1 Words and Word Structure

As speakers of English, we rarely have difficulty segmenting a stream of speech sounds into words or deciding where to leave spaces when writing a sentence. What, though, is a word?

Linguists define the **word** as the smallest **free form** found in language. A free form is simply an element that does not have to occur in a fixed position with respect to neighboring elements; in many cases, it can even appear in isolation. Consider, for instance, the following sentence.

1)

Dinosaurs are extinct.

We all share the intuition that *dinosaurs* is a word here, but that the plural marker *-s* is not. The key observation is that *-s* is not a free form since it never occurs in isolation and cannot be separated from the noun to which it belongs. (Elements that must be attached to another category are written here with a hyphen.)

2)

*Dinosaur are -s extinct.

In contrast, *dinosaurs* is a word since it can occur both in isolation, as in the following example, and in different positions within sentences.

3)

Speaker A: What creatures do children find most fascinating?
Speaker B: Dinosaurs.

4)

a. Paleontologists study *dinosaurs.*
b. *Dinosaurs* are studied by paleontologists.
c. It's *dinosaurs* that paleontologists study.

Some words—like *are*—normally do not occur in isolation. However, they are still free forms because their positioning with respect to neighboring words is not entirely fixed. As shown by the following example, *are* can occur at the beginning of a sentence when a question is called for.

5)

Are dinosaurs extinct? (Compare: Dinosaurs *are* extinct.)

1.1 Morphemes

Like syllables and sentences, words have an internal structure consisting of smaller units organized with respect to each other in a particular way. The most important component of word structure is the **morpheme**, the smallest unit of language that carries information about meaning or function. The word *builder,* for example, consists of two morphemes: *build* (with the meaning of 'construct') and *-er* (which indicates that the entire word functions as a noun with the meaning 'one who builds'). Similarly, the word *houses* is made up of the morphemes *house* (with the meaning of 'dwelling') and *-s* (with the meaning 'more than one').

Some words consist of a single morpheme. For example, the word *train* cannot be divided into smaller parts (say, *tr* and *ain* or *t* and *rain*) that carry information about its meaning or function. Such words are said to be **simple words** and are distinguished from **complex words**, which contain two or more morphemes (see Table 4.1).

Table 4.1 Words consisting of one or more morphemes

One	*Two*	*Three*	*More than three*
and			
boy	boy-s		
hunt	hunt-er	hunt-er-s	
act	act-ive	act-iv-ate	re-act-iv-ate

Free and Bound Morphemes

A morpheme that can be a word by itself is called a **free morpheme**, whereas a morpheme that must be attached to another element is a **bound morpheme**. The morpheme *boy,* for example, is free because it can be used as a word on its own; plural *-s,* on the other hand, is bound.

Concepts that are expressed by free morphemes in English do not necessarily have the same status in other languages. For example, in Hare (an Athapaskan language spoken in Canada's Northwest Territories), morphemes that indicate body parts must always be attached to a morpheme designating a possessor, as shown in Table 4.2. (The diacritic ´ marks a high tone.)

Table 4.2 Some body part names in Hare

Without a possessor		*With a possessor*	
*fí	'head'	sefí	'my head'
*bé	'belly'	nebé	'your belly'
*dzé	'heart'	ʔedzé	'someone's heart/a heart'

In English, of course, these body part names are free morphemes and do not have to be attached to another element.

Conversely, there are also some bound forms in English whose counterparts in other languages are free. For example, the notion 'past' or 'completed' is expressed by the bound morpheme *-ed* in English, but by the free morpheme *lɛɛw* in Thai. As the following sentence shows, this morpheme can even be separated from the verb by an intervening word. (Tone is not marked here.)

6)

Boon	thaan	khaaw	lɛɛw.
Boon	eat	rice	past

'Boon ate rice.'

Allomorphs

The variant forms of a morpheme are called its **allomorphs**. The morpheme used to express indefiniteness in English has two allomorphs—*an* before a word that begins with a vowel sound and *a* before a word that begins with a consonant sound.

7)

an orange	a building
an accent	a car
an eel	a girl

Notice, by the way, that the choice of *an* or *a* is determined on the basis of pronunciation, not spelling, which is why we say *an M.A. degree* and *a U.S. dollar.*

Another example of allomorphic variation is found in the pronunciation of the plural morpheme *-s* in the following words.

8)

cats
dogs
judges

Whereas the plural is /s/ in the first case, it is /z/ in the second and /əz/ in the third. Here again, selection of the proper allomorph is dependent on phonological facts. (For more on this, see Section 6.)

Yet another case of allomorphic variation is found in pairs of words such as *permit/permiss-ive, include/inclus-ive, electric/electric-ity, impress/impress-ion,* and so on. As you will see if you say these words aloud, the pronunciation of the final consonant in the first morpheme changes when a suffix is added.

It is important not to confuse spelling changes with allomorphic variation. For example, the final *e* in the spelling of *create* and *ride* is dropped in *creat-ive* and *rid-ing,* but this is not allomorphic variation since there is no change in pronunciation. On the other hand, there is allomorphic variation in *electric/electric-ity* and *impress/impress-ion,* where the pronunciation of the first morpheme changes even though its spelling remains the same.

1.2 Analyzing Word Structure

In order to represent the internal structure of words, it is necessary not only to identify each of the component morphemes but also to classify them in terms of their contribution to the meaning and function of the larger word.

Roots and Affixes

Complex words typically consist of a **root** morpheme and one or more **affixes**. The root constitutes the core of the word and carries the major component of its meaning. Roots typically belong to a **lexical category**, such as noun (N), verb (V), adjective (A), or preposition (P). These categories will be discussed in more detail in Chapter 5, Section 1.1. For now it suffices to note that nouns typically refer to concrete and abstract things (*tree, intelligence*), verbs tend to denote actions (*depart, teach*), adjectives usually name properties (*nice, red*), and prepositions generally encode spatial relations (*in, near*).

Unlike roots, affixes do not belong to a lexical category and are always bound morphemes. For example, the affix *-er* is a bound morpheme that combines with a verb such as *teach*, giving a noun with the meaning 'one who teaches'. The internal structure of this word can be represented in Figure 4.1. (The symbol *Af* stands for affix.)

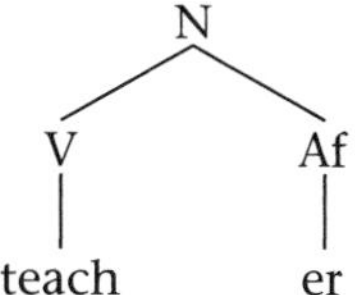

Figure 4.1 The internal structure of the word *teacher*

Figure 4.2 provides some additional examples of word structure.

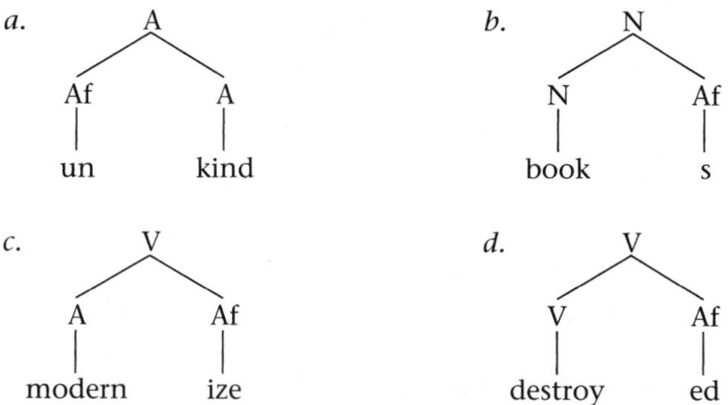

Figure 4.2 Some other words with an internal structure consisting of a root and an affix

The structural diagrams in Figures 4.1 and 4.2 are often called **trees**. The information they depict can also be represented by using labeled bracketing—$[_{A}$ $[_{Af}$ un] $[_{A}$ kind]] for *unkind* and $[_{N}$ $[_{N}$ book] $[_{Af}$ s]] for *books*. (This is somewhat harder to read, though, and we will generally use tree structures in this chapter.) Where the details of a word's structure are irrelevant to the point being considered, it is traditional to use a much simpler system of representation that indicates only the location of the morpheme boundaries: *un-kind, book-s,* and so on.

Bases

A **base** is the form to which an affix is added. In many cases, the base is also the root. In *books,* for example, the element to which the affix *-s* is added corresponds to the word's root. In other cases, however, the base can be larger than a root, which is always just a single morpheme. This happens in words such as *blackened,* in which the past tense affix *-ed* is added to the verbal base *blacken*—a unit consisting of the root morpheme *black* and the suffix *-en.*

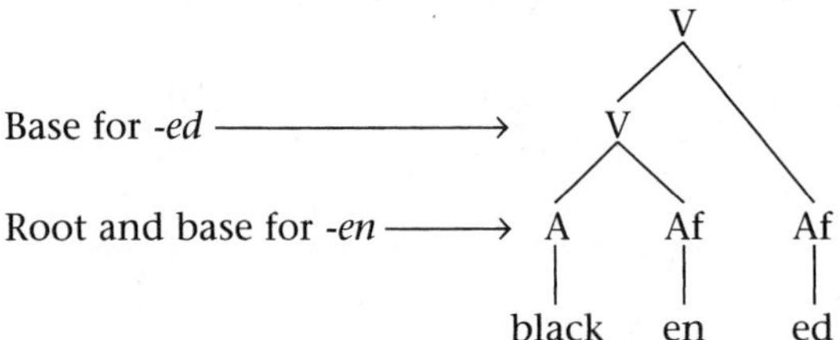

Figure 4.3 A word illustrating the difference between a root and a base

In this case, *black* is not only the root for the entire word but also the base for *-en.* The unit *blacken,* on the other hand, is simply the base for *-ed.*

Types of Affixes

An affix that is attached to the front of its base is called a **prefix**, whereas an affix that is attached to the end of its base is termed a **suffix**. Both types of affix occur in English, as shown in Table 4.3.

Table 4.3 Some English prefixes and suffixes

Prefixes	*Suffixes*
de-activate	vivid-*ly*
re-play	govern-*ment*
il-legal	hunt-*er*
in-accurate	kind-*ness*

We will consider the nature and properties of English affixes in more detail in Sections 2.1 and 4.1.

Far less common than prefixes and suffixes are **infixes**, a type of affix that occurs within another morpheme. The data in Table 4.4 from the Philippine language Tagalog contains examples of the infix *-in-*, which is inserted after the first consonant of the root to mark a completed event.

Table 4.4 Some Tagalog infixes

Base		*Infixed form*	
bili	'buy'	b-*in*-ili	'bought'
basa	'read'	b-*in*-asa	'read' (past)
sulat	'write'	s-*in*-ulat	'wrote'

Beginning students sometimes think that a morpheme such as *-ish* in *boy-ish-ness* is an infix since it occurs between two other morphemes (*boy* and *-ness*), but this is not right. To be an infix, an affix must occur inside another morpheme (as when *-in-* in Tagalog occurs inside *sulat* 'write'). Nothing of this sort happens in the case of *-ish*, which simply occurs between two morphemes.

A very special type of infixing system is found in Arabic, in which a typical root consists simply of three consonants. Affixes consisting of two vowels are then inserted into this root in a manner that intersperses the vowels among the consonants. (In the examples that follow, the segments of the root are written in boldface.)

9)

ka**t**a**b**	**k**u**t**i**b**	a**kt**u**b**	u**kt**a**b**
'write'	'have been written'	'be writing'	'being written'

One way to represent the structure of such words is as follows, with the root and affix assigned to different **tiers**, or levels of structure, that are intercalated in the actual pronunciation of the word (see Figure 4.4).

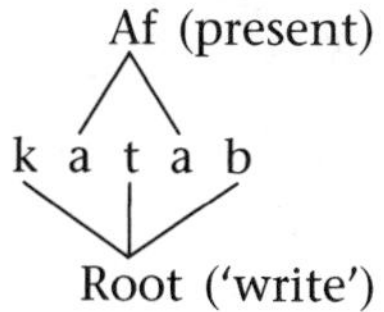

Figure 4.4 Two tiers are used to represent the structure of infixed words in Arabic

Problematic Cases

The majority of complex words in English are built from roots that are free morphemes. In the words *re-do* and *treat-ment,* for example, the root (*do* and *treat,* respectively) is a V that can appear elsewhere in the language without an affix. Because most complex words are formed from a root that can itself be a word, English morphology is said to be **word-based**.

Not all languages work this way, however. In Japanese and Spanish, for instance, verbal roots must always appear with an affix; they never stand alone as separate words.

English too has some bound roots. For example, the word *unkempt* seems to consist of the prefix *un-* (with the meaning 'not') and the root *kempt* (meaning 'groomed'), even though *kempt* cannot be used by itself. There was once a word *kempt* in English (with the meaning 'combed'), and it was to this base that the affix *un-* was originally attached. However, *kempt* later disappeared from the language, leaving behind the word *unkempt* in which an affix appears with a bound root.

Still other words with bound roots were borrowed into English as whole words. *Inept,* for instance, comes from Latin *ineptus* 'unsuited'. Its relationship to the word *apt* may have been evident at one time, but it now seems to consist of a prefix and a bound root.

Another class of words that are notoriously problematic for morphological analysis includes items such as *receive, deceive, conceive,* and *perceive,* or *permit, submit,* and *commit.* These items were borrowed into English from Latin (usually via French) as whole words, and their component syllables have no identifiable meaning of their own. (The *re* of *receive,* for instance, does not have the sense of 'again' that it does in *redo.*) For this reason, we will assume that words of this type consist of a single morpheme.

An interesting fact about these forms is that although *ceive* and *mit* have no identifiable meaning, they undergo certain alternations that suggest that they have a special status in the language. For instance, the *ceive* in words like *receive* and *deceive* becomes *cept* in *receptive* and *deceptive,* while the *mit* in words like *submit* and *permit* becomes *miss* in *submissive* and *permissive.*

2 Derivation

Derivation is an affixational process that forms a word with a meaning and/or category distinct from that of its base. One of the most common derivational affixes in English is the suffix *-er,* which combines with a verb to form a noun with the meaning 'one who does X', as shown in Table 4.5. (Do not confuse this suffix with the *-er* that applies to a noun in cases such as *New Yorker* and *islander* or the *-er* that combines with an adjective in cases such as *taller* and *smarter.*)

Table 4.5 The *-er* affix

Verb base	*Resulting noun*
sell	sell-er
write	writ-er
teach	teach-er
sing	sing-er
discover	discover-er

Words formed by derivation exhibit the type of internal structure illustrated in Figure 4.5.

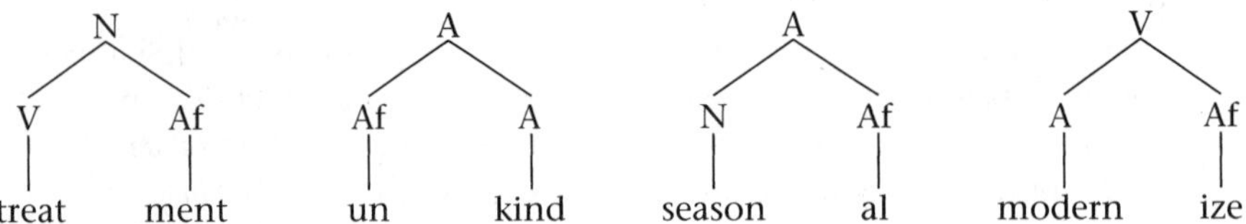

Figure 4.5 Some words formed by derivation

In each of these structures, a suffix or prefix combines with a base of a particular type to give a new word. In the case of *seller,* for instance, the suffix *-er* combines with the verb *sell* to give the noun *seller;* in the case of *unkind,* the prefix *un-* combines with the adjective *kind* to give a new adjective with a different meaning; and so on.

Once formed, derived words become independent lexical items that receive their own entry in a speaker's mental dictionary. As time goes by, they often take on special senses that are not predictable from the component morphemes. The word *writer,* for example, is often used not just for someone who can write but rather for someone who writes for a living (e.g., *He's a writer*); *comparable* (with stress on the first syllable) means 'similar' rather than 'able to be compared'; *profession* usually denotes a career rather than the act of professing; and so on.

2.1 Some English Derivational Affixes

Table 4.6 provides a partial list of English derivational affixes, along with information about the category of their usual base (ignoring bound roots) and of the result-

Table 4.6 Some English derivational affixes

Affix	*Change*	*Examples*
Suffixes:		
-able	V → A	fix-able, do-able, understand-able
-ing$_1$	V → A	the sleep-ing giant, a blaz-ing fire
-ive	V → A	assert-ive, impress-ive, restrict-ive
-al	V → N	refus-al, dispos-al, recit-al
-ant	V → N	claim-ant, defend-ant
-(at)ion	V → N	realiz-ation, assert-ion, protect-ion
-er	V → N	teach-er, work-er
-ing$_2$	V → N	the shoot-ing, the danc-ing
-ment	V → N	adjourn-ment, treat-ment, amaze-ment
-dom	N → N	king-dom, fief-dom
-ful	N → A	faith-ful, hope-ful, dread-ful
-(i)al	N → A	president-ial, nation-al
-(i)an	N → A	Arab-ian, Einstein-ian, Minnesot-an
-ic	N → A	cub-ic, optimist-ic, moron-ic
-less	N → A	penni-less, brain-less
-ous	N → A	poison-ous, lecher-ous
-ize$_1$	N → V	hospital-ize, vapor-ize
-ish	A → A	green-ish, tall-ish
-ate	A → V	activ-ate, captiv-ate
-en	A → V	dead-en, black-en, hard-en
-ize$_2$	A → V	modern-ize, national-ize
-ly	A → Adv	quiet-ly, slow-ly, careful-ly
-ity	A → N	stupid-ity, prior-ity
-ness	A → N	happi-ness, sad-ness
Prefixes:		
anti-	N → N	anti-hero, anti-depressant
ex-	N → N	ex-president, ex-wife, ex-friend
de-	V → V	de-activate, de-mystify
dis-	V → V	dis-continue, dis-obey
mis-	V → V	mis-identify, mis-place
re-	V → V	re-think, re-do, re-state
un$_1$*-*	V → V	un-tie, un-lock, un-do
in-	A → A	in-competent, in-complete
un$_2$*-*	A → A	un-happy, un-fair, un-intelligent

ing new word. The first entry states that the affix *-able* applies to a verb base and converts it into an adjective. Thus, if we add the affix *-able* to the verb *fix,* we get an adjective (with the meaning 'able to be fixed').

It is sometimes difficult to determine the category of the base to which an affix is added. In the case of *worker,* for instance, the base (*work*) is sometimes used as a verb (as in *they work hard*) and sometimes as a noun (as in *the work is time consuming*). How can we know which of these forms serves as the base for *-er*? The key is to find words such as *teacher* and *writer,* in which the category of the base can be unequivocally determined. Because *teach* and *write* can only be verbs, we can infer that the base with which *-er* combines in the word *worker* is also a verb.

Complex Derivations

Since derivation can apply more than once, it is possible to create multiple levels of word structure, as in the following example.

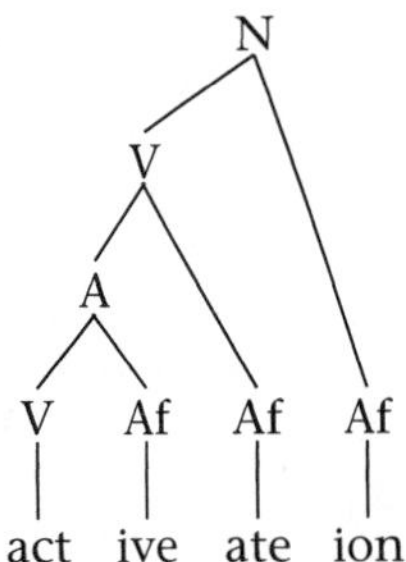

Figure 4.6 A word with a multilayered internal structure

The word *activation* contains several layers of structure, each of which reflects the attachment of an affix to a base of the appropriate type. In the first layer, the affix *-ive* combines with the verbal base *act* to give an adjective. (As noted in Table 4.6, *-ive* is the type of affix that converts a verb into an adjective.) In the next layer, the affix *-ate* combines with this adjective and converts it into a verb (*activate*). At this point, the affix *-ion* is added, converting the verb into a noun and forming the word *activation.*

In some cases, the internal structure of a complex word is not so obvious. The word *unhappiness,* for instance, could apparently be analyzed in either of the ways indicated in Figure 4.7.

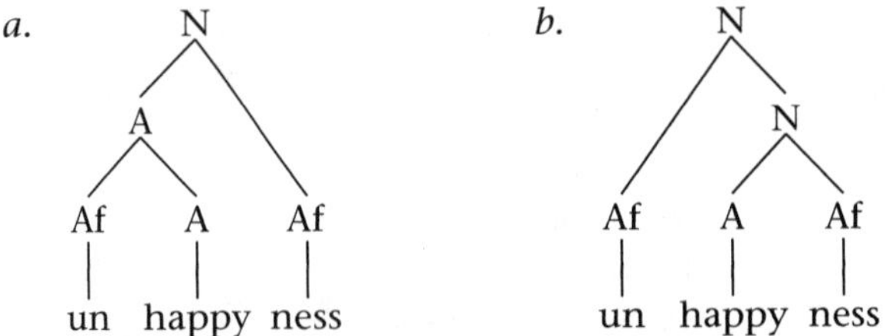

Figure 4.7 Two possible structures for the word *unhappiness*

However, by considering the properties of the affixes *un-* and *-ness,* it is possible to find an argument that favors Figure 4.7a over 4.7b. The key observation is that the prefix *un-* combines quite freely with adjectives but not with nouns, as shown in Table 4.7.

Table 4.7 The prefix *un-*

un + *A*	un + *N*
unable	*unknowledge
unkind	*unhealth
unhurt	*uninjury

This suggests that *un-* must combine with the adjective *happy* before it is converted into a noun by the suffix *-ness,* exactly as depicted in Figure 4.7a.

By contrast, in a word such as *unhealthy,* the prefix *un-* can be attached only *after* the suffix has been added to the root. That is because *-y* turns nouns into adjectives, creating the type of category with which *un-* can combine (see Figure 4.8).

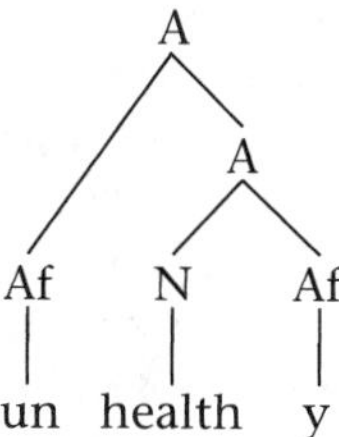

Figure 4.8 The internal structure of the word *unhealthy*

Constraints on Derivation

Derivation is often subject to special constraints and restrictions. For instance, the suffix *-ant* (see Table 4.6) can combine with bases of Latin origin such as *assist* and *combat,* but not those of native English origin such as *help* and *fight.* Thus, we find words such as *assistant* and *combatant,* but not **helpant* and **fightant.*

Sometimes a derivational affix is able to attach only to bases with particular phonological properties. A good example of this involves the suffix *-en,* which can combine with some adjectives to create verbs with a causative meaning as shown in Table 4.8 (*whiten* means roughly 'cause to become white').

Table 4.8 Restrictions on the use of *-en*

Acceptable	*Unacceptable*
whiten	*abstracten
soften	*bluen
madden	*angryen
quicken	*slowen
liven	*greenen

The contrasts illustrated here reflect the fact that *-en* can only combine with a monosyllabic base that ends in an obstruent. Thus, it can be added to *white,* which is monosyllabic and ends in an obstruent. But it cannot be added to *abstract,* which has two syllables, or to *blue,* which does not end in an obstruent.

2.2 Two Classes of Derivational Affixes

It is common to distinguish between two types of derivational affixes in English. **Class 1 affixes** often trigger changes in the consonant or vowel segments of the base and may affect stress placement. In addition, they often combine with bound roots, as in the last of the following examples in Table 4.9.

Table 4.9 Typical effects of Class 1 affixes

Affix	*Sample word*	*Change triggered by affix*
-ity	san-ity	vowel in the base changes from /e/ to /æ/ (cf. *sane*)
	public-ity	final consonant of the base changes from /k/ to /s/; stress shifts to second syllable (cf. *públic* vs. *publícity*)
-y	democrac-y	final consonant of the base changes from /t/ to /s/; stress shifts to second syllable (cf. *démocrat* vs. *demócracy*)
-ive	product-ive	stress shifts to second syllable (cf. *próduct* vs. *prodúctive*)
-(i)al	part-ial	final consonant of the base changes from /t/ to /ʃ/ (cf. *part*)
-ize	public-ize	final consonant of the base changes from /k/ to /s/ (cf. *public*)
-ion	nat-ion	final consonant of the base changes from /t/ to /ʃ/ (cf. *native*)

In contrast, **Class 2 affixes** tend to be phonologically neutral, having no effect on the segmental makeup of the base or on stress placement (see Table 4.10).

Table 4.10 Some typical Class 2 affixes

Affix	*Sample word*	*Change triggered by affix*
-ness	prompt-ness	None
-less	hair-less	None
-ful	hope-ful	None
-ly	quiet-ly	None
-er	defend-er	None
-ish	self-ish	None

As the following examples help illustrate, a Class 2 affix usually cannot intervene between the root and a Class 1 affix.

10)

relat-ion-al	divis-ive-ness	*fear-less-ity	fear-less-ness
ROOT 1 1	ROOT 1 2	ROOT 2 1	ROOT 2 2

Notice that all combinations of Class 1 and Class 2 affixes are found in English words except one—a Class 2 suffix followed by a Class 1 suffix.

3 Compounding

Another common technique for word building in English involves **compounding**, the combination of two already existent words (see Figure 4.9). With very few exceptions, the resulting **compound word** is a noun, a verb, or an adjective. (Possible examples of compound prepositions include the words *into* and *onto*.)

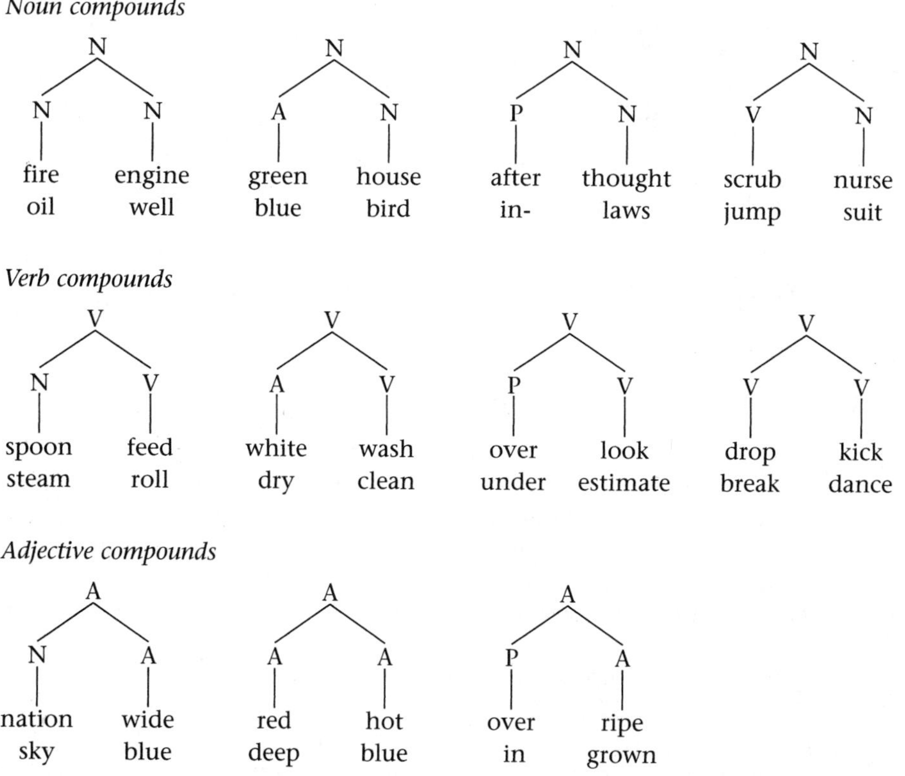

Figure 4.9 Some English compounds

In these and most other compounds of this type, the rightmost morpheme determines the category of the entire word. Thus, *greenhouse* is a noun because its rightmost component is a noun, *spoon-feed* is a verb because *feed* also belongs to this category, and *nationwide* is an adjective just as *wide* is. The morpheme that determines the category of the entire word is called the **head**.

Once formed, compounds can be combined with other words to create still larger compounds, as the examples in Figure 4.10 show.

In addition, compounding can interact with derivation, yielding forms such as *abortion debate,* in which the first word in the compound is the result of derivation, as shown in Figure 4.11.

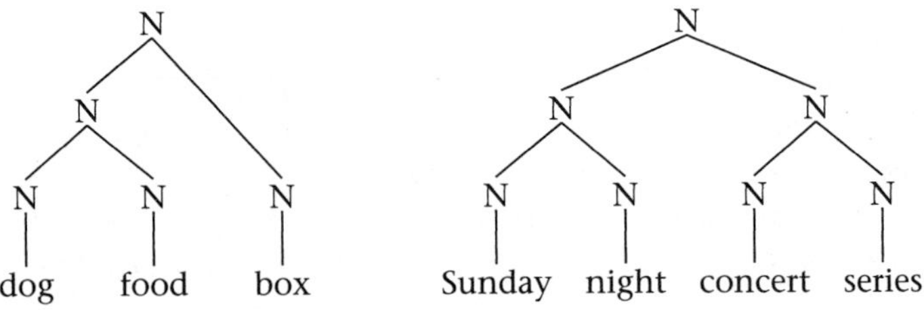

Figure 4.10 Compounds formed from smaller compounds

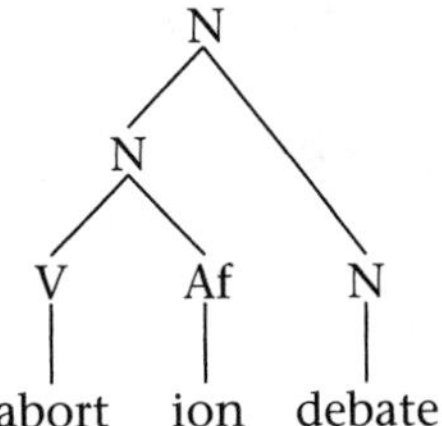

Figure 4.11 The interaction of derivation with compounding

3.1 Properties of Compounds

English orthography is not consistent in representing compounds, which are sometimes written as single words, sometimes with a hyphen, and sometimes as separate words. In terms of pronunciation, however, there is an important generalization to be made (see Table 4.11). In particular, adjective-noun compounds are characterized by more prominent stress on their first component. In noncompounds consisting of an adjective and a noun, in contrast, the second element is generally stressed.

Table 4.11 Compounds versus noncompounds

Compound word		*Noncompound expressions*	
greénhouse	'a glass-enclosed garden'	green hoúse	'a house painted green'
bláckboard	'a chalkboard'	black boárd	'a board that is black'
wét suit	'a diver's costume'	wet suít	'a suit that is wet'

A second distinguishing feature of compounds in English is that tense and plural markers cannot typically be attached to the first element, although they can be added to the compound as a whole. (There are some exceptions, however, such as *swords̲man* and *parks̲ supervisor.*)

11)

*The player [dropped̲ kick] the ball through the goalposts.
The player [drop kick]ed̲ the ball through the goalposts.

12)

*The graduate students go to the pub on [Fridays̲ night].
The graduate students go to the pub on [Friday night]s̲.

3.2 Endocentric and Exocentric Compounds

Compounds are used to express a wide range of meaning relationships in English. Table 4.12 contains examples of some of the semantic patterns found in noun-noun compounds.

Table 4.12 Some noun-noun compounds

Example	*Meaning*
steamboat	'a boat powered by steam'
airplane	'a conveyance that travels through the air'
air hose	'a hose that carries air'
airfield	'a field where airplanes land'
fire truck	'a vehicle used to put out fires'
fire drill	'a practice in the event of a fire'
bathtub	'a place in which to bathe'
bath towel	'a towel used after bathing'

In most cases, a compound denotes a subtype of the concept denoted by its head (the rightmost component). Thus *dog food* is a type of food, a *caveman* is a type of man, *sky blue* is a type of blue, and so on. Such compounds, including all the examples in Table 4.12, are called **endocentric compounds**. In a smaller number of cases, however, the meaning of the compound does not follow from the meanings of its parts in this way. Thus, a *redhead* is not a type of head; rather, it is a person with red hair. Similarly, a *redneck* is a person and not a type of neck. Such compounds are said to be **exocentric compounds**.

A very striking difference between English endocentric and exocentric compounds sometimes shows up in cases where the head is a word like *tooth* or *foot,* which has an irregular plural form. Consider in this regard the examples in Table 4.13.

Table 4.13 Pluralization in English compounds

In endocentric compounds	*In exocentric compounds*
wisdom teeth	saber tooths (extinct species of carnivore)
club feet	bigfoots (mythical creatures; "Sasquatch")
policemen	Walkmans (a type of portable radio)
oak leaves	Maple Leafs (Toronto's NHL hockey team)

Notice that whereas the endocentric compounds employ the usual irregular plural (*teeth, feet,* etc.), the exocentric compounds permit the plural suffix *-s* for words such as *tooth, foot,* and *man.*

3.3 Compounds in Other Languages

Although the rules for forming compounds differ from language to language, the practice of combining words to build a more complex word is very widespread. As the examples in Table 4.14 illustrate, compound nouns are especially common.

Table 4.14 Noun compounds in various languages

Korean		
kot elum straight ice 'icicle'	isul pi dew rain 'drizzle'	nwun mwul eye water 'tears'
Tagalog		
tubig ulan water rain 'rainwater'	tanod bayan guard town 'policeman'	anak araw child sun 'albino'
German		
Gast- hof guest-inn 'hotel'	Wort-bedeutungs-lehre word-meaning- theory 'semantics'	Fern-seher far- seer 'television'
Finnish		
lammas-nahka-turkki sheep- skin- coat 'sheepskin coat'	elin- keino- tulo- vero-laki life's-means-income-tax- law 'income tax law'	
Tzotzil		
piʃ- xól wrap-head 'hat'	méʔ- k'ínobal mother-mist 'rainbow'	ʔóra- tʃón rightaway-snake 'deadly viper'

With the exception of Tagalog, in which compounds are left-headed, the languages exemplified in Table 4.14 all have compounds in which the rightmost element is the head.

A special type of compounding process involves **incorporation**, the combination of a word (usually a noun) with a verb to form a compound verb. The following examples are from Chukchee, spoken in northeastern Siberia, and the Micronesian language Ponapean. (As these examples help illustrate, incorporation often involves phonological adjustments to the noun and/or the verb. Semantically, it usually involves de-emphasis of the noun, whose referents are treated as indefinite or nonspecific.)

13)

a. Chukchee

Without incorporation	*With incorporation*
tə-pelaɹkən qoɹaŋə.	tə-qoɹa-pelaɹkən
I- leave reindeer	I-reindeer-leave
'I'm leaving the reindeer.'	'I'm in the process of reindeer-leaving.'

b. Ponapean

Without incorporation	*With incorporation*
I pahn pereki lohs	I pahn perek-los
I will unroll mats	I will unroll-mats
'I will unroll the mats.'	'I will engage in mat unrolling.'

Incorporation is not a productive word-formation process in English, although signs of it show up in sentences such as *They are housecleaning* and *We have to baby-sit tonight.*

4 Inflection

Virtually all languages have contrasts such as singular versus plural and past versus nonpast. Such contrasts are often marked with the help of **inflection**, the modification of a word's form to indicate grammatical information of various sorts. (The base to which an inflectional affix is added is sometimes called a **stem**.)

4.1 Inflection in English

Affixation is the dominant inflectional process in language, and many languages (e.g., Japanese, Swahili, Inuktitut, and Finnish) have dozens of inflectional affixes. With only eight inflectional affixes (all suffixes), English is not a highly inflected language. Table 4.15 lists the inflectional affixes of English.

Table 4.15 English inflectional affixes

Nouns	
Plural *-s*	the books
Possessive (genitive) *-'s*	John's book
Verbs	
3rd person SG nonpast *-s*	He reads well.
Progressive *-ing*	He is working.
Past tense *-ed*	He worked.
Past participle *-en/-ed*	He has eaten/studied.
Adjectives	
Comparative *-er*	the smaller one
Superlative *-est*	the smallest one

Although most inflection in English involves regular affixation, some words mark inflectional contrasts in less regular ways. This is most obvious in the case of verbs, a number of which indicate past tense by internal changes of various sorts: *come/came, see/saw, fall/fell, eat/ate, drink/drank, lose/lost, is/was,* and so on.

Regular and irregular inflection appear to operate in fundamentally different ways: whereas regular inflected forms are constructed as needed in accordance with a general morphological rule (such as "Add *-ed* to mark the past tense"), irregular forms must be stored permanently in the language user's memory. Evidence for this difference comes from studies of how long it takes speakers to utter the past tense form of a verb when presented with the base. For irregular forms, there is a correlation between response time and frequency of the verb; thus, it takes less time to recall the past form of frequent verbs such as *see* and *find* than it does for infrequent verbs such as *stride* and *bid*—presumably because it takes longer to locate infrequently used forms in one's memory. For regular verbs, in contrast, response time is independent of frequency: because the past tense is formed by a regular rule, there is no need to look up the word in the mental dictionary, and all verbs—frequent ones like *walk* and infrequent ones like *discern*—can be handled with equal speed.

4.2 Inflection versus Derivation

Because inflection and derivation are both commonly marked by affixation, the distinction between the two can be subtle, and it is sometimes unclear which function a particular affix has. Three criteria are commonly used to help distinguish between inflectional and derivational affixes.

Category Change

First, inflection does not change either the grammatical category or the type of meaning found in the word to which it applies, as shown in Figure 4.12.

Figure 4.12 The output of inflection: there is no change in either the category of the base or the type of meaning it denotes.

The form produced by adding the plural suffix *-s* in Figure 4.12a is still a noun and has the same type of meaning as the base. Even though *books* differs from *book* in referring to several things rather than just one, the type of thing(s) to which it refers remains the same. Similarly, a past tense suffix such as the one in Figure 4.12b indicates that the action took place in the past, but the word remains a verb and it continues to denote an action.

In contrast, derivational suffixes characteristically change the category and/or the type of meaning of the form to which they apply. Consider the examples of derivation given in Figure 4.13. As Figure 4.13a shows, *-ize* makes a verb out of an adjective, changing the type of meaning it expresses from a property (*modern*) to an action (*modernize*). Parallel changes in category and type of meaning are brought about by *-ment* (V to N) and *-al* (N to A). Matters are a little different in the case of *-dom*, which does not bring about a category change in the word *kingdom* (since both

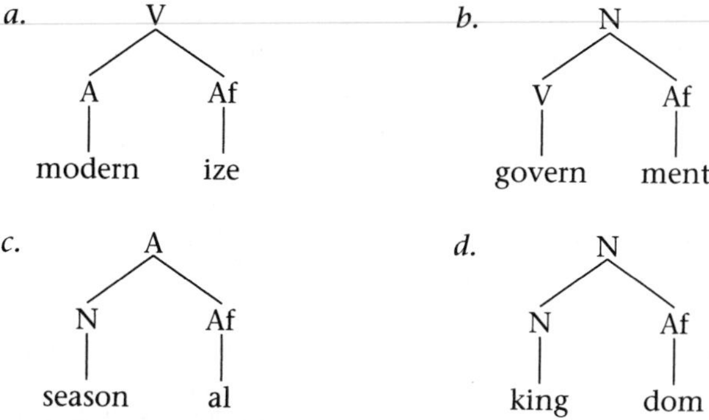

Figure 4.13 The output of derivation: there can be a change in the category of the base and/or the type of meaning it denotes.

the base and the resulting word are nouns). However, *-dom* does modify the type of meaning from 'person' (for *king*) to 'place' (for *kingdom*).

Order

A second property of inflectional affixes has to do with the order in which they are combined with a base relative to derivational affixes. As Figure 4.14 illustrates, a derivational affix must combine with the base before an inflectional affix does (IA = inflectional affix; DA = derivational affix).

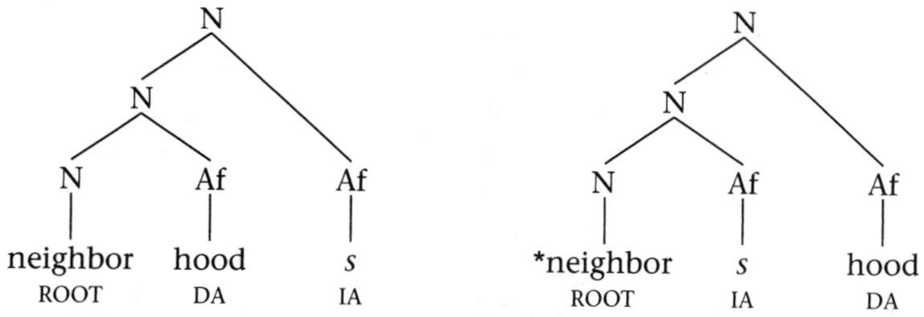

Figure 4.14 The relative positioning of derivational affixes (DA) and inflectional affixes (IA): the derivational affix must be closer to the root.

The positioning of inflectional affixes outside derivational affixes in these examples reflects the fact that inflection takes place after derivation.

Productivity

A third criterion for distinguishing between inflectional and derivational affixes has to do with **productivity**, the relative freedom with which they can combine with bases of the appropriate category. Inflectional affixes typically have relatively few exceptions. The suffix *-s,* for example, can combine with virtually any noun that allows a plural form (aside from a few exceptions such as *oxen* and *feet*). In contrast, derivational affixes characteristically apply to restricted classes of bases. Thus, *-ize* can combine with only certain adjectives to form a verb.

14)

modern-ize	*new-ize
legal-ize	*lawful-ize
final-ize	*permanent-ize

In the case of verbs, matters are somewhat more complicated, since many English verbs have irregular past tense forms (*saw, left, went,* and so on). Nonetheless, the inflectional affix *-ed* is much more generally applicable than a derivational affix such as *-ment.* For example, all the verbs in Table 4.16 can take the regular past tense ending, but only those in the top three rows are able to take the *-ment* suffix.

Table 4.16 Compatibility of verb bases with inflectional *-ed* and derivational *-ment*

Verb	*With* -ed	*With* -ment
confine	confined	confinement
align	aligned	alignment
treat	treated	treatment
arrest	arrested	*arrestment
straighten	straightened	*straightenment
cure	cured	*curement

Sometimes, the same affix can be either inflectional or derivational. For example, there are three *-ing* affixes in English, one inflectional and two derivational. Inflectional *-ing* combines with a verb to give another verb, as in *He is breathing.* One derivational *-ing* combines with a verb to give a noun (*The breathing of the runners*), and the other converts a verb into an adjective (*the sleeping giant*)—see Table 4.6. There are also two types of *-en/-ed* suffix, one inflectional, as noted in Table 4.15, and the other derivational. The latter converts verbs into adjectives so that they can appear in structures such as the *stolen* money or the *escaped* convict.

4.3 How Inflection Is Marked

As the examples above illustrate, the most common type of inflection involves affixation (suffixation in the case of English). However, inflection can be marked in a variety of other ways as well, including by internal change, by suppletion, by reduplication, and by tone placement.

Internal Change

Internal change is a process that substitutes one nonmorphemic segment for another to mark a grammatical contrast, as illustrated in the following pairs of words in Table 4.17. Verbs such as *sing, sink,* and *drive* form their past tense by changing the vowel (e.g., from *i* to *a* in the first two examples). The term **ablaut** is often used for vowel alternations that mark grammatical contrasts in this way.

Some internal changes reflect phonologically conditioned alternations from an earlier stage in the language's history. The irregular plurals *geese* and *feet* came about in

Table 4.17 Internal change in English

sing (present)	sang (past)
sink (present)	sank (past)
drive (present)	drove (past)
foot (singular)	feet (plural)
goose (singular)	geese (plural)

this way: the original vowel in the words *goose* and *foot* was fronted under the influence of the front vowel in the old plural suffix /i/, which was subsequently dropped. This type of change in English and other Germanic languages is known as **umlaut**.

15)

Old singular form of *goose:*	/gos/
Old plural form:	/gos-i/
Umlaut:	/gœs-i/
Loss of the plural suffix:	/gœs/
Other changes (see Chapter 7):	/ges/ and then /gis/ 'geese'

Internal change differs from infixing in important ways. As shown by the Tagalog examples in Table 4.4, the base into which a real infix is inserted typically exists as a separate form elsewhere in the language (compare *sulat* 'write' with *s-in-ulat* 'wrote'). Matters are quite different in the case of alternations such as *foot/feet* or *sing/sang* in English, since we have no form **ft* meaning 'lower extremity of the leg' or **sng* meaning 'produce words in a musical tone'. Moreover, in contrast to the situation in either Tagalog or Arabic, the segments affected by internal change are not themselves morphemes: the *a* of *ran* and the *o* of *drove* do not in general carry the meaning 'past' in English any more than the *ee* of *geese* normally carries the meaning 'plural'.

The existence of internal change and of infixing illustrates an important point about word structure: morphology is not always **concatenative**. That is, not all word structure is built by assembling morphemes in an additive, linear fashion.

Suppletion

Suppletion replaces a morpheme with an entirely different morpheme in order to indicate a grammatical contrast. Examples of this phenomenon in English include the use of *went* as the past tense form of the verb *go,* and *was* and *were* as the past tense forms of *be* (see Table 4.18 for suppletion in some other European languages).

Table 4.18 Suppletion in some European languages

Language	*Basic form*	*Suppletive form*
French	*aller* 'to go'	*ira* '(s/he) will go'
Spanish	*ir* 'to go'	*fue* '(s/he) went'
German	*ist* 'is'	*sind* 'are'
Russian	*xoroʃo* 'good'	*lutʃʃe* 'better' ('more good')

In some cases, it is hard to distinguish between suppletion and internal change. For example, is the past tense of *think* (*thought*) and *seek* (*sought*) an instance of suppletion or internal change? This type of alternation is often treated as an extreme form of internal change, but the term **partial suppletion** is also used by some linguists.

Reduplication

A common morphological process in some languages involves **reduplication**, which marks a grammatical or semantic contrast by repeating all or part of the base to which it applies. Repetition of the entire base yields **full reduplication**, as in the data from Turkish and Indonesian given in Table 4.19.

Table 4.19 Some examples of full reduplication

Base		*Reduplicated form*	
Turkish			
tʃabuk	'quickly'	tʃabuk tʃabuk	'very quickly'
javaʃ	'slowly'	javaʃ javaʃ	'very slowly'
iji	'well'	iji iji	'very well'
gyzel	'beautifully'	gyzel gyzel	'very beautifully'
Indonesian			
oraŋ	'man'	oraŋ oraŋ	'all sorts of men'
anak	'child'	anak anak	'all sorts of children'
maŋga	'mango'	maŋga maŋga	'all sorts of mangoes'

In contrast, **partial reduplication** copies only part of the base. In the data from Tagalog in Table 4.20, for instance, reduplication affects only the first consonant-vowel sequence.

Table 4.20 Reduplication in Tagalog

Base		*Reduplicated form*	
takbuh	'run'	tatakbuh	'will run'
lakad	'walk'	lalakad	'will walk'
piliʔ	'choose'	pipiliʔ	'will choose'

English makes limited use of partial reduplication in diminutive expressions such as *teeny-weeny* and *itsy-bitsy,* but this is not general enough to be counted as an inflectional contrast.

Tone Placement

In the language Mono-Bili (spoken in the Congo in Africa), tone is used to make the distinction between past and future tense. (A high tone is marked by ´ and a low tone by ` in Table 4.21.)

Table 4.21 Past versus future in Mono-Bili

Past		*Future*	
dá	'spanked'	dà	'will spank'
zɨ́	'ate'	zɨ̀	'will eat'
wó	'killed'	wò	'will kill'

As you can see, high tone is associated with the past tense and low tone with the future.

4.4 Other Inflectional Phenomena

Inflection is a very widely used morphological process and its effects can be seen in far more phenomena than can be discussed here. Nonetheless, two additional phenomena are worth mentioning, however briefly, because of their importance and frequency in languages of the world.

Case involves a change in a word's form to indicate its grammatical role (subject, direct object, and so on). A very simple example of this can be seen in English, where the pronoun form *he* is used for subjects and the form *him* is employed for direct objects. There is a comparable contrast between *I* and *me, she* and *her, we* and *us,* and *they* and *them.* (Notice all of these contrasts involve full or partial suppletion rather than affixation.)

16)

He met the new professor. The new professor met him.
↑ ↑
subject direct object

Agreement takes places when one word is inflected to match certain grammatical properties of another word. Especially common is agreement for number (singular vs. plural) and for person (first person—speaker; second person—addressee; third person—anyone else). Here again English offers a simple example: the suffix *-s* appears on a present tense verb when the subject is third person singular.

17)

That man speaks French.

(Compare: *I speak French* or *They speak French,* with no *-s* suffix.)

For a more detailed discussion of these and other inflectional phenomena, go to **bedfordstmartins.com/linguistics/morphology** and click on **inflection** and **case**.

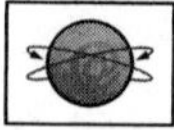

5 Other Morphological Phenomena

No introductory textbook can hope to offer a full survey of the processes that contribute to word formation in human language. The preceding sections have touched upon many of the most common and central processes, but a number of others merit consideration as well.

5.1 Cliticization

Some morphemes behave like words in terms of their meaning and function, but are unable to stand alone as independent forms for phonological reasons. Called **clitics**, these elements must be attached to another word (known as a **host**). A good example of this can be found in English, where certain verb forms have reduced variants (*'m* for *am*, *'s* for *is*, and *'re* for *are*) that cannot stand alone because they no longer constitute a syllable. Cliticization occurs, attaching these elements to the preceding word.

18)

a. I*'m* leaving now.
b. Mary*'s* going to succeed.
c. They*'re* here now.

Cliticization is also common in French, which has a set of unstressed clitic pronouns that must be phonologically attached to the verb. The two are then pronounced as if they formed a single word.

19)

Jean *t'*aime.	Suzanne *les* voit
John you-like	Suzanne them-sees
'John likes you.'	'Suzanne sees them.'

Clitics that attach to the end of their host (as in the English examples) are called **enclitics**; those that attach to the beginning of their host (as in the French examples) are known as **proclitics**.

The effects of cliticization can bear a superficial resemblance to affixation because, in both cases, an element that cannot stand alone is attached to a base. The key difference is that—unlike affixes—clitics are members of a lexical category such as verb, noun (or pronoun), or preposition.

5.2 Conversion

Conversion is a process that assigns an already existing word to a new syntactic category. Even though it does not add an affix, conversion is often considered to be a type of derivation because of the change in category and meaning that it brings about. For this reason, it is sometimes called **zero derivation**. Table 4.22 contains examples of the three most common types of conversion in English. Less common types of conversion can yield a noun from an adjective (*the poor, gays*) and even a verb from a preposition (*down a beer, up the price*).

Conversion is usually restricted to words containing a single morpheme, although there are a few exceptions, such as *propos-ition* (noun to verb), *refer-ee* (noun to verb), and *dirt-y* (adjective to verb).

Table 4.22 Some examples of conversion

V derived from N	*N derived from V*	*V derived from A*
ink (a contract)	(a long) run	dirty (a shirt)
butter (the bread)	(a hot) drink	empty (the box)
ship (the package)	(a pleasant) drive	better (the old score)
nail (the door shut)	(a brief) report	right (a wrong)
button (the shirt)	(an important) call	total (a car)

Conversion in two-syllable words is often accompanied by stress shift in English. As the examples in Table 4.23 show, the verb has stress on the final syllable while the corresponding noun is stressed on the first syllable. (Stress is represented here by ´.)

Table 4.23 Stress placement in English

Verb	*Noun*
implánt	ímplant
impórt	ímport
presént	présent
subjéct	súbject
contést	cóntest

5.3 Clipping

Clipping is a process that shortens a polysyllabic word by deleting one or more syllables. Some of the most common products of clipping are names—*Liz, Ron, Rob, Sue,* and so on. Clipping is especially popular in the speech of students, where it has yielded forms like *prof* for *professor, phys-ed* for *physical education, poli-sci* for *political science,* and *burger* for *hamburger.* However, many clipped forms have also been accepted in general usage: *doc, ad, auto, lab, sub, deli, porn, demo,* and *condo.*

In some cases, speakers may not even realize that a particular word is the product of clipping: the word *zoo,* for instance, was formed in this manner from *zoological garden,* while *fax* is from *facsimile* (meaning 'exact copy or reproduction').

An interesting recent clip is *blog,* from *Web log*—a personal Web site–based log of events, comments, and links. Once formed, *blog* quickly appeared in new compounds (*blog archive, blog template*) and has undergone conversion to a verb (as in 'things to blog about'). The verb in turn has undergone derivation, resulting in the noun *blogger.* No wonder that *blog* was voted the new word most likely to succeed at the 2003 meeting of the American Dialect Society.

5.4 Blends

Blends are words that are created from nonmorphemic parts of two already existing items, usually the first part of one and the final part of the other. Familiar examples include *brunch* from *breakfast* and *lunch, smog* from *smoke* and *fog, spam* from *spiced* and *ham, telethon* from *telephone* and *marathon, aerobicise* from *aerobics* and *exercise, chunnel* (for the underwater link between Britain and the continent) from *channel* and *tunnel,* and *infomercial* from *information* and *commercial.*

In some languages, blending can bring together parts of three words. The following examples are from Malay.

20)

pembangunan lima tahun > pelita 'five-year plan'
development five year

universeti utara malaysia > unitama 'University of North Malaysia'
university north Malaysia

Some blends have become so integrated into the standard vocabulary of English that speakers are unaware of their status. For example, relatively few people know that blending has produced *chortle* (coined by author Lewis Carroll) from *chuckle* and *snort, motel* from *motor* and *hotel, bit* (in computer jargon) from *binary* and *digit,* and *modem* from *modulator* and *demodulator.*

Sometimes, a word is formed by a process that is on the borderline between compounding and blending in that it combines all of one word with part of another. Examples of this in English include *e-mail, perma-press, workaholic, medicare, guesstimate,* and *threepeat* (used by sports fans to refer to the winning of a championship in three successive years).

5.5 Backformation

Backformation is a process that creates a new word by removing a real or supposed affix from another word in the language. *Resurrect* was originally formed in this way from *resurrection.* Other backformations in English include *enthuse* from *enthusiasm, donate* from *donation, orient* or *orientate* from *orientation,* and *self-destruct* from *self-destruction.*

Sometimes backformation involves an incorrect assumption about a word's form: for example, the word *pea* was derived from the singular noun *pease,* whose final /z/ was incorrectly interpreted as the plural suffix.

Words that end in *-or* or *-er* have proven very susceptible to backformation in English. Because hundreds of such words are the result of affixation (*runner, walker, singer,* etc.), any word with this shape is likely to be perceived as a verb + *er* combination. The words *editor, peddler,* and *swindler* were (mis)analyzed in just this way, resulting in the creation of the verbs *edit, peddle,* and *swindle,* as shown in Table 4.24.

Table 4.24 Some examples of backformation

Original word	*Misanalysis*	*Verb formed by backformation*
editor	edit + or	edit
peddler	peddle + er	peddle
swindler	swindle + er	swindle

A more recent backformation of this type is the verb *lase,* produced by backformation from *laser,* which itself had an unusual origin (see Section 5.6).

Backformation continues to produce new words in modern English. For instance, the form *attrit,* from *attrition,* was used by military officials during the 1991 Gulf War (as in *The enemy is 50 percent attritted*). Among the backformations noticed by the authors of this chapter are *liposuct* (from *liposuction,* seen in a magazine article), *orate* (from *oration,* used in a newspaper editorial), and even *tuit* (from *intuition,* heard on the radio).

5.6 Acronyms

Acronyms are formed by taking the initial letters of (some or all) the words in a phrase or title and pronouncing them as a word. This type of word formation is especially common in names of organizations and in military and scientific terminology. Common examples include UNICEF for United Nations International Children's Emergency Fund, NASA for National Aeronautics and Space Administration, NATO for North Atlantic Treaty Organization, and AIDS for acquired immune deficiency syndrome.

Acronyms are to be distinguished from abbreviations such as LA for Los Angeles or U.S.A. for United States of America, which are pronounced as a series of letters rather than a word. A nice intermediate case is *jeep,* from GP (general purpose) vehicle.

In some cases, speakers may not know that a word in their vocabulary originated as an acronym. Three commonly used words of this type are *radar* (from radio detecting and ranging), *scuba* (self-contained underwater breathing apparatus), and *laser* (light amplification by stimulated emission of radiation).

5.7 Onomatopoeia

All languages have some words that have been created to sound like the thing that they name. Examples of such **onomatopoeic words** in English include *buzz, hiss, sizzle,* and *cuckoo.* Since onomatopoeic words are not exact phonetic copies of noises, their form can differ from language to language as shown in Table 4.25.

Table 4.25 Onomatopoeia across languages

English	*Japanese*	*Tagalog*
cock-a-doodle-doo	kokekokko	kuk-kukaok
meow	nyaa	ngiyaw
chirp	pii-pii	tiɾiɾit
bow-wow	wan-wan	aw-aw

English does not always have an equivalent for the onomatopoeic words found in other languages. The Athabaskan language Slavey, for instance, has the onomatopoeic word *sah sah sah* for 'the sound of a bear walking unseen not far from camp', *ðik* for 'the sound of a knife hitting a tree', and *tɬóòtʃ* for 'the sound of an egg splattering'.

5.8 Other Sources of New Words

Sometimes a word may be created from scratch. Called **word manufacture** or **coinage**, this phenomenon is especially common in the case of product names, including *Kodak, Dacron, Orlon,* and *Teflon.* (Notice how the *-on* of the final three words makes them more scientific-sounding, perhaps because an affix of this form occurs in words of Greek origin such as *phenomenon* and *automaton.*)

New words can also sometimes be created from names, including those listed in Table 4.26.

Table 4.26 Some English words created from names

Word	*Name of the person*
watt	James Watt (late 19th-century scientist)
curie	Marie and Pierre Curie (early 20th-century scientists)
fahrenheit	Gabriel Fahrenheit (18th-century scientist)
boycott	Charles Boycott (19th-century land agent in Ireland, who was ostracized for refusing to lower rents)

In still other cases, brand names can become so widely known that they are accepted as generic terms for the product with which they are associated. The words *Kleenex* for 'facial tissue' and *Xerox* for 'photocopy' are two obvious examples of this.

6 Morphophonemics

As we saw in Chapter 3, a word's pronunciation is often sensitive to the particular phonetic context in which phonemes occur. For instance, an /æ/ that occurs in front of a nasal consonant will be nasalized (e.g., [kæ̃nt] 'can't' vs. [kæt] 'cat'), an /æ/ that occurs before a voiced consonant will be longer than one that occurs before a voiceless consonant (e.g., [hæːd] 'had' vs. [hæt] 'hat'), and so on. Pronunciation can also be sensitive to morphological factors, including a word's internal structure. The study of this phenomenon is known as **morphophonemics** (or **morphophonology**).

Morphophonemic phenomena are extremely common in language. A famous example from English involves the way that we pronounce the plural suffix *-s.* As noted in Section 1.1, the morpheme can be pronounced as [s], [z], or [əz].

21)

lip-[s]
pill-[z]
judg-[əz]

There are good reasons for this alternation: voiceless -[s] occurs after voiceless sounds (such as [p]), voiced -[z] occurs after voiced sounds (such as [l]), and the -[əz] form shows up only when a vowel is needed to break up an otherwise illegal consonant cluster (no English syllable ends with the coda [dʒz]). The key point for now, though, has to do with the conditions under which all of this happens. This is a classic example of a morphophonemic alternation for two reasons.

First, it occurs at a morpheme boundary, where a suffix of a particular type is attached to its base. It is perfectly possible to pronounce an [s] sound after an [l] in English when they are both in the same morpheme—as in a word like *else,* for instance. Yet the plural morpheme *-s* has to be pronounced as [z] when it attaches to a base that ends in [l], as happens in *pill*-[z].

Second, the alternation involves sounds that are associated with separate phonemes—/s/ and /z/. In this, it differs from the alternations considered in the preceding chapter, which involved allophones of the same phoneme.

For a more detailed discussion of morphophonemics, go to **bedfordstmartins .com/linguistics/morphology** and click on **morphophonemics**.

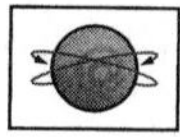

Summing Up

This chapter has focused on the structure and formation of **words** in human language. Many words consist of smaller formative elements, called **morphemes**. These elements can be classified in a variety of ways (**free** versus **bound**, **root** versus **affix**, **prefix** versus **suffix**) and can be combined and modified under various conditions to build words.

The two basic types of word formation in English are **derivation** and **compounding**. Other important morphological phenomena include **cliticization**, **conversion**, **clipping**, **blends**, and **backformation**.

Inflection, a change in the form of a word to convey grammatical information such as plurality or tense, can be expressed via **affixation**, **internal change**, **reduplication**, and **tone placement**.

Key Terms

General terms

allomorphs	lexicon
bound morpheme	morpheme
complex words	morphology
free form	simple words
free morpheme	word

General terms concerning morphological analysis

affixes	root
base	suffix
infixes	tiers
lexical category	trees
prefix	word-based (morphology)

Terms concerning derivation and compounding

Class 1 affixes	endocentric compounds
Class 2 affixes	exocentric compounds
compound word	head
compounding	incorporation
derivation	

Terms concerning inflection

ablaut
agreement
case
concatenative (morphology)
full reduplication
inflection
internal change
partial reduplication
partial suppletion
productivity
reduplication
stem
suppletion
umlaut

Other kinds of morphological phenomena

acronyms
backformation
blends
clipping
clitics
coinage
conversion
enclitics
host
onomatopoeic words
proclitics
word manufacture
zero derivation

Terms concerning the interaction of morphology and phonology

morphophonemics
morphophonology

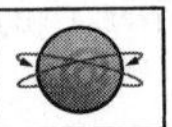

For more information on the sources used in this chapter, go to **bedfordstmartins.com/linguistics/morphology** and click on **Sources**.

Recommended Reading

Anderson, Stephen. 1988. "Morphological Theory." In *Linguistics: The Cambridge Survey*. Vol. 1. Edited by F. Newmeyer, 146–91. New York: Cambridge University Press.

Bauer, Laurie. 1983. *English Word-Formation.* New York: Cambridge University Press.

Bauer, Laurie. 2003. *Introducing Linguistic Morphology.* 2nd ed. Georgetown: Georgetown University Press.

Carstairs-McCarthy, Andrew. 2002. *An Introduction to English Morphology.* Edinburgh: Edinburgh Univeristy Press.

Gleason, Henry Allan. 1955/1961. *An Introduction to Descriptive Linguistics.* New York: Holt, Rinehart and Winston.

Jensen, John. 1990. *Morphology: Word Structure in Generative Grammar.* Amsterdam: John Benjamins Publishing.

Katamba, Francis. 1993. *Morphology.* London: Macmillan.

Spencer, Andrew. 1991. *Morphological Theory.* Cambridge, MA: Blackwell.

Appendix: How to Identify Morphemes in Unfamiliar Languages

An important part of morphological analysis involves identifying morphemes in unfamiliar languages and determining the nature of the information that they carry.

(A number of the problems in the set of exercises that follow this chapter will give you an opportunity to practice this type of analysis.) The key procedure to follow in working on this sort of problem can be stated simply as follows:

- Identify recurring strings of sounds and match them with recurring meanings.

Consider in this regard the following small sample of data in Table 4.27 from Turkish, consisting of four words along with their English translations. (A more realistic data sample would not only be much larger, but also include sentences in which it might well be unclear where the word boundaries should be placed.)

Table 4.27 Some Turkish words

/mumlaɾ/	'candles'
/toplaɾ/	'guns'
/adamlaɾ/	'men'
/kitaplaɾ/	'books'

As you can probably see, the syllable /laɾ/ occurs in all four items in our sample. From the translations of these items, you can see that a particular feature of meaning—namely, plurality—is present in all four cases as well. Using the procedure just stated, we therefore hypothesize that /laɾ/ is the morpheme marking plurality in Turkish. Once this has been determined, we can then infer that /mum/ in /mumlaɾ/ is also a morpheme (with the meaning 'candle'), that /top/ in /toplaɾ/ is a morpheme (with the meaning 'gun'), and so on. A larger sampling of Turkish data would confirm the correctness of these inferences.

In doing morphological analysis in unfamiliar languages, there are a number of pitfalls to avoid. For the type of data normally investigated at the introductory level, the following guidelines are especially important.

- Do not assume that the morpheme order in the language you are analyzing is the same as in English. In Korean, for example, morphemes indicating location (the rough equivalent of 'at', 'in', and so forth) follow rather than precede the noun (*hakkyo-eyse* 'at school' is literally 'school at').

- Do not assume that every semantic contrast expressed in English will also be manifested in the language you are analyzing. In Turkish, for instance, there is no equivalent for English *the* and *a*. In Mandarin Chinese, the same pronoun form can be used to refer to a male or a female (there is no *he-she* distinction).

- Do not assume that every contrast expressed in the language you are analyzing is manifested in English. For example, as discussed at **bedfordstmartins.com/linguistics/morphology** (**inflection**), some languages distinguish more than two number categories (Inuktitut distinguishes singular, dual, and plural); and some languages make multiple tense contrasts (ChiBemba has an eight-way distinction).

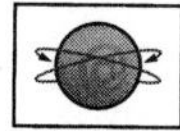

- Remember that a morpheme can have more than one form (allomorph). For example, further study of Turkish would reveal that the plural suffix in this language can also be realized as /leɾ/, depending on the vowel in the base to which the suffix is attached.

Exercises

1. Consider the following words and answer the questions below.

a) fly	f) reuse	k) spiteful	p) preplan
b) desks	g) triumphed	l) suite	q) optionality
c) untie	h) delight	m) fastest	r) prettier
d) tree	i) justly	n) deform	s) mistreat
e) dislike	j) payment	o) disobey	t) premature

i) For each word, determine whether it is simple or complex.
ii) Circle all the bound morphemes. Underline all the roots.

2. All of the following Persian words consist of two or more morphemes. (*Note: xar* means 'buy' and *-id* designates the past tense.)

a) xaridam	'I bought'
b) xaridi	'you (SG) bought'
c) xarid	'(he) bought'
d) naxaridam	'I did not buy'
e) namixaridand	'they were not buying'
f) naxaridim	'we did not buy'
g) mixarid	'(he) was buying'
h) mixaridid	'you (PL) were buying'

i) Try to match each of the following notions with a morpheme in the Persian data.

a) I	e) they
b) you (SG)	f) not
c) we	g) was/were + -ing (CONTINUOUS)
d) you (PL)	

ii) How would you say the following in Persian?
a) They were buying.
b) You (SG) did not buy.
c) You (SG) were buying.

3. Consider the following data from Turkish.

a) lokanta	'a restaurant'	lokantada	'in/at a restaurant'
b) kapɨ	'a door'	kapɨda	'in/at a door'
c) ɾandevu	'an appointment'	ɾandevuda	'in/at an appointment'
d) baʃ	'a head'	baʃta	'in/at a head'
e) kitap	'a book'	kitapta	'in/at a book'
f) koltuk	'an armchair'	koltukta	'in/at an armchair'
g) taɾaf	'a side'	taɾafta	'in/at a side'

i) Does the Turkish morpheme meaning 'in/at' have more than one allomorph?
ii) If so, what are the allomorphs? Describe their distribution as generally as possible.

4. Consider the following words.

   a) desks
   b) untie
   c) invalid (A)
   d) dislike (V)
   e) triumphed
   f) ageless
   g) justice
   h) payment
   i) preplan (V)
   j) fastest
   k) reuse
   l) disobey
   m) optionality
   n) prettier
   o) mistreat
   p) preview (V)

   i) Draw a tree structure for each word.
   ii) For the word *optionality,* what is the base for the affix *-ion*? What is the base for the suffix *-ity*? Are either of these bases also the root for the entire word? If so, which one?

5. The following data from Agta (spoken in the Philippines) illustrates a specific type of affix.

a)	dakal	'big'	dumakal	'grow big, grow up'
b)	darág	'red'	dumarág	'redden'
c)	furáw	'white'	fumuráw	'become white'

   i) What is the affix in Agta meaning 'become X'?
   ii) What type of affix is it?

6. In this chapter, an argument was presented in favor of the following structure for the word *unhappiness.*

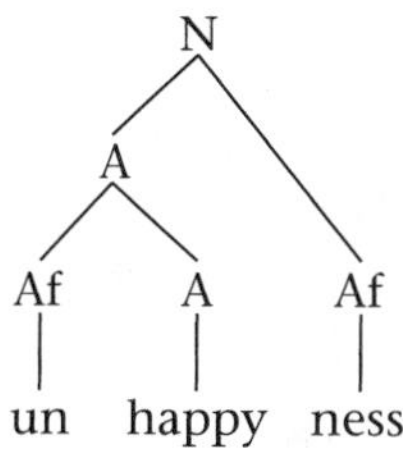

   Using the same type of argument, justify tree structures for the words *inexpensive, redisposal,* and *disinvestment.* (*Hint:* This will involve determining the type of syntactic category with which the affixes in these words can combine; see Table 4.6.)

7. In English, the suffix *-er* can be added to a place name. Examine the words in the two columns below.

Column 1	*Column 2*
Long Islander	*Denverer
Vermonter	*Philadelphiaer
New Yorker	*San Franciscoer
Newfoundlander	*Torontoer
Londoner	*Miamier

   i) In general terms, what does the suffix *-er* mean in these words?
   ii) How is this *-er* different in meaning from the *-er* found in the words *skater* and *walker*?
   iii) As is shown in column 2, the distribution of *-er* in the above data is restricted in some way. State the constraint on the distribution of *-er* illustrated in this data.

iv) Does this constraint also apply to the type of *-er* used in the word *skater*? (*Hint:* What would you call 'one who discovers' or 'one who rows'?)

8. The following words have all been formed by compounding. Draw a tree structure for each word. If you are in doubt as to the lexical category of the compound, remember that the category of the head determines the category of the word.

a) football	i) tree trunk	q) hockey match
b) billboard	j) lead-free	r) coffee table
c) sunspot	k) shortstop	s) flower girl
d) in-crowd	l) girlfriend	t) blueprint
e) fast food	m) city center	u) Greenpeace
f) software	n) fail-safe	v) spaceship
g) freeze-dry	o) potato peel	w) brain-dead
h) overbook	p) bittersweet	x) killjoy

9. Examine the following compounds and answer the questions below.

a) loudmouth	h) cutthroat
b) skinhead	i) pickpocket
c) killjoy	j) spoilsport
d) bath towel	k) crybaby
e) death blow	l) brain-dead
f) airhead	m) blow-dry
g) Walkman	n) armchair

i) For each of the compounds, determine whether it is endocentric or exocentric.
ii) How do you form the plural of *Walkman* and *loudmouth*? (*Hint:* See Table 4.13. Also, pay special attention to the pronunciation of *mouth*. Is it any different here than when it is an independent word?)

10. Indicate whether the words in each of the following groups are related to one another by processes of inflection or derivation.
a) go, goes, going, gone
b) discover, discovery, discoverer, discoverable, discoverability
c) lovely, lovelier, loveliest
d) inventor, inventor's, inventors, inventors'
e) democracy, democrat, democratic, democratize

11. The following sentences contain both derivational and inflectional affixes. Underline all of the derivational affixes and circle the inflectional affixes.

a) The farmer's cows escaped.	e) The strongest rower continued.
b) It was raining.	f) The pitbull has bitten the cyclist.
c) Those socks are inexpensive.	g) She quickly closed the book.
d) Jim needs the newer copy.	h) The alphabetization went well.

12. Each of the following columns illustrates a different type of inflection.

Column 1	*Column 2*	*Column 3*
a) mouse/mice	f) go/went	k) record/recorded
b) dive/dove	g) is/was	l) arrive/arrived
c) take/took	h) good/better	m) start/started
d) man/men	i) she/her	n) discuss/discussed
e) eat/ate	j) am/are	o) try/tried

i) How is inflection expressed in column 1? column 2? column 3?

ii) Think of at least one more English example to add to each column.

13. The following data from Samoan illustrate one of the morphological processes discussed in this chapter.

a)	mate	'he dies'	mamate	'they die'
b)	nofo	'he stays'	nonofo	'they stay'
c)	galue	'he works'	galulue	'they work'
d)	tanu	'he buries'	tatanu	'they bury'
e)	alofa	'he loves'	alolofa	'they love'
f)	taoto	'he lies'	taooto	'they lie'
g)	atamaʔi	'he is intelligent'	atamamaʔi	'they are intelligent'

i) What morphological process is used to express the inflectional contrast between singular and plural here?

ii) Describe how it works in your own words.

iii) If 'he is strong' in Samoan is *malosi,* how would you say 'they are strong' in Samoan?

14. The following words from Chamorro, spoken in Guam and the Mariana Islands, all involve derivation. (Data are presented in the orthography of Chamorro, not in phonetic transcription.)

I.	*Root*		*Derived word*	
a)	adda	'mimic'	aadda	'mimicker'
b)	kanno	'eat'	kakanno	'eater'
c)	tuge	'write'	tutuge	'writer'
II.	*Root*		*Derived word*	
d)	atan	'look at'	atanon	'nice to look at'
e)	sangan	'tell'	sanganon	'tellable'
f)	guaiya	'love'	guaiyayon	'lovable'
g)	tulaika	'exchange'	tulaikayon	'exchangeable'
h)	chalek	'laugh'	chalekon	'laughable'
i)	ngangas	'chew'	ngangason	'chewable'
III.	*Root*		*Derived word*	
j)	nalang	'hungry'	nalalang	'very hungry'
k)	dankolo	'big'	dankololo	'very big'
l)	metgot	'strong'	metgogot	'very strong'
m)	bunita	'pretty'	bunitata	'very pretty'

Like inflection, derivation can be expressed in a variety of ways—including by affixation of various types (prefixation, suffixation, infixation) and by reduplication.

i) How is derivation expressed in I? in II? in III?

ii) What changes in lexical category take place in I? in II? in III?

iii) Formulate a general statement as to how the derived words in I are formed. Do the same for II and III.

iv) One of these derivational processes consists of affixation involving allomorphs. Which process involves allomorphs, and what is the distribution of the allomorphs?

15. The following words can be either nouns or verbs.

a) record	f) outline	k) report
b) journey	g) convict	l) assault
c) exchange	h) imprint	m) answer
d) remark	i) reply	n) import
e) surprise	j) retreat	o) cripple

i) For each word, determine whether stress placement can be used to make the distinction between noun and verb.

ii) Think of two more English examples illustrating the process of stress shift to mark a category distinction.

16. Indicate the morphological phenomenon illustrated by the items in column 2.

	Column 1		*Column 2*
a)	automation	→	automate
b)	humid	→	humidifier
c)	information, entertainment	→	infotainment
d)	love, seat	→	loveseat
e)	prógress	→	progréss
f)	typographical error	→	typo
g)	aerobics, marathon	→	aerobathon
h)	act	→	deactivate
i)	curve, ball	→	curve ball
j)	methamphetamine	→	meth
k)	(the) comb	→	comb (your hair)
l)	beef, buffalo	→	beefalo
m)	random access memory	→	RAM
n)	megabytes	→	megs
o)	Federal Express	→	FedEx
p)	influenza	→	flu
q)	They have finished	→	They've finished

17. Here are five instances where a new word is needed. Create a word for each of these definitions in the manner indicated. Fill in the blanks with your new words.

a) Use an acronym . . . for your uncle's second oldest brother.
"We visited my ____________ at Christmas."

b) Use onomatopoeia . . . for the sound of a dishwasher in operation.
"I can't concentrate because my dishwasher is ___________ing."

c) Use conversion . . . for wrapping something breakable in bubble wrap.
"You'd better ___________ that ornament or else it might break."

d) Use a compound . . . for the annoying string of cheese stretching from a slice of hot pizza to one's mouth.
"As the ______________ hung precariously from my lips, our eyes met!"

e) Use backformation . . . for the action of backformation.
"We had to ________________ words in Linguistics today."

18. Create new words for each of the following situations.

a) Use a product name . . . for the act of scrubbing with Ajax.
"I _________ed the tub after giving Fido a bath."

b) Use a proper name . . . for the act of breaking dishes, which Jonathan does regularly.
"He's going to ____________ all of my best dishes."

c) Use clipping . . . for a course in ovinology (the study of sheep).
"Have you done your ____________ assignment yet?"

d) Use derivation . . . for being able to be contacted.
"The counselor is not very ____________."

e) Use a blend . . . for a hot drink made with chocolate and ginseng.
"I'll have a ____________ and two peanut butter cookies, please."

19. The following data provide the possible forms of the regular past tense morpheme of English.

a)	walked	/wɔkt/	l)	heaved	/hivd/
b)	cracked	/kɹækt/	m)	wheezed	/wizd/
c)	flipped	/flɪpt/	n)	fined	/fajnd/
d)	hissed	/hɪst/	o)	flitted	/flɪtəd/
e)	huffed	/hʌft/	p)	butted	/bʌtəd/
f)	hushed	/hʌʃt/	q)	padded	/pædəd/
g)	munched	/mʌntʃt/	r)	loaded	/lodəd/
h)	drubbed	/dɹʌbd/	s)	collided	/kəlajdəd/
i)	dragged	/dɹægd/	t)	allowed	/əlawd/
j)	jogged	/dʒɑgd/	u)	sowed	/sod/
k)	fudged	/fʌdʒd/			

i) List the alternate forms of the past tense morpheme.
ii) Which alternate makes the best underlying form? Why?
iii) State in words the conditioning factors that account for the presence of the alternate forms of the past tense morpheme.

For the Student Linguist

BAMBIFICATION

Well, of course, language is productive. You can't possibly read this chapter without being completely convinced of how very easy it is to make up new words. Morphological productivity is mildly interesting when you're creating transparent new words, such as when you have a verb like *fax* and create a new verb like *refax* (fax again) or *speed-fax* (fax fast) or an adjective like *faxable* (can be faxed), but it's not exactly earth-shattering.

What amazes me, though, is running across a new word, knowing it's a perfectly good word in English, knowing exactly how to pronounce it, and not having a clue about what it means. I'm not talking about knowing *frete* could be a word because it doesn't break any phonological rules of English. I'm talking about a word whose meaning remains mysterious even though that word can be broken down into recognizable, meaningful parts. Take the word *Brazilification,* which appears in Douglas Coupland's novel *Generation X. Brazilification* might appear in a sentence like "The recent Brazilification seen in the United States will have a large impact on tax reform plans." *Brazilification* could mean 'the replacement of forests with cattle ranches' or 'the improved quality of coffee' or many other things; it actually means 'the widening gulf between the rich and the poor and the accompanying disappearance of the middle classes' (p. 11). From this, the meaning of *Brazilify* is transparent: make the gulf between the rich and the poor wider, thereby causing the disappearance of the middle classes.

Now consider *Bambification,* another morphologically complex word from Coupland's book. It means 'make like X', where X is a variable that can be replaced by *Brazil,* or *Bambi,* or some other noun. *Bambification* doesn't mean 'make like Bambi's economic system', although theoretically it could. It means 'the mental conversion of flesh and blood living creatures into cartoon characters possessing bourgeois Judeo-Christian attitudes and morals' (p. 48).

Morphology is even more interesting when you look at compounds. The four words below, also gleaned from *Generation X,* could each be interpreted in a few ways. For each word, I've given the real definition and my own, made-up definition (Coupland's are made up too, but his were first, so I count them as the real definitions). I've also given the morphological structure that matches one of the definitions. Your task is to figure out if and how the structure would be different for the other definition.

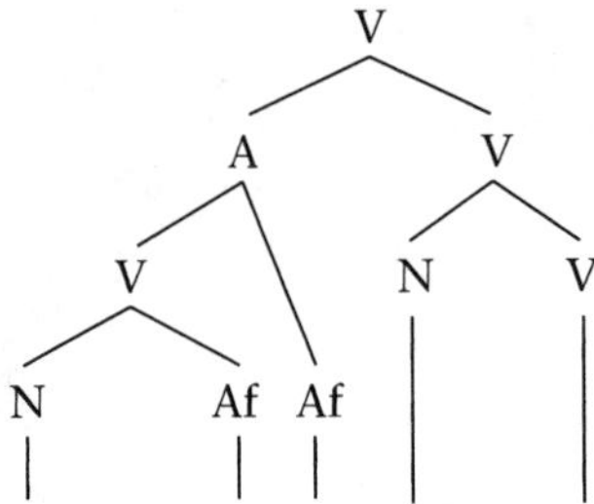

VACCIN ATE D TIME TRAVEL
To fantasize about traveling backward in time, but only with the proper vaccinations. (p. 11)

VACCINATED TIME TRAVEL
To travel freely in time, but only to times and places worth going to.

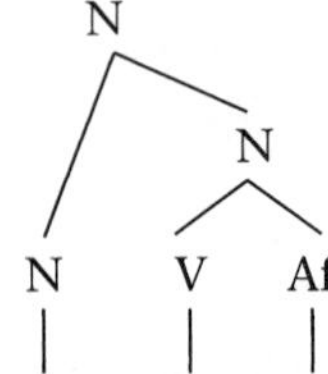

GREEN DIVISION
Sorting waste into chic recycling bins, showing how environmentally aware you are to all your friends.

GREEN DIVIS ION
Knowing the difference between envy and jealousy. (p. 150)

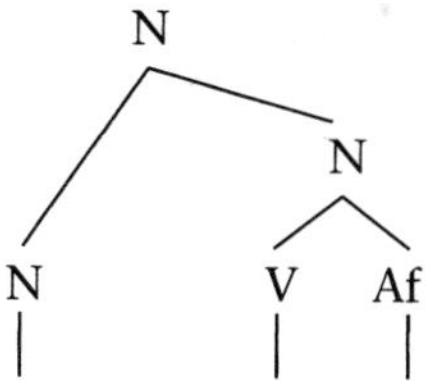

DUMPSTER CLOCK ING
The tendency when looking at objects to guesstimate the amount of time they will take to eventually decompose: *"Ski boots are the worst. Solid plastic. They'll be around till the sun goes supernova."* (p. 162)

DUMPSTER CLOCKING
Reckoning time by the amount and nature of the contents of the dumpster: *"An old couch, three textbooks, and twenty pounds of notebooks beneath a case of empties. Must be late May."*

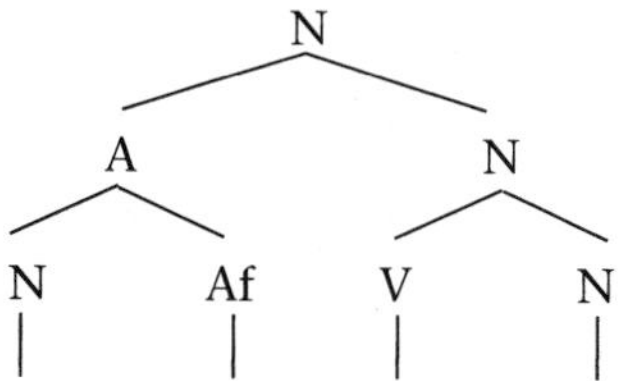

TERMINAL WANDERLUST
The inescapable urge, when seated at a computer, to do *anything* else as long as it involves getting away from the machine. Often involves coffee and cigarettes.

TERMIN AL WANDER LUST
A condition common to people of transient middle-class upbringings. Unable to feel rooted in any one environment, they move continually in the hopes of finding an idealized sense of community in the next location. (p. 171)

five

Syntax: The Analysis of Sentence Structure

William O'Grady

. . . the game is to say something new with old words.
– Ralph Waldo Emerson, *Journals,* 1849

Objectives

In this chapter, you will learn:

- how we categorize words
- how words can be combined into phrases and sentences according to a systematic schema
- that words "choose" what they can combine with in the same phrase
- how questions are derived from statements
- how to diagram the structure of sentences
- how all languages are alike in the way sentences are constructed
- how languages can differ systematically in the way sentences are constructed

Not much can be said with a single word. If language is to express complex thoughts and ideas, it has to have a way to combine words into sentences. In this chapter, we will consider how this is done, focusing on the component of the grammar that linguists call **syntax**.

As noted in Chapter 1, speakers of a language are able to combine words in novel ways, forming sentences that they have neither heard nor seen before. However, not just any combination of words will produce a well-formed sentence. English speakers recognize that the pattern in *1* is not permissible even though the same words can be combined in a different way to form the acceptable sentence in *2*.

1)

*House painted student a the.

2)

A student painted the house.

We say that an utterance is **grammatical** if native speakers judge it to be a possible sentence of their language.

The study of syntax lies very close to the heart of contemporary linguistic analysis, and work in this area is notorious both for its diversity and for its complexity. New ideas are constantly being put forward, and there is considerable controversy over how the properties of sentence structure should be described and explained.

This chapter will introduce a simple version of **transformational** (or **generative**) **grammar**. Although many linguists disagree with various features of this approach, it is very widely used in linguistics and other disciplines concerned with language (especially cognitive science). For this reason, it is the usual point of departure for introductions to the study of sentence structure.

An intriguing aspect of work within transformational syntax is the emphasis on **Universal Grammar (UG)**, the system of categories, operations, and principles that are shared by all languages. The key idea is that despite the many superficial differences among languages, there are certain commonalities with respect to the manner in which sentences are formed. As things now stand, it is widely believed that the syntactic component of any grammar must include at least two subcomponents. The first of these is a **lexicon**, or mental dictionary, that provides a list of the language's words along with information about their pronunciation, their form, and their meaning.

The second subcomponent consists of what can be called a **computational system**, by which we simply mean operations that combine and arrange words in particular ways. As we will see a little later in this chapter, the two principal structure-building operations made available by Universal Grammar are **Merge** (which combines elements to create phrases and sentences) and **Move** (which transports an element to a new position within a particular sentence).

We will begin our discussion of these matters in Section 1 by introducing some of the most common categories of words found in language and by investigating how they can be combined into larger structural units.

1 Categories and Structure

A fundamental fact about words in all human languages is that they can be grouped together into a relatively small number of classes called **syntactic categories**. This classification reflects a variety of factors, including the type of meaning that words express, the type of affixes that they take, and the type of structures in which they can occur.

1.1 Categories of Words

Table 5.1 provides examples of the word-level categories that are most central to the study of syntax.

Table 5.1 Syntactic categories

Lexical categories	*Examples*
Noun (N)	Harry, boy, wheat, policy, moisture, bravery
Verb (V)	arrive, discuss, melt, hear, remain, dislike
Adjective (A)	good, tall, old, intelligent, beautiful, fond
Preposition (P)	to, in, on, near, at, by
Adverb (Adv)	slowly, quietly, now, always, perhaps
Nonlexical categories	*Examples*
Determiner (Det)	the, a, this, these, no (as in *no books*)
Auxiliary verb (Aux)	
Modal	will, can, may, must, should, could
Nonmodal	be, have
Conjunction (Con)	and, or, but
Degree word (Deg)	too, so, very, more, quite

The four most studied syntactic categories are **noun (N)**, **verb (V)**, **adjective (A)**, and **preposition (P)**. These elements, which are often called **lexical categories**, play a very important role in sentence formation, as we will soon see. A fifth and less studied lexical category consists of **adverbs (Adv)**, most of which are derived from adjectives.

Languages may also contain **nonlexical** or **functional categories**, including **determiner (Det)**, **auxiliary verb (Aux)**, **conjunction (Con)**, and **degree word (Deg)**. Such elements generally have meanings that are harder to define and paraphrase than those of lexical categories. For example, the meaning of a determiner such as *the* or an auxiliary such as *would* is more difficult to describe than the meaning of a noun such as *hill* or *vehicle*.

A potential source of confusion in the area of word classification stems from the fact that some items can belong to more than one category.

3)

comb used as a noun:
The woman found a comb.

comb used as a verb:
The boy should comb his hair.

4)

near used as a preposition:
The child stood near the fence.

near used as a verb:
The runners neared the finish line.

near used as an adjective:
The end is nearer than you might think.

How then can we determine a word's category?

Meaning

One criterion involves meaning. For instance, nouns typically name entities, including individuals (*Harry, Sue*) and objects (*book, desk*). Verbs, on the other hand, characteristically designate actions (*run, jump*), sensations (*feel, hurt*), and states (*be, remain*). Consistent with these tendencies, *comb* in *3* refers to an object when used as a noun but to an action when used as a verb.

The typical function of an adjective is to designate a property or attribute of the entities denoted by nouns. Thus, when we say *that tall building,* we are attributing the property 'tall' to the building designated by the noun.

In a parallel way, adverbs typically denote properties and attributes of the actions, sensations, and states designated by verbs. In the following sentences, for example, the adverb *quickly* indicates the manner of Janet's leaving and the adverb *early* specifies its time.

5)

Janet left quickly.
Janet left early.

A word's category membership does not always bear such a straightforward relationship to its meaning, however. For example, there are nouns such as *difficulty, truth,* and *likelihood* that do not name entities in the strict sense. Moreover, even though words that name actions tend to be verbs, nouns may also denote actions (*push* is a noun in *give someone a push*).

Matters are further complicated by the fact that in some cases, words with very similar meanings belong to different categories. For instance, the words *like* and *fond* are very similar in meaning (as in *Mice like/are fond of cheese*), yet *like* is a verb and *fond* is an adjective.

Inflection

Most linguists believe that meaning is only one of several criteria that enter into determining a word's category. As shown in Table 5.2, inflection can also be very useful for distinguishing among different categories of words. (For a discussion of inflection, see Chapter 4, Section 4.)

Table 5.2 Lexical categories and their inflectional affixes

Category	*Inflectional affix*	*Examples*
N (Noun)	plural *-s*	books, chairs, doctors
	possessive *-'s*	John's, (the) man's
V (Verb)	past tense *-ed*	arrived, melted, hopped
	progressive *-ing*	arriving, melting, hopping
	third person singular *-s*	arrives, melts, hops
A (Adjective)	comparative *-er*	taller, faster, smarter
	superlative *-est*	tallest, fastest, smartest

However, even inflection does not always provide the information needed to determine a word's category. In English, for example, not all adjectives can take the comparative and superlative affixes (**intelligenter, *beautifulest*), and some nouns cannot be pluralized (*moisture, bravery, knowledge*).

Distribution

A third and often more reliable criterion for determining a word's category involves the type of elements (especially functional categories) with which it can co-occur (its **distribution**). For example, nouns can typically appear with a determiner, verbs with an auxiliary, and adjectives with a degree word in the sort of patterns illustrated in Table 5.3.

Table 5.3 Distributional properties of nouns, verbs, and adjectives

Category	*Distributional property*	*Examples*
Noun (N)	occurrence with a determiner	a car, the wheat
Verb (V)	occurrence with an auxiliary	has gone, will stay
Adjective (A)	occurrence with a degree word	very rich, too big

Of course, a verb cannot occur with a determiner or degree word in these sorts of patterns, and a noun cannot occur with an auxiliary.

6)

a verb with a determiner:
*the destroy

a verb with a degree word:
*very arrive

a noun with an auxiliary:
*will destruction

Distributional tests for category membership are simple and highly reliable. They can be used with confidence when it is necessary to categorize words you are unsure of.

1.2 Phrase Structure

Sentences are not formed by simply stringing words together like beads on a necklace. Rather, sentences have a hierarchical design in which words are grouped together into successively larger structural units. This section will focus on the structure of **phrases**, which are the units that stand between words and sentences in syntactic structure.

The Blueprint

As a first approximation, it is often suggested that a typical phrase can be broken down into three parts—a **head**, a **specifier**, and a **complement**—arranged as specified in the blueprint or **X' schema** shown in Figure 5.1. (X' is pronounced "X-bar".) X stands for any category (e.g., N, V, A, P), so XP stands for a phrase such as NP, VP, AP, or PP.

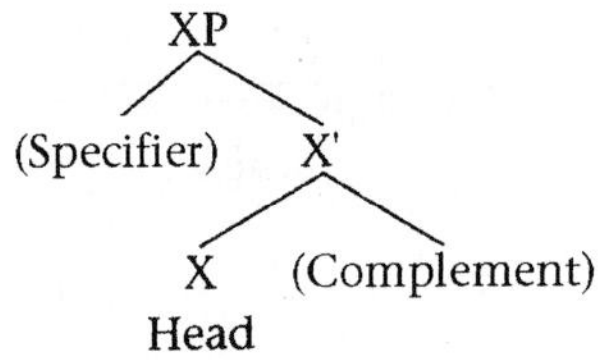

Figure 5.1 The X' schema

Such structures, which are often called (inverted) trees, capture the hierarchical organization of phrases and sentences. In particular, the X' schema captures four generalizations:

1. All phrases have a three-level structure (X, X', and XP).
2. All phrases contain a head, X.
3. If there is a complement, it is attached at the intermediate X' level, as a "sister" of the head.
4. If there is a specifier, it is attached at the XP level.

Let us consider each part of a phrase's architecture in turn.

Heads

The head is the obligatory nucleus around which a phrase is built. For now, we will focus on four categories that can function as the head of a phrase—nouns, verbs, adjectives, and prepositions. Thus, to start out, the X in the X' schema can be N, V, A, or P.

Although phrases usually consist of two or more words, a head may form a phrase all by itself, as shown in the examples in Figure 5.2. When this happens, the resulting structure has a single straight branch from which only the head hangs.

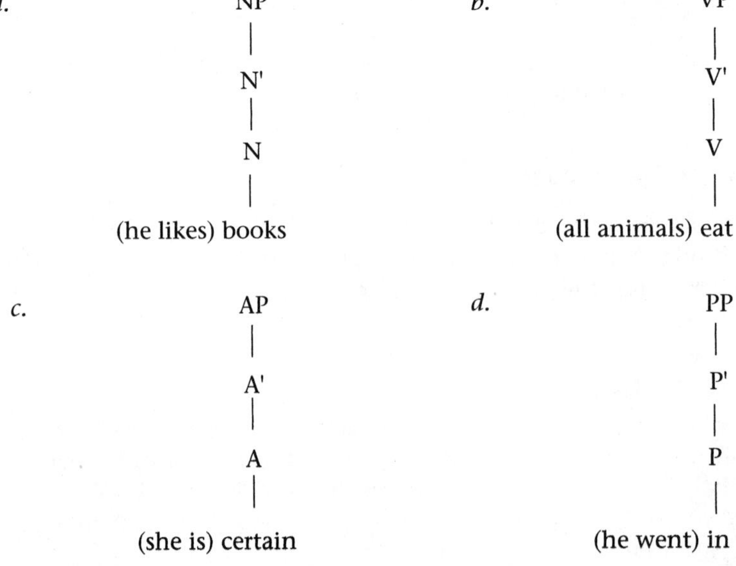

Figure 5.2 Phrases consisting of only a head

Specifiers

The type of specifier that appears in a particular phrase depends on the category of the head. Determiners serve as the specifiers of Ns, while preverbal adverbs typically function as the specifiers of Vs and degree words as the specifiers of As and (some) Ps (see Table 5.4).

Table 5.4 Some specifiers

Category	*Typical function*	*Examples*
Determiner (Det)	specifier of N	the, a, this, those, no
Adverb (Adv)	specifier of V	never, perhaps, often, always
Degree word (Deg)	specifier of A or P	very, quite, more, almost

When a specifier is present, it attaches to XP in accordance with the X' schema. This gives structures such as the ones shown in Figure 5.3.

Syntactically, specifiers typically mark a phrase boundary. In English, specifiers occur at the beginning of their respective phrases, as illustrated in the examples below.

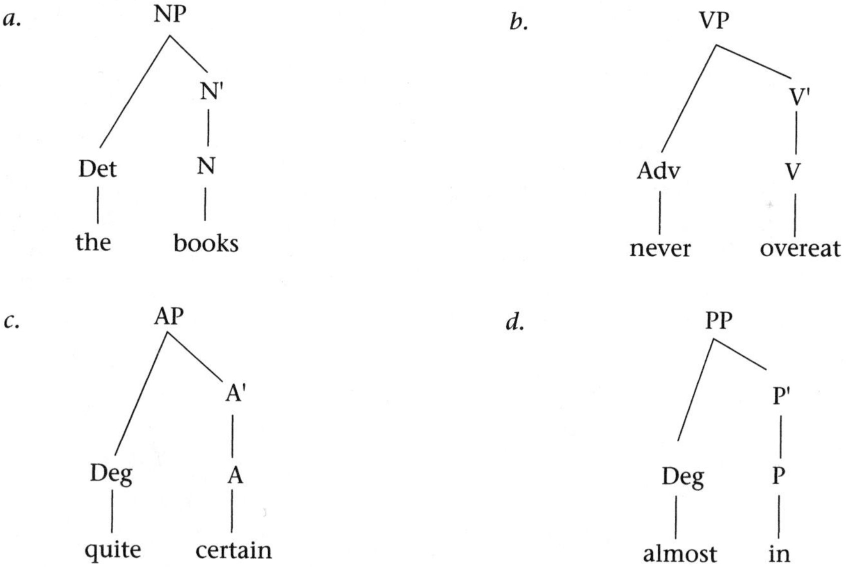

Figure 5.3 Some phrases consisting of a specifier and a head

Semantically, specifiers help to make the meaning of the head more precise. Hence, the determiner (Det) *the* in *a* indicates that the speaker has in mind specific books, the adverb *never* in *b* indicates nonoccurrence of the event, and the degree words (Deg) *quite* and *almost* in *c* and *d* indicate the extent to which a particular property or relation is manifested.

Exercise 3 at the end of the chapter provides practice in identifying specifiers and heads.

Complements

Consider now some examples of slightly more complex phrases. The head is underlined in each phrase.

7)

a. $[_{NP}$ the <u>books</u> about the war]
b. $[_{VP}$ never <u>eat</u> a hamburger]
c. $[_{AP}$ quite <u>certain</u> about Mary]
d. $[_{PP}$ almost <u>in</u> the house]

In addition to a specifier and the underlined head, the phrases in *7* also contain a complement. These elements, which are themselves phrases, provide information about entities and locations whose existence is implied by the meaning of the head. For example, the meaning of *eat* implies an object that is eaten, the meaning of *in* implies a location, and so on.

8)

A vegetarian would never eat [a hamburger].
↑ ↑
head *complement naming the thing eaten*

9)

in [the house]
↑ ↑
head *complement naming a location*

Figure 5.4 illustrates the structure of a phrase consisting of a specifier, a head, and a complement. (The NP serving as complement of a V is often called a **direct object**; a verb taking a direct object is called **transitive**.) As noted above, complements are themselves phrases. Thus, the complement of the V *eat* is an NP that itself consists of a determiner (*a*) and a head (*hamburger*).

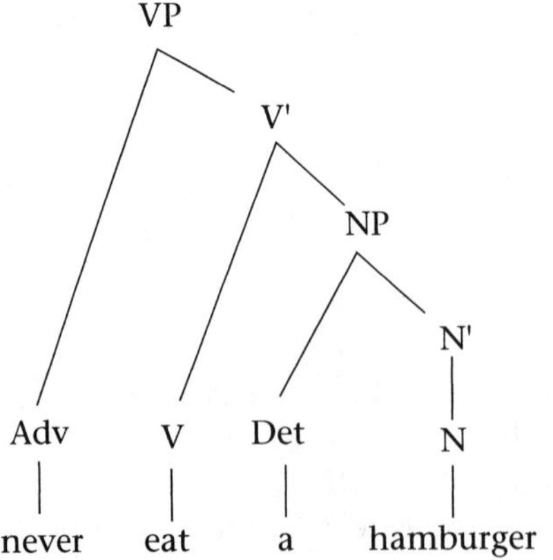

Figure 5.4 A VP consisting of a specifier, a head, and a complement

NPs, APs, and PPs have a parallel internal structure, as the examples in Figure 5.5 illustrate. (In order to save space, we do not depict the internal structure of the complement phrases in these examples. For the full structure of any tree abbreviated in this way go to **bedfordstmartins.com/linguistics/syntax** and click on **trees**.)

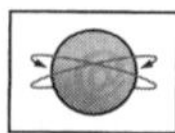

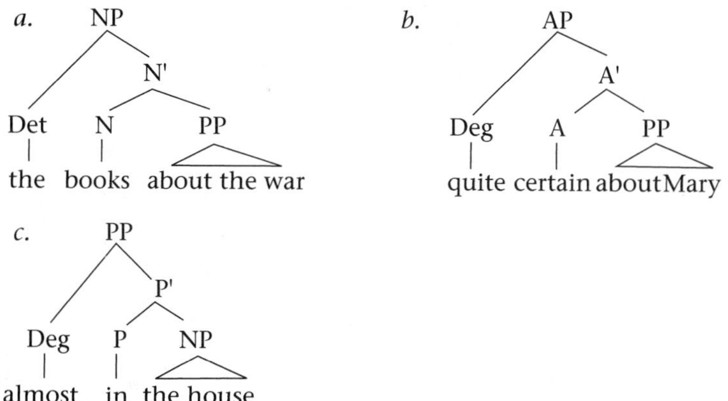

Figure 5.5 Other phrases consisting of a specifier, a head, and a complement

Of course, it is also possible to have phrases that consist of just a head and a complement, with no specifier. This results in the type of bottom-heavy structures depicted in Figure 5.6.

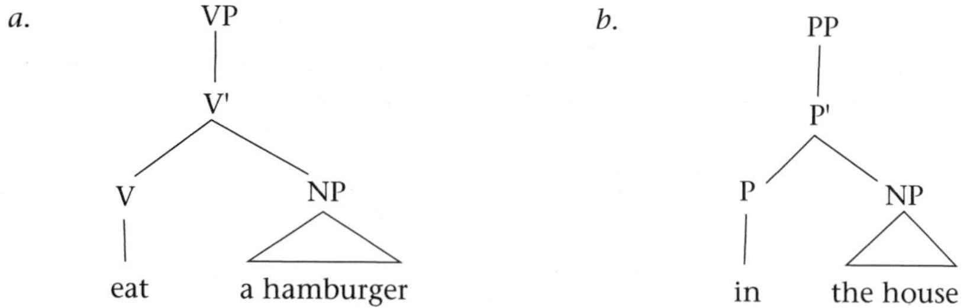

Figure 5.6 Phrases consisting of a head and a complement

Exercise 4 at the end of the chapter provides practice in identifying complements.

The Merge Operation

We can now formulate the following operation for sentence building.

10)

Merge

Combine words in a manner compatible with the X' schema.

The Merge operation is able to take a determiner such as *the* and combine it with an N' consisting of the N *house* to form the NP *the house*. It is then able to take a head such as the preposition *in* and combine it with the NP *the house* to form the P' and PP *in the house* (see Figure 5.7).

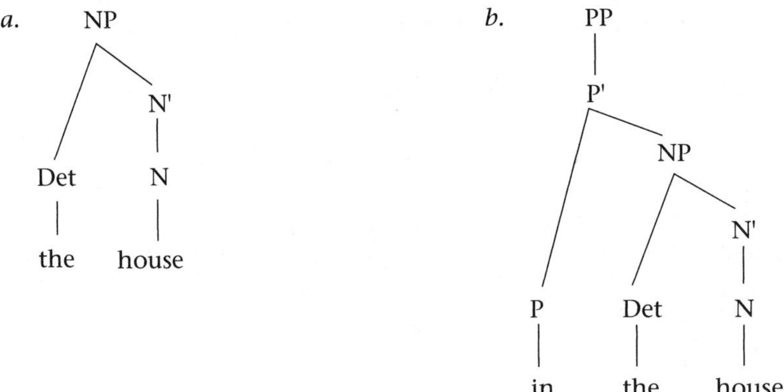

Figure 5.7 The Merge operation in action

Continued application of the Merge operation to additional words can lead to the formation of phrases and sentences of unlimited complexity.

1.3 Sentences

The largest unit of syntactic analysis is the sentence. Sentences have as their head an abstract category dubbed I (or Infl for 'inflection') that indicates the sentence's tense. The I category takes a VP as its complement and the sentence's subject as its specifier. This results in the structure depicted in Figure 5.8 (Pst = Past).

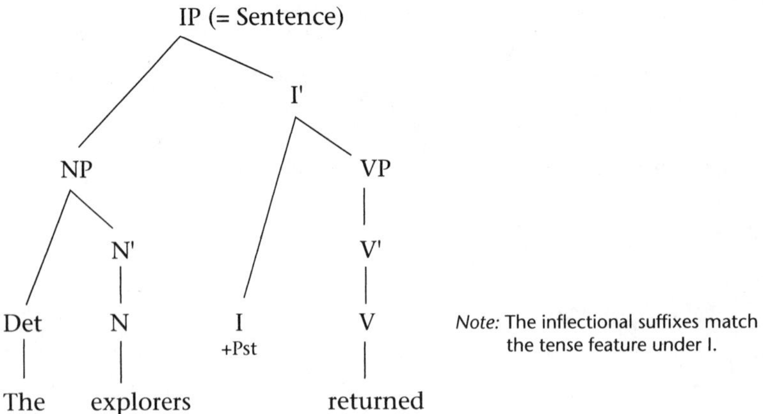

Figure 5.8 The structure of a sentence

The tense feature in I must be compatible with the form of the verb. So a sentence like the one above whose head contains the feature +Pst must contain a verb marked for the past tense.

Although somewhat abstract, this analysis has the advantage of giving sentences the same internal structure as other phrases (with a specifier, a head, and a complement), making them consistent with the X' schema. Moreover, because I, like all heads, is obligatory, we also account for the fact that all sentences have tense (e.g., in English they are all past or nonpast).

The structure in Figure 5.8 also provides us with a natural place to locate modal auxiliaries such as *can, will,* and *must,* most of which are inherently nonpast, as shown by the unacceptability of **He can/will/must work yesterday.* (The auxiliaries *could* and *would* can be either past or nonpast—e.g., *He could swim tomorrow/He could swim when he was three.*) Although traditionally analyzed as auxiliary verbs, these words are treated as instances of the I category in contemporary linguistic analysis, as depicted in Figure 5.9. (We will discuss the status of nonmodal auxiliaries such as *have* and *be* in Section 4.1.)

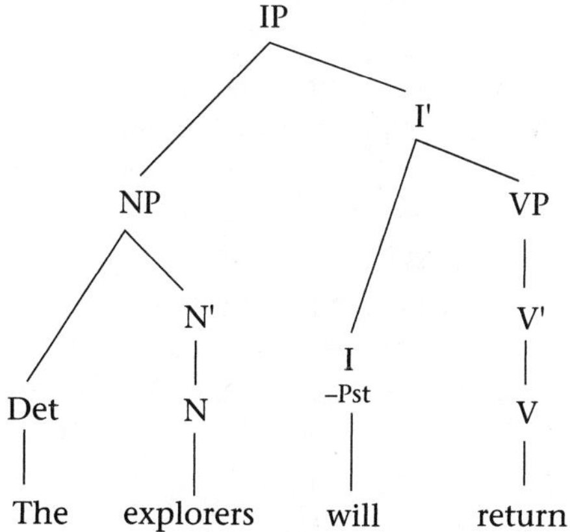

Figure 5.9 An IP with an auxiliary in the I position

This neatly accounts not only for the fact that modals have an inherent tense but also for their occurrence between the subject (the specifier) and the VP (the complement)—in the position reserved for the head of the sentence. (It must be admitted, however, that the use of the term *inflection* by syntacticians to include free morphemes is unfortunate.)

The appendix at the end of the chapter outlines a procedure that should help you assign sentences an appropriate structure. Exercise 5 provides an opportunity to practice this procedure.

1.4 Tests for Phrase Structure

How can linguists be sure that they have grouped words together into phrases in the right way? The existence of the syntactic units, or **constituents**, found in tree structures can be independently verified with the help of special tests. We will briefly consider three such tests here as they apply to XP-level constituents. (Not every test works for every constituent, though.)

The Substitution Test

Evidence that phrases are syntactic units comes from the fact that they can often be replaced by an element such as *they, it,* or *do so.* This is illustrated in *11,* where *they* replaces the NP *the children* and *do so* replaces the VP *stop at the corner.* (This is called a **substitution test**.)

11)

[$_{NP}$The children] will [$_{VP}$ stop at the corner] if *they* see us *do so.*
(*they* = the children; *do so* = stop at the corner)

The substitution test also confirms that a PP such as *at the corner* is a unit since it can be replaced by a single word in a sentence such as *12.*

12)

The children stopped [$_{PP}$ at the corner], and we stopped *there* too.
(*there* = at the corner)

Elements that do not form a constituent cannot be replaced in this way. Thus, there is no word in English that we can use to replace *children stopped,* for example, or *at the.*

The Movement Test

A second indication that *at the corner* forms a constituent is that it can be moved as a single unit to a different position within the sentence. (This is called a **movement test**.) In *13,* for instance, *at the corner* can be moved from a position after the verb to the beginning of the sentence.

13)

They stopped [$_{PP}$ at the corner]. → [$_{PP}$ At the corner], they stopped.

Of course, *at the,* which is not a syntactic unit, cannot be fronted in this manner (**At the, they stopped corner*).

The Coordination Test

Finally, we can conclude that a group of words forms a constituent if it can be joined to another group of words by a conjunction such as *and, or,* or *but.* (This is known as the **coordination test** since patterns built around a conjunction are called **coordinate structures**.) The sentence in *14* illustrates how coordination can be used to help establish that *stopped at the corner* is a constituent.

14)

The children [$_{VP}$ stopped at the corner] and [$_{VP}$ looked both ways].

2 Complement Options

How can we be sure that individual words will occur with a complement of the right type in the syntactic structures that we have been building? Information about the complements permitted by a particular head is included in its entry in a speaker's lexicon. For instance, the lexicon for English includes an entry for *devour* that indicates its syntactic category (V), its phonological representation, its meaning, and the fact that it takes an NP complement.

15)

devour: category: V
phonological representation: /dəvawəɹ/
meaning: 'eat hungrily'
complement: NP

The term **subcategorization** is used to refer to information about a word's complement options.

Subcategorization information helps ensure that lexical items appear in the appropriate types of tree structures. For example, by saying that *devour* belongs to the subcategory of verbs that require an NP complement, we are permitting it to occur in patterns such as *16a* but not *16b*.

16)

a. *devour* with an NP complement:
The child devoured [$_{NP}$ the sandwich].

b. *devour* without an NP complement:
*The child devoured.

2.1 Complement Options for Verbs

Table 5.5 illustrates some of the more common complement options for verbs in English. The subscripted prepositions indicate subtypes of PP complements where this is relevant. *Loc* stands for any preposition expressing a location (such as *near, on, under*).

Table 5.5 Some examples of verb complements

Complement option	*Sample heads*	*Example*
Ø	vanish, arrive, die	The rabbit vanished __.
NP	devour, cut, prove	The professor proved [$_{NP}$ *the theorem*].
AP	be, become	The man became [$_{AP}$ *very angry*].
PP_{to}	dash, talk, refer	The dog dashed [$_{PP}$ *to the door*].
NP NP	spare, hand, give	We handed [$_{NP}$ *the man*] [$_{NP}$ *a map*].
NP PP_{to}	hand, give, send	She gave [$_{NP}$ *a diploma*] [$_{PP}$ *to the student*].
NP PP_{for}	buy, cook, reserve	We bought [$_{NP}$ *a hat*] [$_{PP}$ *for Andy*].
NP PP_{loc}	put, place, stand	She put [$_{NP}$ *the muffler*] [$_{PP}$ *on the car*].
PP_{to} PP_{about}	talk, speak	I talked [$_{PP}$ *to a doctor*] [$_{PP}$ *about Sue*].
NP PP_{for} PP_{with}	open, fix	We opened [$_{NP}$ *the door*] [$_{PP}$ *for John*] [$_{PP}$ *with a crowbar*].

The verbs in the first line of Table 5.5 (*vanish, arrive,* and *die*) occur without any complement, those in the second line occur with an NP complement, and so on.

A word can belong to more than one subcategory. The verb *eat,* for example, can occur either with or without an NP complement and therefore belongs to both of the first two subcategories in our table.

17)

After getting home, they ate (the sandwiches).

Of course, not all verbs exhibit this flexibility. As we have already seen, *devour*—although similar in meaning to *eat*—requires an NP complement and therefore belongs only to the second subcategory in our table.

As the examples in Table 5.5 also show, some heads can take more than one complement. The verb *put* is a case in point, since it requires both an NP complement and a PP complement.

18)

put with an NP complement and a PP complement:
The librarian put [$_{NP}$ the book] [$_{PP}$ on the shelf].

19)

put without an NP complement:
*The librarian put [$_{PP}$ on the shelf].

20)

put without a PP complement:
*The librarian put [$_{NP}$ the book].

The VP *put the book on the shelf* has the structure in Figure 5.10, in which the V' consists of the head *put* and its two complements—the NP *the book* and the PP *on the shelf.*

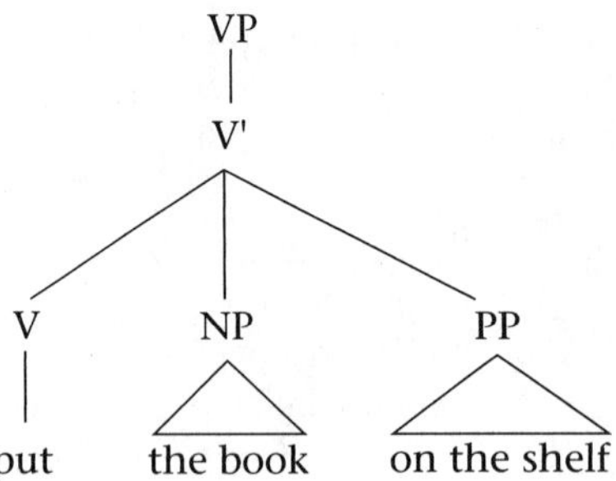

Figure 5.10 A verb with two complements

2.2 Complement Options for Other Categories

Various complement options are also available for Ns, As, and Ps. Tables 5.6, 5.7, and 5.8 provide examples of just some of the possibilities.

Here again subcategorization ensures that particular heads can appear in tree structures only if there is an appropriate type of complement. Thus, the adjective *tired* takes an *of*-PP as its complement, while the adjective *fed up* takes a *with*-PP.

Table 5.6 Some examples of noun complements

Complement option	*Sample heads*	*Example*
Ø	car, boy, electricity	the car __
PP_{of}	memory, failure, death	the memory [$_{PP}$ *of a friend*]
PP_{of} PP_{to}	presentation, gift, donation	the presentation [$_{PP}$ *of a medal*] [$_{PP}$ *to the winner*]
PP_{with} PP_{about}	argument, discussion, conversation	an argument [$_{PP}$ *with Stella*] [$_{PP}$ *about politics*]

Table 5.7 Some examples of adjective complements

Complement option	*Sample heads*	*Example*
Ø	tall, green, smart	very tall __
PP_{about}	curious, glad, angry	curious [$_{PP}$ *about China*]
PP_{to}	apparent, obvious	obvious [$_{PP}$ *to the student*]
PP_{of}	fond, full, tired	fond [$_{PP}$ *of chocolate*]

Table 5.8 Some examples of preposition complements

Complement option	*Sample heads*	*Example*
Ø	near, away, down	(he got) down __
NP	in, on, by, near	in [$_{NP}$ *the house*]
PP	down, up, out	down [$_{PP}$ *into the cellar*]

21)

a. tired [$_{PP}$ of cafeteria food] (compare: *tired with cafeteria food)
b. fed up [$_{PP}$ with cafeteria food] (compare: *fed up of cafeteria food)

A good deal of what we know about our language consists of information about words and the type of complements with which they can appear. Much of this information must be stored in the lexicon, since it cannot be predicted from a word's meaning.

2.3 Complement Clauses

All human languages allow sentence-like constructions to function as complements. A simple example of this from English is given in *22*.

22)

complement clause

[The coach knows [that/whether/if the team will win]].

matrix clause

The smaller bracketed phrase in *22* is called a **complement clause**; the larger phrase in which it occurs is called the **matrix clause**.

Words such as *that, whether,* and *if* are known as **complementizers** (**C**). They take an IP complement, forming the CP (complementizer phrase) depicted in Figure 5.11.

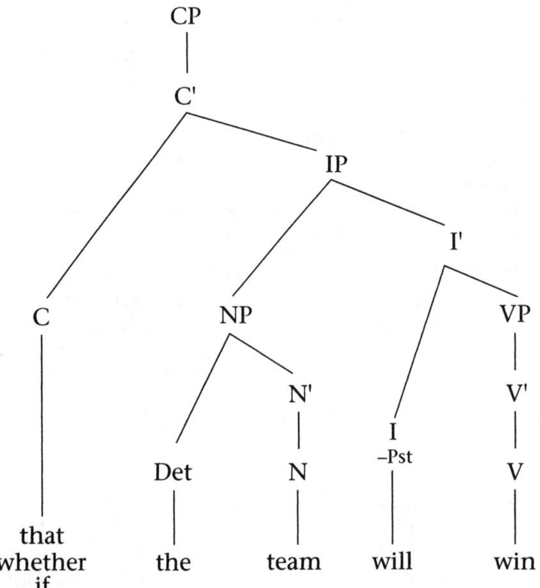

Figure 5.11 The structure of a CP

Given our X' schema, we must also ask about a possible specifier position for CP. As we will see in Section 3.4, there is even a type of element that can occur in the specifier position under CP.

When a CP occurs in a sentence such as *22,* in which it serves as complement of the verb *know,* the entire sentence has the structure shown in Figure 5.12. Table 5.9 provides examples of some of the verbs that are commonly found with this type of complement.

There is no limit on the number of embedded clauses that can occur in a sentence, as *23* helps show.

23)

A man thought $[_{CP}$ that a woman said $[_{CP}$ that Sue reported $[_{CP}$ that . . .

This structure is made possible by the fact that any CP can contain a verb that itself takes a complement CP. The first clause in our example contains the verb *think,* whose complement clause contains the verb *say,* whose complement clause contains *report,* and so on.

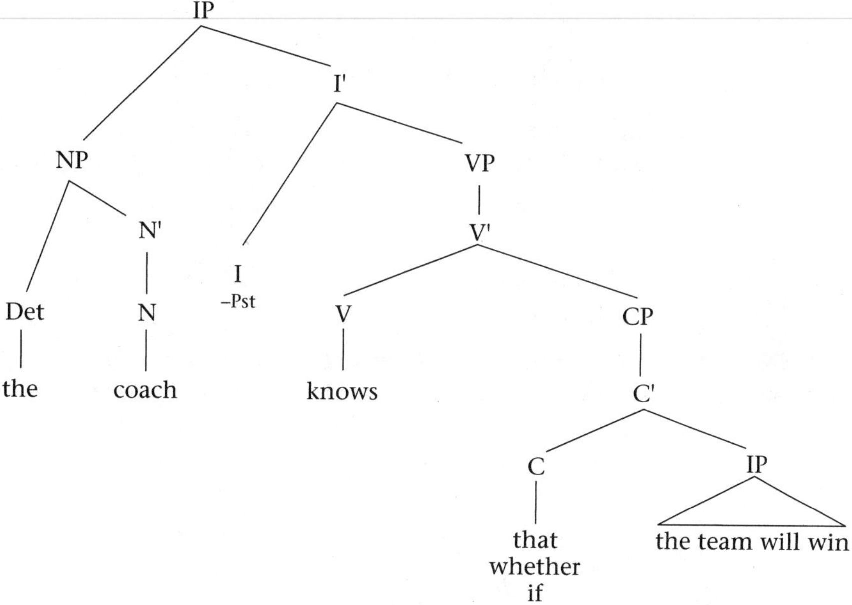

Figure 5.12 The structure of a sentence with an embedded CP

Table 5.9 Some verbs permitting CP complements

Complement options	*Sample heads*	*Example*
CP	believe, know, think, remember	They believe [$_{CP}$ *that Mary left*].
NP CP	persuade, tell, convince, promise	They told [$_{NP}$ *Eric*] [$_{CP}$ *that Mary had left*].
PP_{to} CP	concede, admit	They admitted [$_{PP}$ *to Eric*] [$_{CP}$ *that Mary had left*].

3 Move

As we have seen, it is possible to build a very large number of different sentences by allowing the Merge operation to combine words and phrases in accordance with the X' schema and the subcategorization properties of individual words. Nonetheless, there are still many sentences that we cannot build. This section considers two such patterns and discusses the sentence-building operation needed to accommodate them.

3.1 *Yes-No* Questions

To begin, let us consider the question sentences exemplified in *24.* (Such structures are called ***yes-no* questions** because the expected response is usually "yes" or "no.")

24)

a. *Should* that guy go?
b. *Can* the cat climb this tree?

A curious feature of these sentences is that the auxiliary verb occurs at the beginning of the sentence rather than in its more usual position to the right of the subject, as illustrated in *25*.

25)

a. That guy *should* go.
b. The cat *can* climb this tree.

Given that auxiliary verbs such as *should* and *can* are instances of the I category, the X' schema dictates that they should occur in the position depicted in Figure 5.13.

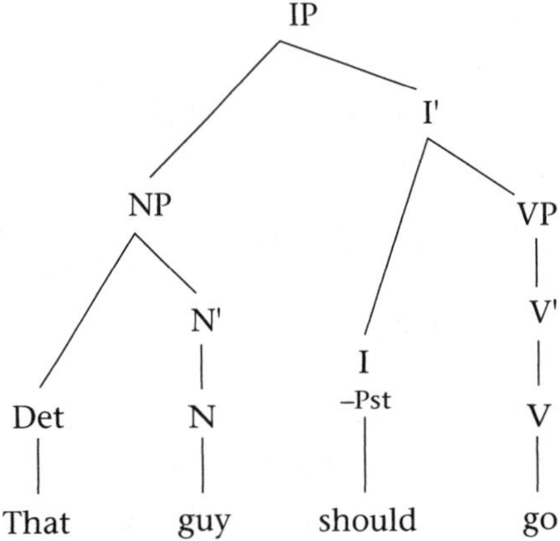

Figure 5.13 *Should* occurring in the head position between the subject (its specifier) and the VP (its complement)

How, then, does the word order in *24* come about?

The formation of question structures requires the use of a structure-building operation that we can call Move. Traditionally known as a **transformation** because it transforms an existing structure, Move applies to structures such as the one in Figure 5.13 and moves the auxiliary verb in the I position to a new position in front of the subject.

26)

Should that guy __ go?

The transformational analysis has at least two advantages. First, it allows us to avoid the conclusion that there are two types of auxiliary verbs in English: one that occurs between the subject and the VP and one that occurs in front of the subject. Under the transformational analysis, all auxiliaries originate inside the sentence. Auxiliaries that occur in front of the subject simply undergo an extra process—the Move operation that transports the I category in front of the subject in order to signal a question.

Second, the transformational analysis automatically captures the fact that the sentence *Should that guy go?* is the question structure corresponding to *That guy should go.* According to the analysis presented here, both sentences initially have the same basic structure. They differ only in that the Move operation has applied to the I category in the question structure.

A Landing Site for I

In what position does the auxiliary verb land when it is moved in front of the subject? This question can be answered if we assume that IPs occur within larger CPs, as depicted in Figure 5.14.

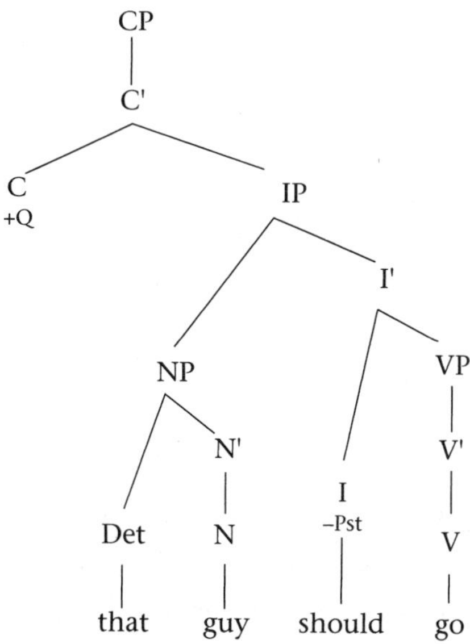

Figure 5.14 An IP inside a CP shell

By adopting this structure, we take the position that all IPs occur within a CP, whether they are embedded or not. It may help to think of the CP category as a shell that forms an outer layer of structure around an IP. When embedded within a larger sentence, the CP can contain an overt complementizer such as *that* or *whether.* Elsewhere, the C position simply contains information about whether the sentence is a statement or a question. For the sake of illustration, we use the symbol +Q to indicate a question; sentences with no such symbol in their C position will be interpreted as statements.

In some languages, the **Q feature** is spelled out as a separate morpheme (for further discussion of this, go to **bedfordstmartins.com/linguistics/syntax** and click on **variation**). In languages like English, where there is no such morpheme, the feature must attract another element to its position. The auxiliary verb in the I position is that element. This is illustrated in Figure 5.15 on page 170, where the Q feature in the C position attracts the auxiliary verb in the I position, causing it to move to the beginning of the sentence.

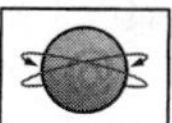

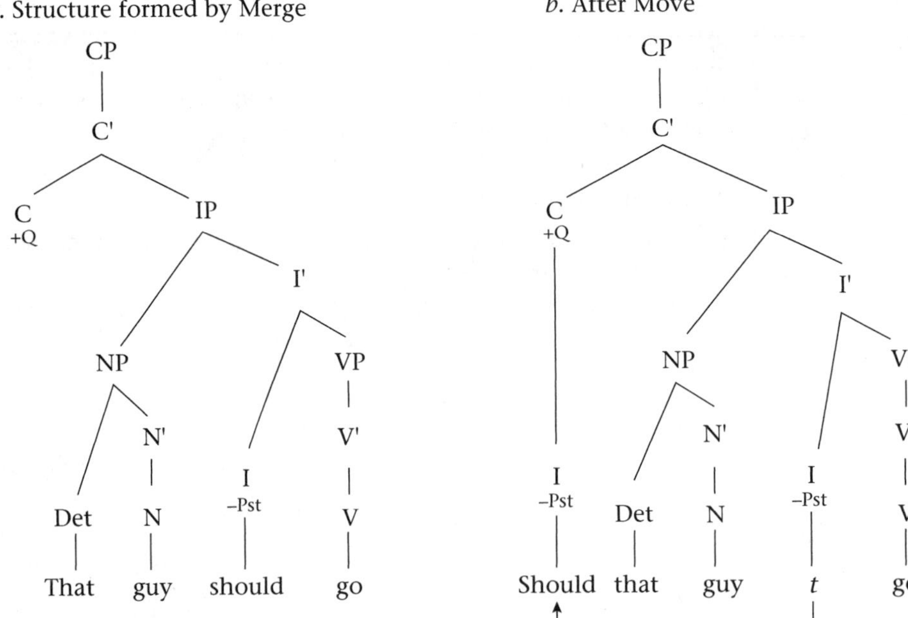

Figure 5.15 Movement of an auxiliary from the I position to the C position

A transformation (i.e., a Move operation) can do no more than change an element's position. It does not change the categories of any words and it cannot eliminate any part of the structure created by the Merge operation. Thus, *should* retains its I label even though it is moved into the C position, and the position that it formerly occupied remains in the tree structure. Called a **trace** and marked by the symbol *t,* it records the fact that the moved element comes from the head position within IP.

The Move operation used for *yes-no* questions is often informally called **Inversion** and is formulated as follows.

27)

Inversion:
Move I to C.

Is there any way to be sure that this idea is on the right track and that the auxiliary verb in the I position really does move to the C position? Some interesting evidence comes from the analysis of the embedded CPs in sentences such as the following.

28)

He asked [$_{CP}$ whether we would return].

Notice that the C position in the embedded clause is occupied by the complementizer *whether.* Assuming that no more than one word can occur in a particular position, we predict that Inversion should not be able to apply in the embedded clause since there is nowhere for the moved auxiliary verb to land. The ungrammaticality of *29* shows that this is correct.

29)

Inversion in an embedded CP that includes a complementizer:
*He asked [$_{CP}$ whether would we *t* return].

Interestingly, the acceptability of Inversion improves quite dramatically when there is no complementizer and the C position is therefore open to receive the moved auxiliary. (This sort of sentence sounds most natural when the embedded clause is interpreted as a sort of quotation.)

30)

Inversion in an embedded CP that does not have a complementizer:
He asked [$_{CP}$ would we *t* return].

Although some speakers prefer not to apply Inversion in embedded clauses at all (especially in formal speech), most speakers of English find *30* to be much more natural than *29*. This is just what we would expect if Inversion moves the auxiliary to an empty C position, as required by our analysis.

To summarize before continuing, we have introduced two changes into the system of syntactic analysis used until now. First, we assume that all IPs occur inside CPs. Second, we assume that the Inversion transformation moves the auxiliary from the I position to an empty C position in front of the subject NP. This not only gives the correct word order for question structures, but also helps explain why inversion sounds so unnatural when the C position is already filled by another element, as in *29*.

3.2 Deep Structure and Surface Structure

The preceding examples show that at least some sentences must be analyzed with the help of two distinct types of mechanisms. The first of these is the Merge operation, which creates tree structures by combining categories in a manner consistent with their subcategorization properties and the X' schema. The second is the Move operation, which can modify these tree structures by moving an element from one position to another. The process whereby a syntactic structure is formed by these operations is called a **derivation**.

In traditional work in transformational syntax, all instances of the Merge operation take place before any instances of the Move operation. As a result, the derivation for a sentence typically yields two distinct levels of syntactic structure, as shown in Figure 5.16. The first, called **deep structure** (or **D-structure**), is formed by the Merge operation in accordance with subcategorization properties and the X' schema. As we shall see in the chapter on semantics, deep structure plays a special role in the interpretation of sentences.

The second level of syntactic structure corresponds to the final syntactic form of the sentence. Called **surface structure** (or **S-structure**), it results from applying whatever other operations are appropriate for the sentence in question.

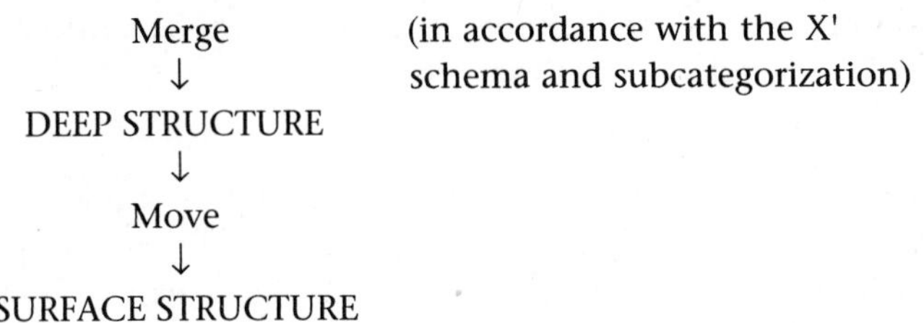

Figure 5.16 How a derivation works

3.3 *Do* Insertion

As we have just seen, formation of *yes-no* questions in English involves moving the I category, and the auxiliary verb that it contains, to the C position. How, then, do we form the questions corresponding to sentences such as those in *31,* which contain no auxiliary verb?

31)

a. The students liked the movie.
b. Those birds sing.

Since the I category in these sentences contains only an abstract tense marker (see Figure 5.17a), applying the Inversion transformation would have no visible effect and there would be no indication that the sentence was being used as a question. English circumvents this problem by adding the special auxiliary verb *do.*

32)

a. *Did* the students like the movie?
b. *Do* those birds sing?

As these examples show, *do* is inserted into sentences that do not already have an auxiliary verb, thereby making Inversion possible. We can capture this fact by formulating an **insertion rule** that adds an element to a tree structure.

33)

***Do* Insertion:**
Insert interrogative *do* into an empty I position.

The sentence in *32b* can now be analyzed as shown in Figure 5.17b. As these tree structures show, the sentence *Do those birds sing?* is built in three steps. In the initial step, the Merge operation interacts with the X' schema to give the D-structure in Figure 5.17a, which contains no auxiliary verb in the I position. The *Do* Insertion rule then adds the special interrogative auxiliary *do,* creating an intermediate level of structure in Figure 5.17b. The Move operation then moves I to the C position, creating the sentence's S-structure in Figure 5.17c.

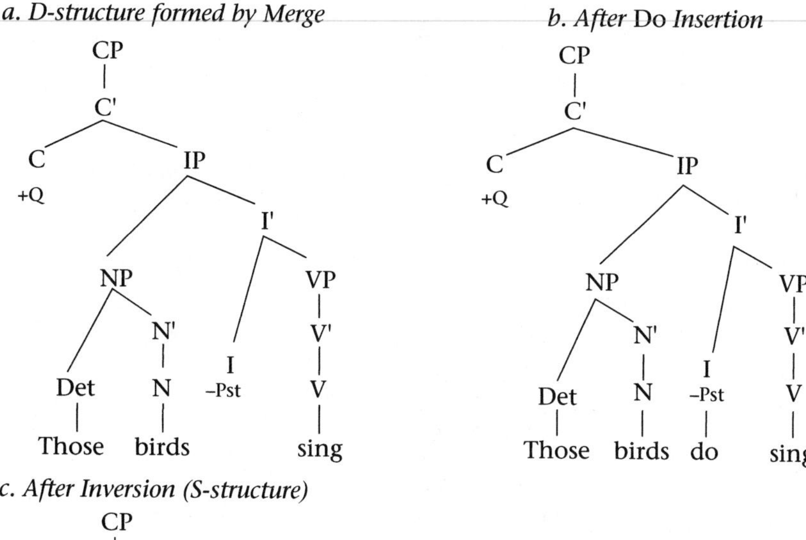

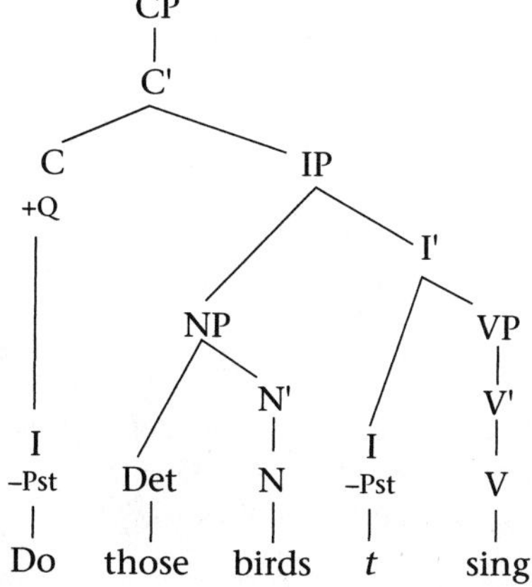

Figure 5.17 A sentence formed with the help of *Do* Insertion

3.4 *Wh* Movement

Consider now the set of question constructions exemplified in *34*. These sentences are called ***wh* questions** because of the presence of a question word beginning with *wh*.

34)

a. Which languages could Aristotle speak?
b. What can the child sit on?

There is reason to believe that the *wh* elements at the beginning of these sentences have been moved there from the positions indicated in Figure 5.18. (We take the question word *which* to be a determiner and *what* to be a noun in these sentences.)

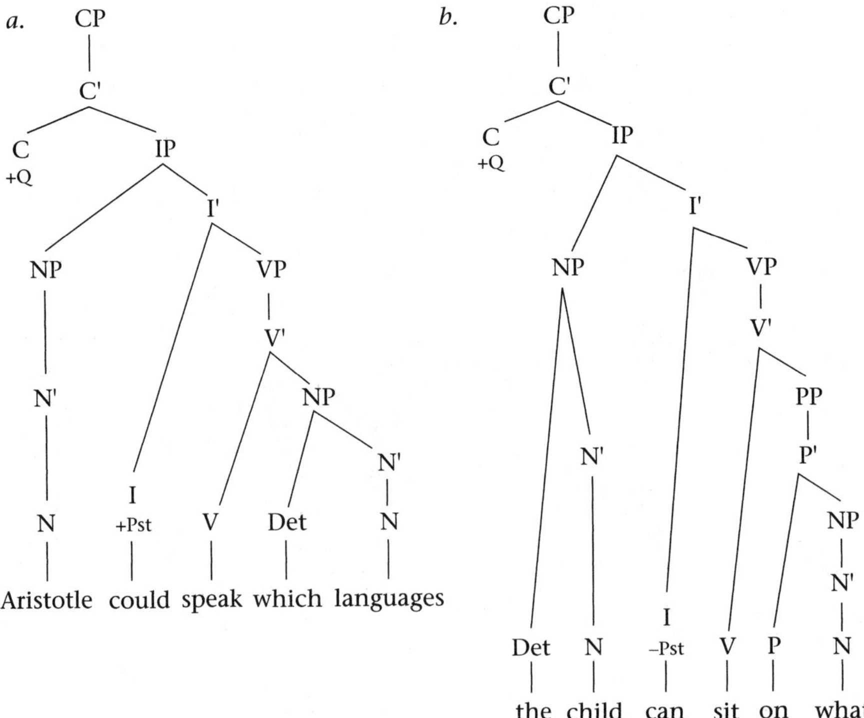

Figure 5.18 D-structures depicting the original positions of the *wh* expressions in *34*

Notice that *which languages* occurs as complement of the verb *speak* while *what* appears as complement of the preposition *on,* in accordance with the subcategorization requirements of these words. As the sentences in *35* show, both *speak* and *on* commonly occur with an NP complement.

35)

a. Aristotle could speak *Greek.*
b. The child can sit on *the bench.*

The structures in Figure 5.18 capture this fact by treating the *wh* phrase as complement of the verb in the first pattern and complement of the preposition in the second.

How then do the *wh* phrases end up at the beginning of the sentence? The answer is that they are attracted there by the Q feature, which results in the application of a second Move operation. (Recall that we have already posited one Move operation, which we have been calling Inversion.)

36)

Which languages could Aristotle *t* speak *t*?

↑ *Move 1*

Move 2

Application of the same two transformations to the structure in Figure 5.18b yields the *wh* question in *37a* or *37b* depending on whether the NP or the PP moves.

37)

a. Movement of the NP *what:*

$[_{NP}$ What] can the child *t* sit on *t*?

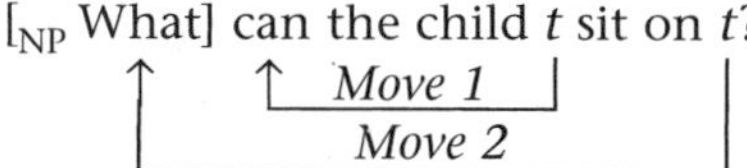

b. Movement of the PP *on what:*

$[_{PP}$ On what] can the child *t* sit *t*?

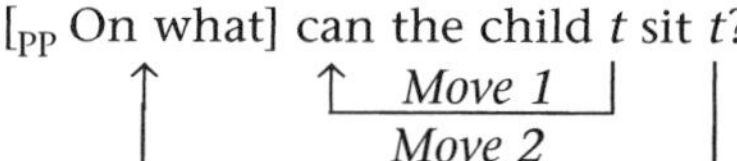

A Landing Site for *Wh* Words

As the examples in *36* and *37* help illustrate, the Move operation carries the *wh* phrase to the beginning of the sentence, to the left even of the fronted auxiliary. But where precisely does the *wh* phrase land?

Given that the moved auxiliary is located in the C position (see Figure 5.18 above, for example), it seems reasonable to conclude that the fronted *wh* phrase ends up in the specifier position of CP. Not only is this the only position in syntactic structure to the left of the C, but it is empty prior to the application of the Move operation.

We can make this idea precise by formulating the Move operation that applies to *wh* phrases as follows.

38)

***Wh* Movement:**
Move a *wh* phrase to the specifier position under CP.

The sentence *Which languages could Aristotle speak?* can now be analyzed in steps, the first of which involves formation of the structure in Figure 5.19 by the Merge operation. Consistent with our earlier assumption, the IP here occurs within a CP shell. *Wh* Movement and Inversion then apply to this structure, yielding the structure in Figure 5.20.

Like other transformations, *Wh* Movement cannot eliminate any part of the previously formed structure. The position initially occupied by the *wh* phrase is therefore not lost. Rather, it remains as a trace (an empty category), indicating that the moved element corresponds to the complement of the verb *speak*.

In the examples considered so far, the *wh* word originates as complement of a verb or preposition. In sentences such as the following, however, the *wh* word asks about the subject (the person who does the criticizing).

39)

Who criticized Maxwell?

In such patterns, the *wh* word originates in the subject position and subsequently moves to the specifier position within CP even though the actual order of the words in the sentence does not change as a result of this movement (see Figure 5.21 on page 177). (For reasons that are not fully understood, there is no *Do* Insertion in this type of question structure except for purposes of emphasis, as in *Who DID criticize Maxwell?*)

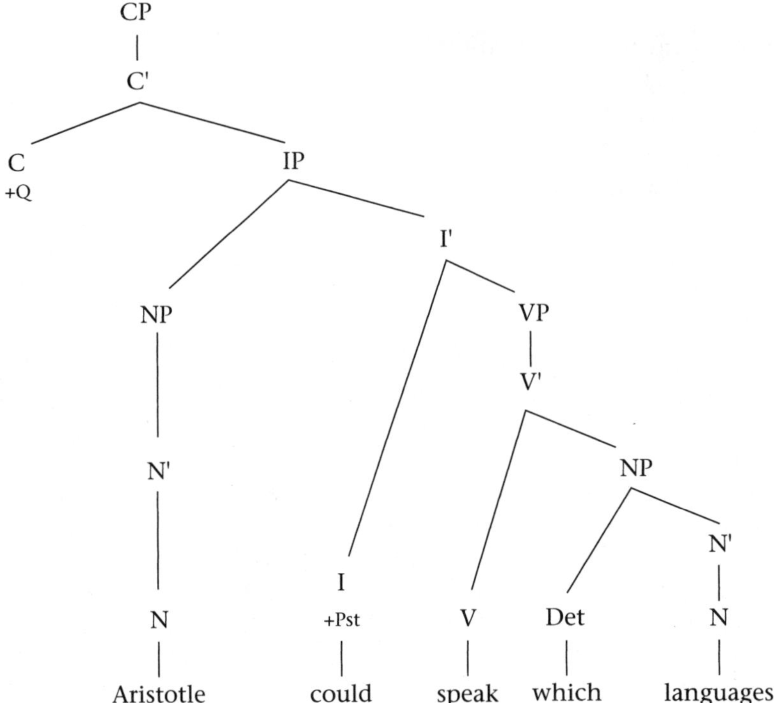

Figure 5.19 Deep structure for *Which languages could Aristotle speak?*

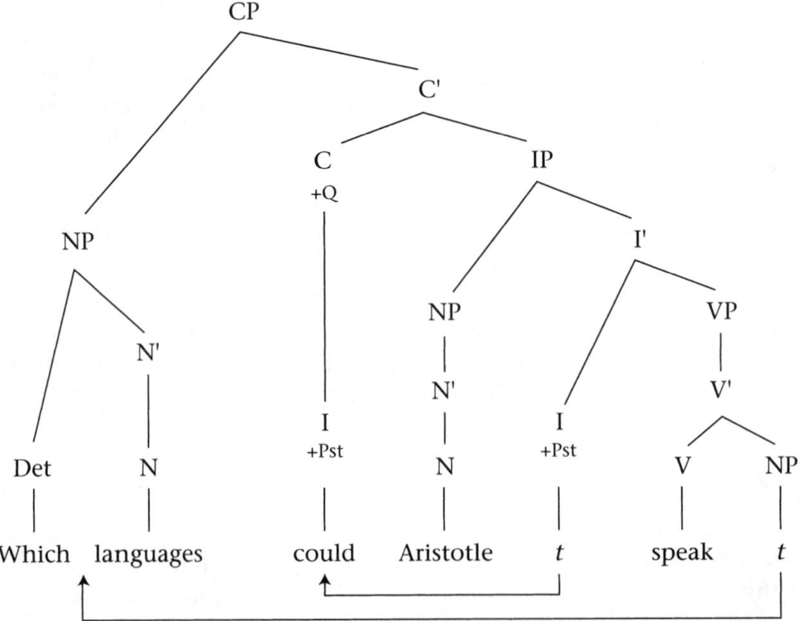

Figure 5.20 Surface structure for *Which languages could Aristotle speak?* The I category moves to the C position and the *wh* phrase moves to the specifier of CP position.

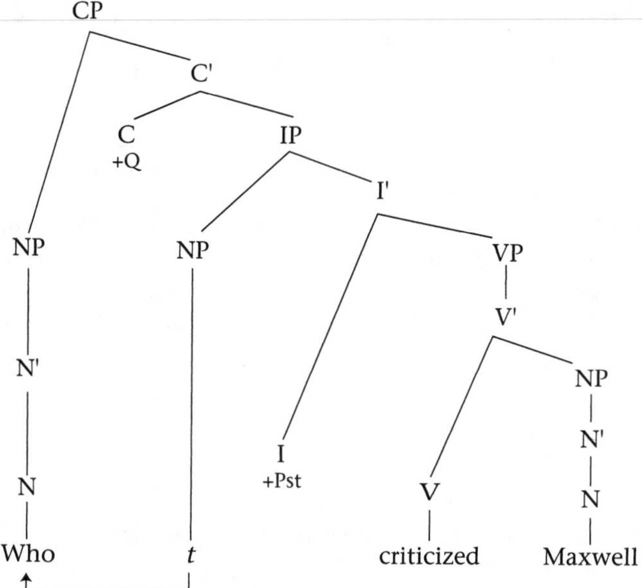

Figure 5.21 Movement of a subject *wh* word. Since there is nothing for the *wh* word to move over in such cases, there is no visible change in word order.

For more about Move, and particularly about limits on its operation, go to **bedfordstmartins.com/linguistics/syntax** and click on **constraints**.

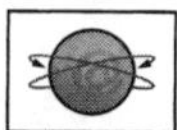

4 Universal Grammar and Parametric Variation

Thus far, our discussion has focused on English. Before looking at any further phenomena in this language, it is important to extend the scope of our analysis to other languages.

As noted at the beginning of this chapter, recent work on Universal Grammar suggests that all languages are fundamentally alike with respect to the basics of syntax. For instance, all languages use the Merge operation to combine words on the basis of their syntactic category and subcategorization properties, creating phrases that comply with the X' schema.

This does not mean that languages must be alike in all respects, though. Universal Grammar leaves room for variation, allowing individual languages to differ with respect to certain **parameters**. (You can think of a parameter as the set of options that UG permits for a particular phenomenon.) We will consider an example of this now that involves the Move operation. Some additional instances of cross-linguistic differences in syntax are considered at **bedfordstmartins.com/linguistics/syntax** (click on **variation**) and in Section 2.3 of Chapter 8.

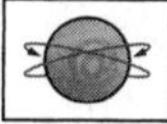

4.1 Verb Raising

Consider the contrast between the following two English sentences.

40)

a. Paul always works.
b. *Paul works always.

The ungrammaticality of the second sentence is expected since the preverbal adverb *always* functions as specifier of the verb and therefore should occur to its left, as in *40a*. Surprisingly, however, the equivalent adverb must follow the verb in French, even though specifiers in French normally precede the head, just as they do in English.

41)

a. The adverb precedes the verb; the sentence is ungrammatical:
*Paul toujours travaille. (= English *40a*)
Paul always works
'Paul always works.'

b. The adverb follows the verb; the sentence is grammatical:
Paul travaille toujours. (= English *40b*)
Paul works always
'Paul always works.'

Why should this be? One possibility is that the tense feature in the I category somehow attracts the verb to that position in French, just as the Q feature can attract verbs to the C position in some languages. As a result, French has the **Verb Raising transformation** outlined in *42*. (It's called "Raising" because the verb moves upward in the tree.)

42)

Verb Raising:
Move V to I.

This Move operation brings about the change depicted in Figure 5.22.

An important piece of independent evidence for the existence of Verb Raising in French comes from the operation of the Inversion transformation. As we have already seen (Section 3.1), this transformation moves the I category to the C position. Now, in English, only auxiliary verbs occur in the I position, which explains why only they can undergo Inversion.

43)

a. Inversion of an auxiliary verb in English:
Will you *t* stay for supper?
↑_____|

b. Inversion of a nonauxiliary verb in English:
*Stay you *t* for supper?
↑_____|

In French, however, regular verbs can occur in the I position, thanks to the Verb Raising transformation. This predicts that Inversion should be able to apply to these Vs in French as well as to auxiliaries. This is correct. Like English, French can form a question by moving an auxiliary leftward, as *44* illustrates.

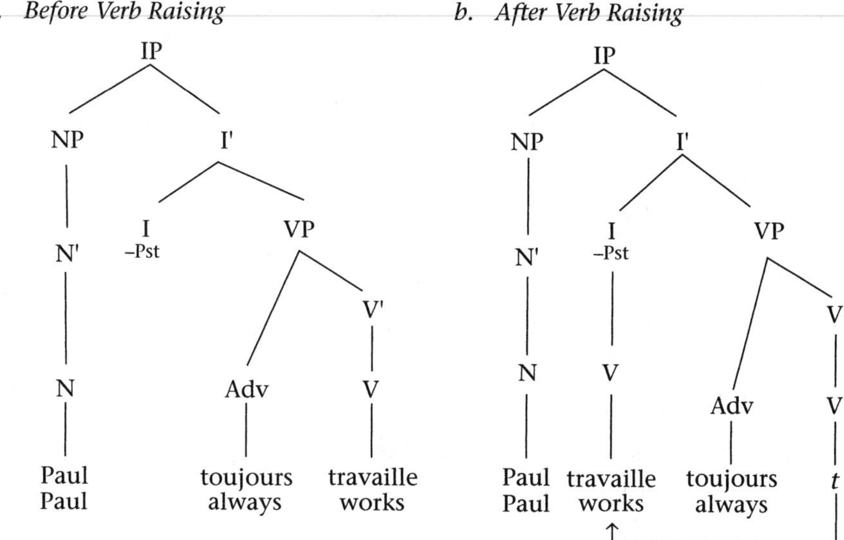

Figure 5.22 Verb Raising in French. The verb moves from within the VP to the I position.

44)

Inversion of an auxiliary:
As-tu *t* essayé?
'Have you tried?'

However, unlike English, French also allows inversion of nonauxiliary Vs.

45)

Inversion of a nonauxiliary verb:
Vois-tu *t* le livre?
see you the book
'Do you see the book?'

Figure 5.23 depicts the interaction between Verb Raising and Inversion needed to form this sentence. As you can see, the V first raises to the I position, and the I category then moves to the C position. (We treat the pronoun *tu* 'you' as a type of N.)

Verb Raising in English

At this point, it might seem that there is a simple Verb Raising parameter with two options—raising (as in French) and no raising (as in English). This neatly accounts for the facts that we have considered so far, but matters are not so simple. As we'll see next, Verb Raising can apply in English, but only to the nonmodal auxiliaries *have* and *be*.

To begin, consider the sentences in *46,* which contain two auxiliaries—one **modal auxiliary** and one **nonmodal auxiliary**.

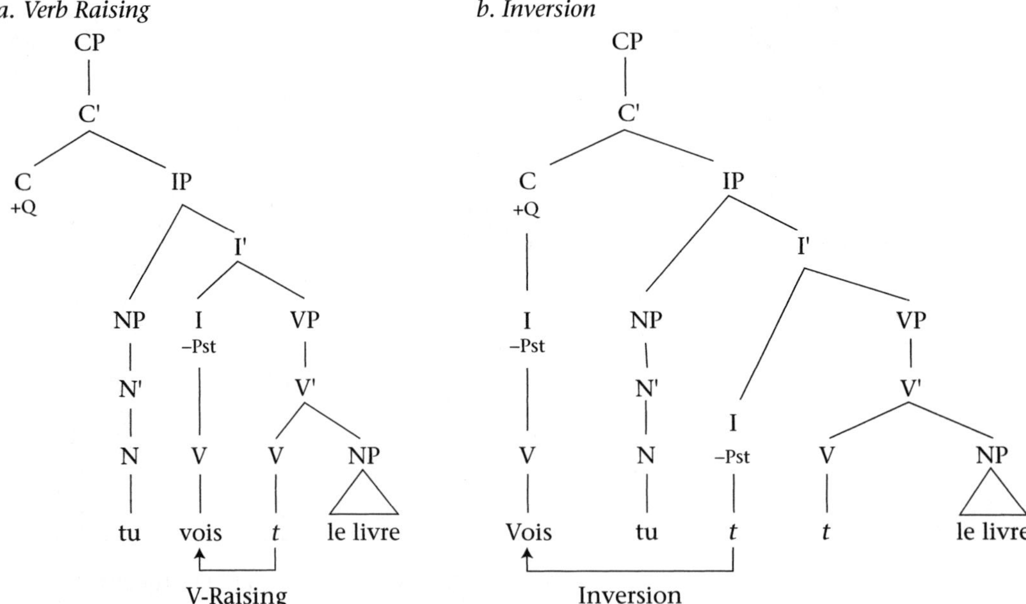

Figure 5.23 The interaction of Verb Raising and Inversion in French

46)

a. The children should have waited.
b. Those guys may be sleeping.

As we have already seen, the modal auxiliary occurs under I, but what of the nonmodal auxiliary? As depicted in Figure 5.24, it is considered to be a special type of V that takes a VP complement. As expected, only the modal auxiliary can undergo inversion in this structure.

47)

a. The modal auxiliary moves to the C position:
[$_{CP}$ Should [$_{IP}$ the children *t* have waited]]

b. The nonmodal auxiliary moves to the C position:
*[$_{CP}$ Have [$_{IP}$ the children should *t* waited]]

Crucially, however, a nonmodal auxiliary can undergo Inversion when there is no modal auxiliary in the sentence.

48)

a. The children have waited for two hours.
b. Have the children *t* waited for two hours?

Since Inversion involves movement from I to C, the auxiliary *have* must have moved to the I position, as depicted in Figure 5.25—an instance of the same V Raising operation

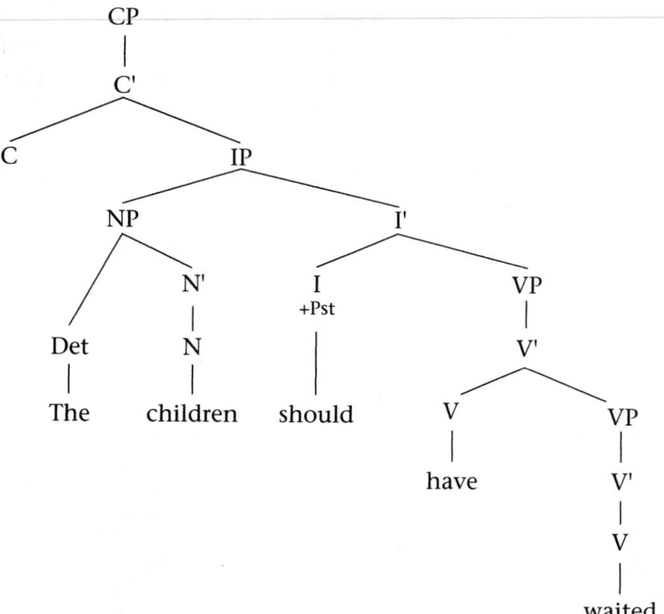

Figure 5.24 A structure containing two auxiliary verbs. The modal auxiliary is treated as an instance of the I category, which takes the VP headed by *have* as its complement. *Have* in turn is a V that takes the VP headed by *wait* as its complement.

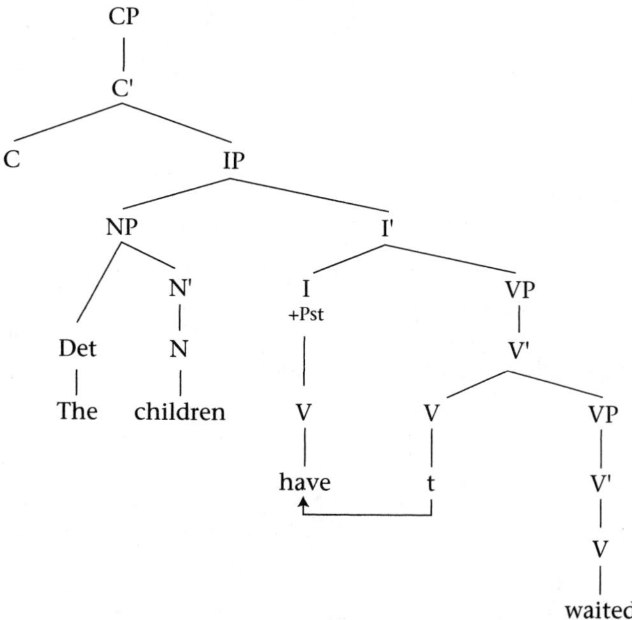

Figure 5.25 The result of V-to-I movement in the sentence *The children have waited*

that is used more generally in French. Once in the I position, *have* can undergo inversion (I-to-C movement), giving the question structure *Have the children waited?*

In sum, then, it appears that the two options permitted by the Verb Raising parameter are: (a) any type of verb raises (the case in French), and (b) only auxiliary verbs raise (the case in English). We discuss other examples of parametric variation, including another one involving Verb Raising, at **bedfordstmartins.com/linguistics/syntax** (click on **variation**).

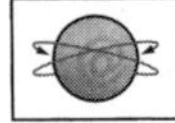

5 Some Additional Structures

Now that we have in place a basic system for forming sentences, it is possible to extend it to encompass various other syntactic phenomena. We will consider three such phenomena here.

5.1 Coordination

A common syntactic phenomenon in English and other languages involves **coordination**—the grouping together of two or more categories with the help of a conjunction such as *and* or *or*.

49)

coordination involving NPs:
$[_{NP}$ the man] and $[_{NP}$ a child]

50)

coordination involving VPs:
$[_{VP}$ go to the library] and $[_{VP}$ read a book]

51)

coordination involving PPs:
$[_{PP}$ down the stairs] and $[_{PP}$ out the door]

Coordination exhibits several important properties, three of which will be considered here. First, a category at any level (a head, an X', or an entire XP) can be coordinated. The preceding examples illustrate coordination of XPs; following are examples involving word-level and X'-level categories.

52)

coordination involving P:
$[_{P}$ up] and $[_{P}$ down] the stairs

53)

coordination involving V:
$[_{V}$ repair] and $[_{V}$ paint] the deck

54)

coordination involving V':
never [$_{V'}$ drink alcohol] and [$_{V'}$ drive a car]

Second, the category of the coordinate structure must be identical to the category of the elements being conjoined. Hence, if NPs are conjoined, the coordinate structure is an NP; if V's are conjoined, the coordinate structure is a V'; if Ps are conjoined, the coordinate structure is a P, and so on (see Figure 5.26).

a. Coordination involving NPs:

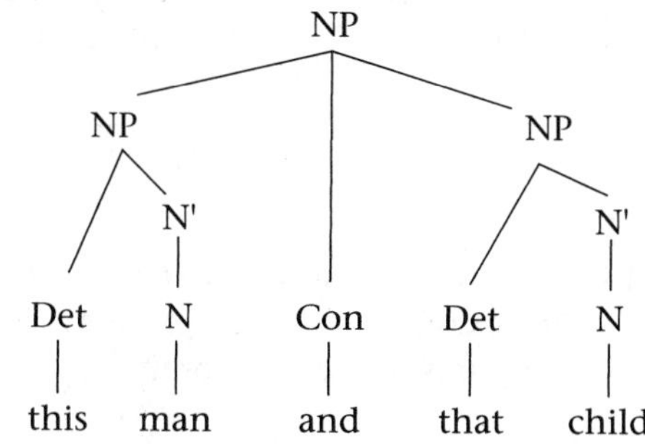

b. Coordination involving V's:

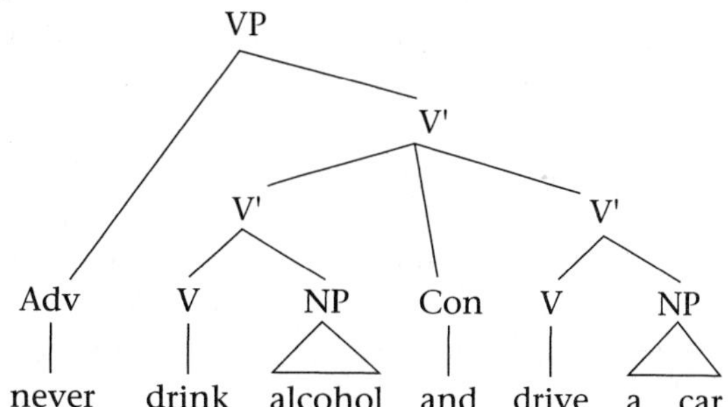

c. Coordination involving Ps:

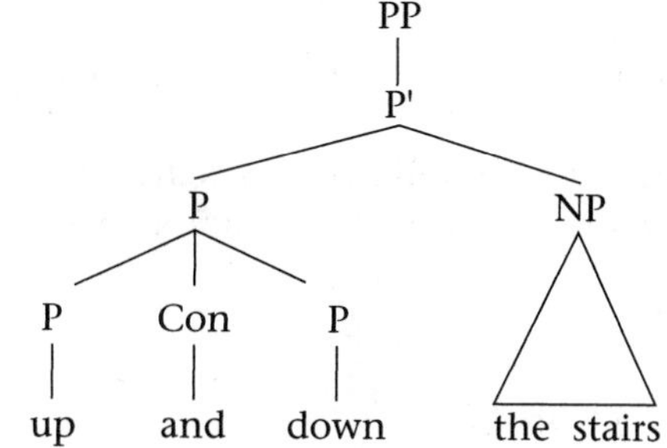

Figure 5.26 Some coordinate structures

Third, conjoined categories must be of the same type—they must both be NPs, or V's, or Ps, and so on. As *55* shows, coordination that involves different categories generally gives a quite unnatural result.

55)

a. coordination involving an NP and a PP:
*He read [$_{NP}$ the book] and [$_{PP}$ in the library]

b. coordination involving an NP and an AP:
*He left [$_{NP}$ the house] and [$_{AP}$ very angry]

We can accommodate these facts if we assume that the X' schema is not the only blueprint guiding the Merge operation. There must also be a **coordination schema**, as depicted in Figure 5.27.

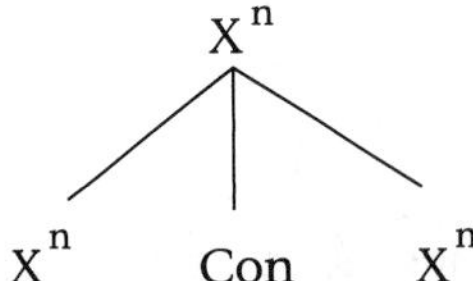

Figure 5.27 The coordination schema

The superscripted symbol ^{n} stands for 'a category at any structural level', indicating that a coordinate structure can involve Xs, X's, or XPs. Moreover, because the symbol X is used to stand both for the categories that are conjoined and for the larger resulting phrase, we neatly capture the fact that the conjoined elements and the resulting phrase must all be of the same type.

5.2 Relative Clauses

Another important syntactic phenomenon involves the use of **modifiers**—words and phrases that denote properties of heads. For example, adjective phrases (APs) commonly serve as modifiers of Ns, while adverb phrases (AdvPs) modify Vs.

56)

a. The [$_{AP}$ very tall] man walked into the room.
b. The guests left [$_{AdvP}$ rather quickly].

The AP *very tall* denotes a property of the man, while the AdvP describes the manner in which the guests left.

Sometimes even CPs can serve as modifiers. In the following sentence, for instance, a special type of CP called a **relative clause** provides information about the N in front of it.

57)

a. The car [$_{CP}$ which Leslie bought _] was a lemon.
b. Harry visited the village [$_{CP}$ which Sue walked to _].

Relative clause structures resemble *wh* questions in two respects. First, they can begin with a *wh* word such as *who* or *which* (a so-called relative pronoun). Second, there is an empty position within the sentence from which the *wh* phrase has apparently been moved. In sentences *57a* and *57b,* for instance, the NP positions following the transitive verb *buy* and the preposition *to* are unfilled in S-structure.

The first step in the formation of the relative clause in *57a* involves the D-structure in Figure 5.28. Like other modifiers, relative clauses are attached at the XP level; the +Rel feature in the C position indicates that the CP is a relative clause (go to **bedfordstmartins.com/linguistics/syntax** and click on **modifiers**). (To save space, we give only the structure for the NP containing the relative clause.) Here, the *wh* word *which* occurs as complement of the verb *buy* since it corresponds to the thing which was bought.

The next step involves the application of the *Wh* Movement rule (triggered by the **+Rel feature** in the C position) to give the structure in Figure 5.29, with the *wh* word in the specifier of CP position.

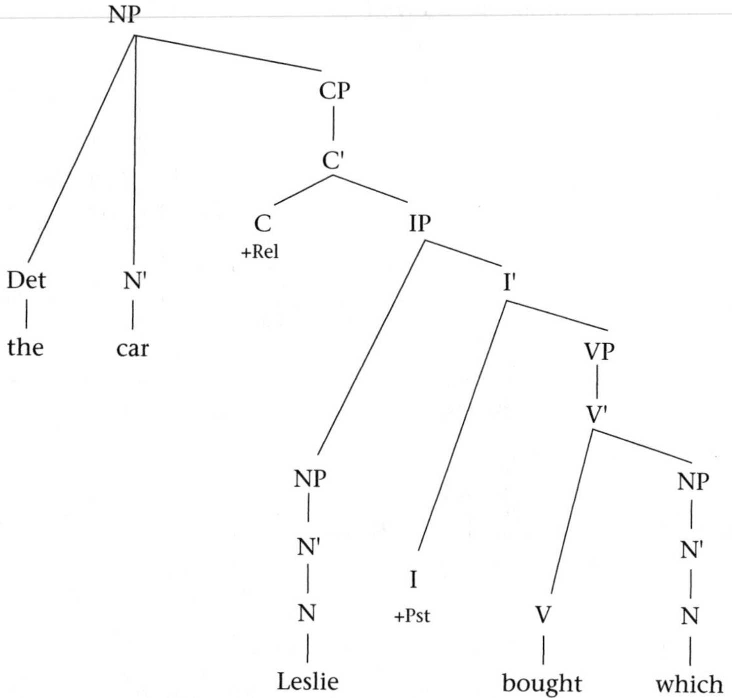

Figure 5.28 The D-structure for a relative clause

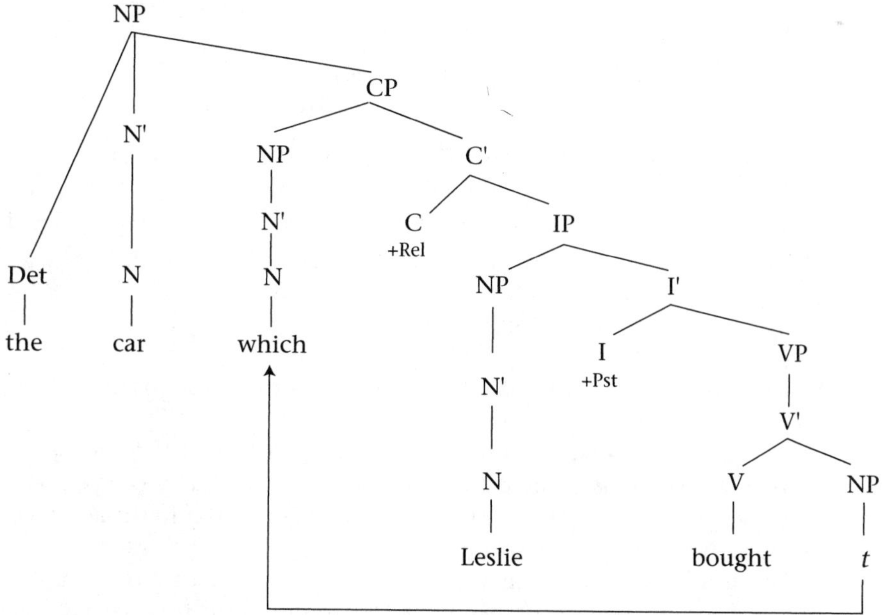

Figure 5.29 The S-structure for a relative clause: the *wh* phrase has moved to the specifier position within CP.

In the preceding example, the *wh* word originates in the direct object position. In *58,* in contrast, it originates in the subject position.

58)

Sue knows the woman [who bought the car].

Here *who* corresponds to the person who bought the car. The deep structure for this sentence therefore corresponds to *59,* in which the *wh* word appears in the subject position.

59)

Sue knows the woman $[_{CP}$ $[_{IP}$ who bought the car]].

Like other *wh* words, *who* subsequently moves to the specifier position within CP even though the actual order of the words in the sentence does not change as a result of this movement.

60)

Sue knows the woman $[_{CP}$ who $[_{IP}$ *t* bought the car]].

5.3 Passives

Another important type of syntactic phenomenon involves the relationship between particular sentences. A famous example of this involves sentences such as the following. (The first type of sentence is called **active** because the subject denotes the agent or instigator of the action denoted by the verb, while the second type is called **passive**.)

61)

a. A thief stole the painting. (active sentence)
b. The painting was stolen (by a thief). (passive sentence)

We will focus here on three key properties of passive constructions.

First, passive constructions involve a major reduction in the importance of the agent. Indeed, whereas the agent serves as subject of an active clause, it is not expressed at all in the vast majority of passive sentences in English.

62)

The painting was stolen.

When it does appear, as in *61b,* it is relegated to a position inside a PP at or near the end of the sentence.

Second, some other NP—usually the direct object of the corresponding active sentence—functions as subject in the passive sentence. This can be seen in example *61* above, where the NP *the painting* serves as direct object in the active sentence and as subject in the passive sentence.

Third, and related to the second point, verbs that cannot occur with a direct object NP in an active sentence typically cannot occur in a passive sentence. Take the verb *arrive,* for instance. It cannot be used in English with an NP complement in an active sentence, nor can it occur in a passive sentence.

63)

a. *Arrive* with an NP complement in an active sentence:
*The tourist arrived Beijing.

b. *Arrive* in a passive sentence:
*Beijing was arrived (by the tourist).

The D-structure for a passive sentence such as *The painting was stolen* is depicted in Figure 5.30. (Note that the nonmodal auxiliary *be* is treated as a V that takes a VP complement. To save space, we drop the CP level here. We include an empty specifier position under IP to capture the fact that all sentences require a subject.)

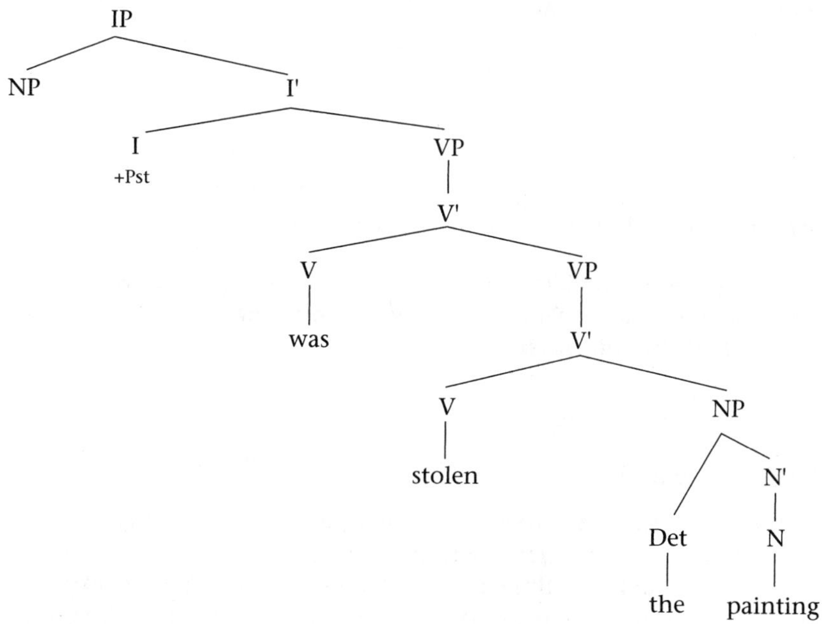

Figure 5.30 D-structure for *The painting was stolen*

This D-structure is admittedly abstract—it does not sound like any sentence that we actually utter. However, it does neatly capture the first and third properties of passive constructions: the agent is not expressed, and the verb occurs with a direct object. (When the agent is expressed as a PP [e.g., *by a thief*], it is attached under the V' headed by *stolen.*)

This leaves just the second property to be accounted for: the NP that functions as direct object in the active sentence becomes the subject in the passive. This is accomplished by moving the direct object NP to the subject position. The Move operation needed to bring about this result can be stated as follows.

64)

NP Movement:
Move NP into the subject position.

This gives the S-structure depicted in Figure 5.31. (Note that the nonmodal auxiliary verb also raises to I for the reasons discussed in Section 4.1.)

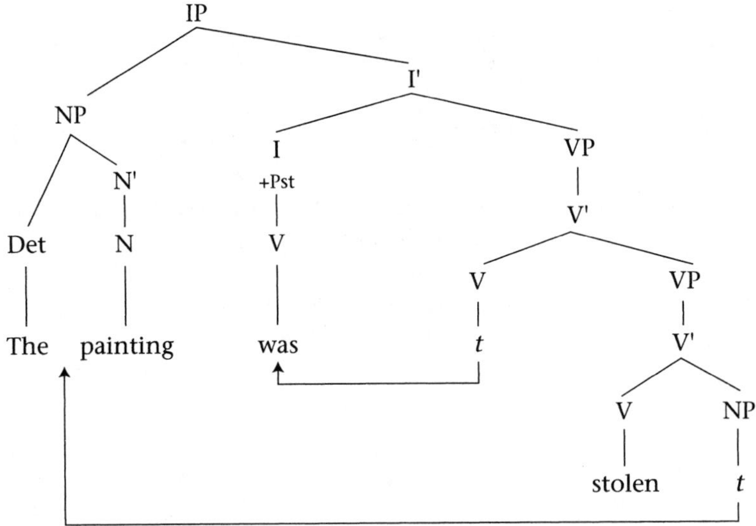

Figure 5.31 S-structure resulting from NP Movement

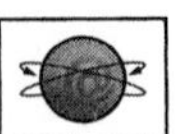

The Web site provides additional information about passives and how other approaches to syntax deal with them; go to **bedfordstmartins.com/linguistics/syntax** and click on **passive**.

Summing Up

Universal Grammar provides all languages with the same general type of syntactic mechanisms. As we have seen, this includes a **Merge** operation that combines words in accordance with their **syntactic category** and their **subcategorization** properties, creating a representation called **deep structure**. Deep structure must comply with the **X' schema**, which stipulates the place of **heads**, **specifiers,** and **complements** in phrase structure. **Move** operations (**transformations**) can modify deep structure by moving words and phrases in particular ways to produce a **surface structure**.

Although the form of sentences can vary considerably from language to language, such differences can for the most part be attributed to a small set of **parameters**, each of which makes available a variety of alternatives from which individual languages may choose.

Key Terms

General terms

computational system
grammatical
lexicon
syntax
transformational (generative) grammar
Universal Grammar (UG)

Terms concerning syntactic categories

adjective (A)
adverbs (Adv)
auxiliary verb (Aux)
conjunction (Con)
degree word (Deg)
determiner (Det)
distribution
lexical categories
modal auxiliary
nonlexical (functional) categories
nonmodal auxiliary
noun (N)
preposition (P)
syntactic categories
verb (V)

Terms concerning combining words into phrases

complement
direct object
head
Merge
phrases
specifier
transitive
X' schema

Terms concerning complement options

complement clause
complementizers (C)
matrix clause
subcategorization

Terms concerning tests for phrase structure

constituents
coordinate structures
coordination test
movement test
substitution test

Terms concerning the Move operation and parametric variation

deep structure (D-structure)
derivation
Do Insertion
insertion rule
Inversion
Move
parameters
Q feature
surface structure (S-structure)
trace
transformation
Verb Raising transformation
Wh Movement
wh questions
yes-no questions

Terms concerning additional structures

active
coordination
coordination schema
modifiers
NP Movement
passive
+Rel feature
relative clause

For more information on the sources used in this chapter, go to **bedfordstmartins.com/linguistics/syntax** and click on **Sources**.

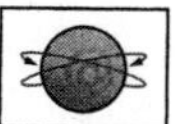

Recommended Reading

Carnie, Andrew. 2002. *Syntax: A Generative Introduction.* Malden, MA: Blackwell.

Haegeman, Liliane. 1994. *Introduction to Government and Binding Theory.* 2nd ed. Cambridge, MA: Blackwell.

Palmer, F.R. 1994. *Grammatical Roles and Relations.* New York: Cambridge University Press.

Payne, Thomas. 1997. *Describing Morphosyntax: A Guide for Field Linguists.* New York: Cambridge University Press.

Radford, Andrew. 1997. *Syntax: A Minimalist Introduction.* New York: Cambridge University Press.

Shopen, Timothy, ed. 1985. *Language Typology and Syntactic Description.* Vols. 1–3. New York: Cambridge University Press.

Appendix: How to Build Tree Structures

In building a tree structure from scratch for a phrase or sentence that you are analyzing, you will probably find it easiest to proceed in steps, working from the bottom up and from right to left. As an illustration, let us first consider the phrase *near the door.*

The first step involves assigning each word to the appropriate category, as depicted in Figure 5.32.

```
 P    Det    N
 |     |     |
near  the  door
```

Figure 5.32 The first step: determining the word-level categories

Then, working from right to left, the appropriate phrasal structure (X' and XP) is built above each head. Thus, we first build an N' and an NP above the N *door.* There is clearly no complement here, but there is a specifier (the determiner *the*), which combines with the N' in accordance with the X' schema.

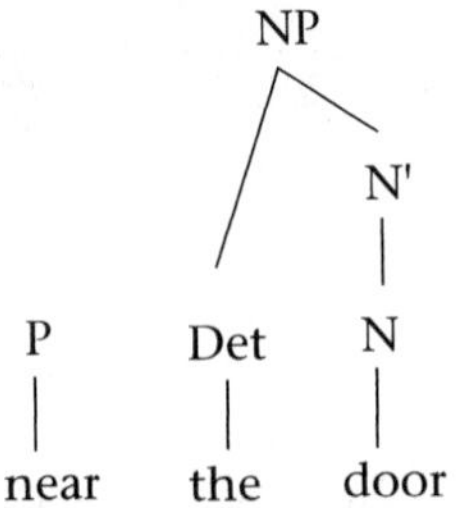

Figure 5.33 Building the NP

Next, we carry out the same procedure for the P *near.* The NP to the right of the P clearly functions as its complement, since it names the location entailed by the meaning of *near.* We therefore combine the P and the NP, forming the P' and PP depicted in Figure 5.34.

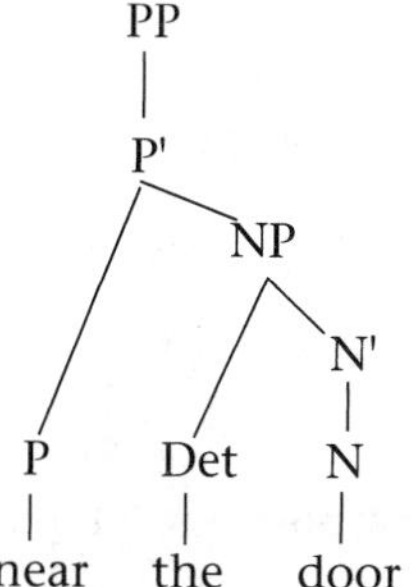

Figure 5.34 The complete PP

A Simplified Tree Structure

In order to abbreviate and simplify, linguists sometimes use tree structures such as the following in which the X' level has been eliminated, so that specifiers, heads, and complements are all attached at the XP level. Your instructor will decide whether this is appropriate in your class.

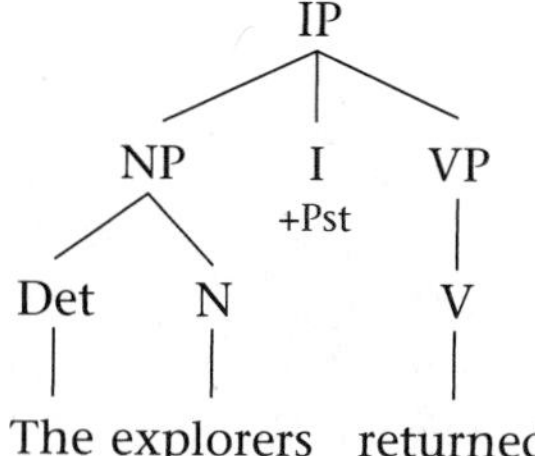

Figure 5.35 A simplified sentence structure

A Sentential Example

Consider now how we proceed in the case of a complete sentence such as *The dog might bite that man.* Assignment of each word to the appropriate category gives the structure depicted in Figure 5.36.

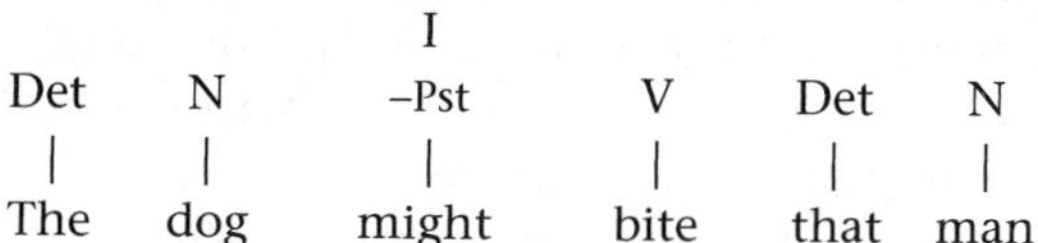

Figure 5.36 The categories for each word in the sentence

Working from right to left, it is easy to see that the noun *man* heads an NP that contains a specifier but no complement, as depicted in Figure 5.37.

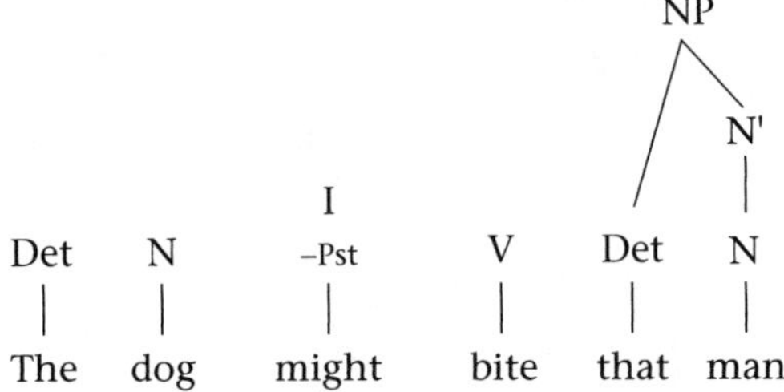

Figure 5.37 The structure of the rightmost NP

Next, we focus on the V *bite,* combining it with the complement NP *that man* and building the required V' and VP, as depicted in Figure 5.38.

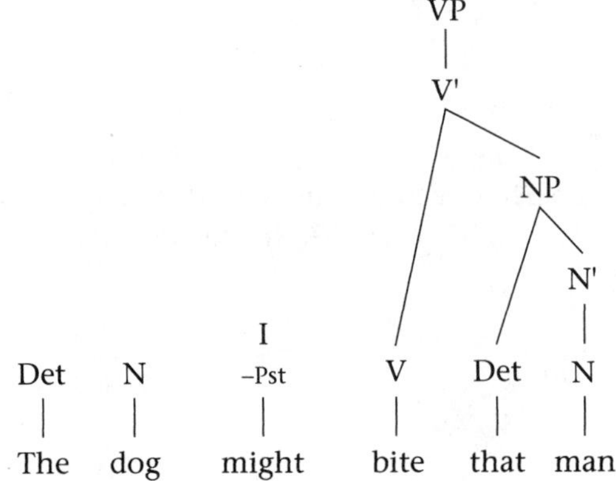

Figure 5.38 Adding the VP level above the V head

As an instance of the I category, the modal auxiliary *might* is the head of IP, with the VP to the right serving as its complement and the NP to the left functioning as its specifier. This yields the complete sentence illustrated in Figure 5.39. The entire sentence is then embedded in a CP shell, giving the tree in Figure 5.40.

Transformations

As explained in Section 3, the syntactic analysis of some sentences involves the Move operation in addition to Merge. It's relatively simple to recognize that one of the transformations described in this chapter has applied: if a sentence contains an auxiliary verb in front of the subject, then Inversion has applied; if it begins with a *wh* word, then *Wh* Movement has applied. In the sentence *What should the farmers plant?*, then, both of these transformations have applied.

In order to determine the deep structure, we must return the auxiliary verb to its position under I and must determine the position from which the *wh* word has been moved. Since the *wh* word in the sentence *What should the farmers plant?* asks about the complement of the verb (the thing that is planted), we place *what* in the com-

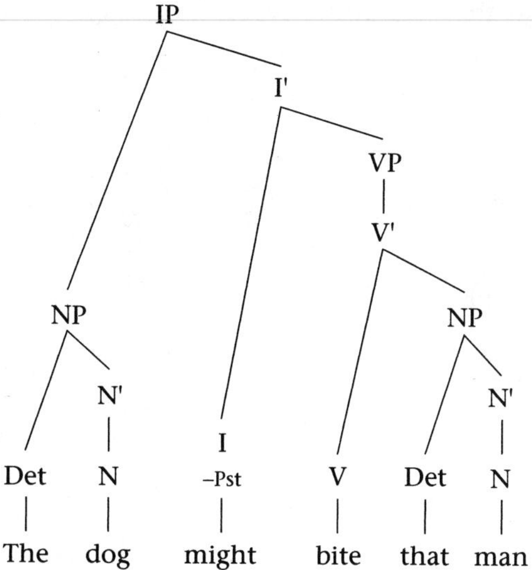

Figure 5.39 The complete sentence

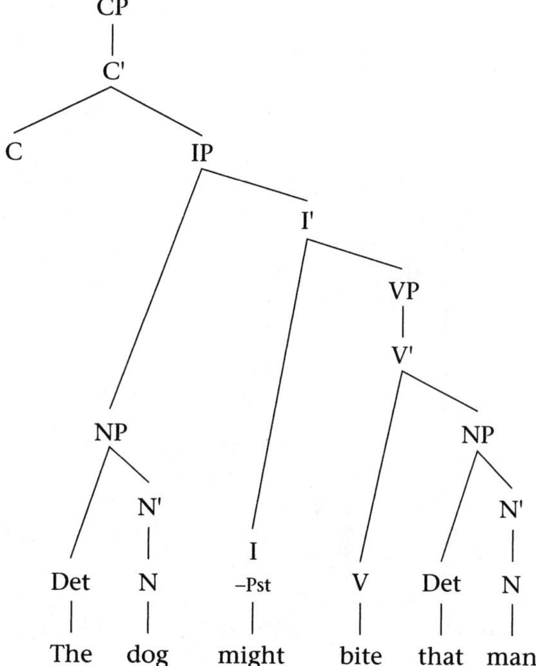

Figure 5.40 The sentence embedded in a CP shell

plement position within VP in the deep structure. This gives the deep structure depicted in Figure 5.41.

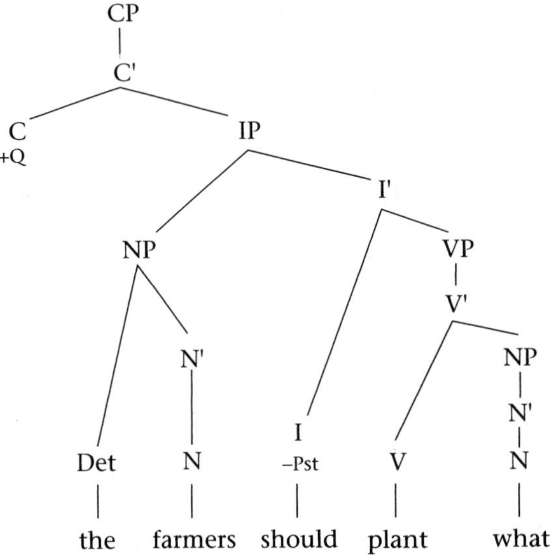

Figure 5.41 The deep structure for the sentence *What should the farmers plant?*

Attracted by the +Q feature, the auxiliary *should* then moves to the C position (Inversion) and *what* moves to the specifier position under CP (*Wh* Movement), yielding the complete surface structure depicted in Figure 5.42.

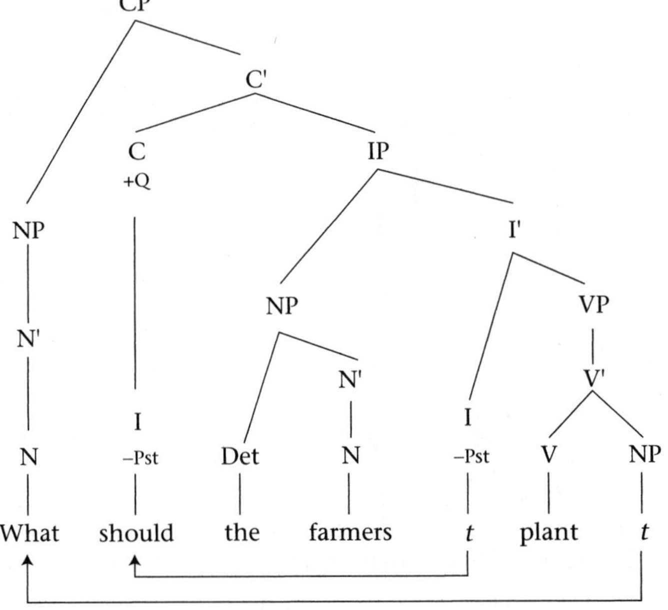

Figure 5.42 The surface structure for *What should the farmers plant?*

Exercises

1. Place an asterisk next to any of the sentences that are ungrammatical for you. What makes these sentences ungrammatical?
   a) The instructor told the students to study.
   b) The instructor suggested the students to study.
   c) The customer asked for a cold beer.
   d) The customer requested for a cold beer.
   e) He gave the Red Cross some money.
   f) He donated the Red Cross some money.
   g) The pilot landed the jet.
   h) The jet landed.
   i) A journalist wrote the article.
   j) The article wrote.
   k) Jerome is fed up of his job.
   l) Jerome is tired of his job.

2. Indicate the category of each word in the following sentences. (It may help to refer back to Section 1.1.)
   a) That glass suddenly broke.
   b) A jogger ran toward the end of the lane.
   c) These dead trees are blocking the road.
   d) The detective hurriedly looked through the records.
   e) The peaches never appear quite ripe.
   f) Jeremy will play the trumpet and the drums in the orchestra.

3. Each of the following phrases consists of a specifier and a head. Build a tree structure for each example that complies with the X' schema.
   a) the zoo
   b) always try
   c) so witty
   d) perhaps pass
   e) less bleak
   f) this house
   g) very competent
   h) quite cheap
   i) never surrender
   j) those books

4. The following phrases include a head, a complement, and (in some cases) a specifier. Build a tree structure for each example that complies with the X' schema. For now, there is no need to depict the internal structure of complements. (See the tree diagrams in Figures 5.5 and 5.6 in the chapter.)
   a) into the house
   b) fixed the telephone
   c) full of mistakes
   d) more toward the window
   e) a film about pollution
   f) always study this material
   g) perhaps earn the money
   h) that argument with Owen
   i) the success of the program

5. Use the X' schema and the process illustrated in the appendix to draw trees for each of the following sentences.
   a) Those guests should leave.
   b) Maria never ate a brownie.
   c) That shelf will fall.

d) The glass broke.
e) The student lost the debate.
f) The manager may offer a raise.
g) The judge often jails shoplifters.
h) The teacher often organized a discussion.
i) A psychic will speak to this group.
j) Marianne could become quite fond of Larry.

6. Apply the substitution test to determine which of the bracketed sequences in the following sentences form constituents. Support your answer by rewriting each sentence with the substitution.
   a) [The tragedy] upset the entire family.
   b) They hid [in the cave].
   c) The [computer was very] expensive.
   d) [The town square and the civic building] will be rebuilt.
   e) Jane has [left town].

7. Apply the movement test to determine which of the bracketed sequences in the following sentences form constituents. Support your answer by rewriting each sentence with the bracketed sequence moved.
   a) We ate our lunch [near the river bank].
   b) Steve looked [up the number] in the book.
   c) The [island has been] flooded.
   d) I love [peanut butter and bacon sandwiches].
   e) The environmental [movement is gaining momentum].
   f) The goslings [swam across] the lake.

8. Lexical categories are divided into subcategories on the basis of their complements. For each of the following words, two potential complement options are given. For each of the words:
   i) Determine which one of the two options better matches its subcategorization requirements.
   ii) Justify your choice by creating a sentence using that complement option.

	Verb	*Options*		*Verb*	*Options*
a)	expire	Ø *or* NP NP	e)	clean	NP PP_{for} *or* NP NP
b)	destroy	NP *or* Ø	f)	mumble	NP *or* NP NP
c)	observe	NP *or* PP_{to} PP_{about}	g)	throw	Ø *or* NP PP_{loc}
d)	discuss	NP *or* Ø	h)	paint	NP PP_{to} *or* NP PP_{for}

	Noun	*Options*
a)	debate	PP_{of} PP_{to} *or* PP_{with} PP_{about}
b)	hammer	Ø *or* PP_{with} PP_{about}
c)	success	PP_{of} PP_{to} *or* PP_{of}
d)	transfer	PP_{with} PP_{about} *or* PP_{of} PP_{to}
e)	sickness	Ø *or* PP_{with} PP_{about}

	Adjective	*Options*
a)	strong	Ø *or* PP_{about}
b)	sick	NP *or* PP_{of}
c)	fed up	PP_{with} *or* PP_{of}
d)	knowledgeable	PP_{to} *or* PP_{about}
e)	small	PP_{of} *or* Ø

9. The following sentences all contain embedded clauses that function as complements of a verb. Draw a tree structure for each sentence.
   a) The reporter said that an accident injured a woman.
   b) The fishermen think that the company polluted the bay.
   c) Bill reported that a student asked whether the eclipse would occur.

10. The derivations of the following sentences involve the Inversion transformation. Give the deep structure and the surface structure for each sentence.
    a) Will the boss hire Hillary?
    b) Can the dog fetch the ball?
    c) Should the student report the incident?
    d) Must the musicians play that sonata?
    e) Might that player leave the team?

11. The following sentences involve the rules of *Wh* Movement and Inversion. Draw the trees to show the deep structure and the surface structure for each of these sentences.
    a) Who should the director call?
    b) Who should call the director?
    c) What can Joanne eat?
    d) Who will the visitors stay with?
    e) What might Terry bake for the party?
    f) What could Anne bring to the gathering?

12. The following data illustrate the formation of *yes-no* questions in German.
    a) Das Kind wird die Schwester lehren.
       the child will the sister teach
       'The child will teach the sister.'
    b) Wird das Kind die Schwester lehren?
       will the child the sister teach
       'Will the child teach the sister?'
    c) Der Mann liebt die Frau.
       the man love the woman
       'The man loves the woman.'
    d) Liebt der Mann die Frau?
       loves the man the woman
       'Does the man love the woman?'

    Assuming that German makes use of the same Inversion transformation as English (i.e., "Move I to the C position"), does the above data tell us whether German employs the Verb Raising transformation? Explain your answer.

13. The following sentences all contain coordinate phrases. Draw a tree structure for each sentence.
    a) The cyclist drank a gallon of water and a liter of cola.
    b) The airplane will land at the airport and taxi to the terminal.
    c) The dog ran down the stairs and out the door.
    d) Jill should recycle that book and this magazine.
    e) Hillary knows that spring will come and that the snow will melt.
    f) Mary is fond of dogs but tired of the fleas.

14. Each of the following sentences contains a relative clause. Draw the deep structure and the surface structure for each.
    a) The animals which Sam saw came from Kenya.
    b) Kyle likes the girl who June befriended.
    c) The woman who Clyde lives with recycles plastics.
    d) Helen recited a poem which Wordsworth wrote.
    e) The canoe which the Scouts built was too heavy.

For the Student Linguist

BACKWARDS

Sometimes poetry frustrates me because of all the seemingly nonsensical sentence bits I get after my brain automatically inserts a dramatic pause at the end of each line. Because I'm stuck, waiting for my eyes to get to the next line as I try to figure out what's so incredibly significant about a line consisting of "Eskimo" or "his amber eyes" or "detritus" and nothing else. But I really like Lesléa Newman's work because the line divisions actually seem meaningful and because she seems to be having so much fun arranging these sentence bits.

Tiff and I*

Tiff and I sit
in Tompkins Square Park
reading poetry
under a sky
full of clapping pigeons.
He calls them flying rats
but I think
the pink and green circles
around their necks
like greasy oil puddles are
beautiful.
Tiff says
all my poems sound better
backwards.

Backwards
all my poems sound better
Tiff says.
Beautiful
like greasy oil puddles
around their necks are
the pink and green circles
but I think
he calls them flying rats.
Full of clapping pigeons
under a sky
reading poetry
in Tompkins Square Park
Tiff and I sit.

If you read the poem as if it were prose, I think the first half sounds pretty bland and the second half is just plain loopy:

> Tiff and I sit in Tompkins Square Park reading poetry under a sky full of clapping pigeons. He calls them flying rats but I think the pink and green circles around their necks like greasy oil puddles are beautiful. Tiff says all my poems sound better backwards.
>
> Backwards all my poems sound better Tiff says. Beautiful like greasy oil puddles around their necks are the pink and green circles but I think he calls them flying rats. Full of clapping pigeons under a sky reading poetry in Tompkins Square Park Tiff and I sit.

In fact, I can't read the second half in prose format without imagining flying poems that have greasy pink and green circles around their necks, a sky that is reading poetry, and two people who've spent the afternoon eating live pigeons.

What is it about the change from prose to poetry that makes this string of words interesting and meaningful? (We've got to drudge through some syntax here, but trust me, it's relatively painless and worth it.) Assume that the first half of the poem has three untransformed sentences, and the second half has sentences that have undergone transformations. Also notice that one word—*are*—gets switched into a different line in the second stanza. It shouldn't be too hard to draw tree structures for the sentences in the first stanza *if* you do it line by line (i.e., first draw the tree for "Tiff and I sit," then for "in Tompkins Square Park," etc., and then hook them together).

The sentences in the second stanza will be harder to draw trees for, but if you do the first stanza line by line, those parts will be the same, except for where the word *are* is switched. So all you really need to do is figure out which parts of the trees got moved, and in which order. Actually, that's not even too hard to do, since only constituents can be moved.

You've probably figured out by now why this poem is in the syntax chapter: it does a good job of showing off what constituents are and of showing how the same words, even the same phrases, can have a different meaning when they're moved. However, this poem does more than show off constituents. I also like the rhythm of the poem—the way some of the lines seem to invite me to pause after them, and other lines lead me quickly on to the next line. Take a look at the subcategorizations of the last word of each line. Some of them lead you to expect a complement and others don't. Try reading the poem again and see if the subcategorization frames make a difference in how much emphasis you put on each line.

Finally, look at some other poetry that you love or hate and see what sort of match there is between grouping in lines or stanzas and grouping into constituents. Look at some different types of writing and their phrase structures; since punctuation is sadly limited in how well it can show pauses or emphasis or any sort of complex tone, the actual structure of the sentence can be crucial if the sentence is to be read with the right emphasis. And look in particular at some of your own writing and at how transformations of sentences could make a difference in their clarity. All of this theory might actually improve your writing.

*Newman, Lesléa, "Tiff and I," in *Sweet Dark Places* (Santa Cruz, CA: HerBooks, 1991).

six

Semantics: The Analysis of Meaning

William O'Grady

. . . in every object there is inexhaustible meaning.

– THOMAS CARLYLE

OBJECTIVES

In this chapter, you will learn:

- how we derive meaning from words and sentences
- how different languages encode concepts in words and sentences
- how we use sentence structure to produce and understand meaning
- how speaker beliefs and attitudes, setting, and context contribute to meaning

Up to now, this book has focused on the form of utterances—their sound pattern, morphological structure, and syntactic organization. But there is more to language than just form. In order for language to fulfill its communicative function, utterances must also convey a message; they must have content. Speaking very generally, we can refer to an utterance's content as its **meaning**.

This chapter is concerned with **semantics**, the study of meaning in human language. Because some work in this complicated area of linguistic analysis presupposes considerable knowledge of other disciplines (particularly logic, mathematics, and philosophy), not all aspects of contemporary semantics are suitable for presentation in an introductory linguistics textbook. We will restrict our attention here to four major topics in semantics: (1) the nature of meaning, (2) some of the properties of the conceptual system underlying meaning, (3) the contribution of syntactic structure to the interpretation of sentences, and (4) the role of nongrammatical factors in the understanding of utterances.

1 The Nature of Meaning

Long before linguistics existed as a discipline, thinkers were speculating about the nature of meaning. For thousands of years, this question has been considered central to philosophy. More recently, it has come to be important in other disciplines as well, including of course linguistics and psychology. Contributions to semantics have come from a diverse group of scholars, ranging from Plato and Aristotle in ancient Greece to Bertrand Russell in the twentieth century. Our goal in this section will be to consider in a very general way what this research has revealed about meaning in human language. We will begin by considering some of the basic analytic notions used in evaluating the meanings of words and sentences.

1.1 Semantic Relations among Words

Words and phrases can enter into a variety of semantic relations with each other. Because these relations help identify those aspects of meaning relevant to linguistic analysis, they constitute a good starting point for this chapter.

Synonymy

Synonyms are words or expressions that have the same meaning in some or all contexts. The following pairs of words in Table 6.1 provide plausible examples of synonymy in English.

Table 6.1 Some synonyms in English

filbert	hazelnut
youth	adolescent
automobile	car
remember	recall
purchase	buy
big	large

Because it would be inefficient for a language to have two words or phrases with absolutely identical meanings, perfect synonymy is rare, if not impossible. For example, although *youth* and *adolescent* both refer to people of about the same age, only the latter word can be used to imply immaturity, as in *Such irresponsible behavior—what an adolescent!*

Antonymy

Antonyms are words or phrases that are opposites with respect to some component of their meaning. The pairs of words in Table 6.2 provide examples of antonymy. In each of these pairs, the two words contrast with respect to at least one aspect of their meaning. For instance, the meanings of *boy* and *girl* are opposites with respect to gender, although they are alike in other respects (both are human). Similarly, *come* and *go* are opposites with respect to direction, although both involve the concept of movement.

Table 6.2 Some antonyms in English

dark	light
boy	girl
hot	cold
up	down
in	out
come	go

Polysemy and Homophony

Polysemy occurs where a word has two or more related meanings. Table 6.3 contains some examples of polysemous words in English.

Table 6.3 Some polysemy in English

Word	*Meaning a*	*Meaning b*
bright	'shining'	'intelligent'
to glare	'to shine intensely'	'to stare angrily'
a deposit	'minerals in the earth'	'money in the bank'

If you consult a reasonably comprehensive dictionary for any language, you will find numerous examples of polysemy. For example, my dictionary lists several related meanings for the word *mark*.

1)

Polysemy in the meaning of *mark*

- a visible trace or impression on something (*The tires left a mark on the road.*)
- a written or printed symbol (*You need a punctuation mark here.*)
- a grade, as in school (*He got a good mark on the math test.*)
- a target (*She hit the mark every time.*)
- an indication of some quality or property (*The mark of a good diplomat is the ability to negotiate.*)

Homophony exists where a single form has two or more entirely distinct meanings (see Table 6.4). In such cases, it is assumed that there are separate words with the same pronunciation rather than a single word with different meanings.

Table 6.4 Some homophones in English

Word	*Meaning a*	*Meaning b*
light	'not heavy'	'illumination'
bank	'a financial institution'	'a small cliff at the edge of a river'
club	'a social organization'	'a blunt weapon'
pen	'a writing instrument'	'an enclosure'

Homophones sound the same but need not have identical spellings—*write* and *right* are homophones, as are *piece* and *peace*.

Polysemy and homophony create **lexical ambiguity**, in that a single form has two or more meanings. Thus, a sentence such as *2* could mean either that Liz purchased an instrument to write with or that she bought an enclosure.

2)

Liz bought a *pen*.

Of course, in actual speech, the surrounding words and sentences usually make the intended meaning clear. The lexical ambiguity in sentences such as the following therefore normally goes unnoticed.

3)

He got a loan from the *bank*.

4)

Because Liz needed a place to keep her goat, she went downtown and bought a *pen* for $100.

The most lexically ambiguous item in English may well be *set,* which has more than 150 entries in the *Oxford English Dictionary.*

1.2 Semantic Relations Involving Sentences

Like words, sentences have meanings that can be analyzed in terms of their relation to other meanings. Three such relations—paraphrase, entailment, and contradiction—are particularly important.

Paraphrase

Two sentences that can have the same meaning are said to be **paraphrases** of each other. The following pairs of sentences provide examples of paraphrase.

5)

a. The police chased the burglar.
b. The burglar was chased by the police.

6)

a. I gave the summons to Erin.
b. I gave Erin the summons.

7)

a. It is unfortunate that the team lost.
b. Unfortunately, the team lost.

8)

a. Paul bought a car from Sue.
b. Sue sold a car to Paul.

9)

a. The game will begin at 3:00 p.m.
b. At 3:00 p.m., the game will begin.

The *a* and *b* sentences in each of the above pairs are obviously very similar in meaning. Indeed, it would be impossible for one sentence to be true without the other also being true. Thus, if it is true that the police chased the burglar, it must also be true that the burglar was chased by the police. (Sentences whose meanings are related to each other in this way are said to have the same **truth conditions**—that is, they are true under the same circumstances.)

For some linguists, this is enough to justify saying that the two sentences have the same meaning. However, you may notice that there are subtle differences in emphasis between the *a* and *b* sentences in *5* through *9*. For instance, it is natural to interpret *5a* as a statement about what the police did and *5b* as a statement about what happened to the burglar. Similarly, *9b* seems to place more emphasis on the starting time of the game than *9a* does. As is the case with synonymy, many linguists feel that languages do not permit two or more structures to have absolutely identical meanings and that paraphrases are therefore never perfect.

Entailment

When the truth of one sentence guarantees the truth of another sentence, we say that there is a relation of **entailment**. This relation is mutual in the case of examples *5* to *9*, since the truth of either sentence in the pair guarantees the truth of the other. In examples such as the following, however, entailment is asymmetrical.

10)

a. The park wardens killed the bear.
b. The bear is dead.

11)

a. Prince is a dog.
b. Prince is an animal.

If it is true that the park wardens killed the bear, then it must also be true that the bear is dead. However, the reverse does not follow since the bear could be dead without the park wardens having killed it. Similarly, if it is true that Prince is a dog, then it is also true that Prince is an animal. Once again, though, the reverse does not hold: even if we know that Prince is an animal, we cannot conclude that he is a dog rather than a horse or a cat.

Contradiction

Sometimes it turns out that if one sentence is true, then another sentence must be false. This is the case with the examples in *12.*

12)

a. Charles is a bachelor.
b. Charles is married.

If it is true that Charles is a bachelor, then it cannot be true that he is married. When two sentences cannot both be true, we say that there is a **contradiction**.

1.3 What Is Meaning?

Although it is relatively easy to determine whether two words or sentences have identical or different meanings, it is much more difficult to determine precisely what meaning is in the first place. In fact, despite many centuries of study, we still know very little about the nature of meaning or how it is represented in the human mind. Nonetheless, it is worthwhile to review briefly some of the better-known proposals and the problems that they encounter.

Connotation

One notion that is closely linked with the concept of meaning is **connotation**, the set of associations that a word's use can evoke. For most Minnesotans, for example, the word *winter* evokes thoughts of snow, bitter cold, short evenings, frozen fingertips, and the like. These associations make up the word's connotation, but they cannot be its meaning (or at least not its entire meaning). The word *winter* does not become meaningless just because it is a mild year or because one moves to Florida in November. We must therefore look beyond connotation for our understanding of what meaning is.

Denotation

One well-known approach to semantics attempts to equate the meaning of a word or phrase with the entities to which it refers—its **denotation**, or **referents**. The denotation of the word *winter,* for example, corresponds to the season between autumn and spring (regardless of whether it is cold and unpleasant). Similarly, the denotation of the word *dog* corresponds to the set of canines, and so on.

Although a word's denotation is clearly connected to its meaning in some way, they cannot be one and the same thing. This is because there are words such as *unicorn* and phrases such as *the present king of France* that have no referents in the real world, even though they are far from meaningless.

A problem of a different sort arises with expressions such as *the Prime Minister of Britain* and *the leader of the Labour Party,* both of which refer (in 2004, at least) to Tony Blair. Although these two expressions may have the same referent, it seems wrong to say that they mean the same thing. Thus, we would not say that the phrase *Prime Minister of Britain* is defined as 'the leader of the Labour Party' or that the definition of the phrase *leader of the Labour Party* is 'Prime Minister of Britain'.

Extension and Intension

The impossibility of equating an element's meaning with its referents has led to a distinction between **extension** and **intension**. Whereas an expression's extension corresponds to the set of entities that it picks out in the world (its referents), its intension corresponds to its inherent sense, the concepts that it evokes. Thus, the extension of *woman* is a set of real world entities (women) while its intension involves notions like 'female' and 'human'. Similarly, the phrase *Prime Minister of Britain* has as its extension an individual (Tony Blair), but its intension involves the concept 'leader of the governing party' (see Table 6.5).

Table 6.5 Extension versus intension

Phrase	*Extension*	*Intension*
prime minister of Britain	Tony Blair	leader of the governing party
World Series champions	Florida Marlins (2003)	winners of the World Series championship
capital of Missouri	Jefferson City	city containing the state legislature

The distinction between intension and extension does not allow us to resolve the question of what meaning is. It simply permits us to pose it in a new way: what are intensions?

One suggestion is that intensions correspond to mental images. This is an obvious improvement over the referential theory, since it is possible to have a mental image of a unicorn or even the king of France, although there are no such entities in the real world. However, problems arise with the meanings of words such as *dog,* which can be used to refer to animals of many different sizes, shapes, and colors. If the meaning of this word corresponds to a mental image, that image would have to be general enough to include Chihuahuas and St. Bernards, yet still exclude foxes and wolves. If you try to draw a picture that satisfies these requirements, you will see just how hard it is to construct an image for meanings of this sort.

Componential Analysis

Still another approach to meaning tries to represent a word's intension by breaking it down into smaller semantic components. Sometimes known as **componential analysis** or **semantic decomposition**, this approach has often been used to analyze the meaning of certain types of nouns in terms of **semantic features**. The analysis in Figure 6.1 for the words *man, woman, boy,* and *girl* illustrates how this works. (Nothing depends on the choice of feature names here; the analysis would work just as well with the feature ±female as ±male.)

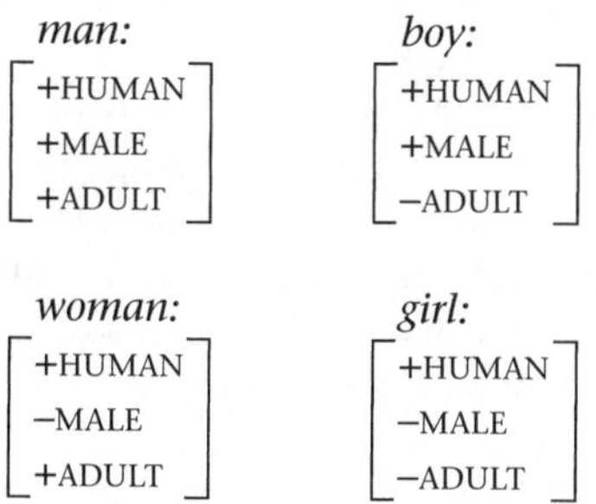

Figure 6.1 Semantic feature composition for *man, woman, boy, girl*

An obvious advantage of this approach is that it allows us to group entities into natural classes (much as we do in phonology). Hence, *man* and *boy* could be grouped together as [+human, +male] while *man* and *woman* could be put in a class defined by the features [+human, +adult].

This in turn can be useful for stating generalizations of various sorts. For instance, there are certain verbs, such as *marry, argue,* and the like, that we expect to find only with subjects that are [+human]. Moreover, within the English pronoun system, *he* is used to refer to [+human] entities that are [+male] while *she* is used for [+human] entities that are [–male].

There are limits on the insights into word meaning offered by componential analysis. What value, for example, is there in characterizing the meaning of *dog* as [+animal, +canine] as long as there is no further analysis of these features? Similarly, do we say that the meaning of *blue* consists of the feature [+color] and something else? If so, what is that other thing? Isn't it blueness? If so, then we have not really broken the meaning of *blue* into smaller components, and we are back where we started.

To date, componential analysis has given its most impressive results in the study of verb meaning. A typical component of verb meaning is the concept GO, which is associated with change of various sorts. (The components of verb meaning tend not to be binary features. We use uppercase letters to represent a semantic concept.)

13)

manifestations of the concept GO:

a. positional change:
Harvey went from Austin to New Orleans.

b. possessional change:
The inheritance went to Marla.

c. identificational change:
Max went from being a rational gentleman to being a stark raving lunatic.

Despite their somewhat different senses, all three uses of the verb *go* have something in common that can be traced to the GO component of their meaning—they typically occur with a phrase that denotes the entity (i.e., the subject in these examples) undergoing change and with a phrase expressing the endpoint of that change (the *to* complements).

The GO concept is manifested in the meaning of verbs other than just *go.* For instance, positional GO is present in the meaning of *fly* 'go through the air', *walk* 'go on foot', *crawl* 'go on hands and knees', and so forth. Possessional GO is manifested in the meaning of *give, buy,* and *inherit,* all of which involve a change of possession, while identificational GO shows up in *become* and *turn into.* Because these verbs all share the abstract GO meaning, they are all typically used with a phrase denoting the entity undergoing the change (marked in *14* by a single underline) and a phrase denoting the endpoint of that change (marked by a double underline).

14)

a. positional GO:
The bird flew to its nest.

b. possessional GO:
The coach gave a new ball to the children.

c. identificational GO:
The caterpillar turned into a butterfly.

Verb Meaning and Subcategorization

Sometimes quite surprising features of verb meaning can be relevant to the choice of accompanying phrases. Consider, for instance, the contrast between the verbs in list *a,* which can occur with two NP complements, and the verbs in list *b,* which cannot.

15)

a. throw [$_{NP}$ the boy] [$_{NP}$ the package]	*b.* *push [$_{NP}$ the boy] [$_{NP}$ the package]
toss	*pull
kick	*lift
fling	*haul

Can you see the semantic difference? The verbs in list *a* all denote ballistic motion that results from the instantaneous application of force to an object at its point of origin. (When we throw something, for example, we thrust it forward and then release it.) In contrast, the verbs in list *b* all denote motion that is accompanied by the continuous application of force to the object as it moves from one point to another. (Pulling, for instance, typically involves the extended use of force as the object moves, rather than a single quick motion.)

Now think about the contrast between the following two sets of verbs.

16)

a. fax [$_{NP}$ Helen] [$_{NP}$ the news]	*b.* *murmur [$_{NP}$ Helen] [$_{NP}$ the news]
radio	*mumble
e-mail	*mutter
phone	*shriek

Once again, componential analysis reveals a subtle semantic contrast. The first group of verbs (*phone, radio,* etc.) have meanings that include the means by which a message was communicated (by phone, by radio, and so on). In contrast, the verbs in the second group all have meanings that describe the type of voice that was used to communicate the message (murmuring, mumbling, shrieking, etc.). For reasons that are not yet fully understood, meaning differences like these help determine the type of complements that particular verbs can select.

2 The Conceptual System

Underlying the use of words and sentences to express meaning in human language is a conceptual system capable of organizing and classifying every imaginable aspect of our experience, from inner feelings and perceptions, to cultural and social phenomena, to the physical world that surrounds us. This section focuses on what the study of this conceptual system reveals about how meaning is expressed through language. We will begin by considering some examples that illustrate the way in which these concepts are structured, extended, and interrelated.

2.1 Fuzzy Concepts

We tend to think that the concepts expressed by the words and phrases of our language have precise definitions with clear-cut boundaries. Some concepts may indeed be like this. For example, the concept expressed by the word *senator* seems to have a clear-cut definition: one is a senator if and only if one is duly elected to a particular legislative body; no other person can be truthfully called a senator.

But are all concepts so straightforward? Consider the concept associated with the word *rich*. How much does a person have to be worth to be called rich? Five hundred thousand dollars? Eight hundred thousand? A million? Is there any figure that we can give that would be so precise that a person who is short by just five cents would not be called rich? It seems not. While one could miss out on being a senator by five votes, it does not seem possible to miss out on being rich by just five cents. Moreover, whereas some people clearly qualify as rich and others uncontroversially do not, an indefinitely large number of people fall into the unclear area at the borderline of the concept, and it is just not possible to say definitively whether or not they count as rich. This is because the notion of 'richness' does not have clear-cut boundaries; it is what we call a **fuzzy concept**.

This type of fuzziness pervades the human conceptual system. With only a little effort, you should be able to think of many everyday concepts whose boundaries are fuzzy—TALL, OLD, PLAYBOY, STRONG, GRAY-HAIRED, GENIUS, CLEAN, and BARGAIN are just a few examples.

Graded Membership

A second important fact about concepts is that their members can be **graded** in terms of their typicality. Consider first a fuzzy concept such as BASEBALL STAR. Even within the set of people who we can agree are baseball stars, some provide better examples of this concept than others. At the time of this writing, for instance, Alex Rodriguez is a better example of a baseball star than is Derrick Jeter. Although baseball fans agree that both players are stars, Alex Rodriguez has hit more runs, won more awards, set more records, endorsed more products on TV, received more media attention, and so on. This makes him a better example of a star than Derrick Jeter.

Even concepts whose boundaries can be scientifically defined exhibit this type of graded membership. A good example of this involves the concept BIRD, as shown in Figure 6.2 on page 211. Even assuming that all English speakers think of birds as 'warm-blooded, egg-laying, feathered vertebrates with forelimbs modified to form wings' (the dictionary definition), they still feel that some of these creatures are more birdlike than others. For instance, robins and magpies are intuitively better examples of birds than are hummingbirds, ostriches, or penguins. Examples like these suggest that concepts have an internal structure, with the best or **prototypical** exemplars (Alex Rodriguez in the case of BASEBALL STARS, robins in the case of BIRDS) close to the core and less typical members arranged in successively more peripheral regions.

The existence of fuzzy concepts and of graded membership provides important insights into the nature of the human conceptual system. In particular, it seems that many (perhaps even most) concepts expressed in language are not rigid all-or-nothing notions with precise and clear-cut boundaries. Rather, they are characterized by an

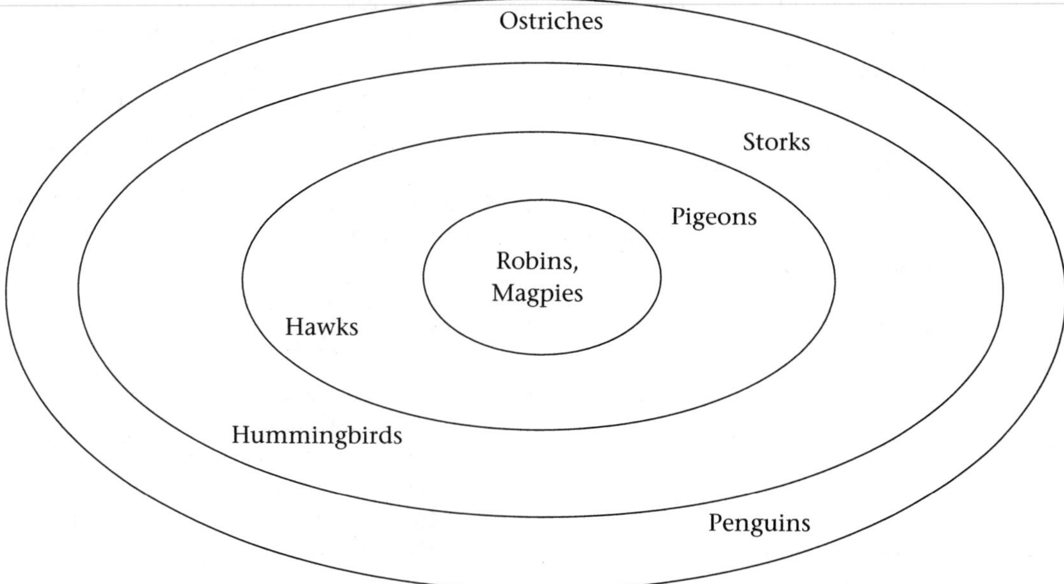

Figure 6.2 Internal structure of the concept BIRD

internal structure that recognizes degrees of typicality as well as by fuzzy boundaries that sometimes overlap with those of other concepts.

2.2 Metaphor

The concepts expressed by language make up a giant network, with many interconnections and associations. A good example of these interconnections involves **metaphor**, the understanding of one concept in terms of another.

Many people think of metaphor as a literary device reserved for the use of authors and poets. In fact, however, it has a prominent place in the conceptual system shared by all human beings. This can be seen in the way that we use language to talk about even commonplace notions such as 'time.'

The dominant metaphor for talking about time involves treating it as if it were a concrete commodity that can be saved, wasted, and invested, just like other valuable things.

17)

a. You're *wasting* my time.
b. This gadget will *save* you hours.
c. How do you *spend* your time these days?
d. I have *invested* a lot of time in that project.
e. You need to *budget* your time.
f. Is that *worth* your while?
g. He's living on *borrowed* time.
h. You don't use your time *profitably.*

What is the basis for this metaphor? There is apparently no objective, inherent similarity between time and commodities such as gold or money. What brings these concepts together is the *perception,* based in part on culture and in part on feelings that all human beings share, that time is like a valuable commodity that can be gained and lost.

A Spatial Metaphor

Another very prevalent metaphor in our language involves the use of words that are primarily associated with spatial orientation to talk about physical and psychological states (see Table 6.6).

Table 6.6 Metaphorical use of spatial terms

Emotions: happy *is up;* sad *is down*	
I'm feeling *up.*	I'm feeling *down.*
That *boosted* my spirits.	He *fell* into a depression.
My spirits *rose.*	Her spirits *sank.*
You're in *high* spirits.	He's feeling *low.*
the *height* of ecstasy	the *depths* of depression
That gave me a *lift.*	
Physical health: health *and* life *are up;* sickness *and* death *are down*	
He's at the *peak* of health.	He's *sinking* fast.
Lazarus *rose* from the dead.	He *fell* ill.
He's in *top* shape.	He came *down* with the flu.
	Her health is *declining.*
	She's feeling *under* the weather.

The basis for these **spatial metaphors** appears to lie in our physical experience. Unhappiness and ill health tend to be associated with lethargy and inactivity, which often involve being on one's back (physically down). In contrast, happiness and good health are often correlated with energy and movement, which involve being on one's feet (physically up).

These few examples illustrate the point that the concepts expressed through language are interrelated in special and intriguing ways. By investigating phenomena such as the use of metaphor to represent abstract concepts in terms of more basic physical and cultural experience, we can gain valuable insights into how language is used to communicate meaning.

2.3 The Lexicalization of Concepts

Do all human beings share the same conceptual system? Do all languages express concepts in the same way? These are questions that have fascinated and puzzled researchers for many decades. At the present time, there is no reason to believe that human beings in different linguistic communities have different conceptual systems. But there is ample evidence that languages can differ from each other in terms of how they express particular concepts.

Lexicalization

A notorious example of how languages can supposedly differ from each other in the expression of concepts involves the number of words for snow in Inuktitut. Sometimes estimated to be in the hundreds, the number is actually much smaller. In fact, one dictionary gives only the four items in Table 6.7 (although other dictionaries give a few more, at least for some varieties of Inuktitut).

As you can see, there is nothing particularly startling about this list of words. In fact, even in English there is more than just one word to describe snow in its various forms—*snow, slush, blizzard,* and *sleet* come to mind.

Table 6.7 Words for 'snow' in Inuktitut

aput	'snow on the ground'
qana	'falling snow'
piqsirpoq	'drifting snow'
qimuqsuq	'snow drift'

These examples illustrate the phenomenon of **lexicalization**, the process whereby concepts are encoded in the words of a language. Inuktitut lexicalizes the concepts 'falling' and 'snow' in a single word (*qana*), while English uses two separate words. While some lexicalization differences may correlate with cultural factors (the relative importance of types of snow in traditional Inuit culture), this is not always so. For example, English has an unusually rich set of vocabulary items pertaining to the perception of light (see Table 6.8).

Table 6.8 Some verbs pertaining to light in English

glimmer	glisten
gleam	glow
glitter	flicker
shimmer	shine
flare	glare
flash	sparkle

Although English speakers know and use the words in this list, it is hard to see how the variety found in this particular area of vocabulary can be correlated with any significant feature of culture.

As we have tried to emphasize throughout this book, linguistic analysis focuses on the *system* of knowledge that makes it possible to speak and understand a language. The fact that a particular language has more words pertaining to snow or light does not in and of itself provide any insight into the nature of the human linguistic system, and therefore does not merit special attention. However, as we shall see in the next subsection, certain lexicalization differences do shed light on how language expresses meaning.

Motion Verbs

All languages have words that can describe motion through space (in English, *come, go,* and *move,* among many others). However, there are systematic differences in terms of how languages express motion and the concepts related to it. In English, for example, there are many verbs that simultaneously express both the concept of motion and the manner in which the motion occurs (see Table 6.9).

Table 6.9 Some verbs expressing motion and manner in English

The rock *rolled* down the hill.
The puck *slid* across the ice.
She *limped* through the house.
The smoke *swirled* through the opening.

Notice how each of these verbs expresses both the fact that something moved and the manner in which it moved (by rolling, sliding, limping, and so on). We describe this fact by saying that English lexicalization includes a **conflation pattern** that combines manner and motion into a single verb meaning.

Interestingly, Romance languages (descendants of Latin) cannot express motion events in this way. Thus, while Spanish has a verb *rodar* with the meaning 'to roll', it does not use this verb to express both manner and motion as English does.

18)

*La botella rodó en la cueva.
'The bottle rolled into the cave.'

Instead, the motion and its manner have to be expressed separately.

19)

La botella entró en la cueva, rodando.
'The bottle entered the cave, rolling.'

Although Spanish does not have the motion plus manner conflation pattern, it does have verbs whose meanings bring together the concepts of motion and path (see Table 6.10). As the English translations show, Spanish verbs of motion express both the concept of movement and the direction of its path—down, up, back, across, out, and so forth. (English too has verbs that can express both motion and path—

Table 6.10 Some verbs expressing motion and path in Spanish

El globo	*bajó*	por la chimenea.
'The balloon moved-down through the chimney.'		
El globo	*subió*	por la chimenea.
'The balloon moved-up through the chimney.'		
La botella	*volvió*	a la orilla.
'The bottle moved-back to the bank.'		
La botella	*cruzó*	el canal.
'The bottle moved-across the canal.'		
La botella	*salió*	de la cueva.
'The bottle moved-out from the cave.'		

descend, ascend, return, and so on—but these words are not part of its native vocabulary. Rather, they were borrowed into English from Latinate sources, usually through French.)

Yet another conflation pattern is found in the Amerindian language Atsugewi (spoken in northern California), in which verbs can express both motion and the type of thing that moves (see Table 6.11).

Table 6.11 Some verb roots expressing motion and the thing moving in Atsugewi

lup	for movement of a small, shiny, spherical object (a hailstone)
t	for movement of a smallish, flat object that can be attached to another (a stamp, a clothing patch, a shingle)
caq	for movement of a slimy, lumpish object (a toad, a cow dropping)
swal	for movement of a limp linear object, suspended by one end (a shirt on a clothesline, a hanging dead rabbit)
qput	for movement of loose, dry dirt
staq	for movement of runny, unpleasant material (manure, guts, chewed gum, rotten tomatoes)

We learn two things from these facts. First, the concept of motion is associated with a number of other concepts, including 'path', 'manner of movement', and 'moving thing'. Second, the way in which these concepts are combined for the purposes of lexicalization can differ systematically from language to language. Languages such as English have verbs that conflate motion and manner, while other languages have verbs that conflate motion and path (Spanish) or motion and the type of thing that moves (Atsugewi).

The general picture that is emerging from this type of work is consistent with the key idea underlying componential analysis (Section 1.3). In particular, it seems that at least within certain semantic domains, there may be a small universal set of concepts (motion, manner, path, thing that moves, and so on) and a small set of options for how these concepts can be combined for purposes of lexicalization (see Figure 6.3).

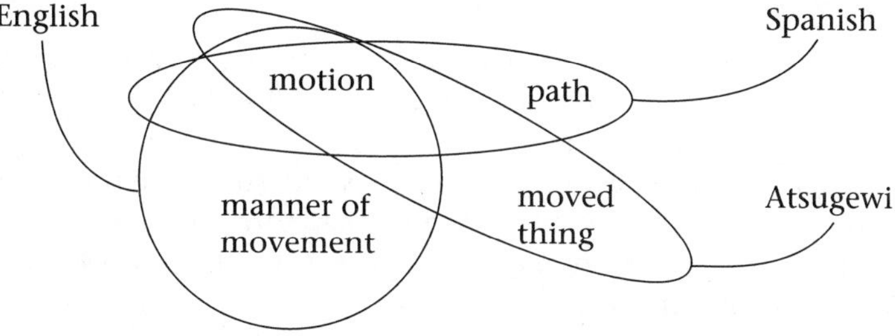

Figure 6.3 Systematic differences in conflation patterns

Unlike the lexicalization differences involving snow and light discussed earlier, these differences appear to be highly systematic and to reveal some general tendencies about the organization of the human conceptual system and the way in which meaning is expressed in language.

2.4 Grammaticization

Of the indefinitely large set of concepts expressible in human language, a relatively small subset enjoys a special status. These are the concepts that are expressed as affixes and nonlexical (functional) categories in one language or another. Some of the concepts that are treated this way in English are listed in Table 6.12.

Table 6.12 Some concepts associated with affixes and nonlexical categories in English

Concept	*Affix*
Past	*-ed*
More than one	*-s*
Again	*re-*
Negation	*in-, un-*
Concept	*Nonlexical category*
Obligation	*must*
Possibility	*may*
Definite, specific	*the*
Indefinite, nonspecific	*a*
Disjunction	*or*
Negation	*not*
Conjunction	*and*

Concepts that are expressed as affixes or nonlexical categories are said to have been **grammaticized**. Some concepts, such as negation, tense, and number, are highly grammaticizable and are expressed as affixes or special nonlexical categories in most languages. But grammaticization is not restricted to just these familiar concepts, as we will see next.

Evidentiality in Hidatsa

In the Siouan language Hidatsa, each statement is accompanied by a morpheme to indicate the evidence for its truth (see Table 6.13). (Morphological contrasts of this sort express **evidentiality**.)

Choice of the appropriate sentence-ender is extremely important in Hidatsa. Speakers who utter a false sentence marked by the morpheme *-ski* are considered to be liars. Had they used the morpheme *-c,* on the other hand, it would be assumed that they simply made a mistake.

While English has ways of indicating these contrasts (by using expressions such as *perhaps, I heard that,* and *I guess*), it does not have a grammatical system of morphemes that obligatorily encodes this information in every sentence. By investigating the grammaticization options found in different languages, it may eventually be possible to identify the factors that determine which concepts are singled out for association with affixes and nonlexical categories.

Table 6.13 Evidentiality morphemes in Hidatsa

ski	THE SPEAKER IS CERTAIN OF THE STATEMENT'S TRUTH Waceo iikipi kure heo -ski. 'The man (definitely) carried the pipe.'
c	THE SPEAKER BELIEVES THE STATEMENT TO BE TRUE Waceo iikipi kure heo -c. 'The man (supposedly) carried the pipe.'
wareac	THE SPEAKER REGARDS THE STATEMENT TO BE COMMON KNOWLEDGE Waceo iikipi kure heo -wareac. 'The man carried the pipe (they say).'
rahe	THE STATEMENT IS BASED ON AN UNVERIFIED REPORT FROM SOMEONE ELSE Waceo wiira rackci heo -rahe. 'The man roasted the goose (it is rumored).'
toak	THE TRUTH OF THE STATEMENT IS UNKNOWN TO BOTH SPEAKER AND LISTENER Waceo cihpa rakci heo -toak. 'The man roasted the prairie dog (perhaps).'

3 Syntax and Sentence Interpretation

The two preceding sections have focused on the meaning conveyed by the individual words and phrases that make up a sentence. In this section, we turn to the problem of sentence interpretation, with an emphasis on how the positioning of words and phrases in syntactic structure helps determine the meaning of the entire sentence, consistent with the following principle.

20)

The **Principle of Compositionality:**
The meaning of a sentence is determined by the meaning of its component parts and the manner in which they are arranged in syntactic structure.

Syntactic structure is relevant to meaning in a variety of ways. For purposes of illustration, we will consider four aspects of its contribution to the interpretation of sentences—constructional meaning, the representation of structural ambiguity, the assignment of thematic roles, and the interpretation of pronouns.

3.1 Constructional Meaning

There is reason to believe that structural patterns are themselves capable of carrying meaning above and beyond the meaning of their component parts. One example of this **constructional meaning** can be seen in "the caused-motion construction" exemplified in *21*.

21)

a. Seymour pushed the truck off the table.
b. Mabel moved the car into the garage.
c. Perry pulled the dog into the swimming pool.

As these examples help illustrate, the caused-motion construction consists of a structural pattern (NP V NP PP) that is used to express the meaning 'X causes Y to go somewhere'. Thus, the first sentence describes a situation in which Seymour causes the truck to go off the table by pushing it; the second sentence is used for situations in which Mabel causes the car to go into the garage; and so on.

22)

The caused-motion construction
Form: NP V NP PP
Meaning: 'X causes Y to go somewhere'

Striking evidence for the existence of a constructional meaning comes from sentences such as the following.

23)

a. Boris sneezed the handkerchief right across the room.
b. The judges laughed the poor guy out of the room.
c. Morley squeezed the shirt into the suitcase.

There is clearly nothing in the meaning of verbs such as *sneeze, laugh,* and *squeeze* that implies caused motion. Yet when they occur in the NP V NP PP pattern, the resulting sentence has a meaning in which X causes Y to go somewhere. Thus, sentence *23a* means that Boris caused the handkerchief to fly across the room by sneezing; *23b* means that the judges forced someone out of the room by laughing at him; and so on.

How can this be? It seems that part of the meaning of these sentences comes from the construction itself: in *23a,* for instance, the verb *sneeze* provides the meaning 'involuntarily expel air from the mouth and nose', while the structural pattern tells us that this action caused the handkerchief to be propelled across the room. Without both types of information, the sentence could not mean what it does.

Another example of constructional meaning can be found in patterns such as the following.

24)

a. Jerry sent Lou a present.
b. The company gave its employees a bonus.
c. The secretary handed Mary a message.
d. Marvin threw Harry the ball.

These sentences are instances of the so-called ditransitive construction that is typically associated with the meaning 'X causes Y to have Z'. Thus *24a,* for instance, describes a situation in which Jerry causes Lou to have a present by sending it to her.

25)

The ditransitive construction
Form: NP V NP NP
Meaning: 'X causes Y to have Z'

An indication that the structure itself contributes part of the meaning associated with ditransitive constructions comes from sentences such as *Jerry baked Lou a cake.* This sentence describes a situation in which Lou ends up with a cake, even though there is clearly nothing in the meaning of *bake* that implies that one person causes another person to have something. This part of the sentence's meaning comes from the structure itself—another example of constructional meaning.

3.2 Structural Ambiguity

Some sentences are **structurally ambiguous** in that their component words can be combined in more than one way. A simple example of this is found in the phrase *wealthy men and women,* where *wealthy* can be seen as a property of both the men and the women or of just the men alone. These two interpretations or **readings** are depicted in Figure 6.4 (Con = conjunction).

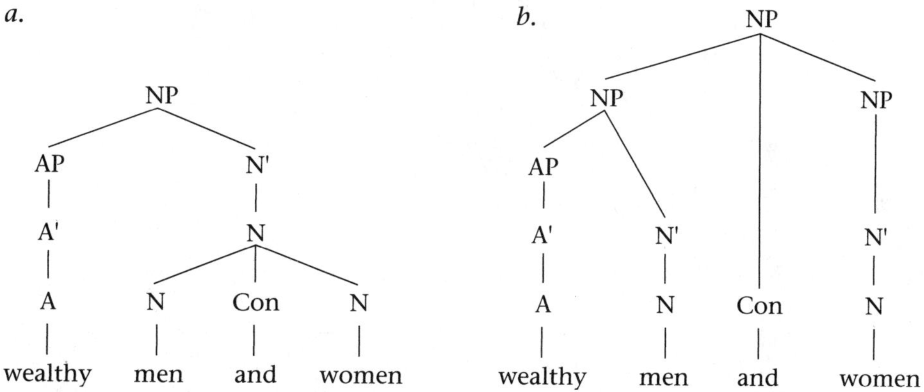

Figure 6.4 An ambiguous phrase. The structure on the left indicates that both the men and the women are wealthy; the structure on the right indicates that only the men are wealthy.

Figure 6.4a corresponds to the reading in which *wealthy* modifies both *men* and *women.* This is shown by having the adjective combine with a category that includes both nouns. In Figure 6.4b, on the other hand, the adjective combines only with the N *men.* This structure corresponds to the reading in which *wealthy* applies only to the men.

Another case of structural ambiguity is found in sentences such as the following.

26)

Nicole saw people with binoculars.

In one interpretation of *26,* the people had binoculars when Nicole noticed them (the phrase *with binoculars* modifies the noun *people*); in the other interpretation, Nicole saw the people by using the binoculars (the PP modifies the verb). These two readings are represented in Figure 6.5.

a.

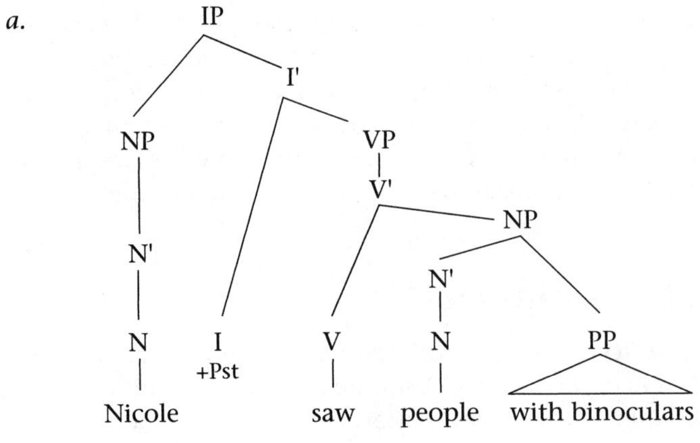

b.

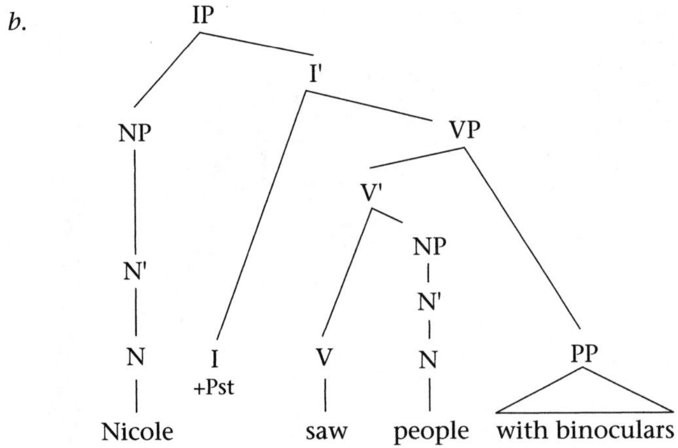

Figure 6.5 An ambiguous sentence. In the first structure, the people have the binoculars; in the second structure, Nicole uses the binoculars to see the people.

In Figure 6.5a, the PP *with binoculars* occurs inside the NP headed by the N *people,* reflecting the first reading for this sentence. In Figure 6.5b, on the other hand, the PP is part of the VP headed by the verb *saw.* This corresponds to the interpretation in which *with binoculars* describes how Nicole saw the people.

In sum, the manner in which words are grouped together in syntactic structure reflects the way in which their meanings are combined. Sometimes, as in the examples we have just considered, identical strings of words can be combined in either of two ways, creating structural ambiguity that can be neatly captured with the help of tree structures.

3.3 Thematic Roles

Another aspect of semantic interpretation involves determining the role that the referents of NPs play in the situations described by sentences. Consider in this regard the sentence in *27*.

27)

The courier carried the document from Boston to Seattle.

It would be impossible to understand this sentence if we could not identify the courier as the person who is responsible for carrying something, the document as the thing that is carried, Boston as the point of origin, and Seattle as the destination. Linguists often use **thematic roles** to categorize the relation between a sentence's parts and the event that it describes. In most linguistic analyses, at least the following thematic roles are recognized (see Table 6.14).

Table 6.14 Thematic roles

Agent	the entity that performs an action
Theme	the entity undergoing an action or a movement
Source	the starting point for a movement
Goal	the end point for a movement
Location	the place where an action occurs

Examples of these thematic roles can be seen in sentences such as the following.

28)

a. The courier carried the document from Boston to Seattle.
agent *theme* *source* *goal*

b. The athletes practiced in the Astrodome.
agent *location*

The notion of movement used in the definition of **theme**, **source**, and **goal** is intended to involve not only actual physical motion but also changes in possession, as in *29*, and identity, as in *30*.

29)

Terry gave the skis to Mary.
agent *theme* *goal*

30)

The magician changed the ball into a rabbit.
agent *theme* *goal*

As you may recall, we observed a similar set of contrasts in the manifestation of the GO concept discussed in Section 1.3. This is no coincidence. Thematic roles can be traced to particular aspects of word meaning, and the presence of GO in a verb's meaning is specifically linked to the presence of a theme role and a goal role.

Thematic Role Assignment

How does the grammar ensure that the appropriate thematic role is associated with each NP in a sentence? As we have just seen, thematic roles originate in word meaning. Thus, if the sentence *Marvin purchased a pen at the bookstore* contains an **agent** and a theme, it is because the verb *purchase* has the type of meaning that implies an entity that does the purchasing (an agent) and an entity that gets purchased (a theme). Similarly, *the bookstore* is taken to denote the **location** of the action because of the meaning of the preposition *at*. Information about the thematic roles assigned by a particular lexical item is recorded in a **thematic grid**, as depicted in Table 6.15.

Table 6.15 Some words and the thematic roles implied by their meanings

purchase	<agent, theme>
walk	<agent>
to	<goal>
from	<source>
at	<location>

The thematic roles implied by the meanings of lexical items are assigned to NPs based on their position in syntactic structure, with each NP receiving a single role. As a first example of this, let us consider the complement of a preposition. In such cases, the process of thematic role assignment can be summarized as follows:

31)

A P assigns a thematic role to its complement NP.

The operation of this convention is illustrated in Figure 6.6.

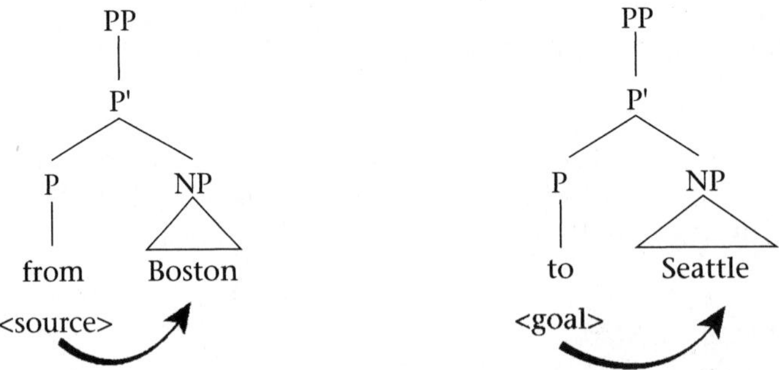

Figure 6.6 Thematic role assignment by prepositions

Matters are slightly more complicated in the case of Vs. Here we must distinguish between the theme role, which is assigned to the verb's complement, and the agent role, which is assigned to its subject.

32)

A V assigns a theme role (if it has one) to its complement NP.
A V assigns an agent role (if it has one) to its subject NP.

This is exemplified in the structures in Figure 6.7. In accordance with *32*, the theme (th) role is assigned to the V's NP complement, while the agent (ag) role is assigned to its subject.

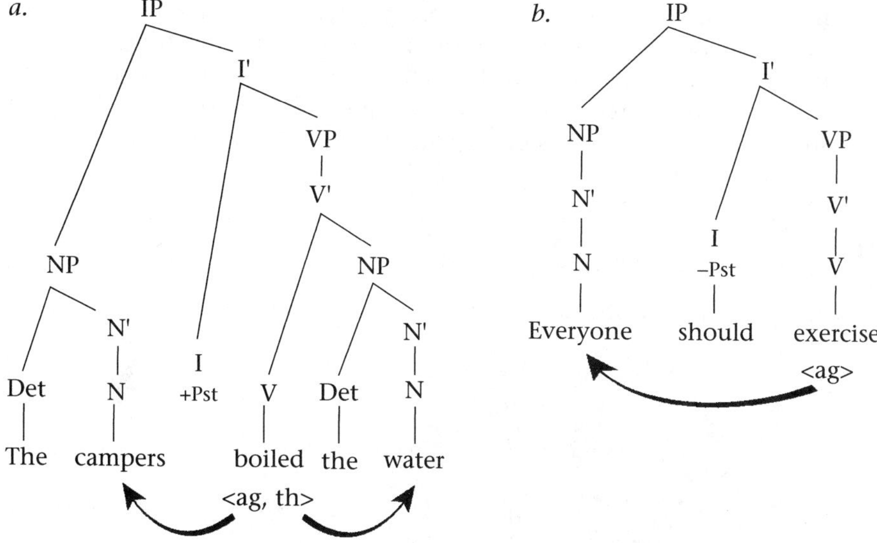

Figure 6.7 Thematic role assignment by verbs

The structure in Figure 6.8 illustrates the assignment of thematic roles in a sentence that contains a P in addition to a V. Here, the P *at* assigns its location (loc) role

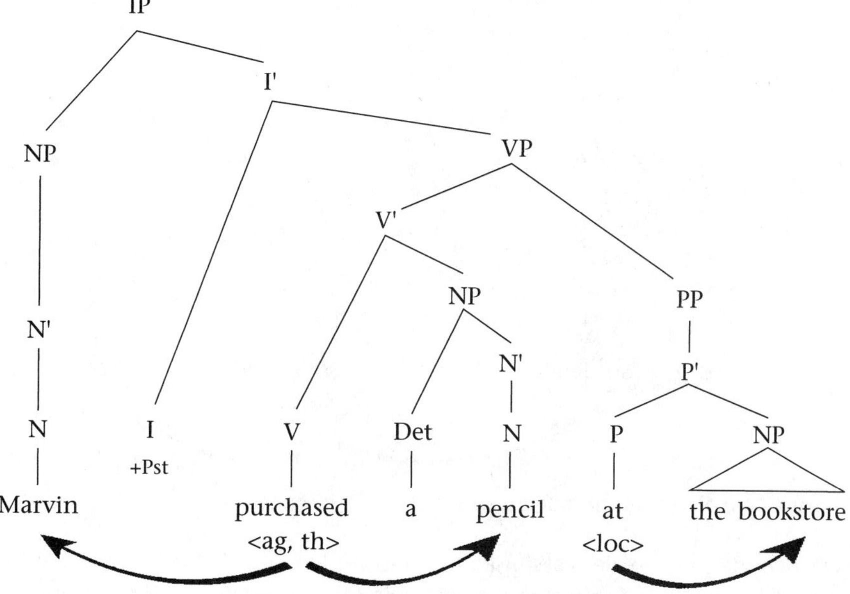

Figure 6.8 Thematic role assignment in a complex sentence

to its complement NP (*the bookstore*), while the verb *purchase* assigns its theme role to the complement *a pencil* and its agent role to the subject *Marvin.*

Deep Structure and Thematic Roles

In the examples considered to this point, it is unclear whether an NP receives its thematic role on the basis of its position in deep structure or surface structure. This is because our example sentences are all formed without the help of the Move operation, so that each NP occupies the same position in both deep structure and surface structure. But now consider a sentence such as *33,* which is formed with the help of *Wh* Movement.

33)

Which book should the students read?

This sentence has the deep structure depicted in Figure 6.9.

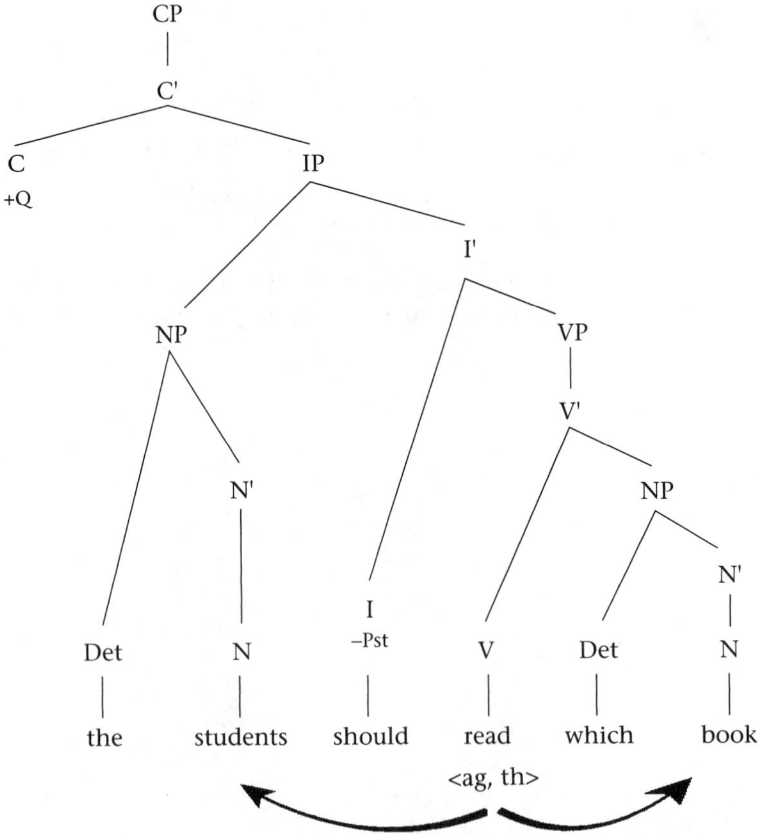

Figure 6.9 Thematic role assignment in a *wh* question

Since the theme role is assigned to the complement of V, it follows that the NP *which book* in the above example receives this role by virtue of its position in deep structure, not surface structure (where it occurs in the specifier of CP position).

In sum, an NP's initial position in syntactic structure (the result of the Merge operation) determines its thematic role. The Move operation may subsequently transport the NP to another position (as is the case with *wh* words), but the original thematic role remains unchanged. The relationship between syntactic structure and the part of a sentence's meaning represented by thematic roles is thus very intricate, reflecting the structural relations manifested in deep structure rather than position in surface structure.

3.4 The Interpretation of Pronouns

Syntactic structure also has an important role to play in the interpretation of **pronouns**, including **pronominals** such as *he, him, she,* and *her* and **reflexive pronouns** such as *himself* and *herself* (see Table 6.16).

Table 6.16 Subject and object pronouns in English

	Pronominals		*Reflexives*	
	SG	*PL*	*SG*	*PL*
1st person	I, me	we, us	myself	ourselves
2nd person	you	you	yourself	yourselves
3rd person	he, him		himself	
	she, her	they	herself	themselves
	it		itself	

A defining property of pronouns is that their interpretation can be determined by another element, called the **antecedent**. As the following sentences help show, pronominals and reflexive pronouns differ in terms of where their antecedents can occur.

34)

a. [$_{IP}$ Claire knew that [$_{IP}$ Alexis trusted *her*]].
b. [$_{IP}$ Claire knew that [$_{IP}$ Alexis trusted *herself*]].

Notice that *her* can refer either to Claire or to someone not mentioned in the sentence, but that *herself* refers only to Alexis. This reflects the fact that a reflexive pronoun must typically have an antecedent in the smallest IP containing it.

A somewhat more abstract feature of syntactic structure enters into the interpretation of the reflexive pronouns in sentences such as *35,* which has the tree structure shown in Figure 6.10. (Pronouns are treated as N-type categories that head NPs; to save space, some word-level category labels are omitted. Possessor NPs occur in the specifier position within larger NPs.)

35)

That boy's teacher admires himself.

Although there are two NPs in the same IP as *himself* (namely, *that boy* and *that boy's teacher*), only one (*that boy's teacher*) can serve as antecedent for the reflexive pro-

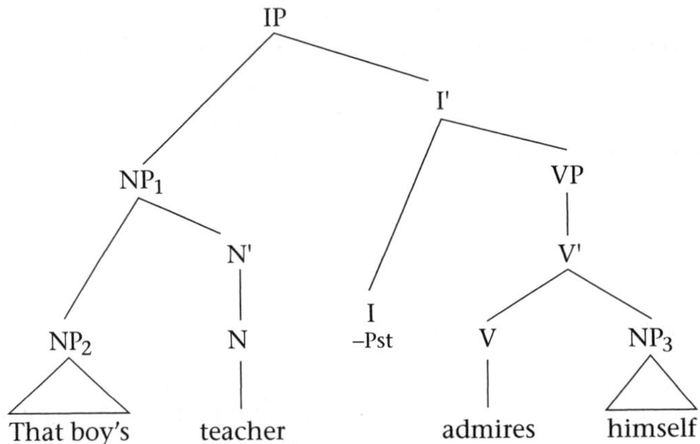

Figure 6.10 Structure containing a reflexive pronoun

noun. Thus, the person who is admired in *35* must have been the boy's teacher, not the boy.

Principles A and B

The principle needed to ensure this interpretation makes use of the notion **c-command**, which is defined as follows.

36)

NP_a c-commands NP_b if the first category above NP_a contains NP_b.

Although c-command might appear to be a rather technical notion, the underlying idea is very simple. Figure 6.11 illustrates the type of configuration in which c-command occurs.

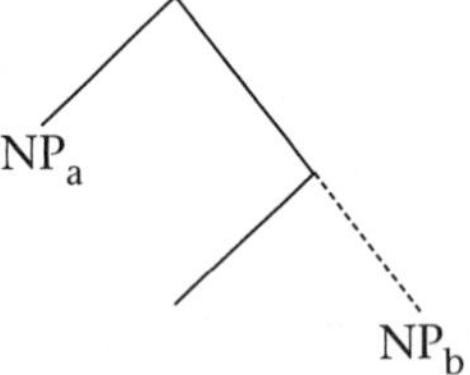

Figure 6.11 The c-command configuration

When trying to determine c-command relations, you can either use the definition in *36* or apply the template in Figure 6.11 to the tree structure being analyzed.

We can now formulate the constraint on the interpretation of reflexives, called **Principle A**, as follows. (The "minimal IP" is just the smallest IP containing the pronoun.)

37)

Principle A
A reflexive pronoun must have an antecedent that c-commands it in the same minimal IP.

When using Principle A, the key step involves determining whether a potential antecedent c-commands the reflexive pronoun. Compare in this regard the status of the NPs *that boy* and *that boy's teacher* in Figure 6.12.

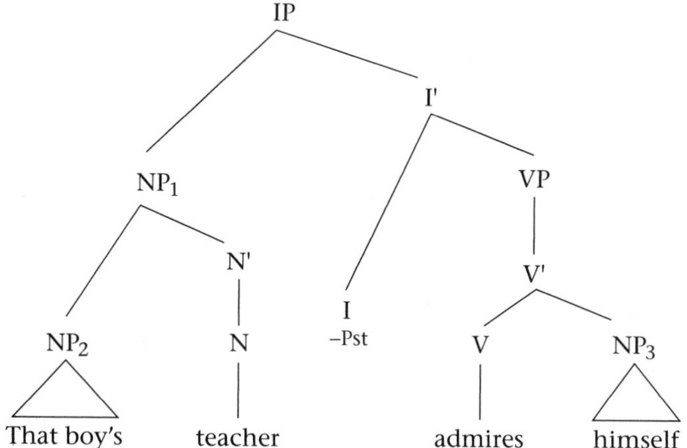

Figure 6.12 Structure illustrating c-command relations. NP_1 c-commands NP_3 but NP_2 does not.

Since the first category above the NP *that boy's teacher* (namely, IP) contains the reflexive, this NP c-commands *himself* according to our definition and can therefore serve as its antecedent. As we have already seen, the sentence has this interpretation.

Now let us consider the interpretation of pronominals. As the following example shows, the interpretation of the pronominal *him* contrasts sharply with that of the reflexive *himself* in the structure that we have been considering. Thus, *him* can refer to the boy, but not to the boy's teacher—the opposite of what we observed for *himself.*

38)

That boy's teacher admires him.

How are we to account for these facts? The relevant constraint, called **Principle B**, is stated in *39*.

39)

Principle B

A pronominal must not have an antecedent that c-commands it in the same minimal IP.

To see how this principle works, consider the structure in Figure 6.13. In this structure, NP_1 (*that boy's teacher*) c-commands *him* since the first category above it (namely, IP) also contains *him.* Principle B therefore prevents NP_1 from serving as antecedent for *him.* In contrast, NP_2 (*that boy's*) does not c-command *him* since the first category above it (namely, NP_1) does not contain the pronoun. Thus, nothing prevents the interpretation in which *him* and *that boy* refer to the same person.

There is much more that can and should be said about the interpretation of pronouns. However, the examples we have just considered suffice to illustrate the crucial

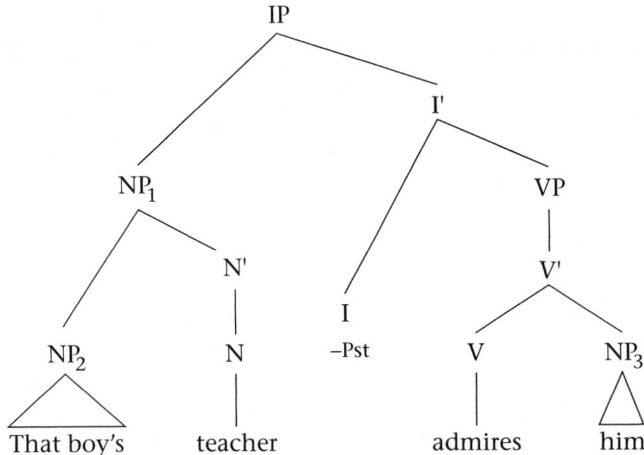

Figure 6.13 Structure containing a pronominal

point in all of this, which is that syntactic structure plays an important role in the interpretation of both pronominals and reflexive pronouns. For more on this subject, go to **bedfordstmartins.com/linguistics/semantics** and click on **pronouns**.

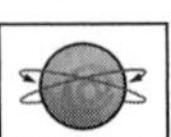

4 Other Factors in Sentence Interpretation

Syntactic structure provides only some of the information needed to interpret a sentence. Other necessary information comes from **pragmatics**, which includes the speaker's and addressee's background attitudes and beliefs, their understanding of the context in which a sentence is uttered, and their knowledge of how language can be used to inform, to persuade, to mislead, and so forth. This section focuses on the role of pragmatics in sentence interpretation.

4.1 The Role of Beliefs and Attitudes

As we saw in the preceding section, the grammar includes a structural principle (Principle B) that regulates the interpretation of pronominals such as *he* and *they*. However, as the following sentences show, nonlinguistic knowledge and beliefs can also play an important role in selecting the antecedent for a pronominal.

40)

a. The judge denied the prisoner's request because he was cautious.
b. The judge denied the prisoner's request because he was dangerous.

These two sentences have identical syntactic structures, differing only in the choice of the adjective in the second clause (*cautious* in the first sentence versus *dangerous* in the second). Yet most people feel that *he* refers to the judge in *40a* but to the prisoner in *40b*. Why should this be?

The crucial factor involves our beliefs about people in our society and their likely characteristics and behavior. All other things being equal, we are more likely to believe that a judge is cautious and a prisoner dangerous than vice versa. This in turn leads us to interpret the pronoun as referring to the judge in the first sentence in *40* but to the prisoner in the second.

Presupposition

There are many other ways in which a speaker's beliefs can be reflected in language use. Compare in this regard the following two sentences.

41)

a. Have you stopped exercising regularly?
b. Have you tried exercising regularly?

Use of the verb *stop* implies a belief on the part of the speaker that the listener has been exercising regularly. No such assumption is associated with the verb *try.*

The assumption or belief implied by the use of a particular word or structure is called a **presupposition**. The following two sentences provide another example of this.

42)

a. Nick admitted that the team had lost.
b. Nick said that the team had lost.

Choice of the verb *admit* in *42a* indicates that the speaker is presupposing the truth of the claim that the team lost. No such presupposition is associated with the choice of the verb *say* in *42b*, where the speaker is simply reporting Nick's statement without taking a position on its accuracy.

Still another type of presupposition is illustrated in *43.*

43)

a. Abraham Lincoln was assassinated in 1865.
b. Abraham Lincoln was murdered in 1865.

Notice that use of the verb *assassinate* in *43a* involves the assumption that Abraham Lincoln was a prominent person, but that no such presupposition is associated with the verb *murder.*

4.2 Setting

As noted at the beginning of this section, the pragmatic factors relevant to sentence interpretation can include knowledge of the context in which a sentence is uttered, including its physical environment or **setting**.

All languages have forms whose use and interpretation depend on the location of the speaker and/or hearer within a particular setting. Called spatial **deictics**, these forms are exemplified in English by words such as *this* and *here* (proximity to the speaker) versus *that* and *there* (proximity to the hearer and/or distance from the speaker). Thus, if Steve and Brian are sitting across from each other at a table, each would refer to a plate directly in front of him as *this plate* and to a plate in front of the other or a plate distant from both as *that plate*. Without an understanding of how the setting in which a sentence is uttered can influence the choice of words such as *this* and *that*, it would be impossible for speakers of English to use or interpret these forms correctly.

As the preceding examples show, English makes a two-way distinction in its expression of deictic contrasts. However, many languages have a three-way system that may be sensitive to distance from the speaker, the addressee, or both (depending on the language). (See Table 6.17.)

Table 6.17 Languages with a three-way deictic distinction

Language	*'this'*	*'that'*	*'that over there'*
Spanish	este	ese	aquel
Japanese	kono	sono	ano
Korean	i	ku	ce
Palauan	tia	tilęcha	se
Turkish	bu	ʃu	o

An even more complex system is found in the Amerindian language Tlingit, which makes a four-way distinction: *yáa* 'this one right here', *héi* 'this one nearby', *wée* 'that one over there', and *yóo* 'that one far off'.

Determiners are not the only type of element whose use and interpretation require reference to features of the setting. In English, for example, deictic contrasts are also crucial to the understanding of such commonly used verbs as *come* and *go*. Notice in this regard the striking difference in perspective found in the following two sentences.

44)

a. The bear is coming into the tent!
b. The bear is going into the tent!

Whereas *come* with a third person subject implies movement toward the speaker (hence we can infer that the person who utters *44a* is in the tent), *go* with the same type of subject suggests movement away from the speaker.

4.3 Discourse

An additional source of contextual information relevant to sentence interpretation can be found in **discourse**, the connected series of utterances produced during a conversation, a lecture, a story, or some other speech act. The importance of discourse stems from the fact that individual sentences commonly include elements whose interpretation can only be determined with the help of information in preceding utterances. For instance, each of the italicized words in the following passage relies for its interpretation on information encoded in a preceding sentence.

45)

A little girl went for a walk in the park. While *there, she* saw a rabbit. Since *it* was injured, *she* took *it* home.

We interpret *there* with reference to *in the park, she* with reference to *a little girl,* and *it* with reference to *a rabbit.*

One of the most important contrasts in the study of discourse involves the distinction between new and old information. **Old** (or **given**) **information** consists of the knowledge that the speaker assumes is available to the addressee at the time of the utterance, either because it is common knowledge or because it has been previously mentioned in the discourse. In contrast, **new information** involves knowledge that is introduced into the discourse for the first time. Consider the contrast between the following two sentences.

46)

a. The man is at the front door.
b. A man is at the front door.

The choice of *the* as the determiner for *man* in *46a* suggests that the referent of the phrase is someone who has already been mentioned in the discourse and is therefore known to the addressee (old information). In contrast, the choice of the determiner *a* in *46b* implies that the referent is being introduced into the discourse for the first time (new information).

Notice that both sentences in *46* use *the* as the determiner for *front door* and that the indefinite determiner *a* would not be natural in this context. This is because the setting for the conversation is likely to include only one front door. Since this information is likely to be known to both the speaker and the addressee (i.e., it is old information), *the* is the right determiner to use in this context.

Topics

Another important notion for the study of discourse is that of **topic**, which corresponds to what a sentence or a portion of the discourse is about. Consider the following passage.

47)

Once upon a time there was a merchant with two sons. The older son wanted to be a scholar. He spent his time reading and studying. As for the younger son, he preferred to travel and see the world.

The first sentence in this passage introduces a merchant and his two sons as new information. A topic (the older son) is selected in the second sentence and maintained in the third, in which *he* refers back to the older son. The final sentence then switches to a new topic (the younger son), providing some information about him. This switch is facilitated by the expression *as for,* which can be used in English to mark new topics.

There is a strong tendency in language to encode the topic as subject of a sentence. This is why (as mentioned in Section 1.2) it is natural to interpret the active sentence in *48a* as being about the police and the passive sentence in *48b* as being about the burglar (see also Section 5.3 of Chapter 5).

48)

a. The police chased the burglar.
b. The burglar was chased by the police.

In some languages, a special affix is used to identify the topic. The following sentences from Japanese illustrate this phenomenon (NOM = nominative, the subject marker; TOP = topic marker; QUES = question marker).

49)

Speaker A:	Dare-ga kimasita-ka? Who-NOM came-QUES?
Speaker B:	John-ga kimasita. John-NOM came.
Speaker A:	John-wa dare-to kimasita-ka? John-TOP who-with came-QUES? 'Who did John come with?'

The topic marker in Japanese (the suffix *-wa*) is distinguished from the subject marker (*-ga*) by its use to mark old or background information. This is why speaker B responds to A's first question by using the subject marker on the NP *John*. Because this NP provides new information (in answer to A's question), the topic marker would be inappropriate. However, once it has been established that John is the person who came, the corresponding NP can then bear the topic marker. This is precisely what happens in speaker A's final utterance, in which the NP *John* (now associated with previously established information) is marked by the topic suffix *-wa*.

4.4 Conversational Maxims

In addition to background beliefs, the setting, and the discourse, there is at least one other major type of information that enters into the interpretation of utterances. This information has to do with the "rules" for conversation—our understanding of how language is used in particular situations to convey a message. For example, if I ask you, *Would you like to go to a movie tonight?* and you respond by saying *I have to study for an exam,* I know that you are declining my invitation even though there is nothing in the literal meaning of the sentence that says so. Moreover, I recognize that this is a perfectly appropriate way to respond. (Notice that the same could not be said of a response like *I have to scratch my arm* or *It's a bit warm in here.*)

As speakers of a language, we are able to draw inferences about what is meant but not actually said. Information that is conveyed in this way is called **conversational implicature**. The ease with which we recognize and interpret implicature stems from our knowledge of how people in our linguistic community use language to communicate with each other.

The general overarching guideline for conversational interactions is often called the **Cooperative Principle**.

50)

The Cooperative Principle
Make your contribution appropriate to the conversation.

More specific **conversational maxims** or guidelines ensure that conversational interactions actually satisfy the Cooperative Principle as shown in Table 6.18. These maxims are responsible for regulating normal conversation but, as we will see, each can be suspended under certain circumstances to create particular effects.

Table 6.18 Some conversational maxims

The Maxim of Relevance Be relevant.
The Maxim of Quality Try to make your contribution one that is true. (Do not say things that are false or for which you lack adequate evidence.)
The Maxim of Quantity Do not make your contribution more or less informative than required.
The Maxim of Manner Avoid ambiguity and obscurity; be brief and orderly.

Relevance

The **Maxim of Relevance** gives listeners a bottom line for inferring the intent of other speakers. For example, it is because of this maxim that we are able to interpret the utterance *I have to study for an exam* (in response to the question *Would you like to go to a movie?*) as a no.

Failure to respect the Maxim of Relevance creates a peculiar effect. For example, if someone asks you *Have you finished that term paper yet?* and you respond *It's been raining a lot lately, hasn't it?* you violate the Maxim of Relevance by not responding in a relevant way. But by giving this response, you signal that you want to change the topic of conversation.

Quality

The **Maxim of Quality** requires that the statements used in conversations have some factual basis. If, for example, I ask *What's the weather like?* and someone responds *It's snowing,* I will normally assume that this statement provides reliable information about the current weather.

In order to achieve irony or sarcasm, however, it is sometimes possible to abandon the Maxim of Quality and say something that one knows to be false. Thus, if two people live in the middle of a sweltering desert and one person insists on asking every morning, *What's the weather like?* it might be appropriate for the other person to respond sarcastically, *Oh, today it's snowing, as usual,* perhaps with a particular facial expression or intonation to indicate that the statement was not intended as a true report of the facts.

Considerations of politeness can also justify suspension of the Maxim of Quality. For instance, in order to avoid hurt feelings, you might congratulate a fellow student on a presentation, even though you thought it was the worst thing you ever heard.

Quantity

The **Maxim of Quantity** introduces some very subtle guidelines into a conversation. Imagine, for example, that someone asks me where a famous American author lives. The nature of my response will depend in large part on how much information I believe to be appropriate for that point in the conversation. If I know that the other person is simply curious about which part of the country the author lives in, it might suffice to respond, *in Mississippi.* On the other hand, if I know that the person wants to visit the author, then much more specific information (perhaps even an address) is appropriate.

The Maxim of Quantity can be suspended in order to mislead a conversational partner. For example, if someone asks me where Mary is and I know that Mary does not want any visitors, I might respond by saying, *I think she went downtown or something,* even though I know precisely where she is. In responding in this way, I am not being untruthful since I have said nothing false, but by giving less information than is appropriate, I am violating the Maxim of Quantity and hence being misleading.

Manner

The **Maxim of Manner** imposes several constraints on language use, two of which will be exemplified here. First, imagine that I refer to a particular person as *the man who Mary lives with.* A listener would be justified in concluding that the man in question is not Mary's husband. This is because, by the Maxim of Manner, a briefer and less obscure description, *Mary's husband,* would have been used if it could have correctly described Mary's companion.

Second, imagine that an employer asks me about a former student of mine who has applied for a job and I say, with some sarcasm, *You will be fortunate indeed if you can get him to work for you.* By using a sentence that can be interpreted in two very different ways (*You will be glad to have him on your staff* versus *It is not easy to get him to do any work*), I violate the Maxim of Manner by using an ambiguous structure. Since the maxims are violated only for specific purposes, the employer would be justified in doubting the sincerity of my recommendation.

Summing Up

The study of **semantics** is concerned with a broad range of phenomena, including the nature of **meaning**, the role of syntactic structure in the interpretation of sentences, and the effect of **pragmatics** on the understanding of utterances. Although much remains to be done in each of these areas, work in recent years has at least begun to identify the type of relations, mechanisms, and principles involved in the understanding of language. These include the notions of **extension** and **intension** in the case of word meaning, **thematic roles** in the case of NPs, and **c-command** in the case of pronouns. Other factors known to be involved in an utterance's interpretation include **constructional meaning**, the speaker's and hearer's background beliefs (as manifested, for example, in **presuppositions**), the context provided by the setting and the **discourse**, and the **maxims** associated with the **Cooperative Principle**.

Key Terms

General terms

meaning
semantics

Terms concerning semantic relations among words

antonyms
homophony
lexical ambiguity
polysemy
synonyms

Terms concerning semantic relations in sentences

contradiction
entailment
paraphrases
truth conditions

Terms concerning meaning

componential analysis
connotation
denotation
extension
intension
referents
semantic decomposition
semantic features

Terms concerning how concepts are encoded

conflation pattern
evidentiality
fuzzy concept
graded (membership)
grammaticized (concepts)
lexicalization
metaphor
prototypical
spatial metaphors

General terms concerning the interpretation of sentences

constructional meaning
Principle of Compositionality
readings
structurally ambiguous

Terms concerning thematic roles in sentences

agent
goal
location
source
thematic grid
thematic roles
theme

Terms concerning the interpretation of pronouns

antecedent
c-command
Principle A
Principle B
pronominals
pronouns
reflexive pronouns

Terms concerning pragmatics

conversational implicature
conversational maxims
Cooperative Principle
deictics
discourse
Maxim of Manner
Maxim of Quality
Maxim of Quantity
Maxim of Relevance
new information
old (given) information
pragmatics
presupposition
setting
topic

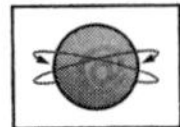

For more information on the sources used in this chapter, go to **bedfordstmartins .com/linguistics/semantics** and click on **Sources**.

Recommended Reading

Chierchia, Gennaro, and Sally McConnell-Ginet. 1990. *Meaning and Grammar.* Cambridge, MA: MIT Press.

Cruse, D.A. 2001. "The Lexicon." In *The Handbook of Linguistics*. Edited by Mark Aronoff and Janie Rees-Miller, 238–264. Malden, MA: Blackwell.

Horn, Laurence. 1988. "Pragmatic Theory." In *Linguistics: The Cambridge Survey.* Vol. 1. Edited by F. Newmeyer, 113–145. New York: Cambridge University Press.

Ladusaw, William. 1988. "Semantic Theory." In *Linguistics: The Cambridge Survey.* Vol. 1. Edited by F. Newmeyer, 89–112. New York: Cambridge University Press.

Lakoff, George, and Mark Johnson. 2003. *Metaphors We Live By.* 2nd ed. Chicago: University of Chicago Press.

Lappin, Shalom (ed.). 1997. *The Handbook of Contemporary Semantic Theory.* Boston: Blackwell.

McCawley, James. 1993. *Everything That Linguists Have Always Wanted to Know about Logic.* 2nd ed. Chicago: University of Chicago Press.

Prince, Ellen. 1988. "Discourse Analysis: A Part of the Study of Linguistic Competence." In *Linguistics: The Cambridge Survey.* Vol. 2. Edited by F. Newmeyer, 164–182. New York: Cambridge University Press.

Saeed, John. 1996. *Semantics.* Boston: Blackwell.

Schiffrin, Deborah. 1993. *Approaches to Discourse: Language as Social Interaction.* Boston: Blackwell.

Schiffrin, Deborah, Deborah Tannen, and Heidi E. Hamilton (eds.). 2001. *The Handbook of Discourse Analysis.* Malden, MA: Blackwell.

Exercises

1. Two relations involving word meanings are antonymy and synonymy. Which relation is illustrated in each of the pairs of words below?
   a) flourish-thrive
   b) intelligent-stupid
   c) casual-informal
   d) young-old
   e) uncle-aunt
   f) intelligent-smart
   g) flog-whip
   h) drunk-sober

2. It was noted in this chapter that a single form can have two or more meanings. Depending on whether these meanings are related to each other, this phenomenon involves polysemy or homophony. Which of these two relations is exemplified by the forms below?
   a) *grass:* herbage used for grazing animals; marijuana
   b) *leech:* a bloodsucking worm; a hanger-on who seeks advantage
   c) *range:* a cooking stove; a series of mountains
   d) *key:* an instrument used to apply to a lock; an answer sheet for a test or assignment
   e) *steal/steel*: rob/a type of metal
   f) *race:* the act of running competitively; people belonging to the same genetic grouping
   g) *flower/flour:* a type of plant/finely ground wheat

3. Three semantic relations among sentences were covered in this chapter: paraphrase, entailment, and contradiction. Which of these relations is exemplified in each of the following pairs of sentences?
   a) I saw Timothy at the anniversary party.
      It was Timothy that I saw at the anniversary party.
   b) Jules is Mary's husband.
      Mary is married.
   c) My pet cobra likes the taste of chocolate fudge.
      My pet cobra finds chocolate fudge tasty.
   d) Vera is an only child.
      Olga is Vera's sister.
   e) It is fifty miles to the nearest service station.
      The nearest service station is fifty miles away.
   f) My cousin Bryan teaches at the community college for a living.
      My cousin Bryan is a teacher.

4. In discussing the nature of meaning, we noted that it is necessary to distinguish between intension and extension. Describe the intensions and the extensions of each of these phrases.
   a) the president of the United States
   b) the queen of England
   c) the capital of Indiana
   d) women who have walked on the moon
   e) my linguistics professor

5. In our discussion of semantic decomposition, we noted that at least some words have meanings that can be represented in terms of smaller semantic features. Four such words are *dog, puppy, cat,* and *kitten.*
   i) Attempt to provide the semantic features associated with each of these words.
   ii) How are the pairs *dog-puppy* and *cat-kitten* different from *man-boy* and *woman-girl*?
   iii) Try to provide semantic features for the words *circle, triangle,* and *quadrangle.* What problems do you encounter?

6. Each of the following words is associated with a concept.

a) island	e) food
b) soft	f) husband
c) white	g) baseball bat
d) wristwatch	h) mountain

i) Determine which of these examples involve fuzzy concepts.
ii) Choose one of the fuzzy concepts above. Name one prototypical member of that concept and one member that is closer to the concept boundary.
iii) Draw a diagram for the concept DWELLING similar to that of Figure 6.2 in this chapter. Do the same for the concept VEHICLE.

7. Examine the following sets of sentences, each of which includes words or phrases used metaphorically.
   a) She gave him an icy stare.
   He gave her the cold shoulder.
   He exudes a lot of warmth toward people.
   They got into a heated argument.
   b) He drops a lot of hints.
   The committee picked up on the issue.
   She dumps all her problems on her friends.
   Although he disagreed, he let it go.
   c) the eye of a needle
   the foot of the bed
   the hands of the clock
   the arm of a chair
   the table legs
   d) This lecture is easy to digest.
   He just eats up the lecturer's words.
   Chew on this thought for a while.
   Listen to this juicy piece of gossip.

   For each set of sentences:
   i) Identify the words or phrases that are used metaphorically in each sentence.
   ii) Determine the basis for each of these metaphor sets.
   Use the pattern: "The metaphors in *x* describe _____ in terms of _____."
   Example: The metaphors in *a* describe human relationships in terms of temperature.

8. The section on lexicalization of concepts discussed how some languages simultaneously express motion and path, motion and manner, and/or motion and thing moving in motion verbs. Can you change the sentence *He moved the goods by truck to the warehouse* so that both the movement and the vehicle used for the move are lexicalized in one verb? Can you think of another verb that expresses a similar combination of concepts?

9. Consider the following Fijian pronouns.

au	1st person singular 'me'
iko	2nd person singular 'you'

koya	3rd person singular 'him/her/it'
kedaru	1st person dual 'you and me'
keirau	1st person dual 'one other (not you) and me'
kemudrau	2nd person dual 'you two'
rau	3rd person dual 'them two'
kedatou	1st person trial 'two others (including you) and me'
keitou	1st person trial 'two others (excluding you) and me'
kemudou	2nd person trial 'you three'
iratou	3rd person trial 'them three'
keda	1st person plural 'us' (more than three, including you)
keimami	1st person plural 'us' (more than three, excluding you)
kemuni:	2nd person plural 'you' (more than three)
ira	3rd person plural 'them' (more than three)

i) Some concepts are grammaticized in the Fijian pronoun system that are not grammaticized in the English pronoun system. Can you identify them?

ii) Which concept is grammaticized in the English pronoun system but not in the Fijian system?

10. Each NP in the following sentences has a thematic role that represents the part that its referent plays in the situation described by the sentence.
    a) The man chased the intruder.
    b) The cat jumped from the chair onto the table.
    c) Aaron wrote a letter to Marilyn.
    d) The governor entertained the guests in the lounge.
    e) Nancy mailed the manuscript from Atlanta.

    Using the terms described in this chapter, label the thematic role of each NP in these sentences and identify the assigner for each thematic role.

    Example: Bill wrote a novel in the park.

11. Each of the following sentences has undergone a movement transformation.
    a) What should Larry give to the bride?
    b) Who will Liane kiss?
    c) Which house will the group leave from?
    d) What might Marvin forget on the bus?

    Write out the deep structure string for each of these sentences and mark all thematic roles and thematic role assigners.

    Example: a) Larry should give what to the bride

12. One of the relations involved in the interpretation of pronouns is that of c-command. Examine the following tree structure for the sentence *Marie's sister gave herself a haircut.*

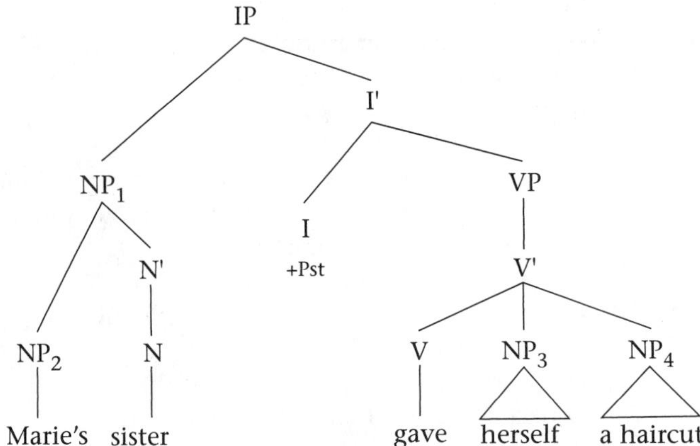

i) Who does *herself* refer to in this sentence?
ii) Does NP_2 c-command NP_3?
iii) How does your answer to *ii* relate to your answer to *i*?
iv) Does the antecedent change if you change *herself* to *her*? Why?

13. In the following sentence, the pronoun *she* could, according to Principle B, refer to either *the architect* or *the secretary.*

    The architect gave the secretary a raise after she typed the report.

    i) Which interpretation for *she* comes to mind first?
    ii) Why?
    iii) What happens to the pronoun's interpretation if you change the word *secretary* to *janitor*?

14. In the following pairs of sentences, one of the two sentences contains a presupposition relating to the truth of the complement clause.
    a) John regrets that Maria went to the graduation ceremony.
    John believes that Maria went to the graduation ceremony.
    b) The captain thought that the ship was in danger.
    The captain realized that the ship was in danger.
    c) It is significant that the criminal was sentenced.
    It is likely that the criminal was sentenced.

    For each pair:
    i) Identify the sentence that contains the presupposition.
    ii) Locate the word that is responsible for the presupposition.

15. In Malagasy, the use of the deictics *ety* 'here' and *aty* 'there' depend on whether the object in question is visible to the speaker.
    a) *Ety ny tranony.* 'Here is his house (visible to the speaker)'.
    b) *Aty ny tranony.* 'There is his house (not visible to the speaker)'.

    How does this differ from the English use of *here/there*?

16. The syntactic construction *It was* _____ *that* _____ is called a cleft construction and is used in certain discourse contexts. Consider the following conversations involving cleft constructions.

a) *A:* Did Sally claim that she saw a flying saucer last night?
B: No, it was a meteorite that Sally claimed she saw last night.

b) *A:* Did Sally claim that she saw a flying saucer last night?
B: No, it was Sally that claimed she saw a meteorite last night.

c) *A:* Did Sally claim that she saw a flying saucer last night?
B: No, it was last week that Sally claimed she saw a flying saucer.

i) In which example is B's response inappropriate?

ii) Focus first on contexts in which B's response is appropriate. How do the underlined parts correspond to new and old information?

iii) Explain why the cleft construction is unacceptable in one of the examples.

17. Each of the following examples contains a conversational implicature.

a) *A:* Have you washed the floor and done the dishes?
B: I've washed the floor.

b) *A:* Did you get hold of Carl yet?
B: I tried to call him yesterday.

c) *A:* What did you think of the movie?
B: Well, the supporting actor was great.

d) *A:* Do you have any pets?
B: I have two cats.

What is the implicature for each example?

For the Student Linguist

ELVIS'S BIGGEST FAN CLEANS OUT BANK— ACCOMPLICE LAUNDERS THE DOUGH

PEORIA—Blanche VanBuren, an old Elvis fan from Oneida, Illinois, cleaned out the Peoria Institution for Savings yesterday with nothing but a sawed-off broom and old shotgun.

Darrel Apley, the owner of Union Electric and a shocked witness who preferred to remain anonymous said, "Blanche should be at home at this time of the day. Her favorite soap is on the TV."

A teller said, "Someone came in a truck. I heard some screams coming from inside. People were rolling on the floor. Then it was over and I smoked a pack of cigarettes on the way home."

By the time the Bureau had been hauled in, the local pigs had decided someone else had done it. But the tip-off, by Oneida Otters star center Billie Jones, was about her partner. "Everyone thought two people were involved from the beginning," Jones claimed. "But it was when I saw the suds in the record store behind the pizzeria that it all came together."

The King could not be reached for comment by press time.

It's surprisingly easy to write an article in which every sentence is ambiguous. It's much harder—maybe even impossible—to write one that isn't ambiguous, or to write anything that isn't ambiguous. Maybe this explains why legal language is so tedious in its attempt to be unambiguous and why our court system is so clogged (obstructed, that is, not filled with Dutch wooden shoes), and why multiple-choice exams are so awful.

To show that the sentences in this article really are ambiguous, I'll attempt to disambiguate the first couple of paragraphs of Blanche's story in painstaking detail. By the time I'm done, you'll probably be able to see ambiguity everywhere you go.

Blanche VanBuren is an elderly Elvis aficionado who resides in Oneida, Illinois. And she's just plain old, all would agree (see tree *1B*). Or, when considering Elvis fans from Oneida, she's getting up in years (see tree *1A*), but in some other context she'd be considered pretty young (because most of the Elvis fans in Oneida are teeny-boppers, whereas Blanche is pushing thirty). Maybe Blanche has been an Elvis fan for a long time (*1B*). Or maybe, just maybe, most Oneidan Elvis fans are new to their admiration of him (it began with the postage stamp), but Blanche has loved Elvis since 1984, when she encountered him on a spaceship, and is therefore, comparatively speaking, an old Elvis-fan-from-Oneida (tree *1A*). Of course, she could also be a fan of only the *old* Elvis—that is, she liked his Vegas days but hated the early stuff. You can figure out the tree for this reading.

Let's assume Blanche is elderly. And a neat freak, because she washed the Peoria Institution for Savings from top to bottom (taking the shotgun to teach a lesson to litterbugs). Then again, she might be an incredibly compulsive cleaner in her own house and spend so much money on lemon-scented antiseptics that she robbed the P.I.S. and took along that sawed-off broom because she was delirious from inhaling ammonia all day. Let's consider her implements. The shotgun was old. The broom was sawed-off. Was the broom old? We don't know; the story doesn't provide information on its age. Was the shotgun sawed-off? This is a classic case of structural ambiguity, made famous by the example "the old men and women," and the answer should be obvious by now (but see trees *2A* and *2B* for confirmation).

The article does make clear that the event of interest took place yesterday, but I'm wondering whether Blanche habitually cleans out banks, and it just happened to be the P.I.S. yesterday, or if this was an out-of-the-blue cleaning or what. Could be that she cleans the P.I.S. every day, but usually she has more equipment than a broom and a gun.

Then there's the possibility that Blanche is an early model electric cooling device (or an antique paper and balsa wood construction), once owned (and affectionately named) by Elvis, which either: (a) blew all the dirt out of the bank or (b) was brought to life and performed the robbery. You never know.

What about Darrel Apley? If the writer of this article had any ethics, he (Darrel) is not the person who owns Union Electric, nor is he (Darrel) a shocked witness who preferred to remain anonymous. If the writer had ethics there would have to have been three different people who all said "Blanche should be at home..." and one of them is Darrel, one's the owner of U.E., and the third is shocked and prefers anonymity (tree *3A*). However, sloppy writing and broken promises are everywhere, and it's quite possible that *the owner of Union Electric* and *a shocked witness who preferred to remain anonymous* are actually intended to describe Darrel (tree *3B*).

"Blanche should be at home at this time of the day." Should? As in, given her normal patterns, the most likely case is that Blanche is at home? Or *should* as in if that lowdown, bank-thieving woman knew what was good for her she'd be at home watching *All My Children*?

"Her favorite soap is on the TV." This one's easy; it's nothing but lexical ambiguity. Her favorite soap could be Ivory Family Size or the aforementioned *All My Children*. If this were spoken instead of written, we'd have to explore the option that her favorite soap is called "On the TV," and actually, considering the doubts you might have about the writer's integrity, that could have been what Darrel (and maybe two others) meant. Of course, "on" is ambiguous between "being broadcast" or "on top of" but enough is enough.

The rest of the article you can disambiguate on your own. It's useful to draw trees for the structurally ambiguous parts and make sure the different interpretations match the trees. Every *written* sentence—every portion of material from one period to another—is ambiguous, but not every *IP* in the technical, linguistic sense is ambiguous. Be sure to look for lexical ambiguity, structural ambiguity, and pronouns that could refer to a few different people. Also look carefully at Jones's quote—this one is hard but interesting. Finally, check out your local newspaper. I predict that many of the sentences in it are as ambiguous as the ones in this article. You could even examine the instructions for your next linguistics homework assignment and (politely) tease your instructor if they're not crystal clear. Be careful, though—he or she might hold you to the same standard in your writing.

TREES:

(*1A*)

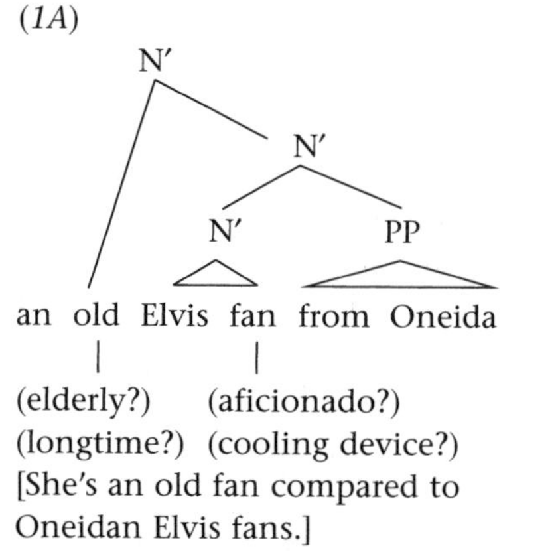

(*1B*)

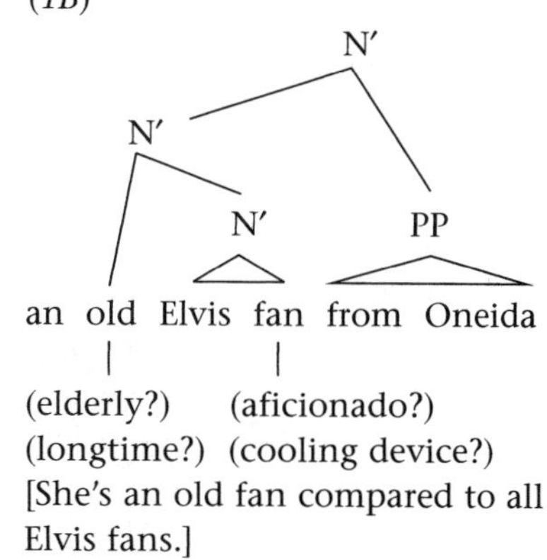

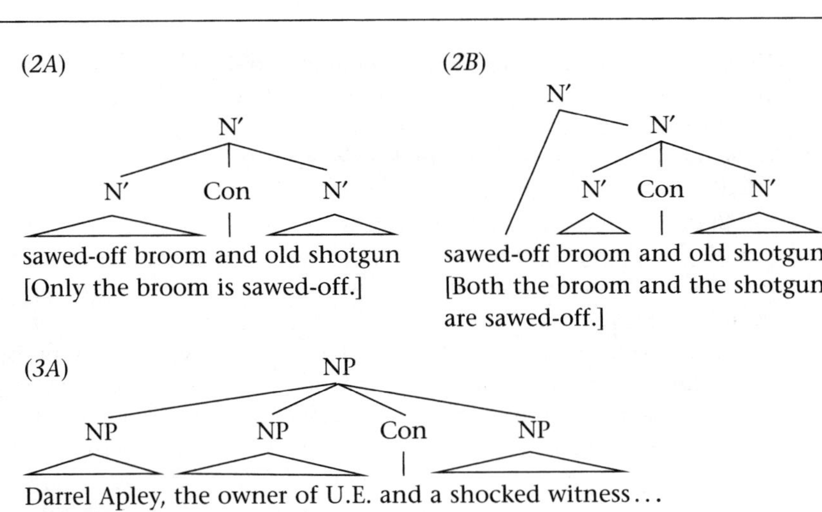

(3B)

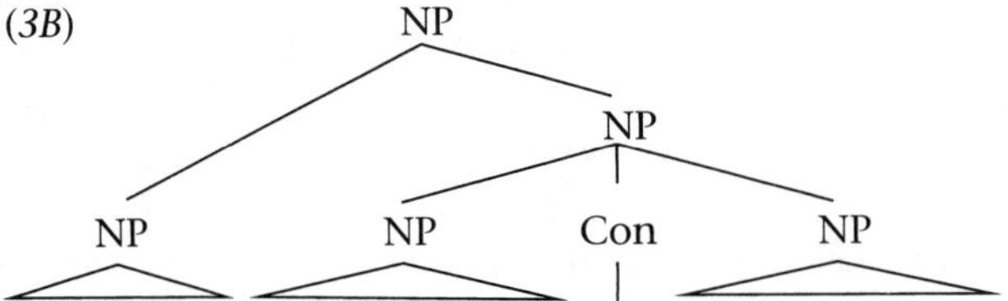

Darrel Apley, the owner of U.E. and a shocked witness...
[One person: "Darrell Apley, (who is) the owner... ," after "who is" has been deleted. Don't worry about the details of this structure.]

seven

Historical Linguistics: The Study of Language Change

Robert W. Murray

Many men sayn that in sweveninges
Ther nys but fables and lesynges;
But men may some swevenes sene
Whiche hardely that false ne bene,
But afterwarde ben apparaunt.

– CHAUCER, *The Romance of the Rose* (c. 1370)

OBJECTIVES

In this chapter, you will learn:

- how and why languages change over time
- how and why sound changes occur
- what kinds of changes occur in morphology and syntax
- ways in which words change
- how linguists can reconstruct languages spoken in earlier times, based on the existing languages that are descended from them

Language change is both obvious and rather mysterious. The English of the late fourteenth century, for example, is so different from Modern English that without special training it is difficult to understand the opening lines to *The Romance of the Rose* cited above. Not only would these sentences have a foreign sound, but words and structures such as *sweveninges, lesynges,* and *false ne bene* are unfamiliar.* The

* The translation for the passage is as follows:
Many men say that in dreams
There is nothing but talk and lies;
But men may see some dreams
Which are scarcely false;
But afterward come true.

existence of such differences between early and later variants of the same language raises questions as to how and why languages change over time.

Historical linguistics is concerned with both the description and the explanation of language change. In this chapter we examine the nature and causes of language change and survey in some detail phonological, morphological, syntactic, lexical, and semantic change. We also explore techniques used to reconstruct linguistic prehistory and briefly discuss interrelated research into language acquisition and linguistic universals.

1 The Nature of Language Change

All languages undergo change over time. English has undergone continuous and dramatic change throughout its three major periods: Old English (roughly from 450 to 1100), Middle English (from 1100 to 1500), and Modern English (from 1500 to the present). Although Chaucer's Middle English is at least partially comprehensible today, Old English looks like a completely foreign language. The following is an extract from an eighth-century Old English document, a translation of Bede's Latin history of England. (The letter <þ>, called 'thorn', represented the phoneme /θ/ in Old English; here and elsewhere in this chapter, the symbol ¯ marks a long vowel in the orthography.)

1)

and Seaxan þā sige geslōgan.
and Saxons the victory won
'And the Saxons won the victory.'

þā sendan hī hām ǣrenddracan.
then sent they home a messenger
'Then they sent home a messenger.'

These Old English sentences differ from their Modern English counterparts in many respects. In terms of pronunciation, for instance, the Old English word *hām* [hɑːm] 'home' in the second sentence became [hɔːm] in Middle English, and then [howm] in Modern English. In its morphology, Old English differed significantly from Modern English. The suffix *-an* on the Old English word for 'sent' indicates both past tense and plurality of the subject (*hī* 'they'). Differences in word order are also readily apparent, with the verb following both the subject and the direct object in the first sentence and preceding both the subject and the direct object in the second. Neither of these word orders would be acceptable in the Modern English forms of these sentences.

In addition, some Old English words have disappeared from use, as the unfamiliar *ǣrenddracan* 'messenger' and *sige* 'victory' indicate. Still other words have been maintained, but with a change in meaning. For example, the Old English word *geslōgan* (which we translated as 'won') is the past tense of the verb *slēan*, the Old English predecessor of our word *slay*. Although the Modern English meaning of this word in normal usage is restricted to the act of killing, the Old English verb could also mean 'to strike, beat, coin (money), and forge (weapons)'. As these examples imply, all components of the grammar from meaning (semantics) to individual sounds (phonology) are subject to change.

1.1 Systematicity of Language Change

A striking fact about language change in general is its regularity and systematicity. For example, the development of a fixed subject-verb-direct object (SVO) word order in English did not affect just a few verbs; all verbs in Modern English appear before rather than after the direct object. Similarly, the changes affecting the vowel in the word *hām* did not occur in that word only; they represent the regular development of the Old English vowel *ā* ([ɑː]) (see Table 7.1).

Table 7.1 Changes affecting Old English [ɑː]

Old English	*Middle English*	*Modern English*	
[bɑːt]	[bɔːt]	[bowt]	'boat'
[ɑːθ]	[ɔːθ]	[owθ]	'oath'
[stɑːn]	[stɔːn]	[stown]	'stone'

1.2 Causes of Language Change

The inevitability of language change is guaranteed by the way in which language is passed on from one generation to the next. Children do not begin with an intact grammar of the language being acquired but rather must construct a grammar on the basis of the available data (see Chapter 11). In such a situation it is hardly surprising that differences will arise, even if only subtle ones, from one generation to the next. Moreover, since all children use the same physiological and cognitive endowment in learning language, it is to be expected that the same patterns of change will be consistently and repeatedly manifested in all languages. Following is a brief overview of the principal causes of language change.

Articulatory Simplification

As might be expected, most sound changes have a physiological basis. Since such sound changes typically result in **articulatory simplification**, they have traditionally been related to the idea of ease of articulation. Although this notion is difficult to define precisely, we can readily identify cases of articulatory simplification in our everyday speech, such as the deletion of a consonant in a complex cluster or, in some dialects, the insertion of a vowel to break up a complex cluster (see Table 7.2).

Table 7.2 Simplification of complex clusters

Deletion of a consonant			
[fɪfθs]	→	[fɪfs]	'fifths'
Insertion of a vowel			
[æθlit]	→	[æθəlit]	'athlete'

For information about spelling pronunciation as a source of change, go to **bedfordstmartins.com/linguistics/historical** and click on **spelling pronunciation**.

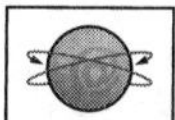

Analogy and Reanalysis

Cognitive factors also play a role in change in all components of the grammar. Two sources of change having a cognitive basis are **analogy** and **reanalysis**. Analogy reflects the preference of speakers for regular patterns over irregular ones. It typically involves the extension or generalization of a regularity on the basis of the inference that if elements are alike in some respects, they should be alike in others as well. Both phonological and semantic characteristics can serve as a basis for analogy. For example, on the basis of its phonological similarity with verbs such as *sting/stung* and *swing/swung,* in some dialects *bring* has developed a form *brung,* as in *I brung it into the house*. The effects of analogy can also be observed in the speech of children, who often generalize the regular *-ed* past tense form to produce forms such as *goed* and *knowed* (see Chapter 11). As we will see shortly, analogy plays a very important role in morphological change as well.

Reanalysis is particularly common in morphological change. Morphological reanalysis typically involves an attempt to attribute a compound or root + affix structure to a word that was not formerly broken down into component morphemes. A classic example in English is the word *hamburger,* which originally referred to a type of meat patty deriving its name from the city of Hamburg in Germany. This word has been reanalyzed as consisting of two components, *ham* + *burger.* The latter morpheme has since appeared in many new forms, including *fishburger, chickenburger,* and even as a free morpheme, *burger.* Note that the resulting reanalysis need not be correct. (There is usually no ham in a burger!)

Language Contact

Another cause of language change is **language contact**. Language contact refers to the situation where speakers of a language frequently interact with the speakers of another language or dialect. As a consequence, extensive **borrowing** can occur, particularly where there are significant numbers of bilinguals or multilinguals. Although borrowing can affect all components of the grammar, the lexicon is typically most affected. English, for example, has borrowed many Native American words, including *Mississippi, moccasin, totem, tomahawk, chinook, moose,* and *skunk.*

Among the effects that borrowing can have on the sound system are the introduction of new phonemes or allophones and changes in their distribution. For example, some English speakers pronounce the name of the classical composer *Bach* with the final velar fricative [x] found in the German pronunciation. If there is a significant number of borrowings from another language, the borrowed foreign segment can eventually become a new phoneme. In the early Middle English period, the London dialect had [f] but not [v] in word-initial position. The [v] was later introduced as a result of contact with other English dialects and with French, in which it did occur word-initially. This contact was a likely factor in the development of a contrast between /f/ and /v/ word-initially, as found in Modern English pairs such as *file* and *vile.*

Language (as well as dialect) contact also results in another minor but nevertheless important source of language change, **hypercorrection**. Hypercorrection occurs when a speaker who is attempting to speak another dialect or language overgeneralizes particular rules. For example, most Americans speak a dialect in which no distinction is made between intervocalic [t] and [d], so that words such as *latter* and *ladder* are both pronounced with an intervocalic flap [ɾ] (see Chapter 2). If a speaker from such a dialect attempts to emulate the pronunciation of a speaker from another dialect who does distinguish the two stops intervocalically, hypercorrection could result in the use of intervocalic [t] in words where [d] should be used—for example, the pronunciation *pro*[t]*igy* for *prodigy*.

Another example of hypercorrection is the use of *I* in constructions such as *He saw John and I.* This usage is an overgeneralization of the rule that only *I* should be used in subject position, never *me*. According to this rule, *John and I are going* is correct but *John and me/me and John are going* is incorrect. For some speakers, hypercorrection has resulted in the inference that all coordinate phrases containing *me* (such as *John and me*) are incorrect, even when they serve as direct object (complement) of the verb. Note that even a person who says *He saw John and I* would not say *He saw I.*

2 Sound Change

Although all components of the grammar are susceptible to change over time, some types of change yield more obvious results than others. Variation and change are particularly noticeable in the phonology of a language. Several common types of sound change can be distinguished.

Most sound changes begin as subtle alterations in the sound pattern of a language in particular phonetic environments. The linguistic processes underlying such **phonetically conditioned change** are identical to the ones found in the phonology of currently spoken languages (see Chapter 2, Section 9). The application of such processes usually brings about an articulatory simplification, and over time significant changes in the phonology of a language can result.

Although all aspects of a language's phonology (e.g., tone, stress, and syllable structure) are subject to change over time, we will restrict our attention here to change involving segments. Since most sound changes involve sequences of segments, the main focus will be on **sequential change**. However, we will also discuss one common type of **segmental change**, involving the simplification of an affricate. In addition, in order to demonstrate that more than just articulatory factors play a role in sound change, we will discuss a case of sound change based on auditory factors. All important sound changes discussed in this section and referred to in this chapter are found in the catalog of sound changes in Table 7.3.

2.1 Sequential Change

Assimilation

The most common type of sequential change is **assimilation**, which has the effect of increasing the efficiency of articulation through a simplification of articulatory movements. We will focus here on the four main types indicated in Table 7.3.

Partial assimilation involving **place or manner of articulation** is a very common change that, over time, can result in total assimilation. In the Spanish and Latin examples in Table 7.4, the nasal assimilated in place of articulation to the following consonant. (In these and other examples throughout this chapter, actual spellings are

Table 7.3 Catalog of sound changes

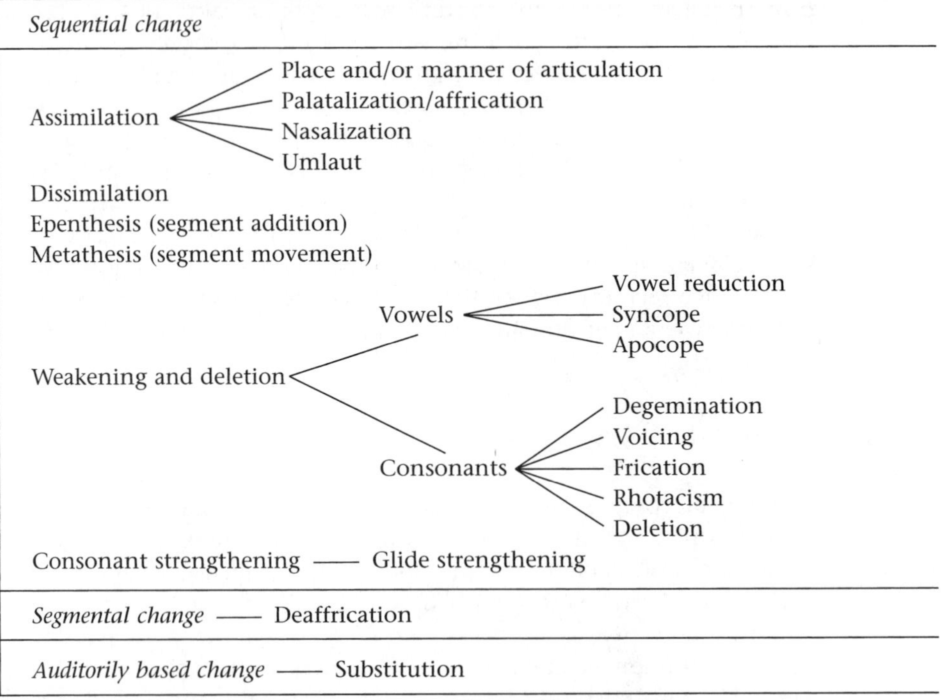

Table 7.4 Assimilation in place of articulation in Spanish and Latin

Old Spanish	semda	Modern Spanish	senda	'path'
Early Latin	inpossibilis	Later Latin	impossibilis	'impossible'

given where these clearly reflect the sound change(s) in question. If required, partial or full phonetic transcriptions are provided.) The first of the Old English examples in Table 7.5 shows voicing assimilation and the second shows the assimilation of nasality.

Table 7.5 Assimilation in manner of articulation in Old English

Early Old English	*Later Old English*	
slǣpde	slǣpte	'slept'
stefn	stemn	'stem' (of a tree)

In the Italian examples in Table 7.6, a stop assimilates totally to a following stop.

Table 7.6 Total assimilation in Italian

Latin	*Italian*	
octo (*c* = [k])	otto	'eight'
septem	sette	'seven'
damnum	danno	'damage'

Another type of assimilation is **palatalization**—the effect that front vowels and the palatal glide [j] typically have on velar, alveolar, and dental stops, making their place of articulation more palatal. If you compare your pronunciation of *keep* as opposed to *cot,* you will notice that the pronunciation of [k] in *keep* is much more palatal than in *cot* due to the influence of [i]. Palatalization is often the first step in **affrication**, a change in which palatalized stops become affricates, either [ts] or [tʃ] if the original stop was voiceless, or [dz] or [dʒ] if the original stop was voiced (see Table 7.7).

Table 7.7 Palatalization/affrication induced by front vowels and [j]

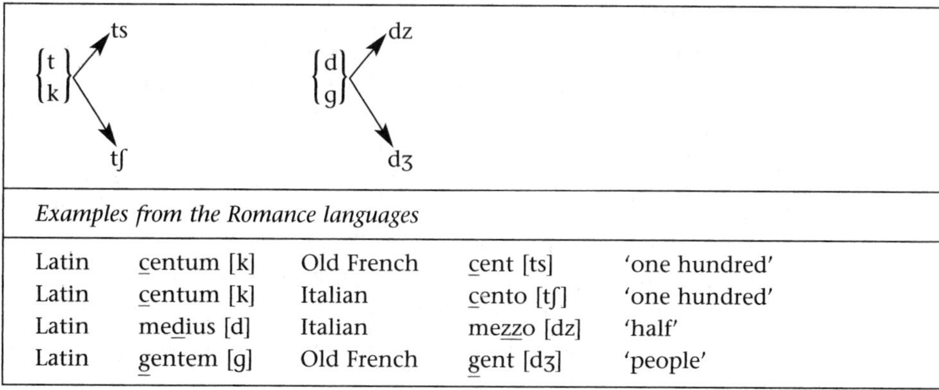

Examples from the Romance languages

Latin	centum [k]	Old French	cent [ts]	'one hundred'
Latin	centum [k]	Italian	cento [tʃ]	'one hundred'
Latin	medius [d]	Italian	mezzo [dz]	'half'
Latin	gentem [g]	Old French	gent [dʒ]	'people'

Nasalization refers to the nasalizing effect that a nasal consonant can have on an adjacent vowel. This change occurred in both French and Portuguese, with the subsequent loss of the nasal consonant. (The pronunciation of the vowels in the examples in Table 7.8 underwent additional changes in height and backness in French.)

Table 7.8 Nasalization in Portuguese and French

Latin	*Portuguese*	*French*	
bon-	bom [bõ]	bon [bɔ̃]	'good'
un-	um [ũ]	un [œ̃]	'one'

Although assimilation is probably most common in the case of adjacent segments, it can also apply at a distance. A case in point is **umlaut**, the effect a vowel or sometimes a glide in one syllable can have on the vowel of another syllable, usually a preceding one. Umlaut (resulting in the front rounded vowels [y] and [ø]) played an important role in Old English and is the source of irregular plurals such as *goose/geese* and *mouse/mice* in Modern English. For example, as Table 7.9 shows, the plural of the pre–Old English words *gōs* 'goose' and *mūs* 'mouse' was formed by adding a suffix -[i]. As a result, umlaut of the vowel in the preceding syllable occurred in the plural forms (see pre–Old English stages 1 and 2) but not in the singular forms. By early Old English, the suffix -[i] had been lost in a separate change, leaving the umlauted vowel as the marker of the plural form. (Subsequent changes included the derounding of the umlauted vowels [ȳ] and [ø̄], yielding [ī] and [ē] respectively by Middle English, and the Great English Vowel Shift as described in Section 2.4.)

Table 7.9 Umlaut in English

Pre-Old English 1		*Pre-OE 2*		*Early OE*		*Subsequent changes*	
[gōs]	>	[gōs]	>	[gōs]	>	[gus]	'goose'
[gōsi]	>	[gø̄si]	>	[gø̄s]	>	[gis]	'geese'
[mūs]	>	[mūs]	>	[mūs]	>	[maws]	'mouse'
[mūsi]	>	[mȳsi]	>	[mȳs]	>	[majs]	'mice'

Note: It is traditional in historical linguistics to use the sign > to mean 'changed into'.

Dissimilation

Dissimilation, the process whereby one segment is made less like another segment in its environment, is much less frequent than assimilation. This type of change typically occurs when it would be difficult to articulate or perceive two similar sounds in close proximity. The word *anma* 'soul' in Late Latin, for example, was modified to *alma* in Spanish, thereby avoiding two consecutive nasal consonants. Like assimilation, dissimilation can also operate at a distance to affect nonadjacent segments. For instance, the Latin word *arbor* 'tree' became *arbol* in Spanish and *albero* in Italian, thereby avoiding two instances of *r* in adjacent syllables. (By contrast, dissimilation did not occur in French, where *arbre* has retained both instances of *r*.)

Epenthesis

Another common sound change, **epenthesis**, involves the insertion of a consonant or vowel into a particular environment (see Table 7.10). In some cases, epenthesis results from the anticipation of an upcoming sound.

Table 7.10 Epenthesis in Old English

Earlier form	*Change*	*Later form*	
ganra	VnrV > VndrV	gandra	'gander'
simle	VmlV > VmblV	simble	'always'
ǣmtig	VmtV > VmptV	ǣmptig	'empty'

In these examples, the epenthetic [d], [b], or [p] has the place of articulation of the preceding nasal but agrees with the following segment in terms of voice and nasality. The epenthetic segment therefore serves as a bridge for the transition between the segments on either side, as is shown in Table 7.11.

Table 7.11 The nature of epenthesis

[m]	[b]	[l]	[m]	[p]	[t]
labial	labial	nonlabial	labial	labial	nonlabial
nasal	nonnasal	nonnasal	nasal	nonnasal	nonnasal
voiced	voiced	voiced	voiced	voiceless	voiceless

In other cases, vowel epenthesis serves to break up a sequence of sounds that would otherwise be difficult to pronounce or even inconsistent with the phonotactic patterns of the language. As shown in Table 7.2, some English speakers avoid [θl] clusters by inserting an epenthetic [ə] in their pronunciation of words such as *athlete* as *ath*[ə]*lete*. In the history of Spanish, word-initial [sk] clusters were avoided by inserting a vowel (see Table 7.12).

Table 7.12 Examples of epenthesis

Latin	schola [sk]	Spanish	escuela [esk]	'school'
Latin	scrībere [sk]	Spanish	escribir [esk]	'write'

Metathesis

Metathesis involves a change in the relative positioning of segments. This change, like assimilation and dissimilation, can affect adjacent segments or segments at a distance (see Table 7.13).

Table 7.13 Metathesis of adjacent segments in Old English

Earlier form	*Later form*	
wæps	wæsp	'wasp'
þridda	þirdda	'third'

Metathesis at a distance is found in the change from Latin *mīrāculum* 'miracle' to Spanish *milagro,* in which [r] and [l] have changed places although they were not adjacent (see Figure 7.1).

Figure 7.1 Metathesis of nonadjacent segments in Spanish

Weakening and Deletion

Both vowels and consonants are also susceptible to outright **deletion** as well as to various **weakening** processes. We will first treat the effects of these processes on vowels and then turn to their effects on consonants.

Vowel deletion commonly involves a word-final vowel (**apocope**) or a word-internal vowel (**syncope**) (see Table 7.14). A vowel in an unstressed syllable is particularly susceptible to deletion, especially when a neighboring syllable is stressed. The effects of syncope are also apparent in the loss of the medial vowel in Modern English words such as *vegetable, interest,* and *family,* which are frequently pronounced as [vέdʒtəbl̩], [íntɹɪst], and [fǽmli].

Vowel deletion is commonly preceded diachronically by **vowel reduction**, in which a full vowel is reduced to a schwa-like vowel (i.e., short, lax, central [ə]). Vowel

Table 7.14 Vowel deletion in French

Note: [y] is a high front rounded vowel; [ʁ] is a voiceless uvular fricative.

Apocope		
Latin	*French*	
cū́ra	cure [kyʁ]	'cure'
ōrnā́re	orner	'decorate'
Syncope		
Latin	*French*	
pḗrdere	perdre	'lose'
vī́vere	vivre	'live'

reduction typically affects short vowels in unstressed syllables and may affect all or only a subset of the full vowels (see Figure 7.2).

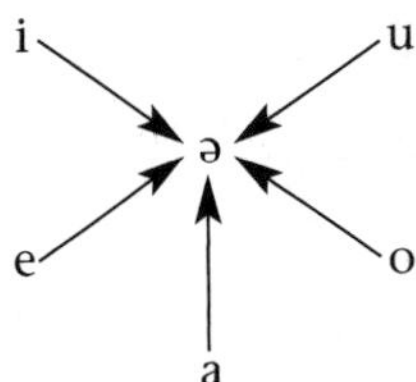

Figure 7.2 Vowel reduction

Vowel reduction with subsequent deletion (syncope and apocope) occurred in Middle English and Early Modern English, as shown in Table 7.15.

Table 7.15 Vowel reduction and deletion in English

Syncope					
Old English		*Middle English (vowel reduction)*		*Early Modern English (word-internal vowel deletion)*	
stānas	[a]	stones	[ə]	stones	Ø
stānes	[e]	stones	[ə]	stone's	Ø
Apocope					
Old English		*Middle English (vowel reduction)*		*Early Modern English (word-final vowel deletion)*	
nama	[a]	name	[ə]	name	Ø
talu	[u]	tale	[ə]	tale	Ø

Consonant deletion is also a very common sound change. For example, the word-initial cluster [kn] was found in Old and Middle English, as the spelling of such words as *knight, knit, knot,* and *knee* implies, but the [k] was subsequently lost, giving us our modern pronunciation. The loss of word-final consonants has played a major role in the evolution of Modern French. The final letters in the written forms of the words in Table 7.16 reflect consonants that were actually pronounced at an earlier stage of the language.

Table 7.16 Consonant loss in French

French spelling (masculine form)	*Current pronunciation*	
gros	[gro]	'large'
chaud	[ʃo]	'warm'
vert	[vɛʁ]	'green'

Just as vowel reduction can be identified as a weakening process, since it represents an intermediate step on the pathway from a full vowel to deletion of the vowel, so too can pathways of **consonant weakening** be identified. The scale of **consonantal strength** in Figure 7.3 can be helpful in identifying cases of weakening.

Consonantal strength

stronger	↑	voiceless stops
		voiceless fricatives, voiced stops
		voiced fricatives
		nasals
		liquids
weaker	↓	glides

(*Note:* Geminate consonants are stronger than their nongeminate counterparts.)

Figure 7.3 Scale of consonantal strength

Accordingly, geminates weaken to nongeminates (**degemination**), stops weaken to fricatives (**frication**), and voiceless stops or voiceless fricatives weaken to voiced stops or voiced fricatives respectively (**voicing**). Weakening can ultimately result in the deletion of the consonant. Figure 7.4 is a typical pathway of consonant weakening.

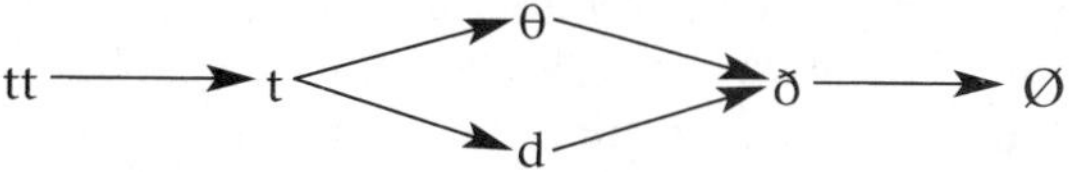

Figure 7.4 Typical pathway of consonant weakening

Consonants are particularly subject to weakening between vowels. Parts of the pathway of consonantal weakening are exemplified with developments from the Romance languages shown in Table 7.17.

Rhotacism is a relatively common type of weakening that typically involves the change of [z] to [r]. Often rhotacism is preceded by a stage involving the voicing of [s] to [z]. Within the Germanic family of languages, for instance, [s] first became [z] in a particular environment between vowels. This [z] remained in Gothic but became /r/ in other Germanic languages such as English, German, and Swedish. The effects

Table 7.17 Consonantal weakening in Romance languages

Degemination (tt > t):	Latin	mittere	Spanish	meter	'to put'
Voicing (t > d):	Latin	mātūrus	Old Spanish	maduro	'ripe'
Frication (d > ð):	Old Spanish	maduro	Spanish	maduro [ð]	'ripe'
Deletion (ð > Ø):	Old French	[maðyr]	French	mûr	'ripe'

of the latter part of this change can be seen in the standard spellings of the words in Table 7.18.

Table 7.18 Rhotacism in English, German, and Swedish

Gothic	*English*	*German*	*Swedish*
maiza	more	mehr	mera
diuzam	deer	Tier	djur
huzd	hoard	Hort	—

In Modern English, rhotacism is the source of the alternation between [z] and [ɹ] in *was* and *were*. The [ɹ] resulted from earlier [z], which was originally intervocalic.

Consonantal Strengthening

Just as consonants weaken, they can also strengthen. **Glide strengthening** (the strengthening of a glide to an affricate) is particularly common, especially in word-initial position. In the Italian examples in Table 7.19, the glide [j] has been strengthened to [dʒ]·

Table 7.19 Glide strengthening in Italian

Latin	iūdicium [j]	Italian	giudizio [dʒ]	'justice'
Latin	iuvenis [j]	Italian	giovane [dʒ]	'young'

2.2 Segmental Change

Segments such as affricates are considered phonologically complex because they represent the fusing of a stop plus a fricative into a single segment, e.g., [ts] or [dʒ]. Such complex segments are commonly subject to simplification. A very common type of segmental simplification is **deaffrication**, which has the effect of turning affricates into fricatives by eliminating the stop portion of the affricate (see Table 7.20).

Table 7.20 Deaffrication in French

Old French	cent [ts]	French	cent [s]	'one hundred'
Old French	gent [dʒ]	French	gent [ʒ]	'people, tribe'

Since deaffrication of [tʃ] (as well as of [dʒ]) has not occurred in English, early borrowings from French maintain the affricate, while later borrowings have a fricative (see Table 7.21).

Table 7.21 Borrowing from French

Early borrowing (before deaffrication occurred in French)	
Old French [tʃ]	*English* [tʃ]
chaiere	chair
chaine	chain
(*Note:* Compare Modern French [ʃ] in *chaire* 'throne, seat' and *chaîne* 'chain'.)	
Later borrowings (after deaffrication occurred in French)	
Modern French [ʃ]	*English* [ʃ]
chandelier	chandelier
chauffeur	chauffeur

2.3 Auditorily Based Change

Although articulatory factors (particularly relating to ease of articulation) are of central importance in sound change, as indicated in the discussion above, auditory factors also play a role. **Substitution** is a type of auditorily based change involving the replacement of one segment with another similar-sounding segment. A common type of substitution involves [f] replacing either [x] (a voiceless, velar fricative) or [θ]. Earlier in the history of English, [f] replaced [x] in some words in standard varieties of English while [f] replaced [θ] in Cockney, a nonstandard dialect spoken in London (see Table 7.22).

Table 7.22 Auditorily based substitution

[x] > [f]	Middle English	laugh [x]	English	laugh [f]
[θ] > [f]	English	thin [θ]	Cockney	[fɪn]

So far we have treated sound changes without consideration of their effect on the sound pattern of the particular language as a whole. All of the foregoing sound changes can lead both to new types of allophonic variation and to the addition or loss of phonemic contrasts. Examples of such cases are presented in the next section.

2.4 Phonetic versus Phonological Change

The sound changes outlined in the previous sections can affect the overall sound pattern (phonology) of a language in different ways. Commonly, the first stage of a sound change results in the creation of a new allophone of an already existing phoneme. The term **phonetic sound change** can be used to refer to this stage.

A good example of phonetic sound change involves the laxing of short high vowels that has developed in Canadian French (see Table 7.23). This change can be seen in closed word-final syllables, among other environments.

Table 7.23 Vowel laxing in Canadian French

Note: [ʁ] is a voiceless uvular fricative.

European French	*Canadian French*	
Closed syllable		
[vit]	[vɪt]	'quick'
[libʁ]	[lɪb]	'free'
[ekut]	[ekʊt]	'listen'
[pus]	[pʊs]	'thumb'
Open syllable		
[vi]	[vi]	'life'
[li]	[li]	'bed'
[vu]	[vu]	'you'
[lu]	[lu]	'wolf'

Whereas Canadian French has the lax vowels [ɪ] and [ʊ] in closed final syllables, European French has kept the tense vowels [i] and [u]. Both dialects of French retain [i] and [u] in open syllables. This suggests that Canadian French has developed the rule in Figure 7.5.

$$\underset{\begin{bmatrix}\text{+high}\\ \text{–long}\end{bmatrix}}{\text{V}} \rightarrow \text{[–tense]} \;/\; \_\_\_\; \text{C (C) \#}$$

Figure 7.5 Vowel laxing rule in Canadian French

Although this rule did introduce an allophone not present in European French, it did not create any new phonemes since there was no contrast between lax vowels and their tense counterparts in Canadian French.

Splits

Sometimes sound change can lead to changes in a language's phonological system by adding, eliminating, or rearranging phonemes. Such **phonological change** can involve **splits**, **mergers**, or **shifts**.

In a phonological split, allophones of the same phoneme come to contrast with each other due to the loss of the conditioning environment, with the result that one or more new phonemes are created. The English phoneme /ŋ/ was the result of a phonological split (see Table 7.24).

Table 7.24 Phonological split resulting in /ŋ/

Original phonemic form	/sɪng/
Original phonetic form	[sɪŋg]
Deletion of [g]	[sɪŋg] > [sɪŋ]
New phonemic form	/sɪŋ/

Originally, [ŋ] was simply the allophone of /n/ that appeared before a velar consonant. During Middle English, consonant deletion resulted in the loss of [g] in word-final position after a nasal consonant, leaving [ŋ] as the final sound in words such as *sing*. The loss of the final [g] in words created minimal pairs such as *sin* (/sɪn/) and *sing* (/sɪŋ/), in which there is a contrast between /n/ and /ŋ/. This example represents a typical phonological split. When the conditioning environment of an allophonic variant of a phoneme is lost through sound change, the allophone is no longer predictable and thus itself becomes phonemic. In Figure 7.6, the original phoneme /n/ splits into two phonemes, /n/ and /ŋ/.

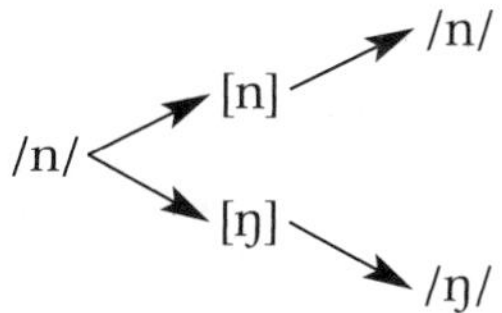

Figure 7.6 A phonological split

Mergers

In a phonological merger, two or more phonemes collapse into a single one, thereby reducing the number of phonemes in the language. The case of auditorily based substitution discussed above has this effect in Cockney English, where all instances of the interdental fricative /θ/ have become /f/ (see Figure 7.7). Consequently, the phonemes /θ/ and /f/ have merged into /f/ and words such as *thin* and *fin* have the same phonological form (/fɪn/). Similarly, /ð/ and /v/ have merged (e.g., /smuv/ for *smooth*).

Figure 7.7 A phonological merger

Shifts

A phonological shift is a change in which a series of phonemes is systematically modified so that their organization with respect to each other is altered. A well-known example of such a change is called the **Great English Vowel Shift**. Beginning in the Middle English period and continuing into the eighteenth century, the language underwent a series of modifications to the long vowels (see Table 7.25).

Table 7.25 The Great English Vowel Shift

Middle English	*Great Vowel Shift*			*Modern English*	
[tiːd]	[iː]	>	[aj]	/tajd/	'tide'
[luːd]	[uː]	>	[aw]	/lawd/	'loud'
[geːs]	[eː]	>	[iː]	/gis/	'geese'
[sɛː]	[ɛː]	>	[iː]	/si/	'sea'
[goːs]	[oː]	>	[uː]	/gus/	'goose'
[brɔːkən]	[ɔː]	>	[oː]	/brokən/	'broken'
[naːmə]	[aː]	>	[eː]	/nem/	'name'

Figure 7.8 illustrates the changes that gradually affected the English long vowels.

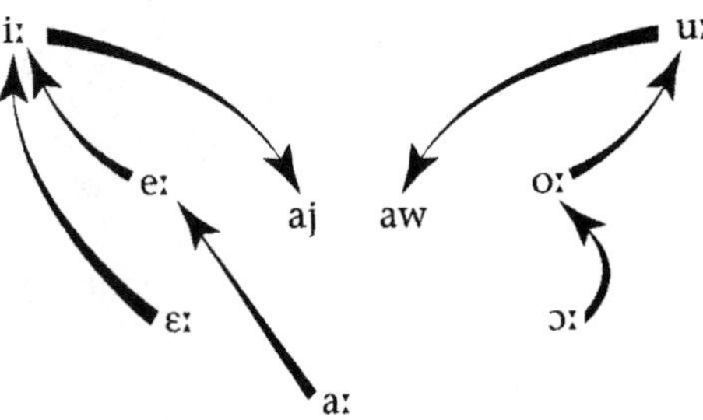

Figure 7.8 Changes brought about by the Great English Vowel Shift

Another well-known shift that occurred much earlier, Grimm's Law, is discussed in Section 6.3.

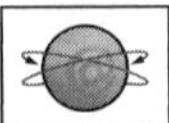

For more information about phonological shifts, go to **bedfordstmartins.com/linguistics/historical** and click on **phonological shifts**.

3 Morphological Change

In this section we discuss morphological changes involving the addition or loss of affixes as well as changes resulting from analogy and reanalysis.

3.1 Addition of Affixes

Borrowing has been a very important source of new affixes in English. During the Middle English period, many French words containing the suffix *-ment* (e.g., *accomplishment, commencement*) made their way into the language. Eventually, *-ment* established itself as a productive suffix in English and was used with bases that were not of French origin (e.g., *acknowledgment, merriment*). The ending *-able,* which converts a verb into an adjective (e.g., *readable, lovable*), followed a similar pattern. Although words with this ending (e.g., *favorable, conceivable*) were initially borrowed into English as whole units, eventually the suffix became productive and was used with new bases.

Not all new affixes are the result of borrowing. Lexical forms can become grammatical forms over time through a process called **grammaticalization**. Grammaticalized forms often undergo dramatic phonological reduction, as well as semantic change in which they can lose much of their original content; for example, the Latin word *habeō* '(I) have, hold, grasp' is the source of the Italian future suffix ō. In the first stage of grammaticalization, *habeō* remained an independent word but underwent semantic reduction and functioned as an auxiliary verb indicating future tense; for example, *amāre habeō* 'I will love'. In the case where two words are frequently adjacent, over time they can become fused together to form a single unit consisting of a base and an affix. **Fusion** refers to this specific type of grammaticalization, where words develop into affixes (either prefixes or suffixes) (see Table 7.26).

Table 7.26 Fusion

word word	>	base + affix (suffixation)
word word	>	affix + base (prefixation)

A number of Modern English suffixes are derived from earlier words by means of fusion (see Table 7.27).

Table 7.27 English suffixes resulting from fusion

Old English word		*Modern English Suffix*
hād	'state, condition, rank'	-hood (childhood)
dōm	'condition, power'	-dom (freedom)
(ge-)līc	'similar, equal, like'	-ly (fatherly)

Fusion is also the source of the future tense suffixes in Italian, which are derived from various forms of the Latin word *habere* 'to have' (see Table 7.28).

Table 7.28 Fusion resulting in a future tense suffix in Italian

Latin	*Italian*	
amāre habeō	amerò	'I will love'
amāre habēmus	ameremo	'we will love'

3.2 Loss of Affixes

Just as affixes can be added to the grammar, they can also be lost. Sometimes affixes simply fall into disuse for no apparent reason. For example, a number of Old English derivational affixes, including *-bǣre* and *-bora,* are no longer used (see Table 7.29).

Table 7.29 Affixes no longer found in English

N + bǣre →	A	(e.g., *lustbǣre* 'pleasant, agreeable' from *lust* 'pleasure' + *bǣre* 'bearing')
N + bora →	N	(e.g., *mundbora* 'protector' from *mund* 'protection' + *bora* 'rules')

It is also very common for affixes to be lost through sound change. For example, Old English had a complex system of affixes marking case and gender. Nouns were divided into three gender classes—masculine, neuter, and feminine. Assignment to a class was not based on sex (natural gender) but on grammatical gender; for example, the word for *stone* (Old English *stān*) and even a word for *woman* (*wīfmann*) were masculine, the word for *sun* (*sunne*) was feminine, and another word for *woman* (*wīf*) was neuter. Each gender class was associated with a different set of case endings (see Table 7.30).

Table 7.30 Old English case affixes

	Masculine		*Neuter*		*Feminine*	
Singular						
	hund	'dog'	dēor	'animal'	gief	'gift'
Nominative	hund		dēor		gief-u	
Accusative	hund		dēor		gief-e	
Genitive	hund-es		dēor-es		gief-e	
Dative	hund-e		dēor-e		gief-e	
Plural						
Nominative	hund-as		dēor		gief-a	
Accusative	hund-as		dēor		gief-a	
Genitive	hund-a		dēor-a		gief-a	
Dative	hund-um		dēor-um		gief-um	

The following Old English sentence contains all four case categories.

2)

Se cniht	geaf	gief-e	þæs hierd-es	sun-e
the youth-NOM	gave	gift-ACC	the shepherd-GEN	son-DAT

'The youth gave a gift to the shepherd's son.'

By the fifteenth century, English case endings had changed radically. Consonant deletion resulted in the loss of the earlier [m] of the dative plural suffix, and through vowel reduction, all the unstressed vowels of the case endings were reduced to the short, lax vowel [ə] (which was later lost through vowel deletion). Consequently, many of the earlier case and gender distinctions were obliterated. (The examples in Table 7.31 also include changes to the stem-internal vowels as the result of various processes, including the Great English Vowel Shift.)

Table 7.31 The loss of case affixes through sound change (in English *hound*)

	Old English	*Middle English (e = [ə])*	*Modern English*
Singular			
Nominative	hund	hund	hound
Accusative	hund	hund	hound
Genitive	hund-es	hund-(e)s	hound's
Dative	hund-e	hund-(e)	hound
Plural			
Nominative	hund-as	hund-(e)s	hounds
Accusative	hund-as	hund-(e)s	hounds
Genitive	hund-a	hund-(e)	hounds'
Dative	hund-um	hund-(e)	hounds

Whereas Old English had five distinct affixes for cases, Middle English had only two suffixes, *-e* and *-es,* which, with the loss of schwa, were ultimately reduced to a single suffix *-s,* still used in Modern English for the plural and the possessive. This represents a typical example of how sound change can result in modification to the morphological component of the grammar.

3.3 From Synthetic to Analytic to Synthetic

Since languages vary greatly in the complexity of their morphology, linguists often make a distinction between **analytic** and **synthetic languages** (see Chapter 8). Whereas some languages like Modern English have very few inflectional affixes, synthetic languages have many (e.g., Latin, Old English).

Even in the absence of borrowing, sound change and fusion ensure that there is an endless transition in the morphology of a language over time. As we have seen, due to the loss of case endings through sound change, English has developed from a synthetic language with many inflectional affixes to a more analytic one with very few, as the above discussion of nouns such as *hound* indicates.

By contrast, fusion ensures the rise of new synthetic forms. Fusion can be observed in some Modern English dialects in forms such as *coulda* (e.g., *I coulda won*), which represents the fusion of *could* and *have.* For many speakers, the *-a* is treated as a suffix that is no longer related to *have,* as evident in spellings such as *could of,* which result from confusion over how to represent the pronunciation of *coulda* in written English. Through fusion, a language with an analytic morphology can become more synthetic over time.

3.4 Analogy

The drastic effects that sound change can have on the morphology of a language are often alleviated through analogy. For example, the plural of Old English *hand* 'hand' was *handa.* Vowel reduction and apocope applying to *handa* would have yielded a Modern English plural form identical to the singular form, namely *hand* (see Table 7.32).

Table 7.32 Sound changes applied to Old English *handa* 'hands'

handa	
handə	vowel reduction
hand	apocope

Obviously, then, the Modern English plural *hands* cannot be the consequence of sound change. Rather, it is the result of earlier analogy with words such as Middle English *hund* 'hound' (see Table 7.31), which did form the plural with the suffix *-s.* This suffix, whose earlier form *-as* was predominant even in Old English, was extended by analogy to all English nouns with a few exceptions (*oxen, men, geese,* etc.). Other plural forms besides *hands* that were created on the basis of analogy include *eyes* (*eyen* in Middle English) and *shoes* (formerly *shooen*).

Continuing analogy along these lines is responsible for the development of the plural form *youse* (from *you*) in some English dialects. Each generation of English-speaking children temporarily extends the analogy still further by producing forms such as *sheeps, gooses,* and *mouses.* To date, however, these particular innovations have not been accepted by adult speakers of Standard English and are eventually abandoned by young language learners.

3.5 Reanalysis

As mentioned in Section 1.2, reanalysis can result in a new morphological structure for a word. It can affect both borrowed words and, particularly in cases where the morphological structure of the word is no longer transparent, native words. Reanalysis can result in new productive patterns (as in the case of *(-)burger*) or it can remain quite isolated, affecting perhaps only one word. Since the type of reanalysis exemplified by *hamburger* is not based on a correct analysis of a word (at least from a historical perspective) and does not usually involve a conscious or detailed study of the word on the part of the speaker, it is often called **folk etymology** (see Table 7.33).

Table 7.33 Folk etymology in English (native words and borrowings)

Modern word	*Source*
belfry	Middle English *berfrey* 'bell tower' (unrelated to *bell*)
bridegroom	Middle English *bridegome* (unrelated to *groom*) (compare Old English *brȳd* 'bride' and *guma* 'man')
muskrat	Algonquian *musquash* (unrelated to either *musk* or *rat*)
woodchuck	Algonquian *otchek* (unrelated to either *wood* or *chuck*)

In the case of *hamburger,* the only evidence of folk etymology is the productive use of *(-)burger* as an independent word and in compounds like *fishburger.* However, in other cases, folk etymology commonly involves changes in pronunciation that reflect the new morphological analysis. For example, our word *earwig* derives from Old English *ēarwicga* [ǣərwidʒɑ], a compound consisting of 'ear' and 'insect'. Taking into consideration sound change alone, the expected Modern English pronunciation of this word would be *earwidge* [irwɪdʒ]. However, the second part of the compound was lost as an independent word by Middle English, so speakers could no longer associate it with the meaning of 'insect'. Subsequently, reanalysis related the second part of the compound to the verb 'wiggle', resulting in Middle English *arwygyll* (literally 'ear' + 'wiggle'). The end result is Modern English *-wig* and not *-widge.*

Although reanalysis of individual words is common, affixes can also be affected, sometimes with new productive morphological rules developing as a result. This is the case of the Modern English adverbial suffix *-ly,* derived from Old English *-lic(e).* In Old English, adjectives could be derived from nouns by adding the suffix *-lic.* Adverbs, in turn, could be derived by adding the suffix *-e* to adjectives (including those derived with *-lic*) (see Table 7.34). At some point, the entire complex suffix *-lic+e* was reanalyzed as an adverbial suffix (rather than as an adjectival suffix *-lic* plus an adverbial suffix *-e*). It was then used by analogy to derive adverbs from adjectives in forms where it was not used before, resulting in Modern English *deeply* and other such words.

Table 7.34 The derivation of Old English adjectives and adverbs

Formation of an adjective from a noun			
$[\text{dæg}]_N$	+ lic →	$[\text{dæglic}]_A$	'daily' (e.g., as in 'daily schedule')
Formation of an adverb from an adjective			
$[\text{dēop}]_A$	+ e →	$[\text{dēope}]_{Adv}$	'deeply'
Formation of an adverb from a derived adjective with -lic			
$[\text{dæg+lic}]_A$	+ e →	$[\text{dæglice}]_{Adv}$	'daily' (e.g., as in 'she ran daily')

4 Syntactic Change

Like other components of the grammar, syntax is also subject to change over time. Syntactic changes can involve modifications to phrase structure (such as word order) and to transformations, as the following examples illustrate.

4.1 Word Order

All languages make a distinction between the subject and the direct object. This contrast is typically represented through case marking or word order. Since Old English had an extensive system of case marking, it is not surprising that its word order was somewhat more variable than that of Modern English. In unembedded clauses, Old English placed the verb in second position (much like Modern German). Thus we find subject-verb-object order in simple transitive sentences such as the following.

3)

S	V	O	
Hē	geseah	þone	mann
'He	saw	the	man.'

When the clause began with an element such as *þa* 'then' or *ne* 'not', the verb preceded the subject, as in the following example.

4)

	V	S		O	
þa	sende	sē	cyning	þone	disc
then	sent	the	king	the	dish

'Then the king sent the dish.'

Although this word order is still found in Modern English, its use is very limited and subject to special restrictions, unlike the situation in Old English.

5)

	V	S			O
Rarely	has	he	ever	deceived	me.

When the direct object was a pronoun, the subject-object-verb order was typical.

6)

S	O	V
Hēo	hine	lǣrde
She	him	advised

'She advised him.'

The subject-object-verb order also prevailed in embedded clauses, even when the direct object was not a pronoun.

7)

	S		O	V	
þa	hē	þone	cyning	sōhte,	hē bēotode
when	he	the	king	visited,	he boasted

'When he visited the king, he boasted.'

After case markings were lost during the Middle English period through sound change, fixed subject-verb-object order became the means of marking grammatical relations. As Table 7.35 shows, a major change in word order took place between 1300 and 1400, with the verb-object order becoming dominant.

Table 7.35 Word order patterns in Middle English

Year	*1000*	*1200*	*1300*	*1400*	*1500*
Direct object before the verb (%)	53	53	40	14	2
Direct object after the verb (%)	47	47	60	86	98

From SOV to SVO

Just as languages can be classified in terms of their morphology, languages can also be grouped on the basis of the relative order of subject (S), object (O), and verb (V) in basic sentences. Almost all languages of the world fall into one of three types: SOV, SVO, or VSO, with the majority of languages being one of the first two types. Just as languages change through time from one morphological type to another, they can also change from one syntactic type to another. A case in point is found in the history of English, which shows the development from SOV to SVO syntax.

Evidence indicates that the earliest form of Germanic from which English descended was an SOV language. One of the earliest recorded Germanic sentences, for example, has this word order. The sentence in *8* was inscribed on a golden horn (now called the Golden Horn of Gallehus) about 1600 years ago.

8)

Horn of Gallehus

S		O	V
ek HlewagastiR	HoltijaR	horna	tawido
I Hlewagastir	of Holt	horn	made

'I, Hlewagastir of Holt, made the horn.'

Another type of evidence for an earlier SOV order is found in morphological fusion (see Section 3.1). Since fusion depends on frequently occurring syntactic patterns, it can sometimes serve as an indicator of earlier syntax. The OV compound, very common in Old English (as well as in Modern English), likely reflects an earlier stage of OV word order (see Table 7.36).

Table 7.36 Old English compounds with OV structure

manslæht	'man' + 'strike'	'manslaughter, murder'
æppelbǣre	'apple' + 'bear'	'apple-bearing'

If the earliest Germanic was SOV and Modern English is firmly SVO, then Old English represents a transitional syntactic type. In developing from SOV syntax to SVO syntax, languages seem to follow similar pathways. For example, Modern German, which developed from the same Germanic SOV source as English, shares two of Old English's distinguishing characteristics. First, the verb is typically placed in the second position of the sentence in main clauses, preceded by the subject or some other element (such as an adverb). Secondly, the SOV order is employed for embedded clauses.

9)

Modern German word order:

a. Verb in second position in unembedded clauses
(Compare the Old English sentence in *4*.)

	V	S	O	
Gestern	hatte	ich	keine	Zeit
yesterday	had	I	no	time

'I had no time yesterday.'

b. SOV in embedded clauses
(Compare the Old English sentence in *7*.)

	S	O	V
Als	er	den Mann	sah . . .
when	he	the man	saw

'When he saw the man . . .'

The change from SOV to SVO is not restricted to English and other Germanic languages. The same change is evident, for example, in completely unrelated languages such as those of the Bantu family of Africa. Since linguists are still not sure why languages change from one syntactic type to another, the causes of such change will undoubtedly remain an important area of investigation, especially since the relative order of verb and object (OV versus VO) has been closely linked with other word-order patterns (see Chapter 8).

4.2 Inversion in the History of English

In Old and Middle English, the Move operation called Inversion (see Chapter 5) involved in the formation of *yes-no* questions could apply to all verbs, not just auxiliaries, yielding forms that would be unacceptable in Modern English.

10)

Speak they the truth?

During the sixteenth and seventeenth centuries, the Inversion rule was changed to apply solely to auxiliary verbs.

11)

Inversion (old form)
The V moves in front of the subject:
They speak → Speak they?
They can speak → Can they speak?

Inversion (new form)
The Aux moves in front of the subject:
They speak → *Speak they?
They can speak → Can they speak?

With this change, structures such as *Speak they the truth?* were no longer possible. The corresponding question came to be formed with the auxiliary *do* as in *Do they speak the truth?*

5 Lexical and Semantic Change

Another obvious type of language change involves modifications to the lexicon. Since we have already dealt with some changes relating to derivational and inflectional morphology in Section 3, the main focus here will be on lexical change involving entire words. Simply stated, there are two possible types of lexical change: addition and loss. The addition or loss of words often reflects cultural changes that introduce novel objects and notions, and that eliminate outmoded ones.

5.1 Addition of Lexical Items

Addition is frequently the result of technological innovations or contact with other cultures. Such developments result in **lexical gaps** that can be filled by adding new words to the lexicon. New words are added either through the word-formation processes available to the language or through borrowing.

Word Formation

The most important word-formation processes are compounding and derivation, although other types, including conversion, blends, backformation, clipping, and acronyms (see Chapter 4), can play a significant role.

Compounding and derivation have always been available to English speakers for the creation of new words. In fact, much of the compounding and derivation in Old English seems very familiar (see Table 7.37). Just as speakers of Modern English can use compounding and derivational rules to create new words (e.g., the N + N compound *airhead*), so could Old English speakers create new words such as the poetic N + N compound *hwælweg,* literally 'whale' + 'path' to mean 'sea'.

Table 7.37 Compounding and derivation in Old English

Noun compounds			
N + N		sunbēam	'sunbeam'
A + N		middelniht	'midnight'
Adjective compounds			
N + A		blōdrēad	'bloodred'
A + A		dēadboren	'stillborn'
Derived nouns			
$[\text{bæc}]_V$ + ere	→	bæcere	'baker'
$[\text{frēond}]_N$ + scipe	→	frēondscipe	'friendship'
Derived adjectives			
$[\text{wundor}]_N$ + full	→	wundorfull	'wonderful'
$[\text{cild}]_N$ + isc	→	cildisc	'childish'

Note however that even though many Old English compounding and derivational patterns have been maintained in Modern English, words that were acceptable in Old English are not necessarily still in use in Modern English, even though many of them are quite understandable (see Table 7.38).

Table 7.38 Old English compound and derived forms that are no longer used

Noun compounds			
N + N	bōccræft ('book' + 'craft')		'literature' (compare *witchcraft*)
A + N	dimhūs ('dim' + 'house')		'prison'
Adjective compounds			
N + A	ælfscīene ('elf' + 'beautiful')		'beautiful as a fairy'
A + A	eallgōd ('all' + 'good')		'perfectly good'
Derived nouns			
$[\text{sēam}]_V$ + ere	→	sēamere	'tailor' (compare *seamster, seamstress*)
$[\text{man}]_N$ + scipe	→	manscipe	'humanity' (compare *friendship*)
Derived adjectives			
$[\text{word}]_N$ + full	→	wordfull	'wordy' (compare *wonderful*)
$[\text{heofon}]_N$ + isc	→	heofonisc	'heavenly' (compare *childish*)

However, not all word-formation processes available to Modern English speakers were found in Old English. For example, conversion (as in Modern English $[\text{summer}]_N$ → $[\text{summer}]_V$) was not possible in Old English. In fact, conversion is typically not available to (synthetic) inflectional languages such as Old English since change in a word category in such languages is usually indicated morphologically, and conversion, by definition, does not involve the use of affixes.

Borrowing

As discussed in Section 1.2, language contact over time can result in an important source of new words: borrowing. Depending on the cultural relationship holding between languages, three types of influence of one language on the other are traditionally identified: **substratum**, **adstratum**, and **superstratum influence**.

Substratum influence is the effect of a politically or culturally nondominant language on a dominant language in the area. American English, Canadian English, and Canadian French, for instance, have borrowed vocabulary items from Native American languages (see examples in Section 1.2). From a much earlier period in the history of English, the influence of a Celtic substratum is also evident, particularly in place names such as *Thames, London,* and *Dover.* Substratum influence does not usually have a major impact on the lexicon of the borrowing language. Borrowed words are usually restricted to place names and unfamiliar items or concepts. This situation reflects the fact that it is usually the speakers of the substratum language who inhabited the area first.

Superstratum influence is the effect of a politically or culturally dominant language on another language or languages in the area. For example, the Athapaskan language Gwich'in (Loucheux, spoken in Alaska and Canada's Northwest Territories) has borrowed a number of governmental terms and expressions from English, including *bureaucratic, constituents, program, business, development,* and *political.*

In the case of English, Norman French had a superstratum influence. The major impact of French on the vocabulary of English is related to a historical event—the conquest of England by French-speaking Normans in 1066. As the conquerors and their descendants gradually learned English over the next decades, they retained French terms for political, judicial, and cultural notions (see Table 7.39). These words were in turn borrowed by native English speakers who, in trying to gain a place in the upper middle class, were eager to imitate the speech of their social superiors. Not surprisingly, borrowing was especially heavy in the vocabulary areas pertaining to officialdom: government, the judiciary, and religion. Other areas of heavy borrowing include science, culture, and warfare.

Table 7.39 Some French loan words in English

Government	tax, revenue, government, royal, state, parliament, authority, prince, duke, slave, peasant
Religion	prayer, sermon, religion, chaplain, friar
Judiciary	judge, defendant, jury, evidence, jail, verdict, crime
Science	medicine, physician
Culture	art, sculpture, fashion, satin, fur, ruby
Warfare	army, navy, battle, soldier, enemy, captain

In some cases, French loan words were used in conjunction with native English words to convey distinctions of various sorts. For a minor crime, for example, the

English word *theft* was employed, but for a more serious breach of the law, the French word *larceny* was used. The English also kept their own words for domesticated animals, but adopted the French words for the meat from those creatures (see Table 7.40).

Table 7.40 French loan words used in conjunction with native English words

English origin	*French origin*
cow	beef
calf	veal
sheep	mutton
pig	pork

Adstratum influence refers to the situation in which two languages are in contact and neither one is clearly politically or culturally dominant. In a city such as Montreal, with its large number of bilingual speakers, English and French inevitably influence each other (see Table 7.41).

Table 7.41 French influence on Montreal English

Montreal English	*American English*
subvention	'subsidy'
metro	'subway'
autoroute	'highway'

Earlier in the history of English, when the Scandinavians settled part of England beginning in A.D. 800, there was substantial contact between the speakers of English and those of Scandinavian, resulting in an adstratum relationship. As evident in the examples in Tables 7.41 and 7.42, adstratum contact usually results in the borrowing of common, everyday words. In fact, without consulting a dictionary, most English speakers could not distinguish between borrowings from Scandinavian and native English words.

Table 7.42 Some loan words from Scandinavian

anger, cake, call, egg, fellow, gear, get, hit, husband, low, lump, raise, root, score, seat, skill, skin, take, their, they, thrust, ugly, window, wing

Borrowed words from many other languages attest to various types of cultural contact and serve often to fill the lexical gaps such contact inevitably brings (see Table 7.43).

Although borrowing has been a very rich source of new words in English, it is noteworthy that loan words are least common among the most frequently used vocabulary items. This reflects a general tendency for highly frequent words to be relatively resistant to loss or substitution (see Table 7.44).

Table 7.43 Some lexical borrowings into English

Italian	motto, artichoke, balcony, casino, mafia, malaria
Spanish	comrade, tornado, cannibal, mosquito, banana, guitar, vigilante, marijuana
German	poodle, kindergarten, seminar, noodle, pretzel
Dutch	sloop, cole slaw, smuggle, gin, cookie, boom
Slavic languages	czar, tundra, polka, intelligentsia, robot
Native American languages	toboggan, opossum, wigwam, chipmunk, Massachusetts, Missouri
Hindi	thug, punch (drink), shampoo, chintz

Table 7.44 Origin of the 5,000 most frequent words in English

Degree of frequency	*Source language (%)*			
	English	*French*	*Latin*	*Other*
First 1,000	83	11	2	4
Second 1,000	34	46	11	9
Third 1,000	29	46	14	11
Fourth 1,000	27	45	17	11
Fifth 1,000	27	47	17	9

5.2 Loss of Lexical Items

Just as words can be added to the lexicon, they can also be lost. Changes in society play an important role in the loss of words, since words are often lost because the object or notion they refer to has become obsolete (see Table 7.45).

Table 7.45 Some Old English words lost through cultural change

dolgbōt	'compensation for wounding'
þeox	'hunting spear'
eafor	'tenant obligation to the king to convey goods'
flȳtme	'a blood-letting instrument'

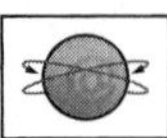

For information on semantic change and how linguistic change spreads, go to **bedfordstmartins.com/linguistics/historical** and click on **semantic change**.

6 Language Reconstruction

When we compare the vocabulary items of various languages, we cannot help but notice the strong resemblance certain words bear to each other. By systematically comparing languages, we can establish whether two or more languages descended from a common parent and are therefore **genetically related** (see Chapter 8). The

comparative method refers to the procedure of reconstructing earlier forms on the basis of a comparison of later forms. By means of such **comparative reconstruction**, we can reconstruct properties of the parent language with a great degree of certainty.

6.1 Comparative Reconstruction

The most reliable sign of family relationships is the existence of **systematic phonetic correspondences** in the vocabulary items of different languages. Many such correspondences can be found in the sample of vocabulary items in Table 7.46 from English, Dutch, German, Danish, and Swedish, all of which are members of the Germanic family of languages.

Table 7.46 Some Germanic cognates

English	*Dutch*	*German*	*Danish*	*Swedish*
man	man	Mann	mand	man
hand	hand	Hand	hånd	hand
foot	voet	Fuß (ß=[s])	fod	fot
bring	brengen	bringen	bringe	bringa
summer	zomer	Sommer	sommer	sommar

Since the relationship between the phonological form of a word and its meaning is mostly arbitrary, the existence of systematic phonetic correspondences in the forms of two or more languages must point toward a common source. Conversely, where languages are not related, their vocabulary items fail to show systematic similarities. This can be seen by comparing words from Turkish, which is not related to the Germanic languages, with their Germanic counterparts (see Tables 7.46 and 7.47).

Table 7.47 Some words in Turkish, a non-Germanic language (phonemic transcription)

adam	'man'
el	'hand'
ajak	'foot'
getiɾmek	'bring'
jaz	'summer'

Words that have descended from a common source (as shown by systematic phonetic correspondences and, usually, semantic similarities) are called **cognates**. Cognates are not always as obvious as the Germanic examples in Table 7.46. Where languages from the same family are only distantly related, the systematic correspondences may be considerably less striking. This is exemplified in the data in Table 7.48 from English, Russian, and Hindi, all of which are distantly related to each other. Forms from the unrelated Turkish are included to emphasize the similarities among the first three languages.

Table 7.48 Some distantly related cognates compared to nonrelated Turkish

Note: [y] is a high front rounded vowel

English	*Russian*	*Hindi*	*Turkish (phonemic transcription)*
two	dva	dō	iki
three	tri	tīn	ytʃ
brother	brat	bhāī	kaɾdeʃ
nose	nos	nahī̃	buɾun

Once the existence of a relationship between two or more languages has been established, an attempt can be made to reconstruct the common source. This reconstructed language, or **protolanguage**, is made up of **protoforms**, which are written with a preceding * (e.g., **hand*) to indicate their hypothetical character as reconstructions of earlier forms that have not been recorded or are not directly observable.

6.2 Techniques of Reconstruction

Reconstruction can be undertaken with some confidence because (as discussed in the previous section) the processes underlying language change are systematic. Once the processes are uncovered by linguists, they can be reversed, allowing us to infer earlier forms of the language. Although it is possible to reconstruct all components of a protolanguage (its phonology, morphology, syntax, lexicon, and semantics), we will focus in the following on phonological reconstruction, the area in which linguists have made the most progress.

Reconstruction Strategies

Reconstruction of a protoform makes use of two general strategies. The most important one is the **phonetic plausibility strategy**, which requires that any changes posited to account for differences between the protoforms and later forms must be phonetically plausible. Secondarily, the **majority rules strategy** stipulates that if no phonetically plausible change can account for the observed differences, then the segment found in the majority of cognates should be assumed. It is important to note that the first strategy always takes precedence over the second; the second strategy is a last resort.

Consider the cognates in Table 7.49 (somewhat simplified) from members of the Romance family.

Table 7.49 Romance cognates

French	*Italian*	*Rumanian*	*Spanish*	
[si]	[si]	[ʃi]	[si]	'yes'; 'and' (Rum.)

The data exemplify a correspondence between [s] and [ʃ] before the vowel [i]. To account for this, we could assume either that Rumanian underwent a change that converted [s] to [ʃ] before [i] or that the other three languages underwent a change converting [ʃ] to [s] before [i], as shown in Figure 7.9.

Hypothesis A	
Protoform	*si
Sound change (Rumanian only)	*s > ʃ / ___ i
Hypothesis B	
Protoform	*ʃi
Sound change (French, Italian, and Spanish)	*ʃ > s / ___ i

Figure 7.9 Romance cognates

Both reconstruction strategies favor Hypothesis A. Most importantly, the phonetic change needed to account for the Rumanian pronunciation involves palatalization before [i]. Since palatalization in this context is a very common phenomenon in human language, it is reasonable to assume that it occurred in Rumanian. It would be much more difficult to argue that the protolanguage contained [ʃ] before [i] and that three languages underwent the change posited by Hypothesis B since depalatalization before [i] would be an unusual phonetic process. (The reconstructed *s posited in Hypothesis A is also compatible with the majority rules strategy since three of the four languages in the data have [s] before [i].)

Reconstruction and the Catalog of Sound Changes

Although there are factors that can confound our attempt to determine the relative plausibility of various sound changes, the changes listed in the catalog in Table 7.3 can generally be considered highly plausible. Table 7.50 lists some plausible versus less plausible or even implausible changes based on that catalog.

Table 7.50 Different rules in terms of their plausibility based on the catalog

Rule	*Name of sound change in catalog*
High probability	
t > tʃ / __ i	palatalization/affrication
n > m / __ b	assimilation (place of articulation)
t > d / V __ V	voicing
k > Ø / V __ st	consonant deletion
Low probability	
tʃ > t / __ i	(does not correspond to any listed change)
m > n / __ b	(does not correspond to any listed change)
d > t / V __ V	(does not correspond to any listed change)
Ø > k / V __ st	(does not correspond to any listed change)

Reconstructing Proto-Romance

Consider now the slightly more complex example in Table 7.51 involving data from several languages of the Romance family. Our goal here is to reconstruct the protoforms for these words in Proto-Romance, which stands very close to Latin, the parent language of the Modern Romance languages. Classical Latin was the literary

Table 7.51 Some Romance cognates

Note: Orthographic *c* represents [k] in all the above examples. Rumanian ă and î represent the central vowels [ə] and [ɨ], respectively. [β] is a voiced bilabial fricative and [ɣ] is a voiced velar fricative. Some details of vowel quality have been ignored.

Spanish	*Sardinian*	*French*	*Portuguese*	*Rumanian*	*Original meaning*
riba [β]	ripa	rive [ʁiv]	riba	rîpă	'embankment'
amiga [ɣ]	amica	amie [ami]	amiga	—	'female friend'
copa	cuppa	coupe [kup]	copa	cupă	'cup, goblet'
gota	gutta	goutte [gut]	gota	gută	'drop'

language of ancient Rome, whereas Proto-Romance represents an attempt to reconstruct the spoken language spread throughout Europe that was the source of the various Romance languages.

Let us first consider the reconstruction of the Proto-Romance form for 'embankment'. Since the first two segments are the same in almost all the cognate languages, we can reconstruct Proto-Romance **r* and **i* on the basis of the majority rules strategy. In the case of the second consonant, however, there are differences between the cognates (see Table 7.52).

Table 7.52 Systematic correspondences in the cognates for 'embankment'

Spanish	*Sardinian*	*French*	*Portuguese*	*Rumanian*
-β-	-p-	-v	-b-	-p-

It is most important that we first think in terms of phonetic plausibility. In the absence of evidence to the contrary, we will assume that one of the segments found in the cognates ([p], [b], [v], or [β]) should be reconstructed for Proto-Romance. Logically possible changes ranked with respect to their phonetic plausibility are found in Table 7.53.

Table 7.53 Changes based on phonetic plausibility

Change in V_V	*Name of change based on catalog*	*Phonetic plausibility*
p > b	voicing	high
p > v	voicing (p > b) and frication (b > v)	high
p > β	voicing (p > b) and frication (b > β)	high
b > p	—	low
β > p	—	low
v > p	—	low

In terms of plausibility, the only possible reconstruction for Proto-Romance is **p*. Proto-Romance **p* underwent no change in Sardinian and Rumanian, but in Portuguese it underwent intervocalic voicing, and in Spanish it underwent both voicing and frication (that is, weakening) (see Table 7.54). (We assume that voicing preceded frication since Portuguese shows voicing but no frication.) If we assume that the final vowel of the protoform was still present in French when the consonant changes took place, we can conclude that voicing and frication occurred in this language as well. (In its written form, *rive* retains a sign of the earlier reduced vowel [ə].) These changes are phonetically plausible and thus expected.

Table 7.54 Summary of the changes affecting Proto-Romance **p*

*p > p /V__V	no change in Sardinian or Rumanian
*p > b /V__V	voicing in Portuguese
*p > b > β /V__V	voicing and frication in Spanish
*p > b > v /V__V	voicing and frication in French

Turning now to the final vowel, we note that three languages have full vowels, Rumanian has [ə], and French has no vowel (see Table 7.55). Since vowel reduction and apocope are identified as phonetically plausible changes in the catalog, it is appropriate to posit a full vowel for the protolanguage. Furthermore, since the three languages with a full vowel all have [ɑ], we can posit this vowel on the basis of the majority rules strategy. Accordingly, the reconstructed protoform is **ripa.*

Table 7.55 Summary of the changes affecting Proto-Romance **a*

Language	*Change (word final)*	*Name of change(s)*
Rumanian	*ɑ > ə	vowel reduction
French	*ɑ > ə > Ø	vowel reduction and deletion

We can now outline the evolution of this word in French, which has the most complicated development of the six languages (see Table 7.56).

Table 7.56 Evolution of French *rive* from **ripa*

Change	**ripa*	*Name of change*
p > b / V__ V	ribɑ	voicing
b > v / V __ V	rivɑ	frication
ɑ > ə / __ #	rivə	vowel reduction
ə > Ø / __ #	riv	apocope

In the case of the cognates for 'female friend' (the second row of Table 7.51), the first three segments are the same in all the languages in the data. According to the majority rules strategy, we can reconstruct the first three segments as **ami-*. In the reconstruction of the second consonant, however, we must appeal to our strategy of phonetic plausibility (see Table 7.57). Once again, since intervocalic voicing, frication, and deletion are phonetically plausible changes, it is most appropriate to posit **k* for the protoform (see Table 7.58).

Table 7.57 Systematic correspondences in the second consonant of the cognates for 'female friend'

Spanish	*Sardinian*	*French*	*Portuguese*	*Rumanian*
-ɣ-	-k-	-Ø	-g-	—

Table 7.58 Summary of the changes affecting Proto-Romance **k*

Language	*Change (in V_V)*	*Name of change(s)*
Portuguese	*k > g	voicing
Spanish	*k > g > ɣ	voicing and frication
French	*k > g > ɣ > Ø	voicing, frication, and deletion

In the case of the final vowel, we have the same situation we had in the previous form. The full vowel is found in Spanish, Sardinian, and Portuguese, but there is no vowel in French. We can therefore assume the full vowel **a* for the protoform, with subsequent vowel reduction and apocope in French. Consequently, we arrive at the protoform **amika*.

Finally, applying the same procedure to the cognates in the final two rows of Table 7.51 yields the protoforms **kuppa* 'cup' and **gutta* 'drop'. All the languages in the data retain the initial consonant of both protoforms. The vowel **u* is reconstructed on the basis of the majority rules strategy, since we have no phonetic grounds for choosing either [u] or [o] as the older vowel. The systematic correspondences involving the intervocalic consonants are given in Table 7.59.

Table 7.59 Systematic correspondences of the medial consonants of **kuppa* and **gutta*

Spanish	*Sardinian*	*French*	*Portuguese*	*Rumanian*
-p-	-pp-	-p	-p-	-p-
-t-	-tt-	-t	-t-	-t-

Regardless of whether we are dealing with original **pp* or **tt,* the same pattern is evident in the case of both geminate types. There is a geminate stop consonant in Sardinian and a single consonant in Spanish, French, Portuguese, and Rumanian. Since degemination is an expected sound change (see the catalog in Table 7.3), we assume that the protoforms contained geminate consonants that underwent degemination except in Sardinian. This is an example of a case where the phonetic plausibility strategy overrules the majority rules strategy (since four of the five languages have [p]/[t], whereas only one language has [pp]/[tt]). As far as the final vowels are concerned, the same pattern found in the previous examples is once again evident. Proto-Romance **a* was retained in Spanish, Sardinian, and Portuguese, reduced to [ə] in Rumanian, and deleted in French (see Table 7.55).

Of the languages exemplified here, Sardinian is considered the most conservative since it has retained more of the earlier consonants and vowels. (In fact, the Sardinian words in the examples happen to be identical with the protoforms, but this degree of resemblance would not be maintained in a broader range of data.) In the case of the other Romance languages and changes we have discussed, the most to least conservative are: Portuguese (degemination and voicing) and Rumanian (degemination and vowel reduction); Spanish (degemination, voicing, and frication); and French (degemination, voicing, frication, consonant deletion, vowel reduction, and apocope).

Although there is no reason to expect Proto-Romance to be identical with Classical Latin, close similarity is expected. Accordingly, the fact that our reconstructions are so close to the Latin words gives us confidence in our methods of reconstruction (see Table 7.60).

Table 7.60 Comparison of Latin and Proto-Romance forms

Latin	*Proto-Romance form*
rīpa	*ripɑ
amīca (c = [k])	*ɑmikɑ
cuppa	*kuppɑ
gutta	*guttɑ

Notice that it is sometimes not possible to reconstruct all the characteristics of the protolanguage. For example, on the basis of our data we were not able to reconstruct vowel length (Latin had a distinction between long and short vowels) since there was no evidence of this characteristic in the cognate forms.

It is also worth noting that we are not always so fortunate as to have written records of a language we expect to be very close to our reconstructed language. In the case of the Germanic languages, for example, there is no ancient written language equivalent to Latin. We must rely completely on our reconstruction of Proto-Germanic to determine the properties of the language from which the modern-day Germanic languages descended. Furthermore, for many languages of the world we have no written historical records at all and for other languages, such as the Native American languages of North America, it is only very recently that we have written records.

In summary, when the forms of two or more languages appear to be related, we can, through a consideration of systematic phonetic correspondences among cognates, reconstruct the common form from which all the forms can be derived by means of phonetically plausible sound changes. Genetically related lexical forms of different languages are called cognates, while the reconstructed forms are protoforms and a reconstructed language, a protolanguage.

Sometimes, reconstruction is done without reference to comparative data. For information on internal reconstruction, go to **bedfordstmartins.com/linguistics/historical** and click on **internal reconstruction**.

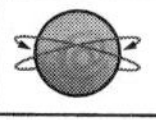

6.3 The Discovery of Indo-European

The late eighteenth-century discovery that Sanskrit (an ancient language of India) was related to Latin, Greek, Germanic, and Celtic revolutionized European linguistic studies.

This discovery led to several decades of intensive historical-comparative work and to important advances in historical linguistics during the nineteenth century. By studying phonetic correspondences from an ever-increasing number of languages, linguists eventually ascertained that most of the languages of Europe, Persia (Iran), and the northern part of India belong to a single family, now called Indo-European. By applying the techniques of the comparative method, they began reconstructing the grammar of the protolanguage from which these languages evolved, **Proto-Indo-European (PIE)**.

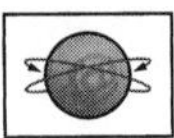

For details of some of the early linguists and their discoveries about Indo-European, go to **bedfordstmartins.com/linguistics/historical** and click on **early linguists**.

In 1822 Jakob Grimm became the first person to explain the relationships among cognates in various Indo-European languages in terms of a **sound shift**, the systematic modification of a series of phonemes. Some of the correspondences on which he based his work are given in Table 7.61.

Table 7.61 Some Indo-European phonetic correspondences

Greek	*Latin*	*English*
patḗr	pater	father
treîs	trēs	three
hekatón	centum [k]	hundred

The crucial observation is that where English has [f], [θ], and [h] (here, in word-initial position), Greek and Latin have [p], [t], and [k]. Grimm tabulated a series of consonant shifts for Proto-Germanic that differentiated it from other Indo-European languages. **Grimm's Law** is the name given to the consonant shifts that took place between Proto-Indo-European and Proto-Germanic (see Table 7.62).

Table 7.62 The sound shifts underlying Grimm's Law

Proto-Indo-European	p	t	k	b	d	g	bh	dh	gh
Germanic	f	θ	x	p	t	k	b	d	g

Note: [x] undergoes a subsequent change to [h].

Some additional examples of the relationships captured by these shifts follow in Table 7.63. The Proto-Indo-European consonants either were maintained in Sanskrit, Greek, and Latin or, in some cases, underwent changes different from those found in Germanic.

Although there appeared to be exceptions to Grimm's Law, they turned out to be systematic and could be traced to specific environments. For example, voiceless stops were not subject to Grimm's Law when they were immediately preceded by *s* (see Table 7.64).

A particularly important discovery was made by Karl Verner, who traced a group of exceptions to Grimm's Law to the original accentual pattern of Proto-Indo-European. In a generalization that came to be known as **Verner's Law**, he proposed that a voiceless fricative resulting from Grimm's Law underwent voicing if the original Proto-Indo-European accent did not immediately precede it. Since stress came to be

Table 7.63 Some examples of the consonant shifts underlying Grimm's Law

Shift in Germanic	*Sanskrit*	*Greek*	*Latin*	*English*
p > f	pād-	pod-	ped-	foot
t > θ	tanu-	tanaós	tenuis	thin
k > x	çatam	hekatón	centum	hundred
b > p	—	—	lūbricus	slippery
d > t	daça	déka	decem	ten
g > k	ajras	agrós	ager	acre
bh > b	bhrātā	phrā́tēr	frāter	brother
dh > d	vidhavā	ēítheos	vidua	widow
gh > g	hansas	khē̃n	(h)ānser	goose

Table 7.64 A systematic exception to Grimm's Law

Original s + voiceless stop			
Latin	<u>st</u>āre	English	<u>st</u>and [st] (not [sθ])

fixed on the root syllable in Germanic subsequent to the changes covered by Verner's Law, the original environment was obscured. However, Sanskrit provides very direct evidence for Verner's claim, since Sanskrit was conservative in its maintenance of the original Proto-Indo-European accent. Although the English forms are complicated by other developments, the effects of Verner's Law are apparent in the Gothic examples in Table 7.65. In the Gothic word for *brother,* PIE **t* becomes [θ] according to Grimm's Law, whereas in the word for *father* it becomes [ð] in accordance with both Grimm's Law and Verner's Law.

Table 7.65 Verner's Law

PIE	*Sanskrit*	*Grimm's Law*	*Verner's Law*	*Gothic*	
*t	bhrā́tā	*t > θ	—	[bro:θar]	'brother'
*t	pitā́	*t > θ	θ > ð	[faðar]	'father'

It should also be noted here that borrowing is an important factor that must be taken into consideration when comparative reconstruction is being carried out. For example, English has many words that do not show the effects of Grimm's Law (see Table 7.66).

Table 7.66 English words not showing the effects of Grimm's Law

Expected by Grimm's Law	*Latin*	*English*
p > f	ped-	pedestrian
t > θ	tenuis	tenuous
k > x	canalis	canal

The apparent failure of Grimm's Law here stems from the fact that the English words were borrowed directly from Latin or French many centuries after the sound shifts described by Grimm's Law had taken place. The task of reconstruction can often be complicated by such borrowings.

Subsequent Developments

By the middle of the nineteenth century, the study of language had made great strides, especially in the field of phonetics, which opened the way for the detailed comparison of linguistic forms. One influential hypothesis at that time was that sound laws operated without exception. A group of linguists known as the Neogrammarians adopted this idea and made many important contributions to the fledgling science of linguistics by applying it to new and more complicated data. Although such factors as social pressures were more or less ignored by the Neogrammarians, their hypothesis represented an important and daring advance in the scientific study of language.

The nineteenth century also saw major advances in the classification of languages. A German scholar, August Schleicher, developed a classification for the Indo-European languages in the form of a genealogical tree. This type of genetic classification is discussed in much more detail in the chapter on language classification that follows.

Work in comparative reconstruction is far from finished. In particular, some linguists are now considering the possibility of superfamilies, although the methods of this line of research have been open to criticism. One such proposed family is Nostratic, which includes Indo-European, Afro-Asiatic (e.g., Arabic, Hebrew), Altaic (e.g., Japanese, Korean, Turkic), and Uralic (e.g., Finnish, Hungarian). (See Chapter 8 for further discussion.) Comparative reconstruction is also playing an important role in determining the genetic relationships of the hundreds of North American indigenous languages, a topic that still remains highly controversial.

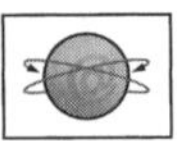

For information about reconstruction and typology as well as language change and naturalness, go to **bedfordstmartins.com/linguistics/historical** and click on **naturalness**.

Summing Up

Historical linguistics studies the nature and causes of language change. The causes of language change find their roots in the physiological and cognitive makeup of human beings. Sound changes usually involve articulatory simplification, as in the case of the most common type, **assimilation**. **Analogy** and **reanalysis** are particularly important factors in morphological change. **Language contact** resulting in **borrowing** is another important source of language change. All components of the grammar, from phonology to semantics, are subject to change over time. Sociological factors can play an important role in determining whether or not a linguistic innovation is ultimately adopted by the linguistic community at large. Since language change is systematic, it is possible, by identifying the changes that a particular language or dialect has undergone, to reconstruct linguistic history and thereby posit the earlier forms from which later forms have evolved. Using sets of **cognates**, **comparative reconstruction** allows us to reconstruct the properties of the parent or **protolanguage** on the basis of **systematic phonetic correspondences**.

Key Terms

General terms and terms concerning the nature of change and its spread

analogy
articulatory simplification
borrowing
historical linguistics
hypercorrection
language contact
reanalysis

General terms concerning sound change

assimilation
consonantal strength
deaffrication
dissimilation
epenthesis
glide strengthening
metathesis
phonetic sound change
phonetically conditioned change
segmental change
sequential change
substitution
weakening

Terms concerning sound change by assimilation

affrication
nasalization
palatalization
place or manner of articulation (assimilation)
umlaut

Terms concerning sound change by weakening

apocope
consonant deletion
consonant weakening
degemination
deletion
frication
rhotacism
syncope
voicing
vowel reduction

Terms concerning phonological change

Great English Vowel Shift
mergers
phonological (sound) change
shifts
splits

Terms concerning morphological, syntactic, and lexical changes

adstratum influence
analytic languages
folk etymology
fusion
grammaticalization
lexical gaps
substratum influence
superstratum influence
synthetic languages

Terms concerning genetic relationships and reconstruction

cognates
comparative method
comparative reconstruction
genetically related (languages)
Grimm's Law
majority rules strategy
phonetic plausibility strategy
protoforms
Proto-Indo-European (PIE)
protolanguage

sound shift
systematic phonetic correspondences
Verner's Law

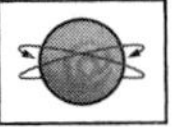

For more information on the sources used in this chapter, go to **bedfordstmartins.com/linguistics/historical** and click on **Sources**.

Recommended Reading

Anttila, Raimo. 1989. *Historical and Comparative Linguistics.* 2nd ed. Amsterdam: John Benjamins.

Blake, N.F. 1996. *A History of the English Language.* Houndmills, Basingstoke, Hampshire: Macmillan.

The Cambridge History of the English Language, 1992–2001. Six volumes. Cambridge, UK: Cambridge University Press.

Campbell, Lyle. 2004. *Historical Linguistics: An Introduction.* 2nd ed. Cambridge, MA: MIT Press.

Hock, Hans Henrich. 1992. *Principles of Historical Linguistics.* 2nd ed. Amsterdam: Mouton de Gruyter.

Hock, Hans Henrich, and Brian D. Joseph. 1996. *Language History, Language Change, and Language Relationship: An Introduction to Historical and Comparative Linguistics.* New York: Mouton de Gruyter.

Hopper, Paul J., and Elizabeth Closs Traugott. 1993. *Grammaticalization.* Cambridge, UK: Cambridge University Press.

Joseph, Brian D., and Richard Janda (eds.). 2003. *The Handbook of Historical Linguistics.* Oxford: Blackwell.

Koerner, E.F., and R.E. Asher, eds. 1995. *Concise History of the Language Sciences: From the Sumerians to the Cognitivists.* New York: Pergamon.

Labov, William. 1994. *Principles of Linguistic Change: Internal Factors.* Oxford: Blackwell.

Lass, Roger. 1997. *Historical Linguistics and Language Change.* Cambridge, UK: Cambridge University Press.

Lehmann, Winfred P. 1992. *Historical Linguistics.* 3rd ed. New York: Routledge.

McMahon, April M.S. 1994. *Understanding Language Change.* Cambridge, UK: Cambridge University Press.

Millward, C.M. 1996. *A Biography of the English Language.* 2nd ed. New York: Holt, Rinehart and Winston.

Smith, Jeremy. 1996. *An Historical Study of English: Function, Form and Change.* New York: Routledge.

Trask, R. L. 1996. *Historical Linguistics.* London: Arnold.

Exercises

1. Identify the following sound changes with reference to the catalog of sound changes provided in Table 7.3. In each pair of examples, focus on the segment(s)

in bold only. The form on the left indicates the original segment(s) before the change, and the form on the right indicates the segment(s) after the change.

a)	Sanskrit	**sn**eha	Pali	**sin**eha	'friendship'
b)	Old English	**hl**āf	English	**l**oaf	
c)	Latin	**i**uvenis [j]	Italian	**gi**ovane [dʒ]	'young'
d)	English	tria**thl**on	dialect	tria**th[ə]l**on	
e)	Latin	vi**du**a [dw]	Spanish	vi**ud**a [wd]	'widow'
f)	Sanskrit	sa**pt**a	Pali	sa**tt**a	'seven'
g)	Latin	tu**r**tu**r**	English	tu**r**t**l**e	
h)		*ve**nr**é	Spanish	ve**ndr**é	'I will come'
i)	Italian	mu**nd**o	Sicilian	mu**nn**u	'world'
j)	Old French	**c**ire [ts]	French	**c**ire [s]	'wax'
k)	Latin	p**ān**-	French	p**ain** [ɛ̃]	'bread'
l)	Latin	**mul**gēre	Italian	**mun**gere	'to milk'
m)	Latin	pa**c**are [k]	Italian	pa**g**are	'to pay'
n)	Old Spanish	ni**d**o	Spanish	ni**d**o [ð]	'nest'
o)	Latin	pe**cc**ātum [kk]	Spanish	pe**c**ado [k]	'sin'
p)		*honō**s**is	Latin	honō**r**is	'honor (GEN SG)'
q)	English	ra**ge**	French	ra**ge** [ʒ]	'rage'
r)	English	co**ff**ee	Chipewyan	[ka**θ**i]	
s)	Latin	mar**e**	Portuguese	mar	'sea'
t)	Latin	vīcīn**i**tās	Spanish	vecindad	'neighborhood'
u)	Gothic	**þ**liuhan [θ]	English	**f**lee	
v)	Old English	(ic) sing**e**	English	(I) sing	
w)	Latin	su**mm**a	Spanish	su**m**a	'sum, gist'
x)	Latin	ōrn**ā**mentum	Old French	orn**e**ment [ə]	'ornament'
y)		*l**ū**si	Old English	l**ȳ**s [yː]	'lice'

2. *i)* Describe the difference in obstruents between the two French dialects in the following data. Assume that the data are in phonetic transcription.
   ii) What sound change would you posit here? Why?
   iii) State the sound change in the form of a rule.

	European French	*Acadian French*	
a)	okyn	otʃyn	'none'
b)	køʁ	tʃør	'heart'
c)	ke	tʃe	'wharf'
d)	kɛ̃ːz	tʃɛ̃ːz	'fifteen'
e)	akyze	atʃyze	'accuse'
f)	ki	tʃi	'who'
g)	kav	kav	'cave'
h)	kɔʁ	kɔr	'body'
i)	kuʁiʁ	kurir	'run'
j)	ɑ̃kɔːʁ	ɑ̃kɔːr	'again'

3. *i)* What sound changes differentiate Guaraní from its parent language, Proto-Tupí-Guaraní, in the following data?
   ii) State these changes in rule form.

	Proto-Tupí-Guaraní	*Guaraní*	
a)	jukɨr	jukɨ	'salt'
b)	moajan	moajã	'push'
c)	puʔam	puʔã	'wet'
d)	meʔeŋ	meʔẽ	'give'
e)	tiŋ	tʃĩ	'white'
f)	potiʔa	potʃiʔa	'chest'
g)	tatatiŋ	tatatʃĩ	'smoke'
h)	kɨb	kɨ	'louse'
i)	men	mẽ	'husband'

4. *i)* Describe the three changes that took place between Proto-Slavic and Bulgarian in the following data. (The symbol ˘ over a vowel indicates that it is short.)
   ii) State these changes as rules and indicate, as far as possible, the order in which they must have applied.
   iii) Apply these rules to the Proto-Slavic word for 'adroit' to show how the Bulgarian form evolved.

	Proto-Slavic	*Bulgarian*	
a)	gladŭka	glatkə	'smooth'
b)	kratŭka	kratkə	'short'
c)	blizŭka	bliskə	'near'
d)	ʒeʒĭka	ʒeʃkə	'scorching'
e)	lovŭka	lofkə	'adroit'
f)	gorĭka	gorkə	'bitter'

5. For each word, list all the sound changes required to derive the later form from the protoform. Where necessary, give the chronology of the sound changes.

a)	*feminam	Old French	femme (final e =[ə])	'woman'
b)	*lumine	Spanish	lumbre	'fire'
c)	*tremulare	Spanish	temblar	'tremble'
d)	*stuppam	Spanish	estopa	'tow'
e)	*populu	Rumanian	plop	'poplar'

6. Taking into consideration the Great English Vowel Shift, give all the changes necessary to derive the Modern English forms from the Old English forms. (*Note:* Assume, simplifying somewhat, that the Old English forms were pronounced as they are written.)

	Old English	*Modern English*
a)	brōde (SG ACC)	brood [brud]
b)	cnotta (c = [k])	knot [nɑt]
c)	wīse	wise [wajz]
d)	hlǣfdige	lady [lejdi]

7. Compare the Old English singular and plural forms:

Singular	*Plural*	
bōc	bēc	'book(s)'
āc	ǣc	'oak(s)'

Although the Old English words have an umlaut plural (as in Old English gōs/gēs 'goose/geese'), the Modern English forms do not. Explain how the change in plural formation could have come about.

8. As evident in the following sentence, Shona, a modern Bantu language, has SVO word order. (*Note:* The morpheme *ano-* marks present tense.)

mwana	anotengesa	miriwo
child	sells	vegetables

'The child sells vegetables.'

By contrast, Shona's morphology reflects a different pattern, as evident in the following examples.

mwana	ano**mu***ona*
child	**him**+*see*

'The child sees him.'

mukadzi	ano**va***batsira*
woman	**them**+*help*

'The woman helps them.'

What do these examples indicate about earlier Shona or possibly Proto-Bantu word order?

9. Look up the following words in a good dictionary. Discuss any semantic changes that have affected the underscored portions since Old English. Do you think speakers of Modern English have reanalyzed any of these forms in terms of folk etymology?

a) wedlock
b) witchcraft
c) steadfast
d) afterward

10. The following line is from *Troilus and Criseyde V* by Geoffrey Chaucer.
His lighte goost ful blisfully is went.
[hɪs liçtə gɔːst fʊl blɪsfʊlli ɪs wɛnt] ([ç] is a voiceless palatal fricative.)
'His light spirit has gone very blissfully.'

i) How has the meaning of the word *ghost* changed since Chaucer's time?
ii) Describe the changes that have taken place in the pronunciation of *light* and *ghost.*

11. Consider the following lyrics from the Middle English song "Sumer is i-cumen in." Compare the Middle English lyrics with the Modern English translation and answer the questions that follow.

Original text	*Transcription*
Sumer is i-cumen in;	[sʊmər ɪs ɪkʊmən ɪn
Lhude sing, cuccu!	luːdə sɪŋg kʊkku
Grōweþ sēd, and blōweþ mēd,	grɔːwəθ seːd and blɔːwəθ meːd
And springþ þe wude nū.	and sprɪŋgθ ðə wʊdə nuː]

Translation
'Summer has come in;

Loudly sing, cuckoo!
Seed grows and meadow blooms
And the wood grows now.'

i) What affix converted the adjective *loud* into an adverb in Middle English?
ii) Why is the vowel in *loud* pronounced differently in Modern English?
iii) What other words in this poem reflect this general shift?
iv) How has the relative ordering of the subject and verb changed since this was written?
v) How has the third person singular present tense suffix changed since Middle English?

12. The following words found in various Cree dialects were borrowed from French as the result of contact between the two groups on the Canadian prairies. (Notice that the French determiner was not treated as a separate morpheme and was carried along with the borrowed word.) Why were these words borrowed?

	Cree	*French*	
a)	labutōn	le bouton	'button'
b)	lībot	les bottes	'boots'
c)	lamilās	la mélasse	'molasses'
d)	lapwīl	la poêle	'frying pan'
e)	litī	le thé	'tea'

13. The following Latin roots are found in words that have been borrowed into English. Since these words were borrowed after Grimm's Law had applied, they do not show its effects. All of these roots, however, do have Germanic cognates that did undergo Grimm's Law. On the basis of your knowledge of this law and the meaning of the borrowing, try to determine the Modern English (Germanic) cognate for each root. Consult a good dictionary if you need help. (*Note:* Focus on the portion of the Latin word in bold only; vowel changes must also be taken into consideration.)

	Latin root	*Related borrowing*	*English cognate*
a)	**ped**is	pedestrian	*foot*
b)	**nep**os	nepotism	________
c)	**pisc**es	piscine	________
d)	**ten**uis	tenuous	________
e)	**corn**u	cornucopia	________
f)	**duo**	dual	________
g)	**ed**ere	edible	________
h)	**gen**us	genocide	________
i)	**ager**	agriculture	________

14. Attempt to reconstruct the Proto-Germanic form for each pair of cognates. Focusing on the vowels, describe the changes that affected the Old English forms. (*Note:* y = [y], œ = [ø], and j = [j].)

	Gothic	*Old English*	
a)	kuni	cyn	'kin'
b)	badi	bed	'bed'

c)	dōmjan	dœ̄man	'to judge'
d)	sōkjan	sœ̄can	'to seek'
e)	bugjan	bycgan	'to buy'
f)	nati	net	'net'

15. Reconstruct the Proto-Romance form for each set of cognates. Give all the changes necessary to derive each of the modern forms from the protoforms. If you are not sure how to proceed, return to Section 6. (*Note:* The Spanish and Rumanian spelling <ie> represents the sequence /je/, and the Rumanian spelling <ia> represents the sequence /ja/.)

	Spanish	*Sardinian*	*Rumanian*	
a)	vida	bita	vită (ă = [ə])	'life'
b)	sí	si	şi (ş = [ʃ])	'yes'; 'and' (Rum.)
c)	riso	rizu	rîs	'laugh'
d)	miel	mele	miere	'honey'
e)	hierro	ferru	fier	'iron'
f)	piedra	pedra	piatră (ă = [ə])	'stone'
g)	hierba	erva	iarbă (ă = [ə])	'grass'
h)	oso	ursu	urs	'bear'
i)	roto	ruttu	rupt	'broken'
j)	lecho	lettu	—	'bed'

eight

The Classification of Languages

Aleksandra Steinbergs

Everything it is possible for us to analyze depends on a clear method which distinguishes the similar from the not similar.
– LINNAEUS, *Genera Plantarum* (1754)

OBJECTIVES

In this chapter, you will learn:

- how different languages can be classified according to similarities in their phonology, morphology, and syntax
- how languages are related to one another genetically
- how languages in the Indo-European family are related
- how language families may be grouped into larger phyla

In the world today there are thousands of different languages, each with its own sound patterns, syntax, and vocabulary. But underlying these differences are similarities of various sorts that allow linguists to arrange languages into groups based on shared features. This chapter describes the methods of classification linguists use, and some of the findings that have resulted from this type of research.

1 Some Preliminaries

We will begin by considering two topics—the problem of distinguishing between a language and a **dialect**, and the chief methods of language classification used in linguistics today.

1.1 Dialect and Language

It is often difficult to determine whether two linguistic communities speak different languages or merely different dialects of the same language. One test that linguists use to decide this involves the criterion of **mutual intelligibility**. Mutually intelligible varieties of the same language can be understood by speakers of each variety. According to this criterion, the English of Milwaukee, the English of Toronto, and the English of London qualify as dialects of the same language. On the other hand, if two speakers cannot understand one another, then linguists normally conclude that they are speaking different languages. The Italian of Florence and the French of Paris are examples of varieties of speech that are not mutually intelligible.

Political, cultural, social, historical, and religious factors frequently interfere when determining linguistic boundaries. (In fact, it is sometimes said that a language is just a dialect with an army and a navy!) For example, Serbs and Croats, with their different histories, cultures, and religions, often claim that they speak different languages. However, even though they use different alphabets, Serbian and Croatian are actually mutually intelligible dialects of the same language, which linguists call Serbo-Croatian. In contrast, we often speak of Chinese as if it were a single language, even though it is actually a number of individual, mutually unintelligible languages (Mandarin, Cantonese, Taiwanese, Wu, and so on), each with a multitude of dialects of its own.

In addition to the problems presented by these nonlinguistic considerations, complications also arise when we try to divide a continuum of mutually intelligible dialects whose two endpoints are not intelligible. Dutch and German, for example, are mutually intelligible around the border area between Germany and Holland; however, the Dutch of Amsterdam and the German of Munich are not. Similarly, Palestinian Arabic and Syrian Arabic are mutually intelligible, but Moroccan Arabic and Saudi Arabian Arabic are not.

The Threat to Human Linguistic Diversity

Taking these considerations into account, how many languages are there in the world today? The best available estimate, from the Ethnologue organization (www.ethnologue.com), places the figure at about 6,800, with the following geographic distribution (see Table 8.1).

Table 8.1 The geographical distribution of the world's living languages

Region	*Number of languages*	*% of the total*
The Americas	1,013	15
Africa	2,058	30
Europe	230	3
Asia	2,197	33
The Pacific	1,311	19
Total	6,809	

Table 8.2 lists the world's twenty most-spoken languages, again using Ethnologue data. (Only native speakers of the languages in question are included in these estimates.)

Table 8.2 The world's twenty most spoken languages (in 2003)

Language	*Estimated number of speakers*
Mandarin	874,000,000
English	341,000,000
Spanish	322,200,000
Bengali (Bangladesh, India)	207,000,000
Hindi	182,000,000
Portuguese	176,000,000
Russian	167,000,000
Japanese	125,000,000
German	100,000,000
Korean	78,000,000
Wu (China)	77,175,000
French	77,000,000
Javanese (Indonesia)	75,500,800
Yue (China)	71,000,000
Telugu (India)	69,660,000
Marathi (India)	68,022,000
Vietnamese	68,000,000
Tamil (India, Sri Lanka)	66,000,000
Turkish	61,000,000
Urdu (India, Pakistan)	60,290,000

These are large numbers, but they are not typical—most languages have fewer than 10,000 speakers, and many are at risk of disappearing altogether.

Ask the average person to name a dead language, and he or she is likely to mention Latin. In fact, Latin did not really die at all. Rather, it evolved over a period of centuries into French, Spanish, Italian, Portuguese, Rumanian, and the other modern-day Romance languages (see Section 3.1).

Contrast this with the situation of Manx, a Celtic language indigenous to the Isle of Man, a small island midway between Ireland and Great Britain. Its last speaker, Ned Madrell, died in 1974. Just one hundred years earlier, 12,000 people had spoken Manx. Now no one does. Manx didn't just change over time; it simply ceased to be spoken.

This sort of language death is increasingly common in the contemporary world, accelerating a process that has been under way for several centuries. Indeed, according to some estimates, 60 percent of the world's languages are currently at risk, with few, if any, children learning them. The situation is grim in many different areas of the world. Of the 300 indigenous languages spoken in the area corresponding to the United States at the time of Columbus, there are now just 175—many of which are on the verge of disappearing. Over half of the languages have fewer than 100 speakers, and only 20 Native American languages in the United States are being transmitted to children. (See Chapter 9 for details.) Ninety percent of Australia's 250 Aboriginal languages are near extinction.

The death of languages is lamentable for a variety of reasons. From a purely linguistic perspective, the loss of linguistic diversity means that we have much less information about how language works and about the different forms that it can take.

For example, when the last speaker of Ubykh (a North Caucasian language spoken in Turkey) died in 1992, linguists lost the opportunity to study a very unusual phonological system—Ubykh had eighty-one consonants and just three vowels. (In contrast, a typical variety of American English has twenty-four consonants and around sixteen vowels and diphthongs—see Chapter 3.)

Just as serious is the loss of cultural knowledge that accompanies language death. A language's vocabulary encodes much of a community's cultural and scientific knowledge, including the distinctions that it makes among the plants and animals in its environment. This knowledge, accumulated over centuries, is not insignificant: many indigenous languages distinguish among thousands of species of plants, fish, and animals based on their appearance, behavior, edibility, and even medicinal properties.

How and why do languages die? In some cases, they die because the people who speak them perish as the result of war or disease. Indeed, according to some estimates, up to 95 percent of the Native population of North America died from diseases brought to their continent by European colonists.

More commonly these days, however, languages die because their speakers gradually use them less and less in favor of a language that appears to offer greater economic or educational opportunities. English, Spanish, and French are obvious examples of international languages that acquire new speakers in this way, but many other languages are dominant on a more local scale: Thai, Bahasa Indonesia, Swahili, and Filipino (among others) are all threats to smaller languages in their respective territories.

The classic pattern of language loss involves three generations: the parents are monolingual, their children become bilingual by adopting a new language, and their children's children grow up monolingual in the new language. They end up unable to speak to their own grandparents.

With more than 6,000 languages in the world today and only about 200 countries, the vast majority of the world's languages do not have the protection of a national government. Nor are smaller language communities well equipped to compete with the larger languages that surround them, tempting their young people to abandon their linguistic heritage.

This ongoing pervasive threat to the world's linguistic diversity is of great concern to linguists, many of whom are actively involved in studying and documenting languages on the verge of extinction. Where feasible, linguists are also seeking ways to improve the prospects for endangered languages by participating in linguistic, social, and educational programs designed to promote and protect the use of indigenous languages.

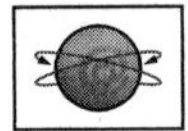

Section 3 of this chapter and our Web site present an overview of a few hundred languages and the families to which they belong (go to **bedfordstmartins.com/linguistics/historical** and click on **families**). First, however, we will turn our attention to some of the methods that are used for classifying languages into a more manageable number of types and groups.

1.2 Types of Classification

Within the field of linguistics, three different approaches to language classification are used.

Genetic classification categorizes languages according to their descent. Languages that developed historically from the same ancestor language are grouped together and are said to be **genetically related**. This ancestor may be attested (that is, texts written in this language have been discovered or preserved, as in the case of Latin), or it may be a reconstructed protolanguage for which no original texts exist (as is the case for Indo-European; see Chapter 7, Section 6.3). Genetic classification is discussed further in Section 3.

Although genetically related languages often share structural characteristics, they do not necessarily bear a close structural resemblance. For example, Latvian and English are genetically related (both are descended from Indo-European), but their morphological structure is quite different. An English sentence like *It has to be figured out* can be expressed in Latvian by the single word *jāizgudro*. Of course, Latvian and English are very distantly related, and languages that are more closely related typically manifest greater similarity.

On the other hand, it is also necessary to recognize that even languages that are totally unrelated may be similar in some respects. For example, English, Thai, and Swahili, which are unrelated to each other, all employ subject-verb-object word order in simple declarative sentences.

1)

Swahili
Maria anapenda Anna.
Maria likes Anna
'Maria likes Anna.'

2)

Thai
roudbuntuk ding roud.
truck push car
'Trucks push cars.'

For this reason, another approach to language classification is useful. Known as **linguistic typology**, it classifies languages according to their structural characteristics, without regard for genetic relationships. Thus, typologists might group together languages with similar sound patterns or, alternatively, those with similar grammatical structures. Typological studies also endeavor to identify **linguistic universals**, that is, structural characteristics that occur in all or most languages. We discuss linguistic typology further in Section 2.

Finally, **areal classification** identifies characteristics shared by languages that are in geographical contact. Languages in contact often borrow words, sounds, morphemes, and even syntactic patterns from one another. As a result, neighboring languages can come to resemble each other, even though they may not be genetically related. Because of space considerations, this chapter will not deal with areal classification specifically; however, borrowing is discussed in Sections 1.2 and 5.1 of Chapter 7.

2 Typological Classification

As just noted, the classification of languages according to their structural characteristics is known as linguistic typology. Typological studies group together languages on the basis of similarities in their syntactic patterns, morphological structure, and/or phonological systems. An important area of research within the study of linguistic typology is the search for linguistic universals. Structural patterns and traits that occur in all languages are called **absolute universals**, while those that simply occur in most languages are known as **universal tendencies**.

Many typological generalizations involve **implicational universals**, which specify that the presence of one trait implies the presence of another (but not vice versa). For instance, languages with fricative phonemes (such as /f/ and /s/) will also have stop phonemes (such as /p/ and /t/), although the reverse is not necessarily true.

Another way to analyze linguistic universals is through **markedness theory**. Within this theory, **marked traits** are considered to be more complex and/or universally rarer than **unmarked** characteristics. In addition, a marked trait is usually found in a particular language only if its unmarked counterpart also occurs. Thus, markedness theory is closely related to the study of implicational universals.

An example may provide some clarification of these terms. Nasal vowel phonemes are more complex than oral vowel phonemes, since they allow the airstream to exit through both the nose and the mouth, rather than just the mouth. Cross-linguistically, we find that all languages have oral vowels, but that only some have nasal vowels. (Moreover, even in languages that have both, there are usually far fewer nasal vowels than oral vowels.) Thus, oral vowels are unmarked—they are both more common and phonologically less complex than nasal vowels, which are marked. We can represent this fact with the help of the following markedness hierarchy, in which the symbol '>' can be read as 'less marked than' or 'is implied by'.

3)

oral vowel > nasal vowel

This, in turn, means that we make the distinction outlined in Table 8.3 between possible and impossible vowel systems in human language.

Table 8.3 Oral and nasal vowels

Oral vowels	*Nasal vowels*	
yes	no	possible
yes	yes	possible
no	yes	**impossible**

The following sections present some of the typological generalizations and universals that have been proposed in the areas of phonology, morphology, and syntax.

2.1 Phonology

In this section, we represent all vowel and consonant systems phonemically. This simplifies their presentation; note, however, that the exact phonetic realization of these systems may vary in the individual languages.

Vowel Systems

Languages are often classified according to the size and pattern of their vowel systems. The most common vowel system has five phonemes—two high vowels, two mid vowels, and one low vowel (see Figure 8.1). The front vowels are unrounded, as is the low vowel, and the back vowels are rounded.

Figure 8.1 The most common vowel system

About half the world's languages, including Basque, Hawaiian, Japanese, Spanish, and Swahili, have such a system.

The majority of the world's other languages have vowel systems with three, four, six, seven, eight, or nine different vowels (disregarding contrasts based on length or nasalization, which can double or triple the number of vowel phonemes). Languages with fewer than three distinctive vowels or more than nine are rare. Some typical vowel systems are presented in Figure 8.2.

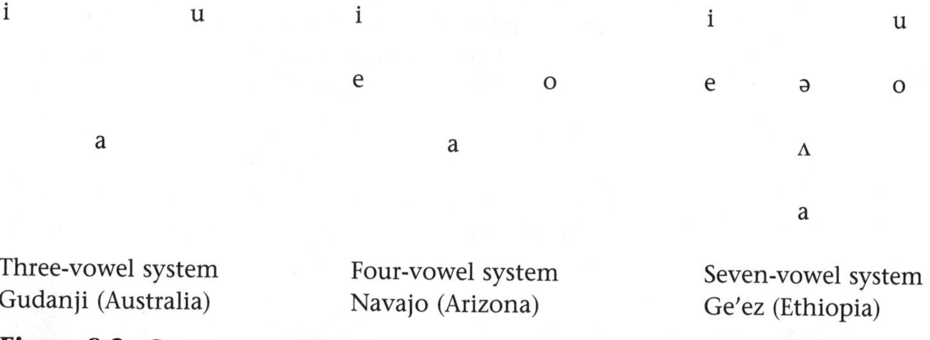

Three-vowel system
Gudanji (Australia)

Four-vowel system
Navajo (Arizona)

Seven-vowel system
Ge'ez (Ethiopia)

Figure 8.2 Common vowel systems

Analysis of many languages has led to the discovery of a number of universal tendencies pertaining to vowel systems. Some of these tendencies are listed here, along with a description of the most commonly occurring vowels.

- The most commonly occurring vowel phoneme is /a/, which is found in almost all the languages of the world. The vowels /i/ and /u/ are almost as common as /a/.
- Front vowel phonemes (/i, e, ɛ, æ/) are generally unrounded, while nonlow back vowel phonemes (/ɔ, o, u/) are generally rounded.
- Low vowels (/æ, a, ɑ/) are generally unrounded.

Although English has an above-average number of vowels, they all conform to the above tendencies. Thus, English has only front unrounded vowels, all the low vowel phonemes are unrounded, and all of the back, nonlow vowels are rounded. The vowel system of American English is represented in Figure 8.3.

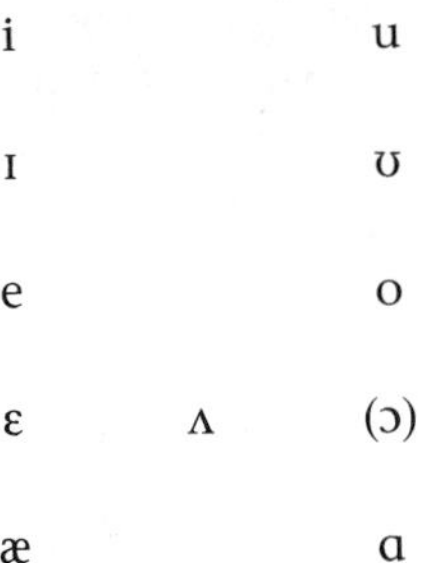

Figure 8.3 The vowel system of American English

The relationship between contrasting vowel types (such as oral versus nasal and long versus short) can also be expressed in terms of implicational universals, since the presence of one vowel phoneme type implies the presence of another (but not vice versa).

- As already noted, if a language has contrastive nasal vowels, then it will also have contrastive oral vowels. For example, French contrasts different nasal vowels—as in *long* /lɔ̃/ 'long' versus *lent* /lã/ 'slow'. And it contrasts oral vowels with nasal vowels, as in *las* /la/ 'weary' versus *lent* /lã/ 'slow'. Predictably, French also contrasts different oral vowels, as in *clos* /klo/ 'shut' versus *clou* /klu/ 'nail'. English shows contrasts among oral vowels but does not contrast nasal vowels with oral vowels. There are no contrasts in English like /bɔt/ 'bought' and */bɔ̃t/.
- If a language has contrasting long vowels, then it will also have contrasting short vowels. For example, Finnish has contrasting long vowels and, predictably, contrasting short vowels (see Table 8.4).

Table 8.4 Finnish vowel contrasts

Long versus long	/viːli/	'junket'	/vaːli/	'election'
Short versus short	/suka/	'bristle'	/suku/	'family'
Short versus long	/tuli/	'fire'	/tuːli/	'wind'

The reverse is not necessarily the case. While English has contrasts based on vowel quality (e.g., *meet* vs. *mate*), it has no long vowel phonemes because length is predictable (see page 90). Its vowels are therefore all considered to be typologically short (see Table 8.5).

Consonant Systems

It is not particularly useful to classify languages according to the number of consonants that they contain, since languages may have as few as eight consonant phonemes (as in Hawaiian) or more than ninety. (!Kung, a language spoken in Namibia,

Table 8.5 Long and short vowels: short vowels > long vowels

Contrasting short vowels	*Contrasting long vowels*	
yes	no	possible (English)
yes	yes	possible (Finnish)
no	yes	**impossible**

has ninety-six consonant phonemes.) Nevertheless, typological analysis of consonant systems has produced a number of well-substantiated universals:

- All languages have stops.
- The most common stop phonemes are /p, t, k/. Very few languages lack any one of these, and there are no languages that lack all three. If any one of these three stops is missing, it will probably be /p/; for example, Aleut, Nubian, and Wichita have no /p/ phoneme. The most commonly occurring phoneme of the three is /t/.
- The most commonly occurring fricative phoneme is /s/. If a language has only one fricative, it is most likely to be /s/. It is the only fricative found in Nandi (a language of Kenya) and Weri (a language of New Guinea). The next most common fricative is /f/.
- Almost every known language has at least one nasal phoneme. In cases where a language has only one nasal phoneme, that phoneme is usually /n/ (as in Arapaho, spoken in Wyoming). If there are two contrasting nasals, they are normally /m/ and /n/.
- The majority of languages have at least one phonemic liquid. However, a small number of languages have none at all; for example, Blackfoot, Dakota, Efik (spoken in Nigeria), and Siona (found in Ecuador). English, of course, has two: /l/ and /ɹ/.

Consonant phonemes are also subject to various implicational universals:

- If a language has voiced obstruent phonemes (stops, fricatives, or affricates), then it will also have voiceless obstruent phonemes (see Table 8.6). The reverse is not necessarily true; for example, Ainu (a language of northern Japan) has only voiceless obstruent phonemes: /p, t, k, tʃ, s/.

Table 8.6 Obstruent voicing: voiceless obstruents > voiced obstruents

Voiceless obstruents	*Voiced obstruents*	
yes	no	possible (Ainu)
yes	yes	possible (English)
no	yes	**impossible**

- Sonorant consonants are generally voiced. Very few languages have voiceless sonorants; those that do always have voiced sonorants as well (see Table 8.7). For example, Burmese contrasts voiced and voiceless nasals and laterals.

Table 8.7 Sonorants: voiced sonorants > voiceless sonorants

Voiced sonorants	*Voiceless sonorants*	
yes	no	possible (English)
yes	yes	possible (Burmese)
no	yes	**impossible**

- If a language has fricative phonemes, then it will also have stop phonemes (see Table 8.8). There are no languages that lack stops; however, there are some languages that lack fricatives. For example, Gilbertese (Gilbert Islands), Kitabal (eastern Australia), and Nuer (southeastern Sudan) have no fricatives.

Table 8.8 Stops and fricatives: stops > fricatives

Stops	*Fricatives*	
yes	no	possible (Nuer)
yes	yes	possible (English)
no	yes	**impossible**

- Languages that have affricates will also have fricatives and stops (see Table 8.9). This is not surprising, since an affricate is, in essence, a sequence of a stop followed by a fricative. However, many languages lack affricates altogether. For example, French has fricative and stop phonemes, but no affricate phonemes. In contrast, English has all three consonant types.

Table 8.9 Types of obstruents: stops > fricatives > affricates

Stops	*Fricatives*	*Affricates*	
yes	yes	yes	possible (English)
yes	yes	no	possible (French)
yes	no	no	possible (Kitabal)
no	yes	yes	**impossible**
no	yes	no	**impossible**
no	no	yes	**impossible**

Suprasegmental Systems

Languages can also be classified according to their suprasegmental (or prosodic) type. Languages that use pitch to make meaning distinctions between words are called **tone languages**. (The phonetics and phonology of tone were introduced in Chapters 2 and 3.)

A great many of the world's languages are tone languages. Mandarin, for instance, has four contrastive tones (see Table 8.10). The other Chinese languages, as well as many languages of Southeast Asia, Africa, and the Americas, are also tone languages. A few tone languages are also found in Europe; for example, one of the dialects of Latvian makes a three-way tonal distinction (see Table 8.11).

Table 8.10 Tone contrasts in Mandarin

High tone	dā	'build'
Low rising tone	dá	'achieve'
Falling-rising tone	dǎ	'hit'
High falling tone	dà	'big'

Table 8.11 Tone contrasts in Latvian

Falling tone	loks	[lùoks]	'arch, bow'
Level (high) tone	loks	[lūoks]	'green onion'
Rising-falling (broken) tone	loks	[lûoks]	'window'

As noted in the chapter on phonetics, there are two types of tones: level tones and contour tones. Tone languages most often contrast only two tone levels (usually high and low). However, contrasts involving three tone levels (such as high, low, and mid tones) are also relatively common. Five or more levels of tonal contrast are practically unknown.

Tone systems, too, exhibit various universal tendencies:

- If a language has contour tones (such as rising tone or falling tone), then it will most likely also have level tones (such as high, mid, or low tone), as outlined in Table 8.12. Burmese, Crow, Latvian, and Mandarin are examples of languages that fit this pattern. The reverse pattern (languages with contour tones but no level tones) is extremely rare (although Dafla, spoken in northern India, has such a system).

Table 8.12 Tones: level tones > contour tones

Level tones	*Contour tones*	
yes	no	possible (Sarcee)
yes	yes	possible (Mandarin)
no	yes	**very rare** (Dafla)

- If a language has complex contour tones (such as rising-falling or falling-rising), then it will also have simple contour tones (like rising or falling), as summarized in Table 8.13. Both the Mandarin and Latvian examples fit this pattern.

Table 8.13 Contour tones: simple contour tones > complex contour tones

Simple contour tones	*Complex contour tones*	
yes	no	possible (Hausa)
yes	yes	possible (Mandarin)
no	yes	**impossible**

Differences in stress are also useful in classifying languages. **Fixed stress languages** are those in which the position of stress on a word is predictable. For example, in Modern Hebrew and K'iché (a Mayan language), stress always falls on the last syllable of a word; in Polish, Swahili, and Samoan, stress falls on the penultimate (second-to-last) syllable of words; while in Czech, Finnish, and Hungarian, the stressed syllable is always the first syllable of a word. In **free stress languages**, the position of stress is not predictable and must be learned for each word. Free stress is also called *phonemic stress* because of its role in distinguishing between words. Russian is an example of a language with free stress, as shown in Table 8.14.

Table 8.14 Stress contrasts in Russian

múka	'torture'	muká	'flour'
zámok	'castle'	zamók	'lock'
rúki	'hands'	rukí	'hand's' (genitive singular)

Syllable Structure

The CV and V syllable types are unmarked. They are simpler than other syllable types (CVC, VCC, and so on), are found in all languages, and are learned first by children (see Chapter 11, Section 2.3).

In any given language, onsets may be structured differently from codas. For example, in English, a nasal + stop sequence is permitted in the coda (in a word like *hand*), but not in the onset (there are no English words that begin with the sequence *nd*). However, Swahili has precisely the opposite restrictions: the *nd* sequence is permitted in onset position (in words like *ndizi* 'banana'), but not in coda position. In fact, Swahili syllables are coda-less—they can only end in vowels.

Differences in syllable structure constraints can have interesting consequences when languages come in contact. For example, in Hawaiian, only V and CV syllables are permitted. Thus, when a word is borrowed from a language like English, which allows more complicated syllable structures, vowels are inserted to produce the only allowed syllable structures. For example, when the phrase *Merry Christmas* was borrowed into Hawaiian, it was reformulated as *mele kalikimaka*. (Of course, some consonant changes were made as well, since Hawaiian lacks /r/ and /s/ phonemes.)

Two examples of implicational universals for syllable structure are presented below. Both deal with the structure of onsets as opposed to codas.

- If a language permits sequences of consonants in the onset, then it will also permit syllables with single consonant onsets and syllables with no onset at all (see Table 8.15).

Table 8.15 Onsets: single consonant onsets > multiple consonant onsets

Single C onsets/no onsets	*Multiple C onsets*	
yes	no	possible (Hawaiian)
yes	yes	possible (English)
no	yes	**impossible**

- If a language permits sequences of consonants in the coda, then it will also permit syllables with single consonant codas and syllables with no coda at all (see Table 8.16).

Table 8.16 Onsets: single consonant codas/no codas > multiple consonant codas

Single C codas/no codas	*Multiple C codas*	
yes	no	possible (Cantonese)
yes	yes	possible (English)
no	yes	**impossible**

2.2 Morphology

Both words and morphemes are found in all languages. However, there are clear differences in the ways in which individual languages combine morphemes to form words. Four types of systems can be distinguished.

The Isolating Type

A purely **isolating** or **analytic language** would contain only words that consist of a single (root) morpheme. In such a language there would be no affixes, and categories such as number and tense would therefore have to be expressed by a separate word. In Mandarin, which is primarily an isolating language, the morpheme *le* is often used to indicate a past or completed action. Although this morpheme is thus semantically similar to a past tense, it acts just like an independent word, since its position in the sentence may vary:

4)

a. Tā chī fàn *le.*
he eat meal past
'He ate the meal.'

b. Tā chī *le* fàn.
he eat past meal
'He ate the meal.'

Other languages that are primarily isolating include Cantonese, Vietnamese, Laotian, and Cambodian.

The Polysynthetic Type

In a **polysynthetic language**, single words can consist of long strings of roots and affixes that often express meanings that are associated with entire sentences in other languages. The following word from Inuktitut illustrates this (3 = 3rd person; SG = singular).

5)

Qasuiirsarvigssarsingitluinarnarpuq.
Qasu -iir -sar -vig -ssar -si -ngit-luinar -nar -puq
tired not cause-to-be place-for suitable find not completely someone 3SG
'Someone did not find a completely suitable resting place.'

Polysynthesis is common in many Native languages of North America, including Inuktitut, Cree, and Sarcee, to name but a few.

The terms *isolating* and *polysynthetic* refer to two extremes: words consisting only of a single morpheme versus words that can be complete sentences. Few if any languages are either purely isolating or purely polysynthetic. Instead, the vast majority of languages are **synthetic languages**, in that they permit multimorphemic words, but one word does not usually mean a whole sentence. There are two types of synthetic languages.

The Agglutinating Type

An **agglutinating language** has words that can contain several morphemes, but the words are easily divided into their component parts (normally a root and affixes). In such languages, each affix is clearly identifiable and typically represents only a single grammatical category or meaning. The following examples are from Turkish.

6)

a. kœj
'village'

b. kœj-leɾ
village-PL
'villages'

c. kœj-leɾ-in
village-PL-GEN
'of the villages'

Turkish words can have a complex morphological structure, but each morpheme has a single, clearly identifiable function. In *6c,* for instance, *-ler* marks plurality and *-in* marks the genitive case, giving the meaning 'of the villages'.

The Fusional Type

Words in a **fusional language** (also called an **inflectional language**) can also consist of several morphemes. However, in contrast to agglutinating systems, the affixes in fusional languages often mark several grammatical categories simultaneously. In Russian, for example, a single inflectional affix simultaneously marks the noun's gender class (masculine, feminine, or neuter), its number (singular or plural), and its grammatical role (subject, direct object, and so on). This is illustrated in *7* for the suffix *-u.*

7)

Mɨ $v^j id^j im$ ruk-u.
we see hand-FEM.SG.ACC
'We see a/the hand.'
Note: ACC stands for 'accusative' and marks the direct object.

The distinction between agglutinating and fusional is sensitive to the number of semantic "bits" of information normally packed into an affix. In an agglutinating language, each affix normally contains only one element of grammatical or lexical meaning, while in a fusional language, affixes often denote several such bits of information.

Mixed Types

Many (perhaps most) languages do not belong exclusively to any of the four categories just outlined. For example, English employs isolating patterns in many verbal constructions, where each notion is expressed by a separate word. The future, for instance, is indicated by the independent word *will* (rather than by an affix) in structures such as *I will leave.* On the other hand, English also exhibits considerable agglutination in derived words, such as *re-en-act-ment,* which consist of a series of clearly identifiable morphemes, each with its own unique meaning and function. However, the English pronoun system is largely fusional, since a single form can be used to indicate person, number, gender, and case. The word *him,* for instance, is used to express a third person singular, masculine direct object.

Since many, if not most, of the world's languages exhibit mixed patterns of this type, it has been suggested that terms like *isolating, agglutinating,* and *fusional* should be used to refer not to a language as a whole but to particular structures within a language.

It is also important to recognize that these classifications do not take into consideration morphological processes such as compounding (e.g., English *greenhouse*), reduplication (e.g., Tagalog *sulat* 'write' versus *susulat* 'will write'), grammatical use of stress or tone (e.g., the noun *présent* versus the verb *presént* in English), and internal word change (e.g., vowel ablaut, as in English *run* versus *ran*).

Implicational Universals: Morphology

A variety of generalizations can be made about word structure in human language.

- If a language has inflectional affixes, it will also have derivational affixes (see Chapter 4, Section 4.2). For example, English not only has inflectional affixes such as the past tense *-ed* and plural *-s,* but also contains derivational affixes like *un-* (*unhappy, unwanted*) and *-ly* (*quickly, slowly*).
- If a word has both a derivational and an inflectional affix, the derivational affix is closer to the root (DA = derivational affix; IA = inflectional affix) (see Table 8.17).

Table 8.17 The ordering of derivational and inflectional affixes

DA = derivational affix	*IA = inflectional affix*
English	
friend-ship-s Root DA IA	*friend-s -ship Root IA DA
Turkish	
iʃ -tʃi -leɾ work -er -PL Root DA IA	*iʃ -leɾ -tʃi work -PL -er Root IA DA

- If a language has only suffixes, it will also have only postpositions. (Postpositions are the equivalent of prepositions in languages that place the head at the end of the phrase.) Turkish, for example, has only suffixes; as expected, it also has postpositions rather than prepositions. This is illustrated in the following sentence.

8)

Ahmet Ajʃe itʃin kitab-ɨ al-dɨ.
Ahmet Ayshe for book-ACC buy-PST
'Ahmet bought a book for Ayshe.'

2.3 Syntax

Because we lack detailed descriptions for most of the world's languages, much of the work on syntactic universals has been restricted to the study of word order in simple declarative sentences such as *The men built the house.* Preliminary classification focuses on the relative order of the subject (S), direct object (O), and verb (V). The three most common word orders (in descending order of frequency) are SOV, SVO, and VSO. Over 95 percent of the world's languages use one of these patterns as their basic word order.

9)

SOV (Turkish):
Hasan œkyz-y al-dɨ.
Hasan ox-ACC bought
'Hasan bought the ox.'

10)

SVO (English):
The athlete broke the record.

11)

VSO (Welsh):
Lladdodd y ddraig y dyn.
killed the dragon the man
'The dragon killed the man.'

SOV, SVO, and VSO patterns all have one common trait: the subject appears before the direct object. The prevalence of the SO pattern may be due to the fact that the subject usually coincides with the topic of the sentence (i.e., what the sentence is about; see Chapter 6, Section 4.3), and therefore is more useful at an early point in the utterance.

While an overwhelming majority of the world's languages place the subject before the direct object in their basic word order, this pattern is not universal. There are a small number of VOS languages, of which the best-known example is Malagasy.

12)

VOS (Malagasy):
Nahita ny mpianatra ny vehivavy.
saw the student the woman
'The woman saw the student.'

As well, there are a very few OVS or OSV languages, all of which seem to be spoken in South America:

13)

OVS (Hixkaryana):
Kana janɨmno bɨrjekomo.
fish caught boy
'The boy caught a fish.'

14)

OSV (Apuriña)
Anana nota apa.
pineapple I fetch
'I fetch a pineapple.'

Word-Order Universals

Sometimes the order of elements within one kind of structure has implications for the order of elements in other structures. Many of these implications concern the relationship between the verb and its (direct) object.

- If a language has VO word order, then it will have prepositions rather than postpositions. Languages of this type include Berber (spoken in Morocco), Hebrew, Maori (spoken in New Zealand), Maasai (spoken in Kenya), Welsh, and Irish Gaelic.

15)

Irish Gaelic

a. VSO pattern:
Chonaic mé mo mháthair.
saw I my mother
'I saw my mother.'

b. Preposition pattern:
sa teach
in house
'in the house'

- If a language has OV word order, then it will probably have postpositions rather than prepositions. Languages with this structural pattern include Basque, Burmese, Hindi, Japanese, Korean, Quechua, Turkish, and Guugu Yimidhirr, an Aboriginal language of Australia (ERG = ergative, a case used for the subject of a transitive verb).

16)

Guugu Yimidhirr

a. SOV pattern:
Gudaa-ngun yarrga dyindaj.
dog-ERG boy bit
'The dog bit the boy.'

b. Postposition pattern:
yuwaal nganh
beach from
'from the beach'

- PPs almost always precede the verb in OV languages, and usually follow the verb in VO languages (NOM = nominative, a case used for the subject; ACC = accusative, a case used for the direct object).

17)

Japanese

a. SOV pattern:
Gakusei-ga hon-o yonda.
student-NOM book-ACC read
'The student read a book.'

b. PP precedes verb:
Taroo-ga [$_{PP}$ nitiyoobi ni] tsuita.
Taroo-NOM Sunday on arrived
'Taroo arrived on Sunday.'

18)

English

a. SVO pattern:
I like candy.

b. PP follows verb:
George left [$_{PP}$ on Sunday].

- Manner adverbs overwhelmingly precede the verb in OV languages and generally follow the verb in VO languages.

19)

Japanese (SOV pattern, as seen in *17a*):
Manner adverb precedes verb:
hayaku hasiru
quickly run
'run quickly'

20)

English (SVO pattern, as seen in *18a*):
Manner adverb follows verb:
John runs well.

- With respect to possessive structures, there is an overwhelming preference for Genitive (possessive) + N order in OV languages, and a (somewhat weaker) preference for N + Genitive order in VO languages.

21)

Japanese (SOV pattern, as seen in *17a*):

Genitive structure precedes head N:
Taroo-no hon
Taroo-GEN book
'Taroo's book'

22)

French

a. SVO pattern:
Pierre aime Marie.
'Pierre likes Marie.'

b. Genitive structure follows head N:
la maison de Marie
the house of (GEN) Marie
'Marie's house'

English, although an SVO language, exhibits both Genitive + N and N + Genitive patterns:

23)

a. Genitive + N pattern:
the country's laws

b. N + Genitive pattern:
the laws of the country

Examples such as this are rare, however, and do not invalidate the universal tendencies we have been considering.

Grammatical Hierarchies

Implicational universals are often stated in terms of **hierarchies** of categories or relations. One of the most important hierarchies of this type refers to the grammatical relations of subject and direct object.

24)

The grammatical relation hierarchy
subject > direct object > other

According to this hierarchy, a process that applies only to subjects is less marked than a process that applies to direct objects, and so on. In other words, if a particular phenomenon applies to direct objects, it should also apply to subjects. In contrast, it would not be surprising to find a process that applies to subjects but not direct objects.

Among the many typological phenomena that conform to this hierarchy is verb agreement, first mentioned in Chapter 4 (Section 4.4). As the following examples show, there are languages in which the verb agrees only with the subject, and there are languages in which it agrees with both the subject and the direct object (3 = 3rd person; SG = singular; PL = plural).

25)

Agreement with subject only (Spanish):

Subject
Juan parti-ó.
Juan leave-3SG.PST
'Juan left.'

26)

Agreement with subject and direct object (Swahili):

Subject *Direct object*
Juma a- li- wa-piga watoto.
Juma 3SG-PST-3PL-hit children
'Juma hit the children.'

However, as predicted by the hierarchy, there are no languages in which the verb agrees only with the direct object.

2.4 Explaining Universals

Linguists are still uncertain about how to explain the existence of many linguistic universals. Nonetheless, a number of interesting proposals have been made, and it is worthwhile to consider some of them here.

Phonology

Perceptual factors play a role in shaping phonological universals. For example, the fact that /s/ is the most commonly occurring fricative may have to do with its acoustic prominence: varieties of /s/ are inherently louder and more strident (Chapter 2, Section 5.4) than other kinds of fricatives.

Vowel systems (discussed in Section 2.1) develop so as to keep vowel phonemes as different from each other as possible. A three-vowel system such as the one in Figure 8.4 allows for plenty of "space" around each vowel, which probably makes each vowel easier to distinguish from the others.

i u

a

Figure 8.4 A three-vowel system

The same holds true for the distribution of stop phonemes. It may be that /p/, /t/, and /k/ are the three most common stops because they occur at three maximally distant places of articulation within the supralaryngeal vocal tract. These three stops are much easier to distinguish perceptually than a sequence of dental, alveolar, and palatal stops, for example, all of which are produced in the central region of the oral cavity.

It has been suggested that consonant systems in general respond to the articulatory pressures that give rise to unmarked sounds and systems. Articulatorily basic obstruents such as [p], [t], and [k] are found much more commonly than more complex articulations such as [tɬ] and [qw]. Table 8.18 shows the set of obstruents that is most widely used across human languages.

Table 8.18 Obstruents most often found cross-linguistically

p	t	k	ʔ
b	d	g	
f	s		h
	tʃ		

Languages tend to have consonant systems that consist of about 70 percent obstruents and 30 percent sonorants no matter what the total size of their consonant inventories may be. These figures reflect the articulatory possibilities available for contrast: more distinctions can be made among obstruents than among sonorants. There are, for example, no nasal fricative sonorants, because the air pressure needed to force air through a narrow opening (which is necessary for the production of fricatives) cannot be built up when so much air is flowing through the nasal passage at the same time. For reasons such as this, the number of obstruent consonants in any language is potentially much larger than the number of possible sonorant consonants. This is just one example of how considerations involving articulation can play a role in the shaping of consonant systems.

Morphology

Other types of explanations are appropriate for morphological universals. For example, the fact that languages with suffixes but no prefixes always have postpositions (Section 2.2) may have a historical explanation. In these languages, some postpositions became attached to a preceding word and were thereby converted into suffixes. Because suffixes in such languages evolved from postpositions, the link between the two elements can be traced to their common origin.

An example of this very phenomenon can be seen in the closely related languages Finnish and Estonian. Their ancestor language (Proto-Baltic-Finnic) contained a postposition **kanssa* 'with', which is still evident in Standard Finnish but has evolved into a suffix in Estonian (see Table 8.19).

Table 8.19 Proto-Baltic-Finnic postposition *kanssa* becomes suffix *-ga*

COM = comitative, a case expressing accompaniment

Standard Finnish: postposition *kanssa* 'with'

poika	'boy'	poja-n	kanssa	'with the boy'
		boy-GEN	with	

Estonian: case suffix *-ga*

poeg	'son'	poja-ga		'with the son'
		son-COM		

The requirement that derivational affixes occur closer to the root than inflectional affixes has another type of explanation. As noted in the morphology chapter, derivation typically forms new words, while inflection marks the subclass (for example, plural for Ns, past tense for Vs) to which a word belongs. Given that a word must be formed before its subclass can be determined, it follows that derivational processes will precede inflection. This is reflected in word structure, where derivational affixes appear closer to the root than inflectional markers. In Figure 8.5, for instance, the verbal root *treat* is converted into a noun by the affix *-ment* before the plural inflectional marker is added.

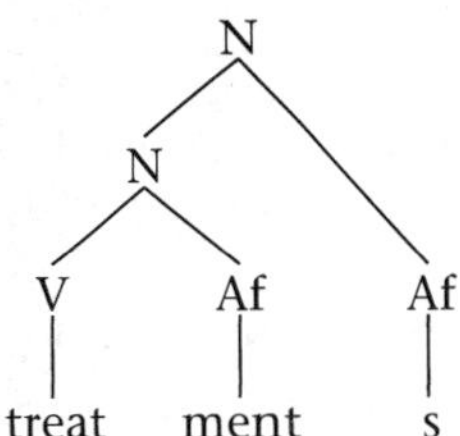

Figure 8.5 The structure of a word containing a derivational affix and an inflectional affix

Syntax

At least some syntactic universals may be explained in terms of the way that the human brain processes sentence structure. Consider the summary of word-order patterns in Table 8.20, which is based on the implicational universals discussed in Section 2.3.

Table 8.20 Word-order patterns

Constituents	*Order in VO language*	*Order in OV language*
P & NP	preposition-NP	NP-postposition
V & PP	verb-PP	PP-verb
V & manner Adv	verb-manner Adv	manner Adv-verb
N & GEN	noun-genitive	genitive-noun

One explanation as to why the word-order properties in the second and third columns cluster together involves the contrast between right-branching and left-branching languages. In right-branching languages, the more elaborate part of a phrase's structure occurs on its right branch; in left-branching languages, it occurs on the left. Thus, a verb-object pattern is right-branching since a phrasal constituent (an XP) appears on its right branch, but an object-verb pattern is left-branching, as shown in Figure 8.6.

As you can easily determine for yourselves, the P-NP, V-PP, V-Adv, and N-Gen patterns commonly associated with VO languages are also all right-branching (both genitives and adverbials are a type of phrase). In contrast, the NP-P, PP-V, Adv-V, and Gen-N patterns typically found in OV languages are all left-branching. In other words, it seems that languages are fairly consistent in using one or the other type of branching structure. This sort of uniformity may make it easier for speakers and hearers to process syntactic structure. Thus, just as some human beings are right-handed and others left-handed, it appears that some languages prefer to use consistently right-branching systems, while others prefer consistently left-branching systems.

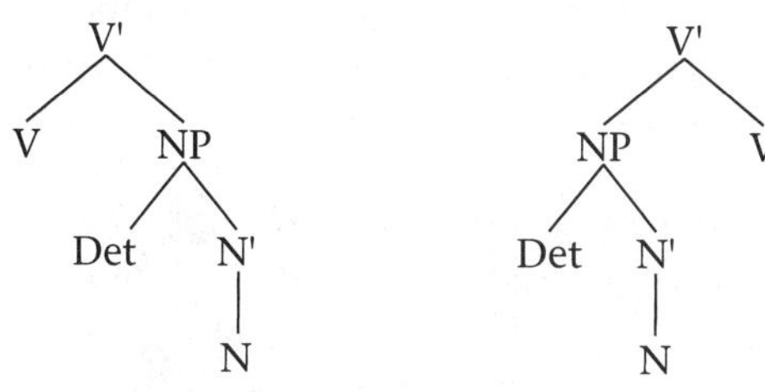

Figure 8.6 Right-branching and left-branching patterns

The study of linguistic typology and language universals is a relatively new field within linguistics. There is obviously much still to be learned about linguistic universals, and it must be admitted that some of the current work is speculative and incomplete. No doubt many interesting new facts will eventually come to light.

3 Genetic Classification

The goal of genetic classification is to group the languages into families based on evidence of a common origin established through use of the comparative method (Chapter 7, Section 6). This work is difficult and challenging for a variety of reasons.

Perhaps the biggest problem is simply the amount of data that must be collected before linguists can be confident about the status of a group of languages. It is only in the last two or three decades, for example, that enough information has been accumulated to propose a detailed classification of the languages of Africa. Moreover, many of the languages of South America, New Guinea, and Australia are still relatively unknown.

Matters are further complicated by the fact that entirely unrelated languages may be similar in various ways. This is particularly likely if the languages have been in contact long enough to have borrowed a large number of words, sounds, morphemes, or syntactic structures from one another.

Moreover, even languages that are related may not look that similar. The more distant the genetic relationship between languages is, the less likely it is that a large number of obvious similarities will be found, especially since sound changes can obscure relationships between cognate words. English and Latin are related (though distantly), but the similarity between cognates like Latin *unda* 'wave' and English *water* is certainly not striking.

Research is also made difficult by the fact that words that may be excellent indicators of a genetic relationship can drop out of the lexicon. For example, Old English had a word *leax* 'salmon' (which was cognate with German *Lachs* and Yiddish *lox*), but this lexical item has since been lost from the native English lexicon. (*Lox* has been borrowed back into some varieties of English as the name for a popular delicatessen food).

Since word loss is a common historical event, linguists prefer to use the oldest available form of a language for their research. Thus, our knowledge of Proto-Indo-

European is drawn from the study of Old English, Sanskrit, Latin, etc., rather than English, Hindi-Urdu, French, and their other modern descendants.

Some language families contain many hundreds of languages. In other cases, only one language may remain to represent a family. In still other cases, families have become extinct. The following section summarizes some of what we know about the Indo-European family of languages. Although it might appear to be overly Eurocentric to focus on this particular family, you will see that the homelands of the various Indo-European languages extend well beyond Europe into the Middle East and India. It is also worth noting that a number of languages spoken in Europe (Finnish, Hungarian, and Basque, to name three) do not belong to the Indo-European family.

3.1 The Indo-European Family

If we consider only living languages, the **Indo-European family** currently has nine branches, which are listed in Table 8.21.

Table 8.21 Main branches of the Indo-European family

Germanic	Hellenic	Baltic
Celtic	Albanian	Slavic
Italic	Armenian	Indo-Iranian

Germanic

The Germanic branch of Indo-European can be divided into three sub-branches: East, North, and West. The East Germanic branch included Gothic, the oldest Germanic language for which written texts exist (dating from the fourth century A.D.). Gothic and any other languages belonging to this branch of Germanic have long been extinct.

The North Germanic (or Scandinavian) branch originally included Old Norse (also known as Old Icelandic), which was the language of the Vikings and the ancestor of modern Icelandic, Norwegian, and Faroese (spoken on the Faroe Islands, north of Scotland). Swedish and Danish are two other familiar North Germanic languages.

The West Germanic branch includes English, German, Yiddish, Dutch, Frisian, and Afrikaans. Afrikaans is descended from the Dutch spoken by seventeenth-century settlers (known as Boers) in South Africa.

Frisian is the language most closely related to English. It is spoken on the north coast of Holland and on the Frisian Islands just off the coast, as well as on the northwestern coast of Germany. English descended from the speech of the Angles, Saxons, and Jutes—Germanic tribes who lived in northern Germany and southern Denmark (in an area just east of the Frisians) before invading England in A.D. 449 and settling there.

The organization of the Germanic family of languages is illustrated in Table 8.22. (In this and other tables, parentheses are used to indicate languages that no longer have any native speakers. The tables are intended to illustrate the membership and organization of the families; they do not necessarily provide a complete list of the languages in each family.)

Although we use tables to represent family groupings in this book, trees of the sort illustrated in Figure 8.7 are widely used as well.

Table 8.22 The Germanic family

(East Germanic)	*North Germanic*	*West Germanic*
(Gothic)	Icelandic	English
	Norwegian	German
	Faroese	Yiddish
	Swedish	Dutch
	Danish	Frisian
		Afrikaans

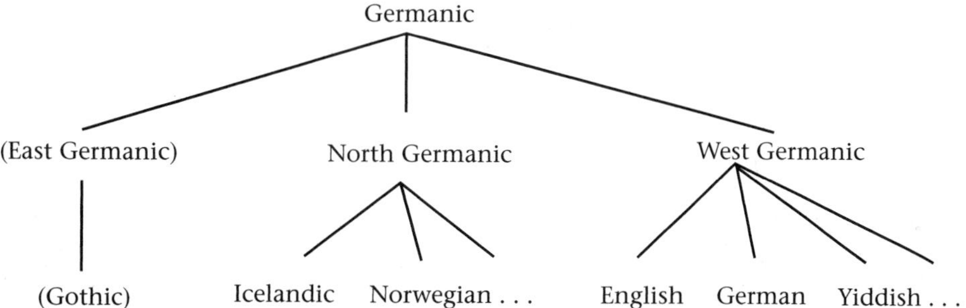

Figure 8.7 Tree depicting the organization of the Germanic family

Celtic

The Celtic branch of Indo-European (see Table 8.23) has two main subbranches: Insular and Continental (now extinct). Gaulish, a member of the Continental branch, was once spoken in France (the Gauls were the tribe Julius Caesar defeated), but it has long been extinct.

Table 8.23 The Celtic family

Insular		*Continental*
Brythonic	*Goidelic*	
Welsh	Irish [= Irish Gaelic]	(Gaulish)
Breton	(Manx)	
(Cornish)	Scots Gaelic	

The Insular subbranch can be subdivided into two groups of languages: Brythonic or British (also called P-Celtic) and Goidelic or Gaelic (also called Q-Celtic). Brythonic languages include Welsh and Breton (which is spoken in northwestern France) as well as Cornish, which was formerly spoken in southwestern Britain but no longer has any native speakers. The Goidelic branch contains Irish (or Irish Gaelic), which is still spoken natively in the western parts of Ireland, the now extinct Manx, and Scots Gaelic, which is spoken in parts of northwestern Scotland (especially the Hebrides Islands) and, to a lesser extent, Cape Breton Island in Nova Scotia.

Italic

The Italic family originally had a number of branches, which included several now-extinct languages spoken in the area corresponding roughly to modern-day Italy. However, the only Italic languages that are presently spoken are all descended from Latin, the language of the Roman Empire (hence the term *Romance languages*).

These languages are commonly divided into four groups. Ibero-Romance includes Portuguese and Spanish, while Gallo-Romance contains French, Catalan (spoken in northeastern Spain, around Barcelona), and Romansch (one of the four official languages of Switzerland). The Italo-Romance branch includes Italian and Sardinian; Rumanian is the best-known language in the Balkano-Romance group (see Table 8.24).

Table 8.24 The Romance family

Ibero-Romance	*Gallo-Romance*	*Italo-Romance*	*Balkano-Romance*
Portuguese	French	Italian	Rumanian
Spanish	Catalan	Sardinian	
	Romansch		

Hellenic

The Hellenic branch of Indo-European has only one living member, Greek. All modern Greek dialects are descended from the classical dialect known as Attic Greek, which was the speech of Athens during the Golden Age of Greek culture (approximately 500 to 300 B.C.).

Hellenic Greek, which was used in subsequent centuries, was the language of commerce throughout the Middle East. (Hellenic Greek was also Cleopatra's native language; she was descended from one of Alexander the Great's generals.)

Albanian

The Albanian branch of Indo-European has only one member, Albanian, which is spoken not only in Albania but also in parts of the former Yugoslavia, Greece, and Italy.

Armenian

The Armenian branch also has only one member, Armenian. This language is centered in the Republic of Armenia (formerly part of the USSR) but is also spoken in Turkey, Iran, Syria, Lebanon, and Egypt.

Baltic

The Baltic branch contains only two surviving languages, Latvian (or Lettish) and Lithuanian. They are spoken in Latvia and Lithuania (located just west of Russia and northeast of Poland). Lithuanian has an elaborate case system, which resembles the one proposed for Proto-Indo-European.

Slavic

The Slavic branch of Indo-European can be divided into three sub-branches: East, West, and South. The East Slavic branch is made up of Russian (also called Great Russian), Ukrainian, and Byelorussian (or White Russian). The latter is spoken in Belarus, which is just east of northern Poland. The West Slavic branch includes Czech, Slovak, and Polish.

The South Slavic branch consists of Bulgarian, Macedonian, Serbo-Croatian, and Slovene (or Slovenian). The latter three languages are all spoken in the former Yugoslavia. Note that although Alexander the Great was king of Macedonia, he spoke Hellenic Greek, not (Slavic) Macedonian; Slavic-speaking tribes did not move into that area until several centuries later.

The organization of the Slavic group of languages is represented in Table 8.25.

Table 8.25 The Slavic family

East Slavic	*West Slavic*	*South Slavic*
Russian	Czech	Bulgarian
Ukrainian	Slovak	Macedonian
Byelorussian	Polish	Serbo-Croatian
		Slovene

Indo-Iranian

The Indo-Iranian branch of Indo-European is divided into the Iranian and Indic sub-branches. The Iranian sub-branch contains about two dozen different languages, including Modern Persian (also called Parsi or Farsi, spoken in Iran), Pashto (the principal language of Afghanistan), and Kurdish (found in Iran, Iraq, Turkey, and Syria). Other Iranian languages are spoken in Pakistan, southern parts of the former USSR, and China.

There are about thirty-five different Indic languages. Most of the languages spoken in northern India, Pakistan, and Bangladesh belong to this branch of Indo-European. Some of the most widespread (in terms of number of speakers) are Hindi-Urdu, Bengali, Marathi, and Gujarati. Although Hindi and Urdu are two dialects of the same language, they have totally different writing systems and are associated with different cultures; Urdu is spoken principally in Pakistan by Muslims, while Hindi is spoken primarily in India by Hindus.

Less well known as an Indic language is Romany, or Gypsy. It is now believed that the Gypsies (or Roma) fled to Turkey from northwestern India during the Middle Ages, after being defeated by Islamic invaders. Subsequently they spread throughout Europe: Gypsies are found as far west as Ireland and as far east as Russia. Many now also live in North America. Romany contains many borrowed words—particularly from Greek, which was the language primarily spoken in Turkey during the Middle Ages.

Table 8.26 depicts the organization of Indo-Iranian.

Table 8.26 The Indo-Iranian family

Iranian	*Indic*
Persian [= Farsi]	Hindi-Urdu
Pashto	Bengali
Kurdish	Marathi
	Gujarati
	Romany [= Gypsy]

The map in Figure 8.8 illustrates the geographic location of the Indo-European families identified in this chapter.

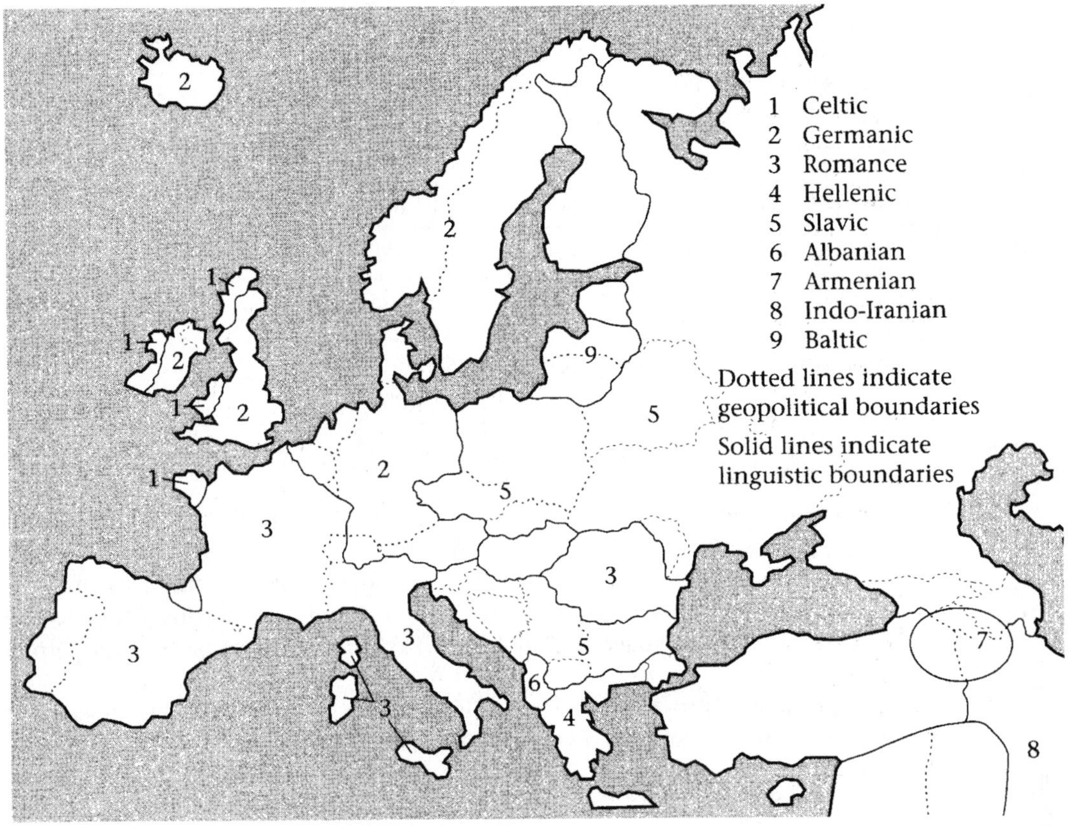

1 Celtic
2 Germanic
3 Romance
4 Hellenic
5 Slavic
6 Albanian
7 Armenian
8 Indo-Iranian
9 Baltic

Dotted lines indicate geopolitical boundaries

Solid lines indicate linguistic boundaries

Figure 8.8 Location of Indo-European languages

3.2 Some Other Families

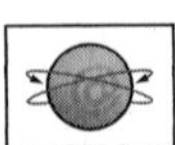

Although no introductory text could hope to present a complete survey of all of the world's language families, you can find additional information on this topic at our Web site—go to **bedfordstmartins.com/linguistics/classification** and click on **families**. Among the families discussed there are Uralic (which includes Finnish and Hungarian), Altaic (Turkish, and possibly Japanese and Korean as well), Austronesian (Samoan, Fijian, Filipino, and Indonesian), Austroasiatic (Vietnamese and Khmer), Afroasiatic (Arabic and Hebrew), and Niger-Congo (Swahili), in addition to the dozens of language families indigenous to the Americas. The maps in Figures 8.9 and 8.10 show the location of some of these language families.

Not all of the world's languages have been placed in families at this point in time. Languages with no known relatives are called **isolates**. Basque (spoken in northern Spain and southwestern France), Ainu (northern Japan), Burushaski (Pakistan), Kutenai (British Columbia), Gilyak (Siberia), Taraskan (California), and Yukagir (Siberia) are among the languages that are widely considered to be isolates.

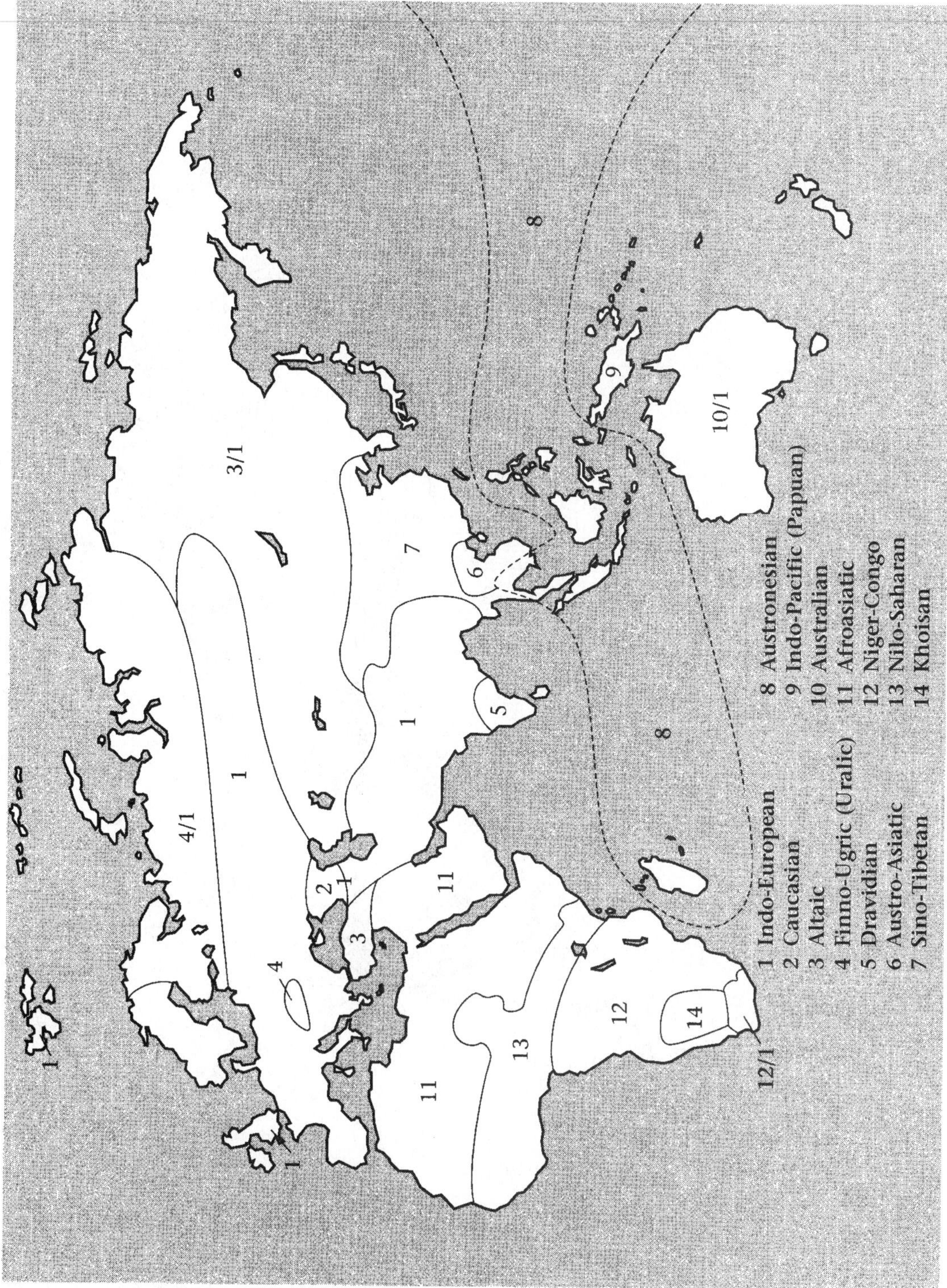

Figure 8.9 Location of some major language families

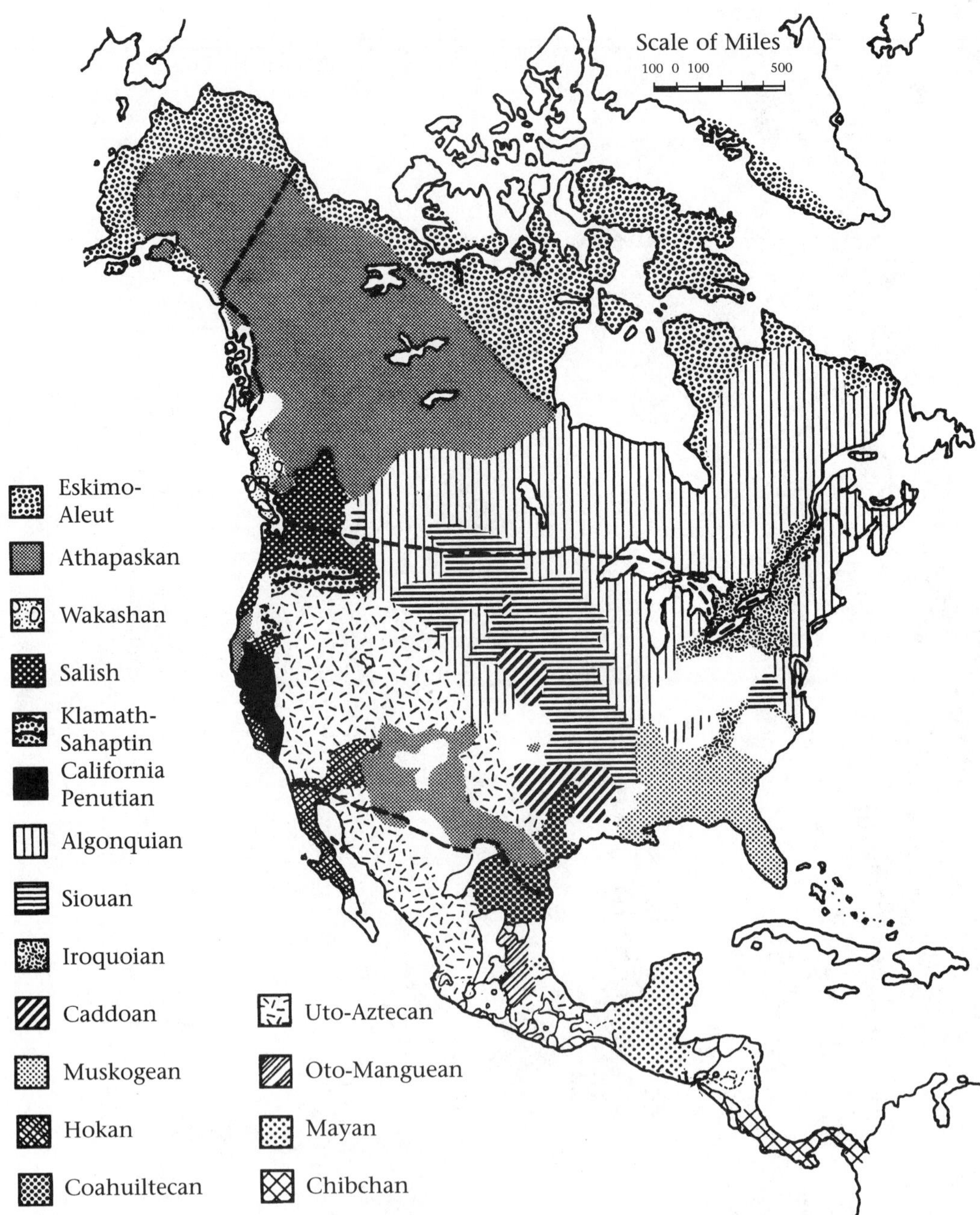

Figure 8.10 North and Central American language groups

3.3 Language Phyla

In recent years, attempts have been made to place many of the world's language families in even larger groupings called **phyla** (singular *phylum*), **stocks**, or **macrofamilies**.

One of the best known of the proposed phyla is Nostratic (also called Eurasiatic). Supposedly dating back 20,000 years, this hypothetical phylum includes Indo-European, Uralic, Altaic, and (depending on the proposal) various other languages and language families as well. This type of work is controversial, however, and most linguists remain very skeptical about the methodology, evidence, and conclusions associated with comparative research involving a time depth greater than eight or ten thousand years. For this reason, we will say nothing more about this topic here.

Summing Up

The focus of this chapter is on the criteria that linguists use to classify languages, and on the enormous variety of languages found throughout the world. Linguistic diversity is severely threatened, however, as many languages are endangered. Linguists sometimes attempt to classify languages solely in terms of their structural similarities and differences (that is, in terms of their **linguistic typology**). Analysis of cross-linguistic data has identified a number of **linguistic universals** in phonology, morphology, and syntax, indicating the most common characteristics of human language. The other major type of classificatory work in linguistics is concerned with **genetic relationships**—establishing language families whose members are descended from a common ancestor. While research in this area is hampered both by the large number of languages involved and the scarcity of the available data, a sizable portion of the world's several thousand languages have been placed in families. Finally, we present the controversial work recently done on linguistic **phyla** or **macrofamilies**. Research in these areas can shed light on the nature of language change, as well as the movement of peoples throughout the world.

Key Terms

General terms and terms concerning types of classification

areal classification
dialect
genetic classification
genetically related (languages)
linguistic typology
linguistic universals
mutual intelligibility

Terms concerning typological classification

absolute universals
agglutinating language
analytic language
fixed stress languages
free stress languages
fusional language
hierarchies
implicational universals
inflectional language
isolating language

marked traits
markedness theory
polysynthetic language
synthetic languages
tone languages
universal tendencies
unmarked

Terms concerning genetic classification and language phyla

Indo-European family
isolates
macrofamilies
phyla
stocks

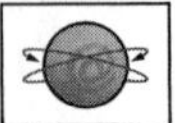

For more information on the sources used in this chapter, go to **bedfordstmartins .com/linguistics/classification** and click on **Sources**.

Recommended Reading

Comrie, Bernard. 1989. *Language Universals and Linguistic Typology.* 2nd ed. Oxford: Blackwell.

Croft, William. 2003. *Typology and Universals.* 2nd ed. New York: Cambridge University Press.

Greenberg, Joseph, ed. 1966. *Universals of Language.* 2nd ed. Cambridge, MA: MIT Press.

Grimes, Barbara, and Joseph E. Grimes. 2004. *Ethnologue.* Vols. 1 and 2. Dallas: SIL International.

Lyovin, Anatole V. 1997. *An Introduction to the Languages of the World.* New York: Oxford University Press.

Ruhlen, Merritt. 1994. *On the Origin of Languages.* Stanford, CA: Stanford University Press.

Shopen, Timothy (ed.). 1987. *Languages and Their Speakers.* Philadelphia: University of Pennsylvania Press.

Shopen, Timothy (ed.). 1987. *Languages and Their Status.* Philadelphia: University of Pennsylvania Press.

Voegelin, C.F., and F.M. Voegelin. 1977. *Classification and Index of the World's Languages.* New York: Elsevier.

Exercises

The data for exercises 1 to 3 are found in *A Guide to the Languages of the World* by M. Ruhlen (Language Universals Project: Stanford University, 1976).

1. Which tendencies and universals are manifested in the following vowel systems? (*Hint:* Look at the pattern of the vowel systems and at rounding.)
   a) Afrikaans (South Africa) ([y] and [ø] are front rounded vowels)

i	y		u
	ø	ə	o
ɛ			ɔ
		a	

b) Squamish (Washington State)

i		u
	ə	
	a	

2. As noted in Section 2.1, the presence of long and nasal vowel phonemes is governed by implicational universals. In what ways do the vowel systems below comply with the implicational universals that make reference to length and nasality?

a) Maltese Arabic

i		u	iː		uː
e		o	eː		oː
	a			aː	

b) Awji (North New Guinea)

i		u	ĩ		ũ
e	ə	o	ẽ	ə̃	õ
	a			a	

3. Consider the following consonant systems. Do these consonant systems comply with the implicational universals mentioned in this chapter?

a) Tahitian (Tahiti)

p	t	ʔ
f		h
v	r	
m	n	

b) Palauan (Palau Islands)

	t	k	ʔ
b			
	ð		
	s		
m		ŋ	
	l, r		

c) Nengone (Loyalty Islands, South Pacific)—stop and nasal system only

p^h	t^h	$ʈ^h$		k^h	ʔ
b	d	ɖ		g	
m	n		ɲ	ŋ	
m̥	n̥			ŋ̊	

(*Note:* [ʈ] and [ɖ] are retroflex consonants; [̥] marks a voiceless nasal; [ɲ] represents a palatal nasal.)

d) Mixe (South Mexico)

p	t		k	ʔ
	d		g	
	ts	tʃ		
	s		x	h
v			ɣ	
m	n			

4. Describe the morphological characteristics of each of the following languages in terms of the four-way system of classification outlined in Section 2.2, namely isolating, polysynthetic, agglutinating, and fusional.
   a) Siberian Yupik
      Angya-ghlla-ng -yug -tuq.
      boat -big -get-want-3SG
      'He wants to get a big boat.'
   b) Latvian

las-u	las-ām	rakst-u	rakst-ām
read-1SG.PRES	read-1PL.PRES	write-1SG.PRES	write-1PL.PRES
'I read'	'we read'	'I write'	'we write'

   c) Japanese
      gakusei-wa homer-are-na-i
      student-TOPIC praise-PASS-NEG-PRES
      'The student is not praised.'

5. Do a morphological analysis of the following data from Latvian. Single out each morpheme and identify its meaning. After you have segmented and identified the morphemes, describe how the data reflects the implicational universals in Section 2.2.
   a) lidotājs 'aviator (NOMINATIVE)'
   b) lidotāju 'aviator (ACCUSATIVE)'
   c) lidotājam 'to the aviator (DATIVE)'
   d) lidot 'to fly'
   e) rakstītājs 'writer (NOMINATIVE)'
   f) rakstītāja 'writer's (GENITIVE)'
   g) rakstīt 'to write'

6. Note the following data from Malagasy, an Austronesian language spoken on the island of Madagascar. The data are from *Malagasy: Introductory Course,* by C. Garvey (Washington: Center for Applied Linguistics, 1964). Does Malagasy comply with all the word-order tendencies mentioned in Section 2.3?
   a) amin' ny restauranta
      'to the restaurant'
   b) Enti'n ny labiera ny mpiasa.
      brings the beer the waiter
      'The waiter brings the beer.'
   c) Avy any Amerika izy.
      come from America he
      'He comes from America.'

nine

Indigenous Languages of North America

Victor Golla

The condition of American languages is . . . an epitome of that of the language of the world in general.
– William Dwight Whitney, *Life and Growth of Language* (1875)

Objectives

In this chapter, you will learn:

- how many indigenous languages there are in North America
- where they may have come from
- what their historical relationships to one another are
- what their important phonetic characteristics are
- what their important grammatical characteristics are
- what is happening to them today

For the purposes of this chapter, North America includes the United States (except for Hawaii), Canada, and Greenland, as well as the northern states of Mexico. The indigenous peoples of North America are usually known as Indians in the United States and First Nations in Canada, except for the Aleuts and the Eskimos (the latter called Inuit in Canada), who are designated separately. In the United States, *Native Americans* is used as the general term for all indigenous peoples, including Indians, Aleuts, Eskimos, and Native Hawaiians.

Of the approximately 6,500 languages in the world, about 325 are (or once were) spoken by the indigenous peoples of North America. Although they account for only 5 percent of the languages of humankind, the impact of North American languages on linguistic theory has been disproportionately great. This is largely due to historical circumstances. Some North American languages were among the few non-European languages for which extensive and relatively accurate information was available to

European scholars before 1800. When the modern disciplines of linguistics and anthropology were established at the beginning of the twentieth century, North American languages continued to be a rich source of data on the diversity and variability of human speech, attracting the research interest of such influential figures as Franz Boas, Edward Sapir, Leonard Bloomfield, and Benjamin Whorf. Sapir's *Language* (1921), which was among the most influential books on language in the first half of the twentieth century, made extensive use of data from the North American languages Sapir had studied, such as Yana (of northeastern California), Takelma (of western Oregon), and Nootka (of Vancouver Island).

Although enormously diverse in their structure, North American languages represent points on the same continuum of variation that is characteristic of all human languages. Taken as a whole, they are no more out-of-the-ordinary than a similar number of languages from New Guinea or the Sudan. However, since many widespread phonetic, morphological, and lexical features that are rare in European languages—for example, glottalization, incorporation, and polysynthesis—were first described in various North American languages, there is a lingering tendency to regard these languages as especially complex and difficult. This is especially true in popular culture, where such myths as the "thousands" of Eskimo words for snow, or the utter impenetrability of Navajo to a nonnative speaker, are deeply rooted. In truth, North American languages are no more and no less peculiar or inaccessible than the languages of Europe—just different.

1 Origin and Classification

1.1 Ultimate Origins

Perhaps the oldest and most persistent question that has been asked about North American languages—and all of the languages of the Western Hemisphere—concerns their ultimate origin. Linked to this is the question of their historical relationship to one another: Is there an all-encompassing "American" linguistic stock?

During the past decade, the origin and historical uniqueness of indigenous American languages have once again become topics of heated debate. On the one hand, a few historical linguists—most notably Joseph Greenberg—have made a number of far-reaching proposals concerning historical connections among the languages of the world (see Chapter 8). In Greenberg's view, all American languages, with the exception of the Eskimo-Aleut and Na-Dene families in northwestern North America, are historically distinct from the rest of the world's languages and constitute a **stock** that he calls **Amerind**. Most other linguists who specialize in American languages believe that the historical diversity of languages in the Western Hemisphere is deep and fundamental, and that they are divided into a number of historically unrelated units. Some see as few as a dozen large stocks; others, using the strictest of criteria for historical relationship, count more than 180 historically distinct **language families** and unclassifiable languages in the hemisphere. Still other estimates lie between these extremes.

These differing interpretations of indigenous American linguistic diversity tend to be allied with different theories of the populating of the New World. Although most archaeologists and biological anthropologists believe that humans have lived in the Western Hemisphere since the end of the Pleistocene (approximately 12,500 years ago), there is no agreement on how long before that date the first humans arrived, or on whether the initial migration from the Eastern Hemisphere was followed by significant secondary migrations. Greenberg's hypothesis of "Amerind" unity appeals to prehistorians who favor a single founding migration, perhaps as recently as 12,500 years ago. On the other hand, the view that the languages of the hemisphere are deeply diverse appeals to prehistorians who favor multiple migrations over a long period, beginning perhaps as early as 35,000 years ago.

At the present time, the evidence is too weak and too susceptible to multiple interpretations to allow these debates to be resolved on purely linguistic grounds. Indeed, many historical linguists believe that any claim of a linguistic relationship older than six to eight thousand years is unprovable by the available tools of historical-comparative linguistics, so that hypotheses such as the Amerind one must always lie beyond scientific validation. On the other hand, since no linguistic relationship between an Asiatic and an American language has yet been shown to exist by these tools, nearly all linguists agree that even the most recent migrations of peoples across the Bering Strait must have taken place well before six thousand years ago.

1.2 Historical Relationships in North America

Whatever their ultimate relationship to one another, the current standard classification of indigenous North American languages as shown in Table 9.1 divides them into 61 groups, including 33 established language families and 28 single-language **isolates**, whose further historical affiliation cannot be readily determined. This classification ultimately derives from the work of John Wesley Powell, the late-nineteenth-century scientist and explorer. Powell's criteria for establishing a language family were strict, and very few of the families he proposed in his 1891 classification have been disproven by later work. However, the possibility of interpreting the data less strictly and arriving at wider schemes of relationship has appealed to many scholars. Scores of stocks and phyla have been proposed since Powell's day, but only a few have gained wide acceptance.

The American linguist Edward Sapir (1884–1939) was especially interested in reducing the number of language families in North America. He proposed six "superstocks": Eskimo-Aleut, Na-Dene, Algonkian-Wakashan, Hokan-Siouan, Penutian, and Uto-Aztecan-Tanoan. Of these, only Eskimo-Aleut has won universal acceptance. Na-Dene (including Haida) and Penutian are still viable hypotheses but are far from universally accepted. The other four of Sapir's proposals are considered unlikely by most scholars today, although some of their components continue to be explored (most importantly, the Hokan component of Hokan-Siouan).

It is useful to make a distinction between language families that are geographically widespread (e.g., Algic, represented on the Pacific and Atlantic coasts, on the Plains, and around the Great Lakes) and those that are confined to one small region (e.g., Wakashan, on Vancouver Island and the adjoining coast of northern British Columbia). The former are often associated with (although not necessarily confined to) areas in which the aboriginal population was sparse and the lifestyle nomadic,

Table 9.1 Standard classification of North American languages (after Goddard 1996)

1. ESKIMO-ALEUT (13)
2. ALGIC
    - ALGONQUIAN (43)
    - RITWAN (2)
3. NA-DENE
    - Tlingit
    - ATHABASKAN-EYAK (46)
4. Haida
5. WAKASHAN (6)
6. CHIMAKUAN (2)
7. SALISHAN (23)

(8–18) Proposed PENUTIAN Superfamily

- 8. TSIMSHIANIC (2)
- 9. CHINOOKAN (3)
- 10. ALSEAN (2)
- 11. Siuslaw
- 12. COOSAN (2)
- 13. TAKELMAN (4)
- 14. WINTUAN (2)
- 15. MAIDUAN (3)
- 16. UTIAN
    - MIWOKAN (7)
    - COSTANOAN (8)
- 17. YOKUTS (6)
- 18. PLATEAU PENUTIAN
    - Klamath
    - SAHAPTIAN (2)
    - Molala

(19–28) Proposed HOKAN Superfamily

- 19. Karuk
- 20. Chimariko
- 21. SHASTAN (4)
- 22. PALAIHNIHAN
    - Achumawi
    - Atsugewi
- 23. POMOAN (7)
- 24. Yana
- 25. SALINAN (2)
- 26. COCHIMI-YUMAN (14)
- 27. Seri
- 28. Washo

29. YUKIAN
    - Yuki
    - Wappo
30. Esselen
31. CHUMASHAN (6)
32. UTO-AZTECAN*
    - NUMIC (7)
    - Tubatulabal
    - TAKIC (7)
    - Hopi
    - TEPIMAN (4)
    - TARACAHITAN (5)
    - Tubar
33. KIOWA-TANOAN (7)
34. KERESAN (2)
35. Zuni
36. Guaicura
37. Coahuilteco
38. COMECRUDAN (3)
39. Cotoname
40. Aranama
41. Solano
42. Maratino
43. Quinigua
44. Naolan
45. Karankawa
46. Kootenai
47. Cayuse
48. SIOUAN-CATAWBA
    - SIOUAN (15)
    - CATAWBAN (2)
49. Tonkawa
50. CADDOAN (6)
51. Adai
52. ATAKAPAN (2)
53. Chitimacha
54. Tunica
55. MUSKOGEAN (7)
56. Natchez
57. Yuchi
58. TIMUCUAN (2)
59. Calusa
60. IROQUOIAN (11)
61. Beothuk

Language families are in capitals, with the number of languages included shown in parentheses.

*Two additional branches of Uto-Aztecan are found only in Mesoamerica and are not included here—CORACHOL (two languages: Cora and Huichol) and AZTECAN (two languages: Nahuatl-Pipil and Pochutec). Nahuatl-Pipil, which was the language of the pre-Columbian Aztecs and was also used for administrative purposes in Colonial Mexico, remains one of the most widely spoken American Indian languages.

while the latter are frequently found in areas that were more heavily populated and characterized by sedentary cultures. Widespread language families can also sometimes be connected with the diffusion of an innovative technology, as with the bow and arrow in the case of the Athabaskan family (within Na-Dene) or the cultivation of squash and maize in the case of the Siouan family (within Siouan-Catawba).

Two regions of the continent—the Pacific Coast from southern Alaska to California, and the Gulf Coast from southern Texas to Florida—are remarkable for the number of unrelated languages and small language families they contained at the time of European contact. This mosaic-like linguistic diversity appears to have been correlated in both regions with village-level societies focused on the use of the rich local resources. On the other hand, many of the Pacific Coast language groups appear to some linguists to be related at a deeper level in the Penutian and Hokan superfamilies, indicating that at an earlier date the population of this area may have been considerably more mobile than in the contact period.

2 Phonetics and Phonology

Several speech sounds that are rare in Europe and Asia are frequently encountered in indigenous North American languages; most of these are consonants.

2.1 Velar, Uvular, and Pharyngeal Articulations

In addition to the velar stop [k] found in most of the world's languages, the majority of North American languages also have the less common velar fricative, often both voiceless and voiced ([x] and [ɣ]). In addition, stops and fricatives articulated with the back of the tongue touching the uvula (see Chapter 2) are found in about one-third of North American language groups, most of them in the northern and western parts of the continent. Uvular sounds have the quality of "deep-throated" velar sounds. In a few languages of the Northwest, most notably Nuuchahnulth (Nootka) of Vancouver Island and some Salishan languages, pharyngeal fricatives (as in Arabic) are also distinguished. (The symbols used for these sounds are shown in Table 9.2. It should be noted that here, and in several other cases, linguists who work with North American languages often use symbols that differ from the standard IPA symbols.)

Table 9.2 Velar, uvular, and pharyngeal consonants

	Velar	*Uvular*	*Pharyngeal*
Stops	k	q	
Fricatives			
Voiceless	x	x̣	ḥ
Voiced	ɣ	ɣ̣	ʕ

2.2 Lateral Fricatives

The lateral fricative [ɬ] is characteristic of the Na-Dene and Salishan families and many other languages of the Northwest, and is also found in Muskogean, Tonkawa, and Zuni. The voiceless affricate formed with the lateral fricative [tɬ] is also frequent in these languages.

2.3 Glottalized Stops and Affricates (Ejectives)

At least half of the language groups of North America have consonants with a complex type of coarticulation (see Chapter 2) known as **glottalization**. The most common glottalized consonants (also called **ejectives**) are voiceless stops or affricates that are articulated simultaneously with a closure of the glottis, accompanied by a constriction of the throat. The oral closure is released slightly before the glottis is opened, so that the sound is characterized by a distinctive "pop" or "crack." As Table 9.3 shows, glottalization is usually represented by an apostrophe above or following the phonetic symbol for the underlying stop or affricate (or other consonant).

Table 9.3 Glottalized (ejective) consonants

	Bilabial	*Dental/ alveolar*	*Lateral*	*Palatal*	*Velar*	*Uvular*
Stops	p'	t'			k'	q'
Affricates		ts'	tɬ' (ƛ̓)	tʃ' (č')		

In a few languages, fricatives, nasals, liquids, and even glides can also be accompanied by a closure of the glottis and throat constriction, and although the phonetic result differs from that heard in glottalized stops and affricates, these articulations are also usually considered to be glottalization.

2.4 Vowels and Suprasegmental Features

In the majority of indigenous North American languages, short and long vowels are phonemically distinct (e.g., [a] vs. [aː]). An oral/nasal distinction is also widespread, particularly in the eastern half of the continent and in the Pueblo Southwest. (Nasal vowels are usually represented in indigenous American languages with a hook beneath the vowel symbol rather than a tilde above—e.g., [ą] rather than [ã].) In some languages, such as Cherokee (of Oklahoma and North Carolina), a single nasal vowel of mid quality—that is, a nasalized schwa [ə̨]—contrasts with the oral vowels. In a number of languages, pitch differences between syllables are structurally significant, although in most cases the tone system is relatively simple—high versus low, or high versus mid versus low. (Phonemic high and low pitch are usually represented in indigenous American languages by acute and grave accents—e.g., [á] high vs. [à] low.) Tone systems are found in many languages of the Athabaskan branch of Na-Dene, in many Iroquoian languages, and in Kiowa-Tanoan.

Of particular typological interest is the tendency in some languages of the Northwest—most notably the Salishan family—to permit words and phrases with long clusters of consonants. These usually result from the morphological juxtaposition of a string of monosyllabic morphemes, with the vowel dropping out of the syllables not stressed. Thus, while the underlying structure of the Thompson Salish word that means 'you point a gun at him' is *čúɬ-aqs-xi-t-exw,* with four (potential) syllables, the word is actually pronounced as a single syllable, *čúɬqsxtxw,* with the only vowel phonetically realized being the one in the underlying stressed syllable.

2.5 Sounds Not Frequently Found

Several speech sounds that are relatively common elsewhere are rarely found among indigenous North American languages. These include all voiced stops and affricates. In several groups—most notably Iroquoian, Na-Dene, Caddoan, and Salishan—the bilabial stop articulation [p] is generally lacking.

3 Morphology and Syntax

3.1 The Structure of Words

Polysynthesis

As far as grammatical structure is concerned, the most distinctive characteristic of many (although far from all) indigenous North American languages is their complex morphology. Unlike the moderately complex (synthetic) morphology of the verbal and nominal word classes in Indo-European languages, the morphological complexity of many North American languages focuses on a single word class, usually identified as the verb although its grammatical function is often like that of a sentence. This type of morphology is often called **polysynthetic**. (See also Chapter 8, Section 2.2.)

Fully inflected complex words in a language with polysynthetic morphology typically have formal markers of grammatical relations such as subject, object, and indirect object; of various adverbial categories (particularly direction of motion); and of various inflectional categories such as tense, mode, and aspect. Such words are often semantically equivalent to sentences in languages such as English.

Yana, a Hokan language of northeastern California, has a typical polysynthetic morphology. Most polysynthetic Yana words are formed by suffixing up to half a dozen derivational and inflectional affixes to a root. Some typical formations are illustrated in Table 9.4.

Nuuchahnulth (Nootka), a Wakashan language of the west coast of Vancouver Island, has an especially well-developed polysynthetic morphology that greatly obscures the distinction between nouns and verbs. Except for a small number of interjections and particles, most Nuuchahnulth words are morphologically complex, consisting of at least two elements—a lexical stem and a word suffix. There are about a dozen of the latter, serving to determine the basic semantic and syntactic function of the word. They fall into two groups: predicational suffixes, which combine with the stem to form verbs; and relational suffixes, which form nouns, adverbs, or subordinate clauses.

Stems are semantically quite diverse. Some stems have meanings that are typically verb-like:

Table 9.4 Polysynthetic words in Yana

puy -ru -walti -si -numa
with.the.feet-into.fine.pieces-down.to.the.ground-PRES-2SG
'You mash it by stepping on it.'

ni:na -ha -nča
mother-PAST-1SG
'My mother is deceased; my late mother.'

pay -ru -tʰpa -si -nča
deer-going.in.pursuit.of-to.the.south-PRES-1SG
'I'm hunting deer to the south.'

ni -wul -ha -numa
one.male.goes-into.the.house-PAST-2SG
'You (a man) went into the house.'

wa -tʰi: -walti -ha -nča
with.the.buttocks-bending.(it)-down.to.the.ground-PAST-1SG
'I bent it down to the ground by sitting on it.'

1)

tɬ'i-	'shoot'
mamo:k-	'work'

Other stems express meanings more frequently associated with nouns, adjectives, prepositions, and adverbs: .

2)

qo:ʔas-	'man'
tɬ'os-	'herring'
ʔiḥ-	'large'
ya:ɬ-	'there'
ʔokwiɬ-	'with respect to'

Although there are some restrictions, there is no general rule specifying which suffixes can be used with which stems. Thus, stems with verbal meanings can take predicational suffixes and form verbs:

3)

tɬ'i-maḥ	'I shoot' (-(m)aḥ, indicative suffix, 1st-person form)
tɬ'i-ḥa	'is he shooting?' (-ḥa, interrogative suffix, 3rd-person form)

But so can stems with much less obviously verbal meanings:

4)

q'oʔoc-aḥ	'I am a man'
ya:ɬ-ḥa	'is he there?'

Similarly, stems with nominal or relational meanings can take relational suffixes and form nouns, adverbs, and other nonverb words:

5)

tɬ'os-ʔi	'(that which is) a herring' (-ʔi, relative subject suffix, 3rd-person form)
q'o:ʔas-qa	'since he is a man; that he is a man' (-qa, general subordinate suffix, 3rd-person form)
ʔo:kwiɬ-ʔi	'with respect to him'

But so can stems with verbal meanings:

6)

tɬ'i-ʔi	'he who shoots; shooter'
mamo:k-qa	'since he works; that he works'

In Nuuchahnulth, furthermore, stems are often complex. Stems can take suffixes that add a verbal idea to a noun-like stem (*-nakw-* 'have', *-ʔis-* 'eat') as well as suffixes that are typically locative or directional in their semantics (*-iɬ-* 'in the house', *-is-* 'on the beach'). Thus:

7)

tɬ'os-ʔis-aḥ	'I am eating herring'
q'oʔac-iɬ-ʔi	'(he who is) a man in the house'
ya:ɬ-is-ḥa	'is he there on the beach?'

To sum up, in Nuuchahnulth, Yana, and many other North American languages, roots and affixes are linked together in "sentence-words" by a word-internal syntax that is the functional equivalent of at least some of the relationships marked in the sentences of European languages. However, there is often no semantic equivalence between the morphological elements that enter into these polysynthetic words and the familiar European word classes—noun, verb, adjective, and so on. While speakers of polysynthetic languages can undoubtedly express all of the concepts expressed by English speakers, they do so by taking a very different structural route.

It should be kept in mind, however, that not all North American languages are polysynthetic, and that among polysynthetic languages there are many—such as those belonging to the Eskimo-Aleut and Iroquoian families—that clearly distinguish nouns and verbs. In a few cases, moreover, polysynthesis occurs only in some languages of a historically related group. Thus, the Chinookan languages are polysynthetic, while many of the other languages that are commonly assigned to the Penutian superfamily more closely resemble European languages in their morphological and syntactic structures.

Noun Incorporation

Compound verbs formed by the combination of a verb root with a noun (or an affix derived from a noun) are found in many of the world's languages (see Chapter 4, Section 3.3). However, this process of deriving complex verb stems, usually called **noun incorporation**, is especially common in North America. Many polysynthetic North American languages use noun incorporation, as do a number of others, including many Siouan languages, Zuni, and Takelma. Some examples from Lakota, a Siouan language of North and South Dakota, are shown in Table 9.5.

Table 9.5 Lakota noun incorporation

šųŋʔakąyąka 'to ride horseback' = 'to on-horse-sit' < šųka 'horse' + aką 'on' + yąka 'sit'
ločʰį 'to be hungry' = 'to food-want' < lo- 'food' (nominal affix) + čʰį 'want'
wakšiyužaža 'to wash dishes' = 'to dish-wash' < wakšiča 'dishes' + yužaža 'wash'
ipuza 'to be thirsty' = 'to be mouth-dry' < i 'mouth' + puza 'be dry'

As the Lakota examples illustrate, the grammatical relationship of the noun to the verb can include that of subject ('mouth [is] dry' = 'be thirsty') and object ('want food' = 'be hungry'), as well as locative and other relationships ('sit on [a] horse' = 'ride horseback'). These morphological constructions, however, differ from the syntactic ones on which they are based in their often idiomatic reference.

3.2 Grammatical Categories

Case Relationships

The major grammatical categories expressed in a sentence—particularly the relationship of participants (subjects, objects, etc.) to states or actions—are encoded in various ways in the languages of the world. In some languages these **case** relationships between an entity and a state or action are marked by an affix on the noun (a case marker). In other languages, other grammatical devices (such as word order) are used to mark these relationships. However they are marked, case relationships usually follow one of three fundamental patterns.

In the **nominative-accusative pattern** (which is found in all the familiar European languages), the subject of a state or an intransitive action ('the man is old', 'the man walks') is formally identified with the **agent** of a transitive action ('the man sees the dog'). This nominative case is formally distinct from the object of a transitive action ('the dog sees the man'), the accusative case. (In English, these case distinctions are marked by word order: the nominative phrase precedes the verb, the accusative follows.)

By contrast, in the **ergative-absolutive pattern**, the agent of a transitive action (the **ergative** case) is formally distinct from the subject of a state or intransitive action, which is marked in the same way as the object of a transitive action (the **absolutive** case). Although relatively rare among the world's languages, the ergative-absolutive pattern is well represented in North America. In the Eskimo languages, an ergative-absolutive case system is marked by suffixes on nouns, illustrated in Table 9.6 with examples from Central Alaskan Yupik (spoken in southwest Alaska).

A third configuration of categories, the **agent-patient pattern**, formally distinguishes the subject of an intransitive action and the agent of a transitive action (the agent case) from the subject of a state and the object of a transitive verb (the **patient** case). The agent-patient pattern is especially widespread in North America,

Table 9.6 Ergative-absolutive case marking in Central Alaskan Yupik

nayiq cikkuuq	'the seal (ABS) is frozen'
nayiq kittuq	'the seal (ABS) sinks'
aŋu:təm nayiq nəɣ̈ɣ̈aa	'the man (ERG) eats the seal (ABS)'
nayim nəqaq nəɣ̈ɣ̈aa	'the seal (ERG) eats the fish (ABS)'
aɣ̥naq ənəmmətuq	'the woman (ABS) is in the house'
aɣ̥nam taŋx̣aa	'the woman (ERG) sees him'

particularly in the languages that Sapir considered to be members of the Hokan-Siouan superstock (see Section 1.2), from the Iroquoian and Muskogean families in the East to Yuki and various Hokan-affiliated languages in California. The basic pattern can be illustrated by the marking of pronominal categories in verbs in Tuscarora, a northern Iroquoian language of New York and Ontario, illustrated in Table 9.7.

Table 9.7 Agent and patient pronominal markers in Tuscarora

k-	1 SG agent	
	k-aʔnà:wę̨s	'I'm swimming'
	k-arè:rúheʔ	'I'm running'
	k-túhar	'I'm washing something'
	k-rì:yus	'I'm killing it'
wak-	1 SG patient	
	wak-ə̨hré:tis	'I'm hungry'
	wak-nə̨́:hraraʔr	'I'm dirty'
	wak-rì:yus	'it's killing me'
	wak-yetkáhneʔ	'it's chasing me'

In some languages with an agent-patient pattern of case relationships, these categories interact with a semantic distinction between actions that are under the control of the participant and those that are uncontrollable. In Central Pomo, a language of northern California, speakers can sometimes indicate the degree of control that a participant has by choosing between agent and patient case marking:

8)

ʔa: maṭ'ém	'I (agent) stepped on it (intentionally)'
to: maṭ'ém	'I (patient) stepped on it (accidentally)'
ʔa: k'lú:k'lu:w	'I (agent) coughed (intentionally)'
to: k'lú:k'lu:w	'I (patient) coughed (involuntarily)'

Evidentials

Many indigenous North American languages have grammatical expressions representing the speaker's source of information for the statement he or she is making. In many languages, these expressions (frequently enclitic particles) are ubiquitous in discourse, if not grammatically obligatory. The most common types of **evidentials** are (1) firsthand personal experience, (2) hearsay (often used to indicate that the speaker is quoting another's words), (3) nonverbal auditory evidence, and (4) inference from other evidence.

In Central Pomo, seven evidential categories are marked by enclitics, as shown in Table 9.8.

Table 9.8 Central Pomo evidential enclitics

čʰé mul=ʔma	'it rained' (it's an established fact)
čʰé mul=ya	'it rained' (I was there and saw it)
čʰé mul=ʔdoː	'it rained' (I was told)
čʰé mul=nmeː	'it rained' (I heard the drops)
čʰé mul=ʔka	'it must have rained' (because everything is wet)
dačéːw=la	'I caught it' (I know because I did it)
dačéːw=wiya	'I got caught' (I know because it happened to me)

Aspect and Tense

A popular misconception about indigenous American languages is that they are "timeless"—that is, that they do not concisely mark the categories of past, present, and future tense that are nearly universal in European languages. This is emphatically not true for a number of North American languages (see the discussion of Wishram Chinook tenses below), although there are many languages on the continent in which grammatical contrasts in **aspect**—the manner in which an action takes place, regardless of whether it is in the past, present, or future—are of equal or greater importance than contrasts in tense.

In the Athabaskan languages, verbs are obligatorily marked for several aspectual categories by intricate combinations of prefixes and stem variation. Typical of the aspectual variants in Hupa (an Athabaskan language of northern California) are the following forms (W represents a voiceless [w]):

9)

yantiW	'you're picking it up' (continuously)
yaːʔantiW	'you pick it up' (habitually)
yaːntaːn	'you pick it up' (at a specific time)
yaːntiWiɬ	'you pick it up' (repeatedly)

In contrast to the morphological complexity of aspectual marking, **tense** is marked only by two optional enclitics, *-neʔin* 'past' and *-te* 'future':

10)

yantiW-neʔin	'you were picking it up' (continuously)
yaːʔantiW-neʔin	'you picked it up' (habitually)
yantiW-te	'you will be picking it up' (generally)
yaːntan-te	'you will pick it up' (at a specific time)

These tense enclitics are not part of the inflectional system of Hupa verbs, but are markers of time past and time yet to come that can also be used with nouns and other parts of speech:

11)

Wiʔad	'my wife'
Wiʔad-te	'my fiancée, my wife-to-be'
Wiʔad-neʔin	'my late wife'

Although aspectual marking is more often emphasized, grammatical contrasts in tense—particularly gradations of past tense—are quite elaborately marked in some North American languages. In Wishram Chinook (of Washington), four past tenses are distinguished by prefixes:

12)

Distant past	ga(l)-:	ga-yúya 'he went (a year or more ago)' (also used in reciting myths)
Indefinite past	ni(g)-:	ni-yúya 'he went (more than a couple of days ago, but less than a year)'
Recent past	na(l)-:	na-yúya 'he went (yesterday)'
Immediate past	i(g)-:	i-yúya 'he went (earlier today)'

A verb without a past tense prefix but with suffixed *-t* refers to an action now going on but soon to be completed:

13)

yúi-t 'he is looking at him (just now)'

There is only one future tense, marked with *a(l)-*:

14)

a-yúya 'he will go'

In addition, Wishram verbs can also take one of two directional prefixes, *u-* 'in that direction, thither' and *t-* 'in this direction, hither'. Speakers commonly make even finer tense distinctions by using these directional markers in combination with the tense markers:

15)

gal-u-yúya	'he went (in the mythic age)'
ga-t-yúya	'he went (a few years ago)'
nig-u-yúya	'he went (last season)'
ni-t-yúya	'he went (last week)'
a-t-yúya	'he will go (immediately)'
al-u-yúya	'he will go (eventually)'

3.3 Noun Classification

The classification of nouns into gender categories or similar selectional classes is a widespread phenomenon. Among North American languages, gender in the European sense (masculine/feminine/neuter) is rarely used to distinguish classes of nouns (the clearest cases are Tunica in the Southeast and Chimakuan, Salishan, and Chinookan in the Northwest), but classification by alienability of possession, animacy, and shape and texture is frequent.

Alienability of Possession

The most common classification of nouns in North American languages—found in the majority of them—divides nouns into two groups: **inalienably possessed nouns**, which must always have a pronominal possessor indicated (usually by an affix), and all other nouns. Inalienably possessed nouns typically refer to things that are inherently connected to the possessor and that cannot be acquired or given away. The class of inalienably possessed nouns is sometimes quite small, but often includes most terms for parts of the body ('my head', 'his head', but never simply 'head') and for kinship relationships ('my father', 'his father', but never simply 'father'). In some languages, inalienably possessed nouns that have no identifiable possessor are marked with a special possessor that is not used with other nouns. This is the case in Yurok, an Algic language of northern California, as shown in Table 9.9.

Table 9.9 Possessed nouns in Yurok

Inalienably possessed		*Other*	
(*lin)		tepo	'tree'
ne-lin	'my arm'	ne-tepo	'my tree'
k'e-lin	'your arm'	k'e-tepo	'your tree'
we-lin	'his, her arm'	we-tepo	'his, her tree'
me-lin	'somebody's arm; an arm'	(*me-tepo)	

Animacy

In some North American languages, the degree of **animacy** of a noun—its relative semantic closeness to a sentient living being—plays an important grammatical role.

In all Algonquian languages, nouns belong to one of two classes, **animate** or **inanimate**, depending on the plural marker they take (*-ak* or *-a*) and which of two sets of verbal subject and object affixes are used to refer to them. Table 9.10 illustrates the animate and inanimate noun classes of Cree, an Algonquian language of Canada. (The conventional spelling of Cree words is used. Vowels with a macron—ā, ī, etc. —are long. Inalienably possessed nouns are shown with an initial hyphen.) The assignment of a Cree noun to one or the other class is often semantically arbitrary, just as with masculine and feminine classes in European languages. In the nouns of group A, there is a clear semantic contrast between the animate and inanimate classes (note how *mistik* changes its meaning—'tree' or 'stick, pole'—according to which class it is treated as belonging to). The nouns of group B, however, show no such obvious contrast.

Shape and Texture Classes

In Athabaskan languages, every noun belongs to one of several classes (in some languages a dozen or more), depending on which of a set of otherwise semantically identical stems is used when it is the object of a verb of moving or handling, or the subject of a stative verb. The verb stems that are matched with these noun classes

Table 9.10 Animate and inanimate nouns in Cree

	Animate class		*Inanimate class*	
A.	atihkamēk	'whitefish'	asiskiy	'mud, clay'
	cīpay	'ghost'	iskotēw	'fire'
	iskwēw	'woman'	kīsikaw	'day'
	ililiw	'person, Indian, Cree'	maskēk	'swamp, muskeg'
	maskwa	'bear'	mēskanaw	'road'
	mistik	'tree'	mistik	'stick, pole'
	mōs	'moose'	nipiy	'water'
	-tōtēm	'friend, guardian spirit'	pihkotēw	'ashes'
	-ōkom	'grandmother'	pīwāpisk	'metal'
	sīsīp	'duck'	sākahikan	'lake'
B.	asām	'snowshoe'	ācimōwin	'story'
	asiniy	'stone, rock'	astotin	'hat'
	askihk	'kettle, pail'	maskisin	'shoe, moccasin'
	āsokan	'wharf, jetty'	mīcim	'food'
	cīstēmāw	'tobacco'	mīnis	'berry'
	kōna	'snow'	-spiton	'arm'
	ospwākan	'(tobacco) pipe'	-tēhi	'heart'
	palacīs	'trousers'	pīskākan	'jacket'
	pīsim	'sun'	wāskāhikan	'house'
	siklētk	'cigarette'	wāwi	'egg'

are usually referred to as **classificatory verbs**. In Navajo, there are eleven basic classificatory categories, illustrated in Table 9.11 by the variants in the stative verb stem. (Each of the verb forms means 'it lies/they lie motionless'. They are cited in the standard Navajo orthography.) As can be seen, the noun classes are primarily distinguished by shape and texture.

Table 9.11 Classificatory categories in Navajo

Category	*'it lies there'*	*Typical nouns in category*
1. Solid or compact roundish object	si-'ą́	rock, box
2. Noncompact matter	shi-jool	wool, wig
3. Mushy matter	si-tłéé'	dough, pitch
4. Single flat flexible object	si-łtsooz	sheet of paper, shirt
5. Slender flexible object	si-lá	string of beads, snake
6. Slender stiff object	si-tą́	log, cigarette
7. Single animate object	si-tį́	baby, grandmother
8. Load, pack, or burden	si-yį́	load of trash, sack of apples
9. Anything in an open container	si-ką́	bowl of soup, box of apples
10. Plural (countable) objects	si-nil	dishes, children
11. Plural (granular) objects	shi-jaa	seeds, dirt

As with the animate/inanimate classification in Cree, not all Navajo nouns fall naturally into one of these classes, and a number of assignments are arbitrary or rest on metaphor or cultural assumptions. Thus, a lake or puddle is assigned to the "load, pack, or burden" class; a word or utterance to the "slender flexible object" class; and anything that comes in pairs (like socks, shoes, and scissors) to the "slender flexible object" class.

4 The Future of Indigenous North American Languages

Although this chapter has been written in the present tense, many indigenous North American languages have become extinct in recent generations (Yana, for example, has not been in use since the 1930s), and nearly all of those that remain are losing speakers and facing extinction. The 2004 edition of *Ethnologue* lists over 160 living Native American languages in the United States and 50 extinct languages. Of the living languages, 92 are "nearly extinct." That means that two-thirds of the Native American languages of the United States have become or will soon become extinct.

According to the 2000 U.S. census, approximately 350,000 Native Americans above the age of five in the United States speak a Native language at home. This figure, however, must be interpreted with some caution as we do not know how often the language is spoken at home nor the range of language employed. Just looking at the number of speakers, however, is not the whole story. Cherokee is a case in point. There are approximately 6,500 speakers of Cherokee in Oklahoma, yet most proficient speakers are of the grandparent generation. If a language is not transmitted to children, then its future is bleak. Only in a few remote communities in the United States and Canada (such as the Crow Reservation in Montana, various Cree settlements in the Canadian north, and in parts of the Navajo Nation) are indigenous languages still being routinely acquired by children as their first tongue. It has been estimated that only 20 Native American languages are now being transmitted to children as a mother tongue. The implication is that within a generation or two, only 10 percent of Native American languages will remain as living languages. For example, in Alaska, of 20 indigneous languages, only two are being transmitted to children in the home. In Oklahoma, where 40 indigenous languages are represented, a recent survey indicated that only one of these was in daily use among children. Even Navajo, which was vigorously prospering as late as 1970, is now the first language of only a minority of Navajo children. A tribal survey in 1992 discovered that only 32 percent of children in kindergarten spoke Navajo well, in contrast with 73 percent who spoke English well.

This trend is part of a worldwide phenomenon (see Chapter 8, Section 1.1). Languages of small and sociopolitically weak communities have been under threat since the beginning of the European expansion in the late fifteenth century, a trend that has accelerated in recent decades with the development of satellite television and the Internet. If any but a handful of the indigenous languages of North America are to survive another century, deliberate efforts will have to be made to transmit them to new speakers. In the face of the bleak outlook for Native American languages, linguists and tribal members have combined their efforts to maintain, preserve, and revitalize endangered languages. One success story seems to be the Hawaiian Language Immersion Program, involving K–12 schools in which Hawaiian is the language of instruction. Before the program was started in 1987, there were only thirty people under the age of eighteen who spoke Hawaiian. Now, there are over one thousand young speakers. Some federal funding has been made available for the development of bilingual education programs for languages such as Navajo in Arizona and Yupik in Alaska. For other indigenous languages, various experimental programs have been instituted, such as ancestral language use in Head Start programs or language immersion camps for children (see Chapter 12, Section 4.4). In California, where all indigneous languages are endangered, a master-apprentice program has been introduced in which a tribal elder is paired with a young tribal member for intensive language learning in a naturalistic setting. The extent to which these various efforts will prove successful remains to be seen. Ironically, the same electronic media that are now speeding the demise of so many languages and cultures may offer the best hope of creating new modes of transmission for these languages—and new, virtual communities in which they can meaningfully thrive.

Meanwhile, the linguistic repertoires of the most fluent surviving speakers should be documented with the best available tools, and analytic work should be carried out on as many languages as possible. Despite several centuries of work by linguists, anthropologists, and other skilled observers, the accumulated record of indigenous North American languages still has many gaps and inadequacies, and the need for well-trained descriptive linguists to work in this field remains acute.

For more information on the status of particular languages mentioned in this chapter, go to **bedfordstmartins.com/linguistics/indigenous** and click on **status**.

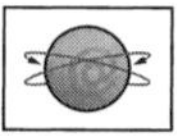

Summing Up

This chapter provides an overview of the approximately 325 languages spoken in North America at the time of European contact. More than sixty **language families** or **isolates** are recognized, and although they have been grouped into a smaller number of **stocks**, these remain controversial. Several otherwise rare speech sounds are common in North America, most notably the **glottalization** of stops and affricates. Many North American languages have a complex morphological structure usually referred to as **polysynthetic**. Many are also characterized by **noun incorporation**, by **ergative-absolutive** or **agent-patient** patterns of case marking, and by the use of **evidentials** to indicate the speaker's source of information. A grammatical distinction between **animate** and **inanimate** nouns is sometimes encountered, as are **classificatory verbs**. Unfortunately, much of this rich heritage of linguistic diversity is in imminent danger of disappearing as languages cease to be spoken.

Key Terms

absolutive
agent
agent-patient pattern
Amerind

animacy
animate
aspect
case
classificatory verbs
ejectives
ergative
ergative-absolutive pattern
evidentials
glottalization
inalienably possessed nouns
inanimate
isolates
language families
nominative-accusative pattern
noun incorporation
patient
polysynthetic (languages)
stock
tense

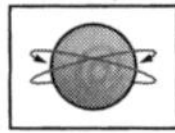

For more information on the sources used in this chapter, please go to **bedfordstmartins.com/linguistics/indigenous** and click on **Sources**.

Recommended Reading

Campbell, Lyle. 1997. *American Indian Languages: The Historical Linguistics of Native America.* Oxford Studies in Anthropological Linguistics, vol. 4. Oxford: Oxford University Press.

Goddard, Ives, ed. 1996. *Handbook of North American Indians.* Vol. 17, *Languages.* Washington: Smithsonian Institution.

Mithun, Marianne. 1999. *The Languages of Native North America.* Cambridge: Cambridge University Press.

Silver, Shirley, and Wick R. Miller. 1997. *American Indian Languages: Cultural and Social Contexts.* Tucson: University of Arizona Press.

ten

Natural Sign Languages

Wendy Sandler
Diane Lillo-Martin

OBJECTIVES

In this chapter, you will learn:

- that sign languages share with spoken languages defining characteristics of human language
- how hand shape, movement, and location can be combined to create meaning
- that sign language has complex morphology
- how sign language sentence structure resembles that of spoken languages
- how poetry is created in sign languages

It has been nearly forty years since serious investigation of natural sign languages began to show that these languages are bona fide linguistic systems, with structures and rules and the full range of expressive power that characterize spoken languages. Researchers have spent most of that time demonstrating, with increasing rigor and formality, the sometimes surprising similarities between languages in the two modalities—spoken and signed. Concomitantly, scholars in related disciplines like language acquisition and neurolinguistics have been discovering significant similarities between spoken and signed languages in these domains as well. It is safe to say that the academic world is now convinced that sign languages are real languages in every sense of the term.

If this were the whole story, however, there would be no need for a chapter on sign languages in an introductory linguistics textbook. Each sign language would be seen as a language like any other—English, Hungarian, Central Alaskan Yupik Eskimo, or Mandarin Chinese—each with its own contribution to make toward understanding the general language faculty of humans. But this is not the case. Rather, sign languages as a group are of special importance, crucial to our understanding of the essential nature of language for two reasons. First, the study of natural languages in a different physical modality confirms in a novel way the hypothesis that all natural human languages are characterized by certain key properties. Second, this study raises fundamental questions about the human language capacity, as well as challenges for language theory that we would never have noticed were it not for the existence of sign languages.

The sign languages under discussion are the languages used by communities of deaf people all over the world. They are natural languages in the sense that they are not consciously invented by anyone but develop spontaneously, wherever deaf people have an opportunity to congregate and communicate regularly with each other. Sign languages are not derived from spoken languages; they have their own independent vocabularies and their own grammatical structures. Although there do exist contrived sign systems that are based on spoken languages (such as Signed English and Signed Hebrew), such systems are not natural languages, and they are not the subject of interest here. Rather, linguists and cognitive psychologists are most interested in the natural sign languages passed down without instruction from one deaf generation to the next, and used by deaf people in their own communities all over the world.

Sign languages exhibit the full range of expression that spoken languages afford their users. Different styles are adopted for different social contexts; storytelling has been heightened to an art in some deaf communities, and deaf poets create artistic poetry in signs, marshaling the formational elements of the languages to convey images, emotions, and ideas. Sign language can "do" everything that spoken language can. In this chapter, we explain how it does so.

Most of the examples we provide here come from American Sign Language (ASL) and Israeli Sign Language (ISL), but the properties they exemplify are common to all sign languages that have been studied so far. This does *not* mean, however, that all sign languages have the same grammatical structure. The common elements described here are selected because they provide useful examples of the linguistic patterning of sign languages in general, and of the ways in which they compare to spoken language patterns.

First we examine the linguistic structure of sign languages, beginning with the structure of the smaller units of language—those that may be compared to the meaningless but identifiable sounds of speech (phonology). Then we move to the structure of words (morphology). We will end the linguistic description with a discussion of the structure of the sentence (syntax). We conclude the chapter with a description of sign language poetry.

1 Phonology

In order to have sentences, one must have words, and words—at least in spoken language—are pronounced as a series of sounds. What about the signs of sign language? Do they have a level of substructure like the spoken word? Since spoken and signed languages are produced and perceived by different physical systems—oral/aural and manual/visual—one might expect to find the least amount of similarity across the two modalities at this level of analysis. Yet here, there is much common ground.

1.1 Formational Elements

In 1960, William Stokoe published a monograph in which he demonstrated that the words of American Sign Language are not holistic gestures but analyzable as a combination of three meaningless yet linguistically significant categories: hand shape, location, and movement. That is, by changing some feature of any one of those three categories, themselves meaningless, one could change the meaning of the sign. For example, by changing only the configuration of the hand, the signs CANDY and APPLE are distinguished. (Conventionally, uppercase is used to represent signs.) In these two signs, the location and movements are the same; only the hand configuration is different. Similar pairs exist that are distinguished only by their locations or only by their movements.

a. CANDY

b. APPLE

Figure 10.1 ASL minimal pair

The example in Figure 10.1 is analogous to the English pair *pan, tan,* in which the first sound of each word—[p] and [t]—is different. The sounds are themselves meaningless, but they are linguistically significant because they make a difference in meaning when put in a word. In the sign language pair CANDY, APPLE, the hand configurations are also meaningless, yet they too make a difference in meaning. The other formational elements—location and movement—can, like hand configurations, independently make a difference in meaning, though they are themselves meaningless.

This finding was of supreme importance. Ever since its discovery, it has no longer been possible to assume, as most people previously had, that signs are fundamentally different from spoken words, that they are simple iconic gestures with no substructure. Rather, ASL is characterized by a defining feature of language in general: **duality of patterning**. This duality is between the meaningful level (consisting of morphemes, words, phrases, sentences) and the meaningless level, which in spoken languages is the level of the sounds that make up the meaningful expressions. The meaningless elements of spoken language are linguistically significant (i.e., they independently make a difference in meaning); they obey constraints on their combination within morphemes and words, and may be systematically altered in different contexts. This is the domain of phonology. The list of hand shapes, locations, and movements are the formational elements of sign language phonology, comparable to the list of consonants and vowels in spoken language. We will now show that sign language phonology is also characterized by constraints on the combination of these elements, and by systematic changes in "pronunciation" under certain circumstances.

1.2 Combining Formational Elements

All languages have constraints on the co-occurrence of sounds in syllables and words. For example, English does not allow the sequences **sr* or **chl* at the beginning of a syllable or word (although other languages do permit such combinations). Sign languages as well have constraints on the combination of elements at this same level of structure. For example, only one group of fingers may characterize the hand shape within any morpheme. While either the finger group (all fingers) or the group (index plus middle finger) may occur in a morpheme, a sequence of the two shapes, *, is prohibited in a morpheme in the native signs of ASL and other sign languages.

Similarly, all languages have **assimilation** processes, in which sounds borrow some or all aspects of neighboring sounds. For example, in the English compound words *greenback* and *beanbag,* the nasal sound [n] often assimilates the labial place of articulation from the [b] that follows it: *gree[m]back, bea[m]bag.* In many common ASL compounds, part of the hand configuration may similarly assimilate from one part of the compound to the other. The example shown in Figure 10.2 is from the compound that means OVERSLEEP, made from the two words SLEEP and SUNRISE. Just as the [n] borrowed one of the features of [b] (the LABIAL feature) in the English examples above, in the ASL compound the hand configuration of SLEEP borrows a feature from the following sign, SUNRISE, when forming the compound—the orientation feature. That is, rather than being oriented toward the face, as in the citation form of SLEEP, the dominant, signing hand in the compound OVERSLEEP is oriented sideways, as in the sign SUNRISE.

The phonology of sign languages has been shown to be similar to that of spoken languages at even more surprising levels of analysis. For example, it has been demonstrated that the phonological elements of ASL words are not all simultaneously organized but have significant sequential structure, just as spoken languages have one sound after another. A sign language equivalent of the syllable has even been argued for.

1.3 Prosody

An aspect of language structure that involves both phonology and syntax is **prosody**. Prosody involves rhythm, to separate the parts of a sentence; prominence, to empha-

a. SLEEP

b. SUNRISE

c. OVERSLEEP

Figure 10.2 ASL signs SLEEP and SUNRISE, and the compound OVERSLEEP with orientation assimilation

size selected elements; and intonation, to communicate other important information, such as the discourse function of the sentence (e.g., whether an utterance is a plain declarative sentence or a question). Recent work argues that sign languages have the equivalent of prosody. While spoken languages use the rise and fall of the pitch of the voice, volume, and pause to achieve these effects, sign languages employ facial expressions, body postures, and rhythmic devices in similar ways and for similar functions. Examples are the Israeli Sign Language facial expressions for *yes/no* questions and for information designated as shared by the signer and addressee (shown in Figure 10.3).

a. yes/no question

b. shared information

Figure 10.3 Facial expressions accompanying an ISL *yes/no* question and "shared information" in a sentence

Sign language facial "intonation" is different from the facial expressions used by hearing people in their communication, which are affective and not mandatory or systematic. Rather, sign language facial expressions are like the intonational pitch patterns of spoken language. Both tonal melodies and facial melodies are **grammaticalized**—that is, fixed and systematic. For example, the intonational melody used in spoken language to ask a question requiring an answer of yes or no is systematically different from the one used to make a declarative statement. The same is true of the facial intonations for these two types of sentences in sign language.

In the next subsection, the element that is perhaps the most central aspect of language is examined: the word.

2 Morphology

Most languages have both simple words, such as *teach,* and complex words, such as *teach+er.* Knowing English entails understanding the internal structure of its complex words, as well as the ability to create and understand new complex words that exploit those internal structures.

2.1 Word Formation

For example, given a new verb *scaff,* as in *The purpose of this machine is to scaff computers against viruses,* we can also create or analyze the internal structure of the word *scaffer* and can deduce something about its meaning in the sentence *The company* *purchased several expensive scaffers last year.* We would also immediately judge the nonce word **er+scaff* to be impossible in English. Speakers of English know the form and function of the meaningful word component *-er,* and they know that it is a suffix rather than a prefix. Although users of a language are usually not conscious of their linguistic knowledge, their use of language clearly reveals the existence of this underlying system.

Another type of complex word formation can be thought of as relating words to each other within a sentence. For example, the word *walk* has two different suffixes in the following sentences, *-s* and *-ed*. The *-s* in sentence *1a* is an agreement marker; it shows that the subject of the sentence, *Hadar,* is third person singular (*he* or *she*). The *-ed* in sentence *1b* is a tense marker, showing that the event described by the sentence took place in the past.

1)

a. Hadar walk<u>s</u> to school sometimes.
b. Stephanie walk<u>ed</u> to her friend's house.

The existence of complexity of structure within words is a typical property of spoken language, though many different kinds of word formation can be found in the languages of the world. Most (though not all) languages have complex words, and many languages have far more complex morphology than English has.

What about sign languages? While one might expect any communication system to have syntax, one might not necessarily expect sign languages to have internal structure to their words. Rather, one might expect—as naive early descriptions of sign language used to claim—that signs are holistic gestures, each one representing a unitary concept. Concomitant with this view is the belief that the vocabulary of sign languages is purely iconic, that there is a one-to-one relationship between the form of a word or concept and its meaning. The ASL sign for AIRPLANE looks something like an airplane; the sign for GIVE looks something like the act of handing something to someone. If these sign words are iconic wholes, then adding grammatical complexity to them in a systematic way might seem counterintuitive.

Yet sign languages do have a great deal of morphological complexity. Such complexity is one of many sources of evidence that systematic grammatical structuring strongly dominates the presumably iconic origins of these languages. We will describe two kinds of word complexity here: verb agreement, and verbs of motion and location, as expressed through classifier constructions.

2.2 Verb Agreement

We begin with verb agreement. In many spoken languages, verbs have some kind of marking on them that gives information about their subjects, objects, or other nouns directly related to them in the sentence. Example *1a* above shows the only agreement marker that English has on main verbs, the *-s* that indicates third person and singular in the present tense. Other languages have far richer agreement systems. For example, Swahili has both subject and object agreement markers that indicate person (*I, you, s/he*), gender (*he* or *she*), and number (singular or plural).

2)
Swahili
a. *atakupenda*
à -ta -ku -penda
he (SUBJ)-(FUTURE)-you (OBJ)-like
'he will like you'
b. *utampenda*
u -ta -m -penda
you (SUBJ)-(FUTURE)-him (OBJ)-like
'you will like him'

All sign languages investigated so far show a comparable kind of verb agreement. Consider for example the ISL verb SHOW, shown in Figure 10.4. To say 'I show you', the motion of the sign is from a point near the signer toward the addressee. To say 'you show me', the beginning and endpoints of the sign are just the opposite, beginning at a point near the addressee and ending near the signer. The beginning and endpoints of the sign are markers for the subject and object of the verb it represents. To say 'I show you (plural)', the hands move in a horizontal arc in front of the signer. In the first example, 'I show you', the first position of the hand corresponds to the prefix *à* in the Swahili example in *2a* above: it marks agreement with the person of the verb's subject—third person (*he*) in the Swahili example, and first person (*I*) in the ISL example. The second position of the hand corresponds to the morpheme *ku* in the same Swahili example, agreeing with the person of the object of the verb—second person (*you*) in Swahili, and second person in ISL. The beginning and endpoints of the second example in Figure 10.4 similarly mark agreement with subject and object—here, *you* and *me.* To agree with the second person plural—'I show you (plural)', the shape of the movement is altered. To see animated video clips of these three examples, go to **bedfordstmartins.com/linguistics/signlanguage** and click on **I show you**, **you show me**, and **I show you (pl)**.

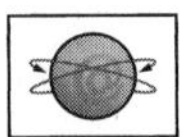

This kind of phenomenon can be described as **subject-object agreement**; in particular, sign language verbs agree in person and in number with their subject and object. In this way, the verb agreement found in sign languages is similar to that found in many spoken languages.

A characteristic of verb agreement systems in sign languages is that different categories of verbs participate in different ways. For example, in addition to the subject-object agreement just described, some verbs, commonly called backwards verbs, have the opposite agreement pattern. In these verbs, the movement of the hand is from the object to the subject rather than from subject to object. This class includes verbs such as INVITE, TAKE, COPY, and ADOPT—essentially the same list in ASL and ISL, and possibly in all sign languages. Other verbs agree with points in space denoting specific locations rather than with the verb's subject and object. Still others do not agree at all.

2.3 Classifier Constructions

A more complex type of morphology in sign languages is found in classifier predicates. In these constructions, hand shapes that stand for classes of nouns combine

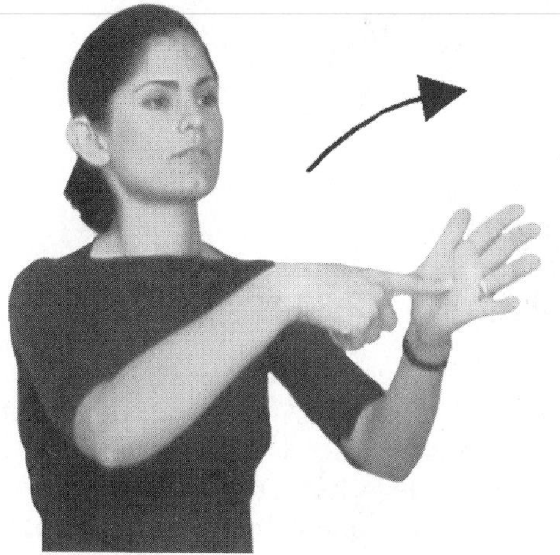

a. 'I show you.'

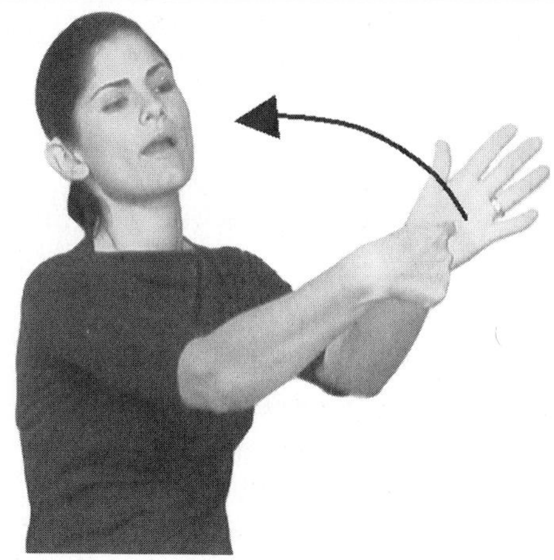

b. 'You show me.'

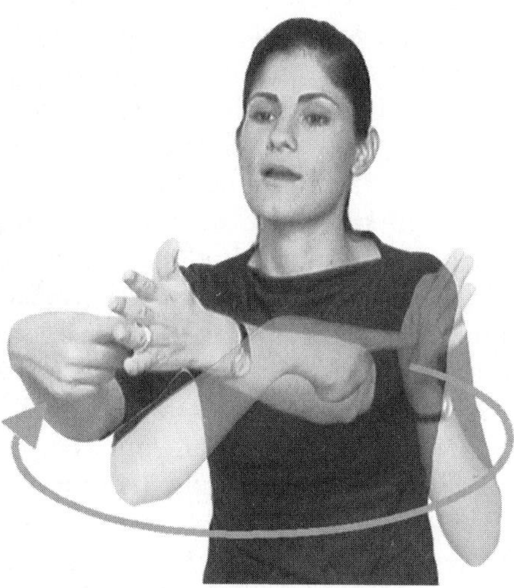

c. 'I show all of you.'

Figure 10.4 ISL verb agreement

with different types and manners of movements and with locations in space. The hand shapes of **classifier constructions** often classify nominal referents according to physical properties. These complex forms differ from the morphologically simple signs of the language exemplified in the phonology subsection above because in the classifier subsystem, each of the formational parameters—hand shape, location, and movement—is meaningful. In fact, classifier predicates in sign languages, which we will exemplify on page 352, are so visually and spatially motivated that one might be tempted to think that they are different from anything found in spoken language. But this is not so; even these constructions can be fruitfully compared with structures found in many spoken languages (see Chapter 9, Section 3.3). For example, Diegueño, a Hokan language spoken in California and Mexico, signifies physical properties of objects with classifier affixes, as shown in *3*.

3)

Diegueño

a'*mi*	'to hang (a long object)'
tu*mi*	'to hang (a small round object)'
a·*xi*·¬	'to drag (a long object)'
c' *xi*·¬	'to drag (a bunch of objects)'

In this language, the prefix is a classifier of some physical property of a nominal: 'a long object', 'a small round object', or 'a bunch of objects', in these examples. Studies that have compared sign language and spoken language classifiers have found significant parallels in the categories that classifiers categorize in the two language modalities.

Size and Shape Classifiers (SASSes)—one of three kinds of sign language classifiers—represent the size and shape of an object, such as 'cylindrical object', 'flat object', or 'small round object'. These hand shapes may combine with one of a short list of motion morphemes (e.g., 'straight', 'pivot'), location morphemes, and manner of movement morphemes, each with a meaning of its own. The classifier system is used to represent the type of referent engaged in an activity; its location; and the direction, shape, and manner of motion it manifests. The different combinations of elements of each type contribute to a system in which expressions can become very complex morphologically. In the following examples from ISL, classifiers for 'cylindrical object' and 'flat object' or 'vehicle' are combined with locations and motions to form complex structures. Figure 10.5a means that a cylindrical object is placed next to a flat object, or 'A cup is next to a piece of paper'. Figure 10.5b means that two vehicles approached from opposite directions and passed each other. To see animated video clips of these two examples, go to **bedfordstmartins.com/linguistics/signlanguage** and click on **a cup is next to . . .** and **two cars pass**.

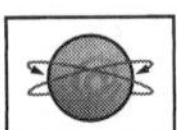

A classifier may correspond to any of a long list of regular words. For example, the word for CAR is shown in Figure 10.5c. Objectively speaking, the phonetic forms of Figure 10.5b and Figure 10.5c are of roughly equal *phonetic* complexity. But the *morphological* complexity of each form is very different. Phonetically, both forms involve two hands with the same hand shape moving in opposition to one another, either by approaching and moving in opposite directions (as in Figure 10.5b) or by moving in up-and-down arc shapes alternately, one hand after the other (as in Figure 10.5c). Yet morphologically, Figure 10.5b is quite complex, involving two entities as well as their locations and movements relative to one another, while Figure 5c is morphologically simple, meaning just CAR. Classifiers and lexical words have different uses and privileges of occurrence in the grammars of sign languages as well.

It is very important to note that classifier predicates are linguistic entities—that is, morphologically complex forms. They are neither pantomime nor otherwise strictly analogic to real-world things and activities. Furthermore, this type of morphology, which incorporates nouns, verbs, and other lexical categories into single expressions, is not uncommon in the world's spoken languages. As we have seen, there are spoken languages such as Diegueño that incorporate into verbs the particular type of size and shape classifiers that are incorporated into sign languages.

a. 'A cup is next to a piece of paper.'

b. 'Two cars pass each other.'

c. CAR

Figure 10.5

3 Syntax

3.1 Recursion

One of the fundamental properties of human language is that it can be used to create an unlimited number of utterances given a limited number of pieces. At the syntactic level, this property follows directly from a mathematical property of language called recursiveness. We're all familiar with recursiveness (even if not with the term). It is found in language, in computer programs, and even in children's stories, as in *4*.

4)

This is the farmer sowing the corn,
That kept the cock that crowed in the morn,
That waked the priest all shaven and shorn,
That married the man all tattered and torn,
That kissed the maiden all forlorn,
That milked the cow with the crumpled horn,

That tossed the dog,
That worried the cat,
That killed the rat,
That ate the malt
That lay in the house that Jack built.

In *4,* the process or rule that creates a **relative clause** (here, the clauses beginning with *that*) has applied repeatedly to the noun phrases inside other relative clauses (see Chapter 5, Section 5.2). This repeated application of the same rule to create more and more complex sentences is an example of recursiveness. The children's story is amusing precisely because we all know that there is no theoretical limit to the application of this rule. Any speaker of English can add to the story by generating another relative clause at the beginning, as in *5.*

5)

This is the banker, his honor forsworn,
That foreclosed on the farmer sowing the corn, . . .

The only limitations on the number of relative clauses are practical and not linguistic: the speaker may run out of things to say, or out of breath or time or memory. It is because the rules of syntax are allowed to apply recursively that language is nonfinite: there is no limit to its expressive power. It is important that this recursiveness applies to create structures that are *embedded* inside other structures, to create **subordinate clauses**, such as the *that* relative clauses in *4.* These embedded subordinate clauses involve more complex structure than coordinate clauses, which are illustrated in *6.*

6)

This is the dog, and the dog worried the cat, and the cat killed the rat, and the rat ate the malt, and the malt lay in the house, and Jack built the house.

Embedding distinguishes subordinate clauses of the sort exemplified in "The House that Jack Built" from simple coordination. A simplified diagram of the structure of recursive subordinate clauses versus coordinate clauses is given in Figure 10.6 (see Chapter 5, Section 5). The rule that makes a relative clause produces a structure in which one sentence is inside another sentence. This is the key to **recursion**: by putting one phrase inside another of the same type, there is in principle no limit to the length of a sentence.

Human language is not limited to simple conjunction of one phrase after another (like that in *6*); it has both coordination and subordination. If someone found a human language that allowed only coordination, it would shake our fundamental assumptions about what human language is. Thus, it should be rather surprising that exactly this was claimed about ASL in the early days of its study. In 1977, H. Thompson attempted to discover the mechanisms for subordination in ASL and, not finding what he considered to be evidence for it, decided that it was systematically missing. If this were correct, then either the character and structure of human language would not be as has been commonly assumed, or signed languages would be significantly different from spoken languages—missing recursivity, which is often taken to be a defining property of language.

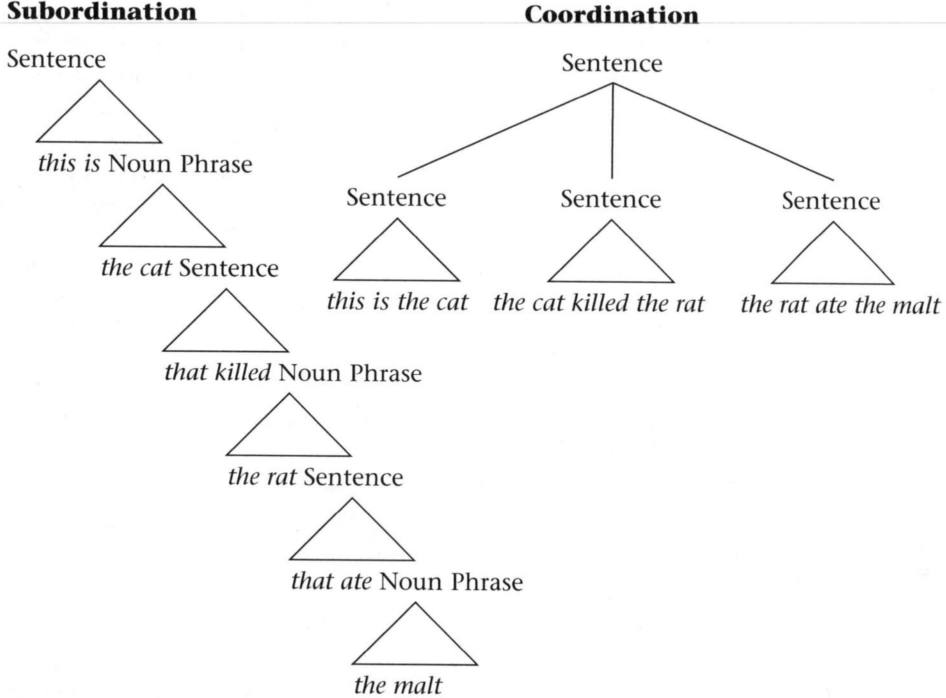

Figure 10.6 Simplified phrase structure diagrams of subordination and coordination

Later research has made it unnecessary to choose between these two puzzling options. Thompson had looked for several kinds of indications that ASL has subordination. For example, he looked for overt complementizers—an analogue to English *that* in *I know that Susan will win*—and found none in ASL. He looked for relative clauses (like those in *4* and *5*) and instead found sequences of signs, as in *7*. ('IND' stands for 'index', a pointing gesture.)

7)

English target: The girl whom Asa gave the dog to is pretty.
ASL response: ASA GIVE DOG GIRL IND PRETTY IND
[roughly: Asa gave the dog to the girl and she is pretty.]

He looked for clausal complements to adjectives like *happy* (e.g., *He's happy that she passed*) and found instead unembedded sequences, as in *8*.

8)

English target: I regret that Asa had to leave.
ASL response: MUST ASA MUST GO / SORRY
[roughly: Asa must go. I'm sorry.]

In some ways, these and other observations of Thompson's were correct. However, his conclusion that ASL had no grammatical means of embedding to create subordinate clauses was incorrect. Later work showed that relative clauses are indeed grammatically marked in ASL, contrary to Thompson's claims—not by function words such as *that,* but by **nonmanual grammatical markers**.

The nonmanual marker of relative clauses consists of raised brows, a backward head tilt, and a tensed upper lip. This nonmanual marker co-occurs with the material of the relative clause. In addition, relative clauses in ASL are not like those of English. In particular, the noun that is modified by the relative clause occurs inside the clause in ASL, as in spoken languages like Diegueño, rather than outside the clause, as in English. While in English the subordinating word *that* indicates a relative clause, in ASL the nonmanual markers that extend over the clause perform essentially the same role. A comparison of these aspects of relative clauses in ASL and English can be observed in *9.*

9)

a. English relative clause: modified noun (underlined) outside the relative clause; relative marker *that*
<u>The dog</u> that chased the cat came home.

b. ASL relative clause: modified noun (underlined) inside the relative clause; nonmanual relative marker 'rc'
$\overline{\text{RECENTLY }{}_{a}\underline{\text{DOG}}\text{ CHASE }{}_{b}\text{CAT}}^{\text{rc}}$ ${}_{a}$COME HOME.

In the notation, the line marked 'rc' indicates the scope of the relative clause nonmanual marker. The lowercase subscripts are indices for DOG and CAT. The 'a' index on DOG and COME are expressed formationally in the language, indicating that it was the dog and not the cat that came home.

Clearly, the reason why Thompson thought ASL has no relative clauses was that he expected them to look more like English. However, once the characteristics of relative clauses in languages other than English are considered, it becomes clear that ASL does have relative clauses, formed by a rule of subordination that allows recursion. Syntactic tests can be used to differentiate embedded clauses from main clauses. Other researchers have provided additional evidence of subordination in ASL, and all current work assumes it.

3.2 Word Order

A controversy over word-order properties in ASL was similarly resolved by more careful analysis and by looking beyond English. Since basic word order is very flexible in ASL, some early researchers argued that only pragmatic considerations—such as emphasis of some part of the sentence—and not linguistic structure dictate word order in ASL sentences. These researchers proposed that there are no syntactic rules for ordering words in ASL. However, since then, many researchers have collected evidence to support the point of view that ASL—like Japanese, Russian, and other spoken languages that allow for relative flexibility in surface word order—has an underlying structure and word order that can be modified by rules of the grammar. In the case of ASL, the underlying word order is subject-verb-object. Here too, most researchers now assume the basic order argued for in these works, and current work concentrates on the rules and principles that generate this order and its many variants.

3.3 Sign Language and Universal Grammar

Using the tools of linguistic analysis, it is possible to go far beyond the observation that ASL has recursion and subordination and a basic word order. Of crucial concern to proponents of the **Universal Grammar** hypothesis is whether or not ASL adheres to constraints hypothesized to characterize all languages. According to this hypothesis, the decisive constraints are those that are found to be operative across languages, but for which overt evidence in the linguistic environment does not seem to be available. If some knowledge that adults are shown to possess is not accessible to the language learner, it is hypothesized to be in some sense part of the innately determined universal human language capacity. For example, consider the paradigm in *10.*

10)

a. Steve likes beer with pizza.
b. What does Steve like beer with?
c. Yoav likes wine and cheese.
d. *What does Yoav like wine and?

Although the relationship between *10a* and *10b* is very similar to the relationship between *10c* and *10d,* only the first pair are both grammatical. Making a question out of the noun phrase following a preposition is usually grammatical in colloquial English, but making a question out of a noun phrase that is coordinated with another noun phrase is not. In fact, the restriction on questions like *10d,* which disallows extraction of material out of a coordinated structure, is virtually universal, and it has been proposed that a general universal constraint—the **Coordinate Structure Constraint**—prohibits it.

Whether or not one accepts the hypothesis that such constraints are innately specified, the fact that they are not easily deducible from the input but appear to be ubiquitous in spoken languages makes them key exemplars of the human language capacity. It is therefore important to determine whether or not they hold for sign languages as well. If so, we may conclude that the constraints are truly universal, and that sign languages have the same properties as any other natural language. In fact, several researchers have argued that this is the case.

The Coordinate Structure Constraint demonstrated in *10* provides the clearest example. As illustrated in *11,* coordinate structures are allowed in ASL.

11)

${}_{i}$INDEX ${}_{i}$GIVE$_{1}$ MONEY, ${}_{j}$INDEX ${}_{j}$GIVE$_{1}$ FLOWERS
'He gave me money, but she gave me flowers.'

Furthermore, ASL, like English, clearly prohibits violations of the Coordinate Structure Constraint, as illustrated in *12.* The 't' on the line over FLOWER in *12* indicates a nonmanual marker for **topicalization**, the process by which the topic, FLOWER, is extracted and moved out of the coordinated structure to the beginning of the sentence.

12)

________t
*FLOWER, ${}_{2}$GIVE$_{1}$ MONEY, ${}_{j}$GIVE$_{1}$
'Flowers, he gave me money but she gave me.'

In several domains of syntax, the constraints proposed to be universal (including the Coordinate Structure Constraint) can be demonstrated to apply to ASL as well as to spoken languages, and it is expected that other signed languages will also show adherence to these constraints.

The properties we have described at each level of grammatical structure—phonology, morphology, and syntax—provide strong evidence that certain basic characteristics of language are indeed universal, belonging to language in either of the two natural modalities available to humans.

4 Language as an Art Form: Sign Language Poetry

Poetry takes language far beyond its primary task of everyday communication. By artfully manipulating the forms and meanings of language, the poet conveys a particular or heightened understanding of human experience. Devices such as meter, rhyme, and alliteration may filter the meaningful content of a poem in order to create an impression or focus an image in the mind of the audience. A conventional meaning may be intentionally distorted in such a way as to enhance the perspective the poet wishes to present.

This union of language, culture, and art is found in some signing communities. We know of several accomplished deaf poets in the United States and Holland, and bring as an example of sign language poetry some work of Wim Emmerik from Amsterdam.

Among the devices used by this poet—and observed in ASL poetry as well—are reiterative use of hand shape and a fluidity of style resulting from the elimination of transitional movements. Entire poems may be characterized by one or two basic hand shapes, such as the extended index finger or a shape that extends all fingers. The aesthetic effect is similar to that of rhyme or alliteration in spoken poetry. While the movements that are part of signs are retained or modulated in some way, lines of poetry are skillfully constructed so as to omit the movements that result from the transition between the end of one sign and the beginning of another, creating flowing verse.

The explicitly poetic, somewhat paradoxical device of disrupting or distorting conventional meanings in order to enhance the intended meaning is also recruited by Emmerik. In his poem "Member of Parliament," Emmerik presents a picture of the governmental representative as jaded and cut off from the occurrences and sensations of the real world. The closest that the member of parliament gets to events in his country is through reading the newspaper as he eats lunch. To convey the idea that the politician crudely ingests the news through his body rather than experiencing events spiritually or intellectually, the poet portrays him "eating" the news. As he eats and reads, he alters the usual sign for *eat* (Figure 10.7a) by changing its location to the eyes rather than the mouth (Figure 10.7b). Intermittently, the member of parliament eats food and ingests news of the world.

The value of the work of Emmerik and other deaf poets is first and foremost artistic. But the fact that poetry arises in established deaf communities is instructive as well. It teaches us that the desire and ability to mold the formational elements of

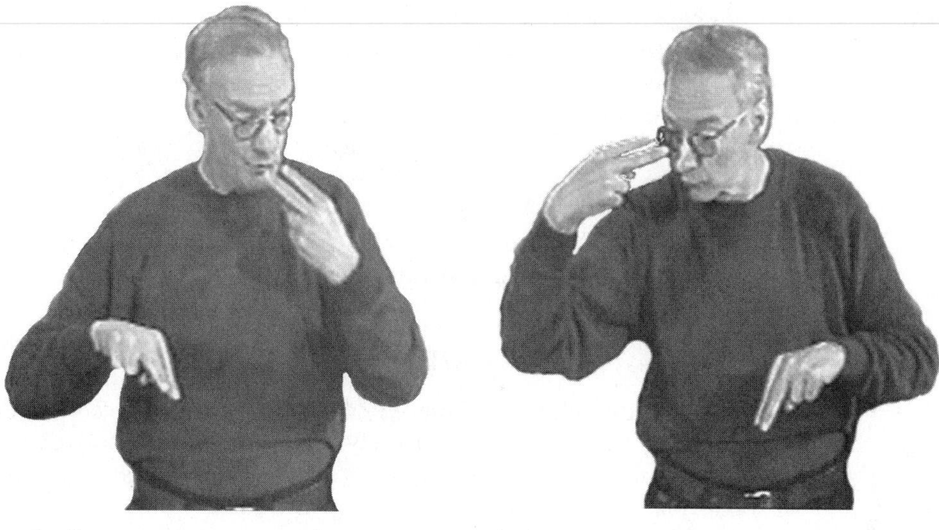

a. 'eat' *b.* 'eat with the eyes'

Figure 10.7 Sign language poetic form

language into an artistic expression of its content is a hallmark of human culture. It also shows clearly that sound is unnecessary, not only for communicative use of language but for artistic use of language as well.

Summing Up

Sign languages are full linguistic systems that share with spoken languages defining characteristics of human language. While sign languages do not use speech sounds, hand shape, location, and movement are the arbitrary formational elements that can be combined to create meaningful morphemes and words. There are constraints on how these formational elements can be combined, and **assimilation** is common. **Prosody** is achieved through facial expression and body postures. Sign languages show complex morphology, for example in word formation, verb agreement, and **classifier constructions**. Like spoken languages, the syntax of sign languages allows **recursion**, but sign languages use **nonmanual grammatical markers** to signal a **subordinate clause**. There is a predominant word order in sign languages, and sign languages exhibit a number of characteristics that support the notion of **Universal Grammar**. Like spoken languages, sign languages have the power to express the full range of human experience, including poetry.

Key Terms

Terms concerning phonology of sign languages

assimilation
duality of patterning
grammaticalized
prosody

Terms concerning morphology and syntax in sign languages

classifier constructions
Coordinate Structure Constraint
nonmanual grammatical markers
recursion
relative clause
Size and Shape Classifiers (SASSes)
subject-object agreement
subordinate clauses
topicalization
Universal Grammar

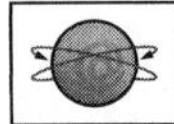

For more information on the sources used in this chapter, please go to **bedfordstmartins.com/linguistics/signlanguage** and click on **Sources**.

Recommended Reading

Brentari, Diane. 1995. "Sign Language Phonology." In *The Handbook of Phonological Theory.* Edited by J. Goldsmith, 615–639. Cambridge, MA: Blackwell.

Emmorey, Karen. 2002. *Language, Cognition, and the Brain: Insights from Sign Language Research.* Mahwah, NJ: Lawrence Erlbaum Associates.

Emmorey, Karen, ed. 2003. *Perspectives on Classifier Constructions in Sign Languages.* Mahwah, NJ: Lawence Erlbaum Associates.

Klima, Edward, and Ursula Bellugi. 1979. *The Signs of Language.* Cambridge: Harvard University Press.

Liddell, Scott K. 1980. *American Sign Language Syntax.* The Hague: Mouton.

Lillo-Martin, D. 1991. *Universal Grammar and American Sign Language: Setting the Null Argument Parameters.* Dordrecht: Kluwer Academic Publishers.

Lillo-Martin, Diane. 1999. "Modality Effects and Modularity in Language Acquisition: The Acquisition of American Sign Language." In *Handbook of Language Acquisition.* Edited by T. K. Bhatia and W. C. Ritchie, 531–567. San Diego: Academic Press.

Meir, Irit. 2002. "A Cross-Modality Perspective on Verb Agreement." *Natural Language and Linguistic Theory* 20, 2: 413–450.

Nespor, Marina, and Wendy Sandler. 1999. "Prosodic Phonology in Israeli Sign Language," *Language and Speech* 42, 2 and 3: 143–176.

Padden, Carol A. 1988. *Interaction of Morphology and Syntax in American Sign Language.* New York: Garland.

Sandler, Wendy. 2000. "One Phonology or Two? Sign Language and Phonological Theory." In *GLOT International State-of-the-Article Book.* Edited by R. Sybesma and L. Cheng, 349–384. The Hague: Holland Academie Graphics.

Sandler, Wendy, and Diane Lillo-Martin (forthcoming). *Sign Language and Linguistic Universals.* Cambridge, UK: Cambridge University Press.

Stokoe, William C. 1960. *Sign Language Structure.* Silver Spring, MD: Linstok Press.

Supalla, Ted. 1986. "The Classifier System in American Sign Language." In *Noun Classes and Categorization.* Edited by C. Craig, 181–214. Philadelphia: John Benjamins.

eleven

First Language Acquisition

William O'Grady
Sook Whan Cho

Human brains are so constructed that one brain responds in much the same way to a given trigger as does another brain, all things being equal. This is why a baby can learn any language; it responds to triggers in the same way as any other baby.

– D. HOFSTADTER

OBJECTIVES

In this chapter, you will learn:

- how first language acquisition is studied
- how children learn to understand and pronounce the sounds of their language
- how children develop a vocabulary
- how children's morphology develops
- what stages children go through in their production of sentences
- what factors influence first language acquisition

Nothing is more important to a child's development than the acquisition of language. Most children acquire language quickly and effortlessly, giving the impression that the entire process is simple and straightforward. However, the true extent of children's achievement becomes evident when we compare their success with the difficulties encountered by adults who try to learn a second language (see Chapter 12). Understanding how children the world over are able to master the complexities of human language in the space of a few short years has become one of the major goals of contemporary linguistic research.

This chapter provides a brief overview of the progress that has been made in this area. We will begin by considering the research strategies used by linguists and psychologists in the study of linguistic development. We will then describe some of the major findings concerning children's acquisition of the various parts of their language—phonology, vocabulary, morphology, syntax, and semantics. The chapter concludes with a brief examination of the contribution of the linguistic environment to language acquisition, the relationship between the emergence of language and cognitive development, and the possible existence of inborn linguistic knowledge.

1 The Study of Language Acquisition

Although we commonly refer to the emergence of language in children as "language acquisition," the end result of this process is actually a **grammar**—the mental system that allows people to speak and understand a language. There are at least two reasons for believing that the development of linguistic skills must involve the acquisition of a grammar.

First, as noted in Chapter 1, mature language users are able to produce and understand an unlimited number of novel sentences. This can only happen if, as children, they have acquired the grammar for their language. Simple memorization of a fixed inventory of words and sentences would not equip learners to deal with previously unheard utterances—a basic requisite of normal language use.

A second indication that children acquire grammatical rules comes from their speech errors, which often provide valuable clues about how the acquisition process works. Even run-of-the-mill errors such as **doed, *runned,* and **goed* can be informative. Since we know that children don't hear adults produce words like these, such errors tell us that they have formulated a general rule that forms the past tense by adding *-ed* to the verb stem.

Because language acquisition involves the emergence of a grammar, its study is closely tied to the type of linguistic analysis with which we have been concerned in preceding chapters. Indeed, linguists and psychologists studying language acquisition must often look to the study of phonology, syntax, and other components of the grammar for help in identifying and describing the grammatical system that children acquire during the first years of life.

1.1 Methods

The majority of research on the acquisition of language focuses on children's early utterances, the order in which they emerge, and the kinds of errors they contain. Two complementary methods of data collection are used—naturalistic observation and experimentation.

Two Approaches

In the **naturalistic approach**, investigators observe and record children's spontaneous utterances. One type of naturalistic investigation is the so-called **diary study**, in which a researcher (often a parent) keeps daily notes on a child's linguistic progress. Alternatively, a researcher may visit individual children on a regular basis and record (or videotape) a sample of their utterances. In both cases, attention is paid to the context in which children's speech occurs, the toys they are playing with, the pictures they are looking at, and the like.

Naturalistic data collection provides a great deal of information about how the language acquisition process unfolds, but it also has its shortcomings. The most serious of these is that particular structures and phenomena may occur rarely in children's everyday speech, making it difficult to gather enough information from natural speech samples to test hypotheses or draw firm conclusions. This problem is further compounded by the fact that speech samples from individual children capture only a small portion of their utterances at any given point in development. (Because of the amount of time required to transcribe and analyze recordings, researchers typically have to be content with hour-long samples taken at weekly or biweekly intervals.)

In **experimental studies**, researchers typically make use of specially designed tasks to elicit linguistic activity relevant to the phenomenon that they wish to study. The child's performance is then used to formulate hypotheses about the type of grammatical system acquired at that point in time.

Experimental research is typically **cross-sectional** in that it investigates and compares the linguistic knowledge of different children (or groups of children) at a particular point in development. A typical cross-sectional study might involve conducting a single experiment with a group of two-year-olds, a group of four-year-olds, and a group of six-year-olds, taking each of these groups to be representative of a particular stage or "cross-section" of the developmental process.

In contrast, naturalistic studies tend to be **longitudinal** in that they examine language development in a particular child or group over an extended period of time (sometimes as long as several years). As the name suggests, longitudinal studies take a long time to conduct, but unlike cross-sectional studies they have the advantage of permitting researchers to observe development as an ongoing process in individual children.

Types of Experimental Studies

Experimental studies usually employ tasks that test children's comprehension, production, or imitation skills. One widely used method for testing children's comprehension makes use of a picture selection format. For example, in order to test the interpretation of reflexive pronouns, an experimenter might show children a picture of Big Bird scratching himself as Cookie Monster looks on and a picture of Big Bird scratching Cookie Monster, and then ask which picture goes with the sentence *Big Bird is scratching himself.* A second method involves supplying children with an appropriate set of toys and then asking them to act out the meaning of a sentence—perhaps a passive structure such as *The truck was bumped by the car.* Children's responses can provide valuable clues about the type of grammatical rules being used to interpret sentences at particular stages of development.

In a typical production task, the child is shown a picture and asked to describe it. Although production tasks can be useful for assessing certain types of linguistic knowledge, there are many structures (such as passives) that are hard to elicit even from adults since they are used only in special contexts. Moreover, because children's ability to comprehend language is often more advanced than their ability to produce sentences of their own, production tasks can provide an overly conservative view of linguistic development unless they are accompanied by other types of tests.

Experiments that have children imitate model sentences can also provide important clues about children's grammatical development. Although imitation might appear to be easy, it has been found that children's ability to repeat a particular structure provides a good indication of how well they have mastered it. For instance, a child who has not yet acquired auxiliary verbs can be expected to have difficulty repeating a sentence such as *The doggie has been barking a lot.*

The principal advantage of the experimental approach is that it allows researchers to collect data of a very specific sort about particular phenomena or structures. Experimentation is not without its pitfalls, however. In addition to the difficulty of designing a good experiment, there is always the possibility that children's performance will be affected by extraneous factors, such as inattention, shyness, or a failure to understand what is expected of them. Nonetheless, by using experimental techniques together with naturalistic observation, linguists and psychologists have made significant progress in the study of the language acquisition process. Much of this chapter is devoted to a survey of this progress, beginning with the development of speech sounds.

2 Phonological Development

Children seem to be born with a perceptual system that is especially designed for listening to speech. Newborns respond differently to human voices than to other sounds, they show a preference for the language of their parents over other languages by the time they are two days old, and they can recognize their mother's voice within a matter of weeks.

From around one month of age, children exhibit the ability to distinguish among certain speech sounds. In one experiment, infants were presented with a series of identical [ba] syllables. These were followed by an occurrence of the syllable [pa]. A change in the children's sucking rate (measured by a specially designed pacifier) indicated that they perceived the difference between the two syllables, and that they were therefore able to distinguish between [p] and [b].

Even more amazing is the fact that infants are able to distinguish between sounds in unfamiliar languages. In one experiment, for instance, six- to eight-month-old infants who were being raised in English-speaking homes could hear contrasts among unfamiliar consonants in Hindi and Nthlakampx (a Native American language spoken on parts of Canada's west coast). By the time they are ten to twelve months old, though, this ability has begun to diminish.

Despite this early sensitivity to contrasts among speech sounds, children initially cannot distinguish between meaningful words. The emergence of this ability has been examined in a task in which children are presented with two toy animals named *bok* and *pok* (for instance) and are asked to respond to sentences such as *Show me pok*. To respond correctly, children must not only hear the difference between [p] and [b] but also recognize that it is linguistically significant—that it is used to distinguish between words in their language. Children under eighteen months have little success in this type of task.

2.1 Babbling

The ability to produce speech sounds begins to emerge around six months of age, with the onset of **babbling**. Babbling provides children with the opportunity to experiment with and begin to gain control over their vocal apparatus—an important prerequisite for later speech. Children who are unable to babble for medical reasons (because of the need for a breathing tube in their throat, for example) can subsequently acquire normal pronunciation, but their speech development is significantly delayed.

Despite obvious differences among the languages to which they are exposed, children from different linguistic communities exhibit significant similarities in their babbling. The tendencies in Table 11.1 are based on data from fifteen different languages, including English, Thai, Japanese, Arabic, Hindi, and Mayan. (We focus here on consonant sounds, for which the data is somewhat more reliable than for vowels.)

Table 11.1 Cross-linguistic similarities in babbling

Frequently found consonants	*Infrequently found consonants*
p b m	f v θ ð
t d n	ʃ ʒ tʃ dʒ
k g	l r ŋ
s h w j	

Such cross-linguistic similarities suggest that early babbling is at least partly independent of the particular language to which children are exposed. In fact, even deaf children babble, although their articulatory activity is somewhat less varied than that of hearing children.

2.2 The Developmental Order

Babbling increases in frequency until the age of about twelve months, at which time children start to produce their first understandable words. Babbling may overlap with the production of real words for several weeks before dying out. By the time children have acquired fifty words or so, they begin to adopt fairly regular patterns of pronunciation.

Although there is a good deal of variation from child to child in terms of the order in which speech sounds are mastered in production and perception, the following general tendencies seem to exist.

- As a group, vowels are generally acquired before consonants (by age three).
- Stops tend to be acquired before other consonants.
- In terms of place of articulation, labials are often acquired first, followed (with some variation) by alveolars, velars, and alveopalatals. Interdentals (such as [θ] and [ð]) are acquired last.
- New phonemic contrasts manifest themselves first in word-initial position. Thus, the /p/-/b/ contrast, for instance, will be manifested in pairs such as *pat-bat* before *mop-mob*.

By age two, a typical English-speaking child has the inventory of consonant phonemes shown in Table 11.2.

Table 11.2 Typical consonant inventory at age two

Stops	Nasals	Fricatives	Other
p b	m	f	w
t d	n	s	
k g		h	

By age four, this inventory is considerably larger and typically includes the sounds shown in Table 11.3.

Table 11.3 Typical consonant inventory at age four

Stops	Nasals	Fricatives	Affricates	Other
p b	m	f v	tʃ dʒ	w j
t d	n	s z		l ɹ
k g	ŋ	ʃ		
		h		

Still to be acquired at this age are the interdental fricatives [θ] and [ð] and the voiced alveopalatal fricative [ʒ].

In general, the relative order in which sounds are acquired reflects their distribution in languages of the world (see Chapter 8). The sounds that are acquired early are generally found most widely in the world's languages, while the sounds that are acquired late tend to be less common across languages.

2.3 Early Phonetic Processes

Children's ability to perceive the phonemic contrasts of their language develops well in advance of their ability to produce them. So even children who are unable to produce the difference between words like *mouse* and *mouth, cart* and *card,* or *jug* and *duck* may nonetheless be able to point to pictures of the correct objects in a comprehension task. Moreover, as the following experimenter's report vividly illustrates, children distinguish phonemes they hear even when they cannot yet produce them.

> One of us, for instance, spoke to a child who called his inflated plastic fish a *fis.* In imitation of the child's pronunciation, the observer said: "This is your *fis?*" "No," said the child, "my *fis.*" He continued to reject the adult's imitation until he was told, "That is your fish." "Yes," he said, "my *fis.*"

The child's reaction to the adult's initial pronunciation of *fish* shows that he could perceive the difference between /s/ and /ʃ/ and that he had correctly represented the word as /fɪʃ/ in his lexicon even though he could not yet produce it himself.

What precisely is responsible for the special character of the sound patterns in children's early speech? The key seems to lie in the operation of a limited number of universal phonetic processes that replace certain sounds with others that children find easier to produce and/or perceive.

Syllable Deletion

Because syllables bearing primary or secondary stress are more noticeable than their unstressed counterparts, they tend to be more salient to children in the early stages of the language acquisition process. As a result, they are retained in children's pronunciation while unstressed syllables are often deleted (see Table 11.4).

Table 11.4 Deletion of unstressed syllables

Word	*Child's pronunciation*
hip po pó ta mus	[pɑs]
spa ghé tti	[gɛ]
hé li còp ter	[ɛlkɑt]
kan ga róo	[wu]

However, unstressed syllables in final position tend to be retained, probably because the ends of words are easier to notice and remember (see Table 11.5).

Table 11.5 Retention of unstressed syllables in final position

Word	*Child's pronunciation*
po tá to	[tejdo]
ba ná na	[ænə]
to má to	[mejdo]
él e phant	[ɛlfən]

Syllable Simplification

Another frequent process in children's speech involves the systematic deletion of certain sounds in order to simplify syllable structure. In the data in Table 11.6, typical

Table 11.6 Reduction of consonant clusters

[s] + stop (strategy: delete [s])
stop → [tɑp]
small → [mɑ]
desk → [dɛk]

stop + liquid (strategy: delete liquid)
try → [taj]
crumb → [gʌm]
bring → [bɪŋ]

fricative + liquid (strategy: delete liquid)
from → [fʌm]
sleep → [sip]

nasal + voiceless stop (strategy: delete nasal)
bump → [bʌp]
tent → [dɛt]

of the speech of two- and three-year-old children, consonant clusters are reduced by deleting one or more segments.

Yet another common deletion process in early child language involves the elimination of final consonants, as in the following examples.

1)

dog	[dɑ]
bus	[bʌ]
boot	[bu]

Both the reduction of consonant clusters and the deletion of final consonants have the effect of simplifying syllable structure, bringing it closer to the CV template that is universally favored by children and that is the most widely found pattern in human language in general.

Substitution

One of the most widespread phonetic processes in early language involves substitution—the systematic replacement of one sound by an alternative that the child finds easier to articulate (see Table 11.7). Common substitution processes include **stopping**, the replacement of a fricative by a corresponding stop; **fronting**, the moving forward of a sound's place of articulation; **gliding**, the replacement of a liquid by a glide; and **denasalization**, the replacement of a nasal stop by a nonnasal counterpart.

Table 11.7 Substitution in early speech

Process	*Example*	*Change*
Stopping	sing → [tɪŋ]	s → t
(continuant → stop)	sea → [ti]	s → t
	zebra → [dibɹə]	z → d
	thing → [tɪŋ]	θ → t
	this → [dɪt]	ð → d, s → t
	shoes → [tud]	ʃ → t, z → d
Fronting	ship → [sɪp]	ʃ → s
	jump → [dzʌmp]	dʒ → dz
	chalk → [tsɑːk]	tʃ → ts
	go → [dow]	g → d
Gliding	lion → [jajn]	l → j
	laughing → [jæfɪŋ]	l → j
	look → [wʊk]	l → w
	rock → [wɑk]	r → w
	story → [stowi]	r → w
Denasalization	spoon → [bud]	n → d
	jam → [dæb]	m → b
	room → [wub]	m → b

Assimilation

Still another widespread phonetic process in child language is assimilation—the modification of one or more features of a segment under the influence of neighboring sounds. In the following examples, initial consonants have been voiced in anticipation of the following vowel.

2)

tell	[dɛl]
pig	[bɪg]
push	[bʊs]
soup	[zup]

Assimilation is also observed in children's tendency to maintain the same place of articulation for all of the consonants or vowels in a word. This can lead to the pronunciation of *doggy* as [gagi] (with two velar stops). Other examples include [fɛlf] for *self* (with identical consonants), [bibi] for *baby* (with identical vowels in both syllables), [kæklin] for *Cathleen* (with identical velar stops), and [næns] for *dance* (with identical nasal consonants).

3 Vocabulary Development

By age eighteen months or so, the average child has a vocabulary of fifty words or more. Common items include the words listed in Table 11.8.

Table 11.8 Common items in the first fifty words

Entities
Words referring to people: *daddy, mommy, baby* food/drink: *juice, milk, cookie, water, toast, apple, cake* animals: *dog, cat, duck, horse* clothes: *shoes, hat* toys: *ball, blocks* vehicles: *car, boat, truck* other: *bottle, key, book*
Properties
hot, all-gone, more, dirty, cold, here, there
Actions
up, sit, see, eat, go, down
Personal-social
hi, bye, no, yes, please, thank-you

As this table shows, noun-like words make up the single largest class in the child's early vocabulary, with verb- and adjective-like words being the next most frequent category types. Among the most frequent words are expressions for displeasure or rejection (such as *no*) and various types of social interaction (such as *please* and *bye*). Over the next months, this vocabulary grows rapidly, sometimes by as much as ten or twelve words a day. By age six, most children have mastered about thirteen thousand words.

Children seem to differ somewhat in the types of words that they focus on, especially in the early stages of language acquisition. One of these differences is reflected in the number of nouns in early vocabulary. Whereas some children have a relatively high proportion of such words (75 percent or more) by age two, other learners exhibit a much lower percentage of nouns (50 percent or less). Making up for the smaller number of nouns is a larger vocabulary of socially useful expressions such as *bye, go-away, stop-it, thank-you, I-want-it,* and so on. (Hyphens are used here to indicate that these expressions are not yet segmented into their component words.)

3.1 Strategies for Acquiring Word Meaning

Children seem to draw on special strategies when trying to determine the meaning of a new word. This is perhaps easiest to illustrate in the case of noun-type meanings, for which the following strategies seem to be employed.

3)

Three strategies for learning the meanings of new words:

The Whole Object Assumption
A new word refers to a whole object.

The Type Assumption
A new word refers to a type of thing, not just to a particular thing.

The Basic Level Assumption
A new word refers to types of objects that are alike in basic ways.

To see how these strategies work, imagine that a mother and her eighteen-month-old daughter are driving through the countryside and they encounter a sheep munching on the grass. The mother points to the animal and says "sheep." What does the child think that the word means? Does it mean 'white'? Or does it mean 'woolly'? Does it refer to the animal? Or does it refer to parts of the animal? Or does it refer to the fact that a particular animal is munching on grass?

The Whole Object Assumption allows the child to infer that the word *sheep* refers to the animal itself, not to its parts, not to whiteness, and not to woolliness. The Type Assumption allows her to infer that *sheep* refers to a type of animal, not to just one particular sheep. And the Basic Level Assumption leads her to guess that *sheep* is used to refer just to white, four-legged, woolly animals, not animals in general.

The fact that so many of children's first words are names for types of whole objects suggests that language learners rely heavily on strategies such as these in the early stages of word learning. Of course, these strategies don't always give the right result. Some words do in fact refer to parts of things (*toe, fingernail, eyeball*), to properties (*white, woolly*), to individuals (*Susie, Mr. Jones*), and to broad classes (*animal, plant*). Nonetheless, the strategies we have been considering provide children with a good way to get started, postponing the acquisition of certain types of words in favor of more basic vocabulary items.

Contextual Clues

Another major factor in vocabulary development is the child's ability to make use of contextual clues to draw inferences about the category and meaning of new words. For instance, from early in the language acquisition process, children can use the presence or absence of determiners to distinguish between names and ordinary nouns. Two-year-old children who are told that a new doll is a *dax* will apply this label to similar-looking dolls as well. However, if they are told that the new doll is *Dax*, they will restrict use of the new word to the doll they have actually been shown. Like adults, these children treat *dax* as an ordinary noun when it is preceded by *a* but as a name when there is no determiner.

In another experiment, three- and four-year-old children were asked to act out the meaning of sentences such as *Make it so there is* tiv *to drink in this glass (of water).* The only clues about the interpretation of the nonsense word *tiv* came from the meaning of the rest of the sentence and from the child's understanding of the types of changes that can be made to a glass of water. Not only did more than half the children respond by either adding or removing water, but some even remembered what *tiv* meant two weeks later!

3.2 Meaning Errors

The meanings that children associate with their early words sometimes correspond closely to the meanings employed by adults. In many cases, however, the match is less than perfect. The two most typical semantic errors involve overextension and underextension.

Overextensions

In cases of **overextension**, the meaning of the child's word is more general or inclusive than that of the corresponding adult form. The word *dog,* for example, is frequently overextended to include horses, cows, and other four-legged animals. Similarly, *ball* is sometimes used for any round object, including a balloon, an Easter egg, a small stone, and so on. As many as one-third of children's words may be overextended at the fifty-word stage of vocabulary development (see Table 11.9). The evidence collected to date suggests that perceptual properties are the single most important factor in children's first hypotheses about word meanings. As a result, children often overextend a word to include a set of perceptually similar objects that they know to have diverse functions. For example, one child used the word *moon* for the moon, grapefruit halves, and a crescent-shaped car light. Another child used the word *money* for a set of objects ranging from pennies to buttons and beads. If you reconsider the examples of overextension given in Table 11.9, you will see that they too are more plausibly explained in terms of perceptual similarities than a shared function.

Table 11.9 Additional examples of overextension

Word	First referent	Subsequent extensions
ticktock	watch	clocks, gas meter, fire hose on a spool, scale with round dial
fly	fly	specks of dirt, dust, small insects, child's toes, crumbs of bread
quack	duck	all birds and insects, flies, coins (with an eagle on the face)
candy	candy	cherries, anything sweet
apple	apples	balls, tomatoes, cherries, onions, biscuits
turtle	turtles	fish, seals
cookie	cookies	crackers, any dessert
kitty	cats	rabbits, any small furry animal
box	boxes	elevators
belt	belts	watch strap

There is reason to believe that many overextensions may be deliberate attempts to compensate for vocabulary limitations. One indication of this is that particular overextensions often disappear as soon as children learn the right word for the objects that they have been mislabeling. For example, two-year-old Allen was using the word *dog* for dogs, cats, sheep, and other four-legged mammals, but he stopped doing so as soon as he learned the words *cat* and *sheep*. If he thought that *dog* meant 'animal', he could still have sometimes referred to cats and sheep as *dogs* (just as adults sometimes refer to them as animals). The fact that he didn't suggests that he never thought *dog* meant 'animal'; he had just been "borrowing" it until the right word came along.

A further indication that many overextensions are designed to compensate for vocabulary limitations comes from the fact that children seem to overextend more in their production than in their comprehension. In one study, for instance, five children who were overextending words were given a naming task in which they were shown pictures and asked to name them. Overextensions were identified and then used to design a comprehension test. For example, if the child overextended *dog* to include cows and horses on the naming test, the comprehension test would include pictures of these animals as well as a dog. The child would then be asked "Show me the dog," "Show me the cow," and so on. The results were quite dramatic, revealing that overextensions in comprehension were much less frequent than in production. This is not the result that one would expect if children thought that *dog* meant 'animal'.

Underextensions

Another possible type of word-meaning error in early language involves **underextension**, the use of lexical items in an overly restrictive fashion. Thus, *kitty* might be used to refer to the family pet, but not to any other cats. Or the word *dog* might be used for collies, spaniels, and beagles, but not for Chihuahuas.

Underextension errors often reflect children's propensity to focus on prototypical or core members of a category. As noted in Section 1.3 of Chapter 6, the potential referents of many words differ in terms of how well they exemplify the properties associated with a particular concept. For example, among the potential referents of the word *dog,* collies and spaniels have more of the properties associated with the concept DOG (long hair, relative size, type of bark, and so on) than do Chihuahuas. While the preference for a prototype can be overruled by factors such as the presence of a nontypical category member in the child's everyday experience (e.g., a Chihuahua as a family pet), the internal structure of concepts can have an important influence on semantic development.

Verb Meanings

Meaning errors also occur with verbs. For example, some preschool children believe that *fill* means 'pour' rather than 'make full'. So, when asked to decide which of the two series of pictures in Figure 11.1 is an example of filling, they choose the second series—even though the glass remains empty.

Figure 11.1 Sample pictures used to test children's understanding of *fill.* Some children believe that the action depicted in the bottom series of pictures involves filling, even though the glass remains empty.

Not surprisingly, there is a tendency for children who make this sort of mistake to use *fill* in the wrong syntactic patterns as well.

4)

I filled the grain up. (Adam, at age 4 yrs., 11 mos.)
And fill the little sugars up in the bowl. (Mark, at age 4 yrs., 7 mos.)
I didn't fill water up to drink it. (E, at age 4 yrs., 1 mo.)
Can I fill some salt into the [salt shaker]? (E, at age 5 yrs.)

These errors disappear as children come to realize that *fill* means 'make full' rather than 'pour'.

Dimensional Terms

Terms describing size and dimensions are acquired in a relatively fixed order, depending on their generality (see Table 11.10). The first adjectives of this type to be acquired, *big* and *small,* are the most general in that they can be used for talking about any aspect of size (height, area, volume, and so on). In contrast, the second group of adjectives to emerge—*tall, long, short, high,* and *low*—can only be used for a single dimension (height-length). The remaining modifiers (*thick-thin, wide-narrow,* and *deep-shallow*) are still more restricted in their use, since they describe the secondary or less-extended dimension of an object. For instance, the dimension of a stick that we describe in terms of width or thickness is almost always less extended than the dimension that we describe in terms of height or length, which tends also to be perceptually more salient.

Table 11.10 Order of acquisition for dimensional adjectives

Step	*Words*	*What they descriibe*
1	*big-small*	any aspect of size
2	*tall-short, long-short, high-low*	a single dimension
3	*thick-thin, wide-narrow, deep-shallow*	a secondary dimension

The difficulty of dimensional adjectives for children is also evident on experimental tasks. For instance, in one experiment, children aged three to five were shown pairs of objects—sometimes a big one and a tall one and sometimes a big one and a long one (see Figure 11.2).

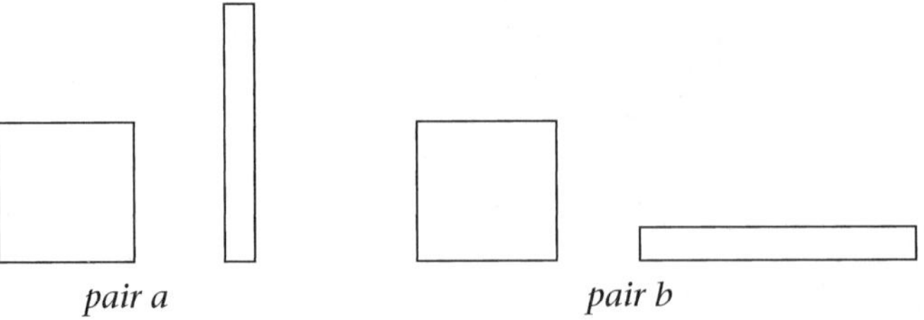

Figure 11.2 *big–tall* versus *big–long*

Younger children did well when asked to choose "the big one." However, when asked to choose "the tall one" or "the long one," they often picked the big one instead.

This suggests that they are initially more sensitive to overall size than to a single dimension like height or length.

4 Morphological Development

As is the case with the sound pattern of language and with vocabulary, the details of morphological structure emerge over a period of several years. Initially, the words produced by English-speaking children seem to lack any internal morphological structure. Affixes are systematically absent and most words consist of a single root morpheme.

4.1 Overgeneralization

Because English has many examples of irregular inflection (*men* as the plural of *man, ran* as the past of *run*), children sometimes begin by simply memorizing inflected words on a case-by-case basis, without regard for general patterns or rules. As a result, they may initially use irregular forms such as *men* and *ran* correctly. However, when they subsequently observe the generality of *-s* as a plural marker and *-ed* as a past tense marker (usually around age two and a half), they sometimes use these suffixes for the irregular forms—producing words such as *mans* and *runned.* (Errors that result from the overly broad application of a rule are called **overgeneralizations** or **overregularizations**.) Even occasional mixed forms such as *felled,* a blend of *fell* and *falled,* may occur during this period (see Table 11.11).

Table 11.11 The development of affixes

Stage 1:	case-by-case learning (*boys, men*)
Stage 2:	overuse of general rule (*mans*)
Stage 3:	mastery of exceptions to the general rule (*men*)

One of the best indications that children have mastered an inflectional rule comes from their ability to apply it to forms they have not heard before. In a classic experiment, children were shown a picture of a strange creature and told, "This is a wug." A second picture was then presented to elicit a plural form (see Figure 11.3).

This is a wug.

Now, there's another wug.
There are two of them.
Now, there are two . . . ?

Figure 11.3 The "wug" test

Even four- and five-year-old children did well with the plural forms of "wug" words, demonstrating that the general rules for inflection have been learned by that time, despite the occurrence of occasional errors.

Recent work has shown that inflectional overgeneralization, which can last into the school years, is much less frequent than previously thought: preschool children seem to overregularize verbs less than 25 percent of the time at any point in development. This suggests that the overgeneralization errors observed in early speech reflect lapses in accessing the appropriate irregular form from the lexicon rather than the failure to learn irregular forms per se.

4.2 A Developmental Sequence

An important result of child language research during the 1970s was the discovery that the development of bound morphemes and functional categories (such as determiners and auxiliaries) takes place in an orderly fashion that is quite similar across children. In a pioneering study of three children between the ages of twenty and thirty-six months, the **developmental sequence** in Table 11.12 was found to be typical.

Table 11.12 Typical developmental sequence for nonlexical morphemes

1. *-ing*	5. past tense *-ed*
2. plural *-s*	6. third person singular *-s*
3. possessive *-'s*	7. auxiliary *be*
4. *the, a*	

An interesting feature of this developmental sequence is that it seems to be largely unrelated to the frequency of the different morphemes in the speech heard by children (see Table 11.13). For example, the determiners *the* and *a* are the most frequent morphemes in the children's environments even though they are acquired relatively late.

Table 11.13 Typical relative frequency of morphemes in parental speech

1. *the, a*	5. possessive *-'s*
2. *-ing*	6. third person singular *-s*
3. plural *-s*	7. past tense *-ed*
4. auxiliary *be*	

This shows that frequency by itself cannot explain developmental order, although it may have some role to play in conjunction with other factors. (It's also clear that pronunciation by itself is not the key factor either, since the three *-s* morphemes are acquired at different times.)

Some Determining Factors

What, then, determines the order of acquisition of nonlexical categories and bound morphemes? Research on a variety of languages suggests that several factors are involved.

1. ***Frequent occurrence in utterance-final position*** Children show a greater tendency to notice and remember elements that occur at the end of the utterance than those found in any other position.

2. ***Syllabicity*** Children seem to take greater notice of morphemes such as *-ing,* which can constitute syllables on their own, than the plural or possessive suffix *-'s,* whose principal allomorphs (/s/ and /z/) are single consonants.

3. ***Absence of homophony*** Whereas the word *the* functions only as a determiner in English, the suffix *-s* can be used to mark any one of three things: plural number in nouns, third person singular in verbs, or possession. The resulting complication in the relationship between form and meaning may impede acquisition.

4. ***Few or no exceptions in the way it is used*** Whereas all singular nouns form the possessive with *-'s,* not all verbs use *-ed* to mark the past tense (*saw, read, drove*). Such exceptions hinder the language acquisition process.

5. ***Allomorphic invariance*** Whereas the affix *-ing* has the same form for all verbs, the past tense ending *-ed* has three major allomorphs—/t/ for verbs such as *chase,* /d/ for forms such as *crave,* and /əd/ for verbs such as *recite.* This type of allomorphic variation, which also occurs with the plural, possessive, and third person singular affixes in English, slows morphological development.

6. ***Clearly discernible semantic function*** Whereas morphemes such as plural *-s* express easily identifiable meanings, some morphemes (such as the third person singular *-s*) make no obvious contribution to the meaning of the sentence. Acquisition of this latter type of morpheme is relatively slow.

4.3 Word-Formation Processes

The major word-formation processes in English—derivation and compounding—both emerge early in the acquisition of English. The first derivational suffixes to show up in children's speech are the ones that are most common in adult language (see Table 11.14).

Table 11.14 Suffixes in the speech of Damon prior to age four

Ending	*Meaning*	*Example*
-er	'doer'*	walker
-ie	'diminutive'	doggie
-ing	'activity'	Running is fun.
-ness	'state'	bigness

Note: *-*er* also has an 'instrument' meaning, as in *cutter* 'something used for cutting', but this is less frequent in children's early speech.

Children as young as three demonstrate an ability to use derivation to make up names for agents and instruments when presented with questions such as the following:

"I've got a picture here of someone who crushes things. What could we call someone who crushes things? Someone who crushes things is called a . . ."

"I've got a picture here of something that cuts things. What could we call something that cuts things? Something that cuts things is called a . . ."

Children also exhibit a propensity for forming compounds, especially of the N-N type, both in experimental settings where they are asked to make up words (e.g., "What would you call a boy who rips paper?") and in their own spontaneous speech. Some of the compounds found in the speech of three- and four-year-olds do not follow the usual pattern for English compounds (e.g., **open man* for someone who opens things and **cutter grass* for 'grass cutter'), but these disappear by age five. Other early compounds have the right structure but are inappropriate because English already has words with the intended meaning (see Table 11.15).

Table 11.15 Some innovative compounds

Child's word	*Intended meaning*
car-smoke	'exhaust'
cup-egg	'boiled egg'
firetruck-man	'firefighter'
plant-man	'gardener'
store-man	'clerk'

Children's creativity with compounds points to a preference for building words from other words, perhaps because this places less demand on memory than does learning a new simple word for each concept.

Even the subtlest properties of word formation seem to be acquired in the preschool years. One such property, first discussed in Section 3.1 of Chapter 4, involves the fact that an inflectional suffix such as the plural cannot occur inside compounds (compare **dogs catcher* with *dog catcher*). In one study, children as young as three years of age produced compounds that obeyed this constraint. Thus, when asked a question such as "What do you call someone who eats cookies?" they responded by saying *cookie eater* rather than **cookies eater.*

5 Syntactic Development

Like phonological and morphological development, the emergence of syntactic structure takes place in an orderly manner and reveals much about the nature of the language acquisition process. We will briefly survey some of the milestones in this developmental process here.

5.1 The One-Word Stage

As noted earlier, children begin to produce one-word utterances between the ages of twelve and eighteen months. A basic property of these one-word utterances is that they can be used to express the type of meaning that is associated with an entire sentence in adult speech. Thus, a child might use the word *dada* to assert 'I see Daddy', *more* to mean 'Give me more candy', and *up* to mean 'I want up'. Such utterances are called **holophrases** (literally 'whole sentences').

In forming holophrastic utterances, children seem to choose the most informative word that applies to the situation at hand. A child who wanted a candy, for example, would say *candy* rather than *want* since *candy* is more informative in this situation. Similarly, a child who notices a new doll would be more likely to say *doll* than *see,* thereby referring to the most novel feature of the situation he or she is trying to describe.

Table 11.16 lists some of the semantic relations that children commonly express during the **one-word stage**.

Table 11.16 Semantic relations in children's one-word utterances

Semantic relation	*Utterance*	*Situation*
Agent of an action	*dada*	as father enters the room
Action or state	*down*	as child sits down
Theme	*door*	as father closes the door
Location	*here*	as child points
Recipient	*mama*	as child gives mother something
Recurrence	*again*	as child watches lighting of a match

5.2 The Two-Word Stage

Within a few months of their first one-word utterances, children begin to produce two-word "mini-sentences." Table 11.17 provides a sampling of these utterances and the types of meaning they are commonly used to express. (Although these examples are from English, similar patterns are found in the early development of all languages.)

Table 11.17 Some patterns in children's two-word speech

Utterance	*Intended meaning*	*Semantic relation*
Baby chair	'The baby is sitting on the chair.'	agent-location
Doggie bark	'The dog is barking.'	agent-action
Ken water	'Ken is drinking water.'	agent-theme
Hit doggie	'I hit the doggie.'	action-theme
Daddy hat	'Daddy's hat'	possessor-possessed

It is unclear whether children have acquired syntactic categories such as noun, verb, and adjective at this point in their development. This is because the markers that help distinguish among syntactic categories in adult English (e.g., inflection such as the past tense suffix and minor categories such as determiners and auxiliary verbs) are absent during this period. To complicate matters still further, the relative shortness of the utterances produced during the **two-word stage** means that the positional differences associated with category distinctions in adult speech are often not manifested. Thus, words such as *busy* (an adjective in adult speech) and *push* (a verb) may appear in identical patterns.

5)

Mommy busy.
Mommy push.

While this does not show that children lack syntactic categories, it makes it difficult to demonstrate that they possess them. For this reason, researchers are split over whether to describe children's utterances in terms of the semantic relations that they express (as shown in Table 11.17) or the syntactic categories of adult speech.

A notable feature of children's two-word utterances is that they almost always exhibit the appropriate word order. This suggests a very early sensitivity to this feature of sentence structure, but there is reason to believe that children do not initially have a general word-order rule. Rather, they may have a separate rule for each verb (e.g., "Put the subject in front of *push*"; "Put the subject in front of *read*"; and so on). In one experiment, for instance, children aged two to four were taught made-up verbs (such as *tam, gop,* and *dack*) for novel actions involving puppet characters. Each verb was presented in one of the following orders:

6)

subject-verb-object order: Elmo tammed the apple.
subject-object-verb order: Elmo the apple gopped.
verb-subject-object order: Dacked the apple Elmo.

The two- and three-year-old children were willing to learn word-order patterns not found in English and would often employ the subject-object-verb and verb-subject-object order for new verbs if that was what they had been exposed to. In contrast, the four-year-olds used the subject-verb-object order regardless of what the experimenter had said, which suggests that they had acquired a general word-order rule for English that they automatically extended to new verbs.

5.3 The Telegraphic Stage

After a period of several months, during which their speech is limited to one- and two-word utterances, children begin to produce longer and more complex grammatical structures (see Table 11.18). Some representative utterances from the first part of this period are given in *7*.

7)

Chair broken.
Daddy like book.
What her name?
Man ride bus today.
Car make noise.
Me wanna show Mommy.
I good boy.

Table 11.18 The development of phrase structure

Stage	*Approx. age*	*Developments*
Holophrastic	1–1.5 yrs.	single-word utterances; no structure
Two-word	1.5–2 yrs.	early word combinations; presence of syntactic categories unclear
Telegraphic	2–2.5 yrs.	emergence of phrase structure, especially head-complement and subject-VP patterns

At first, these utterances lack bound morphemes and most nonlexical categories. Because of the resemblance to the style of language found in telegrams, this acquisitional stage is often dubbed the **telegraphic stage**.

The telegraphic stage is characterized by the emergence of phrase structure. As the examples in *7* help show, children can form phrases consisting of a head and a complement (*like book, ride bus, show Mommy*), phrases that include a modifier (such as *today* and *good*), and even full-fledged sentences.

Language development from this point onward is rapid. As the examples in Table 11.19 on page 382 help illustrate, children move from relatively primitive two- and three-word utterances at the beginning of the telegraphic stage to a broad range of syntactically intricate sentence types that include affixes and nonlexical categories in the space of just a few months.

5.4 Later Development

In the years following the telegraphic stage, children continue to acquire the complex grammar that underlies adult linguistic competence, including the Move operations outlined in Chapter 5.

Inversion

In the very early stages of language acquisition, children signal *yes-no* questions by means of rising intonation alone. (Recall that auxiliary verbs are a relatively late development.)

8)

See hole?
I ride train?
Ball go?
Sit chair?

Even after individual auxiliary verbs appear in child language, there is often a delay of a few months before they appear at the beginning of the sentence in *yes-no* questions. In one study, for example, a young boy began using the auxiliary verb *can* at age two years, five months, but he did not use it in inversion patterns until six months later.

An interesting—but infrequent—error in children's early use of Inversion in both *yes-no* and *wh* questions is exemplified in *9*.

Table 11.19 Sample utterances from a child's speech over a 12-month period

Age	*Sample utterances*
28 mos.	Play checkers. Big drum. I got horn. A bunny-rabbit walk.
30 mos.	Write a piece of paper. What that egg doing? I lost a shoe. No, I don't want to sit seat.
32 mos.	Let me get down with the boots on. Don't be afraid of horses. How tiger be so healthy and fly like kite? Joshua throw like penguin.
34 mos.	Look at that train Ursula brought. I simply don't want put in chair. Don't have paper. Do you want little bit, Cromer? I can't wear it tomorrow.
36 mos.	I going come in fourteen minutes. I going wear that to wedding. I see what happens. I have to save them now. Those are not strong mens. They are going sleep in wintertime. You dress me up like a baby elephant.
38 mos.	So it can't be cleaned? I broke my racing car. Do you know the lights went off? What happened to the bridge? Can I put my head in the mailbox so the mailman can know where I are and put me in the mailbox?

Source: Steven Pinker, *The Language Instinct* (New York: Morrow, 1994), pp. 269–270.

9)

Can he *can* look?
What *shall* we *shall* have?
Did you *did* came home?

In these sentences, the auxiliary verb occurs twice—once to the left of the subject (in the position that it occupies after Inversion) and once to the right (in the position it occupies in deep structure). It has been suggested that this pattern reflects an error in the application of the Inversion transformation in that a copy of the moved auxiliary is left behind in its original position.

Wh Questions

Wh questions emerge gradually between the ages of two and four. The first *wh* words to be acquired are typically *what* and *where,* followed by *who, how,* and *why; when, which,* and *whose* are relatively late acquisitions.

10)

Where that?
What me think?
Why you smiling?
Why not me drink it?

With the acquisition of auxiliary verbs, Inversion becomes possible. Interestingly, some children appear to find it easier to carry out the Inversion operation in *yes-no* questions, where it is the only Move operation, than in *wh* questions, where *Wh* Movement must also apply. They go through a stage where Inversion is more common in the former pattern than in the latter.

11)

Yes-no questions (with Inversion):
Did Mommy pinch her finger?
Can't you fix it?
Do I have it?
Will you help me?
Is Mommy talking to Robin's grandmother?

12)

Wh questions (no Inversion):
What I did yesterday?
Why Kitty can't stand up?
Where I should put it?
Where I should sleep?
Why you are smiling?

5.5 The Interpretation of Sentence Structure

As noted in Chapter 6, the interpretation of sentences draws heavily on various features of syntactic structure. In this section we will briefly consider some aspects of the acquisition of two interpretive phenomena that rely on information about syntactic structure.

Passives

Children learning English are able to associate thematic roles with particular structural positions at a very early point in the acquisition process. By the time their average utterance length is two words, they are able to respond correctly about 75 percent of the time to comprehension tests involving simple active sentences such as the one in *13*, in which *the truck* is the agent and *the car* is the theme.

13)

The truck bumped the car.

However, children find it much harder to interpret certain other types of sentences correctly. This is especially true for passive sentences such as the one in *14*, which contains no semantic clues about which NP is agent and which one is theme. (Note that it makes just as much sense for the car to bump the truck as it does for the truck to bump the car. Such sentences are said to be "reversible.")

14)

The car was bumped by the truck.

Although children produce passive sentences in their own speech from around age three, they have continuing difficulty responding appropriately to passive constructions in comprehension tests (see Table 11.20).

Table 11.20 Comprehension of reversible passive constructions

Group	*Percentage correct*
Nursery school	20
Kindergarten	35
Grade 1	48
Grade 2	63
Grade 3	88

Why should this be so? One possibility is that children expect the first NP in a sentence to bear the agent role and the second NP to bear the theme role. This is sometimes called the **Canonical Sentence Strategy** (see Figure 11.4).

NP ... V ... NP is interpreted as:
agent – action – theme

Figure 11.4 The Canonical Sentence Strategy

The Canonical Sentence Strategy works for active, transitive sentences but not for passive sentences, where the first NP is the theme and the second NP is the agent.

15)

Active sentence:	The truck *agent*	bumped	the car. *theme*
Passive sentence:	The car *theme*	was bumped	by the truck *agent*

Children employing this strategy treat the first NP in passive sentences as the agent and the second NP as the theme, so they think the car bumps the truck.

As the data in Table 11.20 show, this strategy is applied much less consistently by first graders, who have evidently begun to realize that there is no simple correlation between linear position and thematic role. A year or so later, children's scores start to rise dramatically, indicating that they have come to recognize the special properties of the passive construction.

Reflexives and Pronominals

In Chapter 6, we saw that a reflexive pronoun (*myself, himself, herself,* and so on) must have a "higher" (i.e., c-commanding) antecedent in the minimal clause containing it.

16)

a. Reflexive pronoun with a higher antecedent in the same clause:
I hurt *myself* with the knife.

b. Reflexive pronoun without a higher antecedent in the same clause:
*You hurt *myself* with the knife.

In contrast, a pronominal (*me, him, her*) cannot have a higher antecedent in the same minimal clause.

17)

a. Pronominal with a higher antecedent in the same clause:
*I hurt *me* with the knife.

b. Pronominal without a higher antecedent in the same clause:
You hurt *me* with the knife.

Despite the intricacy of the principles involved here, children appear not to have trouble distinguishing between pronominals and reflexive pronouns in their own speech. In one study of the use of *me* and *myself* in speech transcripts from three children aged two to five, researchers found a few errors of the following type.

18)

Sample pronoun errors:

Mistake involving *me:* I see *me.* (Adam, age 34 mos., looking through a telescope)

Mistake involving *myself:* Don't you drop me . . . you hurt *myself.* (Abe, age 34 mos.)

Overall, though, the children misused *me* only about 5 percent of the time and made mistakes using *myself* less than 1 percent of the time. We will return to this point in Section 6.4.

6 What Makes Language Acquisition Possible?

In the preceding sections, we have seen that the language acquisition process extends over a period of several years. It is relatively easy to describe what takes place during these years, but it is much more difficult to explain *how* it happens. The sections that follow focus on some of the factors that may contribute to an eventual understanding of how the language acquisition process works.

6.1 The Role of Adult Speech

At one time, it was widely believed that children learn language simply by imitating the speech of those around them. This cannot be right, however. Not only do children tend not to repeat the speech of others, but they are typically unable to imitate structures that they have not yet learned. For instance, a child who has not yet acquired the Inversion operation will imitate sentence *19a* by producing *19b*.

19)

a. Model sentence: What can you see?
b. Child's imitation: What you can see?

A child's own grammar, not the model provided by adult speech, determines what she or he will say at any given point of development.

Of course, language learners must be sensitive in some way to the language in their environment. After all, children who are exposed to English learn to speak English, those exposed to Navajo learn Navajo, and so forth. It seems, though, that the relationship between input (the language children hear) and acquisition is subtler and more complicated than one might think.

Caregiver Speech

A good deal of work has been devoted to the search for a possible relationship between language acquisition and the type of speech that is typically addressed to young language learners. Such speech is often called **motherese** or **caregiver speech**. Table 11.21 summarizes the principal features of the caregiver speech used by middle-class English-speaking mothers with their children.

Table 11.21 Some features of English caregiver speech

Phonetic	Slow, carefully articulated speech Higher pitch Exaggerated intonation and stress Longer pauses
Lexical and semantic	More restricted vocabulary Concrete reference to here and now
Syntactic	Few incomplete sentences Short sentences More imperatives and questions
Conversational	More repetitions Few utterances per conversational turn

Caregiver speech could be helpful to children in a variety of ways. For example, exposure to slow, carefully articulated speech may make it easier for children to pick out words and to learn their pronunciation. (Remember that sentences consist of a continuous stream of speech sounds; there are no pauses between words.) Moreover, the acquisition of meaning may be facilitated by the fact that caregiver speech tends to concentrate on the here and now, especially the child's surroundings, activities, and needs. The examples in Table 11.22 help illustrate this.

Table 11.22 Some examples of caregiver speech

Mother's utterance	*Context*
That's right, pick up the blocks.	the child is picking up a box of building blocks
That's a puppy.	the child is looking at a young dog
The puppy's in the basket.	the child is examining a puppy in a basket

Exposure to language of this type may well make it easier to match morphemes, words, and phrases with meanings—a major part of the language acquisition process.

Although potentially *helpful,* caregiver speech may not actually be *necessary* to the language acquisition process. In some cultures, for instance, children are not considered to be potential conversational partners until they are fluent speakers. Little speech is addressed directly to them, although they do spend a lot of time with their mothers and are exposed to a good deal of conversation among adults. The fact that these children learn language in a normal fashion indicates that exposure to the speech style typical of middle-class mothers in North American society is not necessary for language acquisition.

Moreover, even in cultures where it is common, caregiver speech seems to have very selective effects on child language. For instance, the number of *yes-no* questions in caregiver speech seems to be correlated with the rate at which auxiliary verbs develop—apparently because auxiliaries occur in the salient sentence-initial position in *yes-no* questions (*Can Jennifer go?*). At the same time, though, many other features of caregiver speech seem not to affect child language. As we saw earlier (Section 4.2), for example, the relative frequency of bound morphemes and nonlexical categories in caregiver speech apparently does not determine their order of acquisition.

In and of itself, then, caregiver speech cannot explain how language acquisition occurs. However, research into this subject may contribute to this goal in less direct ways by helping determine the types of linguistic experience that are most valuable to children. This in turn could help linguists identify the types of mechanisms and strategies involved in language acquisition.

6.2 The Role of Feedback

It is sometimes suggested that parents provide children with direct linguistic training by correcting ill-formed utterances. However, studies of actual interactions between parents and children point in a quite different direction. In general, parents tend to be more concerned with the truth of children's utterances than with their grammaticality—one transcript of a parent-child conservation includes *That's right* as a response to the grammatical monstrosity *Mama isn't boy, he's a girl!*

Moreover, even when adults do attempt to correct children's grammatical errors, their efforts often have little effect. The following exchange between a child and his father is typical in this regard.

20)

Child:	Want other one spoon, Daddy.
Father:	You mean, you want the other spoon.
Child:	Yes, I want other one spoon, please Daddy.
Father:	Can you say 'the other spoon'?
Child:	other . . . one . . . spoon.
Father:	Say 'other'.
Child:	other.
Father:	'spoon.'
Child:	spoon.
Father:	'other spoon.'
Child:	other . . . spoon. Now give me other one spoon?

Interestingly, however, some research suggests that subtler forms of feedback may have a role to play in the language acquisition process.

Recasts

Adults often respond to a child's utterance by repeating it, making adjustments to its form and/or content. (Responses of this sort are called **recasts**.)

21)

Child:	Daddy here.
Mother:	Yes, Daddy is here.
Child:	Him go.
Mother:	Yes, he is going.
Child:	Boy chasing dog.
Mother:	Yes, the boy is chasing the dog.
Child:	The dog is barking.
Mother:	Yes, he is barking at the kitty.

Recasts provide children with potentially useful information—adding a missing verb (*is* in the first example), changing the form of a pronoun (*him* to *he* in the second example), and so on. On the other hand, parents sometimes modify their children's grammatical utterances too (as in the final example), so recasts also have the potential to be misleading.

It is not yet clear what role recasts play in language learning, and studies to date have yielded conflicting results. For instance, a study of the acquisition of *the* and *a* by three children revealed no link between the frequency of recasts and the rate at which their use of determiners increased; no matter how many recasts children heard, it didn't seem to speed up their learning.

On the other hand, a quite different result emerged from an experiment in which four- and five-year-olds were taught made-up verbs that have irregular past tense forms—for example, *pell* (with *pold* as its past tense). When the children first learned what the verbs meant (they were linked to various funny actions, such as hitting someone with a beanbag attached to a string), they heard only the *-ing* forms ("This is called *pelling*"). They therefore had no idea what the past tense forms should be and often produced "mistakes" such as *pelled* when using the new verbs to describe actions in the past tense. Interestingly, a single recast was often enough to permit learning of the "correct" form *pold*—which suggests that feedback of this type may have a role to play in the language acquisition process after all.

6.3 The Role of Cognitive Development

Because there are dramatic changes in both linguistic and nonlinguistic abilities during the first years of life, it is tempting to think that the two are somehow linked. Indeed, prominent psychologists have suggested both that general cognitive development shapes language acquisition (a view put forward by the late Swiss psychologist Jean Piaget) and that language acquisition is crucial to other aspects of cognitive development (a position associated with the late Russian psychologist Lev Vygotsky).

There are many suggestive similarities between language acquisition and cognitive development. During the first two years of life, for example, several cognitive advances that could facilitate language acquisition take place. One of these involves the development of **object permanence**, the ability to recognize that objects have an existence independent of one's interaction with them. Prior to the development of this ability, children seem to assume that an object ceases to exist when it moves out of sight, and that it is a different entity when it reappears. They therefore do not know where to look for an object that they observe being hidden; from their perspective, it has apparently simply ceased to exist. Object permanence emerges around the age of eighteen months, just prior to a period of rapid growth in the child's vocabulary. The relative timing of these two events suggests a possible connection: children's ability to learn the names for objects increases dramatically once they understand that those objects have an independent existence.

Another possible link between cognitive development and language acquisition involves **seriation**, the ability to arrange elements (such as sticks) in order of increasing or decreasing size. Children who are unable to perform this type of task typically describe the objects on which they are working simply as *long* or *short*. In contrast, children who are capable of seriation (age five and older) use comparative terms such as *longer* and *shorter*. Here again, there is an apparent connection between an aspect of language (the *-er* suffix for adjectives) and a more general cognitive skill (seriation).

Just as cognitive development may influence language acquisition, so the emergence of linguistic skills may have an effect on cognition. At the very least, language seems to provide its users with an enhanced capacity for complex reasoning. It is also conceivable that language may help draw children's attention to certain conceptual distinctions that would otherwise develop more slowly. For instance, in the course of learning words such as *father, mother, brother,* and *uncle,* children may make discoveries about family relationships that would otherwise develop more slowly.

Selective Impairment

These examples notwithstanding, there is good reason to believe that language acquisition is to a large extent independent of other types of cognitive development. One source of evidence for this conclusion comes from the study of individuals whose general cognitive development is deficient but whose language is highly developed.

One important study of this type focused on Rick, a severely retarded fifteen-year-old whose performance on a variety of nonlinguistic tasks suggests that his general cognitive level is that of a preschool child. Yet, as the following examples illustrate, Rick's speech shows signs of syntactic and morphological sophistication—with appropriate use of affixes, nonlexical categories, and word order.

22)

She must've got me up and thrown me out of bed.
She keeps both of the ribbons on her hair.
If they get in trouble, they'd have a pillow fight.
She's the one that walks back and forth to school.
I wanna hear one more just for a change.

Another celebrated case involves Christopher, a linguistic savant. Although mentally impaired due to early brain damage (his IQ is 56) and unable to care for himself, he has shown an obsession for language since he was six years old. Thanks solely to his own efforts, he is able to read, write, and communicate in fifteen to twenty different languages, taking particular delight in learning complex morphological paradigms.

On the other hand, there are also documented cases of people whose IQ is perfectly normal but who nonetheless have great difficulty with inflection for the past tense and plural, as illustrated by the examples in *23.* (There is reason to believe that this particular disorder is inherited.)

23)

The boys eat four cookie.
It's a flying finches, they are.
The neighbors phone the ambulance because the man fall off the tree.

Case studies such as these suggest that certain aspects of language (in particular, morphology and syntax) are independent of nonlinguistic types of cognitive development. This in turn implies that the mental mechanisms responsible for the acquisition of those parts of the grammar are relatively autonomous and that their operation neither follows from nor guarantees general cognitive development.

6.4 The Role of Inborn Knowledge

There can be no doubt that there is something special about the human mind that equips it to acquire language. The only real question has to do with precisely what that special thing is. A very influential view among linguists is that children are born with prior knowledge of the type of categories, operations, and principles that are found in the grammar of any human language. They therefore know, for example, that the words in the language they are acquiring will belong to a small set of syntactic categories (N, V, and so on) and that they can be combined in particular ways to create larger phrases (NP, VP, IP, etc.). The set of inborn categories, operations, and principles common to all human languages makes up **Universal Grammar (UG)**, first mentioned in Chapter 5.

The view that certain grammatical knowledge is inborn is known as **nativism**. Although nativism has roots in philosophy that date back thousands of years, its popularity in linguistics is due largely to the influence of Noam Chomsky, a linguist at the Massachusetts Institute of Technology. Chomsky's basic claim is that the grammars for human language are too complex and abstract to be learned on the basis of the type of experience to which children have access. Therefore, he argues, significant components of the grammar must be inborn. To illustrate this, we must consider a relatively complex example involving the notion of c-command, introduced in Chapter 6 (Section 3.4).

Principles A and B

The interpretation of pronouns such as *himself* and *him* is regulated by the following two principles.

24)

Principle A
A reflexive pronoun must have an antecedent that c-commands it in the same minimal IP.

Principle B
A pronominal must not have an antecedent that c-commands it in the same minimal IP.

These principles have played an important role in the study of language acquisition, and three arguments have been put forward in support of the claim that they are inborn.

First, the notion of c-command is quite abstract. It is not the type of concept that we would expect young children to discover simply by listening to sentences. Since we also know that no one teaches them about c-command, it makes sense to think that this notion is inborn and therefore does not have to be discovered or taught.

Second, the c-command relation seems to be universally relevant to pronoun interpretation. Thus, there appears to be no language in which the equivalent of English *himself* can refer to the boy rather than the boy's father in sentences such as the following (see Chapter 6 for discussion).

25)

The boy's father overestimates himself.

The universality of this restriction would be explained if Principles A and B were innate and hence part of the inborn linguistic knowledge of all human beings.

Third, as we saw earlier in this chapter, Principles A and B seem to be available to children from a very early stage in their development—even three-year-olds appear to have mastered the distinction between reflexives and pronominals. Given the complexity of these principles, this provides additional evidence for the claim that they are inborn.

Parameters

Of course, not every feature of a language's grammar can be inborn. Its vocabulary and morphology must be learned, and so must at least part of its syntax. In the case of phrase structure, for example, UG stipulates that an XP constituent can include a head and its complements, but it does not specify the relative order of these elements. This differs from language to language, so that a child acquiring English must learn that heads precede their complements, whereas a child acquiring Japanese must learn the reverse order. UG includes a **parameter** for word order that offers a choice between head-initial and head-final order. (We ignore the positioning of specifiers for the purposes of this illustration in Table 11.23.)

Table 11.23 The word-order parameter

Stipulated by UG	*Resulting options*
X' consists of X and a complement	Head-initial order: X Complement Head-final order: Complement X

There are also phonological parameters: for example, languages can differ from each other in terms of whether they allow two or more consonants in the onset of a syllable—English does (e.g., *gleam, sprint*), whereas Japanese does not.

Part of the language acquisition process involves **parameter setting**—that is, determining which of the options permitted by a particular parameter is appropriate for the language being learned.

6.5 Is There a Critical Period?

One of the most intriguing issues in the study of language acquisition has to do with the possibility that normal linguistic development is possible only if children are exposed to language during a particular time frame or **critical period**. Evidence for the existence of such a period comes from the study of individuals who do not experience language during the early part of their lives.

One such individual is the much-discussed Genie, who was kept in a small room with virtually no opportunity to hear human speech from around age two to age thirteen. After many years of therapy and care, Genie's nonlinguistic cognitive functioning was described as "relatively normal" and her lexical and semantic abilities as "good." In terms of syntax and morphology, however, many problems remained, as evidenced in the sample utterances in Table 11.24. As these examples show, Genie makes word-order errors (the first two examples), and her speech does not contain nonlexical categories or affixes.

Table 11.24 Some of Genie's utterances

Utterance	*Meaning*
Applesauce buy store	'Buy applesauce at the store.'
Man motorcycle have	'The man has a motorcycle.'
Want go ride Miss F. car	'I want to go ride in Miss F.'s car.'
Genie have full stomach	'I have a full stomach.'
Mama have baby grow up	'Mama has a baby who grew up.'

Another revealing case study involved Chelsea, a deaf child who was misdiagnosed as retarded and emotionally disturbed. Chelsea grew up without language and was not exposed to speech until the age of thirty-one, when she was finally fitted with hearing aids. After intensive therapy, she is able to hold a job and to live independently. However, her vocabulary consists of only 2,000 words, and her sentences are badly formed, as the following examples help show.

26)

The woman is bus the going.
Combing hair the boy.
Orange Tim car in.
The girl is gone the ice cream shopping buying the man.

Based on case studies such as these, it is now widely believed that the ability to acquire a first language in an effortless and ultimately successful way begins to decline from age six and is severely compromised by the onset of puberty.

Summing Up

This chapter has been concerned with the problem of how children acquire the **grammar** of their first language. Research in this area deals with two major issues: the nature of the **developmental sequence** leading to the emergence of mature linguistic competence in the areas of phonology, vocabulary, morphology, and syntax, and the factors that make it possible for children to acquire a complex grammar. A number of factors may contribute to the child's acquisition of language, including the properties of **caregiver speech**, **recasts**, the effects of general cognitive development, and inborn linguistic knowledge (**Universal Grammar**). We look to future research for deeper insights into the precise role of these and other factors.

Key Terms

General terms and terms concerned with research methods

cross-sectional
diary study
experimental studies
grammar
longitudinal
naturalistic approach

Terms concerning phonological development

babbling
denasalization
fronting
gliding
stopping

Terms concerning vocabulary, morphological, and syntactic development

Canonical Sentence Strategy
developmental sequence
holophrases
one-word stage
overextension
overgeneralizations
overregularizations
telegraphic stage
two-word stage
underextension

Terms concerning factors contributing to language acquisition

caregiver speech
critical period
motherese
nativism
object permanence
parameter
parameter setting
recasts
seriation
Universal Grammar (UG)

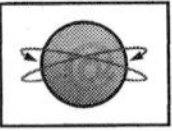

For more information on the sources used in this chapter, go to **bedfordstmartins.com/linguistics/firstlanguage** and click on **Sources**.

Recommended Reading

Clark, Eve. 1993. *The Lexicon in Acquisition.* New York: Cambridge University Press.

Clark, Eve. 2002. *First Language Acquisition.* New York: Cambridge University Press.

Gallaway, Clare, and Brian Richards. 1994. *Input and Interaction in Language Acquisition.* New York: Cambridge University Press.

Ingram, David. 1989. *First Language Acquisition: Method, Description and Explanation.* New York: Cambridge University Press.

O'Grady, William. 1997. *Syntactic Development.* Chicago: University of Chicago Press.

Piattelli-Palmarini, Massimo (ed.). 1980. *Language and Learning: The Debate between Jean Piaget and Noam Chomsky.* Cambridge, MA: Harvard University Press.

Vihman, Marilyn. 1996. *Phonological Development: The Origins of Language in the Child.* Cambridge, MA: Blackwell.

Exercises

1. One piece of evidence that children acquire a grammar is their production of forms like *doed, leaved,* and *goed.* From recollections of your experience with children, what are some other forms (not related to the past tense rule) that children produce that indicate they are acquiring and overgeneralizing grammatical rules?

2. In one naturalistic study, a search for passive structures in a sample of 18,000 utterances from sixty children yielded only nineteen examples produced by twelve of the children.

i) Is this evidence that the other forty-eight children had not yet learned the passive structure? Why or why not?

ii) How are the disadvantages of the naturalistic method exemplified here?

3. The following transcriptions represent the pronunciation of a two-year-old child. Indicate which phonetic processes have applied in each case.

a)	skin	[kɪd]	h)	tent	[dɛt]
b)	spoon	[bun]	i)	teddy	[dɛdi]
c)	zoo	[du]	j)	brush	[bʌt]
d)	John	[dɑn]	k)	bump	[bʌp]
e)	bath	[bæt]	l)	play	[pwej]
f)	other	[ʌdə]	m)	breakfast	[brɛkpəst]
g)	Smith	[mɪt]			

4. Drawing on the phonetic processes posited for the preceding exercise, predict one or more plausible immature pronunciations for each of the following words.

a)	show	e)	juice
b)	please	f)	thumb
c)	spit	g)	zebra
d)	under	h)	ring

5. Consider the following examples of overextensions, all of which have actually been observed in children's speech. What is the basis for each of these overextensions?

	Word	*First referent*	*Overextensions*
a)	sch	sound of a train	music, noise of wheels, sound of rain
b)	bow-wow	dog	sheep, rabbit fur, puppet
c)	baby	baby	people in pictures
d)	sizo	scissors	nail file, knife, screwdriver, spoon
e)	policeman	policeman	mailman, sailor, doctor
f)	strawberry	strawberry	grapes, raspberry
g)	fireworks	fireworks	matches, light, cigarette
h)	Batman	Batman logo on a T-shirt	any logo on a T-shirt

6. Since children have a tendency to focus on the prototypical members of categories in the acquisition of words, how might you expect children to underextend the following words? What members of the category might you expect children not to include?
   a) car
   b) tree
   c) ball

7. Children acquire certain spatial terms like *behind* and *in front of* relatively late. They also acquire words like *those, this, here,* and *there* relatively late. What do all of these words have in common that delays their acquisition?

8. The allomorphic variation associated with the third person singular verbal ending *-s* is identical to that found with plural *-s*.

   i) Make up a test parallel to the "*wug* test" discussed in Section 4.1.

   ii) If possible, give your test to children between the ages of three and seven. Are your results similar to the ones discussed in the chapter?

9. Based on the discussion in Section 4.2 about the developmental sequence of morpheme acquisition, consider the acquisition in other languages of the morphemes corresponding to those listed in Table 11.12. Would you predict that these morphemes would be acquired in exactly the same order as their English equivalents? Why or why not?

10. Considering children's tendency to overgeneralize morphological rules, what might we expect a young child to use in place of the following adult words? Justify your choice in each case.

a) fish (plural)	f) geese
b) went	g) brought
c) mice	h) hit (past tense)
d) ate	i) himself
e) has	j) women

11. Each of the following utterances is from the speech of a child in the two-word stage. Identify the semantic relation expressed by each of these utterances.

Child's utterance	*Intended meaning*
a) Jimmy swim.	Jimmy is swimming.
b) Ken book	Ken's book
c) Daddy office.	Daddy is at his office.
d) Push baby.	You push the baby.
e) Mommy read.	Mommy is reading.

12. Consider the following data from Jordie, a two-and-a-half-year-old child, in light of the list of morphemes in Table 11.12.

Jordie's utterance	*Intended meaning*
a) Where my blanket?	Where's my blanket?
b) Go right here, Mommy?	Does it go right here, Mommy?
c) Running over.	It's running over.
d) Here, go here.	Here, it goes here.
e) No, that mine.	No, that's mine.
f) Dinosaur say gronk.	Dinosaurs say gronk.
g) There more.	There's more.

i) Which of the morphemes in Table 11.12 are missing in Jordie's sentences but present in the intended meaning?

ii) List the morphemes that are present in both the intended meaning and in Jordie's speech.

13. Now consider the following utterances from a child named Krista.

Krista's utterance	*Intended meaning*
a) Mine name Krista.	My name is Krista.
b) Last name Pegit.	My last name is Pegit.
c) Tape right there.	The tape is right there.
d) Daddy book	Daddy's book
e) I'm got a book.	I've got a book.
f) Read me story.	Read me a story.
g) I'm do it.	I'll do it.

h) He went outside.	He went outside.
i) Open a gate, please.	Open the gate, please.
j) Gramma's house	Gramma's house
k) Smell flowers.	Smell the flowers.
l) Shoes on	Shoes on
m) Wee boy fell down.	The wee boy fell down.
n) That's mines ball.	That's my ball.

i) Which morphemes are missing in Krista's speech, but present in the intended meaning?

ii) Krista uses the past tense twice in the above utterances. Do you think this is evidence that she has acquired the past tense morpheme? Why or why not?

iii) Comment on Krista's difficulty with the first person singular possessive pronouns.

iv) Do you think she has acquired possessive *-'s*? Why or why not?

14. The following utterances were produced spontaneously by Holly, age three years.
    a) I learned about loving moms.
    b) Put him in the bathtub.
    c) We eated gummy snakes.
    d) Thank you for giving these books us.
    e) I don't know.
    f) He bited my finger. (When corrected, she said: He bitted my finger.)
    g) I runned in the water.
    h) I rided on a elephant.

    i) Has Holly acquired the past tense morpheme? How do you know?

    ii) What is the evidence in Holly's speech that she has learned phrases that consist of a head, a complement, and/or a specifier?

    iii) What is the evidence that words such as *eat, know* and *ride* are verbs for Holly and that words such as *bathtub, books,* and *water* are nouns for her?

15. Consider the following speech sample from a child.
    a) What Evan will read?
    b) Where Evan will read?
    c) Why you see seal?
    d) Why she want to?

    i) Determine the stage of development of this child in terms of his acquisition of question structures.

    ii) What do we expect to happen next?

16. It has been reported that hearing children growing up in homes with nonspeaking deaf parents cannot learn spoken language from radio or even television (see p. 278 of *The Language Instinct* by S. Pinker [New York: Morrow, 1994]).

    i) Can you think of any reasons for this?

    ii) What are the implications of these findings for our understanding of the type of experience that is required for language acquisition?

twelve

Second Language Acquisition

John Archibald

When we talk about acquisition in SLA research, we are not talking about acquisition in the sense that one acquires polo ponies, Lladró figurines, or CBS, but rather in the sense that one acquires vicious habits, a taste for Brie, or a potbelly.

– Kevin R. Gregg

Objectives

In this chapter, you will learn:

- how the learner's first language and the language being learned interact to influence changes in the learner's grammar as he or she progresses
- what characterizes the phonology, syntax, and morphology of a second language learner's grammar
- how nonlinguistic factors may influence second language acquisition
- how second language classrooms help the learner by modifying language and focusing on form
- what alternatives exist for English language learners in U.S. schools

The field of **second language acquisition (SLA)** research investigates how people attain proficiency in a language that is not their mother tongue. Whether we are looking at someone learning to read Greek in college, someone becoming fluent in a fifth language in their forties, or a child acquiring a new language after moving to a new country, we refer to it as second language acquisition. The interesting phenomenon of children simultaneously acquiring two languages is generally investigated in the field known as **bilingualism** (which may be thought of as a subdiscipline of SLA research). In this chapter, we will primarily be concerned with second language acquisition in adults.

Over the years, the study of second language acquisition has been undertaken from a variety of different perspectives. In the 1950s and 1960s, the primary objective was pedagogic. Researchers were interested in trying to improve the way in which second languages were taught. Therefore, they were interested in discovering how those languages were learned. From the 1970s on, the focus shifted from the teacher to the learner and the field of L2 (second language) instruction became somewhat separate.

The reason for this has something to do with what was going on in linguistics, psychology, and first language acquisition research. All three of these areas shifted focus from the external to the internal in the 1960s. Linguistics became concerned with the mental grammar of the speaker, not just the description of the linguistic structures of a given language. Psychology shifted from behaviorism (which denied the importance of mental representations) to cognitive psychology, and research on first language acquisition focused on children's internal grammars. These fields are also crucial to the study of SLA. Linguistics gives us a sophisticated and accurate description of what people are trying to learn (the second language), and what they already know (the first language). Psychology can provide us with a learning theory to account for how people acquire knowledge. Finally, the field of first language acquisition (which has been around longer than the field of second language acquisition) offers various findings that can be productively applied to SLA. For example, we know that children who are acquiring their first language (L1) have grammars that are systematic and that their utterances are not just bad imitations of the adult target. As we will see, second language learners, too, are developing a grammar that is systematic even if it is not nativelike.

1 The Study of Second Language Acquisition

In the case of first language acquisition, we may ascribe the difference between child and adult grammars to either cognitive or biological immaturity in the child. In the case of second language learning by adults, however, we cannot say that the learners are either cognitively or biologically immature. Rather, they are subject to an influence that is absent from the child's situation: the first language itself. Let us diagram the situation as shown in Figure 12.1.

L1 → interlanguage grammar ← L2

Figure 12.1 Influences on an interlanguage grammar

This diagram illustrates the fact that second language learners have a systematic **interlanguage (IL)** grammar—so called because it is a system of mental representations influenced by both the first and the second language and has features of each.

1.1 The Role of the First Language

One of the most easily recognizable traits of a second language learner's speech is that it bears a certain resemblance to the first language. Thus, someone whose first language is French is likely to sound different from someone whose first language is German when they both speak English. Consider in this regard the typical pronunciation of the English word *have* by speakers of French and German shown in Table 12.1.

Table 12.1 Phonological transfer

English target	*French speaker*	*German speaker*
have [hæv]	[æv]	[hæf]

The form in Table 12.1 produced by the French speakers reflects the fact that French lacks the phoneme /h/, while the pronunciation associated with German speakers can be traced to the fact that German includes a rule of Syllable-Final Obstruent Devoicing (which changes the [v] to a [f]). The term **transfer** is used to describe the process whereby a feature or rule from a learner's first language is carried over to the IL grammar. Other examples can be seen in Table 12.2.

Table 12.2 More phonological transfer

L1	*L2*	*Example*	*Comment*
Spanish	English	I espeak Espanish.	Spanish does not allow *s* + consonant sequences word-initially.
English	French	[ty] 'you' → [tu]	English does not have the front, rounded vowel [y]. The English speaker substitutes the [u] sound.
Quebec French	English	Over dere.	The [ð] sound is replaced by [d].
European French	English	Over zere.	The [ð] sound is replaced by [z].
English	Spanish	[paɾa] 'for' → [paɹa]	As English does not have the tapped [ɾ], a [ɹ] is substituted.

The speech of second language learners can exhibit nonnativelike characteristics in any linguistic domain, as can be seen in Table 12.3 on page 402.

1.2 The Nature of an Interlanguage

The first language is not the only influence on the interlanguage grammar, since some properties of the IL grammar can be traced to aspects of the L2. In the case of a German speaker who is learning English, for example, the IL grammar will contain some features of both German and English. Consider how a German speaker learning Canadian English might pronounce the word *eyes* (see Table 12.4 on page 402). Here, the learner first applies the rule of Syllable-Final Obstruent Devoicing (transferred from German), changing /ajz/ to [ajs]. But the learner also has acquired some knowledge of the target language—in this case, the rule of Canadian Raising (discussed in Chapter 3)—that states that [aj] becomes [ʌj] before a voiceless consonant

Table 12.3 Types of errors found in the acquisition of English

L1	*Example*	*Error type*	*Comment*
Spanish	My wife is embarrassed (meaning 'pregnant').	lexical	Spanish *embarazada* = 'pregnant'
Various	I live in a two-bedroom department.	lexical	Sometimes the wrong word can be chosen.
Various	I didn't took the car.	morphological	English doesn't mark the past tense on both auxiliary and main verbs.
Various	She get ups late.	morphological	The speaker adds the agreement marker to the particle, not the verb.
French	He drinks frequently beer.	syntactic	French places the main verb before the adverb.
Various	There's the man that I saw him.	syntactic	Some languages (e.g., Arabic, Turkish) allow pronouns in this position in a relative clause.

Table 12.4 One possible pronunciation of the English word *eyes* by a German-speaking learner

Target form	*Result of Final Obstruent Devoicing*	*Result of Canadian Raising*
/ajz/	[ajs]	[ʌjs]

in the same syllable. Thanks to application of the Syllable-Final Obstruent Devoicing Rule, the input form now ends in a voiceless consonant ([s]), which triggers Canadian Raising. This example serves to show us something about the nature of an interlanguage: it contains features of both the L1 and the L2. When the interlanguage grammar stops changing, it is said to have **fossilized**.

1.3 The Final State

So far we have been talking about the characteristics of the intermediate grammar. But a discussion of what an IL grammar looks like must consider the **target**, that is, what is to be acquired. The field of SLA, then, must address the issue of actual proficiency or **communicative competence**. Although knowledge of a language's grammar allows us to distinguish between grammatical and ungrammatical sentences, successful communication requires much more than this. The learner must also be able to use the language in a way that is appropriate to the situation or context. As Figure 12.2 helps illustrate, both grammatical accuracy and communicative ability are part of communicative competence.

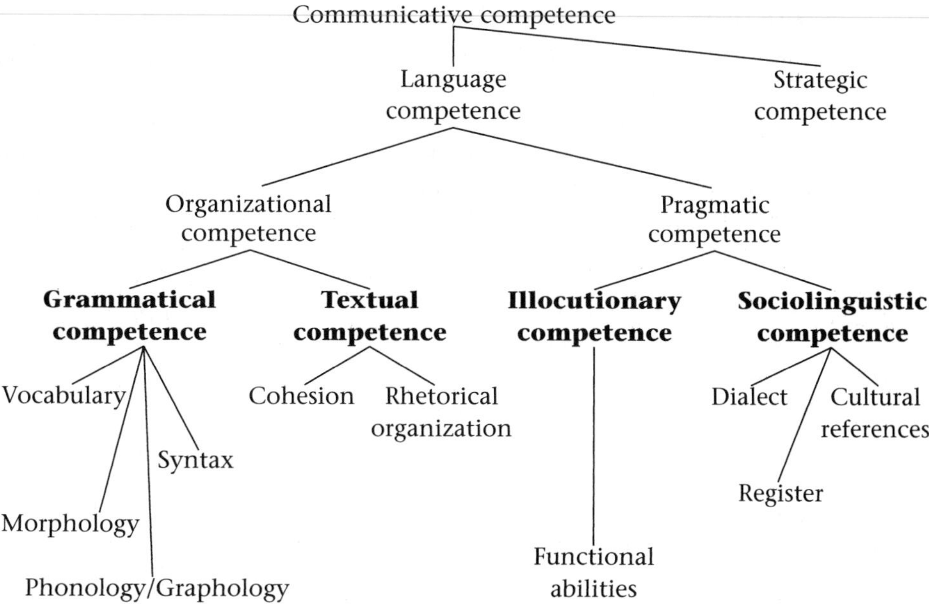

Figure 12.2 A model of communicative competence

Let us now briefly consider each of the major subparts of the model.

Grammatical Competence

Grammatical competence has to do with knowledge of the core components of the grammar: phonetics, phonology, morphology, syntax, and semantics. We will address some of these areas in detail in Section 2.

Textual Competence

Textual competence involves knowledge of well-formedness above the sentence level, including the rules that string sentences together to make a well-formed text in the spoken or written language. As the following examples help show, a text is not just a sequence of grammatical utterances.

1)

MGs can be very temperamental. MGs won't start if they are wet. When they work, MGs are fun to drive. They do not work often.

2)

Like most roadsters, MGs can be very temperamental. For example, they won't start if they are wet. However, on the rare days when they work, they are fun to drive.

The difference between the two texts does not involve the grammaticality of individual sentences, but relates to differences in the use of linking words such as *like, for example,* and *however.* To be proficient, second language learners have to acquire the ability to organize and link sentences in this way.

Illocutionary Competence

The meaning of an utterance is not always directly reflected in its surface structure. For example, when uttering the sentence *Have you ever considered professional help?*, a speaker could have in mind a variety of intended meanings. He might mean 'I can't help you, but maybe somebody else could' or 'I think you are a truly disturbed individual; seek help.' The speaker's intent in producing an utterance is referred to as **illocutionary force**. **Illocutionary competence**, then, refers to the ability to comprehend a speaker's intent, and to produce a variety of sentence types to convey a particular intent in various circumstances (e.g., *Are you cold?, Could I close the window?, Why on earth is the window open?*). This, too, is something that second language learners need to acquire.

Sociolinguistic Competence

As we will see in Chapter 15, language use can vary according to the context. For example, we use a different style of language in informal situations than we do in formal ones. This can affect phonology, syntax, and lexical choice, as can be seen in the following two utterances.

3)

I assume we will be working late again this evening? What a shame!

4)

We gotta work late again? Dammit!

In order to have **sociolinguistic competence**, second language learners need to be able to produce and comprehend a variety of social dialects.

In sum, communicative competence is a model of proficiency that allows us to measure second language knowledge and ability, to construct second language proficiency tests, and to design balanced second language courses.

1.4 Variation in Performance

An important goal of L2 research is to integrate the study of **competence** (linguistic knowledge) and **performance** (actual language use in particular situations). One of the characteristics of the output of second language learners is that it is quite variable. For example, a learner might well produce the following sentence:

5)

I **didn't** like **th**at movie so I told her I **no** want to go **d**ere.

In this (hypothetical) example, the learner is inconsistent, getting one of the two negatives right and correctly pronouncing one of the interdental fricatives. The question that intrigues researchers has to do with what causes this sort of variation. We usually think of knowledge as fairly stable within an individual. So, for example, if you make a mistake while speaking in your native language, you tend not to question your competence in that language but to assume that you made some kind of performance error. So how do we account for learners who behave as if they know how to negate a verb or pronounce [ð] on some occasions but not others? Do they have the knowledge or don't they?

It is difficult to answer this question, in part because of considerations involving error frequency. If a second language learner gets something wrong 10 percent of the time, is it the same (in terms of competence) as getting it wrong 60 percent of the time? We would probably say that a nonnative speaker who gets the English past tense correct 10 percent of the time does not know it, and that someone who gets it right 90 percent of the time does. But what of someone who gets it right somewhere between those two scores? This is a complex research question. The (admittedly simplistic) view adopted in this chapter is that variation falls into the realm of linguistic performance.

Linguistic performance clearly involves the interaction of a number of cognitive systems and has much in common with other skills. A crucial notion for the study of how skills develop involves the distinction between controlled and automatic processing. When acquiring a new skill (e.g., playing golf), we begin by having to devote a lot of conscious or controlled processing to the activity: feet apart, head down, elbow straight, and so on. Once we become proficient, we just hit the ball; the activity has become automatic.

We need to shift processing from controlled to automatic because, as humans, we have a fixed processing capacity. We can't consciously process everything at once. Shifting some material into automatic processing frees up space for more controlled processing. Consider an example from reading. When we first learn how to read, we devote much of our cognitive processing to determining what the written symbols stand for. When we are focusing on decoding the letters, we do not have the processing capacity to deal with things like reading for prejudice or bias. After a time, though, letter recognition happens automatically in our first language and learners can devote more of their cognitive capacity to higher-level skills.

That native speakers do this kind of thing automatically can be seen by the difficulty we have in proofreading. It is hard to suppress the information we're getting from the context since the mind tries to make sense of what it's reading. Conversely, when we are forced by exceptional circumstances to devote a lot of energy to decoding the print (e.g., a bad photocopy or fax), our higher-level processing slows down; we can't focus as much on the message when we are focusing on the form.

All this is relevant to second language acquisition in that it can help explain the variable performance of L2 learners. When learners are focusing on the form of the L2 utterance, they may be able to produce it accurately. However, when there are extra demands, such as trying to communicate a complex thought or carry on a conversation in a noisy room, errors may occur. This suggests that the learner has a mental representation of the form in question (say, a negated verb or a [ð]) but can have difficulty implementing or accessing it under certain conditions.

2 Interlanguage Grammars

Let us turn now to a discussion of the specifics of what is acquired when learning the phonology, morphology, and syntax of a second language. The general question we are trying to answer here is, *What is the structure of an interlanguage?* Second language learners are acquiring grammars, and those grammars involve mental representations. Therefore we can investigate the nature of those representations within the various subdomains of linguistic theory. We begin with phonology.

2.1 L2 Phonology

Let us consider what is to be acquired in the domain of phonology. Broadly speaking, we can distinguish between segmental and prosodic phonology. Segmental phonology has to do with the characteristics of phonological segments, like consonants (C) and vowels (V). Prosodic phonology, on the other hand, has to do with phonological phenomena that affect more than a single segment (e.g., syllables and stress).

Segmental Phonology

As we saw in Chapter 3, languages vary in their segmental inventory in that they choose a subset of the sounds found in human languages. There is thus a good chance that a second language learner will have to learn to produce and perceive some new sounds when acquiring a second language.

One of the most obvious characteristics of adult second language speech is that it is accented as the result of phonological and phonetic transfer from the native language. This is why native speakers of English can usually distinguish Italian-accented English from German-accented English. Consider the examples in Table 12.5.

Table 12.5 Italian- and German-accented English

English target	*Italian speaker*	*German speaker*
[ðə] 'the'	[də]	[zə]

As both Italian and German lack the interdental fricative [ð], native speakers of those languages substitute a sound from their L1 wherever English has that sound. Generally, the learners substitute a sound that shares some features with the target sound. In Table 12.5, the Italian speaker substituted a voiced alveolar (coronal) stop, while the German speaker substituted a voiced alveolar (coronal) fricative for the English voiced, interdental (coronal) fricative. Particularly at a beginning level of proficiency, L2 learners pronounce words using their L1 phonological system.

A similar phenomenon can be seen in the phonology of loan words. When a language borrows a word from another language, it makes the word fit into its own phonological system. For example, when English borrowed the word *pterodactyl* from Greek, it reduced the onset cluster [pt], which is well formed in Greek but not English. However, no such change was made in the word *helicopter* (with the same Greek root *pter* 'wing'), since it already complied with the phonological pattern of English.

Markedness

One question that has received a lot of attention in SLA research is why some sounds are harder to acquire in a second language than others. Perhaps some sounds are simpler than others. Or perhaps some sound systems are easier for speakers of a certain language to acquire. Would it be easier for a Japanese speaker to acquire English or Vietnamese? As might be expected, these are not simple issues. We cannot talk about the ease or difficulty of entire languages, but we may have something to say about individual sounds.

When linguists try to deal with the notions of ease or simplicity, they make use of the notion of **markedness**. Structures that are simple and/or especially common in human language are said to be **unmarked**, while structures that are complex or less common are said to be **marked**. So, we might say that a sound that is found in relatively few of the world's languages (e.g., [θ]) is marked, while a sound that occurs in many of the world's languages (e.g., [t]) is unmarked.

Markedness is commonly approached from the perspective of language typology, which is concerned with the comparative study of similarities and differences among languages. As noted in Chapter 8, researchers have discovered certain implicational universals of the form "if a language has *x,* it will also have *y.*" For example, if a language has nasal vowels (e.g., [ã]), then it will also have oral vowels (e.g., [a]). Crucial to the understanding of implicational universals is the fact that the implication is unidirectional. Thus a language that has oral vowels does not necessarily have nasal vowels. This allows us to identify [a] as less marked than [ã], in accordance with the following generalization.

6)

X is more marked than *y* if the presence of *x* implies the presence of *y, but not vice versa.*

It is interesting to ask whether IL grammars obey such implicational universals and whether this can tell us something about the question of ease and difficulty of learning.

The **Markedness Differential Hypothesis** investigates second language acquisition by comparing the relative markedness of structures in the L1 and the L2. Remember the earlier example of Syllable-Final Obstruent Devoicing in German, which explains why a word like *hund* 'dog' is pronounced with a [t] at the end. German speakers learning English typically transfer Syllable-Final Obstruent Devoicing into their IL (producing [hæt] for [hæd] 'had') and must learn to make the contrast between [t] and [d] at the ends of words. We might be tempted to think that the principle underlying this phenomenon is something like "it's hard to learn to make contrasts that your L1 doesn't make." But when we look at another set of data, we see that this is not the case.

French makes a contrast between [ʃ] and [ʒ] in places where English does not, as Table 12.6 on page 408 indicates. (Note that [ʒ] does not generally occur in English in word-initial position, except in a few words, such as *genre* and *gendarmes,* which have been borrowed from French.) If it were invariably difficult for second language learners to make contrasts that are not found in their L1, we would expect English speakers to have difficulty learning to produce [ʒ] at the beginning of words, but they don't. English speakers seem able to learn to pronounce French words like *jaune* 'yellow' and *jeudi* 'Thursday' without trouble.

The notion of markedness can be used to explain why German speakers have difficulty making a new contrast in English, while English speakers don't have difficulty making a new contrast in French. The typological situation is as follows:

Table 12.6 The [ʃ]/[ʒ] contrast in English and French

	English [ʃ]/[ʒ]	*French [ʃ]/[ʒ]*
Initial	sure [ʃ]/* [ʒ]	chant ([ʃ])/gens ([ʒ]) 'song' 'people'
Medial	assure ([ʃ])/azure ([ʒ])	boucher ([ʃ])/bouger ([ʒ]) 'to fill up' 'to budge'
Final	leash ([ʃ])/liege ([ʒ])	hache ([ʃ])/age ([ʒ]) 'h' 'age'

- There are languages that have a voicing contrast initially, medially, and finally (e.g., English).
- There are languages that have a voicing contrast initially and medially, but not finally (e.g., German).
- There are languages that have a voicing contrast initially, but not medially or finally (e.g., Sardinian).

These generalizations allow us to formulate the following implicational universal.

7)

The presence of a voicing contrast in final position implies the presence of a voicing contrast in medial position, which in turn implies the presence of a voicing contrast in initial position.

We can represent this universal graphically as follows:

8)

initial > medial > final
C B A

The presence of A implies the presence of B (but not vice versa), and the presence of B implies the presence of C (but not vice versa). Therefore A is the most marked and C is the least marked. This markedness differential explains the differing degrees of difficulty exhibited by the German and English L2 learners. The German speakers learning English are attempting to acquire a contrast in a universally more marked position (final) whereas the English speakers learning French are attempting to acquire a contrast in a universally unmarked position (initial).

Another way of looking at the similarity/difference question, though, is not in terms of ease or difficulty of acquisition but in terms of *rate* of acquisition. The **Similarity Differential Rate Hypothesis** (SDRH) makes the claim that the rates of acquisition for dissimilar phenomena are faster than for similar phenomena. In other words, all other things being equal, learners will learn something that is unlike their first language structure *faster* than something that is similar to (and hence could be confused with) their first language structure. The data shown in Figure 12.3 describe the acquisition of English [ɹ] (in word-initial position) and English velarized

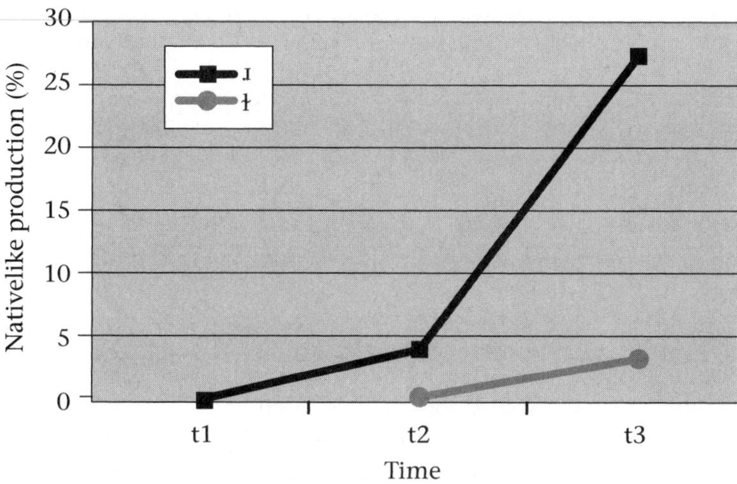

Figure 12.3 Differential rates of acquisition

[ɫ] (in word-final position) by a native speaker of Haitian creole, which has a uvular [ʁ] and only a clear alveolar [l]. Note that there is virtually no acquisition of the velarized [ɫ] and little change in rate, whereas the rate of change for [ɹ] is much more dramatic. The dissimilar [ɹ] is acquired at a faster rate than the similar [ɫ].

Of course, the question of how to determine whether two features are similar or dissimilar is not always straightforward. To really test this hypothesis, we would need to look at perceptual, phonetic, phonological, and even orthographic factors that could affect this judgment. Here we will just accept that the two *l*s are more similar than the two *r*s.

In addition to the segmental inventory, second language learners also have to acquire the prosodic phonology of the target language. For example, they have to acquire the principles of syllabification and stress assignment. We will now look at each in turn.

L2 Syllabification

We saw in Chapter 3 that syllables have the hierarchical structure shown in Figure 12.4.

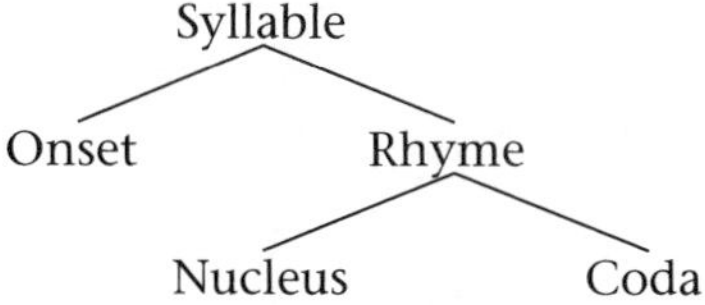

Figure 12.4 The internal structure of the syllable

The languages of the world vary according to such things as whether syllabic nodes can be complex. Some languages (e.g., Japanese) do not allow clusters in onsets or codas. Ignoring some complexities, let us assume that all syllables in these languages must be CV or CVC. More complex syllables such as CCVCC are not allowed. A common phenomenon in second language learning involves modifying an L2 word so that it fits the L1 syllable structure. Consider the following words spoken by someone whose L1 is Arabic:

9)

English target	*Nonnative speaker's version*
plant	pilanti
Fred	Fired
translate	tiransilet

Arabic does not allow clusters in onsets or codas, so an English word like *plant* cannot be mapped onto a single Arabic syllable. A characteristic of Arabic is that illicit consonant clusters are broken up by an epenthetic [i]. With this in mind, let us look at the steps that an Arabic speaker of one dialect would go through in syllabifying *plant.*

Step 1 Initial syllabification: Assign vowels to a nucleus (N) and the nucleus to a rhyme (R).

Step 2 Assign allowable onset (O) consonants (in Arabic, one).

Step 3 Assign allowable coda (Co) consonants (in Arabic, one).

Step 4 Insert an epenthetic [i] after an unsyllabified consonant.

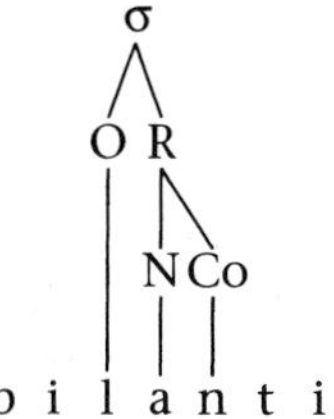

Step 5 Assign vowels to a nucleus and the nucleus to a rhyme.

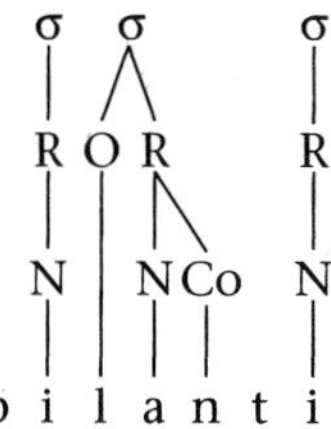

Step 6 Assign allowable onset consonants (in Arabic, one).

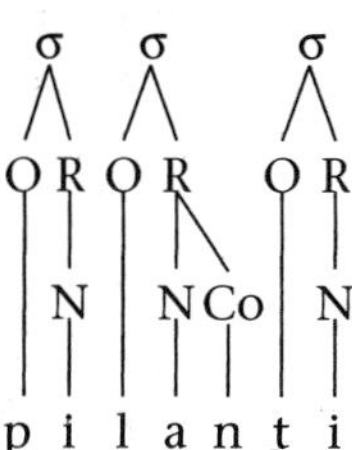

As this example helps show, we can explain why Arabic speakers pronounce English words in the way that they do by investigating the principles of syllabification in the L1. Especially at the beginning levels of proficiency, the structure of the IL grammar is influenced by the structure of the L1.

Stress Assignment

L2 learners also have to acquire the stress patterns of the language they are trying to learn. Consider an example from Polish. Polish is a language in which word-level stress is always assigned to the penultimate syllable. These L1 principles transfer and result in one of the characteristics of a Polish accent in English: the tendency to place stress on the penultimate syllable of English words. The following examples illustrate a nonnative stress pattern in which the second-to-last syllable is always stressed.

10)

English target	*Nonnative form*
astónish	astónish
maintáin	máintain
cábinet	cabínet

2.2 L2 Syntax

L2 learners also have to acquire the syntax of their new language. In this section, we will look at two facets of syntactic structure: the null subject parameter and verb movement.

Null Subjects

As we saw in Chapter 5, Universal Grammar includes universal principles (which account for what all natural languages have in common) as well as parameters (which account for cross-linguistic variation). Parameters are like linguistic switches (often binary) that can be set to a particular value as a result of the linguistic input. One of the first parameters to be proposed was the **Null Subject** (or pronoun-drop) **Parameter**. Essentially, this parameter is designed to account for the contrast between languages like French and English, which require overt grammatical subjects (e.g., *He speaks French/*Speaks French*), and languages like Spanish and Italian, which allow subjects to be omitted (e.g., Spanish *Él habla español/Habla español* '[S/he] speaks Spanish').

11)

The Null Subject Parameter
The subject of a clause with a verb marked for tense {may/may not} be null.

Languages that allow null subjects tend to have other grammatical traits associated with them. For one, they tend to allow declarative sentences with the word order verb + subject as well as subject + verb, as in the following examples from Spanish.

12)

a. Juan llegó.
John arrived.

b. Llegó Juan.
Arrived John.

Secondly, they tend to allow sentences like the following, in which a complementizer (here *que* 'that') is immediately followed by the trace of a moved *wh* word.

13)

Quién dijo usted que *t* llegó?
who said you that arrived
'Who did you say that arrived?'

As the following example shows, such sentences are unacceptable in Standard U.S. English.

14)

*Who did you say [$_{CP}$ that [$_{IP}$ *t* arrived]]?
(deep structure = *you did say that who arrived*)

In other words, languages like English ([–null subject]) do not allow *that*-trace sequences, whereas languages like Spanish ([+null subject]) do.

Studies on L2 learners of English show that Spanish speakers are more likely to judge subjectless English sentences to be grammatical than are French speakers. This is consistent with the assumption that L1 parameter settings are transferred into the IL grammar, at least in the early stages. Learning a second language can be seen as involving the resetting of parameters that have different values in the L1 and the L2.

Moreover, when Spanish subjects are given a task that requires them to change a declarative sentence into a question, they are more likely to produce a sentence that contains a *that*-trace sequence than are French subjects. For example, if Spanish subjects are given a sentence like *Joshua believed that his father would be late* and have to form a question asking about the underlined element, they are more likely than French subjects to produce a sentence like *Who did Joshua believe that* t *would be late?* This points toward the possibility that the admissibility of null subjects and the acceptability of *that*-trace sequences are somehow both related to the Null Subject Parameter (i.e., speakers of null subject languages are more likely to permit *that*-trace sequences).

However, there are complications. Remember that the study just described had the Spanish and French speakers form new sentences. Another study had both French and Spanish subjects judge the grammaticality of English sentences with a *that*-trace violation. Both groups were quite able to reject those sentences as ungrammatical. For some reason, there is a stronger L1 influence when learners have to form new sentences themselves.

Verb Movement

French and English differ in the setting of the **Verb Movement Parameter**.

15)

The Verb Movement Parameter
A verb marked for tense {raises/does not raise} to I.

We saw in Chapter 5 that the transformation of verb movement takes a verb from within the VP and moves it to I (see Figure 12.5).

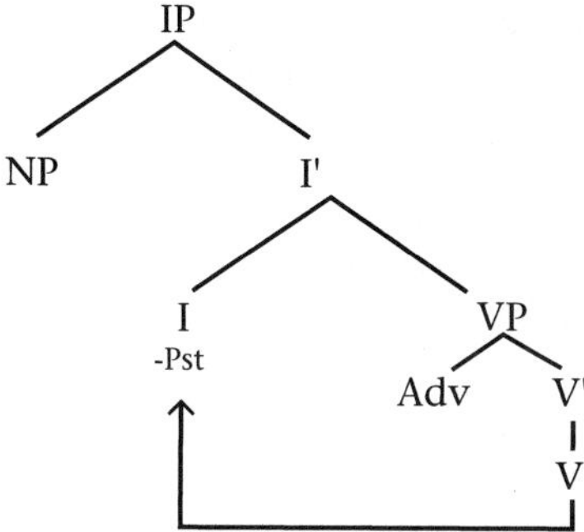

Figure 12.5 Verb movement

Simplifying slightly, let us say that English does not allow verb movement but French does. Thus, in French the verb raises to I past a preverbal adverb, but in English it does not. This difference can be seen in the sentences in *16,* in which movement of the verb over the adverb separating it from the I position gives a bad result in English but a good result in French.

16)

a. *Marie watches often *t* television.
b. Marie regarde souvent *t* la télévision.

Studies have shown that French speakers learning English initially assume that English allows verb raising. In order to learn English, they have to reset the value of their verb-raising parameter.

Markedness and the Subset Principle

Another interesting facet of a parameter-setting approach to SLA has to do with whether adult L2 learners can reset their parameters, and whether the notion of directionality of difficulty captured by the Markedness Differential Hypothesis (see Section 2.1) can be captured in a parameter-setting model. The Null Subject Parameter can be used to address these questions. To understand how, we must first consider how a parameter-setting model instantiates the notion of markedness.

If we consider the two settings of the Null Subject Parameter (+/–), we can see that the different values generate different grammars, as shown in the following sentences from English and Spanish.

17)

[–null subject]:	I	speak	Spanish.
[+null subject]:	Yo	hablo	español.
		Hablo	español.

As you can see, the [+null subject] setting generates more grammatical utterances than the [–null subject] setting does. Therefore the [–] setting is said to be a subset of the [+] setting. Graphically, this can be represented as shown in Figure 12.6.

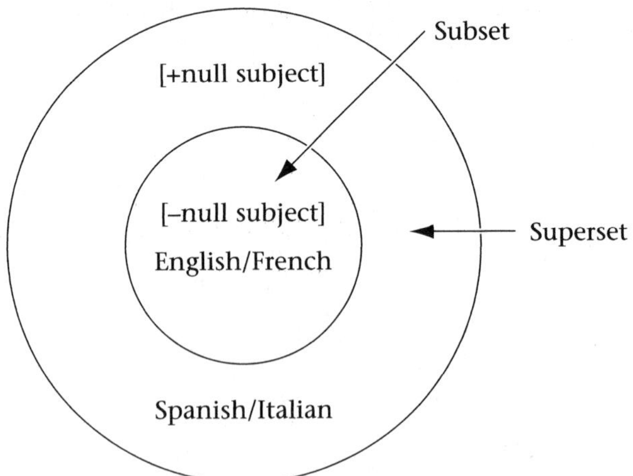

Figure 12.6 Subset/superset relation for the Null Subject Parameter

The **Subset Principle** stipulates that for first language learners, the initial or default setting will be the subset value (i.e., [–null subject] in the case of the Null Subject Parameter). Second language learners may have to reset their parameters.

When attempting to reset from subset to superset or from superset to subset, learners need access to different types of evidence. Imagine a speaker of English (who has the [–] setting) trying to learn Spanish. The learner's initial assumption will be the L1 parameter setting, which leads to the expectation that all sentences will have overt subjects. When faced with Spanish input, the learner will be exposed to grammatical utterances in the L2 that do not have overt subjects (e.g., *Hablo español* '[I] speak Spanish'), which indicates that the L1 setting is incorrect and needs to be reset. Data like this, which involve grammatical utterances to which one is actually exposed, is referred to as **positive evidence**.

Now imagine a learner whose L1 is Spanish ([+]) trying to learn English ([–]). The learner's initial assumption will be that English should be [+null subject], like the L1. The learner's IL grammar will allow both sentences with overt subjects and sentences without. Crucially, there will be no positive evidence in the English input directed at this learner to show that the L1 parameter setting is wrong. The learner will hear sentences with overt subjects, which are sanctioned by the current IL grammar, but there will be no direct indication that sentences with null subjects are not allowed. There is no pressure to reset the parameter. In this case, the learner will have to rely on **negative evidence** (i.e., observations about what is missing or ungrammatical in the data) to reset the parameter. In particular, the learner would have to either be explicitly told what is ungrammatical (**direct negative evidence**) or infer that it is ungrammatical on the basis of the fact that no one else ever says it (**indirect negative evidence**).

Given that direct positive evidence is available in one case (English → Spanish) and negative evidence is required in the other (Spanish → English), we might predict that it is harder for Spanish speakers to learn the English value of the Null Subject Parameter than vice versa. In fact, the prediction is borne out. Studies have shown that it is easier for English speakers to reset to the Spanish value of the Null Subject Parameter than it is for Spanish speakers to reset to the English setting.

Let us now consider how an approach based on typological universals would treat the same phenomenon. The presence of null subjects implies the presence of overt subjects, but not vice versa.

18)

overt subjects > null subjects

Null subjects would therefore be thought of as more marked and, consequently, more difficult to acquire. The Markedness Differential Hypothesis predicts that structures that are more marked typologically will cause difficulty in SLA. The Subset Principle, on the other hand, predicts that structures that are more marked will not cause difficulty because there will be clear evidence that the L1 setting is wrong. Although only the Subset Principle seems to make the correct prediction in the case of the null subjects, further research is necessary in order to see which approach is better able to handle a wider range of data.

2.3 L2 Morphology

The study of second language morphology has a slightly different flavor than the study of either L2 phonology or L2 syntax. L2 phonology has been studied for a long time, though the analyses have changed to reflect changes in linguistic theory. L2 syntax is a much younger field, and much of it has been informed by current linguistic theory. By contrast, L2 morphology has been studied more or less in a theoretical vacuum. In the 1970s, a number of studies collected data on the accuracy of second language learners with a variety of morphemes. This research drew on previous studies in the field of first language acquisition that had attempted to determine the order of acquisition of morphemes in L1 development. The **developmental sequence** in Table 12.7 was found. Research on second language acquisition focused on whether the developmental sequence in L2 learning was the same as for L1 learning. The order in Table 12.8 was found.

Table 12.7 Developmental order for first language acquisition

1. *-ing*	The present participle affix (e.g., she is work*ing*)
2. Plural *-s*	(e.g., bottle*s*)
3. Irregular past	(e.g., she *taught* French)
4. Possessive *-s*	(e.g., a child'*s* toy)
5. Copula *be*	(e.g., I *am* happy)
6. Articles	(e.g., *a, the*)
7. Regular past	(e.g., she walk*ed* quickly)
8. 3rd person *-s*	(e.g., she walk*s* quickly)
9. Auxiliary *be*	(e.g., she *is* working)

Table 12.8 Developmental order for second language acquisition

1. *-ing*	4. Auxiliary *be*	7. Regular past
2. Copula *be*	5. Plural *-s*	8. 3rd person *-s*
3. Articles	6. Irregular past	9. Possessive *-s*

There are many similarities but there are also some differences. For example, note that auxiliary and copula *be* are acquired at a relatively earlier point in L2 than in L1, and that the possessive morpheme *-'s* is acquired later in L2 than in L1. To attempt to explain these patterns, we need to look a little more closely at the structures that implement inflectional morphology. In English, main verbs do not raise to I, but the copula verb *be* does raise to I if no modal is present. The three structures are shown in *19.*

19)

a. If no modal is present: the auxiliary verb moves from inside the VP to I.
He is [$_{VP}$ probably *t* eating].

b. If a modal is present: the auxiliary verb does not raise.
He should [$_{VP}$ probably be eating].

c. Main verbs do not raise.
He [$_{VP}$ probably likes eating] vs. *He likes [$_{VP}$ probably *t* eating].

Children acquire *be* as a main verb before they acquire *be* as an auxiliary verb. So, children start by producing sentences that are simpler in that they have only a copula verb (e.g., *He is hungry*) before they produce sentences that include an auxiliary plus a main verb (e.g., *He was working*), as shown in Figure 12.7

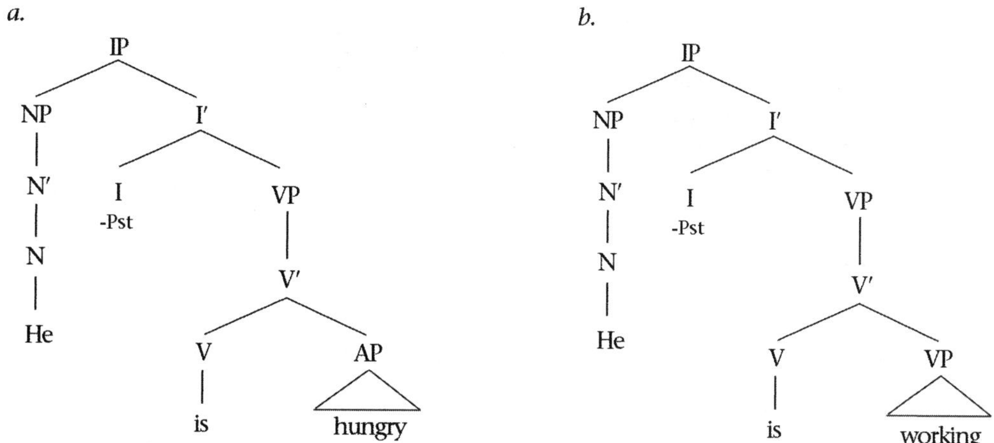

Figure 12.7 Copula versus auxiliary *be*

The structure in *b* has an extra level of complexity in that it has a complex verb phrase (one VP within another). Adult second language learners, in contrast, appear to be able to use both the simple copula and auxiliary verbs quite early on. Differences in the L1 and L2 acquisition of *be* seem to arise from the complexity of the structure.

How can we account for the patterns of *-s* acquisition? Remember that children whose first language is English acquire the three *-s* morphemes in the order plural, possessive, third person. Phonetically, these morphemes have the same realization, so we can't say that the order reflects phonological complexity. The order might be explained by noting that plural is a word-level phenomenon (e.g., *dogs*), possessive is a phrase-level phenomenon (e.g., [*the king of England*]*'s horse,* not **the* [*king*]*'s of England horse*), and third person marking involves a relation between the verb and a phrase (the subject) elsewhere in the sentence (e.g., [*That man*] *usually watches TV*). Like the pattern noted for the development of copula and auxiliary *be,* children seem to be acquiring structures in order of complexity, as shown in Figure 12.8 on page 418.

In contrast, adult L2 learners acquire the plural quite early, but then seem to get both the possessive and the third person marking quite late—perhaps for reasons involving processing. (When concentrating on getting the words right, we do not always have the processing capacity to produce well-formed higher-level structures.) Interestingly, the adults do not seem to find interphrasal morphology (like third person marking) more difficult than phrasal morphology (like possessives). This may be because the adults have already acquired the grammar for their first language, and that grammar most likely has both phrase-level and interphrasal morphological phenomena. In contrast, children could conceivably be building a sentence's structure from the bottom up (words → phrases → sentences).

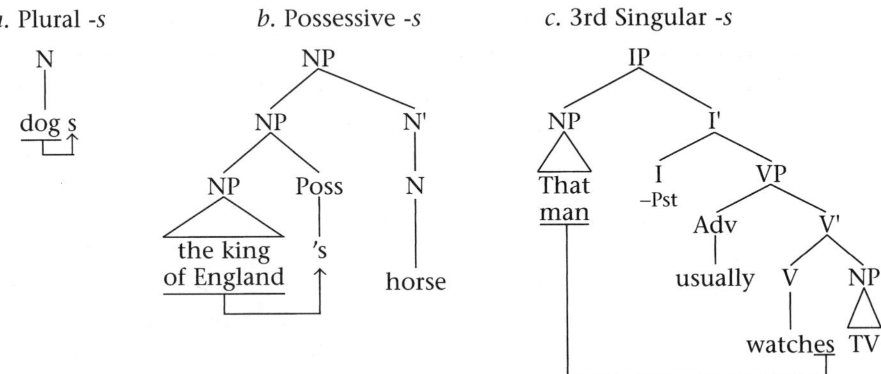

Figure 12.8 Three types of /s/ affix

In summary, we note that the order-of-acquisition data are intriguing in both first and second language acquisition, even though we await a conclusive explanation of the facts.

2.4 Morphology and Syntax

We conclude this section with a discussion of a recent theoretical approach that looks at the interaction of morphology and syntax in second language learners in an attempt to answer one of the questions we have already posed in this chapter: If someone leaves something out, does it really mean they don't have a representation for it? To answer this question, we will consider what second language learners know about tense. It is well known that nonnative speakers often make mistakes with the tense of a sentence.

20)

You know, I *call* Bill this morning and nobody *answer*. And I *start* to worry . . . He either *stay* in Eliotville, because he said he *call* me last night, and he never did.

The absence of overt tense marking on the italicized verbs in *20* might lead us to believe that this learner lacks knowledge of tense. Two theoretical positions have been put forward. The first is the **Impaired Representation Hypothesis**, which argues that the learners have some sort of underlying representation deficiency (i.e., problems with the representation of tense). The second is the **Missing Surface Inflection Hypothesis**, which argues that the learners have the correct underlying functional categories (e.g., tense) but have difficulty relating these categories with their surface inflection (*-ed*).

How can we decide between these two hypotheses? We will use the data from a longitudinal case study to build our argument for the Missing Surface Inflection Hypothesis. The subject, known as Patty in the literature, is a native Chinese speaker who first acquired English as an adult. An example of her English is given in *20* above. At the time of the first recording, she had been in the United States for about ten years. She was recorded three times over the next nine years. During that period, she was virtually immersed in English and yet, as shown in Table 12.9, she often

Table 12.9 Patty's past tense marking in obligatory contexts

Recording #	*Past tense/Obligatory contexts*	*%*
1	24/69	34.78
2	191/548	34.85
3	46/136	33.82

does not mark her past tense forms in finite obligatory contexts (i.e., in those contexts that require tense marking). Note that she supplies the past tense marking in about 34 percent of the contexts in which native speakers must supply the tense marking.

Although Patty is clearly not placing the proper inflectional morphology on her finite verbs (verbs that should have tense), we will argue that she does have knowledge of the tense feature that is targetlike—i.e., we will see that her knowledge of nominative case marking depends on her knowledge of tense.

The subject of a finite clause in English receives nominative case; conversely, the subjects of nonfinite clauses do not receive nominative case. (Go to **bedfordstmartins .com/linguistics/syntax** and click on **case**.) Compare the pronouns in the sentences in *21.*

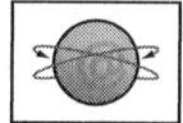

21)

a. I believe that he is a liar.
NOM [finite]

b. I believe him to be a liar.
ACC [nonfinite]

In *21a* the second verb (*is*) is finite (has tense), so the pronoun has nominative case, whereas in *21b* the second verb (*to be*) is infinitival (has no tense), so the preceding pronoun does not receive nominative case. Note that *him* is not the object of the verb *believe*—you don't believe him; in fact, you think he's a liar. The point is that there is a connection between finiteness and nominative case marking.

Let us return to our two hypotheses about Patty. One (the Impaired Representation Hypothesis) says that she lacks a fundamental category (finiteness) because she does not mark tense on her verbs, and the theory therefore predicts that we should not expect her to have the connection between finiteness and nominative case marking. The second (the Missing Surface Inflection Hypothesis) says that she has the underlying category of tense and finiteness but lacks the overt morphological marking and therefore predicts that she will demonstrate a connection between finiteness and case marking. So, what does she do? The data in Table 12.10 clearly show that Patty correctly assigns nominative case to all the pronominal subjects of her finite clauses.

Table 12.10 Patty's use of nominative case on pronominal subjects

Recording #	*Nominative subject pronouns/Finite past contexts*	*%*
1	49/49	100
2	378/378	100
3	76/76	100

Furthermore, she does not *incorrectly* mark pronouns in other contexts; the sentences in *22* demonstrate that Patty correctly uses *me* (instead of nominative *I*) in nonfinite contexts.

22)

It's best for *me* to stay in Shanghai.
It is possibility for *me* to get out.
That doesn't have anything to do with *me* leaving home.

This argument suggests that Patty does have a mental representation of finiteness that governs her grammatical knowledge with respect to case assignment, even though she has fossilized with respect to the morphological expression of tense on verbs.

3 Factors Affecting SLA

So far, we've looked at some of the characteristics of an IL grammar. Now let's turn to a variety of factors that can influence second language acquisition. It is clear that there is much more variation in the grammars of people learning second languages than in the grammars of people learning first languages. This brings us to the question of what factors might help to account for that variation.

3.1 Age

One of the obvious ways that language learners vary is in their age. People start learning second languages at different points in their lives. Could the age of onset of L2 learning cause different levels of final proficiency?

This is a question usually considered under what is known as the **Critical Period Hypothesis** (see Chapter 11, Section 6.5). We know that biologically based critical periods exist in other species. For example, some birds learn the song of their species only if exposed to it during a particular window of opportunity. If they only hear the song too early or too late, then learning will not take place. (See Chapter 17 for further discussion.)

Is second language learning like this? Is there an optimal time (or critical period) to acquire a second language? The answer appears to be yes and no. Proficiency in a language is a remarkably complex thing (see the discussion of communicative competence in Section 1.3). Usually, discussion of a possible critical period focuses on the area of phonological competence. While people who begin SLA as adults tend to retain nonnativelike phonology in the target language, it is much more difficult to predict knowledge or ability in any of the other areas of communicative competence (syntax, cohesion, sociolinguistics, etc.) based on age of acquisition.

In fact, even L2 phonology is not so straightforward as it might first appear to be. We can predict with fair certainty that people who start learning their L2 before the age of seven will have nativelike L2 speech and that people who start learning after fourteen or fifteen will probably not have nativelike speech. But the results for people who start learning between the ages of seven and fourteen are much more varied. Some end up with native accents, and some do not.

There is no current evidence of anything biological that prevents adults from acquiring proficiency in a second language. Factors that have been considered in the past (e.g., brain lateralization; see Chapter 14) are now thought to be of little predictive value in determining L2 ability. There is recent research that demonstrates that people who start learning their second language as adults *are* able to reach a final state that is indistinguishable from native speakers. In one study in the syntactic domain, it has been shown that near-native speakers perform like native speakers when it comes to speed and accuracy in grammaticality judgment tasks (of sentences such as "*Who did Mary meet the man after she saw *t*?").

Similarly, studies have shown that there are some people (admittedly a minority, but they do exist) who can start learning their second language as adults and perform within the range of native speakers when it comes to their pronunciation. When native speaker judges listen to tapes of both native and nonnative speakers (not knowing which is which) and give a global accent rating, there are always some native speakers who do not get a perfect rating and some nonnative speakers who score higher than these subjects. Currently, the critical period debate in SLA research is usually couched in terms of the question, do adults have access to Universal Grammar? Rather than looking for changes in the brain that coincide with aging, researchers now look to see whether IL grammars are governed by the same constraints as primary languages (e.g., Russian and Yoruba).

If adults are engaged in the same kind of development process as children, then we would expect their IL grammars to be describable in terms of the same principles and parameters of UG that we use to describe primary languages. Conversely, if adults are acquiring their second languages using qualitatively different learning mechanisms than are used to acquire an L1 (e.g., if they use general problem-solving abilities), then we might expect them to adopt hypotheses that are not sanctioned by Universal Grammar. Something like this may in fact happen in the acquisition of gender in French.

Children learning French as a first language seem to have very little trouble learning gender as they learn the words themselves (e.g., *le livre* 'the book' is masculine, *la table* 'the table' is feminine). On the other hand, adults whose first language does not have gender often have great difficulty learning French gender. They seem to set up complex (but incorrect) rules for predicting the gender of a given noun. For example, they may assume that words naming colors (or some other semantic category) are of one gender, or that words that end with a certain sound sequence are of another. Rules like this sometimes allow nonnative speakers to guess the gender correctly, but they still perform significantly less accurately than native speakers. This is an example of how adults' greater capacity to formulate general rules can sometimes lead them down the wrong path.

3.2 Individual Differences

Learners vary in ways other than age. Broadly speaking, the researcher asks the question, "If learners have a particular quality *x*, does this make them better at second language acquisition?" For example, we might look at the effect of inhibition, left-handedness, or some other individual trait on L2 ability. As intuitively appealing as this avenue is, it is one that must be taken carefully. In particular, there are three points on which we must be explicit:

1. how we define and measure *x*,
2. what it means to be *better*,
3. what aspect of communicative competence we are referring to.

Consider in this regard a trait like empathy. It has been argued that people who are empathetic are better language learners. This is an intuitively appealing notion. People who are empathetic can imagine what it feels like to be in someone else's shoes and they can look at things from another perspective. And second language learning certainly involves looking at things from a different perspective. But in SLA research, we need to find a more precise way to evaluate this hypothesis.

There are tests that claim to measure a person's empathy, but is this notion really a well-defined construct? Is one simply empathetic or not, or are there degrees of empathy? If there are degrees, do we see a correlation between degree of empathy and degree of success? And what does it mean for empathetic learners to be better language learners than people who aren't empathetic? Do they make fewer errors? Less serious errors? Should we expect people with greater empathy to be better at everything in the L2? Or maybe just at phonology and sociolinguistic competence? On what basis could we make a prediction? These are not simple issues. We raise them not to argue that research in individual variation is misguided, but to show some of the complex areas that need to be addressed before we can hope to establish a causal connection between a particular personality trait and success at second language learning.

We can distinguish between two kinds of factors in terms of which individuals can vary: affective factors and cognitive factors. First we will look at the role of affect.

Affective Factors

Affective factors have to do with the emotional side of learning a second language. Clearly there can be a great deal at stake emotionally when learning a second language, and it is possible that emotions affect how successful a second language learner is. Affective factors that have been studied include empathy, anxiety, inhibition, and risk-taking. In this section we will look at one such factor: motivation.

Learners can vary with respect to the amount or type of motivation they have to learn a second language. If someone is highly motivated to learn, will that person do better at learning? In order to answer this question, we need to say a bit more about what it means to be motivated.

Traditionally, two types of motivation have been proposed: **instrumental** and **integrative**. Instrumental motivation involves wanting to learn the L2 for a specific goal or reason. For example, someone might need to pass a language requirement in order to get a graduate degree or a job with a government agency. Integrative motivation, on the other hand, involves wanting to learn the L2 in order to learn more about a particular culture or fit into it better. For instance, someone might want to learn Japanese in order to learn more about a fascinating culture.

Studies have shown that the degree of integrative motivation correlates with the degree of success in language learning. That is to say, subjects who score highly on tests of integrative motivation do better on certain language tests than comparable subjects who score poorly on the same tests. However, subjects with instrumental rather than integrative motivation can also do well if their level of motivation is high. One study found that subjects who were offered a cash reward if they obtained a certain score on a language test performed much the same as subjects with high integrative motivation. All this seems to suggest that degree of motivation is a better predictor of future learning success than is type of motivation.

Cognitive Factors

While affective factors have something to do with the emotional side of learning, cognitive factors involve the mechanics of how an individual learns something. Different people seem to learn via different cognitive styles and different learning strategies. We will first address cognitive style.

As individuals, we tend to tackle mental tasks using a particular **cognitive style**. In contrast with an affective factor like motivation, which may vary from domain to domain (e.g., someone might be more motivated to learn French cooking than to learn the French language), cognitive style is a stable trait across domains.

The study of cognitive style often focuses on a contrast between **field dependence** and **field independence**. Learners who are field independent are not distracted by irrelevant background information when trying to learn something. These are people who can see the trees without being distracted by the forest. On the other hand, learners who are field dependent tend to see the forest but may miss the characteristics of individual trees. Of course, this is not to say that, overall, one trait is good and the other is bad. Field-dependent learners are probably able to synthesize the overall picture better than field-independent learners, but field-independent learners are probably better able to pick out relevant facts.

In terms of second language acquisition, it seems that field-independent learners do better on language tests that focus on analytic tasks such as providing the correct grammatical form in a given sentence:

23)

Yesterday, we ___ the kids to the zoo. (take)

In contrast, field-dependent learners tend to do better on tasks that involve synthesizing their knowledge. For example, they may demonstrate broader communicative competence in that they are more concerned with getting the message across than with the grammatical accuracy of the sentences they use to form their message.

Ultimately, the proficient L2 learner needs to be concerned with both **accuracy** and **fluency**. Broadly speaking, accuracy has to do with whether the learner has the correct representation of a particular linguistic structure (i.e., it involves *knowledge*). Fluency, on the other hand, has to do with the rapid retrieval or processing of those representations (i.e., it involves *skills*). Someone who is not fluent may have accurate representations but may take considerable time and energy to retrieve them. Different learners, though, are probably going to have a natural affinity to emphasize either accuracy or fluency, depending perhaps on their individual cognitive style.

While cognitive styles appear to be relatively stable traits in an individual, there are elements of learning that we have some control over. Each of us has certain

learning strategies that we can employ to try to fill the gaps in our linguistic knowledge. These learning strategies can be contrasted with **communication strategies**, which are designed to keep communication happening in spite of gaps in knowledge—as when someone uses paraphrase to describe an object for which he or she has no vocabulary item (e.g., *Could you pass me the thing you use for hitting nails?*). In contrast, a learning strategy is used to discover something new about the L2.

Many different learning strategies have been proposed. For example, using the strategy of directed attention, learners may decide in advance to focus on particular aspects of a task and to ignore others. So, when reading a text or listening to a lecture, they might decide to focus only on the main points. Another strategy involves repetition; to retain a lexical item or to improve the pronunciation of a sequence of sounds, the learner may repeat a word or phrase over and over. A third strategy makes use of clarification requests (to the teacher, a peer, or the others in a conversation) about something that is not understood (e.g., How come *stood* does not rhyme with *food*? What's a *liege*?). Under this view, learners have a variety of strategies at their disposal and have to discover which ones work best for them.

This brings us to the interesting question of second language learning in classrooms and the effect that instruction has on L2 learning. Is it really possible to teach someone a second language? Or can you just create an environment in which second language learning can take place? We turn now to the research that has looked specifically at L2 classrooms.

4 The L2 Classroom

It has been flippantly said that people have been successfully acquiring second languages for thousands of years, but when teachers get involved, the success rate plummets. This comment is probably more a reflection of people's unfortunate experience in certain types of language classrooms (which may have been dull or even physically threatening, depending on the century) than a statement about general pedagogic utility. However, the fact remains that language classrooms can be sheltered environments where students can benefit from being given the opportunity to learn and practice without being subject to the penalties for failure that can be imposed outside the classroom. 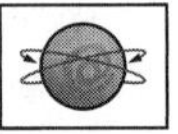 For more discussion of L2 pedagogy, go to **bedfordstmartins.com/linguistics/secondlanguage** and click on **L2 pedagogy**.

We should acknowledge at this point that there is really no such thing as *the* second language classroom. In reality, all classrooms are different because they have different people in them (both students and teachers). Nevertheless, there are certain statements that can be made. There are three relevant characteristics of a second language classroom that we wish to explore:

1. modified input,
2. modified interaction,
3. focus on form.

4.1 Modified Input

In Chapter 11 it was noted that adults do not talk to children in the same way that they talk to other adults. Just as the input directed to children has certain simplifying characteristics, so speech directed at nonnative speakers tends to be simplified compared to the speech directed at native speakers. In all communicative situations—whether dealing with a child or an adult, a nonnative speaker or a native speaker—we seem to make a rapid assessment of the level of proficiency or background knowledge of the listener, and adjust the input accordingly.

The input aimed at nonnative speakers is referred to as **foreigner talk**. The subset of this speech that takes place in classrooms is known as **teacher talk**. Teacher talk (or teacher language) tends not to be as evenly matched to the proficiency of the listener as foreigner talk is, for the simple reason that teachers are usually addressing a class rather than an individual. As a result, some learners may find the modified speech too hard or too easy.

The pedagogic goal of teacher talk is crystal clear: make sure the students know what is being talked about by providing **comprehensible input**. Perhaps surprisingly, this idea has generated an extraordinary amount of conflict in the field of SLA research. Although it seems to be useful to provide learners with comprehensible input, teachers must guard against simplifying too much, which might give the appearance of patronizing the learners or talking to them as if they were stupid rather than on the way to becoming bilingual.

4.2 Modified Interaction

Second language classrooms also differ from the outside world in terms of the kind of interactions that go on there. However, the difference appears to be mainly one of degree, not quality. Inside a classroom, the teacher may engage in the following kinds of strategies:

- more comprehension checks, e.g., *Do you understand?; OK?*
- more prompting, e.g., *Who knows where Council Bluffs is?*
- more expansions, e.g., Student: *Me red sweater.*
Teacher: *Yes, you're wearing a red sweater, aren't you?*

This modified interaction appears to be one of the characteristics that differentiates classrooms from other communicative settings. While all these devices (e.g., comprehension checks) occur in nonclassroom discourse as well, they appear to occur more frequently in second language classrooms. Assuming that the teacher realizes that the purpose of the classroom is to prepare the student to understand input and interaction outside of the classroom as well, modified interaction is beneficial.

4.3 Focus on Form

The final characteristic of the second language classroom to be discussed here involves **focus on form**. The term *focus on form* encompasses two distinct practices that tend to occur in most L2 classrooms: instruction about the language and explicit correction.

Most second language classes present the students with some sort of information about the language—noting, for example, "The English sound [θ] is produced by placing the tongue tip between the teeth," or "The *on* in French *bon* is produced as a nasal vowel." Instruction of this type is designed to improve the form (or accuracy) of the student's L2. In all likelihood, other activities that happen in the class will focus on giving the student a chance to improve fluency or particular sociolinguistic skills.

Error correction is also designed to improve the form of the student's L2. Regardless of the methodology used, in most classes today there is some focus on form and some error correction. The interesting research question is whether either of these practices can be shown to have a positive effect on the learner. Do students who get corrected do better than students who don't?

The question may not be as straightforward as it appears. Remember that it has frequently been argued in first language acquisition research that attempts at error correction are relatively infrequent and don't really affect children's grammars. Could it be different for adult second language learners? The learning environment is different in that adult learners (unlike children) are usually exposed to a fair amount of error correction. But does that make a difference? Not surprisingly, this question is difficult to answer. Some studies have argued that second language learners who receive correction develop at about the same pace as those who do not. Other studies have shown certain increases in accuracy as the result of correction.

These results may not be as contradictory as they seem. The areas where correction seems to be most useful involve lexical items. When students try to learn the properties of a certain lexical item, they benefit from feedback. However, feedback concerning certain structural phenomena may not be as effective. For example, the previously mentioned study of French speakers learning about the lack of verb movement in English (see Section 2.2) found that while there were short-term improvements in the subjects who were explicitly taught the relevant facts, there were no significant long-term effects. When the subjects were tested a year later, they were found to have reverted to their preinstructional performance.

This doesn't necessarily mean that students should not be corrected or that there should be no focus on form in the second language classroom. If a balance is struck between classroom activities that focus on form and those that focus on meaningful communication, then there is certainly no evidence that feedback causes any problems. Indeed, to the contrary, there is evidence that students in classes that focus primarily on communication but also include some instruction on form are significantly more accurate than students who are exposed only to instruction that focuses on communication.

Most of the studies to date have considered focus on form within a pedagogical framework (i.e., how does it affect the learner or the classroom), but there are more recent studies that are couched within a cognitive framework. Under this approach, the following questions could be asked:

1. *The noticing issue:* Do learners have the cognitive resources to notice the gap between their IL utterances and the TL (target language) utterances around them?

This is a very complex question that involves the details of how memory (working, short-term, and long-term) works. Learners would have to have the coordinated working and long-term memory resources to enable the cognitive comparison of the IL and TL sentences. This sort of comparison eventually leads to knowledge restructuring. Studies suggest that learners do have the cognitive resources to engage in this type of comparison, especially if they are comparing TL utterances that have occurred recently in the discourse.

2. *The interruption issue:* Is pedagogical intervention that does not interrupt the learner's own processing for language learning even possible?

   Focus on form should be carried out in response to the learner's needs. If (a) the primary focus of the lesson is on meaning, (b) the focus-on-form targets arise incidentally, and (c) the learner shifts attention briefly, then the focus-on-form activity will be relatively unobtrusive. Indeed, rather than being an unwanted interruption, focus on form may allow the learner to pay selective attention to a structure for a short period of time, which would be beneficial.

3. *The timing issue:* If so, then precisely when, in cognitive terms, should the pedagogical intervention occur?

   Learners appear to benefit from being prepared in advance for some focus-on-form activities. If they know what is coming, it helps them to notice the relevant features in the input. One of the most promising types of intervention is an immediate recast. A corrective recast involves the repetition of an error plus a recast, as shown below:

   Student: *I think that the worm will go under the soil.*
   Teacher: *I <u>think</u> that the worm <u>will</u> go under the soil? . . . I <u>thought</u> that the worm <u>would</u> go under the soil.*

In sum, adult students usually expect error correction, and teachers are accustomed to providing it. Assuming that the class is not devoted entirely to instruction that focuses on form (with no opportunity for meaningful practice), error correction doesn't seem to cause any harm. In a class with activities that focus on both form and fluency, the students tend to emerge with greater accuracy. Certain types of classroom activities seem to be able to engage the cognitive abilities of adult second language learners and allow them to continue to advance their L2 proficiency.

4.4 Education in a Bilingual Environment

Nonnative speakers of English are the fastest growing segment of the school population, comprising almost 10 percent of school-aged children in the United States. These students, called **English language learners (ELLs)**, represent a wide diversity of academic backgrounds. Some of these students come to school in the United States with a strong academic background in their first language. Others, however, may have had limited formal schooling. A third group comprises students born in the United States who speak a language other than English at home. The following sections will describe programs that have been developed to address these diverse needs. Not all the programs are bilingual education, in the sense of offering instruction in two languages. But among bilingual programs, it is useful to distinguish **one-way bilingual education** from two-way (bilingual) immersion programs. One-way bilingual education programs offer instruction only to language minority students in their first language and in English, while two-way programs offer instruction to language majority and language minority students together.

One-Way Bilingual Education

When a school has enough ELLs sharing the same first language, it is possible to provide either **developmental bilingual education** or **transitional bilingual education**. Generally, one-way bilingual education is offered at the elementary school level and introduces instruction in literacy in the first language to students whose primary language is not English. Developmental bilingual education usually lasts for five or six years and has the goal of promoting bilingualism and literacy in both languages in addition to academic achievement for ELLs. In contrast, transitional bilingual education does not aim for full bilingualism or biliteracy but is intended instead to provide instruction in the first language only for as long as it takes the student to acquire enough English to take part in mainstream classes taught in English. Transitional bilingual education provides ELLs with a foundation of literacy skills and content knowledge comparable to that of native English-speaking children, and research with Spanish speakers indicates that there is positive transfer of literacy skills from the first language to the second language.

English-Only ESL

For some schools with ELLs from many different first language backgrounds, it may not be practical to offer bilingual education. In addition, one-way bilingual education is less likely to receive federal funding under the No Child Left Behind Act of 2002. Even before 2002, voters in California and Arizona had already mandated English-only instruction for ELLs in preference to one-way bilingual education. In such cases, English as a Second Language (ESL) is offered using only English as the medium of instruction. One type of English-only ESL is **sheltered instruction**, which refers to English as a Second Language programs taught through academic content. Based on the theory that second language acquisition is more effective when learners *use* the language to interact with content material (rather than learn *about* the language), these programs combine instruction in content courses with English-language instruction. Although English is the language of instruction, the language may be simplified for easier understanding of content in courses such as science, social studies, and math.

Newcomer Programs

According to one estimate, 12 percent of ELLs in middle school and 20 percent in high school have missed two or more years of schooling since the age of six. **Newcomer programs** are designed to meet the needs of recently arrived middle school or high school students with low proficiency in English and/or little prior schooling before their arrival in the United States. The newcomer programs provide intensive language instruction, literacy development, cultural orientation, and some content instruction. These programs are designed to be of limited duration, not lasting more than two years.

Immersion Programs

Another kind of program, which is relatively rare in the United States, is an immersion program in which language majority students are taught through the medium of a minority language. French immersion programs in Canada are an example. To read about these programs, go to **bedfordstmartins.com/linguistics/secondlanguage** and click on **French immersion programs**.

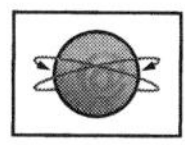

Two-Way Immersion (TWI)

Two-way immersion (TWI) programs (also known as **dual-language programs**) provide bilingual education for native speakers of English and ELLs together. As of early 2004, the Center for Applied Linguistics listed 289 TWI programs in twenty-four states and Washington, D.C. The vast majority of programs are Spanish-English, although other languages taught with English include Chinese, French, Korean, and Navajo.

Three criteria are used to classify a program as a TWI program. First, language minority and language majority students must be integrated academically and socially for at least half of the day. Second, content and literacy instruction must be given in both languages to all students; for example, in a Spanish TWI program, Spanish speakers and English speakers would be taught together in both English and Spanish. Third, the number of language minority and language majority students must be balanced, with neither group comprising more than two-thirds of the class. Typically, these programs are used in elementary school rather than high school, and students join the program when they start school. In some programs, the minority language is used 80 to 90 percent of the time for the first year, with gradual transitioning to a balanced use of both languages by the time students reach fourth grade. Other programs provide balanced instruction in both languages from the start.

Although a few TWI programs have been in existence for decades, the number of TWI programs increased dramatically in the 1990s. One attraction of TWI programs is that, unlike one-way bilingual education, they offer bilingualism for all students, language majority and language minority students alike. Furthermore, because the students are learning each other's native languages, language learning is enhanced by social interactions with native speakers, and academic excellence is promoted in both languages.

Effectiveness

With recent emphasis being put on accountability in education, it is necessary to note that in order for ELLs to show good progress, they must not only learn English but also learn the same content as native speakers of English. If an ELL does not understand what the teacher is saying or cannot read the textbook, he or she cannot make progress in the content subjects, with the result that the ELL falls further and further behind academically. One recent study examined student records of standardized test scores in reading, language arts, and math from over 200,000 students who had participated in various forms of bilingual education, English-only ESL, or English-language mainstream education with no special language support. Students who had participated in bilingual programs (either one-way bilingual education or two-way immersion) were the only ones to reach the fiftieth percentile in both the first and second languages and to maintain their achievement over time. This group also had the fewest dropouts. On first exiting from the bilingual program in elementary school, bilingual education students did not perform as well as English-only ESL students, but bilingual education students caught up in middle school and surpassed the English-only students in high school. The group with the lowest scores were those students who had entered the English-language mainstream with no language support programs; this group also accounted for the largest percentage of dropouts.

Heritage Language Programs

Heritage language programs are designed to maintain, preserve, or revive heritage languages of indigenous people, immigrants, or refugees. This section will describe heritage programs for Native American languages, which are particularly endangered (see Chapter 9, Section 4). Heritage language programs for Native Americans have taken a number of different forms, some more successful than others in encouraging heritage language use among children. At one extreme are programs that include a few minutes of language instruction per day in a heritage language that children no longer speak; such programs, although well intentioned, have generally provided students with some possible sense of pride in the heritage language but little in the way of language skills, other than a handful of vocabulary words. Experimental programs have been introduced in Head Start to enable caregivers to use the heritage language as part of the Head Start instruction. Another model for preschoolers is a **language nest**, a term originally coined in New Zealand for preschool language-immersion programs for Maori children, and now being tried in a variety of settings in the United States.

Among groups with a larger base of native speakers of the heritage language within the surrounding community, bilingual programs have been developed in schools. Recent work in the Navajo Nation has drawn on qualified bilingual speakers from the community to combine instruction in Navajo with instruction in English. The program has garnered community support because students have demonstrated progress in English and in academic achievement as well as maintenance of Navajo. Similarly in the scattered Yupik-speaking villages of Alaska, various forms of bilingual education have been developed to encourage Yupik language maintenance among English-dominant students or to encourage acquisition of English along with initial content instruction in Yupik for Yupik-speaking students. In Hawaii, an immersion program has been developed for K–12 students, with Hawaiian used exclusively in the first years and English gradually introduced in fifth grade and onward. Evaluation of ninth grade students in this program reveals that they score as highly on English-language standardized tests as their peers in nonimmersion programs and are attaining mastery of the Hawaiian language as well.

Summing Up

This chapter has dealt with a number of issues in the field of second language acquisition. We investigated the notion of an **interlanguage grammar** and the influence of both the source and target languages on this grammar. Proficiency in a second language requires both knowledge and ability, something captured in a model of **communicative competence**. Someone must acquire knowledge in all linguistic domains (phonetics, phonology, morphology, syntax, and semantics) as well as the ability to use that knowledge in a variety of social contexts.

What is easy or difficult to acquire in a second language has been investigated from a variety of perspectives. We focused on **Universal Grammar** (the **Subset Principle**) and **typological universals** (the **Markedness Differential Hypothesis**). However, it is not just universals that influence second language learning; the specific characteristics of an individual can also affect the process. **Affective factors** and cognitive factors both influence second language learning. So too do factors such as modified input, modified interaction, **focus on form**, and the available educational opportunities.

The field of second language acquisition is remarkably diverse, in part because of what is involved in L2 learning. Someone who is attempting to learn an additional language must develop new mental representations, and develop facility at accessing those representations in a variety of circumstances. The field of SLA research must therefore draw on philosophy (theories of mind), psychology (theories of learning, theories of performance), linguistics (theories of linguistic structure), and pedagogy (theories of instruction). This is probably the main reason why we have not established anything like a comprehensive theory of how second languages are learned. But bit by bit, we're starting to put together some pieces of the puzzle.

Key Terms

General terms concerning the study of second language acquisition

bilingualism
fossilized
interlanguage (IL)
second language acquisition
target
transfer

Terms concerning second language proficiency

communicative competence
competence
grammatical competence
illocutionary competence
illocutionary force
performance
sociolinguistic competence
textual competence

Terms concerning interlanguage grammars

developmental sequence
direct negative evidence
Impaired Representation Hypothesis
indirect negative evidence
marked
markedness
Markedness Differential Hypothesis
Missing Surface Inflection Hypothesis

negative evidence
Null Subject Parameter
positive evidence
Similarity Differential Rate Hypothesis
Subset Principle
unmarked
Verb Movement Parameter

Terms concerning other factors affecting second language acquisition

accuracy
affective factors
cognitive style
communication strategies
Critical Period Hypothesis
field dependence
field independence
fluency
instrumental (motivation)
integrative (motivation)
learning strategies

Terms related to the second language classroom

comprehensible input
focus on form
foreigner talk
teacher talk

Terms related to education in a bilingual environment

developmental bilingual education
dual-language programs
English language learners (ELLs)
heritage language programs
language nest
newcomer programs
one-way bilingual education
sheltered instruction
transitional bilingual education
two-way immersion (TWI) programs

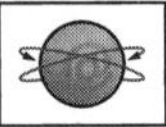

For more information on the sources used in this chapter, go to **bedfordstmartins.com/linguistics/secondlanguage** and click on **Sources**.

Recommended Reading

Archibald, J. (ed.). 2000. *Second Language Acquisition and Linguistic Theory.* Oxford: Blackwell.

Cummins, J., and M. Swain. 1986. *Bilingual Education.* London: Longman.

Flynn, S., G. Martohardjono, and W. O'Neil (eds.). 1998. *The Generative Study of Second Language Acquisition.* Mahwah, NJ: Lawrence Erlbaum.

Hawkins, Roger. 2001. *Second Language Syntax: A Generative Introduction.* Oxford: Blackwell.

Leather, J., and A. James. 2002. *New Sounds 2000.* Klagenfurt, Austria: University of Klagenfurt Press.

Long, M., and D. Larsen-Freeman. 1991. *Second Language Acquisition Research.* London: Longman.

Sharwood Smith, M. 1994. *Second Language Learning: Theoretical Foundations.* London: Longman.

White, L. 2003. *Second Language Acquisition and Universal Grammar.* Cambridge: Cambridge University Press.

Exercises

1. Some dialects of Arabic break up clusters by inserting an epenthetic vowel in front of an unsyllabified consonant (unlike the dialect discussed in this chapter). How would a speaker of this dialect pronounce the words *plant, transport,* and *translate*? Draw the necessary syllable structures.

2. The following is a sample of nonnative writing. The assignment was to write about whether you prefer to live in the city or the country. Look through the sample and "correct" the errors. Compare your corrected copy with that of someone else in the class and see if you agree on the corrections. What are three or four problems this learner should work on?

> Are you among the number of people who have to choose their place to live? Whenever they have to move from another country, they even change the profession, they want to have a house outside the big city, or they can't find a place in Downtown.
>
> Its possible to move as well as you are supported by some essential condition of life I've mention in the following lines.
>
> Most of people are living in the Big city to have many of the opportunities that offer the Downtown lifestyle, jobs, studies, activities or whatever but nowadays for instance in TO [Toronto] its really difficult to find a place to live because the percentage of vacancy is slightly under 0% so many people are constrained to move on the suburb, by this way some of these get along this phenomene because they want to avoid the noise, the smog of the city and even they try to find their own place to live with garden and everything, actually to invest money to owe their house which is better than to rent an apartment in downtown, therefore they have to consider the transportation problem to reach the city even to have a car or use the public transportation.
>
> to have your own house outside the city required a great initial capital that you have to draft from any bank or you dispose in your account but afterwhat the house become your possession with the years and couple of more will increase the house value, although it is expensive furthermore it should be a great benefit for the owner even though he decided to rent the unoccupied room into the house.
>
> Moreless the frienship beetween the person in the subrub is closer they are ore contact with each other and maybe can meet themselves doing yardwork or other kind of activities belong to the suburb lifestyle.
>
> But in another [illegible] it should be difficult for the people who haven't ever lived in the suburb to move from th big city because they have to adapt their habits but they can fin amonst a great number of things that they use to have in the city. Otherwise during the last 15 years the business activites has developing around the city quickly in the North America also the supermarket company, manufacture and so on offered the job opportunity to the people outside the big aglomeration in that way it was created some apartments vacaint in the city.
>
> For me I don't even care where I have to live but I will observe which part could be the less expensive as well as transportation to reach my job but I will be sure that I'd like to live outside the downtown.

3. Given what you know about implicational universals, do you think it would be easier for an English speaker to acquire French nasal vowels (e.g., *gant* [gã] 'glove') or for French speakers to acquire English oral vowels?

4. What explanation would you give for a native speaker of French who produced the English sentence *I drink frequently coffee*? How could you explain the fact that when the same speaker produces the sentence *He is frequently late,* it is grammatical? Do any other English verbs have the same properties as *be*?

5. Which of the following sentences would you classify as positive evidence and which as negative evidence for the learner?
   a) Nonnative Speaker (NNS): He study a lot.
      Native Speaker (NS): He *studies* a lot.
   b) NS: What kind of books do you like to read?
      NNS: Mysteries.
   c) NNS: I was born in Munich.
      NS: Pardon me?
   d) NNS: I goed to Chicago on the weekend.
      NS: Remember that *go* has an irregular past.

6. Discuss why second language learners, regardless of their first language, might produce forms such as *goed, sheeps,* and *could decided* given that they never hear these forms in input from native speakers of English. Give some other forms analogous to the above that might be generated.

7. What factors can you think of that might influence fossilization? In other words, do you think that some people are more likely to fossilize than others? Do you think it can be reversed? How?

8. Acquiring a second language involves both knowing something about the language and being able to do something with the language. Do you think that knowledge and skills are related? Can you see any trade-off between accuracy and fluency?

9. Why do you think that nonnative speakers of English would be more at risk of leaving the education system than native speakers?

10. Respond to the following statement:

    > It's the school system's job to make sure that nonnative speakers of English learn English. They need English in order to be able to succeed in this country. We want them to succeed. If we encourage them to speak their own language, then ghettoes will form and they'll never learn English. And if we want them to learn English, then obviously they need to be exposed to more English. What good is it knowing how to speak another language in America? What they need is English, English, and more English.

thirteen

Psycholinguistics: The Study of Language Processing

Gary Libben

Leaving one still with the intolerable wrestle
With words and meanings

– T.S. Eliot

Objectives

In this chapter, you will learn:

- what methods psycholinguists use to study language processing
- how linguistic concepts and principles contribute to understanding language comprehension and production
- how psycholinguistic models are used to explain language processing

We engage in language processing almost every day of our lives. This processing takes place when we watch television, listen to the radio, read a passing billboard while driving, or discuss the weather. Usually these language activities are carried out with great ease and in a completely subconscious manner. We might sometimes be aware that we are searching for a word, composing a sentence, or straining to understand someone else, but we are never aware of the actual mechanisms and operations involved in producing and understanding language.

Psycholinguistics is the study of these language-processing mechanisms. Psycholinguists study how word meaning, sentence meaning, and discourse meaning are computed and represented in the mind. They study how complex words and sentences are composed in speech and how they are broken down into their constituents in the acts of listening and reading. In short, psycholinguists seek to understand *how language is done.*

This chapter introduces the field of psycholinguistics by first discussing some methods used by psycholinguists to probe language representation and processing in the mind. This is followed by a summary of recent research on language processing in the domains of phonetics, phonology, morphology, and syntax. Finally, we will discuss how these various aspects of linguistic processing work together to make the everyday acts of speaking, listening, and reading appear so simple and effortless.

1 Methods of Psycholinguistic Research

The key fact that guides psycholinguistic methodology is that language users are unaware of the details of language processing. Simply paying attention to what you are doing will not provide reliable insights into how you access words or build sentences. Perhaps the reason for this is that, in normal use, language processing must occur very quickly. By shielding mental linguistic operations from the conscious mind, it is possible that the language-processing system is maximizing its ability to operate with speed and efficiency.

In order to get a sense of just how subconscious language processing is, you might try the following exercise: Give a friend a page of text to read silently and sit opposite him or her. Carefully observe your friend's eyes as they move across the text. You will notice that the eyes do not move smoothly from left to right but rather proceed in a series of jerks called **saccades**. Like most of us, your friend probably has the subjective impression that his or her eyes are moving very evenly across the page. But that subjective impression is incorrect. It seems that we are simply not constructed to be able to monitor many of our automatic activities, including language processing.

A substantial additional challenge for the psycholinguistic researcher comes from the fact that most of language processing does not involve observable physical events such as eye movement, but involves mental events that cannot be observed directly. Research in this field therefore requires that mental language-processing events be inferred from observable behavior. Consequently, a large part of psycholinguistic research is concerned with the development of new (and often very clever) techniques to uncover how language processing is accomplished. Some of these techniques are presented in the following sections.

1.1 Slips of the Tongue

Some of the earliest and most influential studies of language processing examined the spontaneous slips of the tongue produced during speech. One kind of slip of the tongue is known as a **spoonerism**, after Reverend William A. Spooner, who was head of New College Oxford between 1903 and 1924. Reverend Spooner was famous for producing a great many, often humorous, speech errors. Some of his more well-known mistakes are presented below.

1)

What he intended:	You have missed all my history lectures.
What he said:	You have hissed all my mystery lectures.

2)

What he intended: Noble sons of toil
What he said: Noble tons of soil

3)

What he intended: You have wasted the whole term.
What he said: You have tasted the whole worm.

4)

What he intended: The dear old Queen
What he said: The queer old dean

Beginning in the 1960s, Victoria Fromkin began to study these and other naturally occurring slips of the tongue and noted that they can be very revealing of the manner in which sentences are created in speech. For instance, as can be seen in the examples, the characteristic pattern in Reverend Spooner's errors is a tendency to exchange the initial consonants of words in the utterance. When these segment exchanges create new words (as opposed to nonwords as in *fire and brimstone→bire and frimstone*), the result is often humorous. But here's the important psycholinguistic point: In order for these exchanges to occur, the sentence would have to be planned out before the person begins to say it. Otherwise, how would it be possible in example *1* for the first segment of the sixth word *history* to be transported backward so that it becomes the first segment of the third word (*missed→hissed*)?

Another important observation that Fromkin made was that speech errors also often involve mixing and matching morphemes within words. Consider the following slips of the tongue:

5)

Intended: rules of word formation
Produced: words of rule formation

6)

Intended: I'd forgotten about that.
Produced: I'd forgot aboutten that.

7)

Intended: easily enough
Produced: easy enoughly

All these errors involve morphemes being exchanged within a sentence. As is the case for sound-exchange errors, these slips of the tongue provide evidence that a sentence must be planned out before speech begins. They also provide evidence that the morpheme, rather than the word, is the fundamental building block of English sentence production. Note how in example *5* the inflectional suffix *-s* remains in its original place, while the nouns *rule* and *word* reverse positions. In examples *6* and *7*, it is the suffixes that move while the stems remain in their original positions. These examples all suggest that morphological components of words can function independently during sentence planning (and of course also in sentence misplanning).

As can be seen from these examples, slips of the tongue can offer a fascinating window to the mechanisms involved in language production and to the role that linguistic units such as phonemes and morphemes play in that production. But because slips of the tongue are naturally occurring events, the researcher has no control over when and where they will occur and must simply wait for them to happen. In this way, the analysis of slips of the tongue is a **field technique** and differs from the **experimental paradigms** discussed in the following sections. In these experimental paradigms, the researcher takes an active role in controlling the circumstances under which language is processed, the stimuli to which the experimental subjects are exposed, and the ways in which subjects may respond to these stimuli.

1.2 Experimental Methods: Words in the Mind

One of the most intense areas of psycholinguistic research has been the investigation of how words are organized in the mind. We are all in possession of a vocabulary that forms the backbone of our ability to communicate in a language. In many ways, this vocabulary must be used as a normal dictionary is used. It is consulted to determine what words mean, how they are spelled, and what they sound like. But the dictionary in our minds—our mental lexicon—must also be substantially different from a desktop dictionary. It must be much more flexible, accommodating the new words that we learn with ease. It must be organized so that words can be looked up extremely quickly—word recognition takes less than one-third of a second and the average adult reads at a rate of about 250 words per minute. It must allow us to access entries in terms of a wide variety of characteristics. **Tip-of-the-tongue phenomena**, in which we are temporarily unable to access a word, are particularly revealing with respect to how flexible access to the mental lexicon can be—we have all experienced episodes in which we eventually retrieve words on the basis of their meaning, sound, spelling, or first letter, or even what they rhyme with.

Many psycholinguists conceive of the mental lexicon as a collection of individual units, as in Figure 13.1. In this figure, the lexicon is shown as a space in which entries of different types are stored and linked together. The main questions that are asked about the mental lexicon are: (1) How are entries linked? (2) How are entries accessed? (3) What information is contained in an entry?

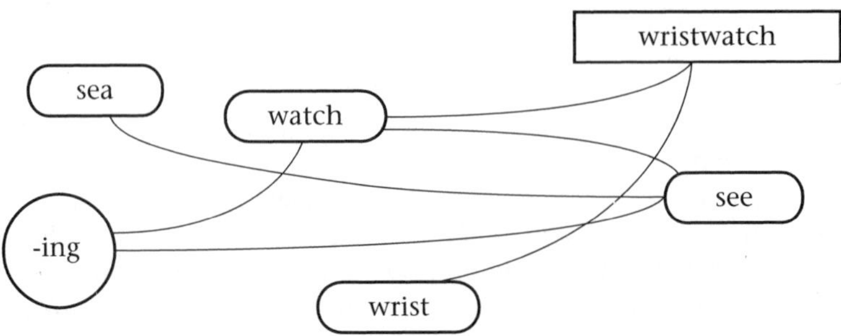

Figure 13.1 Units in the mental lexicon

Although these questions are simple and straightforward, there is no way to answer them directly because the human mental lexicon cannot be observed. So the psycholinguist must use special experimental methods to understand how words are organized, accessed, and represented in the mind. We will briefly discuss the two most common of these methods—**lexical decision** and **priming**.

Lexical Decision

In the lexical decision paradigm, the experimental subject (in this example, a native speaker of English) is seated in front of a computer screen. A word appears in the middle of the screen and the subject must judge as quickly as possible whether or not the word is a real English word by pressing a button labeled "yes" or a button labeled "no" (see Figure 13.2).

Figure 13.2 A lexical decision experiment

This task is very easy for subjects to carry out. They typically see and judge hundreds of words in a single fifteen-minute lexical decision experiment. In most lexical decision experiments, there are two **dependent variables**—that is, things that are being measured: the time that it takes for a subject to respond (**response latency**) and whether or not the subject's judgment is correct (**response accuracy**). A response is judged as correct if a subject responds "yes" to a real word such as *glove* or *sadness* and "no" to a nonword such as *blove* or *sadding*.

Lexical decision experiments usually involve comparing subjects' performance on one set of stimuli (e.g., nouns) to their performance on another set of stimuli (e.g., verbs). The key to the importance of the experimental paradigm is that in order for a subject to respond "no" to a stimulus such as *blove* or "yes" to a real word such as *glove,* the subject's mental lexicon must be accessed. The lexical decision task can therefore be used to measure the speed and accuracy with which words in the mental lexicon are accessed. It has been found in many experiments that subjects take about half a second (500 milliseconds) to press the "yes" button for frequently used words such as *free* but almost three-quarters of a second to press the "yes" button for less common words such as *fret.* This finding has been called the **frequency effect**. Assuming that longer response times reflect processing that is more difficult or complex, this finding suggests that our mental dictionaries are organized so that words that we typically need more often (the frequent words) are more easily and quickly available to us.

Another way in which the lexical decision task can be used to explore language representation and processing is to investigate the speed and accuracy with which subjects press the "no" button for different types of stimuli. It has been found, for example, that pronounceable nonwords such as *plib* show slower "no" response times than unpronounceable nonwords such as *nlib.* Thus subjects' lexical decisions seem to take into account the phonotactic constraints of the language. It has also been found that nonwords that sound like real words (e.g., *blud, phocks*) take longer to reject than stimuli that are nonwords both visually and phonologically. Again this tells us that aspects of phonology are automatically activated during word reading (note that in the lexical decision task, the subject never has to pronounce the word aloud).

Priming

The priming paradigm very often involves the lexical decision task and can be considered an extension of it. Recall that in lexical decision tasks different categories of stimuli (e.g., concrete versus abstract words) are compared in terms of subjects' response latency and accuracy. Priming experiments typically involve the same procedure as the lexical decision task except that the word to be judged (now called the **target**) is preceded by another stimulus (called the **prime**). What is measured is the extent to which the prime influences the subject's lexical decision performance on the target stimulus.

The priming paradigm is an excellent technique for probing how words are related in the mind. One of the first experiments using this paradigm showed that response time is faster when a target is preceded by a semantically related prime (e.g., *cat-dog*) as compared to when it is preceded by an unrelated prime (e.g., *bat-dog*). Results of this sort lead us to the view that words are related in the mind in terms of networks. On the basis of evidence from these priming experiments, psycholinguists reason that when a word such as *cat* is seen, its image is activated in the mind and that activation spreads to other words in the lexical network that are semantically related (e.g., *dog*). Now, because the mental representation for *dog* has already been activated through the prime, it is in a sense "warmed up" so that when the subject later sees it on the screen as the target, response time is faster than it otherwise would have been. This is called the **priming effect** (as shown in Figure 13.3).

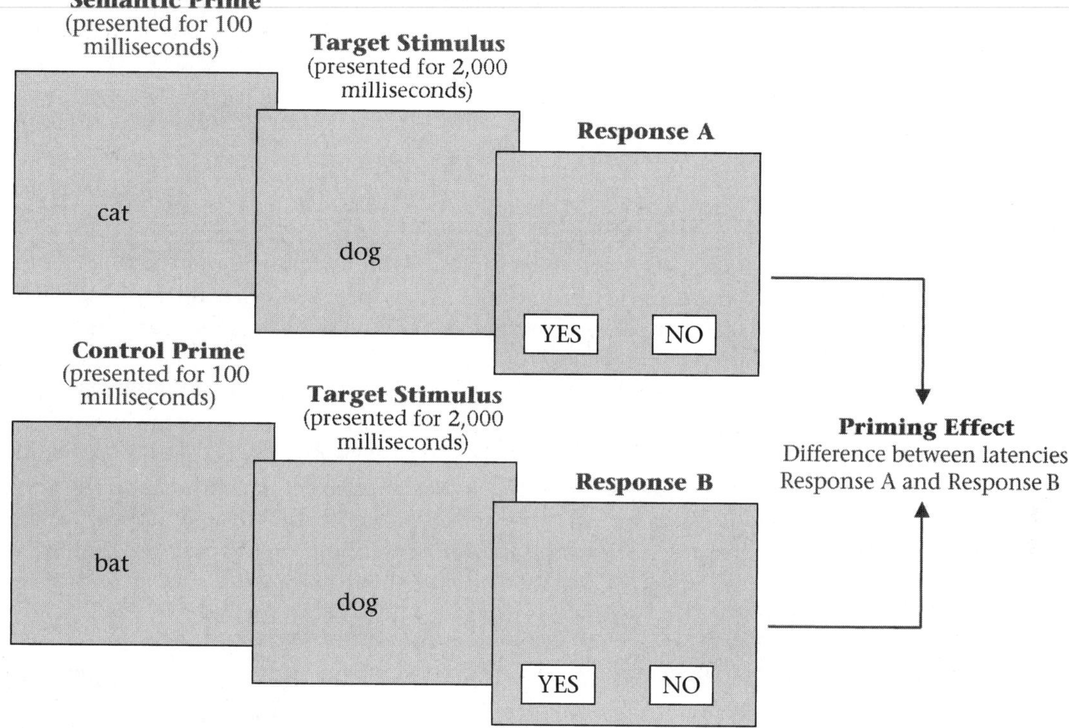

Figure 13.3 The structure of a lexical decision experiment with semantic priming

In recent years, the priming paradigm has been used to explore many aspects of the representation of words in the mind, and researchers have explored many types of priming in addition to the semantic priming above. For example, priming effects have been found for orthographically related words (e.g., *couch-touch*), for phonologically related words (e.g., *light-bite*), and between word roots and complex forms (e.g., *legal-illegality*). This last finding, which suggests that words are represented in the mind in terms of their constituent morphemes, will be discussed further in Section 2.2.

1.3 Experimental Methods: Sentence Processing

The lexical decision and priming paradigms discussed so far offer interesting insights into how words are processed, but are of limited use in exploring the processing of sentences. The main reason for this is that the types of questions asked about sentence processing tend to be different from those asked about the mental lexicon. The vast majority of the sentences that we hear are unique events. Therefore, sentence processing must fundamentally be a process that relies on a particular type of computation (as opposed to a particular type of storage, in the case of words). It is presumed that in sentence processing (i.e., in reading or listening), a sentence is understood through the analysis of the meanings of its words and through the analysis of its syntactic structure. Psycholinguists refer to this type of unconscious automatic analysis as **parsing**. Much of the research on sentence processing is concerned with the principles and steps in sentence parsing, the speed of parsing, and the manner and conditions under which parsing can break down.

In this section, we review two groups of experimental paradigms that have been used extensively to study sentence processing. These are timed-reading experiments and eye-movement experiments.

Timed-Reading Experiments

Timed-reading experiments begin with the assumption that the more difficult sentence processing is, the longer it should take. Therefore, by timing how long it takes subjects to read particular sentence types or parts of sentences, we can study the determinants of sentence-processing difficulty.

One of the more common and revealing timed-reading experimental paradigms is the bar-pressing paradigm in which subjects are seated in front of a computer screen and read a sentence one word at a time. The subject begins by seeing the first word of the sentence in the middle of the screen. When the subject presses a bar on the keyboard, the first word disappears and the second word of the sentence appears in its place. This process continues until the subject has read all the words in the sentence.

The dependent variable in these experiments is the amount of time it takes subjects to press the bar after seeing a particular word (i.e., the amount of time they need to process that word).

Bar-pressing experiments can be very revealing about the manner in which sentence processing occurs. Subjects do not show equal bar-pressing times across a sentence, but rather a pattern that reflects the syntactic structure of the sentence. An example of such a pattern for the sentence is shown in Figure 13.4, which displays bar-pressing times for the sentence *The Chinese, who used to produce kites, used them in order to carry ropes across the rivers.*

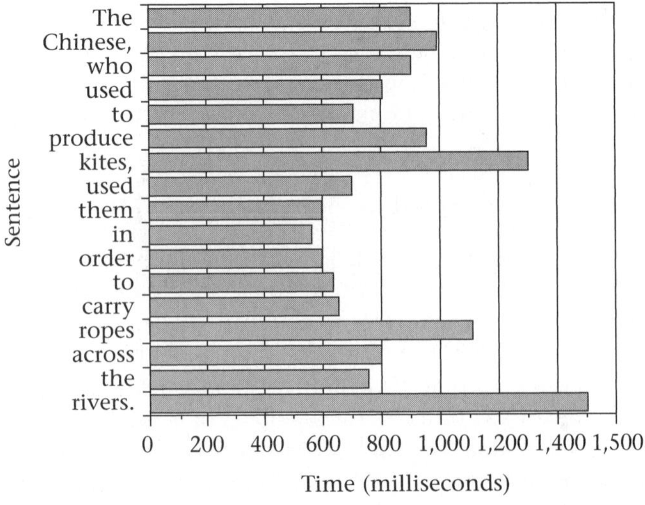

Figure 13.4 Bar-pressing times in sentence reading

As can be seen in Figure 13.4, subjects show longer bar-pressing times for processing content words such as nouns and verbs and relatively less time for function words such as determiners, conjunctions, and prepositions. What is particularly interesting is how subjects pause at the end of clause boundaries. This increased processing time is interpreted as reflecting the extra amount of time required to integrate preceding information into a complete clause structure. Thus the greatest bar-pressing time is required for *rivers,* the final noun in the sentence.

Eye-Movement Studies

We have already noted that sentence reading involves a series of jerky eye movements called saccades. A number of events occur during these jerky movements. When the eyes are at rest, they take a "snapshot" of two or three words. These snapshots usually last from 200 to 250 milliseconds. While the snapshot is being taken, the language-processing system calculates where to jump to next. During a jump to the next fixation location (usually about eight letters to the right), the subject is essentially blind.

The details of eye movements in sentence reading are studied with sophisticated laboratory procedures in which a subject is seated in front of a computer screen on which text is displayed. A low-intensity infrared beam of light is bounced off the subject's eyeball and registered on a video camera. The image from the video camera is fed to a computer that calculates where on the screen the subject is currently fixating.

This technique has revealed that fixation times are typically longer for less-frequent words and that the points of fixation are typically centered on content words, such as nouns and verbs, rather than on function words, such as determiners and conjunctions. Difficult sentence structures create longer fixation times as well as many more **regressive saccades**. Regressive saccades are backward jumps in a sentence and are usually associated with misparsing or miscomprehension. On average, backward saccades make up 10 to 15 percent of the saccades in sentence reading. But syntactically complex sentences and semantically anomalous sentences (e.g., *The pizza was too hot to drink*) create many more regressive saccades. It has also been found that poor readers jump back and forth through sentences much more often than good readers do.

1.4 Brain Activity: Event-Related Potentials

Perhaps the most exciting new technique to be used in psycholinguistic research is the study of **event-related potentials (ERPs)** produced by the brain during language processing. As a research technique, the ERP paradigm has the same basic advantage as eye-movement studies. The subject simply sits in front of a computer screen and reads. This is a relatively natural language-processing activity that, unlike lexical decision activities or bar pressing, is similar to what subjects do in normal language-processing situations.

ERP experiments measure electrical activity in the brain. Electrodes are placed on a subject's scalp and recordings are made of voltage fluctuations resulting from the brain's electrical activity. The difference between ERP recordings and the more familiar EEG recordings is that in the EEG, all the electrical activity of the brain is recorded.

This electrical activity results from a very large number of background brain activities that are always going on. The advantage of the ERP approach is that it uses a computer to calculate what part of the electrical brain activity is related to a stimulus event (in our case, words or sentences on a screen). This is done by a process of averaging. The computer records the instant at which a stimulus is presented and compares the voltage fluctuation immediately following the stimulus presentation to the random background "noise" of the ongoing EEG. By repeating this process many times with stimuli of a particular type, random voltage fluctuations are averaged out and the electrical potentials related to that stimulus type can be extracted. The resulting wave forms are the event-related potentials.

The ERP pattern is typically shown in terms of a line graph in which time is shown from left to right and voltage is shown on the vertical axis with negative values on top and positive values on the bottom. An example of an ERP graph is provided in Figure 13.5.

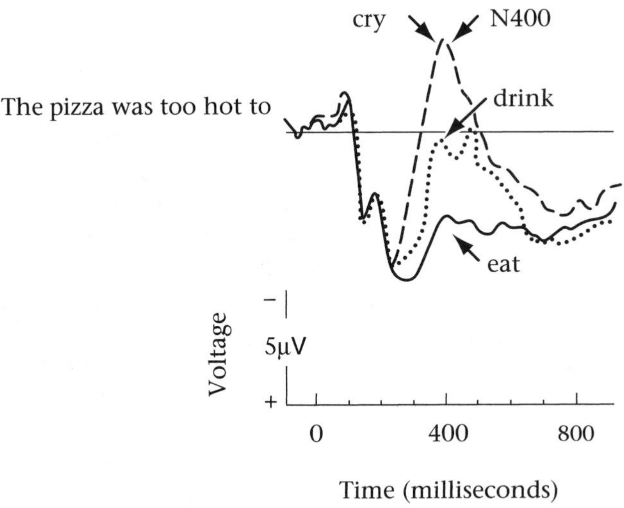

Figure 13.5 ERPs elicited by sentence-final words that are congruent, incongruent, and very incongruent with the sentence context

Figure 13.5 also displays one of the most interesting psycholinguistic findings using ERPs. It turns out that in the processing of implausible sentences, the brain displays a characteristic ERP sign of surprise. Consider the following sentences:

8)

a. The pizza was too hot to eat.
b. The pizza was too hot to drink.
c. The pizza was too hot to cry.

The sentences in *8* are arranged in order of semantic plausibility. In the first case, the last word fits in perfectly well with the sentence and would typically be expected by the reader. As can be seen in Figure 13.5, the ERP for this sentence shows a positive voltage associated with the last word. In the case of *8b,* however, in which the last word does not make sense (people do not drink pizza), the ERP is much more negative. As is shown in the horizontal axis, this negative spike occurs 400 milliseconds after the onset of the word. For this reason, this signal of semantic anomaly is called the N400 (negative spike at 400 milliseconds after stimulus presentation). Note how the N400 is even stronger in the case of sentence *8c,* which is less congruent with the sentence context (*drink* is at least associated with food).

The N400 effect can be obtained not only at the ends of sentences but in any sentence position. This fact suggests that sentence processing is immediate and on-line. When reading a sentence, we do not wait until the entire string is complete but are constantly building interpretations of the sentence as it unfolds. Whenever what we see or hear contradicts our expectations based on our ongoing interpretative processes, an N400 ERP spike is observed.

2 Language Processing and Linguistics

In the preceding sections, we discussed some of the methods that psycholinguists use to investigate how language is processed. One of the most important results of such psycholinguistic investigations has been that many of the concepts and principles used by linguists to describe and understand the structure of language in terms of phonetics, phonology, morphology, and syntax have been found to also play an important role in the understanding of how language is produced and comprehended during activities such as speaking, listening, reading, and writing. In this section, we will focus on these points of contact between theoretical linguistics and psycholinguistics. In doing so, we will also highlight the correspondence between the study of language processing and the concepts discussed in Chapters 1 through 5 of this book.

2.1 Phonetics and Phonology

The study of phonetics and phonology reveals that the sound system of language is richly structured and contains different levels of representation. Thus, as discussed in Chapters 2 and 3, individual segments can be characterized in terms of place and manner of articulation or with respect to a matrix of phonological features. Sequences of sounds can be grouped into syllabic structures, and allophonic variation can be described in terms of underlying phonemes and surface allophones. How much of this structure plays a role in language processing? The simple answer to this question is: "All of it!" The more complex answer is that language processing shows evidence that features, phonemes, and syllable structure all capture some aspects of the way in which we process language, but that speech production and perception is a complex activity that involves much more than these phonetic and phonological representations.

To see why this is the case, consider what might occur when you hear the sentence *The dog bit the cat.* Because the utterance unfolds in time, you will first hear the segment [ð] and then the segment [ə]. (In fact, you do not hear these segments separately but create them out of a continuous sound stream.) As soon as these segments are identified, you have already accessed the representation for the word *the* in your mental lexicon. When the next segment comes up in the sound stream, you already know that it is the beginning of a new word and you also know that this word will probably be a noun. The phonetic analysis that follows identifies the segments *d-o-g* and the corresponding lexical entry. Now come the first segments of the word *bit.* In principle, the first two phonemes /bɪ/ could be the first two segments of the word *believe,* but you are not likely to consider this possibility because your developing interpretation of the sentence is biasing you toward the word *bit,* which is associated in your mind with *dog.*

As can be appreciated from this example, language processing involves the interplay of information that develops simultaneously at many different levels of analysis. The person hearing the sentence *The dog bit the cat* is performing a phonetic analysis to isolate phonemes and word boundaries, and to relate these to representations in the mental lexicon. This inductive analysis is referred to as **bottom-up processing**. But we do not wait until we have analyzed all the phonemes in a sentence before we begin to try to understand it. Rather, we begin interpretation of a sentence spontaneously and automatically on the basis of whatever information is available to us. For this reason, by the time we get to the word *bit,* we are not only recognizing it using bottom-up processing but also employing a set of expectations to guide phonetic processing and word recognition. This is called **top-down processing**. In normal language use, we are always engaged in both bottom-up and top-down activities. We never just process features or phonemes or syllables; we process language for the purposes of understanding each other.

In Section 3 of this chapter, we will discuss how phonetic and phonological analysis fits into other processes involved in speaking and listening. For now, however, we will concentrate on three levels of linguistic structure that seem fundamental to phonetic and phonological representation: features, phonemes, and syllables.

Features

In both linguistics and psycholinguistics, the term *feature* is used to refer to the most basic level of representation. It is therefore always associated with bottom-up processing in language. In the processing of sound, it refers to characteristics of individual phonemes (e.g., ± voice, ± continuant). The most straightforward evidence concerning the role of such features comes from the analysis of slips of the tongue. Some examples of these slips are presented in Table 13.1.

Table 13.1 The role of features in speech errors

Intended	*Actually produced*
a. big and fat	pig and vat
b. Is Pat a girl?	Is bat a curl?
c. Cedars of Lebanon	Cedars of Lemanon

The errors in Table 13.1 follow a pattern. But that pattern can only be understood with reference to a system of phonological features. In all three examples in this table, the errors involve a phonological feature. In example *a* the feature [voice] has been exchanged between the words *big* and *fat* to create the new words *pig* and *vat* (note that /b-p/ and /f-v/ only differ in the feature [voice]).

This same pattern of voice feature exchange can be seen in example *b,* where *Pat* becomes *bat* and *girl* becomes *curl.* Finally, the error in *c* is particularly intriguing because we normally think of /b/ and /m/ as completely different phonemes. In fact, however, they are both voiced bilabial stops that only differ in terms of the feature [± nasal]. Changing the /b/ in *Lebanon* from [–nasal] to [+nasal] creates the error *Lemanon.* These examples offer evidence that language production makes use of the individual feature components of phonemes and that the phonemes that we produce in speech may actually be put together "on the fly" out of bundles of such features.

Phonemes

We have seen in Section 1.1 that Spoonerisms show evidence of entire phonemes being misplaced during sentence planning. The phonemic unit of representation also plays a central role in psycholinguistic models of speech processing, such as the **cohort model** proposed by William Marslen-Wilson. This model states that in word comprehension, words are analyzed by hearers from beginning to end. So, for example, when we hear the word *glass,* we initially consider all the words that begin with the sound [g]. When the next sound [l] is recognized, the number of possible words (the **cohort**) is reduced to those words that begin with [gl]. This process continues until the cohort of possible words is reduced to one—the word that is being recognized. In a number of experiments, Marslen-Wilson investigated whether this beginning-to-end analysis of spoken words proceeds one phoneme at a time, one cluster at a time, or one syllable at a time. He and his colleagues found that the phoneme seems to be the fundamental unit of auditory word recognition.

Syllables

Although in the cohort model, the phoneme rather than the syllable seems to be the fundamental unit of auditory word recognition, there is other evidence that the syllable plays an important role in speech perception. In one study, subjects were presented with disyllabic words (e.g., *bullet*) and disyllabic nonwords (e.g., *sullet*) and were asked to press a button if a particular target unit was in the stimulus. The target units were either syllables (e.g., *let*) or segments (e.g., *t*). It was found for both words and nonwords that subjects were significantly faster at identifying syllable targets than at identifying single segment targets. It was concluded that syllable identification was faster because in normal auditory analysis, subjects first break down stimuli into syllables and then into individual segments as the situation demands.

Another source of evidence on the role of the syllable in language processing comes from observing subjects' performance on word-blending tasks. In such tasks, subjects are given two words—such as *bug* and *cat*—and are required to blend the words together to make a new word. Now, what sounds better: *bug + cat = bat* or *bug + cat = but*? The difference between these two possibilities is that the first one takes the onset of the first syllable and combines it with the rhyme of the second syllable. The other possibility does not split the words in a natural point of English syllable structure. As you might expect, subjects are much better at creating word blends that correspond to the syllable structure of their language and prefer such blends when presented with a choice. The fact that English speakers find such onset-rhyme divisions easier and more natural suggests that the sound of words is represented in speakers' minds in terms of their syllables and syllable constituents (e.g., onset and rhyme).

2.2 Morphological Processing

Morphology is the study of word structure. It seeks to characterize the system of categories and rules involved in word formation and interpretation. The psycholinguistic study of morphological processing seeks to understand how this word structure plays a role in language processing. In the following sections, we will summarize some psycholinguistic research that reveals how morphological structures and principles play a substantial role both in the representation of words in the mind and in word recognition.

Morpheme Activation

Words such as *blackboard, happiness,* and *watching* are made up of two morphemes. In the case of the compound *blackboard,* both morphemes are roots. In the case of *happiness,* one morpheme is a root and the other is a derivational suffix. Finally, in the case of *watching,* one morpheme is a root and the other is an inflectional affix. The first question we will address is whether the individual morphological components of words play a role in processing.

The answer to this question seems to be a straightforward yes. For most multimorphemic words, individual morphemes are automatically activated during word recognition. One source of evidence for this conclusion comes from priming experiments in which it is found that multimorphemic words will prime semantic associates of their constituents in a lexical decision experiment. Thus, when a subject is exposed to a multimorphemic word such as *suntan,* the activation of that word in the mind will facilitate the recognition of *moon,* which is highly associated to the initial morpheme of *sun* but not to the whole word *suntan.* The facilitation, therefore, must arise from independent activation of the morphemes within a word.

There are two ways in which this activation of morphemes could occur. The first is that it derives from structured morphological representations in the mind. Under this view, multimorphemic words such as *happiness* and *blackboard* are represented in the mind as [happy+ness] and [black+board], respectively. When we access such words, both their whole-word forms and their constituent morphemes are automatically activated. This view is termed **postlexical decomposition**, because the constituents of a multimorphemic word are activated through the representation of the whole lexical item. An alternative view is that the activation of constituent morphemes results from a computational mechanism that scans a word and isolates individual morphemes in much the same way as individual words are isolated when we see or hear sentences. This view is termed **prelexical decomposition**, because the constituent morphemes are activated through a computational process (called **morphological parsing**) rather than through the morphological representation of the word in the mind. These alternative views are presented in Figure 13.6.

Interestingly, recent research has shown that both these views are correct. Words such as *barking* were presented to participants as prime words in a semantic priming experiment. The word *bark* is ambiguous: It can be a noun that means 'the outside of a tree' or a verb that means 'the sound that a dog makes'. In the multimorphemic word *barking,* however, it can only have the verb meaning. The researchers asked the question: Will *barking* affect the processing of both *dog* (an associate of the verb) and *tree* (an associate of the noun)? If the latter occurred, this would be evidence for prelexical morphological decomposition because there would be no reason for the

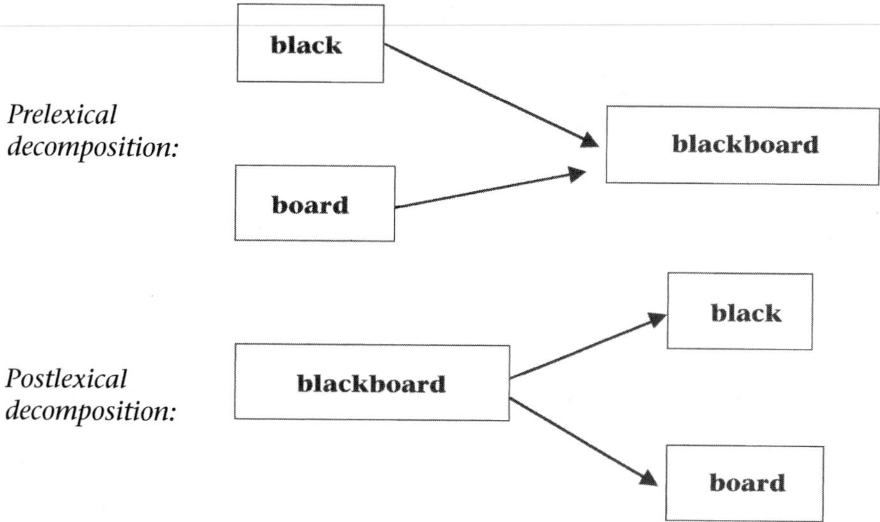

Figure 13.6 Prelexical and postlexical decomposition

meaning of the noun to be part of the morphological representation of *barking*. Indeed, both the semantic associates *dog* and *tree* were affected by the prime word *barking*. However, activation of the incorrect one (*tree*) was inhibited (hence the negative priming effect) rather than increased (see Figure 13.7). This led to the conclusion that during prelexical decomposition, *bark* and *-ing* were accessed separately,

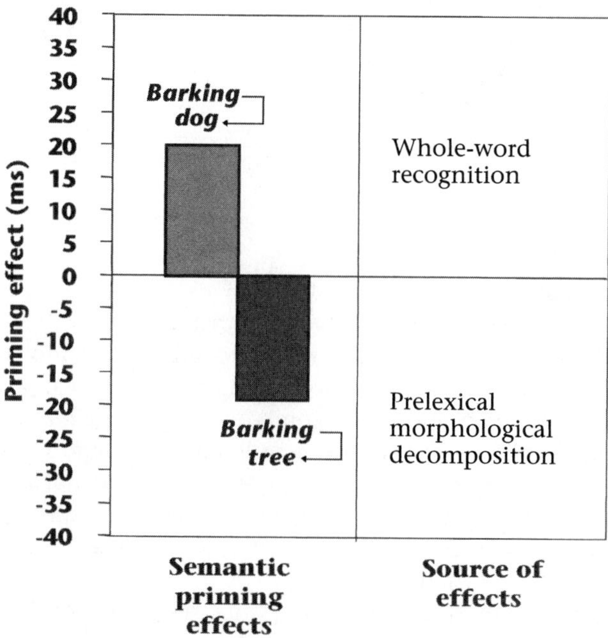

Figure 13.7 Whole-word processing and prelexical morphological decomposition can have opposite effects in a semantic priming experiment.

allowing both meanings of *bark* to be activated. As depicted in Figure 13.8, it was claimed that the competing activations create a need to inhibit the incorrect results of automatic prelexical activation, so that eventually (actually, in under a second) the correct meaning for the word is achieved.

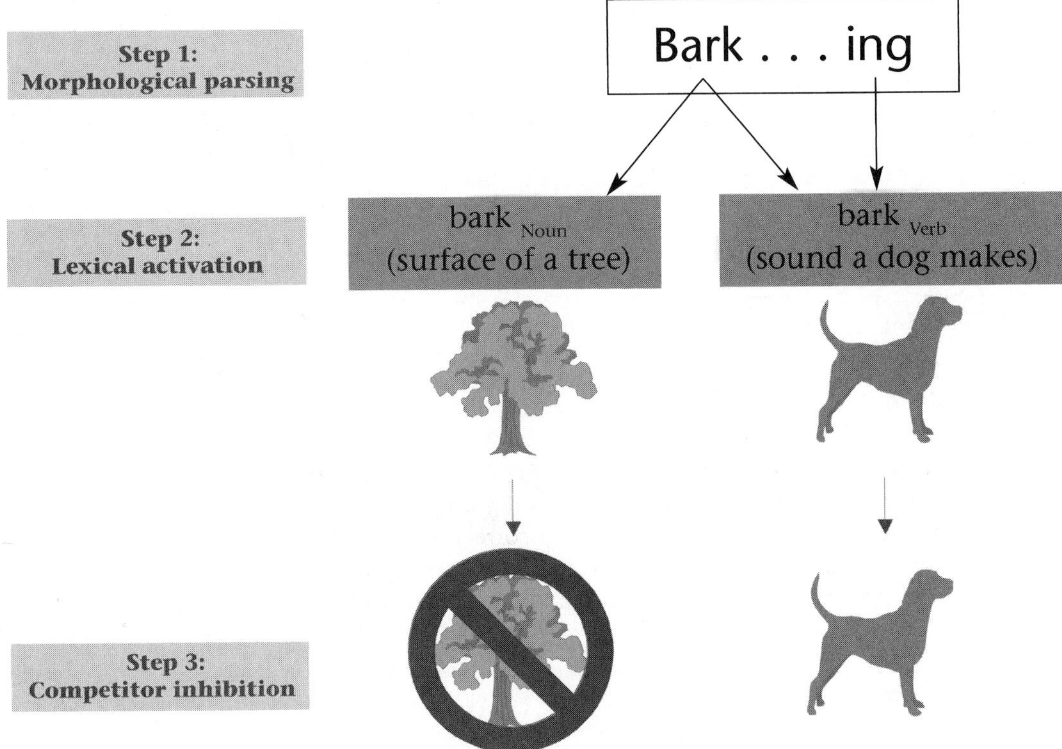

Figure 13.8 Activation and deactivation in the processing of multimorphemic words

Selectional Restrictions

The study we have reviewed above points to the view that even for apparently simple multimorphemic words, a considerable amount of mental computation is involved in working out how morphemes do and do not fit together. To complete our brief discussion of this issue, we return to a phenomenon discussed in Chapter 4 of this book—namely, that not all roots and affixes combine freely in the formation of new words. For example, the suffix *-ize* attaches to only adjectives and nouns to form verbs; for this reason, English morphological constraints would not allow a word such as **understandize* because *understand* is already a verb. The question for psycholinguistic research is: Do these formal restrictions play a role in the way in which native speakers of English process new words?

In another experiment in morphological processing, subjects were presented with nonsense roots (e.g., *birm*) that had prefixes and suffixes attached to them. Because they contained nonsense roots, none of these words made much sense (e.g., *re-birmable, re-birmize, re-birmity*). But notice that, as is shown in Figure 13.9, *re-birmable* and *re-birmize* are morphologically legal, whereas *re-birmity* violates a morphological constraint—the prefix *re-* must attach to a verb and the suffix *-ity* must attach to an adjective (see Table 4.6 in Chapter 4). The construction is illegal because the nonsense root *birm* cannot be both at the same time. In experiments with these sorts of stimuli, it was found that processing times were significantly longer for the illegal nonsense words than for the morphologically legal words. These results suggest that knowledge of the selectional restrictions of affixes does indeed form part of the word-processing system and that violation of these restrictions creates difficulty for automatic lexical processing, which would of course go unnoticed by the language user, but is discernible through psycholinguistic techniques.

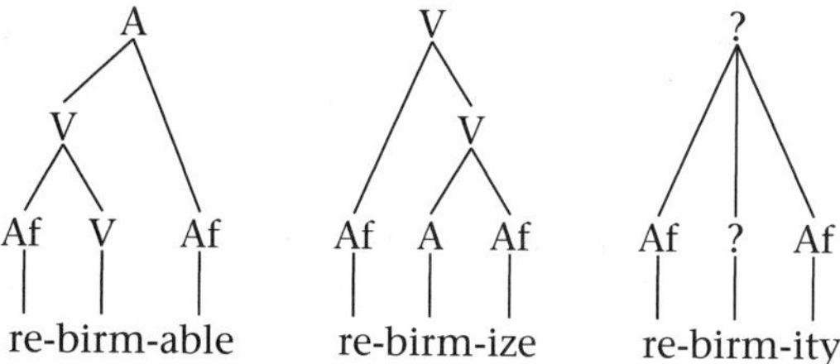

Figure 13.9 Morphologically legal and illegal affixed nonsense roots

2.3 Syntax

Syntax is the system of rules and categories that underlies sentence formation in human language. One of the fundamental insights in the study of syntax is that sentences are unique events. That means that virtually all the sentences that you read in this chapter are sentences that you have never encountered before. They are typically made up of familiar words, but the arrangement of those words into a syntactic structure is unique to each sentence. The question that we will consider in this section is: How are these syntactic structures created during sentence processing?

The Syntax Module

One very simple possibility for how sentences are processed is that production and comprehension employ the system of rules that are used by syntacticians to describe sentence structure. This possibility suggests that speakers would begin with deep structure representations and employ a series of transformations to derive the surface structure characteristics of a sentence. Many psycholinguistic experiments examined this possibility by testing, for example, whether sentences with many transformations take longer to process than sentences with fewer transformations. It turned out that the number of transformations in a sentence did not predict processing time. Researchers concluded that there is at least some difference between the rules that native speakers use to generate and comprehend sentences and the rules that linguists use to characterize the linguistic knowledge of native speakers. It was therefore necessary to postulate a special module for sentence processing and another for grammatical knowledge. This processing module is called the **syntactic parser**.

The parser is understood to be a system that makes use of grammatical knowledge, but which also contains special procedures and principles that guide the order in which elements of a sentence are processed and the manner in which syntactic structure is built up. Because our parsing ability is based on our grammatical knowledge of our language, it is usually the case that there is a close correspondence between sentence parsing and grammatical structure. However, because the parsing module has its own set of principles, sentences that are grammatically complex are not necessarily difficult to parse, and some sentences with relatively simple syntactic structure can create substantial parsing problems.

It should be noted that in discussing how processing takes place, the term **module** has a special meaning. It refers to a unit of processing that is relatively autonomous from other processing units. The idea of processing modules has been very important and controversial in many domains of human information processing. To get a sense of how processing may involve the coordination of separate modules, consider what occurs when you watch a movie. The movie director, in order to obtain a variety of effects, relies on processing modularity. The director knows that in watching an adventure film, your stomach will take a dip when the airplane on the screen goes into a dive or when the canoe goes over the falls. He or she knows that you cannot stop this from happening even though you are aware that you are sitting in a chair that is not moving. Similarly, you will be frightened by the sudden appearance of a monster, even though you know that you are really in no danger. All these effects result from processing modularity. The bottom-up information that comes from processing modules cannot be turned off by the top-down information that you are seated in a stationary and safe movie-theater environment.

A variety of psycholinguistic studies have investigated whether this same sort of modularity is present in syntactic processing. In other words, they look at whether syntactic parsing operates in an automatic and obligatory manner that is relatively independent of the activity of other processing systems. Two sources of evidence have been very important in the exploration of the principles of modularity of sentence processing. These are garden path sentences and sentence ambiguity, which are discussed below.

Garden Path Sentences

Some sentences are extraordinarily difficult to understand even though they are not very complex syntactically. These sentences are called **garden path sentences** because they lead the syntactic parser down the garden path to the wrong analysis. Perhaps the most famous garden path sentence is the one given in *9* below.

9)

The horse raced past the barn fell.

This sentence is perfectly grammatical, but almost impossible to understand. The reason for this is that as we read the sentence, we build up a syntactic structure in which *the horse* is the subject of the sentence and *raced past the barn* is the main VP. When we get to the word *fell,* we are surprised because the sentence we have built up has no room for an extra VP. The correct interpretation for the sentence requires that *fell* be the head of the main VP and that *raced past the barn* be a clause (a reduced version of "that was raced past the barn") that attaches to the NP *the horse* (see Figure 13.10).

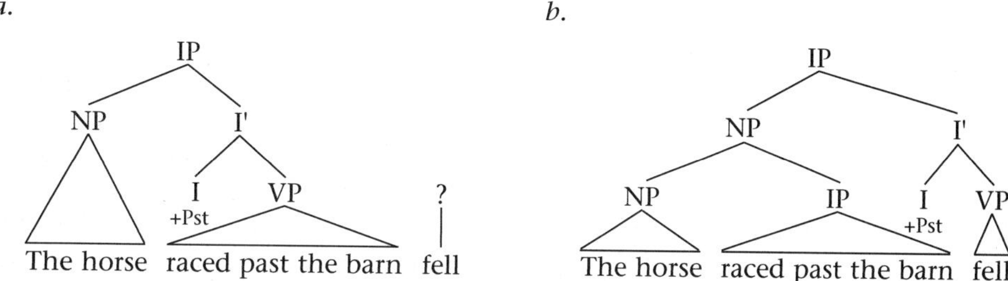

Figure 13.10 A garden path sentence. The garden path effect is shown in *a*. The correct interpretation is represented in *b*.

The ways in which native speakers misunderstand garden path sentences reveal how the parser might work. It seems that we construct syntactic representations from the beginning of the sentences to the end and that our sentence parsers are organized so that we make a number of assumptions about how a sentence will proceed. This can be seen by considering the garden path sentence in *10*.

10)

Since Jay always walks a mile seems like a short distance to him.

This sentence is not as difficult to process as the sentence in *9*, but you probably noticed yourself having to backtrack after an initial misanalysis. Your parser is inclined to build a single VP out of the string *walks a mile,* when in fact the words belong to different clauses. This tendency has been extensively studied by psycholinguists. The backtracking that you might have noticed in your own reading shows up significantly in eye-movement studies, in which it is found that subjects show more regressive saccades for these sentences as well as longer fixation times.

It has been claimed by Lynn Frazier and her colleagues that the garden path effect results from two principles of parsing. These are **minimal attachment** and **late closure**. The principle of minimal attachment states that we do not postulate new syntactic nodes (like the extra embedded IP in Figure 13.10b) unless it is clear that we absolutely have to. The principle of late closure states that we prefer to attach new words to the clause currently being processed as we proceed through a sentence from beginning to end. The result of late closure can be discerned in sentence *10,* where we are inclined to add the NP *a mile* to the VP headed by *walk* rather than beginning a new clause.

There is one last point to be made concerning what garden path sentences can tell us about how people process sentences. Try reading the sentence in *10* again. You should find that although you now know the correct analysis for the sentence, you misread it the second time just as you did the first time. This suggests that the parsing system is in fact a module that operates automatically and independently.

Sentence Ambiguity

Another important clue to how syntactic processing is accomplished comes from the study of **sentence ambiguity**. Consider the sentence in *11*.

11)

They all rose.

In fact, the last word in *11* is ambiguous. The word *rose* can be either related to *stand* or related to *flower.* However, the sentence context leads us clearly to favor the *stand* version of the word. Does the sentence context therefore inhibit activation of the other meaning of *rose*? This question was investigated in a lexical decision experiment in which the sentence in *11* served as the prime. After seeing the sentence, subjects were presented with either the word *flower* or the word *stand.* The researchers found that the sentence facilitated lexical decision response times to both words. That is, both meanings for the word *rose* in the sentence were activated, even though the sentence clearly presented a bias in favor of one reading over the other.

This experimental finding is one of many that reveal a fundamental property of human language processing. We create all representations possible and then discard the ones that are either incorrect or unnecessary. This last characteristic was found in a follow-up priming experiment identical to the one just described except that there was a pause of several hundred milliseconds between the prime and the target. When the pause was present, the priming effect disappeared for the meaning that was unrelated to the sentence context (i.e., *flower*). This suggests that, in fact, sentence processing proceeds in two stages. In the first stage, all possible representations and structures are computed. In the second stage, one of these structures is selected and all others are abandoned. Of course all this happens very quickly and subconsciously so that we as native speakers of a language are never aware that for a sentence such as *12,* we compute two possible interpretations.

12)

The tuna can hit the boat.

In reading this sentence, you either ended up imagining:

a. tuna meat that is packed in a small round can
b. a large fish swimming toward a boat

The point of the psycholinguistic experiments just described is this: No matter which interpretation you arrived at (*a* or *b*), you probably considered both of them, chose one, discarded the other, and forgot about the whole thing in less than a second.

3 Putting It All Together: Psycholinguistic Modeling

Up to this point, our discussion of psycholinguistic research has been restricted to examining characteristics of phonetic, phonological, morphological, and syntactic processing and the relation between the concepts used in theoretical linguistics and those in psycholinguistics. It is important to note, however, that research in language processing seeks to discover not only which types of representations play a role in language processing but also how these representations and processes fit together to make activities such as speaking, listening, reading, and writing possible.

Psycholinguistic researchers present their ideas of *how language is done* in terms of models. A **psycholinguistic model** incorporates the results of experiments into a proposal about how processing takes place. In other words, it is a statement of what happens when. Suppose, for example, we wished to present the finding discussed in Section 2.3 that a sentence such as *They all rose* will prime both *flower* and *stand*. The model might look like Figure 13.11.

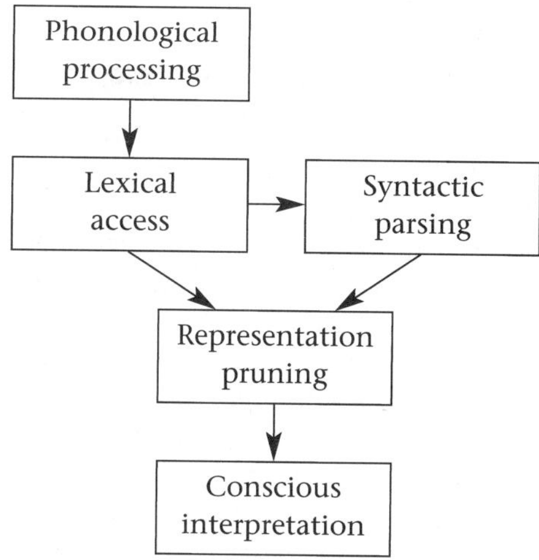

Figure 13.11 A serial psycholinguistic model of sentence processing

For our present purposes, it is not important whether this model is actually correct. The purpose of the model is simply to illustrate how psycholinguistic statements can be represented. This model, which looks very much like a computer flowchart, shows that when processing a sentence such as *They all rose,* we first perform phonological processing. This is followed by lexical access, in which all words with matching phonological representations are accessed (including the two words *rose*). Information from lexical access "feeds" the syntactic parsing module, and information from both the lexical access module and the parsing module are fed to the representation pruning module (the module that discards multiple representations). Finally, the model states that an interpretation becomes conscious only in the final stage of analysis and that there is only one-way information flow to conscious interpretation (in other words, the conscious mind cannot "peek" at how things are going).

You will note that in creating this model, we have taken two kinds of shortcuts. First, we have created a novel name (e.g., pruning) to describe an operation that has been deduced from the results of psycholinguistic experimentation. Second, our model uses the box notation as a shorthand for a constellation of processes. Thus, it is understood that as the model becomes more elaborate, each one of the boxes in Figure 13.11 would be expanded into a flowchart of its own.

As you inspect the model in Figure 13.11, you should find that it is really very inadequate. It is missing much important detail, it seems to characterize only one aspect of sentence processing, and it avoids any mention of how meaning is accessed or how sentence interpretation actually takes place. In other words, to be a model of any real value, it would have to be much more elaborate.

Indeed, the types of psycholinguistic models that have been proposed in recent years are very elaborate. This is a good thing. We want models to be as detailed and comprehensive as possible, to take a great deal of experimentation into account, and, perhaps most importantly, to show how linguistic and nonlinguistic operations work together in the processing of language.

3.1 The Use of Metaphors in Psycholinguistic Modeling

Perhaps the most important characteristic of the model presented in Figure 13.11 is the fact that it obviously could not reflect what really happens in the mind of a language user. It is exceedingly unlikely that our minds possess boxes and arrows (or their equivalents). This model, like all psycholinguistic models, employs metaphors for language representations and language processing. The value of these metaphors is that they allow researchers to make specific claims about how language processing works, which can then be tested. For example, through its architecture, the model in Figure 13.11 claims that phonological processing precedes lexical access, which in turn precedes syntactic parsing. This claim can easily be tested in an experiment that investigates whether all phonological processing is complete before syntactic parsing begins.

We see then that psycholinguistic models have dual functions. They summarize specific research findings and generate specific hypotheses. They also have the very important function of embodying general perspectives on how language processing works. This is again accomplished through the use of metaphors. These metaphors have the effect of shaping how we conceive of language in the mind and what kinds of questions are asked by psycholinguistic researchers. Finally, these metaphors provide the means by which major families of models can be contrasted in order to test which most accurately describes language processing. In the following sections, we review three of the most important current issues in psycholinguistic modeling: serial versus parallel processing models; single-route versus dual-route models; and, finally, symbolic versus connectionist models.

Serial versus Parallel Processing Models

Let us return to Figure 13.11. By employing the metaphor of a computer program that operates sequentially, the **serial processing model** in Figure 13.11 not only makes a claim about sentence processing but also claims that language processing proceeds in a step-by-step manner. In contrast, a **parallel processing model** would claim that phonological, lexical, and syntactic processes are carried out simultaneously. Figure 13.12 represents an example of a parallel processing model. Here information does not flow in a sequential manner. Rather, all modules operate simultaneously and share information. The model in Figure 13.12 claims, therefore, that when we hear a sentence, we begin phonological, lexical, and syntactic processes at the same time. As each type of processing proceeds, it informs the other.

In recent research, serial and parallel processing models have been central in our ability to understand the extent to which bottom-up and top-down processing interact. Serial models correctly characterize those aspects of language processing that are

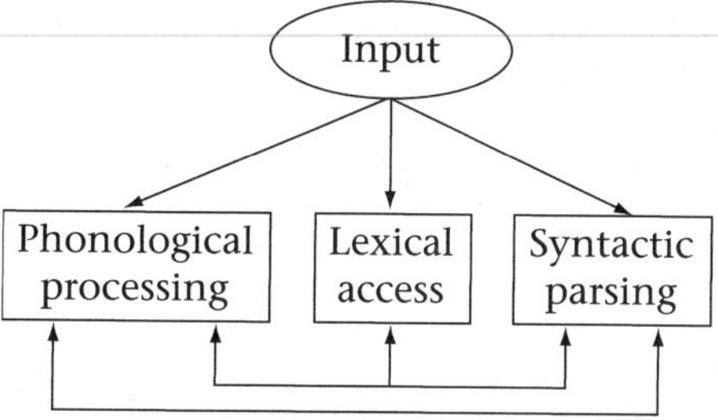

Figure 13.12 A parallel psycholinguistic model of sentence processing

modular and are driven by strict bottom-up procedures, such as phonetic perception. Parallel processing models, on the other hand, are more effective than serial models at characterizing complex processes such as sentence comprehension.

Single-Route versus Dual-Route Models

Put most directly, **single-route models** claim that a particular type of language processing is accomplished in one manner only. **Dual-route models**, on the other hand, claim that a language-processing task is accomplished through (usually two) competing mechanisms. Consider, for example, the task of reading English words. Here there are three possibilities: (1) we always read a word by looking it up in our mental lexicon directly based on its visual characteristics; (2) we convert a visual input into phonological representations first, and this phonological representation becomes the basis for comprehension; and (3) we do both at the same time. Options 1 and 2 represent single-route models in the sense that they claim that reading is accomplished in one way. Option 3, which is represented in Figure 13.13, represents a dual-route model in that it claims that both mechanisms are employed. Usually such dual-route models employ the additional metaphor of a horse race by claiming that for some words (e.g., very frequent short words), the direct route is faster, but for others (e.g., rare words), the phonological conversion route is faster and "wins the horse race."

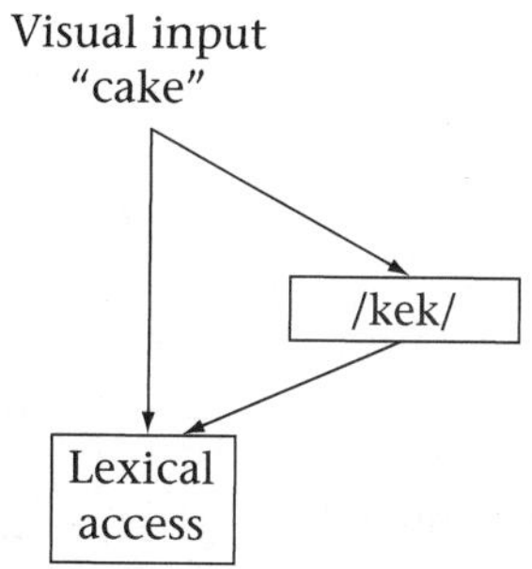

Figure 13.13 A dual-route model of word reading

In recent psycholinguistic investigations, the dual-route model has been very influential in modeling whether multimorphemic words are decomposed into their constituent morphemes during word recognition or are accessed as whole words. It has been found that although both procedures are active all the time, the whole-word recognition route wins the race for frequent bimorphemic words such as *blackboard*. However, in the case of less frequent words such as *breadboard* or novel multimorphemic forms such as *blueboard,* the morphological decomposition route is the one that provides the basis for comprehension.

Symbolic versus Connectionist Models

The final modeling contrast that we review in this section is the contrast between symbolic and connectionist models. These types of models represent fundamentally different views about the nature of mental representations. **Symbolic models** (which include all the ones we have discussed so far) claim that models of linguistic knowledge must make reference to rules and representations consisting of symbols, such as phonemes, words, and syntactic category labels. **Connectionist models**, on the other hand, claim that the mind can be best modeled by reference to large associations of very simple units (often called **nodes**) that more closely approximate the kinds of processing units (i.e., neurons) that we know the brain to be composed of. Connectionist models do not typically contain direct representations for language units such as words, but represent these as an association of nodes. This difference is exemplified in Figure 13.14.

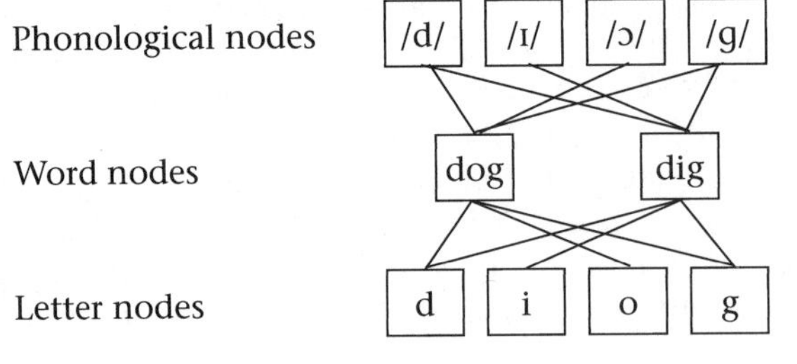

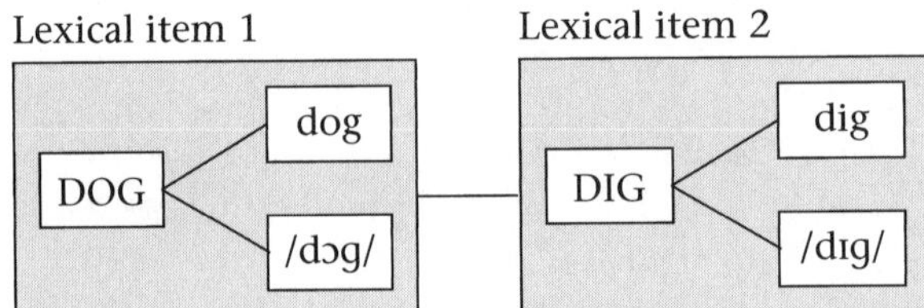

Figure 13.14 Connectionist versus symbolic representations for the words *dog* and *dig* in the mind

In one sense, the two kinds of representations in Figure 13.14 represent exactly the same information—namely, the graphemic and phonological makeup of the words *dog* and *dig*. In another sense, however, they are very different. The connectionist representation shows words as having "reality" only in the sense that they are bundles of associations between phonological and graphemic nodes. (In some connectionist approaches, the word nodes would not exist at all.) In the symbolic representation, on the other hand, words do indeed have discrete representations in the mind, and each representation contains information regarding the word's sound and spelling.

3.2 Which Model Is Right?

Almost certainly, none of the models that we have discussed is correct. All models represent a researcher's claim about the most current version of the truth. Because psycholinguistics is a very young field, we can expect that any "current version of the truth" will be very far from the real truth (if there is one). Perhaps this is the reason that psycholinguistic models are so important; they give us the vocabulary with which to ask major questions about mental processing. For example, do our representations consist of symbols corresponding to phonemes, words, and phrases, or are mental representations distributed over a large number of nodes? Does the mind settle into a best way to perform a task, or are all processes horse races between alternative ways to solve a problem? Do mental operations proceed in a step-by-step manner?

These are all big questions and big issues. Language research is at the center of them. The more we investigate the details of language processing, the more we realize it offers us the best clues to the secrets of human cognition and the more we appreciate how well guarded those secrets are. In the past quarter-century of psycholinguistic research, we have learned a great deal about language representation and processing. In the first part of this chapter, we concentrated on the research techniques that have made these advances possible. In this final section of the chapter, we have focused on the yet unresolved major issues. Although we do not yet know which models are right or which hybrids will be most effective in our evolving understanding of human cognition, the research we have reviewed points to a view of language processing that is characterized by massive storage of language forms and by extensive connections among these forms. Language processing also seems to involve automatic and obligatory computational procedures that break down complex language structures into their phonological, morphological, and syntactic constituents during language comprehension, and build them up again during production. So, we are able to conclude that the language system is paradoxically fast and automatic, but not necessarily efficient. The reason for this is probably that the language-processing system is designed to exploit all the linguistic resources of the human brain—its massive storage ability, its apparently unlimited capacity for associations among representations, and its ability to carry out complex computation within modular subsystems. So, whereas theoretical characterizations of language structure strive, quite appropriately, for elegance and simplicity, the language-processing system might strive for exactly the opposite, namely extensive redundancy. The exact manner in which different and perhaps redundant methods of "doing language" might coexist in a single human brain has been the subject of a great deal of recent reseach and debate among psycholinguists and constitutes the next big research challenge in the field.

Summing Up

Psycholinguistics is the study of language processing. The field is defined both by an area of subject matter and a particular methodology. Psycholinguists study how people perform the functions of language comprehension and production. They seek to discover the nature of the mental representations that serve these functions and the nature of the cognitive operations and computations that are employed when we understand and produce language.

Because language processing involves computations and representations that cannot be observed and measured directly, psycholinguists have devised special experimental techniques to investigate language processing. Some of these techniques, such as **lexical decision** and **priming**, measure a subject's response time and response accuracy to linguistic stimuli. Other techniques measure eye movement while subjects are reading silently, and others measure electrical activity in the brain during language processing.

Language processing involves many processing modules that are specialized for a particular language-processing task and interact with other modules in restricted ways. Thus, language processing involves a constant interplay between **bottom-up** and **top-down processing**. We process phonetic features, phonemes, and words all at the same time. We construct syllable representations, morphological representations, and syntactic representations in a spontaneous and obligatory manner. As conscious beings, we are aware of the results of our processing but not of the processing itself.

In general, psycholinguistic studies have revealed that many of the concepts employed in the analysis of sound structure, word structure, and sentence structure also play a role in language processing. However, an account of language processing also requires that we understand how these linguistic concepts interact with other aspects of human processing to enable language production and comprehension.

Psycholinguists typically present their views of how language production and comprehension are achieved in terms of processing models. These models are at the heart of research in psycholinguistics and allow researchers to express the significance of particular research findings, to predict the outcomes of future experiments, and to debate the fundamental characteristics of human cognition.

Key Terms

General terms and terms concerning psycholinguistic methods

dependent variables
event-related potentials (ERPs)
experimental paradigms
field technique
frequency effect
lexical decision
parsing
prime
priming
priming effect
psycholinguistics
regressive saccades
response accuracy
response latency
saccades
Spoonerism
target
tip-of-the-tongue phenomena

Terms concerning language processing

bottom-up processing
cohort
cohort model
garden path sentences
late closure
minimal attachment
module
morphological parsing
postlexical decomposition
prelexical decomposition
sentence ambiguity
syntactic parser
top-down processing

Terms related to psycholinguistic models

connectionist models
dual-route models
nodes
parallel processing model
psycholinguistic model
serial processing model
single-route models
symbolic models

For more information on the sources used in this chapter, go to **bedfordstmartins .com/linguistics/psycholinguistics** and click on **Sources**.

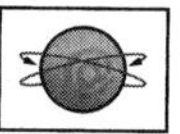

Recommended Reading

Berko-Gleason, Jean, and Nan Bernstein Ratner. 1998. *Psycholinguistics*. Philadelphia: Harcourt Brace.
Gernsbacher, M.A. 1994. *Handbook of Psycholinguistics*. New York: Academic Press.
Kess, J. 1992. *Psycholinguistics*. Philadelphia: John Benjamins.

Exercises

1. How do psycholinguistic investigations of language differ from theoretical linguistic investigations?

2. Consider the following slips of the tongue. What does each reveal about the process of language production?
   a) They *laked* across the *swim*.
   b) The spy was *gound* and *bagged*.
   c) I will *zee* you in the *bark*.

3. Imagine that you read that a psycholinguist has reported an experiment in which a priming effect was found for morphological roots on suffixed past tense forms in a lexical decision task.
   a) State the dependent variable in the experiment.
   b) Give an example of a prime stimulus.
   c) Give an example of a target stimulus.

4. Complete the following sentences by filling in the blanks. In each case, what type of top-down processing and bottom-up processing guided your decision?
   a) The children ______ running in the park.
   b) All ______ movies I like have happy endings.
   c) He tends to see everything as ______ and white.

5. Recall that according to the cohort model, a word is recognized from beginning to end, one phoneme at a time. According to the cohort model, how many phonemes of each of the following words would have to be processed before a hearer would be sure which word had been spoken?
   a) giraffe
   b) splat
   c) computerize

6. Write the garden path sentences in examples *9* and *10* of this chapter on separate index cards. Take a few other cards and write an unambiguous sentence on each of them. Now, have some friends try to read aloud the sentences on the cards. Do they show evidence that the garden path sentences are more difficult to process?

7. What is a processing model? Try to describe the process of reading single words in terms of a processing model that contains specific modules.

8. In this chapter, parsing has been discussed in the context of sentence processing. The notion of parsing, however, can also be used to describe how morphologically complex words are parsed. Describe, in terms of parsing, how you think the following multimorphemic words would be processed.
   a) bookmark
   b) unredoable
   c) overbearing

9. Imagine yourself as a psycholinguist trying to devise experiments to investigate how people do language. What experiments would you make up to address the following questions? Be as specific as possible about how you would interpret the question and about what you would do to try to find an answer through psycholinguistic experimentation.
   a) Are semantically abstract words easier to process than semantically concrete ones?
   b) Are simple clauses more difficult to understand than conjoined clauses?
   c) Do people read words from beginning to end?
   d) Do people with different levels of education process language in fundamentally different ways?
   e) Does the way you parse a sentence depend on what language you speak?

fourteen

Brain and Language

Gary Libben

The goal of neurology is to understand humanity.

– WILDER PENFIELD

OBJECTIVES

In this chapter, you will learn:

- how the human brain is structured as it relates to language
- how neurolinguists have investigated the brain and language
- what studies of brain damage tell us about the brain and language

In this chapter we will be concerned with the branch of neuroscience that has as its goal the understanding of how language is represented and processed in the brain. This field of study is called **neurolinguistics**. Although the study of the relationship between brain and language is still in its infancy, much has already been learned about which parts of the brain are involved in various aspects of language production and comprehension. The field of neurolinguistics has also done much to deepen the way we think about the nature of linguistic competence.

The chapter provides a brief survey of brain structure and the methods that are currently available to study the brain. This is followed by a discussion of the different types of language disturbance that result from brain damage and a discussion of how phonology, morphology, syntax, and semantics may be represented in the brain. The chapter concludes by reviewing the current answers to the important neurolinguistic question, Where is language?

1 The Human Brain

Contained within your skull is about 1,400 grams of pinkish-white matter. It may be the most complex 1,400 grams in the galaxy. For most of human history, however, the role of the brain as the center of mental life remained completely unknown. Even the Greek philosopher Aristotle believed that its primary function was to cool the blood.

We now know much more about the structure and functioning of the brain. But in many ways we are still quite like Aristotle, finding it hard to believe that this wrinkled mass of nerve cells could be the stuff that dreams, fears, and knowledge are made of. Nevertheless, it is, and the task of brain science (or **neuroscience**) is to understand how the breadth and depth of human experience is coded in brain matter.

The brain is composed of nerve cells or **neurons** that are the basic information-processing units of the nervous system. The human brain contains about 10 billion neurons that are organized into networks of almost unimaginable complexity. This complexity results from the fact that each neuron can be directly linked with up to ten thousand other neurons. But the brain is not simply a mass of interconnected neurons; it is composed of structures that seem to play specific roles in the integrated functioning of the brain. The following sections provide a brief overview of these structures.

1.1 The Cerebral Cortex

The brain encompasses all the neurological structures above the spinal cord and appears to have evolved from the bottom up. The lower brain structures are shared by almost all animals. These structures are responsible for the maintenance of functions such as respiration, heart rate, and muscle coordination that are essential to the survival of all animals. As we move farther away from the spinal cord, however, we begin to find structures that have developed differently in different species. At the highest level of the brain, the **cerebral cortex**, the differences are most pronounced. Reptiles and amphibians have no cortex at all, and the progression from lower to higher mammals is marked by dramatic increases in the proportion of cortex to total amount of brain tissue. The human brain has the greatest proportion of cortex to brain mass of all animals.

In humans, the cortex is a grey wrinkled mass that sits like a cap over the rest of the brain. The wrinkled appearance results from the cortex being folded in upon itself. This folding allows a great amount of cortical matter to be compressed into the limited space provided by the human skull (in much the same way as the folding of a handkerchief allows it to fit into a jacket pocket). It has been estimated that up to 65 percent of the cortex is hidden within its folds.

It is the human cortex that accounts for our distinctness in the animal world, and it is within the human cortex that the secrets of language representation and processing are to be found. The remainder of our discussion of brain structure, therefore, will focus on the features of the cerebral cortex.

1.2 The Cerebral Hemispheres

The most important orientation points in mapping the cortex are the folds on its surface. The folds of the cortex have two parts: **sulci** (pronounced /sʌlsaj/; singular:

sulcus), which are areas where the cortex is folded in, and **gyri** (singular: **gyrus**), which are areas where the cortex is folded out toward the surface.

Figure 14.1 shows a human brain as seen from above, illustrating the many sulci and gyri of the cortex. A very prominent feature is the deep sulcus (in this case called a **fissure** because of its size) that extends from the front of the brain to the back. This fissure, which is known as the **longitudinal fissure**, separates the left and right **cerebral hemispheres**. In many ways, the cerebral hemispheres can be considered to be separate brains and indeed are often referred to as the left brain and the right brain. There are two main reasons for this.

First, the hemispheres are almost completely anatomically separate. The main connection between them is a bundle of nerve fibers known as the **corpus callosum**, whose primary function is to allow the two hemispheres to communicate with one another.

The other reason for considering the hemispheres to be separate brains is that they show considerable functional distinctness. In terms of muscle movement and sensation, each hemisphere is responsible for half the body—oddly enough, the opposite half. Thus, the left hemisphere controls the right side of the body and the right hemisphere controls the left side of the body. These **contralateral** (contra = opposite, lateral = side) responsibilities of the cerebral hemispheres account for the fact that people who suffer damage to one hemisphere of the brain (as a result of a stroke or accident) will exhibit paralysis on the opposite side of the body.

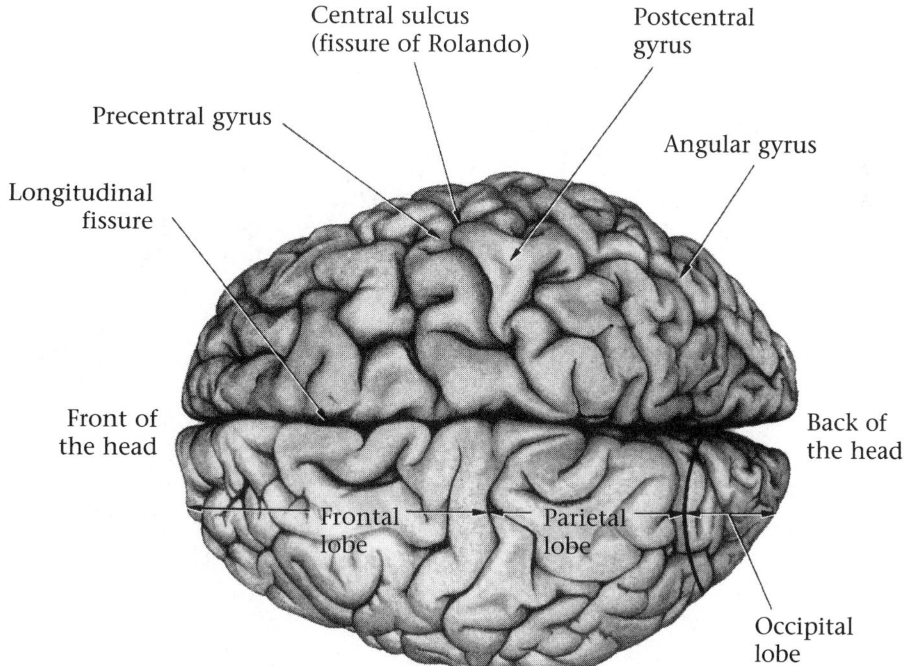

Figure 14.1 The cerebral hemispheres seen from above the head. Note the many fissures and gyri of the cortex and the prominence of the longitudinal fissure that separates the left and right hemispheres.

The hemispheres also show functional distinctness with respect to higher cognitive functions. In general, the left hemisphere seems to excel in analytic tasks such as arithmetic, whereas the right hemisphere excels in tasks that require an overall appreciation of complex patterns, such as the recognition of familiar faces and melodies.

Despite the fact that the hemispheres show such specialization, we should be cautioned against sweeping generalizations about left brain versus right brain abilities or strategies. In all probability, complex mental activities involve the coordinated functioning of both hemispheres. The representation of language in the brain provides a useful example of this.

Most right-handed individuals have language represented in the left cerebral hemisphere and are therefore said to be left **lateralized** for language. But not every aspect of language is represented in the left hemisphere of right-handers. Adults who have had their left cerebral hemispheres surgically removed lose most but not all of their linguistic competence. They typically lose the ability to speak and process complex syntactic patterns but retain some language comprehension ability. Clearly, it must be the right hemisphere that is responsible for whatever language-processing ability remains (see Figure 14.2).

It has also been reported that right-handed patients who suffer damage to the right cerebral hemisphere exhibit difficulty in understanding jokes and metaphors in everyday conversation. These patients are able to provide only a literal or concrete interpretation of figurative sentences such as *He was wearing a loud tie.* They frequently misunderstand people because they cannot use loudness and intonation as cues to whether a speaker is angry, excited, or merely joking. Thus, the right hemisphere has a distinct role to play in normal language use.

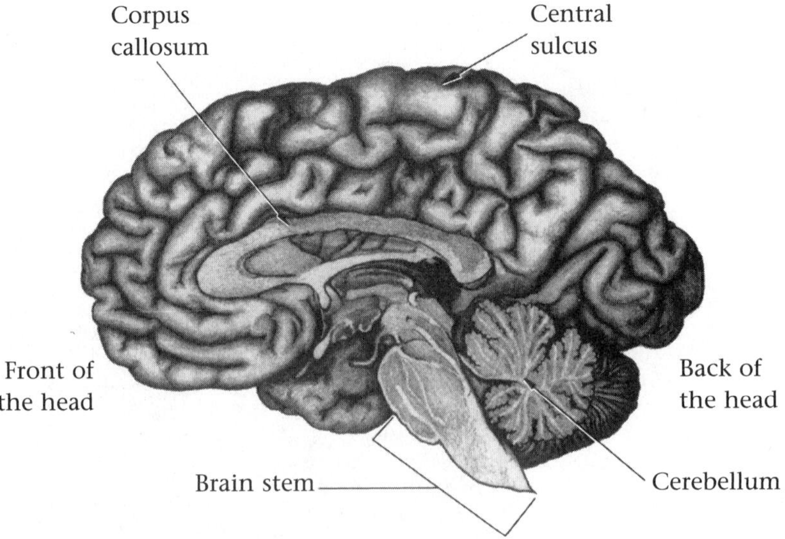

Figure 14.2 The right hemisphere seen from the inside. In this picture the corpus callosum has been cut so that one hemisphere may be separated from the other. Note how the grey cortex caps the lower structures (the brain stem and cerebellum), which are whitish in color.

Finally, consideration of language representation in the brains of left-handers makes matters even more complex. Contrary to what might be expected, few left-handers have a mirror image representation for language (that is, language localization in the right hemisphere). Rather, they tend to show significant language representation in both hemispheres. Thus, left-handers are generally less lateralized for language.

To sum up, although the left and right hemispheres have different abilities and different responsibilities, complex skills such as language do not always fall neatly into one hemisphere or the other. Research into why this is the case constitutes an important part of neuroscience. This research promises to reveal much about the cerebral hemispheres and about the individual representations and processes that comprise language.

1.3 The Lobes of the Cortex

We have seen that the cerebral hemispheres make distinct contributions to the overall functioning of the brain. In addition, each hemisphere contains substructures that appear to have distinct responsibilities. The substructures of the cortex in each hemisphere are called **lobes**. Like the hemispheres, the lobes of the cortex can be located with reference to prominent fissures, sulci, and gyri, which are useful as orientation points in much the same way that rivers and mountain ranges are useful in finding particular locations on a map. As can be seen in Figure 14.3, the **central sulcus** (also called the fissure of Rolando) extends from the top of the cortex to another groove known as the **lateral fissure** (also called the Sylvian fissure). These

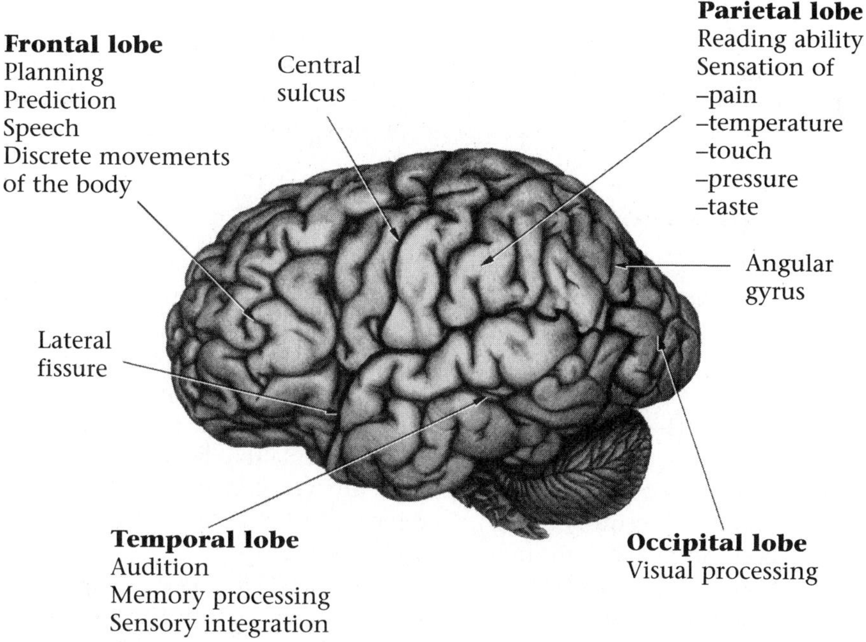

Figure 14.3 The left hemisphere seen from the outside

two features are important in the delineation of the cerebral lobes. The **frontal lobe** lies in front of the central sulcus and the **parietal lobe** lies behind it. The **temporal lobe** is the area beneath the lateral fissure. The fourth lobe, the **occipital lobe**, is not clearly marked by an infolding of the cortex, but can be identified as the area to the rear of the **angular gyrus** (which has been found to play an important role in reading).

Figure 14.3 shows the left hemisphere of the brain. It indicates the location of each lobe and its specialized functions. Assuming that this is the brain of a right-hander, it is also possible to identify those areas of the cortex that have a particular role to play in language processing, as we will see.

2 Investigating the Brain

Imagine that you could open the top of a living human being's skull and observe the brain while the individual is engaged in activities such as reading, writing, watching a hockey game, or having a heated argument. What would you see? The answer is—nothing! To the outside observer, the working brain shows no evidence of its activity. This is clearly a problem for the field of neurolinguistics, which requires the use of special investigative techniques to uncover the secrets of where and how language is processed in the brain. In addition, these special techniques must meet the ethical requirements of research with human subjects. While other neuroscientists are able to do much of their research using animal subjects, this option is not available to neurolinguists.

Imposing as they may be, the problems of investigating the processing of language in the brain are not insurmountable. Recent decades have seen a number of technological advances that have greatly facilitated the investigation of the question, What is going on in the brain when people are engaged in language behavior? In the following sections, we discuss some of the techniques of neurolinguistic investigation.

2.1 Autopsy Studies

Until recently, the only way to study the brain was through **autopsy studies**. This technique was most often carried out with patients who were admitted to hospitals displaying a neurological disorder. Careful observations were made of a patient's behavior, and subsequent to his or her death, the brain was examined to determine which areas were damaged. By comparing the area of brain damage and the type of disorder the patient displayed while alive, neurologists could develop theories about the role of the damaged brain parts in normal brain functioning.

A famous example of this type of analysis comes from the work of Paul Broca, a nineteenth-century French neurologist. In 1860, Broca observed a patient who had been hospitalized for more than twenty years in Paris. For most of his hospitalization, the patient was almost completely unable to speak, but appeared to understand everything that was said to him. Toward the end of his life (he died at age fifty-seven), he also developed a paralysis of the right arm and leg. Immediately after the patient's death (as a result of an unrelated infection), Broca examined the brain. It showed severe damage (called a **lesion**) in the lower rear area of the left frontal lobe. Broca concluded that because the patient was unable to speak, this part of the frontal lobe must normally be responsible for speech production. Since that time, many other autopsy studies have supported Broca's conclusions. This lower rear portion of the left frontal lobe is now called **Broca's area** (see Figure 14.4, which shows this and other language-processing areas of the left hemisphere). As will be discussed in Section 3.1, the impairment of the ability to speak as a result of brain damage is called **Broca's aphasia**.

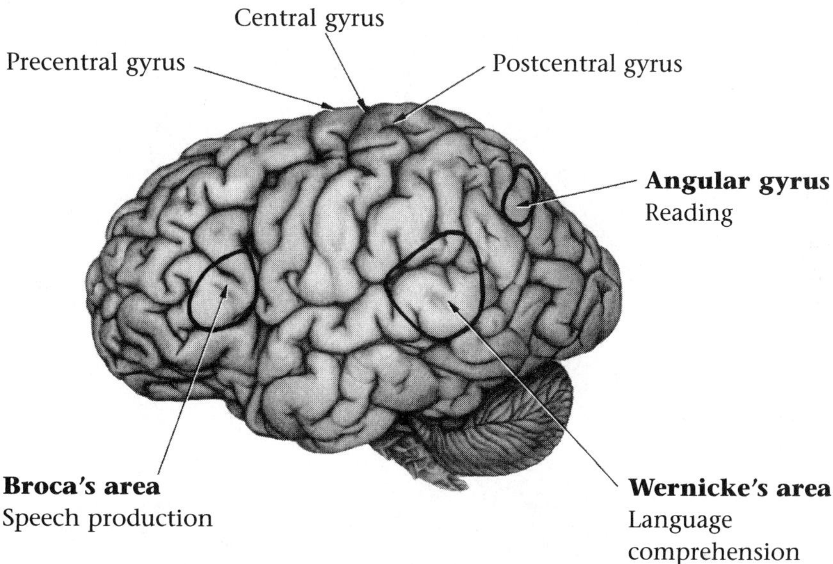

Figure 14.4 Language processes in the left hemisphere. Damage to Broca's area is usually associated with nonfluent speech and difficulty processing complex syntactic patterns. Damage to Wernicke's area (see Section 3.2) is usually associated with comprehension disturbances. Damage to the area around the angular gyrus results in reading impairment.

2.2 Images of the Living Brain

Autopsy analysis has been and continues to be an important tool in the understanding of the brain. But an autopsy can be carried out only after the patient's death. Therefore, whatever information it reveals about the nature and extent of the patient's brain damage can no longer be of any use in treatment of that patient.

Computerized axial tomography (also called **CT scanning**) is a technique that uses a narrow beam of X-rays to create brain images that take the form of a series of brain slices. CT scans have offered neuroscientists their first opportunity to look inside a living brain. However, like autopsy, CT scanning provides a static image of the brain. It is most useful in identifying brain lesions and tumors.

A number of new techniques have recently emerged that make it possible to study the brain in action. One such technique is **positron emission tomography** (also called **PET**). The technique capitalizes on one of the brain's many interesting properties—it is extremely hungry for glucose and oxygen. Although the brain accounts for only about 2 percent of total body weight, it consumes about 20 percent of the oxygen the body uses while at rest. This oxygen is, of course, carried to the brain by the blood.

In the PET technique, positron-emitting isotopes, which function as radioactive tracers, are injected into the arteries in combination with glucose. The rate at which the radioactive glucose is used by specific regions of the brain is recorded while the subject is engaged in various sorts of cognitive activities. These recordings are used to produce maps of areas of high brain activity associated with particular cognitive functions. Examples of such PET maps are represented in Figure 14.5.

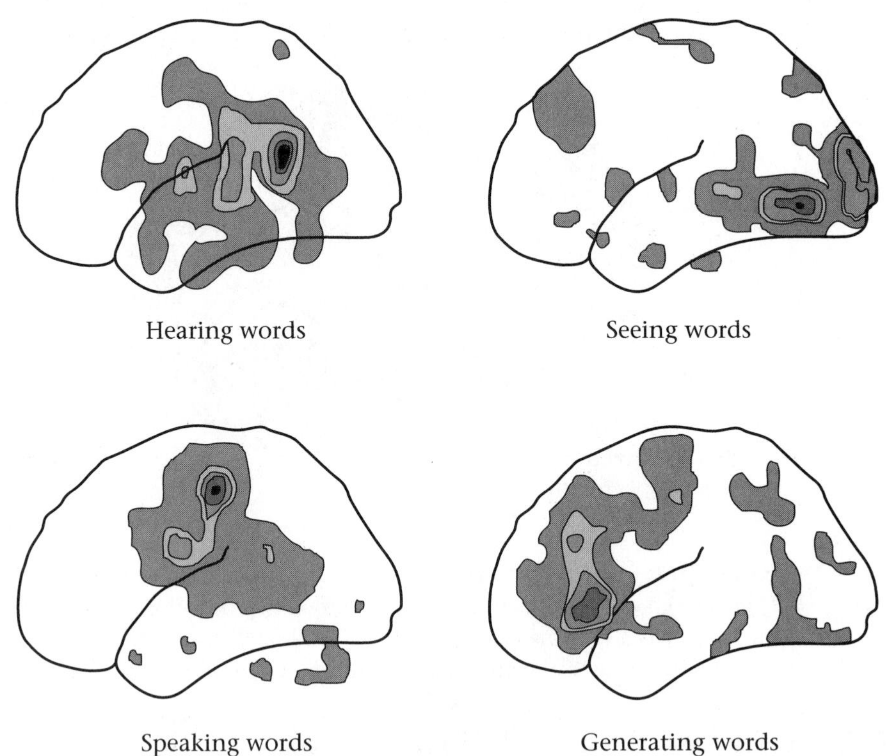

Figure 14.5 PET scans show how blood flow to the brain shifts to different locations depending on which task is being performed.

Another dynamic brain-imaging technique that has become increasingly important over the past few years is **functional magnetic resonance imaging (fMRI)**. This technique yields information on areas of high brain activity during the performance of cognitive tasks but is somewhat less invasive than PET because it does not require the injection of radioactive compounds. The fMRI technique allows many measurements to be taken in a single testing session and offers a good measure of how brain activity changes during language comprehension and production. At present, however, the best fMRI machines employ high-field permanent magnets and require expensive installations not currently available at most research centers.

A final extremely promising technique for the study of how language is processed in the brain is **magnetoencephalography** (**MEG**). The MEG technique records very subtle changes in the magnetic fields generated within the brain. Although MEG currently requires a very expensive apparatus, it has advantages over all the other techniques discussed so far. In contrast to PET, it is noninvasive, and like fMRI, it provides detailed information on which parts of the brain are involved in a language-processing activity. Its key advantage is that it also provides excellent time resolution. Using the MEG technique, researchers are able to gain a millisecond-by-millisecond record of how the brain responds to a stimulus event, such as the presentation of a single word. In this way, MEG combines the time-resolution advantages of event-related potentials (ERP) (discussed in Chapter 13) and the spatial resolution advantages of fMRI.

Modern brain-imaging techniques have greatly increased our knowledge of where language processing takes place in the brain. It has been found, for example, that when subjects speak, much blood flows to the left hemisphere of the cortex and to Broca's area in particular. When subjects read, much blood flows to the occipital lobe (because it is responsible for visual processing), to the angular gyrus (which has a special role to play in reading), and to other areas of the left hemisphere. These observations support the view that the left hemisphere is primarily responsible for language and that there are specific language areas within the left hemisphere.

Finally, fMRI studies are playing an important role in increasing our understanding of the differences that might exist between language processing in a mother tongue and language processing in a second language. Second language processing has been shown to involve a wider variety of cortical sites. This supports the view that the less automatic nature of language use in a second language requires the involvement of diverse mental processes in addition to those specifically dedicated to language.

2.3 Learning from Hemispheric Connections and Disconnections

In the techniques that have been described, information about language representation in the brain is gained through an investigation of the brain itself. In this section, we review an alternative approach—one that examines behavior that can be associated with a particular brain hemisphere.

Dichotic Listening Studies

Dichotic listening studies have been extremely important in the accumulation of the knowledge we possess about the specialization of the cerebral hemispheres. The technique capitalizes on the property of the brain that we discussed in Section 1.2—namely, that each hemisphere is primarily wired to the opposite side of the body (including the head). So, most of the input to your right ear goes to the left hemisphere of your brain. Now, if the left cerebral hemisphere is indeed specialized for language processing in right-handers, these individuals should process language better through the right ear.

If you are right-handed, you will most probably be able to verify this by observing the difference between holding a telephone receiver to your right ear and holding it to your left ear during a conversation. When the receiver is held to the right ear, it will appear that the speech is louder and clearer. This phenomenon is known as the **right ear advantage** (**REA**). In the laboratory technique, stereo earphones are used and different types of stimuli are presented to each ear. In general, the right ear shows an advantage for words, numbers, and Morse code, whereas the left ear shows an advantage for the perception of melodies and environmental sounds such as bird songs.

Split Brain Studies

If the left hemisphere is wired to the right ear, why is it possible to understand speech presented to the left ear? There are two reasons for this. The first is that the auditory pathways to the brain are not completely crossed—there are also secondary links between each hemisphere and the ear on the same side of the body. The second is that after the right hemisphere receives information from the left ear, that information can be transferred to the left hemisphere via the corpus callosum—the bundle of fibers that connects the two hemispheres.

Evidence concerning the crucial role that the corpus callosum plays in normal brain functioning comes from the study of patients who have had this pathway surgically severed. Studies that have investigated the effects of this surgery on cognition are referred to as **split brain experiments**. They have provided dramatic illustrations of what happens when the hemispheres cannot communicate with one another.

It appears from the behavior of split brain patients that although the right hemisphere does show some language understanding, it is mute. In one of the many split brain experiments, a patient is blindfolded and an object (e.g., a key) is placed in one hand. When the key is held in the right hand, the patient can easily name it, because the right hand is connected to the left hemisphere that can compute speech output. However, when the key is placed in the left hand, the patient cannot say what it is. The right hemisphere, which receives information from the left hand, knows what is there, but it can neither put this into words nor transfer the information across the severed corpus callosum to the left hemisphere.

Split brain experiments have presented new and important knowledge about the functioning of the brain. In terms of overall investigative methodology, however, they are not quite as exotic as they seem. In fact, the logic of split brain experiments is identical to the logic employed by Broca in 1860. In both cases the researcher endeavors to learn how the normal brain works by examining which functions are lost as a result of the brain damage. In the case of split brain studies, the damage is surgically induced. In the case of Broca's aphasia, disease caused an "experiment in nature." In the following section, we return to these experiments in nature and examine what they reveal about language representation in the brain.

3 Aphasia

The term **aphasia** refers to the loss of language ability as a result of damage to the brain. The most common cause of aphasia is **stroke** (also called a **cerebrovascular accident**). A stroke occurs when the normal flow of blood to the brain is disrupted, preventing neurons from receiving oxygen and nutrients. Aphasia can also be caused by blows to the head, brain infection, brain tumors, and brain hemorrhage. Currently, aphasia affects more than one million people in North America. The syndrome is equally common in men and women, and is most likely to occur in persons over the age of fifty.

In general, the amount and type of aphasic disturbance that a patient will exhibit depends on how much the brain is damaged and where it is damaged. Most individuals who suffer aphasic impairment experience a mixture of deficits in speaking, listening, reading, and writing. However, some other forms of aphasia are much more specific. In these more specific forms, particular skills are lost and others remain intact. The study of these specific aphasias can tell us much about the building blocks of language in the brain. Sections 3.1 and 3.2 discuss the two most important specific aphasias.

3.1 Nonfluent Aphasia

Nonfluent aphasia (also called **motor aphasia**) results from damage to parts of the brain in front of the central sulcus. Recall that an important part of the frontal lobe is concerned with motor activity and that the bottom rear portion of the left frontal lobe (Broca's area) is responsible for the articulation of speech (see Figure 14.4 on page 469). Not surprisingly, therefore, nonfluent patients show slow, effortful speech production (hence the term *nonfluent*). The most severe form of nonfluent aphasia is **global aphasia**. In this type of aphasia, the patient is completely mute. Of the less severe forms, Broca's aphasia is the most important.

The speech of Broca's aphasics is very halting. Patients have great difficulty in accurately producing the needed phonemes to say a word. For example, a patient who wishes to produce the sentence in *1a* would be likely to produce the utterance in *1b*.

1)
a. It's hard to eat with a spoon.
b. . . . har eat . . . wit . . . poon

The ellipsis dots (. . .) between the words in *1b* indicate periods of silence in the production of the utterance. Sentences produced at this slow rate tend to also lack normal sentence intonation. This is a common characteristic of the speech of Broca's aphasics and is called **dysprosody**. Note how the patient simplifies the consonant clusters in the words *hard* and *spoon* and changes the /θ/ to /t/ in the word *with.* The speech errors that result from these sorts of phonemic errors are called **phonemic paraphasias**.

It is tempting to think that the impairment of speech production in Broca's aphasia is caused by the fact that Broca's area is adjacent to the motor strip that controls movement of the facial muscles. The problem with this hypothesis is that damage to Broca's area usually produces only mild weakness of the muscles on the opposite side of the face and no permanent damage. Yet, for some reason, even people who can still control the muscles used in speech cannot use language properly after damage to Broca's area. This suggests that Broca's area has a language-specific responsibility.

Broca's Aphasia as a Syntactic Disorder

Returning to the utterance in *1b,* note that the patient also omits a number of words that would normally be used in this utterance. The words that are omitted include *it, is, to, a*—the sort of words that we too would be likely to omit if we were writing a telegram (for example, *I will meet you in the airport lounge*→*Meet you in airport lounge*). These "little words" are often called **function words**, and their omission in the speech of Broca's aphasics has been referred to as **telegraphic speech**. (We will return to the problem of determining which items belong to the set of function words in Section 5.)

One possible account of the speech of Broca's aphasics is that it results from an economy of effort. As speech production is very effortful for these patients, they use as few words as possible because, like telegram writers, they are "paying" by the word. But there are other characteristics of their linguistic abilities that point to a deeper cause—the disturbance of syntactic competence.

In addition to omitting function words, Broca's aphasics tend to omit inflectional affixes such as *-ing, -ed,* and *-en* in words such as *running, chased,* and *broken.* They also show difficulty judging the grammaticality of sentences. For example, given sentences such as the ones in *2,* Broca's aphasics will not always be able to determine which ones are grammatical and which ones are not.

2)

a. The boy ate it up.
b. *The boy ate up it.
c. *Boy ate it up.
d. The boy ate up the cake.

Finally, a close examination of the comprehension of Broca's aphasics offers further support to the view that there is a syntactic component to the disorder.

3)

a. The mouse was chased by the cat.
b. The dog was chased by the cat.
c. The cat was chased by the mouse.

Broca's aphasics tend to interpret sentences such as *3a* correctly. In a sentence such as this, knowledge about the behavior of cats and mice helps the patient guess correctly at the meaning of the sentence. For sentences such as *3b,* however, in which knowledge of the world is not a reliable guide to comprehension, patients are unsure about the meaning. Finally, Broca's aphasics tend to interpret a sentence such as *3c* as though it had the same meaning as *3a.* When we read a sentence like *3c,* we recognize it as describing an unlikely event, but our interpretation is driven by the syntax of the sentence, not by our knowledge of the world. Many Broca's aphasics appear not to have this ability.

These sorts of observations have led many neurolinguists to reconsider the traditional view that Broca's aphasia is simply a production deficit. The possibility that Broca's aphasia also involves some central disturbance of syntactic competence is intriguing and may lead to a deeper understanding of how syntactic knowledge is represented in the brain. We will return to this question in Section 4.

A final point about Broca's aphasia is of a less technical nature but is of great importance to the understanding of the syndrome as a whole. Most Broca's aphasics are acutely aware of their language deficit and are typically very frustrated by it. It is as though they have complete understanding of what they should say but, to their constant dismay, find themselves unable to say it. This plight of Broca's aphasics is consistent with our understanding of the role of the frontal lobe, which is usually the site of lesions in the syndrome. Broca's area of the frontal lobe plays an extremely important role in language; however, it does not seem to be involved in the semantic relationships between words and the relationship between units of language and units of thought. The neurological basis of these meaning relationships remains almost entirely unknown. From the analysis of nonfluent aphasia in general and Broca's aphasia in particular, however, we suspect that these semantic relationships are the responsibility of areas of the brain that lie behind the central sulcus—in the temporal and parietal lobes of the brain (see Figure 14.3). This suspicion is supported by the type of language deficits associated with damage to the temporal-parietal lobes.

3.2 Fluent Aphasia

The type of aphasia that results from damage to parts of the left cortex behind the central sulcus is referred to as **fluent aphasia** (or **sensory aphasia**). This type of aphasia stands in sharp contrast to nonfluent aphasia. Fluent aphasics have no difficulty producing language, but have a great deal of difficulty selecting, organizing, and monitoring their language production.

The most important type of fluent aphasia is called **Wernicke's aphasia**. The syndrome is named after the German physiologist Carl Wernicke, who, in 1874, published a now famous report of a kind of aphasia that was almost the complete opposite of Broca's aphasia. It was determined from autopsy data that this type of aphasia was associated with a lesion in the temporal lobe just below the most posterior (rear) portion of the lateral fissure. In severe cases, the lesion could also extend upward into the lower portion of the parietal lobe. This area of the brain is now known as **Wernicke's area** (see Figure 14.4).

In contrast to Broca's aphasics, Wernicke's aphasics are generally unaware of their deficit. Their speech typically sounds very good: there are no long pauses; sentence intonation is normal; function words are used appropriately; word order is usually syntactically correct. The problem is that the patient rarely makes any sense. The following is a conversation between an examiner (E) and a Wernicke's patient (P).

4)

E: How are you today, Mrs. A?
P: Yes.
E: Have I ever tested you before?
P: No. I mean I haven't.
E: Can you tell me what your name is?
P: No, I don't I . . . right I'm right now here.
E: What is your address?
P: I cud /kʌd/ if I can help these this like you know . . . to make it.
We are seeing for him. That is my father.

The patient in this conversation produces a number of errors. But note that most of these errors are different from the kinds of errors made by Broca's aphasics. While the patient is able to produce some well-formed structures (e.g., *no, I don't*), these structures appear intermittently amid various unrelated fragments. Not only are these constructions unrelated to each other, but they are also unrelated to the examiner's questions. It appears that the patient has no understanding of the questions being asked.

This patient displays a significant but not severe form of Wernicke's aphasia. Her speech appears to result from a semirandom selection of words and short phrases. In very severe cases of this syndrome, phonemes are also randomly selected, and the result is speech that has the intonational characteristics of English but actually contains very few real words of the language. This is termed **jargonaphasia**.

The type of deficit found in Wernicke's aphasia leads us to a greater understanding and a deeper consideration of the nature of language comprehension. Wernicke's aphasia is primarily a comprehension deficit. But as we have seen, when comprehension breaks down, most of what we call language ability breaks down with it. Patients cannot express themselves because they cannot understand what they have just said and use that understanding in the planning of what to say next. In a very real sense, these patients have lost contact with themselves (and therefore with the rest of the world). Wernicke's patients cannot have coherent trains of thought—the brain damage does not allow the elements of the train to be connected.

In summary, our discussion of nonfluent and fluent aphasia has demonstrated how normal language use is a marriage of content and form. In the case of nonfluent aphasia, form is compromised but the content of language remains relatively intact. In contrast, fluent aphasia is characterized by a rapid flow of form with little content.

4 Acquired Dyslexia and Dysgraphia

Reading and writing skills involve a complex array of perceptual and motor skills. In this section, we will consider impairments of reading and writing that are caused by damage to the brain. The impairment of reading ability is called **acquired dyslexia** (or **acquired alexia**). The impairment of writing ability is called **acquired dysgraphia** (or **acquired agraphia**). In both cases the term *acquired* indicates that the patient possessed normal reading and/or writing ability prior to brain damage and distinguishes the syndromes from developmental dyslexia and developmental dysgraphia, which deal with disturbances of reading and writing development in children.

4.1 Reading and Writing Disturbances in Aphasia

Acquired dyslexia and dysgraphia typically accompany the aphasic syndromes that we considered in Section 3. Most Broca's aphasics show writing disturbances that are comparable to their speaking deficits. In other words, a patient who cannot pronounce the word *spoon* will also not be able to write it correctly. The resulting error in writing (e.g., *poon*) is called a **paragraphia**. In spontaneous writing, Broca's aphasics also tend to omit function words and inflectional affixes. Finally, while the silent reading of Broca's aphasics is very good, their reading aloud shows the same telegraphic style as their spontaneous speech. These observations reinforce the view that the deficit in Broca's aphasia is much more than a speech articulation deficit. It is a production deficit at a very deep level of language planning.

Wernicke's aphasics also show reading and writing deficits that match their deficits in speaking and listening. The writing of Wernicke's aphasics is formally very good. They typically retain good spelling and handwriting. However, like their speaking, what they write makes little sense. Reading comprehension is also severely impaired in Wernicke's aphasia. Patients can see the letters and words, but cannot make any sense of them. Again the conclusion to be drawn is that Wernicke's aphasia, like Broca's aphasia, involves a central disturbance of language competence—the knowledge that underlies language functioning. In such cases of central language disturbance, whatever impairment the patient has in listening and speaking will be matched in reading and writing.

4.2 Acquired Dyslexia as the Dominant Language Deficit

In addition to the reading and writing deficits that accompany aphasia, there are many cases in which the disruption of reading and writing ability is the dominant symptom. This typically follows damage in and around the angular gyrus of the parietal lobe. An analysis of these types of disabilities has led to some very interesting theories about the nature of reading (at least in English).

Before we proceed to discuss two contrasting types of acquired dyslexia, it might be worthwhile to reflect on the abilities involved in the reading of words. Up to this point in the chapter you have read over five thousand words. Some of these words (such as the function words) are very familiar to you and you probably recognized them as wholes. But others, such as *angular gyrus,* are words that you probably read for the first time. How then could you know how to pronounce them? Many theorists believe that readers maintain a set of spelling-to-sound rules that enable them to read new words aloud. These rules are important in the development of reading ability and in the addition of new words to our reading vocabulary.

Phonological dyslexia is a type of acquired dyslexia in which the patient seems to have lost the ability to use spelling-to-sound rules. Phonological dyslexics can only read words that they have seen before. Asked to read a word such as *blug* aloud, they either say nothing or produce a known word that is visually similar to the target (e.g., *blue* or *bug*).

Surface dyslexia is the opposite of phonological dyslexia. Surface dyslexics seem unable to recognize words as wholes. Instead, they must process all words through a set of spelling-to-sound rules. This is shown by the kinds of errors they make. Surface dyslexics do not have difficulty reading words such as *bat* that are regularly spelled. They read irregularly spelled words such as *yacht,* however, by applying regular rules and thus producing /jætʃt/. The most interesting aspect of surface dyslexics' reading ability is that they understand what they produce, not what they see. For example, a surface dyslexic would be likely to read the word *worm* as

/wɔrm/ (and not /wərm/). When asked what the word means, the patient would answer: the opposite of *cold.*

Data from acquired dyslexia allow researchers to build models that specify the components of normal reading ability and their relationship to each other. Clearly, this type of analysis plays a very important role in the development of our understanding of language, the mind, and the brain.

5 Linguistic Theory and Aphasia

Looking at aphasia in terms of linguistic theory gives us a new perspective on language in the brain. Linguistic theory has been traditionally concerned with the structure of language, not with how it is used in the processes of listening, speaking, reading, and writing. In contrast, the traditional way of looking at aphasia has been in terms of what the patient can and cannot do. The involvement of theoretical linguists in the study of aphasia has caused a minor revolution in the field. Aphasia researchers have begun to think about the deficit in terms of the loss of semantic features, phonological rules, and perhaps syntactic tree structures. Theoretical linguists have also found that the study of aphasia offers an important area for testing theoretical distinctions, such as the one between derivational suffixes and inflectional suffixes. In this section, we will look at some of the areas in which the marriage of theoretical linguistics and neurolinguistics has been most fruitful. This fruitfulness has usually meant an increase in the sophistication of the questions that are asked about aphasia. It has also meant the discovery of new and often bizarre aphasic phenomena.

5.1 Features, Rules, and Underlying Forms

In the area of phonology, we have found that the phonemic paraphasias of Broca's aphasics usually differ from the target phoneme by only one distinctive feature (recall example *1* in Section 3.1: *with*→/wɪt/) and can therefore be easily described by phonological rules. Observations such as these lead us to believe that phonological features and rules might be good tools to characterize how language is represented and produced.

In the area of morphology, the study of aphasia has offered empirical support for the theoretical distinction between inflection and derivation. As we have discussed, Broca's aphasics show a sensitivity to this distinction in their omission of affixes in speech. Inflectional affixes are commonly dropped, but derivational affixes are usually retained. Perhaps most interesting is the tendency of some aphasics to produce underlying forms of morphemes in reading and repetition. Asked to repeat the word *illegal,* for example, some aphasics will produce *inlegal,* using the underlying form of the negative prefix rather than the allomorph that should occur before a base beginning with /l/. Again, errors such as these point to the possibility that phonological processes such as nasal assimilation and the notion of underlying form are not only an elegant way to represent linguistic competence but also relevant to the processing of language in the brain.

The study of aphasia also stands to shed light on the nature of semantic representations. Most of the work in this area has concentrated on the many subvarieties of acquired dyslexia. In a syndrome known as **deep dyslexia**, patients produce reading errors that are systematically related to the word that they are asked to read (in the sense that they share some semantic features but not others). Given the word *mother,* for example, a deep dyslexic is likely to read *father.*

The detailed study of semantic deficits associated with brain damage has also led to some very surprising discoveries. Most aphasics and dyslexics find abstract words much more difficult to process than concrete words. But there have been reports of concrete word dyslexia in which the patient shows exactly the opposite problem (having difficulty with concrete words such as *table*). There has even been a report of a patient who shows a selective inability to read words that refer to fruits and vegetables.

5.2 Agrammatism

In Section 3.1, we observed that many theorists now believe that Broca's aphasia involves a central syntactic deficit. The syndrome that is characterized by telegraphic speech has been given the name **agrammatism**—to indicate that grammatical ability has been lost. Agrammatism is the aphasic disturbance that has been most studied by linguists. As was discussed in Section 3.1, it is characterized by the omission of function words such as *it, is, to,* and *a,* by the omission of inflectional affixes, and by comprehension deficits in cases where the correct interpretation of a sentence is dependent on syntax alone.

In recent years, many linguists have become involved in the problems of characterizing the agrammatic deficit. These problems have raised specific questions such as, What exactly is a function word? and general questions such as, Is it possible to lose syntax? The involvement of linguists has also generated cross-linguistic studies of agrammatism that provide interesting insights into the interaction between characteristics of the syndrome and characteristics of particular languages.

5.3 Function Words

Intuitively, function words are grammatical words that can be distinguished from content words such as nouns, verbs, and adjectives. In terms of formal syntax, however, they are quite heterogeneous. They include pronouns, auxiliaries, determiners, and prepositions—items that do not fall into any single syntactic category. Much of the recent work in this area by linguists has concentrated on working out what exactly the so-called function words have in common. Some researchers have suggested that they form a phonological group—they are all words that do not normally take stress. Others have pointed to the fact that function words do not normally take affixes and therefore form a morphological group. Still others have suggested that syntactic theory should be modified so that all the words that are lost in agrammatism fall under the heading functional category (this would involve changing the status of prepositions, which are currently treated as lexical categories—see Chapter 5).

Whatever the outcome of this debate, it is clear that neurolinguistic evidence has presented a new set of challenges to the field of formal linguistics. One of these challenges is to build bridges between normal and pathological linguistic competence by finding units of analysis that are appropriate to both.

5.4 The Loss of Syntactic Competence

Another much more general challenge is to define what it means to possess syntactic competence such that we can speak of its loss. This challenge has forced researchers to address the question, What is the essence of syntactic knowledge? Is it the hierarchical arrangement of elements? Is it the representation of abstract entities such as +Q features and traces?

Some researchers have suggested that agrammatism involves the loss of the ability to deal with the details of syntactic structure, especially when there has been movement. They claim that agrammatics rely on word order rather than structure to interpret sentences and that they employ a default strategy that treats the first NP as the agent. This strategy works reasonably well for simple sentences in which the first NP can be assigned the thematic role of agent and the second NP can be assigned the role of theme, as in sentence *5a*. It results in miscomprehension, however, for sentences such as *5b* and *5c,* where the first NP does not have the role of agent.

5)

a. The girl kissed the boy.
b. The girl was kissed.
c. It was the girl that the boy kissed.

Other researchers have argued that agrammatism does not involve the loss of syntactic competence but rather an alteration of that competence. They have claimed that agrammatics have hierarchical syntactic structures but can no longer represent the traces that indicate an NP's position in deep structure. As a result, they are unable to recognize that the subject NP in *5b* bears the theme role since they do not realize that it is the complement of the verb in deep structure (see Section 3 of Chapter 6).

5.5 Agrammatism in Other Languages

Data from other languages have suggested that the original characterization of agrammatism as a syndrome in which function words and inflectional affixes are lost may not reflect the true nature of the deficit but rather the fact that the English language normally allows such deletions.

In English, affixes are typically attached to a base that is itself a free form. The past form of the verb *watch,* for example, is created by the addition of *-ed;* the third person singular is created by the addition of *-s*. However, not all languages work this way. In Semitic languages, such as Hebrew, the base is typically a string of three consonants, which is unpronounceable in its uninflected form. Inflections are produced by inserting vowels into this triconsonantal "skeleton." For example, the Hebrew root for the verb *to write* is /ktv/. The masculine third person present form of the verb is /kɔtɛv/, and the masculine third person past form is /katav/. If Hebrew agrammatics simply "lose" inflectional affixes the way they do in English, they should not be able to produce any verbs. As it turns out, Hebrew agrammatics do produce verbs, but instead of dropping inflectional forms, they choose randomly among them. This sort of evidence has provided a convincing argument against the view that agrammatic language results from a simple economy of effort. Rather, it seems that it is a linguistic deficit that involves the mis-selection of linguistic forms. It is only in languages such as English, where the base is also a legal free form, that the agrammatism is characterized by affix omission.

5.6 Where Is Language?

In this chapter we have outlined some important findings that have greatly increased our understanding of the types of language disturbances that result from damage to the brain, as well as our understanding of the association between specific areas of the brain and particular language functions. We have seen that Broca's area plays a crucial role in the articulation of speech and in the ability to create syntactic representations. Wernicke's area plays a key role in language comprehension, and the area surrounding the angular gyrus plays a special role in reading.

On the other hand, we have seen that, in an important sense, normal language use involves the integrated functioning of the entire cortex. Even right-handers who are strongly left lateralized for language show some language deficit in cases of damage to the right hemisphere. Finally, virtually all forms of aphasia are accompanied by word-finding difficulties. This observation suggests that the storage and retrieval of word forms may be diffusely represented in the brain.

There is, therefore, no simple answer to the question, Where is language? Even if there were, the task of neurolinguistics would be far from done, for the truly important question concerning language in the brain is not Where is it? but What is it? Indeed, the answer to the first question may have little to do with the answer to the second question. Consider, by analogy, the goal of understanding the American Congress: to what extent does the knowledge that Congress is to be found in Washington advance the understanding of how Congress works?

Ultimately, the goal of neurolinguistics is to understand, in neurological terms, what language is. The field of neurolinguistics is still a long way from being able to specify how syntax is coded in brain matter, or even how a word is represented. Nevertheless, as our discussion of agrammatism has revealed, recent work by neurolinguists has resulted in important new perspectives on the nature of language competence.

Summing Up

This chapter is concerned with how language is represented and processed in the human brain. **Dichotic listening studies** and **split brain experiments** have shown that the left hemisphere of the brain carries most of the responsibility for language processing in right-handed individuals. Neuroscientists have also used **autopsy studies**, **computerized axial tomography**, **positron emission tomography**, **functional magnetic resonance imaging**, and **magnetoencephalography** to determine the relationship between particular areas of the left hemisphere and specific language functions. It has been found that **Broca's area** is primarily responsible for speech production, **Wernicke's area** is primarily responsible for language comprehension, and the area surrounding the **angular gyrus** plays an important role in reading. Most of our knowledge concerning language representation in the brain comes from the study of **aphasia**—language disturbance resulting from damage to the brain. Neurolinguists, trained in both linguistics and **neuroscience**, carefully examine the manner in which linguistic competence is affected by brain damage. Their goal is to increase our understanding of how linguistic knowledge is coded in brain matter and how this knowledge is used in the processes of language comprehension and production.

Key Terms

General terms

neurolinguistics	neuroscience

Terms concerning the structure of the brain

angular gyrus	lateral fissure
Broca's area	lateralized
central sulcus	lobes
cerebral cortex	longitudinal fissure
cerebral hemispheres	neurons
contralateral	occipital lobe
corpus callosum	parietal lobe
fissure	sulcus/sulci
frontal lobe	temporal lobe
gyrus/gyri	Wernicke's area

Terms concerning how language in the brain is studied

autopsy studies	lesion
Broca's aphasia	magnetoencephalography (MEG)
computerized axial tomography (CT scanning)	positron emission tomography (PET)
dichotic listening studies	right ear advantage (REA)
functional magnetic resonance imaging (fMRI)	split brain experiments

Terms concerning language deficit caused by brain damage

acquired dysgraphia (*or* agraphia)	jargonaphasia
acquired dyslexia (*or* alexia)	motor aphasia
agrammatism	nonfluent aphasia
aphasia	paragraphia
Broca's aphasia	phonemic paraphasias
cerebrovascular accident	phonological dyslexia
deep dyslexia	sensory aphasia
dysprosody	stroke
fluent aphasia	surface dyslexia
function words	telegraphic speech
global aphasia	Wernicke's aphasia

For more information on the sources used in this chapter, go to **bedfordstmartins .com/linguistics/brainandlanguage** and click on **Sources**.

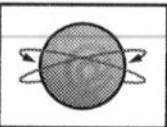

Recommended Reading

Caplan, D. 1987. *Neurolinguistics and Linguistic Aphasiology.* New York: Cambridge University Press.

Caplan, D. 1993. *Language: Structure, Processing, and Disorders.* Cambridge, MA: MIT Press.

Caplan, D. 2001. "Neurolinguistics." In *The Handbook of Linguistics.* Edited by Mark Aronoff and Janie Rees-Miller, 582–607. Malden, MA: Blackwell.

Coltheart, M., J. Patterson, and J.C. Marshall (eds.). 1980. *Deep Dyslexia.* London: Routledge & Kegan Paul.

Patterson, K.E., J.C. Marshall, and M. Coltheart (eds.). 1986. *Surface Dyslexia.* Hillsdale, NJ: Lawrence Erlbaum.

Rosenbek, J.C., L.L. Lapointe, and R.T. Wertz. 1989. *Aphasia: A Clinical Approach.* Boston: College-Hill Press.

Segalowitz, S. 1983. *Two Sides of the Brain.* Englewood Cliffs, NJ: Prentice-Hall.

Stemmer, B., and Whitaker, H.A. (eds.). 1988. *Handbook of Neurolinguistics.* San Diego, CA: Academic Press.

Exercises

1. What distinguishes the human brain from a nonhuman brain?

2. In what ways can the cerebral hemispheres be considered to be two separate brains?

3. Below is an unlabeled diagram of the left hemisphere. Choose four contrasting colors and color each lobe of the cortex. Use arrows to point to the central sulcus, the lateral fissure, and the angular gyrus. Finally, use a pencil to indicate areas of lesion that would result in Broca's aphasia, Wernicke's aphasia, and acquired dyslexia. Label these lesions.

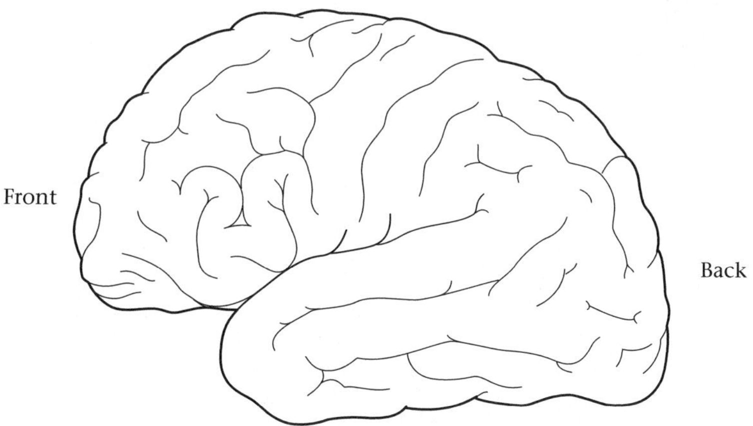

4. What are the relative advantages and disadvantages of the various techniques used to investigate the brain? Consider ethics, cost, intrusiveness, and type of information yielded.

5. What do dichotic listening tests tell us about the specialization of the cerebral hemispheres? Can you think of types of stimuli that would be interesting to present dichotically?

6. Do you think it is possible to learn how the normal brain functions by studying brain-damaged patients? What can the study of aphasia tell us about normal language competence?

7. Contrast the differences in behavior between fluent and nonfluent aphasics. What could explain these differences?

8. Describe the differences between phonological and surface dyslexia.

9. Many researchers have claimed that agrammatism involves a loss of syntactic knowledge. Imagine a type of aphasia that involves a loss of *phonological* knowledge. How would patients with this type of aphasia behave?

fifteen

Language in Social Contexts

Marjory Meechan
Janie Rees-Miller

The real linguistic fact is the full utterance within its context of situation.

– Bronislaw Malinowski

Objectives

In this chapter, you will learn:

- how social conventions influence speech interactions, and how these interactions are studied
- how speech marks a speaker's social identity
- how factors such as region, social class, and ethnicity affect American speech
- what happens to languages when they come into contact

Language is a tool for social interaction, and it should not be surprising to learn that it can be affected by different social contexts. The study of language in social contexts, termed **sociolinguistics**, focuses on the relationship between linguistic behavior and social situations, roles, and functions. Rather than concentrating on individuals, sociolinguistics is centered on the **speech community**, defined as any group of people who share some set of social conventions, or **sociolinguistic norms**, regarding language use.

Speech communities may be distinguished by differing sociolinguistic norms at almost any level of language. Distinctions may be limited to minor phonetic differences in pronunciation, as when two groups have different **accents**, or when differences in grammatical structure may be evident. For example, in some parts of the eastern United States, the words *caught* and *cot* contain two different vowel phonemes, while in Canada and most of the western United States, they are homophones. In other words, where the phoneme inventory of one community has two vowels, the other has only one. Differences in norms between communities may also show up as different preferences for particular morphemes or words or even different orderings of words. Where there is a systematic difference between varieties, the two varieties are generally considered to be different **dialects**.

There are cases where the degree of structural difference between dialects is so extensive that speakers from each community no longer have **mutual intelligibility**. In other words, they can no longer understand one another. Although it might seem that in these cases the dialects should be classified as different languages, their speakers may disagree, perhaps because they are all citizens of the same country or members of the same ethnic group. In these cases, even radically distinct varieties may also be classified as dialects of the same language. This situation holds for many varieties of Chinese.

Of course, groups will vary widely as to the degree to which they differ, and where it is not clear whether their speech involves an accentual, dialectal, or even language difference, the term **speech variety** is used as a cover term to indicate that some set of sociolinguistic norms are present. It can refer to accentual differences, dialect differences, or language differences. Essentially, a dialect shows systematic linguistic distinctions from some other variety of the same language and is spoken by a socially identifiable subgroup of some larger speech community. Dialects that are strongly associated with some social group are referred to as **sociolects**. An **ethnic dialect**, where the accent is associated with a particular ethnic group, is a type of sociolect. **Regional dialects** occur when the speakers are associated with a particular geographical area.

Sociolinguistic norms not only are important for distinguishing speech communities but may also be relevant to language behavior within the community. There are two aspects of the social context that are important. On the one hand, sociolinguistic norms can determine how language is structured depending on the social circumstances in which it is used. This can be referred to as the **sociolinguistics of language**. On the other hand, differing sociolinguistic norms can serve to express a speaker's social identity or membership in the community. This can be referred to as the **sociolinguistics of society**.

1 Sociolinguistics of Language

Conventions associated with social situations can have an influence on the structure of individual speech interactions. These can include anything from conventions for beginning a casual conversation to those for asking a question of a teacher in a formal classroom setting or even those for writing a technical manual or a novel. Almost any interaction can be the focus of sociolinguistic study. No matter what sort of interaction is involved, it is a representation of some type of **discourse**.

1.1 Discourse Analysis

Analysis of the structure of discourse concentrates on how **utterances** are put together by speakers in individual interactions. Language in natural conversations is not always produced in complete sentences (*Do you want a cookie?*), so elliptical sentences (*Want a cookie?*) and even single words (*Cookie?*) can also be considered utterances. Both written and spoken discourse can be subjected to **discourse analysis** using one of various methods. Among these are analyses using **speech act theory** and the study of pragmatics, which have been described in previous chapters and will not be expanded on here. Other methods include **ethnography of communication, ethnomethodology**, and **text analysis**.

Ethnography of Communication

The ethnography of communication is a methodology for analyzing discourse that uses the approach that anthropologists might use to study other cultural institutions, such as medical or religious practices. Discourse studied using this approach is called a **speech event** and appears within a **speech situation**, which is any circumstance that may involve the use of speech. Speech events are subject to cultural rules of usage that are determined by the speech situation.

Ethnography of communication analysis involves the identification of individual components of the speech event and how they are realized. Eight basic components relevant to every speech event have been identified using the mnemonic SPEAKING, as shown in Table 15.1 on page 488, which also includes a sample analysis of a local telephone call.

Comparisons of these components across speech events show that in order for speakers to function effectively in any speech situation, they must be aware of more than just the grammatical rules for language; they must also have access to all the rules of communication, or **communicative competence** (as discussed in Chapter 12). For example, if the receiver in the example in Table 15.1 had failed to answer the caller's complaint with an apology, the goal of the caller would have been compromised. Conversely, if the receiver's goal had been to get rid of the caller in the most expeditious way, an apology might not have been called for.

Instrumentalities can also be important for achieving specific outcomes and goals. For example, if the receiver wishes to appease the caller, it is important for her to show the caller that she views her with respect and takes her concerns seriously. To achieve this in American society, she adopts a formal **style** or **register** during the conversation. Although these two terms are very similar in meaning and are often used interchangeably, they do differ. A speech style is defined in terms of formality of situation, and its values range along a continuum—from relatively informal to formal. A register is more often directly associated with a specific speech situation, which may or may not also be associated with some specific degree of formality. In both cases, they are characterized by a range of phonological, lexical, and syntactic properties. As example *1a* shows, the register used in newspaper headlines tends to omit small function words such as the determiners *the* or *a* and the copula *be*. Ritualistic register, as in *1b,* often includes archaic forms such as *ye* and *thou*. Recipes, as in *1c,* also have a recognizable structure, with frequent omission of both subject and object pronouns as well as determiners. All these stand in contrast to other standard registers, such as the technical writing in *1d*.

1)

a. *Newspaper headlines*
Psychics "scared" after murder
Drink helps active dogs replace bodily fluids
School levy needed to protect future

Table 15.1 SPEAKING mnemonic indicating components of a speech event, including sample analysis of a telephone call

Component	*Explanation*	*Sample analysis*
Setting or locale	Specific information about when and where it occurred (place, time)	Seattle at ten a.m. on May 3, 2005
Scene or situation	Generic information about the social occasion	Telephone call
Participants	Who was there (addressor/ addressee, performer/audience, questioner/answerer)	Caller: Ms. J. Smith Receiver: Ms. E. Jones, manager of a department store
Ends Outcomes:	Purpose of the event (transfer of knowledge, exchange of goods)	Complaint
Goals:	Purpose of the participants (impart knowledge, minimize price)	Caller: to register a complaint Receiver: to appease the caller
Act sequences	Content and forms particular to its use	Content: complaint about a mal-functioning toaster Form: tirade
Key	Tone or mood	Angry, sarcastic
Instrumentalities	Type of discourse or channel (spoken, written, recitation, etc.)	Spoken over a telephone line (only speech communication cues)
	Types of speech (dialect, style)	Formal standard business English
Norms Interaction:	Conventions of the interaction	After the conventional greeting, the caller speaks first giving complaint, receiver says she is sorry and offers to refund the money, etc.
Interpretation:	Normal interpretation	Receiver recognizes that the caller is angry and must be appeased, while the caller recognizes that the receiver is making an attempt to do so.
Genres	Category of event (poem, story, conversation)	Conversation

b. *Rituals*
With this ring, I thee wed.
Hear ye, hear ye, the court of Judge John Smith is now in session.

c. *Recipes*
DINO-GETTI ON TOAST:
INGREDIENTS:
2 slices bread (white or brown, must fit in toaster)
butter or margarine
1 16 oz can dino-getti

INSTRUCTIONS:

Pour contents of dino-getti tin into medium size saucepan. Place on medium heat. Stir ever so gently, so as not to disfigure any of the dinosaur pasta shapes. Taste occasionally, and remove from heat when desired temperature is reached. While the dino-getti is being heated, carefully place bread in the toaster and press down on the handle. Bread will automatically pop up when done. At this time, delicately spread a small amount of butter on *one* side of the toast. Place toast on plate (butter side up), and gingerly pour dino-getti on top.

d. Technical writing

Developers used several different languages to generate project code.

Patients who recovered either through cognitive-behavior therapy (CBT; N = 25) or through pharmacotherapy (PT; N = 29) completed self-reported ratings of dysfunctional attitudes before and after a negative mood induction procedure.

When a register is connected to a particular profession or activity, it may also be characterized by specific vocabulary items known as **jargon**. Jargon may involve specialized meanings for existing lexical items, as in the specialized use of the word *language* to mean programming language in *1d*. There also may be new terms coined specifically for that register, such as *pharmacotherapy* for a treatment involving drugs. Jargon is interesting because although it is generally developed to facilitate communication within the group, it can also be used to indicate membership in the group and even work to exclude nonmembers. Jargon is not always viewed positively by all members of the community. For example, in the computer field, advanced developers will often dismiss jargon-filled sales and managerial reports with little real technical content as "technobabble."

Slang, a common register found in a number of languages, is also a well-known vehicle for demarking group membership. The term *slang* refers to the use of faddish or nonstandard lexical items. Since slang is sensitive to current styles, it changes rapidly. Most slang terms—such as those in Table 15.2—will either disappear from use within a generation or become standardized and, therefore, no longer slang. Words like *dwindle, fan,* and *mob* were all once slang terms.

Table 15.2 Selected slang terms

Term	*Definition*
sweet	good
crib	house, apartment, residence
sick	good, great, generally positive
hot	attractive
sketch	a strange or weird person (also *sketchy:* strange, scary)
kickass	very good
hella	very
stick	someone who lives in a rural area
to bite	be bad, awful
tight	fantastic, wonderful, superlative

Slang is generally considered to be a low or vulgar form of the language and is most consistently associated with younger speakers. The form of any particular slang will differ according to the interests of the group that employs it. For example, high school students usually group themselves according to their interests and goals. Most high school communities include a popular group sometimes called Jocks (or also Preppies, Collegiates, or Socs [sowʃəz]) and a rebellious group sometimes called Burnouts (or Hoods or Greasers). Anyone not falling into either group can be considered a Lame. Of course, some high schools are not necessarily limited to these three although, in some sense, they do tend to be universal.

For example, in one Calgary (Canada) high school in the early 1980s, as many as seven groups could be identified (Jocks, Freaks or Heads, Punks or Rockers, Snobs, Preppies, Brownnoses or Homework Gang, and Nerds or Hosers). Special high school cliques can be formed on the basis of whatever brings the group together, and in most cases, they will employ some slang. Slang is always an informal register and its use in a speech situation requiring a more formal register would be viewed negatively by other participants in the speech event.

Ethnomethodology

Ethnomethodology, also called **conversation analysis**, is another approach to the study of discourse interactions. By identifying different types of utterances and isolating recurring patterns for their distribution in large corpora of tape-recorded natural conversations, many rules for the organization of conversation have been discovered.

One very common structure that has been identified is the **adjacency pair**. This is an ordered pair of adjacent utterances spoken by two different speakers. Once the first utterance is spoken, a second utterance is then required. A few of the many adjacency pairs that have been identified are shown in *2*.

2)
Summons—answer
Can I get some help here?
On my way.

Offer—refusal
Sales clerk: May I help you find something?
No, thank you; I'm just looking.

Compliment—acceptance
Your hair looks lovely today.
Thank you. I just had it cut.

Conversation analysis also tries to identify discourse units within a conversation. For example, most conversations will include an **opening**, or a beginning section, and these frequently include the "greeting—response" adjacency pair, as in example *3*.

3)
How are you?
Fine, thank you.

How these pairs are structured can determine if the conversation will proceed. It affects which participant will introduce the first topic of conversation and even if the conversation will proceed at all. For example, speakers will conventionally respond by saying they are fine even if they are not. Someone who responds with a detailed description of their health has taken control of the conversation. Another common part of conversation is a **closing** section, which signals the end of the conversation.

Between the opening and closing, speakers participate in the conversation in turns. The study of **turn-taking** is a central interest in conversation analysis. Three basic rules for turn-taking have been isolated based on the observation that at the end of a turn, a speaker may either select the next speaker (for example, by asking him or her a question) or may not.

4)

a. If the next speaker in the conversation is selected, then only that person has either a "right" or an "obligation" to speak.
b. If no particular speaker is selected, then any other participant in the conversation may "self-select."
c. If no other speaker opts to take a turn, then the original speaker may continue.

Conversation analyses have shown that there are cues in the discourse that tell speakers where potential transition points occur in conversation. Besides direct questions, transition points can also be identified by intonational cues and even pause durations. For example, in *5,* the tag question *don't you think* followed by a pause invites other participants to take a turn. If the discourse marker *but* occurs before another speaker takes a turn, the speaker shows that she is continuing the turn.

5)

He's a nice guy, don't you think, . . . but I don't think I'll go out with him.

Interestingly, cross-linguistic studies have shown that there are culture-specific conventions for turn-taking. For example, in some communities, as is generally the case for standard North American varieties of English, turns generally do not overlap. In other communities, where speakers show a **high involvement style**, such as Eastern European Jews in New York, beginning a turn before the previous speaker is finished is not only acceptable but desired. In these cases, turns are not so much offered as taken, using strategies such as finishing another's sentence or other **cooperative overlaps**. Failure to do so may give the initial speaker the impression that the other participants are not involved or interested in the conversation.

Even where overlaps are desired, there are culture-specific differences in the meaning of transition point cues. For example, the pause signaling a transition point in Apache discourse is far longer than that found in standard English. Someone using standard English pause lengths as cues for transition points in other communities would either fail to take their turn when obligated (as in New York conversation) or be constantly interrupting other speakers' turns (as in Apache conversation). In both of these cases, the conversational flow would be disrupted.

Text Analysis

The types of discourse analysis mentioned so far focus on the roles and obligations of speakers in conversation as controlled by aspects of their social and cultural environments. Text analysis, both written and oral, concentrates on the linguistic structure of discourse, both within and between utterances. These kinds of studies include analyses of pragmatics and speech act theory discussed in earlier chapters. A prominent sociolinguistic approach to text analysis uses variationist methodology. The variationist approach to discourse operates under the assumption that although a variety of structures may be used to fulfill any one discourse function, patterns in the variation found in natural conversational speech show that there is structure in discourse.

An important tool in variationist analysis is the **sociolinguistic variable**, which, roughly speaking, encompasses alternative ways of saying something. In example *6,* the variable involves questions, which can have a variety of forms. Following the standard convention in variationist sociolinguistics, the label *Questions* is placed in parentheses to indicate that it is a variable.

6)

(Questions)
Wanna drive?
You want to drive?
Do you want to drive?

In the study of structure in discourse, any set of utterances with equivalent discourse functions can constitute a variable. To determine which utterances are functionally equivalent, utterances in specific types of discourse units—such as narratives or lists—are analyzed to isolate their function.

This approach can also focus on the role and function of **discourse markers**. Discourse markers are expressions such as *well, oh,* and *you know* that are used by speakers to bracket utterances, to signal the speaker's feelings about the utterance, and to involve the listener. The discourse marker *oh* marks a shift in the way the speaker looks at information in the discourse. It is used, for example, when the speaker incorporates into the conversation new or unexpected information, such as an unanticipated answer. The expression *you know,* on the other hand, is used by a speaker to establish solidarity with the listener, to confirm shared knowledge, and to invite the hearer's acknowledgment or agreement.

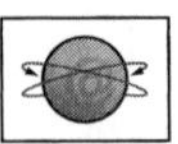

For an example of narrative analysis and a focus on discourse markers, go to **bedfordstmartins.com/linguistics/socialcontexts** and click on **narrative analysis**.

1.2 Solidarity and Power

Language use can reflect not only the identity of a speaker but also relationships of **solidarity** or **power** between speakers. Solidarity can be expressed by using forms of language that emphasize some degree of closeness or intimacy, whereas power differences can be registered by avoiding such forms. Solidarity and power are frequently invoked as explanations for linguistic behavior. An examination of politeness in language can illustrate how this occurs.

Politeness

Politeness can be expressed in many ways in language and is culturally specific, although there may be common elements that extend across cultures. One dominant theory of politeness holds that our use of polite language is based on every person's need both to belong to a group and to be free from imposition. These contradictory needs are called **positive face** (the need to belong to a group) and **negative face** (the need to be free from imposition). According to this theory, some speech acts by their very nature are **face-threatening acts** because they create distance between people, thus disrupting solidarity, or they impose on the freedom of action of the participants. Some examples of face-threatening acts are requests, complaints, advice, and disagreement. According to this theory, speakers choose whether to perform a face-threatening act at all and what language to use in a face-threatening act by weighing the relative power of the participants, the social distance of participants, and the ranking of the imposition of the speech act in the particular culture. For example, because of the difference in power, a student making a request of a professor would probably use somewhat different language than he would use if making the same request of a classmate. Similarly, if the speaker knows the addressee very well, she will use different language than if her addressee is merely an acquaintance. In terms of rank of imposition on the addressee, asking to borrow someone's pen, for instance, is quite different from asking to borrow someone's car and would require different language.

If a speaker wishes to perform a face-threatening act, she may choose language that expresses either **positive politeness** or **negative politeness**. The language of positive politeness increases the solidarity between the **interlocutors** (the participants in the exchange), and includes such things as using the first person plural, using humor, expressing token agreement, or using generally informal language. Using positive politeness shows that the speaker and addressee share the same needs and outlook. Professors, for example, may use positive politeness when correcting or disagreeing with students in order to encourage them; instead of saying, "No, that's wrong," a professor might offer token agreement and follow with the first person plural: "That's *an interesting idea,* but *let's* look at it another way. . . ." On the other hand, the language of negative politeness distances the interlocutors from the imposition on the addressee; such language includes hedges, questions, impersonal pronouns, and other types of formality in order to lessen the imposition on the addressee. A student who wants to ask his professor to give him an extension on a paper might use a question along with impersonal reference and a hedge: "*Would it be* possible for me to have *just* a couple more days for the paper?"

It is important to note that what is considered an appropriate choice of politeness strategies varies cross-culturally. Certain speech acts may be more or less face-threatening depending on the culture; for example, in the United States, it is not considered particularly face-threatening for a student to ask questions of her professor in class. Such behavior in some West African cultures, however, is considered extremely rude, since the less powerful student is imposing on the more powerful professor by requiring a response on a topic of the student's choosing; furthermore, the student's question implies that the professor has not been clear in his explanation. Levels of directness that are considered polite are also subject to cultural convention. For instance, in Israel, direct disagreement and direct requests are considered to be marks of closeness and respect for the addressee, since the speaker considers the addressee worthy of "straight-talking." Of course, if a speaker chooses not to be polite, then he or she may flout shared cultural conventions of politeness. A West African student who asks his professor a lot of questions in class, for instance, would be considered rude; similarly, an Israeli who used a question and a number of hedges to ask her friend for a favor might be perceived as cold or sarcastic.

Another effect of politeness on language use is the avoidance of certain topics of conversation that are deemed by societal convention to be impolite. Words used to refer to these are frequently considered **taboo** by some or all members of the community. What is considered taboo is culture-specific. For example, in Western society, speakers will frequently avoid words relating to bodily functions. This results in the use of **euphemisms** (words used to avoid taboo items), as shown in *7,* where the top word is the most taboo and the bottom is the least.

7)

piss
pee
urinate

Euphemisms are also used when the common word for some item or activity has possible negative associations that the speaker wishes to avoid. For example, after a Stealth fighter crashed during the NATO bombing of Belgrade in 1999, U.S. military spokesmen suggested that at the time when the airplane went down, the pilot was *task saturated.* In fact, the pilot was merely busy. Euphemisms can change relatively quickly. Although the term *downsizing* was only introduced in the 1970s as a euphemism for *layoffs,* in a 2002 television interview, Jack Greenberg of McDonald's Corporation, when asked about plans for *downsizing* the company, responded with the new euphemism *corrections.*

Perhaps a more obvious example of the role of politeness and avoidance strategies in discourse is found in the employment of different forms of address.

Forms of Address

Address terms are the forms that speakers use to address and refer to each other. Some types of address in English are shown in Table 15.3.

Table 15.3 Types of address terms in English

Term	*Example*
First name (N)	Mary
Title + last name (TLN)	Mr. Jones
Title alone (T)	Nurse
Last name (LN)	Jones

Forms of address are heavily dependent on the power and solidarity relationship between speakers as well as on conventions for usage in each culture. For example, the use of a particular form indicates the degree of solidarity the speaker feels with the addressee (person spoken to). With a friend, speakers are more likely to be on a first name basis while more distant relationships involve the use of a title and last name. In the case of a friendship, speakers are likely to address each other reciprocally, each using the other's first name. In relationships where there is a perceived power distinction, such as between age groups or work associates, addressing may be nonreciprocal. For example, students will usually refer to their teachers as Miss Smith or Professor Smith whereas the teacher will use the students' first names. In some cases, power and solidarity relationships between individuals can conflict for the use of address forms. For example, newlyweds will often have difficulty deciding what to call their in-laws. *Mother* may seem too familiar while the use of a first name might seem disrespectful. However, title and last name is too formal; it implies that the speaker is unwilling to form a close relationship. In this situation, the speaker may engage in what is called **no-naming**. They avoid naming their in-laws at all in order to not explicitly take a particular power stance.

For English speakers, it may be easier to conceal power relationships because unlike other European languages, English has lost a formality distinction in the pronoun system. In languages where formality distinctions in pronouns still exist, it is more difficult to conceal one's stance. For example, in most French communities, the standard rule is that between speakers of roughly equal status, reciprocal pronouns are used. To express solidarity, as in relationships between family members and friends, the form *tu* is used. If the addressee is someone of roughly equal status with whom the speaker shares no feeling of solidarity, then the form *vous* is used. Where one speaker is in a position of power over another, pronouns are employed nonreciprocally, with the more powerful participant addressed as *vous* and the less powerful as *tu*.

Studies of *tu/vous* usage patterns in Quebec French found that rural areas showed more usage of nonreciprocal *vous* within the family than urban areas. In other words, in rural families, elders were more likely to be addressed as *vous* and younger people as *tu*. It has been suggested that increased use of pronouns as solidarity markers rather than markers of power in urban areas may indicate that there is a de-emphasis of the power relationship in modern society. However, variationist studies comparing *tu/vous* use in Montreal over a period of thirteen years found that there was no clear evidence that *vous* was disappearing, indicating the continued use of *tu/vous* as markers of both power and solidarity.

Pronoun usage to express solidarity is not restricted to Indo-European languages. In Bislama, a creole spoken in the Republic of Vanuatu, there is a distinction between inclusive and exclusive first person pronouns (pronouns that distinguish whether the hearer is included or not), as shown in Table 15.4.

Table 15.4 Some pronoun contrasts in Bislama

	Singular	*Plural*
1st (exclusive)	mi	mifala
1st (inclusive)	—	yumi
2nd	yu	yufala

In addition to marking addressee participation in the event described, these pronouns are also used as signals of solidarity between the speaker and addressee. Speakers of Bislama will use inclusive forms like *yumi* in the presence of someone with whom they want to show solidarity, even if they were not actually a participant in the activity described, and an exclusive form like *mifala* to express distance.

In Javanese discourse, solidarity marking is not limited to address terms or pronoun choice but involves sharp morphological and lexical differences across registers. Table 15.5 shows examples of high and low registers found in the most standard dialect. In fact, these do not exhaust all of the distinctions available to a speaker of Javanese for indicating differences of solidarity and power.

Table 15.5 Dialect of the Prijajis (Javanese)

Level	*are*	*you*	*going*	*to eat*	*rice*	*and*	*cassava*	*now*
High	menapa	pandjenengan	baḍé	ḍahar	sekul	kalijan	kaspé	semanika
Low	apa	sampéjan	arep	neda	sega	lan	kaspé	saiki

As with address terms, speakers can either show reciprocal use of the low register (indicating strong solidarity and equivalent status), reciprocal use of higher registers (showing distance but equivalent status), or nonreciprocal use (where each speaker uses forms that reflect the status of the addressee). In other words, a lower status person would address a higher status person using the higher form and would be answered in the lower form.

Address forms are also a commonly noted source of distinction between the sexes in a number of societies. For example, in Japanese, there are differences in the pronoun systems of the speech of men and women, as shown in Table 15.6.

Table 15.6 Japanese nonformal personal pronouns

	Men's speech	*Women's speech*
First person	boku	watasi
Second person	kimi	anata

Language and Sex

In most societies, the language of men and women differs. Among the Gros Ventre tribe in Montana, women consistently pronounce some words differently than men. For example, the word for *bread* is pronounced /kjá tsa/ by the women and /dʒá tsa/ by the men. In Koasati, a Muskogean language found in Louisiana, verb forms differ depending on the sex of the speaker, as shown in Table 15.7.

Table 15.7 Gender-exclusive verb forms in Koasati

Women	*Men*	*Gloss*
lakawwíl	lakawwís	'I am lifting it'
lakáwtʃ	lakáwtʃ	'You are lifting it'
lakáw	lakáws	'He is lifting it'
lakáwwilit	lakáwwilitʃ	'I lifted it'

Types of differences such as those found in Koasati and Japanese have been called **gender-exclusive** in that there seem to be strong social prohibitions against using forms associated with the opposite sex. However, recent work among the Lakota, whose language has women's and men's clitics, indicates that choosing to use the clitics or switching to the forms associated with the opposite sex is governed by complex considerations of context. Women may choose to use the women's clitics if they want to convey intimate friendliness or concern, while men may use the men's clitics to assert certainty. However, both women and men may also choose not to use the clitics at all. Speakers may use the opposite form if they are quoting or joking, and atypical use in other contexts allows speakers to construct identity by their choice of form. For example, women who are in traditionally male occupations such as work in the criminal justice system may choose to use the men's forms to assert authority. Thus, the term *gender-exclusive* may capture a linguistic fact but miss the more important social facts of language use.

Differences between sexes have also been noted in European languages. In most cases, these are exhibited as tendencies rather than categorical distinctions. For example, women in North American society tend to possess a wider variety of color terms than men. Men, on the other hand, tend to have more terms relating to sports. Men and women may also differ in rates of usage of variable grammatical forms, as discussed later in the chapter. This kind of differentiation is called **gender-variable** because it involves overall rates rather than absolute distinctions.

Despite the strong correlation between sex of the speaker and language differences, the wide variety of distinctions argues against a biological explanation. There is no genetic reason for men and women to be different in terms of how they use language. Clearly, these differences are related to gender roles in these societies. There are two basic views for explaining the relationship between language and gender. One claims that these differences reflect the inherent differences between the sexes in society; the other claims that these differences may indicate that language operates as a tool for one group to establish and maintain power over another group. This latter view is often held by feminists.

This is a classic point of contention in linguistics. Does language shape society or does society shape language? Some linguists have found that women are more likely to use **verbal hedges** such as *perhaps, you know, sort of,* etc., than are men. It has been suggested that this indicates unassertiveness of women as a result of their relatively powerless position in society. However, a study of the verbal hedge *you know,* which distinguished between its use as an expression of uncertainty—as in example *8a,* where there is rising intonation (´)—and its use as a mark of confidence—as in *8b,* where there is falling intonation (`)—found that women are more likely to use *you know* to express confidence than are men.

8)

a. well it was all very embarrassing *you knów.*

b. and that way we'd get rid of exploitation of many by many all that stuff *you knòw* you've heard it before.

Thus, the existence of increased numbers of verbal hedges in women's speech is not necessarily proof that they are unassertive. Furthermore, other studies of gender-variable differences in language have found that upper-middle-class speakers tend to show the greatest differences across genders. Since upper-middle-class women are arguably the *most* powerful women in society, power differential is probably an overly simplistic explanation for gender differences.

Even so, it is undoubtedly the case that women, as a group, *do* occupy less powerful positions in most societies. On average, women in full-time employment earn less than men, and more men hold managerial positions than women. This difference between the sexes is reflected both in the way women's speech is described and in how men and women are referenced. In English, what is considered "correct" can be frequently traced back to an androcentric (male-oriented) bias on the part of grammarians in that characteristics of men's speech have been considered desirable and those of women are traditionally denigrated. While unrelated to the speech of men and women, a fourteenth-century grammar of English went so far as to comment on the proper ordering of words related to men and women, noting that the NP in *9a,* which places the woman before the man, should be considered less "correct" than that in *9b.*

9)

a. My mother and father
b. My father and mother

Difference in speech as it correlates with gender of the speaker is only one side of the coin. There are numerous examples in language relating to differences in how men and women are referred to.

Correlation of language behavior with gender roles is also connected to another kind of gender in language—that of grammatical gender. In particular, the use of masculine gender as a generic or unmarked form shows a male bias. As mentioned in earlier chapters, many languages use a noun classification system that puts nouns into different classes; in European languages this is called gender, partly because nouns with female referents take one grammatical gender and those with male referents take another—although as the Spanish data in *10* shows, sex is not the only consideration.

10)

Feminine		*Masculine*	
la mujer	'the woman'	**el** hombre	'the man'
la casa	'the house'	**el** edificio	'the building'

English has lost most of its grammatical gender with only a few vestiges of the system remaining, particularly in the pronoun system. However, androcentric grammatical "correctness" influences pronoun choice in situations where the sex of the referent is not specified. For instance, *11a,* which uses the masculine pronoun, is traditionally considered more correct by prescriptive grammarians than *11b,* which uses a gender-neutral pronoun.

11)

a. Someone left a message, but he forgot to leave his name.
b. Someone left a message, but they forgot to leave their name.

Of course, not all gender distinction in language is the result of androcentric bias. Gender differences in many languages may have arisen due to differences in what was considered taboo for each sex. The avoidance of taboo words by one sex and not the other may have led to differences in word choice. In any case, the study of gender differences in language can provide a revealing glimpse into the structure of any society.

Accommodation

Another important aspect of interpersonal relationships related to solidarity and power is that of linguistic **accommodation**, in which speakers modify their language patterns in interactions to make them more like those of the people with whom they are speaking. Speakers' language may **converge** syntactically, morphologically, and even phonologically during the course of the conversation. For example, a study comparing conversations between a travel assistant in Wales and several of her clients according to the social class of the client to whom she was speaking found that the assistant tended to use phonological characteristics such as /h/ deletion, *-in'* versus *-ing,* etc., more often when speaking to clients of lower socioeconomic classes whose speech is also characterized by these forms. In other words, her speech became more like that of the client with whom she was speaking.

Conversely, speakers may also make modifications that cause their language patterns to **diverge** or become more unlike each other. Studies in Catalonia (in Spain) and Japan have found that some speakers, when addressed in their native language by foreigners, will often shift into the foreigner's language even though the foreigner's speech may be perfectly understandable and even technically "correct." Accommodation theory suggests that speakers converge in order to show solidarity and diverge to show distance. This is important for analyzing style differences between speakers but may also be related to how they express their identity linguistically in relation to others in society.

2 Sociolinguistics of Society

Sociolinguistics of society relates to the way language behavior operates as a mark of a speaker's social identity. Since any individual speaker may at the same time have any number of identities related to sex, age, ethnic background, or social class, the investigation of the sociolinguistics of society can be complex. A central issue is the notion of what sociolinguistic norms are guiding speakers with respect to their choices for linguistic behavior.

2.1 Sociolinguistic Norms

Numerous studies have found that patterns within individual social groups reflect perceived societal norms for the entire community. How subgroups pattern for mainstream norms may reflect their participation (or lack of it) in the society. Linguistic patterns across social groups form an **orderly heterogeneity** in that even though subgroups show varying degrees of use of particular variants, similar overall patterns of variability within each group reveal shared linguistic systems and social norms. Distinct behavior can reveal both distinctions in linguistic systems as well as the ways language use can construct social barriers.

Standard Varieties

Most speech communities feature more than one language variety. In a number of situations, prescriptive grammarians and other language purists may hold up one variety as the "correct" or **standard** way of speaking. Language standardization is largely limited to international and colonial languages such as English or French and classical languages such as Arabic. Despite the strong belief in the "correctness" of the standard, it is an idealization created as a result of social and historical pressures associated with the growth of nation-states and colonial empires.

The intangibility of the standard is most clearly shown by the fact that when linguists have come together to define standard American English, the attempt has failed because of lack of agreement on how a standard variety arises and how it should be defined. This situation also holds with French in North America, where the principal debate concerns the existence of a standard form of Quebec French that is distinct from standard European French. Is the standard merely the most frequent form, or that which most people consider most prestigious, or is it some collection of grammatical rules imposed on a community by "experts"?

In fact, the standard variety, as defined by grammarians, does not really exist. Speakers in any community will adopt more or less of its features according to their social status, their level of education, and the situation in which they find themselves; even in the written form, any sizable stretch of discourse may violate someone's idea of correct or standard language since prescriptive grammarians often disagree. For example, a survey of English professors found that there was quite a bit of disagreement about the acceptability of some commonly noted grammatical "errors," as shown in Table 15.8.

Table 15.8 Sample results: survey of English professors

	Frequency (%) (as estimated by the English professors)				*Acceptability (%)*		
	Rare	*Moderately frequent*	*Very frequent*	*Can't say*	*Yes*	*No*	*Can't say*
Everyone volunteered but they all failed to appear. (agreement error)	0	25	62	13	19	81	0
Jane Austen now feels that it is necessary to partially clarify Frank Churchill's relationship to Jane. (split infinitive)	0	16	74	10	17	72	11
Considering how little satisfaction she obtained from it, it was just a waste. (dangling participle)	12	47	35	6	35	59	6

A more reasonable way of thinking of the standard is to consider it to be that variety that has the most features conventionally believed in society to be prestigious. In fact, in popular use, the standard variety is usually the one that is taught in the schools, and its features are found more frequently in the speech of the upper classes, politicians, and the news media. In this sense, there are a number of ways of establishing what features characterize the standard of any given speech community.

Language Attitudes

One way of determining which variety is looked on as more standard in any community is through attitude studies. Generally, people tend to believe that they use more standard forms than they actually do in practice. However, in some cases, speakers are painfully aware of the gap between the way they speak and the standard. For example, a study of **linguistic insecurity** in New York City used a list of words with variable pronunciations to test the relationship between usage and speakers' intuitions of "correctness," or standard language. Table 15.9 shows the list of items tested.

Participants were asked to listen to two possible pronunciations and mark on a questionnaire which one was "correct" and which one they usually used. Interestingly, lower-middle-class speakers (as opposed to working-class, lower-class, and upper-middle-class speakers) were most likely to show a high degree of linguistic insecurity, since they were much more likely than other groups to identify a difference between what they said and what they perceived as correct. Similarly, women were more likely than men to manifest linguistic insecurity in this way. A similar study conducted in Winnipeg in Canada confirmed the relatively higher degree of linguistic insecurity for lower-middle-class speakers.

Table 15.9 Items on the linguistic insecurity test given to New Yorkers

Token	*Form 1*	*Form 2*	*Token*	*Form 1*	*Form 2*
Joseph	[dʒowsɪf]	[dʒowzɪf]	length	[lɛnθ]	[lɛŋθ]
catch	[kætʃ]	[kɛtʃ]	February	[fɛbɹuɛɹi]	[fɛbjuɛɹi]
tomato	[təmejto]	[təmɑto]	ketchup	[kætʃəp]	[kɛtʃəp]
diapers	[dajpɹ̩z]	[dajəpɹ̩z]	escalator	[ɛskəlejtɹ̩]	[ɛskjəlejtɹ̩]
aunt	[ɑnt]	[ænt]	new	[nu]	[nju]
often	[ɔftən]	[ɔfən]	tune	[tjun]	[tun]
garage	[gəɹɑdʒ]	[gəɹɑːʒ]	avenue	[ævənu]	[ævənju]
humorous	[hjuməɹəs]	[juməɹəs]	because	[bikɔs]	[bikɔz]
vase	[vejz]	[vɑːz]	half	[hæf]	[haf]

Another method for determining speakers' attitudes to particular varieties and languages is the **matched guise test**. In this test, participants are asked to listen to recordings of two speakers and then rate the speakers according to characteristics such as intelligence, likability, and social class. In reality, the participants are listening to the same speaker speaking two different varieties. Studies in Britain found that, as expected, the variety taught in school—received pronunciation (RP)—was ranked as most standard. The RP-accented speaker was felt to have more characteristics associated with success, such as intelligence, height, and high socioeconomic status. Matched guise tests have been used extensively since the early sixties to investigate attitudes toward English and French in Quebec. Early studies found that both anglophone and francophone Canadians ranked speakers more positively when they were speaking English.

Another type of attitude test that originated in the Netherlands and Japan but is also used in both the United States and Canada asks participants to rate the accents of different geographical areas according to perceptual categories such as "pleasantness," "correctness," and "similarity" to the participants' own speech. In the United States, residents of Michigan rated their own speech highest with respect to values connected to "correctness" but ranked the speech of southerners higher for categories connected to "pleasantness."

Nonstandard Varieties

The existence of the term *standard* form of a language might seem to imply that all other forms are somehow *substandard.* However, this is not the case. Many forms that are proscribed by grammarians are commonly used throughout the community without stigma. An excellent example is the use of the pronoun *they* to refer to referents that are unspecified for gender. Widely used forms that carry no negative connotations are not necessarily **nonstandard**. The use of the term *nonstandard* merely indicates that the form lacks positive prestige in the community. However, in no way does it mean that the forms are somehow defective.

Prescriptivists often claim that nonstandard forms show an inherent illogic or lack of systematicity. The so-called double negative, seen in *12a,* is a prime example.

12)

a. She didn't see nobody.
b. She didn't see anybody.
c. She saw somebody.
d. She saw nobody.

From a prescriptivist point of view, where a sentence is marked for negation twice, as in *12a,* the double negative will give the sentence an affirmative meaning, as in *12c.* However, as everyone knows, this is patently false. Both *12a* and *12b* are universally recognized by even highly standard speakers as having the meaning in *12d.* In fact, both negative sentences, standard and nonstandard, show parallel grammatical marking. It is just the form that differs. In *12a,* the pronoun is marked with *no-,* and in *12b,* it is marked with *any-*. In both cases, the negative pronoun differs from that found in an affirmative sentence such as *12c.* Neither *12a* nor *12b* is any more or less logical than the other. Furthermore, while the double negative construction is considered nonstandard in modern English, it is the standard form in many other languages, such as Spanish, as shown in *13.*

13)

Ella	no	vio	nada.
She	NEG	saw	nothing

'She didn't see anything.'

In other words, nonstandard varieties are not grammatically less valued, but since they generally represent the speech of a politically less powerful group, they may be socially less valued. However, it is possible that two relatively standard varieties can coexist in one community.

Where two varieties are used in sharply distinguished situations or **domains of use** in a particular speech community, the relationship between varieties is known as **diglossia**. One variety is used in more formal situations or in the written form and is called the high variety, while the other is used in less formal situations and is referred to as the low variety. Table 15.10 shows some uncontroversial cases of diglossia.

Table 15.10 Recognized situations of diglossia

Country	*High*	*Low*
Switzerland	Standard German	Schweizerdeutsch (Schwyzerdütsch)
Haiti	French	Haitian creole
Greece	Katharévusa	Demotic Greek

Official Languages and Language Planning

The issue of standard and nonstandard varieties is also connected to the notion of **official language**. An official language differs from a standard language in that it has been declared the language of a particular region or country as a result of legislation. Designation of an official language has implications for the political and economic power of ethnic groups and is often a reaction to a perceived increase in power of a minority group by the majority. Currently, about half of the United States has some sort of law giving English official status. In Canada, there are two designated official languages at the federal level—English and French. However, most individual provinces conduct official business in one or the other. Governments are not the only institutions concerned with language use. Use of particular languages can be dictated by the official policies of any organization; determining what policies are to be followed is called **language planning**.

Official language designation usually puts speakers of nonofficial languages at a disadvantage because their access to legal or other documents and their participation during official business may be restricted if they have a reduced ability in the official language. They may have less access to educational opportunities and hence fewer chances for advancement in society. In the past, language planning has even resulted in speakers being banned from using their languages at all. This was the case in the early part of the twentieth century when native languages such as Lakota or Apache were banned at residential schools for Native Americans, with harsh punishments dealt out to offenders. In more recent years, attempts have been made to ban languages other than English. For example, in 1988, Spanish-speaking clerks of the municipal court in Huntington Park, California, challenged the English-only rule in their workplace. Although the clerks involved were hired because of their expertise in Spanish and ability to deal with Spanish-speaking members of the public, they were forbidden to use Spanish among themselves. The case was heard by a U.S. Court of Appeals, and the English-only rule was struck down. The court cited Equal Employment Opportunity Commission guidelines that prohibit language restrictions except in narrowly defined cases of business necessity.

Restricting language use is not the only possible outcome of language planning. For example, regulations can also be enacted to increase minority language rights, such as access to education in the minority language as well as access to official government services such as voting materials and driver's license examinations. The 2000 U.S. census forms, for example, were available in Spanish, Chinese, Korean, Tagalog, and Vietnamese, and assistance guides in more than forty languages were available on the Internet.

Language planning is not restricted to multilingual situations. It can also have an effect on which variety of a language is deemed acceptable for official use. For example, in 1961, the *Office de la langue française* was formed in Quebec to regulate the use of Quebec French, protect a standardized Quebec French, and give advice to Quebecers and others on the correct use of the language. A similar watchdog on the French language also exists in France. Although there are no equivalent government regulators on the quality of the English language, recognized authorities on English such as the *Oxford English Dictionary* and numerous published grammars and style manuals serve a similar purpose.

Language planning can be a particularly hot issue in the field of education. There has been a great deal of debate over whether it is preferable to educate minority groups using their native languages, at least at the primary levels, or to force assimilation of the group by eliminating minority language education. This is the main issue surrounding the debate over the use of **ebonics**, or **African American Vernacular English (AAVE)**, as a tool for minority education in the Oakland, California, school system. Many people mistakenly believed that in 1997 the Oakland school system was considering *teaching* students to speak ebonics rather than merely *recognizing* the variety and incorporating it into the teaching of standard English (among other topics). In other words, they were proposing an attempt to reduce the disadvantage of speaking a nonstandard variety. A portion of the official statement of the Linguistic Society of America on the issue is shown in *14*.

14)

> There is evidence from Sweden, the U.S., and other countries that speakers of other varieties can be aided in their learning of the standard variety by pedagogical approaches which recognize the legitimacy of the other varieties of a language. From this perspective, the Oakland School Board's decision to recognize the vernacular of African American students in teaching them Standard English is linguistically and pedagogically sound.

Wherever nonstandard or nonofficial languages exist side-by-side with a standard national language, this issue arises. For example, many African nations have adopted a colonial language such as English or French as their official language, partly because of access to international trade and partly because in many of these countries, there are a number of ethnic languages, and by choosing an international language, they avoid ethnic disputes. Despite the fact that most of their citizens are native speakers of an indigenous language, in many countries, most education takes place in the colonial language. This issue is also highly relevant to addressing possible education problems among Native Americans who may speak Navajo, Blackfoot, or any one of a number of indigenous languages as their first language. Proponents of minority language education argue that teaching subjects such as mathematics, science, etc., in the first language fosters academic growth regardless of students' ability to acquire a second language (see Chapter 12, Section 4.4).

The status of a language variety can affect which form of the language is spoken in any given situation and which form is considered standard. What is considered prestigious for one community may not be so considered for another. Speakers will vary their language depending on the situation and their need to express their social identity. In order to properly determine how language is structured as a function of these social considerations, special methodologies have been developed for the study of variation.

For more information on methods for studying variation, go to **bedfordstmartins.com/linguistics/socialcontexts** and click on **variation**.

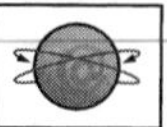

2.2 Social Influence on Variation

Although almost any social characteristic that plays a role in the formation and maintenance of group identities could hypothetically be a factor in variation, there are six main types of social influence that have been studied extensively. These are: geographical or regional location, socioeconomic class, social network, age, gender, and ethnicity.

Regional Variation

Perhaps the best-known factor affecting variation is geographical location. Most early work in sociolinguistics was in the field of **dialectology**, which allowed historical linguists to track sound changes across space, although it quickly expanded to the study of differences in other levels of grammar—particularly the lexicon.

Dialectology studies usually involve **atlas surveys** of large numbers of speakers over wide areas, designed to establish the geographical range and distribution of dialect difference. There are a number of methods by which data is collected for an atlas survey. The predominant method is a personal interview conducted by a field-worker. Based on available information regarding social practice and likely areas of distinction between regions, the field-worker follows an interview schedule constructed to elicit terms and pronunciations considered of interest. The interview includes both casual conversation on preselected topics and specific language questions like those in *15*.

15)

a. Do you pronounce *news* like *cues* or *coos*?
b. *There is a chicken in the yard.* Please repeat this sentence substituting the phrase *three chickens* for *a chicken.*

Since the main goal of a regional dialect study is to speak to people from as many areas as possible, a limited number of speakers are interviewed in each area. In early studies, only one male lifelong resident of the area was chosen. Unfortunately, this resulted in problems related to representativeness, since it ignored or disregarded many social influences in the community. For example, it provided little data on the speech of women. More recent studies include at least one woman and one man from each area, and other possible social influences are noted. For example, *The Phonological Atlas of North America,* a study currently under way at the University of Pennsylvania, samples two speakers from cities with populations under 1,000,000 and four from larger centers. Prior to the widespread use of tape recorders, data were hand-transcribed by trained field-workers. Now, all interviews are tape-recorded.

Direct interviews are not the only way that researchers can gather data. The *Phonological Atlas of North America* uses **telephone survey** methods for some data collection. In cases where the interview schedule does not require access to recordings of the speakers, other methods can be used. For example, written questionnaires can be sent out in a **postal survey**. Although the lack of direct contact with each speaker is a drawback, it has the advantage of more easily reaching a larger number of people than is possible with face-to-face interviews. Some questions from a dialect survey are shown in *16.*

16)

a. Do you pronounce these words the same or differently?
pin/pen
crayon/crown

b. What do you call a nonalcoholic fizzy drink?

Surveys done over the Internet are also valuable, but since Internet access is still somewhat limited to more affluent, educated people, **Internet surveys** do not reach the entire population, and there are questions about how representative they are. To see an actual Internet survey, visit the site at **www.hcs.harvard.edu/~golder/dialect/**.

Once the data have been collected, it is reported in a document called a dialect atlas. This document summarizes the responses to each item of interest from the interviews and plots them on a map such as that shown in Figure 15.1. Maps show either that different communities share features or that they are distinguished by different features. The map in Figure 15.1 shows that there are similarities in vocabulary between francophone fishing villages in Atlantic Canada and a dialect in western France.

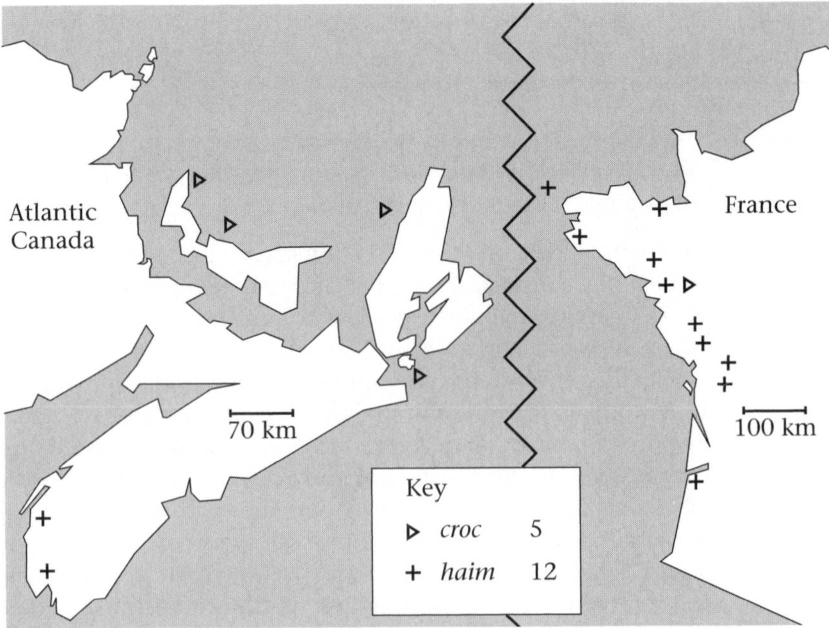

Figure 15.1 Words for 'fishhook' in French dialects of Atlantic Canada and western France

In many cases, it is possible to find distinct boundaries between areas shown on maps in the form of lines called **isoglosses**. A single isogloss indicates one point of distinction between areas. Where several isoglosses occur in roughly the same area on the map, it is referred to as an **isogloss bundle**, as in Figure 15.2.

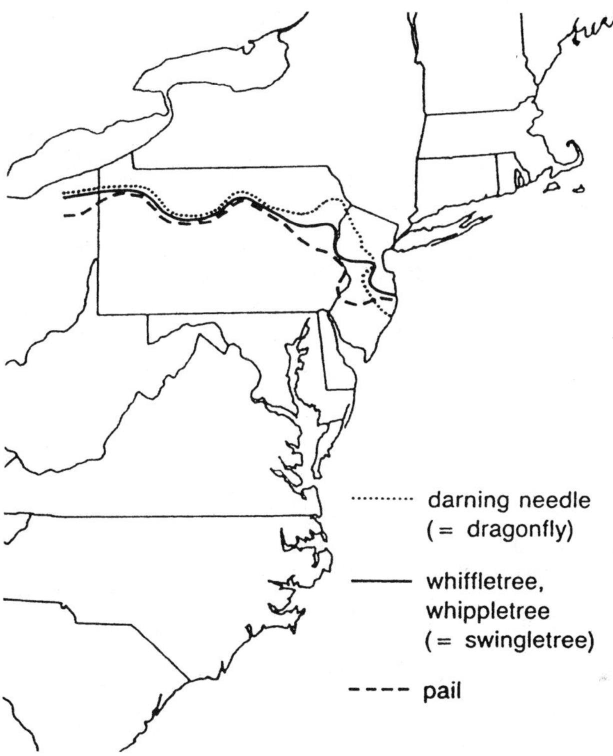

Figure 15.2 An isogloss bundle across eastern Pennsylvania

The larger the isogloss bundle, the more likely a true systematic difference among areas exists, and in that case, there are usually two distinct regional dialects. Isogloss bundles are also interesting for historical reasons, because they often reveal a great deal about changing patterns of movement and communication among communities. For example, a study of isogloss bundles in Louisiana found that earlier patterns corresponded to the river systems, consistent with the fact that most transportation in that area of North America was along the water. In contrast, modern patterns correspond to road systems.

Similarities between areas indicate some relationship between speakers, either because one community migrated from the other area or because the areas are in close contact due to connecting trade routes or other lines of communication. In fact, many of the existing dialect patterns in North America can be traced to routes of trade and immigration. Figure 15.3 on page 508 shows the major dialect areas of the United States and routes of immigration.

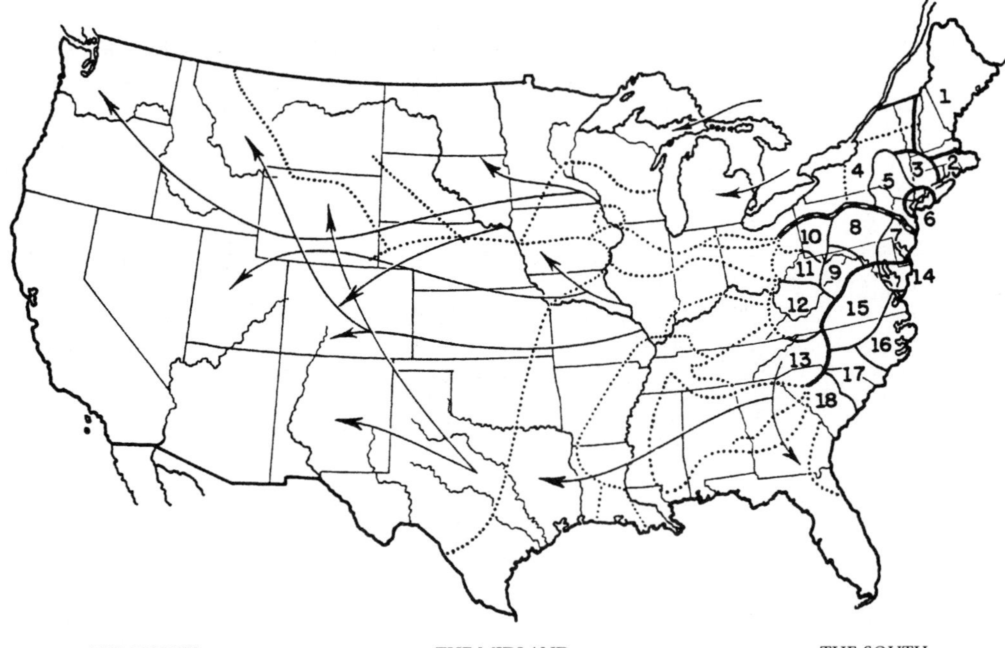

THE NORTH

1. Northeastern New England
2. Southeastern New England
3. Southwestern New England
4. Inland North
5. The Hudson Valley
6. Metropolitan New York

THE MIDLAND

North Midland

7. Delaware Valley (Philadelphia)
8. Susquehanna Valley
10. Upper Ohio Valley (Pittsburgh)
11. Northern West Virginia

South Midland

9. Upper Potomac & Shenandoah
12. Southern West Virginia & Eastern Kentucky
13. Western Carolina & Eastern Tennessee

THE SOUTH

14. Delmarva (Eastern Shore)
15. The Virginia Piedmont
16. Northeastern North Carolina
17. Cape Fear & Peedee Valleys
18. The South Carolina Low Country

Figure 15.3 Regional dialects of American English. Eastern dialects are numbered; other (more tentative) dialect boundaries are indicated by dotted lines. Arrows indicate direction of major migrations.

The northern dialect area reflects patterns of migration and settlement from western New England and northern New York State along the southern shores of the Great Lakes. This route followed the Erie Canal west across New York State to the area around Cleveland known as the Western Reserve and westward to Detroit. From there, settlement fanned out into the upper Midwest and the West. The North Midland region follows the migration route from Philadelphia and the Delaware Valley across Pennsylvania and west along the old National Road (along the approximate route of present-day Interstate 70). The South Midland region spreads out from the Upper Potomac and Shenandoah Valley into the mountains of southern West Virginia, eastern Kentucky, and Tennessee. The dividing line between North and South Midland is roughly the Ohio River, with South Midland extending northward into Indiana in what is known as the Hoosier Apex. The southern dialect area reflects migration and settlement patterns starting in the Chesapeake Bay and tidewater Virginia and sweeping southward through western North Carolina and north Georgia. Another source of migration began on the coast, especially around Charleston, South Carolina, and spread westward across Georgia, Alabama, and Mississippi.

Regional Variation in Lexical Items

In the first half of the twentieth century, when a majority of the U.S. population lived in or close to rural areas, dialectologists believed that isolated rural speech was purer and more interesting than urban speech. Numerous questions on dialect surveys elicited agricultural terms, such as names for farm equipment, terms for livestock, and words used when calling horses, sheep, and cattle. For example, a dialect boundary was drawn across eastern Pennsylvania based on a bundle of isoglosses, including an isogloss separating alternative terms for the pivot bar on a horse-drawn wagon (shown in Figure 15.2). Today, however, most Americans would probably not even be able to visualize parts of a horse-drawn wagon, much less name the pivot bar with a regionally distinctive word such as *whiffletree, whippletree,* or *swingletree.*

Nevertheless, regional differences in lexical items certainly exist today. For example, a carbonated soft drink is called *soda* in the Northeast, *pop* in the inland and Northwest, *tonic* in eastern New England, and *soda pop* in parts of the southern Midland. Similarly, a sandwich on a large roll with a variety of meats and cheeses may be called a *grinder,* a *hero,* a *sub(marine),* a *hoagie,* or a *poorboy,* depending on the region of the country. Some other lexical variants are displayed in Table 15.11.

Table 15.11 Some regional variants

North	*Midland*	*South*	*Meaning*
angleworm	fishing worm	mud worm, wiggler	worm used as fishing bait
darning needle	snake feeder	mosquito hawk	dragonfly
mud wasp (NE)	mud dauber	dirt dauber	wasp that builds a mud nest
bag (upper North)	sack, poke (Appalachian)	sack	paper container

On the basis of lexical variation, it has been suggested that there are really only two main dialect areas: North and South, with the dividing line roughly along the Ohio River. The North is further divided into the upper North and New England, the lower North (previously North Midland), and the West. The South is divided into lower South and upper South (previously South Midland). These divisions and dialect layers are illustrated in Figure 15.4 on page 510.

Regional Variation in Phonology

One distinctive characteristic that distinguishes North from South is the pronunciation of the word *greasy.* In the North, it is said with [s], whereas in the South, it is

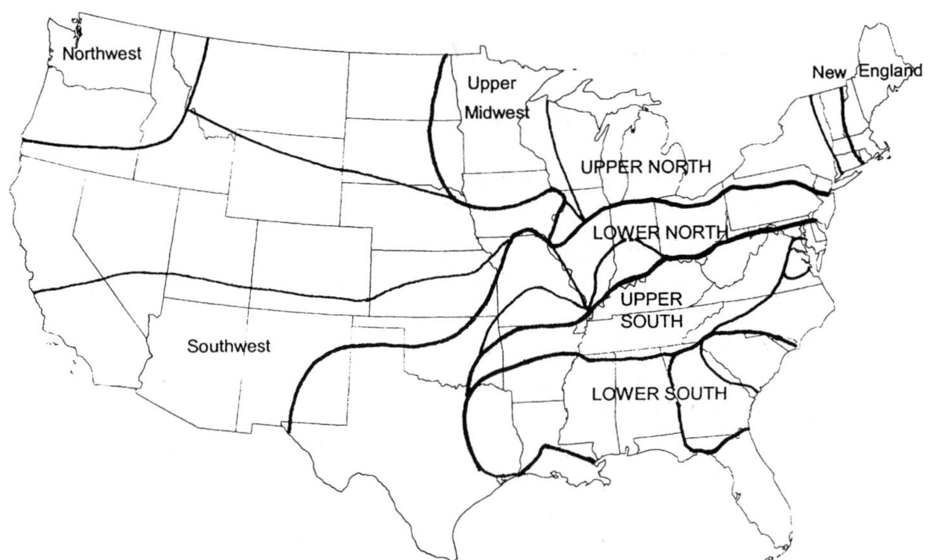

Figure 15.4 Dialect regions of the United States based on lexical items

pronounced with [z]. This distinction, while long recognized, does not suggest any systematic differences, and it is to more systematic differences that we now turn.

One of the most notable regional differences is the presence or absence of **postvocalic *r***. In parts of the South, in New England, and as a stigmatized variant in the New York metropolitan area, [ɹ] is deleted when it is in the syllable coda following a vowel. Where postvocalic *r* is deleted, words such as *car* [kɑɹ] and *cork* [kɔɹk] become [kɑ] and [kɔk], respectively. The [ɹ] is retained but somewhat weakened and less retroflex in a broad swath extending northwest from Texas to Washington State.

In fact, liquids and nasals systematically affect the preceding vowels in ways that are dialectally distinctive. For instance, there is considerable dialectal variation in how orthographic <e> and <a> are pronounced when followed by [ɹ] in words such as *Mary, merry*, and *marry*. Some speakers have a two-way distinction, others have a three-way distinction, while in much of the Midwest, the distinction is neutralized to [ɛ] when the vowel is followed by [ɹ]. Thus, *Mary, merry*, and *marry* all sound the same, as do *Harry* and *hairy, Barry* and *berry, fairy* and *ferry.*

Another dialectal difference is the effect that a nasal has on preceding vowels. Throughout the South and into southern Ohio, central Indiana, Illinois, Missouri, and Kansas, the vowels [ɪ] and [ɛ] have merged as [ɪ] before [n] or [m]. Thus, both *him* and *hem* are pronounced as [hɪm], and one must specify whether a [pɪn] is for sticking (*pin*) or for writing (*pen*). This merger of [ɪ] and [ɛ] before a nasal had its origins in the southern states, and seems to be in the process of spreading northward and westward.

Another dialectal change in progress is the merger of [ɔ] and [ɑ] in words such as *caught* and *cot, hawk* and *hock,* and *dawn* and *Don.* Although the two sounds remain distinct in much of the Midwest, the South, and the mid-Atlantic states, they have merged in northeastern New England, in western Pennsylvania and central Ohio, in northern Minnesota, and throughout the West (with the possible exception of the large cities of San Francisco, Los Angeles, and Denver). One sign that this merger is in the process of expanding is that it is more strongly represented by younger speakers than older speakers.

Finally, two separate vowel shifts have been tracked over the past quarter century. A **vowel shift** occurs when a series of vowel phonemes undergo reorganization (see Chapter 7, Section 2.4). The **Northern Cities Shift** began in the metropolitan areas of Chicago, Detroit, Cleveland, and Buffalo, and may now be spreading to smaller cities around the Great Lakes. In order to understand the changes taking place in the Northern Cities Shift, see Figure 15.5.

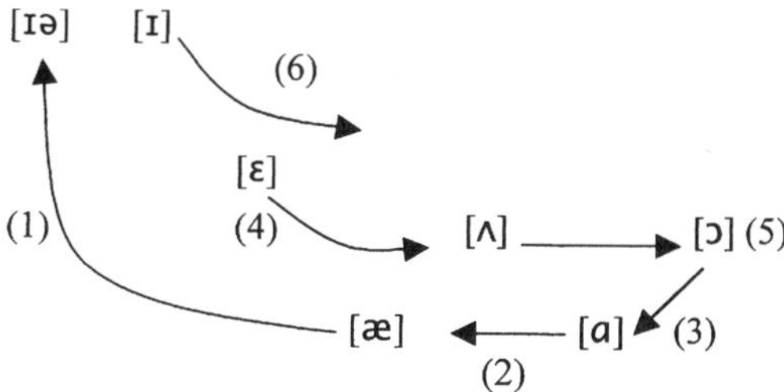

Figure 15.5 The Northern Cities Shift

First, the [æ] in words like *cad* was raised and diphthongized to become [ɪə]. Then, the [ɑ], as in *cod, Don, pop,* and *hot,* was fronted to become closer to [æ]. The [ɔ], as in *dawn* and *cawed,* was then lowered to become more like [ɑ]. The [ɛ], as in *Ked,* was backed, which in turn pushed the [ʌ], as in *cud,* farther back. In parallel with the backing of [ɛ], [ɪ], as in *kid,* also moved back.

A quite different vowel shift is in progress in the South and extends northward through eastern Tennessee and Kentucky and into southern West Virginia. In this shift, known as the **Southern Shift**, the vowels are rotating quite differently from those in the Northern Cities Shift (see Figure 15.6).

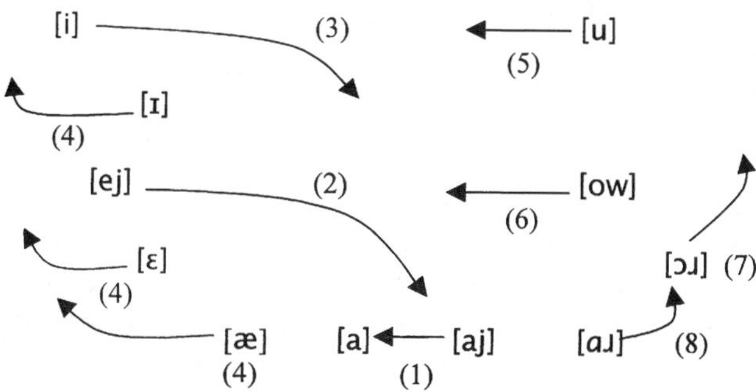

Figure 15.6 The Southern Shift

In the Southern Shift, the [aj] in words like *I* and *time* is monophthongized to [a] and fronted. The [ej], as in *made,* is lowered and backed to sound almost like [aj]. In parallel, the [i], as in *heed,* is also lowered and backed. The remaining front vowels are raised and in some cases become diphthongized so that *bed,* for example, sounds more like [bɪəd]. The nonlow back vowels [u] and [ow] are fronted, and [ɑɹ] and [ɔɹ] move upward.

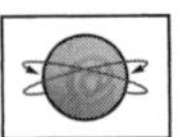

For more information on dialectal differences in phonology, go to **bedfordstmartins.com/linguistics/socialcontexts** and click on **American dialects**.

When dialectal differences based on lexicon are superimposed on dialectal differences based on phonology, the results are actually remarkably similar, as is shown in Figure 15.7.

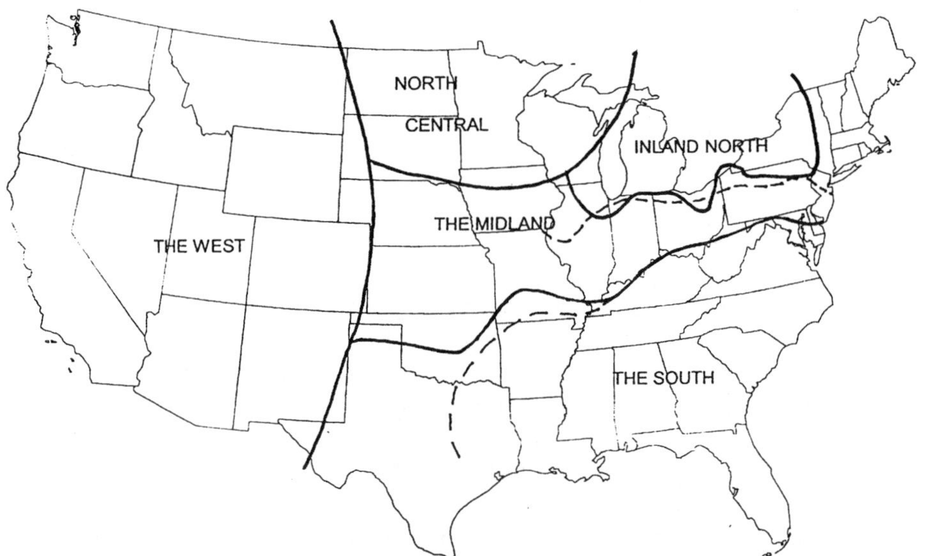

Figure 15.7 Dialect boundaries based on lexical items and a phonological survey. (The solid line represents dialect boundaries found in the Phonological Atlas survey; the dashed line represents dialect boundaries based on lexical items.)

Regional Differences in Morphology and Syntax

Regional differences in morphology and syntax are relatively few, and this section will present examples primarily from southern English and Appalachian English. Two distinctive markers of southern English are the use of double modals and the extension of the pronoun system to include a second person plural. Whereas most dialects of American English have but one *you* to denote both singular and plural, southern English distinguishes between *you* (singular) and *you-all* or *y'all* (plural). Another distinctive grammatical feature in the South is the use of double modals such as *might could* or *might should,* where *might* is used to mean 'perhaps'.

Appalachian English shares a number of features with southern English but also preserves some **relic forms**—forms of older English that have become obsolete in standard American English (although Appalachian English is not unaltered Elizabethan English, as is sometimes claimed!). One such relic form is **a-prefixing** on verbs in the progressive aspect or on adverbial complements to V, as in *17.*

17)

The dog came up just a-prancin'.
The wind was a-comin' on strong.

Other forms in Appalachian English include counterfactual *liketa,* as in *I laughed so hard I liketa died,* and the use of *right* as a degree word, as in *It's right nice weather today.* A couple of interesting syntactic differences exist between standard American English and Appalachian English in relative clauses. In most dialects of American English, the complementizer *that* and the trace of a *wh-* element moved from subject position are not acceptable in sentences such as *18.*

18)

* Who did you say that *t* called?

However, this type of structure is perfectly acceptable in Appalachian English. Interestingly, in some areas of Appalachia and in other southern-based dialects, it is possible to delete the relative pronoun even when it is the subject of a relative clause:

19)

That man lives down the road is crazier than a loon.

As this discussion shows, geographical area can be a factor in explaining patterns of variation. However, other factors within regional dialects can also play a role.

Socioeconomic Class

Patterning of variants according to socioeconomic class can give valuable clues to how language behavior reflects social mobility. The theory is exemplified by studies of variation in New York City and rests on two basic findings: (1) the upper classes tend to use linguistic variants with higher prestige; and (2) speakers from the lower middle class show the most linguistic insecurity. Because lower-middle-class speakers may not have internalized norms of "correctness," they tend to adopt variants that they believe to be "correct," even though these variants are not standard. This pattern is called **hypercorrection**. Table 15.12 shows some examples of hypercorrection.

Table 15.12 Examples of hypercorrection

Standard	*Hypercorrection*
often pronounced as [ɔfən]	spelling pronunciation [ɔftən]
Who did you say was calling?	Whom did you say was calling?
between you and me	between you and I

Certain phonological and grammatical variants may be associated with socioeconomic class. In a now famous study entitled "The Social Stratification of r in New York City Department Stores," William Labov hypothesized that the presence or absence of postvocalic *r* in New York City speech was linked to social class. To test his hypothesis, he chose three department stores catering to different clientele: Saks Fifth Avenue for the upper end of the social scale; S. Klein, a now defunct bargain basement, for the lower end; and Macy's for middle-class shoppers. In each store, Labov asked employees questions that would elicit the response "fourth floor." When he tabulated the percentages of employees who pronounced postvocalic *r* some or all of the time in their responses, he indeed found social stratification: 62 percent of the employees at Saks produced postvocalic *r* all or some of the time and 51 percent of Macy's employees did so, but only 20 percent of the employees of S. Klein pronounced the postvocalic *r*.

However, just because a society can be grouped into classes on the basis of some objective socioeconomic criteria does not indicate that social class is necessarily the prime factor in determining the behavior of individuals. Effects of social class may also be traceable to the fact that people associate more with those in their own socioeconomic class. To examine possible effects of social association, a more direct approach uses social network analysis.

Social Network

Individual social relationships can be examined as an explanation for patterns of variation by counting the ties between speakers according to relevant social network clusters such as family, neighborhood, employment, religion, and friendships. This is called **social network analysis** and is depicted in Figure 15.8.

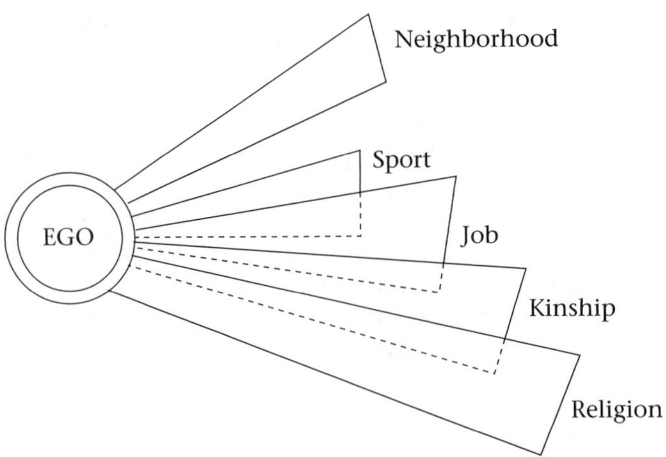

Figure 15.8 Social networks

The basic idea behind social network analysis is that people who talk to one another often are more likely to have the same speech patterns. Speakers are given individual network scores according to both the kinds of network ties they have and the density of the networks in which they are involved. **Dense social networks** are those in which a large number of the speakers are interconnected. **Multiplex networks** are those in which the relationships are formed on the basis of several clusters or kinds of relationships. In Northern Ireland, dense social networks act to enforce community norms, so that speakers who are most closely integrated into the network show the highest rate of variants associated with it. Their relationships constrain their linguistic behavior in much the same way as those in closely knit communities act to restrain other types of social behavior, such as moral values and work ethics. Recent work on the island of Ocracoke on North Carolina's Outer Banks has shown that select distinctive features of the endangered local dialect are most strongly maintained by a group of middle-aged men with dense multiplex networks. They play poker together several times a week, generally work in fishing or other marine activities, and share strong local loyalty and pride. In the face of loss of the island dialect through contact with tourists and with the mainland, the poker players assert their island identity through their speech.

The precise calculation of social network scores varies depending on the community, since some types of network ties may be more important in one community than in another. For example, a study of a small Newfoundland fishing village found that ties related to traditional employment associations, such as fishing or shopkeeping, were the most important for predicting language behavior, whereas in Northern Ireland, personal relationships and neighborhood associations were the most important for maintaining local forms.

Age

Differences across age groups are another important social factor. When younger speakers use more new variants than older speakers, it may indicate the presence of natural changes in the language. However, differences associated with age may have other explanations. In some cases, differences are merely the result of **age-grading**. Speakers may have different language behavior depending on social situations associated with age. For example, as noted earlier, slang expressions are more closely associated with younger speakers. Furthermore, there may be differences associated with the aging process. Age also interacts with sex in cases where the language is changing.

Gender

One of the most widely reported social factors in linguistic variation is that of sex. Cross-linguistically and cross-culturally, we find that the speech of men and women tends to differ. Two tendencies have been frequently observed:

20)

I. When variation is stable (no change is occurring), men use more nonstandard forms than do women.

II. When variation is leading to a change in the language, women use more of the incoming forms than do men.

In general, it has been observed that women are most often associated with greater use of variants that carry prestige, but agreement has not been reached as to the explanation for these tendencies. A number of theories have been suggested.

One possibility is that sex differences result from local network density. However, this is difficult to uphold since social groups almost always include members of both sexes. Even so, men and women will often form distinct social networks within social groups. As discussed earlier, linguistic differences related to sex may also be the result of power differentials in society associated with gender roles.

One extremely compelling explanation is associated with the observation that women tend to lead in situations where change is in progress. This is attributed to their role as child caregivers. Small children in the early stages of acquisition are more likely to hear innovative forms produced by women than by men; thus, the change is advanced because it is transmitted to the younger generation. Where men are in the lead, their limited contact with the next generation in their formative years diminishes the probability that male speech patterns will be passed on.

Ethnicity

In multicultural settings, ethnicity can be expressed linguistically either by the use of different languages or by means of phonological or other grammatical distinctions among varieties in the same language. A group's ancestral language or dialect may have an effect on its variety. The speech of ethnic groups may feature speech markers due to direct influences from the substrate language or dialect. The study of ethnic variation in the English of Irish and Italian Americans in Boston, Cajuns in Louisiana, and Hispanic Americans in other parts of the United States has confirmed this.

However, appeal to linguistic origin does not explain why ethnic variation persists. It has been suggested that the persistence of ethnic languages and dialects is related to their degree of **ethnolinguistic vitality**. Such factors as the number of speakers in a community; the degree to which the ethnic group and the language it speaks has institutional support from government, school, church, mass media, and culture; as well as pride in the community may result in retention of ethnic varieties in a community.

The study of ethnicity is complicated because it is frequently entangled with a complex of social characteristics, any or all of which may influence variation. For example, proposing ethnicity to explain African American Vernacular English (AAVE) as a distinct variety of American English has been confounded by the possible effects of geographical distribution and social class.

AAVE (African American Vernacular English)

Despite the caveat against generalizing about AAVE as a distinct variety of American English, some common characteristics of AAVE are agreed upon. However, the origins of AAVE are still a topic of vigorous debate among linguists. Among the questions under investigation are the possible origins of AAVE as a creole (see Section 2.3), the extent to which present-day features can be traced to origins in African languages, and the extent to which AAVE both influenced and was influenced by white southern speech.

Some of the characteristics of AAVE, particularly where phonology is concerned, are shared with other dialects of American English, and it is difficult to point to single features as characteristic of AAVE and AAVE only. However, the list in Table 15.13, while not exhaustive, is illustrative of some of the phonological features of AAVE. Consonant cluster reduction word-finally is quite regular and depends on voicing of the final two consonants. The second element in a cluster is deleted word-finally if it shares the same [± voice] feature with the preceding consonant. Thus, *test* becomes *tes, desk* becomes *des, hand* becomes *han,* but *pant* does not become **pan.* The deletion rule operates before the addition of the plural suffix, since the plural of *tes* is *tesses* and the plural of *des* is *desses.* Although other varieties of English simplify

Table 15.13 Some phonological features of AAVE

Phonological feature	*Example*
Consonant cluster reduction word-finally	test → tes, desk → des
Deletion of postvocalic liquids	help → [hɛp], ball → [bɔ], car → [kɑ]
Stopping of ð word-initially	the man → [də] man
Change of θ to f, and ð to v word-medially and word-finally	mouth → [mawf] the brother → [də bɹʌvə] smooth → [smuv]

consonant clusters word-finally, AAVE is more likely than other varieties to delete the second consonant even when a vowel follows, as in *lif up* (for *lift up*).

The morphosyntactic features of AAVE illustrate the rule-governed and systematic nature of AAVE. Some of these features are listed in Table 15.14.

Table 15.14 Some morphosyntactic features of AAVE

Morphosyntactic feature	*Example*
absence of possessive *-s*	John hat, Byron car
absence of 3 SG present *-s*	she talk, he sing
absence of PL *-s* when quantifier given	three dog, some cat
multiple negation	He don' know nothin'.
inversion with indefinite negative subject	Don' nobody talk like that.
stressed *bín* for state begun in remote past and still continuing	She bín married. I bín known him.
habitual *be*	The coffee be cold (= always). He be tired out (= habitually).
copula deletion	She nice. He in the kitchen. He tired out (= temporarily).
come to express indignation	She come goin' in my room.

The -*s* morph marking the possessive, the third person singular present, and the plural may be absent. AAVE shares with some other varieties of English (including the English written by Chaucer) the possibility for multiple negation, but it also allows inversion when the subject of the sentence is an indefinite negative:

21)

Don't nobody talk like that.
'Absolutely no one talks like that.'
*Don't John talk like that.
*Don't everybody talk like that.

As the starred examples in *21* show, when the subject of the sentence names a specific person, the inversion is unacceptable; likewise, it is unacceptable when the subject is not a negative.

AAVE has a much richer aspectual system (the forms that indicate duration or type of activity of the verb) than standard English, and the examples listed in Table 15.14 are not exhaustive. In AAVE, the stressed *bín* denotes a state, condition, or activity begun in the remote past and continued to the present. It is not simply a deletion of the standard English auxiliary verb *have* with the same meaning as in standard English *have/has been*. For an AAVE speaker, *She bín married* means that she got married a long time ago and is still married, whereas most non-AAVE speakers would interpret it as meaning that she is no longer married.

The use of **habitual (invariant) *be*** to mark a habitual or repeated state, condition, or action is illustrated in *22*.

22)

a. This room be cold.
*This room be cold today.

b. He be tired out.
*He be tired out right now.

As the starred examples show, the use of habitual *be* means that the state is constant or habitual, not one that is a temporary condition or onetime occurrence. Conversely, copula deletion may be used for a temporary or onetime state of affairs. Thus, *He tired out* can mean that he is tired out today or right now, but not necessarily as a habitual state.

Another aspectual marker in AAVE is *come* used to express indignation. Although other varieties of English have similar structures with *come,* it is obviously not a verb of motion in this AAVE structure when it is used as in *23*.

23)

She come goin' into my room without knockin'.

As this sentence illustrates, *come* and *go* cannot both be verbs of motion. Instead, *come* expresses the speaker's annoyance.

The lists given here of AAVE features are not meant to be exhaustive, nor are they meant to suggest that all speakers of AAVE use exactly these forms. Just as speakers of Appalachian English will differ according to their specific geographical origin, level of education, and socioeconomic status, so too will speakers of AAVE. Similarly, it must be remembered that speakers of any variety of English may be bidialectal or multidialectal and will accommodate to a greater or lesser extent to the setting in which they find themselves and the interlocutors with whom they are speaking.

2.3 Languages in Contact

Lingua Franca

Wherever there is social and commercial interaction between groups of people who speak different languages, we frequently find that speakers maintain their own languages for interaction within the group and designate one semiofficial language for the purpose of communicating between groups. A language used for this purpose is called a **lingua franca**. A lingua franca may be the native language of one of the interacting groups or it may be a "neutral" language in that none of the groups speaks it natively. For example, in many colonized countries where more than one language group exists, a European language—spread by traders and then adopted by local groups—may operate as the lingua franca. However, there are other ways for a lingua franca to arise.

Pidgins

Contact situations where speakers have restricted access to each other's language can sometimes lead to the formation of a **pidgin**—a rudimentary language with minimal grammatical rules and a small lexicon. By definition, a pidgin has no native speakers, and many pidgins are predominantly used as a lingua franca. In fact, the term *lingua franca* comes from the name of a pidgin trade language spoken in the eastern Mediterranean from the Middle Ages to the nineteenth century. Example *24* shows three examples of English-based pidgins.

24)

a. Neo-Melanesian
mi stap lɔŋŋ bɪglajn, mi kətɪm kopra
'I was in the work-group, cutting copra.'

b. Chinese Pidgin English
Before my sell-um for ten dollar.
PAST 1 SG sell-TRANSITIVE for ten dollar
'I sold it for ten dollars.'

c. Nauru Pidgin English (spoken on the Pacific island of Nauru)
Mi hasɪbən flɛn no waɪfu.
my husband friend no wife
'My husband's friend has no wife.'

The examples in *24* illustrate some linguistic features of pidgins. Pidgins are distinguished from other languages in that they have only a small number of grammatical categories and very little grammatical complexity. For example, pidgins do not generally have complement clauses nor do they have bound morphemes to mark agreement, tense, or number. As *24b* illustrates, past tense meaning is conveyed with the use of an adverb of time, *before,* and the word *dollar* is not marked for plurality. All three examples in *24* show use of invariable pronouns; in other words, instead of different pronouns *I, me, my* for subject, object, and possessive, there is just one form. Another feature of English-based pidgins, shown in *24a* and *24b,* is the use of *-um* or *-im* to mark a transitive verb (a verb that takes an object). Typically, too, the lexicon of a pidgin will be relatively limited. As a result, one word may have multiple meanings. In Chinese Pidgin English, for example, *pay* had the meaning of both 'pay' and 'give'. In Chinook Jargon, a Native American pidgin of the Northwest coast, *muckamuck* meant 'eat' as well as 'drink' and even 'bite'. Pidgin phonology also tends to be simplified. For example, the Fijian fricatives /β/ and /ð/ become the corresponding stops /b/ and /d/ in Pidgin Fijian. Pidgins do not generally use tone phonemically, even when the speakers of a particular pidgin have tones in their native languages. And as *24c* shows in the words for *husband* and *wife,* epenthesis may be used to create CV syllables and avoid obstruent codas.

Exactly how pidgins emerge is a controversial question. Some have suggested that pidgins arise as a result of foreigner talk (discussed in Chapter 12), which is also a simplified form of language. This assumes that native speakers of the **lexifier language** (from which the pidgin takes most of its words) who came into contact with speakers of other languages used foreigner talk to speak to them rather than the standard form of their language.

Pidgins tend to originate in two main social situations. One common situation is in areas where there is a great deal of trade between groups of people who speak different languages. Maritime pidgins were used by sailors in communicating with coastal peoples with whom they traded. One example is Russenorsk, which arose in the early 1800s as the result of contact between Russian and Norwegian fishermen working on the Arctic coast of Norway. Russenorsk had dual variants for many words, some lexified from Russian and some from Norwegian, as well as a few words of Dutch or English origin. Australian Pidgin English, Chinese Pidgin Portuguese, and Pidgin Arabic are examples of trade languages lexified by international languages. There are also several examples of pidgins formed from non-European languages as a result of trade, such as the Chinook Jargon mentioned earlier, and Sango, a pidgin form of Ngabandi—a language of west central Africa.

Pidgins have also frequently been found in situations in which people from a large number of language backgrounds come together as hired laborers, slaves, or indentured workers. In the past, these pidgins were found on large agricultural plantations. One modern-day workforce pidgin in extensive use is Fanagalo, a Zulu-based pidgin used by mine workers in southern Africa.

Although some pidgins remain in use for centuries, pidgins are often relatively short-lived. Two main reasons can account for the temporary nature of many pidgins. First, they are generally held in great disdain by native speakers of the lexifier language, so it is socially advantageous for pidgin speakers to learn the standard form of the language when communicating with its speakers. Only in situations where the pidgin operates as a lingua franca between speech communities does it tend to endure for some time. Second, in cases where speakers of different languages come together (for reasons varying from voluntary urbanization to involuntary segregation), their children may learn the pidgin as a first language, and it may be adopted as the native language of the new community. When this happens, the pidgin becomes a full-fledged language known as a **creole**.

Creoles

When a pidgin becomes a creole, its inventory of lexical items and grammatical rules expands dramatically, usually in only one or two generations. One word-formation process used extensively in creoles is conversion (also known as zero derivation; see Chapter 4). For example, in Berbice Dutch—a nearly extinct creole of the coast of Guyana—*kapu* can mean 'to cut', 'a cut', and 'operation'; *kurkuru* means 'black, become black, blacken'; and *sara* can be used to mean both 'to fall' and 'to drop'.

Creoles also frequently use compounding to create new words, as illustrated in *25* by Tok Pisin—the creole that is the official language of Papua New Guinea.

25)

mausgras	(mouth + grass)	'moustache'
gras nogut	(grass + no good)	'weed'
daiman	(die + man)	'corpse'

Reduplication is also very common in creoles and can be used to indicate a variety of meanings, as shown in *26* by Sranan—an English-based creole of Surinam—and by Fa d'Ambu—a west African Portuguese-based creole spoken on an island off the coast of Equatorial Guinea.

26)

a. Sranan

fatu	'fat'	fat(u)fatu	'a bit fat'
ferfi	'paint'	ferfiferfi	'to paint a lot'

b. Fa d'Ambu

kitsyi	'small'	kitsyikitsyi	'very small'
gavu	'good'	gagavu	'very good'

Creoles worldwide also share remarkably similar grammatical characteristics. Creoles betray their pidgin origins by commonly having invariable pronouns and limited bound morphology. However, unlike pidgins, which can have a variety of word orders, creoles almost universally adhere to an SVO word order. Also, in contrast with pidgins, which do not mark tense except with a time adverb, creoles have a number of preverbal elements used to mark tense and aspect (e.g., duration of the action of the verb). The examples in *27* serve to illustrate some of the common features of creoles.

27)

a. Australian Roper River Creole

de bin alde luk dat big tri
3PL PAST always look that big tree
'They always looked for a big tree.'

b. Sranan

a ben e sidon fow en anu na ondro en kakumbe
3SG PAST PROG sit fold 3SG hand LOC under 3SG chin
'He was sitting as usual with his chin on his hands.'

c. Saramaccan

di buku aki mi bi ta lesi
the book here 1SG PAST PROG read
'The book here I have been reading.'

All three examples in *27* mark the past tense with a preverbal particle—*bin, ben, bi.* The examples in *27b* and *27c* illustrate marking of progressive aspect, with *e* in the case of Sranan and *ta* in the case of Saramaccan. The example in *27c* also illustrates a syntactic feature common in many creoles—that of fronting, in which new information is moved to the front of the sentence to focus attention on it.

There are two basic theories to account for the common features of creoles found worldwide. On the one hand, some people believe that creoles either (l) originated from a single, common protopidgin, with different lexical items taken from each individual lexifier language; or (2) are based on one or more of the native languages originally spoken by the founders of the community. The fact that creoles have many similarities simply reflects universal features of language, and differences are accounted for by differences in the **substrate**, or base, languages. This is called the **relexification hypothesis**.

Another prevailing theory is the **language bioprogram hypothesis**, which claims that similarities among creoles reflect universal properties of an innate biological program that guides language acquisition. This theory has evolved, and more recent versions are similar to the Universal Grammar (UG) hypothesis (see Chapter 5). The bioprogram hypothesis is supported by studies of Tok Pisin—a recently formed creole in New Guinea—which have shown that there is a sharp difference in grammatical structure between the generation that speaks the pidgin and the one that speaks the creole. According to the theory, since the first generation of children who acquired the creole must have done so on the basis of an impoverished input, any grammatical structure found in the newly formed creole must have come from their innate language program.

Both these theories have been criticized, and the available evidence is not sufficient to decide unequivocably between the two. Critics of relexification note that there are too many differences across the possible substrate languages to account for the similarities in creoles. Furthermore, in slave populations, people who spoke a common language were often separated from each other to avoid rebellion, casting doubt on the possibility that one base language would have predominated. However, there have been studies of Pacific creoles that are consistent with the relexification hypothesis. The main problem in resolving the issue is that there are no current situations where both the resulting creole and the pidgin input can be observed, so even conclusions based on detailed quantitative comparative analysis are still subject to doubt.

Grammatical features of some creoles may also have arisen from contact with the lexifier language. In most areas, creoles exist alongside a local version of the standard language, which is termed the **acrolect**. As in most other nonstandard language situations, the creole is highly variable, and a number of stages or varieties of the creole can be identified. The variety that is least like the standard is called the **basilect**, while varieties intervening between the basilect and acrolect are termed **mesolects**. For example, the basilectal variety of Jamaican creole uses *nyam* for 'eat', *no ben* for 'didn't', and /d/ in place of /ð/. The acrolect uses *eat, didn't,* and /ð/. One mesolectal variety might use *eat, no ben,* and /d/, while another mesolectal variety with fewer creole features would use *eat, didn't,* and /d/.

In all the previous situations described, it is the speakers of each individual language who are in contact, so that while elements of two languages may combine in a resulting variety, there is no clear indication that any "mixing" of languages is taking place. In the day-to-day use of bilinguals, however, two languages are used by a single speaker who may or may not combine languages in a number of ways.

Code-Switching

In bilingual speech communities, speakers often adopt a speech variety that involves alternating between languages in the same discourse, as in example *28*. This is called **code-switching**.

28)

a. Acadian French-English
Pis, elle est toute seule, comme c'est ('well, it is all alone as if it's') *in the middle of nowheres.*

b. Puerto Rican Spanish-English
Why make Carol *sentarse atras pa' que* ('sit in the back so') everybody has to move *pa' que se salga* ('for her to get out')?

c. Fongbe-French

mɛ́ḍé	lɛ́	nɔ́	ḍò	*gravement*	*blessés.*
someone	PL	HAB	be	seriously	hurt

'Some are seriously hurt.'

Not all utterances that contain elements from two languages necessarily involve code-switching. In example *29,* where a single word from one language is embedded in the syntax of another language, the speaker may merely be **borrowing** a word from one language (L1) into another (L2).

29)

a. French-English

J'ai ramassé une *bathtub,*	pis	j m'ai viré de bord	avec la *bathtub.*
I picked up a bathtub,	then I	fell over	with the bathtub

'I picked up a bathtub and then I fell over with the bathtub.'

b. Finnish-English

Näitä	kaks,	kolme	*bypassia*	sillä	on.
these-PL	two	three	bypass-PL	he-AD	is

'He has two, three bypasses.'

c. Arabic-French

dartha	f'	l'	*couloir*	u	ɣadi
put it (I)	in	the	hallway	and	left (I)

'I put it in the hallway and I left.'

This is particularly true when the word in question shows phonological, morphological, and syntactic properties of the L2, although borrowing does not always involve full integration on all these levels.

Another important question in the study of code-switching has to do with why it occurs in the first place. In some communities, the mere act of code-switching operates as a discourse mode and can signal solidarity between speakers in the same way as any other register of language. This is the case in the Puerto Rican Spanish-English community in New York City and may also be true of French-English bilinguals in New Brunswick. In this case, code-switching may operate metaphorically to express solidarity with or distance from one community. When this occurs, it is called **metaphorical code-switching**.

When people switch from one code to another for clearly identifiable reasons, it is referred to as **situational code-switching**. For example, in some bilingual societies, one language may be more closely associated with government functions while the other is more closely associated with casual conversations. A speaker may begin a conversation with an acquaintance at a government office in one language and when the conversation turns to more bureaucratic topics, the participants may switch to another language.

Studies of code-switching as a discourse mode have found that, contrary to popular belief, the ability to produce code-switching smoothly requires a great deal of language ability. This counters any suggestion that code-switching is somehow degenerate and not *real* language, as derogatory terms like *Franglais* and *Spanglish* may imply.

Summing Up

The study of **sociolinguistics** is concerned with language in its social context within the **speech community**. As such, it involves both the **sociolinguistics of language** and the **sociolinguistics of society**. How language is used in discourse is affected by the **speech situation** and its components. Any given discourse can be analyzed and its overall structure identified. These structures can provide clues to the function of linguistic behavior. Language is an important tool in the expression of **solidarity** and **power** between individuals. **Sociolinguistic norms** for language use can also give indications of how power is distributed in society in general.

The relationship between language and society is clearly shown by the existence of **standard** and **nonstandard** language varieties. Whether or not a language or structure is considered standard is dependent on attitudes of speakers and not on any inherent notion of "correctness." Factors such as region, social class, social network, age, gender, and ethnicity may all have an effect on whether or not a form is considered nonstandard. The designation of **official languages** and **language planning** are political ways for either reducing the disadvantages experienced by speakers of nonstandard varieties or promoting standard varieties in the interest of increasing the power of their speakers. Speakers can also vary between varieties for political reasons. A **lingua franca** can be used to communicate between groups in societies where many languages are spoken. Where communication is limited, a **pidgin** or **creole** language may arise. In groups where speakers are multilingual, speakers may **code-switch** between languages for a number of reasons. At the very least, a language contact situation usually results in the **borrowing** of words between linguistic groups.

By confronting variation and studying its properties (both linguistic and social), over thirty years of research has confirmed that linguistic variation is not "free" but rather shows complex, probabilistic patterns of social and linguistic conditioning that reflect the sociolinguistic competence and, in most cases, the social identity of speakers. Speakers behave in a manner consistent with their own identity and according to the perceived identity of others.

Key Terms

General terms

accents
dialects
ethnic dialect
mutual intelligibility
regional dialects
sociolects
sociolinguistic norms
sociolinguistic variable
sociolinguistics
sociolinguistics of language
sociolinguistics of society
speech community
speech variety

Terms concerning discourse analysis and ethnography of communication

communicative competence
discourse
discourse analysis
ethnography of communication
jargon
register
slang
speech act theory
speech event
speech situation
style
text analysis
utterances

Terms concerning ethnomethodology and text analysis

adjacency pair
closing
conversation analysis
cooperative overlaps
discourse markers
ethnomethodology
high involvement style
opening
turn-taking

Terms concerning politeness

face-threatening acts
interlocutors
negative face
negative politeness
positive face
positive politeness

Terms concerning power and solidarity

accommodation
address terms
converge
diverge
euphemisms
gender-exclusive
gender-variable
no-naming
power
solidarity
taboo
verbal hedges

Terms concerning the standard and linguistic attitudes

diglossia
domains of use
linguistic insecurity
matched guise test
nonstandard
orderly heterogeneity
standard

Terms concerning language planning

African American Vernacular English (AAVE)
ebonics
language planning
official language

Terms concerning methods of studying variation

atlas surveys
dialectology
Internet surveys
postal survey
telephone survey

Terms concerning regional variation

a-prefixing
isogloss bundle
isoglosses
Northern Cities Shift
postvocalic *r*
relic forms
Southern Shift
vowel shift

Terms concerning language and social class, age, and ethnic variation

age-grading
dense social networks
ethnolinguistic vitality
habitual (invariant) *be*
hypercorrection
multiplex networks
social network analysis

Terms related to languages in contact

acrolect
basilect
borrowing
code-switching
creole
language bioprogram hypothesis
lexifier language
lingua franca
mesolects
metaphorical code-switching
pidgin
relexification hypothesis
situational code-switching
substrate (language)

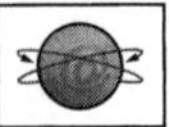

For more information on the sources used in this chapter, go to **bedfordstmartins .com/linguistics/socialcontexts** and click on **Sources**.

Recommended Reading

Chambers, J.K. 1995. *Sociolinguistic Theory.* Oxford: Blackwell.
Downes, W. 1998. *Language and Society.* Cambridge, UK: Cambridge University Press.
Fasold, R. 1984. *The Sociolinguistics of Society.* Oxford: Blackwell.
Fasold, R. 1990. *Sociolinguistics of Language.* Oxford: Blackwell.
Green, L. 2002. *African American English: An Introduction.* Cambridge: Cambridge University Press.
Holmes, J. 1992. *An Introduction to Sociolinguistics.* New York: Longman and Brown.
Schiffrin, D. 1994. *Approaches to Discourse.* Oxford: Blackwell.
Wolfram, W., and N. Schilling-Estes. 1998. *American English: Dialects and Variation.* Oxford: Blackwell.

Exercises

1. Choose a speech situation and analyze it using the components discussed in the section on ethnography of communication.

2. Focusing on a particular adolescent or young adult social group in your community, make a list of the slang terms that they use. Using this list, question an older member of the community and determine how the use of terms differs and how it is the same.

3. Using the adjacency pair greeting–response, choose a specific situation and question four people from different cultural backgrounds to determine if there are any differences in the kinds of utterances they use. State the rules for each different cultural background.

4. Observe the way people around you close conversations. Make a list of some examples of closings. What made a closing particularly effective or ineffective? Why?

5. Examine newspaper articles or television news reports and isolate any examples of euphemisms. Suggest a reason why they were employed.

6. Considering the discussion of language and gender, look for two examples where androcentric bias might be found in three books on the prescriptive rules of English grammar (see Section 1.2 on language and sex). Try to choose books from three different time frames, such as a book from the early 1900s as opposed to books that have been published more recently. Are all three books in agreement regarding the rules you have isolated? What might this indicate about the representation of gender in language?

7. *i.* The examples given in Table 15.9 in the section on language attitudes were given to subjects in New York City. Make your own list of ten words with alternative pronunciations that could be used to test linguistic insecurity. Justify your choice of each word.

   ii. Ask ten people to give you their preferred pronunciation of the words. Then, ask each person which is more "correct." Are there any discrepancies in their answers? What do the results say about the possible linguistic insecurity of the people you talked to?

8. Based on observation of people in your community, construct a questionnaire for eliciting terms, structures, and pronunciations that you have noticed are variable.

For the Student Linguist

WHEN LANGUAGE GOES BAD

Nothing shows more clearly how many rules and norms we have about language use than when something goes awry. The following example, from Tom

Stoppard's *Rosencrantz and Guildenstern Are Dead,* would probably be an interactional sociolinguist's worst nightmare.

In case you haven't read the play or seen the movie, Rosencrantz and Guildenstern (whom you may recall as two minor characters from *Hamlet*) are killing time and decide to play a game. The rules of the game are actually straightforward. Unfortunately for the poor interactional sociolinguist, the guys aren't too consistent with their application of the rules. Thus, some of the statements they make about the game (e.g., "Cheating!") aren't scored as part of the game while others are (e.g., "I hadn't started yet").

The speech norms seem even more dubious when you look at Rosencrantz and Guildenstern's decisions about what does (and does not) count as a synonym, as a non sequitur, or as rhetoric. However, it's surprising to me that many of the components of this speech situation are relatively easily identifiable in spite of this being such an absurd discourse. After you've identified the components, you might want to experiment with making just one or two of them absurd (choosing different ones than Stoppard did) while keeping the others logical, and see if there's any sort of system or pattern to effective humor. Then again, too much analysis always kills a joke. Maybe you should just rent the video, make some popcorn, and put off your homework for tonight.

ROS: We could play at questions.
GUIL: What good would that do?
ROS: Practice!
GUIL: Statement! One-love.
ROS: Cheating!
GUIL: How?
ROS: I hadn't started yet.
GUIL: Statement. Two-love.
ROS: Are you counting that?
GUIL: What?
ROS: Are you counting that?
GUIL: Foul! No repetitions. Three-love. First game to . . .
ROS: I'm not going to play if you're going to be like that.
GUIL: Whose serve?
ROS: Hah?
GUIL: Foul! No grunts. Love-one.
ROS: Whose go?
GUIL: Why?
ROS: Why not?
GUIL: What for?
ROS: Foul! No synonyms! One-all.
GUIL: What in God's name is going on?
ROS: Foul! No rhetoric. Two-one.
GUIL: What does it all add up to?
ROS: Can't you guess?

GUIL: Were you addressing me?
ROS: Is there anyone else?
GUIL: Who?
ROS: How would I know?
GUIL: Why do you ask?
ROS: Are you serious?
GUIL: Was that rhetoric?
ROS: No.
GUIL: Statement! Two-all. Game point.
ROS: What's the matter with you today?
GUIL: When?
ROS: What?
GUIL: Are you deaf?
ROS: Am I dead?
GUIL: Yes or no?
ROS: Is there a choice?
GUIL: Is there a God?
ROS: Foul! No non sequiturs, three-two, one game all.
GUIL: (*seriously*) What's your name?
ROS: What's yours?
GUIL: I asked you first.
ROS: Statement. One-love.
GUIL: What's your name when you're at home?
ROS: What's yours?
GUIL: When I'm at home?
ROS: What home?
GUIL: Haven't you got one?
ROS: Why do you ask?
GUIL: What are you driving at?
ROS: (*with emphasis*) What's your name?
GUIL: Repetition. Two-love. Match point to me.
ROS: (*seizing him violently*) WHO DO YOU THINK YOU ARE?
GUIL: Rhetoric! Game and match!

sixteen

Writing and Language

Michael Dobrovolsky
William O'Grady

Outside of a dog, a book is man's best friend; inside of a dog, it's too dark to read.

– GROUCHO MARX

OBJECTIVES

In this chapter, you will learn:

- how different types of writing systems have developed from earliest times
- how different types of alphabetic systems emerged
- how various types of non-European writing systems developed
- how historical factors have led to the modern English spelling system
- how writing and reading are related

Speaking and writing are different in both origin and practice. Our ability to use language is as old as humankind, and reflects the biological and cognitive modification that has occurred during the evolution of our species. **Writing**, the symbolic representation of language by graphic signs or symbols, is a comparatively recent cultural development, having occurred within the past five thousand years and only in certain parts of the world. The contrast between speech and writing comes into sharper focus when we consider that spoken language is acquired without specific formal instruction, whereas writing must be taught and learned through deliberate effort. There are entire groups of people in the world today, as well as individuals in every literate society, who are unable to write. While spoken language comes naturally to human beings, writing does not.

1 Types of Writing

As different as they are, speech and writing share one major characteristic: just as spoken language shows an arbitrary link between sound and meaning, written language exhibits an arbitrary link between symbol and sound.

All writing can be grouped into two basic types—logographic and phonographic—depending on the technique that it uses to represent language.

1.1 Logographic Writing

The term **logographic** (from Greek *logos* 'word') refers to a type of writing in which symbols called **logograms** represent morphemes or even entire words.

Logograms

Logographic writing is the oldest type of genuine writing. Ancient Mesopotamian **cuneiform** inscriptions, Egyptian **hieroglyphs**, and primordial Chinese **characters** were all highly logographic in their early stages. In fact, all writing systems maintain some logographic writing. Conventional abbreviations such as &, %, $, and the like are logographic, as are the symbols for numerals. To a certain extent, logographic writing can be read independently of its language of origin. For example, the Arabic numbers 1, 2, 7, 10, and so on can be read in any language.

1.2 Phonographic Writing

No writing system is purely logographic, however. Nor can it be, since using a separate symbol to write each word in a language is simply too cumbersome. Throughout human history, writing systems have always evolved signs that represent some aspect of pronunciation. In **phonographic writing** (from Greek *phōnē* 'sound'), symbols represent syllables or segments. There are two principal types of phonographic writing systems—syllabic and alphabetic.

Syllabic Writing

As the name suggests, **syllabic writing** employs signs to represent syllables (a set of syllabic signs is called a **syllabary**). Languages with relatively simple syllabic structures such as CV or CVC (Japanese and Cherokee, for example) are well suited to this type of writing, since they contain a relatively limited number of syllable types. In Japanese, for example, the word *kakimashita* '(s/he) wrote' can be written with the five syllabic signs か, き, ま, し, and た: かきました.

Alphabetic Writing

Alphabetic writing represents consonant and vowel segments. Unlike the International Phonetic Alphabet, which is devised expressly to represent details of pronunciation, ordinary alphabets generally ignore nonphonemic phenomena. Thus, the spelling of the English words *pan* and *nap* represents the phonemes /p/, /n/, and /æ/ but ignores consonant aspiration, vowel nasalization, and other subphonemic variation. As we will see in Section 4 of this chapter, some spelling systems also capture certain morphophonemic alternations.

Writing systems emerged and spread around the world over a long period of time. Though we can trace the spread of some systems over a wide area, writing may have emerged independently in several different places. The next sections trace the development of some writing systems from their pictorial origins.

2 The Early History of Writing

It is surprising that we cannot say with certainty how a comparatively recent cultural phenomenon like writing originated. We do know that the precursors of writing involved direct representation of objects. This is sometimes called **prewriting**.

2.1 Prewriting

Figures and scenes depicted on cave walls and rock faces in the Americas, Africa, and Europe as much as fifteen thousand years ago may have been forerunners of writing. Some of these petroglyphs (scenes painted on stone) may represent a type of preliterate stage that did not evolve into a full-fledged writing system.

These drawings depict a wide range of human and animal activity, and may even have been intended for purposes of linguistic communication. Some illustrations were doubtless a form of religious magic to guarantee a successful hunt or other benefits. Perhaps some were purely aesthetic expression. Still others, such as those depicting the phases of the moon, may have been part of some form of record keeping. For example, the cave paintings of Lascaux, France, dating back to 15,000 B.C., have been interpreted as religious magic. Among the realistic paintings of animals are hundreds of abstract signs. As Figure 16.1a shows, some are feather or branchlike signs, others are parallel marks suggesting animal tracks, and others are box-shaped signs, possibly representing traps or enclosures. Figure 16.1b shows an incised eagle bone from Le Placard, France, that dates back some 13,000 to 15,000 years. The incisions, which vary subtly, have been analyzed as a record of lunar phases. Pictorial records thus link the origins of writing with the history of representative art.

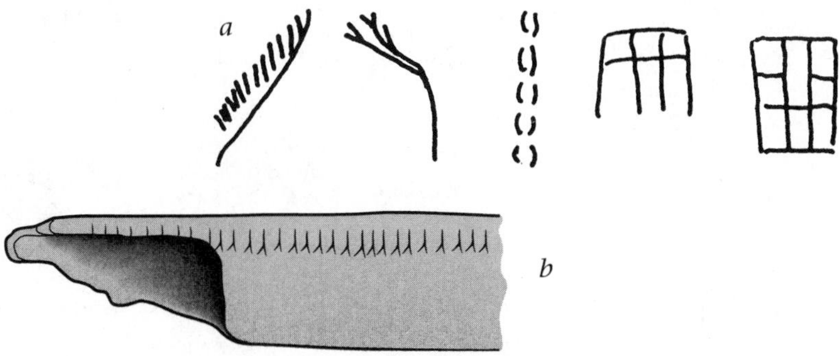

Figure 16.1 *a.* Abstract signs, Lascaux cave; *b.* Le Placard eagle bone

An even more direct connection may link the origin of writing with record keeping. Small clay tokens or counters such as those shown in Figure 16.2 have been recovered from prehistoric sites throughout the Near East. It has been suggested that these tokens were used for thousands of years before the invention of writing for record keeping and business transactions. These tokens were in use at the end of the fourth millennium B.C., along with clay tablets incised with numerical signs as well as seal impressions stamped on clay to indicate ownership.

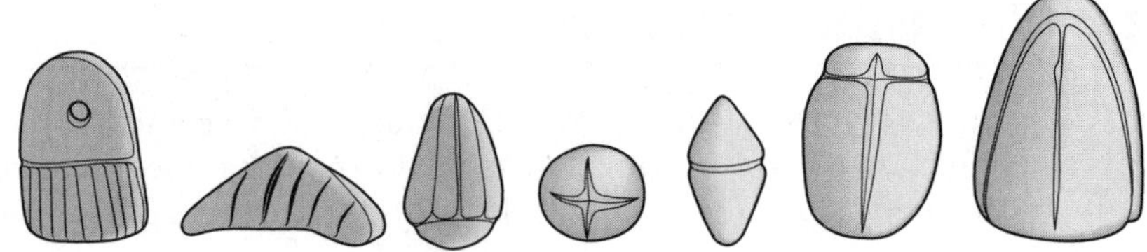

Figure 16.2 Ancient Mesopotamian tokens

2.2 Pictograms

Early writing systems made use of pictorial representations called **pictograms**, or picture writing. Each pictogram was an image of the object or concept that it represented and, as far as we know, offered no clues to pronunciation. Pictorial representations of this sort have been found among people throughout the ancient and modern world. Figure 16.3 is an example of Native American picture writing taken from a record kept by a Dakota named Lonedog; these pictures served as a kind of memory aid and not as a detailed record of events.

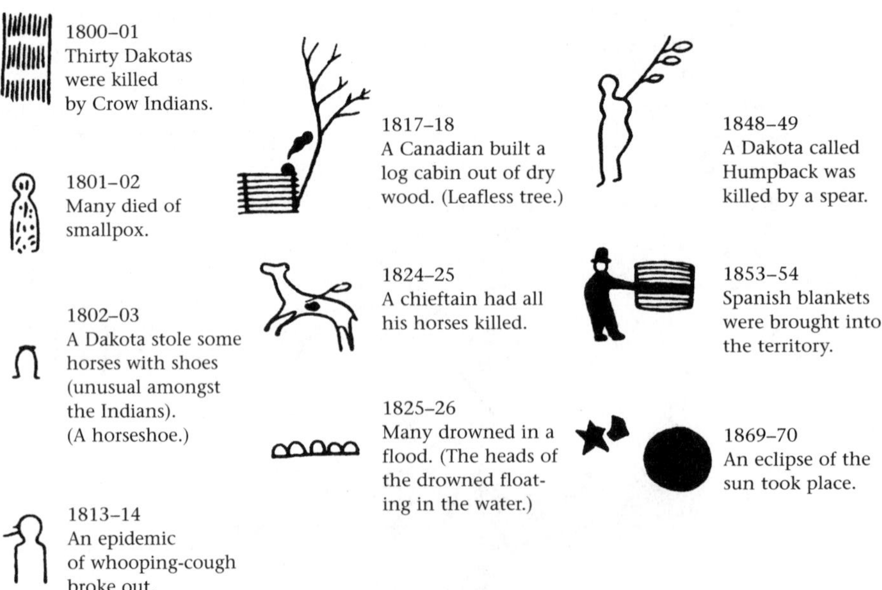

Figure 16.3 Native American pictography: a Dakota record of significant events

Like any other product of culture, pictography requires a knowledge of the conventions used by the author. Lonedog's record, for example, lists thirty Dakotas killed, but there are only twenty-four short vertical lines. To interpret the record correctly, it is necessary to know that the frame around the short lines consists of six additional joined lines.

Pictograms are still used today, often reflecting the function of this form of prewriting as a memory aid. Signs indicating roadside services or information in parks are all pictographic in nature, as are the standardized set of symbols developed by the Olympic Association to indicate sporting events (see Figure 16.4).

Figure 16.4 Contemporary pictograms: Olympic signs for sporting events

For another contemporary example of pictograms, go to **bedfordstmartins .com/linguistics/writingandlanguage** and click on **pictograms**.

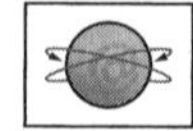

As we consider developments that emerge from pictographic representation, it is important to remember that pictograms are not writing in any sense of the word. They do not represent linguistic elements such as segments, syllables, morphemes, or words; they are not written in a sequence that matches the language's word order; and they typically lend themselves to more than one interpretation, often providing only limited clues about their intended meaning.

3 The Development of Writing

The earliest known writing appeared in Sumer about five thousand years ago and spread from there to surrounding areas. This early writing included numerical signs used for accounting and approximately nine hundred signs used in writing words. Some signs, such as those for 'barley' and 'ox', were clearly pictograms. Other signs, however, were arbitrary. For example, the sign meaning 'sheep' was a cross inside a circle, and the word for 'mother' was a star sign inside a box. Over time, inherently ambiguous pictograms came to be used to represent abstract notions, as their use was extended to include related concepts. For example, as shown in Figure 16.5, the

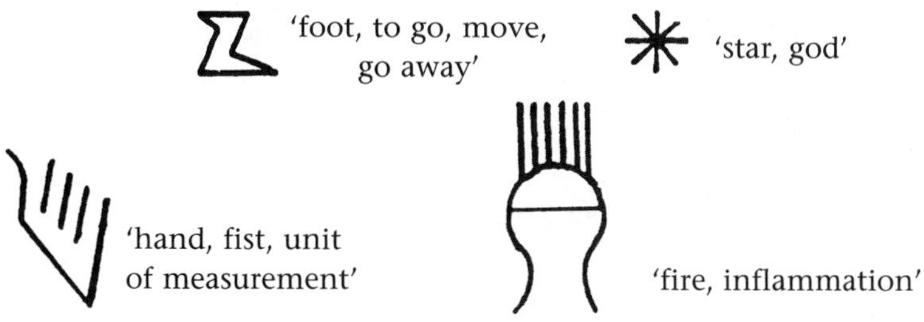

Figure 16.5 Sumerian logograms

pictogram for 'fire' was also used for 'inflammation', the pictogram for 'hand' was employed to signify 'fist' as well as a particular unit of measurement, and the symbol for 'foot' came to stand for 'go', 'move', and 'go away'. Sumerian writing also combined signs to express abstract meanings. For example, a head with fire coming out of the crown indicated 'anger', as shown in Figure 16.6.

Figure 16.6 The Sumerian logogram for 'anger'

3.1 Rebuses

Phonographic writing made its appearance at the end of the fourth millennium B.C. with the use of Sumerian symbols to represent sound rather than just meaning. This major development in the history of writing was made possible by the use of the **rebus principle**, which allows a sign to be used for any word that is pronounced like the word whose meaning it originally represented. In the inscription of an economic transaction in Figure 16.7, for example, the symbol in the upper left-hand corner, which was originally used to represent the word *gi* 'reed', here represents a homophonous word with the meaning 'reimburse'.

Figure 16.7 Sumerian rebus inscription (c. 3000 B.C.)

Thanks to the rebus principle, concepts that could not be directly depicted by a pictogram/logogram could be represented in writing. Thus, the sign for the word *ti* 'arrow', →, was also used for the word *ti* 'life'.

3.2 Toward Syllabic Writing

As Sumerian writing developed, signs that clearly represented not just homophonous words but parts of words—specifically, syllables—became well established. For example, the word *kir* was represented by the syllabic signs for *ki* and *ir,* written in sequence. (By allowing the function of the symbols to overlap in this way, the need for a special sign for *r* was avoided.) Figure 16.8 illustrates this with the help of Sumerian cuneiform signs, which are discussed in more detail in the following section. Sumerian writing never developed into a pure syllabary. Logographic elements were interspersed with syllabic ones, and many syllabic signs were used to represent syllables with other pronunciations as well.

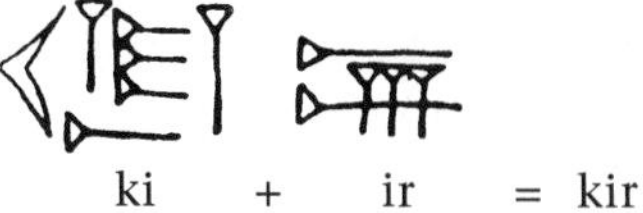

Figure 16.8 Overlapped Sumerian syllabic signs

Cuneiform

Over the centuries, Sumerian writing was simplified and eventually came to be produced with the use of a wedge-shaped stylus that was pressed into soft clay tablets. This form of writing, initiated in the fourth millennium B.C., has come to be known as cuneiform (from Latin *cuneus* 'wedge'). In time, a change in writing practices led the cuneiform signs to be modified so that they ended up bearing even less resemblance to their pictographic origins than before. Figure 16.9 illustrates this development.

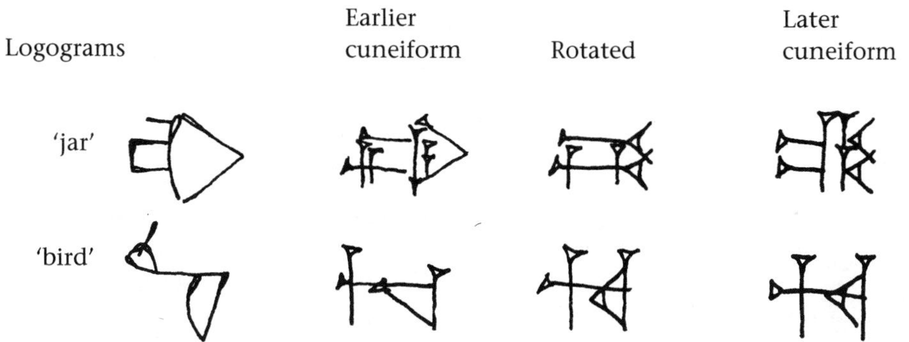

Figure 16.9 Changes in cuneiform writing

The cuneiform system was borrowed by the Elamites and Akkadians in the third millennium B.C., a little later by the Persians, and in the second millennium B.C. by the Hittites far to the north in the ancient region of Anatolia (modern Asian Turkey).

Cuneiform writing persisted until about the first few centuries of the Christian era in some areas, and then disappeared from use, not to be rediscovered until the nineteenth century. It was first deciphered from Old Persian texts, a breakthrough that led to the deciphering of Akkadian, Sumerian, and Hittite, among other languages that employed it. This script was used for thousands of years but then was generally replaced by systems of writing employed by the Semitic peoples of the eastern Mediterranean.

3.3 Another Middle Eastern Writing System: Hieroglyphs

At about the time Sumerian writing was emerging, a system of picture-based writing was in use in Egypt. The Egyptian signs have become known as hieroglyphs (meaning 'sacred inscriptions' in Greek). Hieroglyphic writing seems to have emerged as a complete system, with no evidence yet recovered of evolution from earlier forms.

Although hieroglyphs were pictures, they could be used as pictograms, as phonograms, or as **determinatives**—signs that indicated the meaning of a word and how the previous signs were to be interpreted. For example, the sign for the heart and trachea was: ; this represented the word itself: *nfr.* (Only the consonants of words represented by hieroglyphs are known with certainty. The Egyptians did not represent vowels—these can only be partially reconstructed from transcriptions in Greek and other languages that were made much later.) In addition, a sign such as this one could be disassociated from the word it represented and used to transcribe other words that consisted of or included the same sounds, such as the word for 'good', which also contained the consonants *nfr.*

Hieroglyphic symbols could be used to represent individual consonant phonemes by application of what is called the **acrophonic principle** (from Greek *acros* 'extreme'): sounds are represented by pictures of objects whose pronunciation begins with the sound to be represented. In this way, the first consonant of a word-sign came to be what the sign stood for. For example, the hieroglyph for 'horned viper':

is read logographically as *f-t.* Thanks to the acrophonic principle, this sign is also used to represent the phoneme /f/ in spellings such as *fen* 'pleasant'.

As we will see in Section 3.4, the acrophonic principle was crucial to the development of true alphabets. In Egyptian writing, however, it was only part of a system that mixed logographic and phonographic elements.

Figure 16.10 provides some additional examples of hieroglyphs. Hieroglyphs continued in decreasing use to Christian times. By the second century A.D., Egyptian began to be written with Greek letters, and by the third century A.D., hieroglyphs had been replaced by the Greek alphabet.

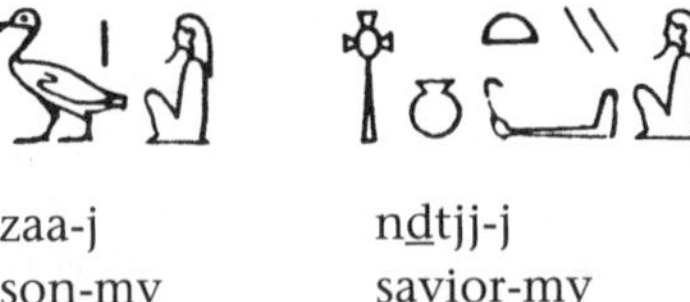

Figure 16.10 Egyptian hieroglyphs (c. 1500 B.C.)

3.4 The Emergence of Alphabets

The Semitic peoples of ancient Phoenicia (modern Lebanon) devised a writing system of twenty-two consonantal signs as early as 1000 B.C. This system was written horizontally, right to left, as had been common in earlier scripts. It ultimately led to the development of many alphabetic writing systems, including the Greek and Latin alphabets.

The pictorial (and eventually logographic) origins of the Phoenician alphabet are evident in some of its symbols. Figure 16.11 illustrates the development of logograms for a stylized ox's head, a throwing stick, and a wavy flow of water into alphabetic symbols. (Throughout this chapter, a macron indicates a long vowel.)

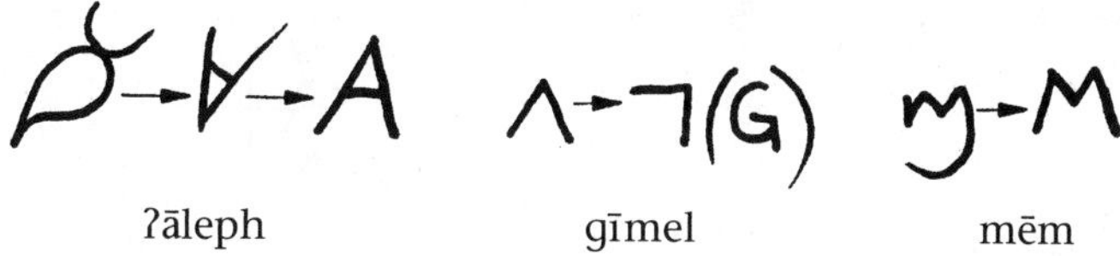

Figure 16.11 Pictorial and logographic origins of some signs in the Phoenician alphabet

These symbols came to be used to represent the consonant phonemes of words by application of the acrophonic principle (see Section 3.3). In this way, *ʔāleph* was used to represent a glottal stop; *gīmel*, a /g/; and *mēm*, an /m/. The Phoenicians were a trading people, and their alphabetic writing spread to adjacent countries and beyond. Eventually, the Greeks acquired and adapted the Phoenician alphabet.

The Greek Alphabet

The Greeks developed the Phoenician writing system into a full alphabet: each sign represented one phoneme, and all phonemes were recorded by a sign. The Greeks were aware that some of the Phoenician symbols represented consonant sounds that were not found in Greek. Some of these symbols were adapted to represent Greek vowels, and other unneeded consonant signs were eventually dropped. Figure 16.12 on page 540 illustrates the evolution of the Classical Greek and ultimately the Latin alphabet from the original Phoenician consonantal signs.

As we have seen, Phoenician *ʔāleph* represented a glottal stop. Since Greek had no such phoneme, the *ʔāleph* was employed to represent the vowel /a/ in Greek. Phoenician /h/ was used to represent the Greek vowel /e/, and other signs were added to the system by the Greeks, including Φ/p^{h}/, X/k^{h}/, Ψ/ps/, and Ω/ō/.

The Semitic names for the letters (*aleph, beth, gimel, daleth,* and so on) were maintained by the Greeks (as *alpha, beta, gamma, delta,* and so on), but the possible pictorial origins had been lost, and the names carried no other meaning. The writing system itself gained its name from the first two letters of the series: alphabet.

Unlike Phoenician, which was written right to left, the earliest inscriptions in ancient Greek reversed the direction of writing at the end of each line. If the first line of a text was written right to left, the next line continued left to right, then right to left, and so on. This practice was typical of many old writing systems and is known as **boustrophedon** (Greek for 'as the ox turns'), since it was said to resemble the pattern made by plowing a field. Eventually, this practice was abandoned, and Greek was written left to right.

The Roman Alphabet

When Greek colonists occupied southern Italy in the eighth and seventh centuries B.C., they took their alphabet with them. It was in turn taken up and modified by

Symbols			Greek			Latin	
Phoenician	Hebrew name	Phonetic value	Early	Classical	Name	Early	Monumental (Classical)
𐤀	'Aleph	ʔ	Α	Α	Alpha	A	A
𐤁	Beth	b	Β	Β	Beta		B
𐤂	Gimel	g	𐤂	Γ	Gamma		C
𐤃	Daleth	d	Δ	Δ	Delta	D	D
𐤄	He	h	Ǝ	Ε	Epsilon	Ǝ	E
𐤅	Waw	w	Ϝ		Digamma	Ϝ	F
							G
𐤆	Zayin	z	I	Ζ	Zeta		
𐤇	Ḥeth	ħ	日	Η	Ēta	日	H
𐤈	Teth	ŧ	⊗	Θ	Theta		
𐤉	Yod	j	𐤉	Ι	Iota	I	I (J)
𐤊	Kaph	k	𐤊	Κ	Kappa	K	K
𐤋	Lamed	l	𐤋	Λ	Lambda		L
𐤌	Mem	m	𐤌	Μ	Mu	M	M
𐤍	Nun	n	𐤍	Ν	Nu	N	N
𐤎	Samekh	s					
𐤏	'Ayin	ʕ	Ο	Ο	Ŏmicron	O	O
𐤐	Pe	p	𐤐	Π	Pi		P
𐤑	Tsade	ṣ	Ϻ		San		
𐤒	Qoph	q	Ϙ		Qoppa		Q
𐤓	Reš	r	𐤓	Ρ	Rho		R
𐤔	Šin	ʃ-s	Σ	Σ	Sigma	S	S
𐤕	Taw	t	X		Tau		T
				Υ	Upsilon	V	V
				Χ	Chi		X
							Y
				Ω	Omega		Z

Figure 16.12 Evolution of the Greek and Latin alphabets

the Etruscan inhabitants of central Italy—a non-Latin-speaking people who were a political and cultural power before the rise of Rome. It is believed that the Romans acquired their alphabet through the Etruscans. As the Romans grew in power and influence during the following centuries, first as masters of Italy and later of Europe, the Roman alphabet spread throughout their Empire.

Under the Romans, the Greek/Etruscan alphabet was again modified, this time with some symbols influenced by the Etruscans. The *G* in Greek writing developed into both *C* for the phoneme /k/ and *G* for /g/. The oldest inscriptions also retained *K* for /k/ in some words, but it was generally replaced by *C*. Similarly, *Q* was retained before /u/. Roman script also employed Greek *U* (= V), *X, Y,* and *Z* and moved *Z* to the end of the alphabet. The symbols Φ, Θ, Ψ, and Ω were among those discarded, and *H* was converted back to a consonant symbol.

Some subsequent changes were made in the alphabet as it was adapted by various peoples of the Roman Empire. In English, for example, *W* was created from two juxtaposed *V*s. Spanish employs a tilde (˜) over *n* (ñ) to signify a palatal nasal, as in *año* /aɲo/ 'year', and French uses a cedilla under *c* (ç) to indicate the dental fricative /s/, as in the spelling of *français* /frãsɛ/ 'French'.

Many alphabetic systems other than those of Greece and Rome flourished in Europe and the Middle East. You can find a brief discussion of these systems at **bedfordstmartins.com/linguistics/writingandlanguage** (click on **world writing systems**).

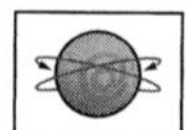

4 Some Non-European Writing Systems

This section focuses on the nature and development of writing systems that originated outside the Middle East. While some of these systems emerged in response to external influences, others seem to have been entirely independent innovations. We will focus here on the writing systems of China, Japan, and Korea as well as on a script developed for use with Cherokee. For a discussion of writing systems found in other parts of the world, including the Americas, Africa, and India, go to the Web site at **bedfordstmartins.com/linguistics/writingandlanguage** and click on **world writing systems**.

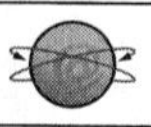

4.1 Chinese Writing

The Chinese system of writing developed out of pictograms that eventually came to represent morphemes (most of which are also words). The oldest inscriptions are the oracle texts, written on animal bones and tortoise shells and dating back to about twelve hundred B.C. These include many recognizable images, such as ⊙ 'sun' and ☽ 'moon'.

A change toward more **symbolic signs** began at an early date as more abstract notions were symbolized, such as ⌣ 'above' and ⌢ 'below'. Symbols were also combined to extend meanings metaphorically. For example, the sign for 'to tend' 牧 is composed of 牛 'cow' and 攴 'hand and whip'. 'To follow' 从 is two men in sequence, and so on. In time, the characters became more abstract. Figure 16.13 shows the historical development of the symbol for 'dog'.

Figure 16.13 Historical development of the Chinese symbol for 'dog'

Calligraphy is an ancient and respected art in China, and Chinese writing exists in a number of styles. The script is usually written from left to right along a horizontal axis, although newspapers and older texts begin in the right-hand margin and are read downward.

The units of contemporary Chinese writing are called characters. Many monosyllabic words are presented in true logographic fashion by a character consisting of a single symbol. For example, the Mandarin words [ʃǒw] 'hand' and [mǎ] 'horse' are written 手 and 馬, respectively. However, the overwhelming majority of characters (one estimate is 99 percent) consist of two parts.

The main component of a multielement character, called the **phonetic determinative**, provides information about the pronunciation of the corresponding morpheme. Although about 4,000 different phonetic determinatives are used in Chinese writing, they represent pronunciation very imperfectly. Tone, which is contrastive in Chinese (see Chapter 2), is not represented at all, and many phonetic determinatives indicate only part of the morpheme's pronunciation. For instance, the determinative is used for a wide variety of words ending in *ao* without regard for whether the initial consonant is *j, n, r,* or some other element. Furthermore, due to sound changes over the last centuries, about one-third of all phonetic determinatives provide little or no useful information about current pronunciation. Finally, because Chinese has many homophones, even the most informative phonetic determinatives can be used for many different words.

Chinese characters also include a semantic component, called the **radical**, or key, which provides clues about the morpheme's meaning. There are about 200 different radicals in contemporary Chinese writing. Table 16.1 provides examples of some of the characters that can be formed by combining phonetic determinatives with radicals.

Table 16.1 Some Chinese characters

		Phonetic determinatives			
		A	B	C	D
	Semantic radical	敖 (*áo*)	參 (*cān*)	堯 (*yāo*)	甫 (*fū*)
1	亻 'person'	傲 (*ào:* 'proud')	傪 (*cān:* 'good')	僥 (*jiǎo:* 'lucky')	俌 (*fù:* 'help')
2	扌 'hand'	擙 (*ào:* 'shake')	摻 (*shǎn:* 'seize')	撓 (*nǎo:* 'scratch')	捕 (*bǔ:* 'catch')
3	木 'wood'	㯠 (*āo:* 'barge')	槮 (*shēn:* 'beam')	橈 (*náo:* 'oar')	𣐤 (*fú:* 'trellis')
4	氵 'water'	滶 (*ào:* 'stream')	滲 (*shèn:* 'leak')	澆 (*jiāo:* 'sprinkle')	浦 (*pǔ:* 'creek')

Notice that only the phonetic determinative in column A indicates the precise pronunciation (ignoring tone) of the four characters in which it appears. The other determinatives supply helpful, but incomplete, phonetic information. For instance, the determinative *yao* (column C) has a pronunciation that rhymes with that of the four morphemes it helps to represent.

The usefulness of the information supplied by the radicals also varies. The characters in row 1 represent morphemes whose meaning is at best indirectly associated with that of the radical ('person'), but the radicals in rows 2, 3, and 4 are much more informative: the characters in row 2 all denote actions involving the hand, those in row 3 all refer to things made of wood, and those in row 4 all have something to do with liquids.

Although neither phonetic determinatives alone nor semantic radicals alone suffice to identify the morphemes that they are used to represent, they are more than adequate when used in conjunction with each other. Despite these complexities—one authority has described the system as "outsized, haphazard, inefficient, and only partially reliable"—Chinese writing provides its users with an effective way to represent the words and morphemes of the language. Moreover, the lack of efficiency is offset by the fact that the same literary script can be understood by speakers of different Chinese languages. Although a speaker of Mandarin and a speaker of Cantonese may pronounce the word for 'fire' differently—/xwǒ/ and /fɔ̀/, respectively—both can read it from the same character (火), since Chinese writing does not directly represent a word's phonemic segments.

In recent times, the government of the People's Republic of China has introduced simplified characters (some newly invented) in an attempt to promote literacy. At the same time, a system of writing Mandarin with a modified Latin alphabet, called **pinyin**, has been introduced. Pinyin is used as a subsidiary system for writing such things as street signs, addresses, and brand names as well as for teaching children how to pronounce characters. It is also used for word processing and other computer-related activities, including e-mail.

4.2 Japanese Writing

The writing system of modern Japanese is arguably the most complicated in the entire world. Its use requires knowledge of three distinct scripts, including a pair of syllabaries—**hiragana** and **katakana**—that were created by modifying Chinese characters. Although Japanese can be written exclusively with either syllabary, normal writing involves use of Chinese characters (called **kanji** in Japanese) in addition to hiragana and katakana. Kanji symbols are typically used to represent all or part of a word's root while affixes are represented by hiragana symbols. The phrase *the man's car,* for example, can be written as in Figure 16.14, with the roots 'man' and 'car' represented by kanji, and the possessive morpheme *no* written in hiragana.

Figure 16.14 A phrase written in a mixture of kanji and hiragana

The katakana syllabary, whose symbols are less rounded than their hiragana counterparts, is used to write onomatopoeic words as well as words borrowed into Japanese from other languages. In addition, it is employed in advertising and in telegrams (see Figure 16.15).

Hiragana chart

COLUMN / LINE	A	I	U	E	O
SINGLE VOWEL	あ A	い I	う U	え E	お O
K	か KA	き KI	く KU	け KE	こ KO
S	さ SA	し SHI	す SU	せ SE	そ SO
T	た TA	ち CHI	つ TSU	て TE	と TO
N	な NA	に NI	ぬ NU	ね NE	の NO
H	は HA	ひ HI	ふ FU	へ HE	ほ HO
M	ま MA	み MI	む MU	め ME	も MO
Y	や YA		ゆ YU		よ YO
R	ら RA	り RI	る RU	れ RE	ろ RO
W	わ WA				を O
N (in a coda)	ん N				

Katakana chart

COLUMN / LINE	A	I	U	E	O
SINGLE VOWEL	ア A	イ I	ウ U	エ E	オ O
K	カ KA	キ KI	ク KU	ケ KE	コ KO
S	サ SA	シ SHI	ス SU	セ SE	ソ SO
T	タ TA	チ CHI	ツ TSU	テ TE	ト TO
N	ナ NA	ニ NI	ヌ NU	ネ NE	ノ NO
H	ハ HA	ヒ HI	フ FU	ヘ HE	ホ HO
M	マ MA	ミ MI	ム MU	メ ME	モ MO
Y	ヤ YA		ユ YU		ヨ YO
R	ラ RA	リ RI	ル RU	レ RE	ロ RO
W	ワ WA				ヲ O
N (in a coda)	ン N				

Figure 16.15 Hiragana and katakana syllabaries and their phonetic values. (The conventions for representing voicing, vowel length, and gemination are not indicated here.)

Finally, it should be noted that the Roman alphabet, which the Japanese call *romaji,* is also making inroads. It is not unusual to see all four writing systems used together, especially in advertising (see Figure 16.16 on page 545).

New Tomato

ほんのり 甘味 さらっと あと 味
(honnori amami saratto ato aji)
'Subtle sweetness and light after taste.'

トマト の 新しい ジュース です
(tomato no atarashii juusu desu)
'It's a new tomato juice.'

——— --Hiragana
〰〰〰 --Katakana
═══ --Kanji

Figure 16.16 Kanji, hiragana, katakana, and romaji in a Japanese advertisement

Learning to read Japanese is a formidable task, in part because of the way the various scripts are intermingled and in part because of complexities in the use of kanji symbols, which can have more than one pronunciation depending on whether they are used to represent a word of Chinese origin or Japanese origin. (For example, Japanese has two morphemes with the meaning 'mountain'—/san/, which is of Chinese origin, and the native Japanese /yama/. Both are written with the kanji character 山.)

4.3 Korean Writing

Korean was once written with Chinese characters, which had been introduced in the first centuries A.D. However, Korean suffixes could not be easily represented by Chinese writing. Various devices were used to alleviate this problem, but inadequacies persisted. Finally, King Sejong (1419–1452) commissioned an alphabetic script called **hangul**. After some modifications over the centuries, it became the standard Korean writing system. An especially interesting feature of hangul is that symbols are grouped together into syllable-sized clusters (see Figure 16.17 on page 546).

Like Japanese, Korean also makes use of Chinese characters (called **hanja**), although in a more restricted way. Slightly more than half the vocabulary of contemporary Korean is of Chinese origin, and many words of this type are written with the help of Chinese characters in newspapers and in scientific articles. However, this practice has been reduced somewhat in recent years in South Korea and eliminated entirely in North Korea.

Hangul symbols

ㅂ	ㅜ	ㄹ	ㄱ	ㅗ	ㅣ
/p/	/u/	/l/	/k/	/o/	/i/

Grouped symbols

불	고기
'fire' /pul/	'meat' /koki/

Written form

불고기

'barbecued meat' *pulkoki*

Figure 16.17 Korean hangul

4.4 Cherokee Writing

Some American writing systems are of more recent origin. After the colonization of North America by Europeans, a number of scripts were developed to provide native peoples with a form of written communication. In one well-known case, the Cherokee leader Sikwayi (Sequoia) devised a syllabic script of more than eighty symbols, some based on the shapes of English letters and others newly invented (see Table 16.2).

Table 16.2 Some Cherokee syllabic symbols

Symbol	Value	Symbol	Value	Symbol	Value	Symbol	Value	Symbol	Value
Ꭰ	*a*	Ꭱ	*e*	Ꭲ	*i*	Ꭳ	*o*	Ꭴ	*u*
Ꭶ	*ga*	Ꭸ	*ge*	Ꭹ	*gi*	Ꭺ	*go*	Ꭻ	*gu*
Ꭽ	*ha*	Ꭾ	*he*	Ꭿ	*hi*	Ꮀ	*ho*	Ꮁ	*hu*
Ꮃ	*la*	Ꮄ	*le*	Ꮅ	*li*	Ꮆ	*lo*	Ꮇ	*lu*
Ꮉ	*ma*	Ꮊ	*me*	Ꮋ	*mi*	Ꮌ	*mo*	Ꮍ	*mu*

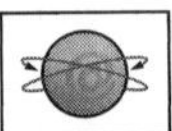

A syllabary was also created for Cree. For information about it, go to **bedfordstmartins.com/linguistics/writingandlanguage** and click on **Cree**.

5 English Orthography

The set of conventions for representing language in written form is called an **orthography**. English employs an alphabetic orthography in which symbols are used to represent individual consonants and vowels rather than syllables or words. In this section, we will consider the nature and history of English orthography. Section 6 examines the relationship between writing and reading.

5.1 Irregularities

A frequently expressed complaint about English orthography is that it does not establish a one-to-one relationship between symbols and phonological segments. Table 16.3 lists some well-known examples of this.

Table 16.3 Some problems with English orthography

Problem	*Examples*
Some letters do not represent any segments in a particular word.	through, sign, give, palm
A group of two or more letters can be used to represent a single segment.	think /θ/, ship /ʃ/, philosophy /f/
A single letter can represent a group of two or more segments.	saxophone /ks/, exile /gz/
The same letter can represent different segments in different words.	*o* in on /ɔ/, bone /ow/, son /ʌ/, one /wʌ/
The same segment can be represented by different letters in different words.	/u/ in rude, loop, soup, new, sue, to, two

The following excerpt from a poem by Richard Krogh vividly illustrates the extent to which English orthography departs from the principle of one sound, one letter (one segment, one symbol).

Beware of heard, a dreadful word
That looks like beard and sounds like bird.
And dead; it's said like bed, not bead;
For goodness sake, don't call it deed!
Watch out for meat and great and threat
(They rhyme with suite and straight and debt).
A moth is not a moth in Mother,
Nor both in bother, broth in brother.

Historical Factors

The relationship between symbol and segment in English orthography has not always been so indirect. In fact, the spelling system used throughout England during the Old English period provided a regular set of direct symbol-segment correspondences. The foundation for today's system, it lacked the symbols *j, v,* and *w,* but made use of four symbols that are not part of our current alphabet (see Table 16.4 on page 548).

Table 16.4 Old English symbols not found in Modern English spelling

Symbol	*Name*	*Segment(s) it represented*
æ	ash	[æ]
ð	eth	[θ] and [ð]
þ	thorn	[θ] and [ð]
ƿ	wynn	[w]

The relationship between symbol and segment in English orthography was significantly disturbed in the Middle English period, as the phonological pattern of the language began to change. To see an example of this, we need only consider the Great English Vowel Shift, which dramatically altered the pronunciation of long vowels—converting /iː/ into /aj/, /eː/ into /i/, /aː/ into /e/, and so on (see Chapter 7). Because Old English orthography used the same symbol for long and short vowels, complications arose when the former vowels changed. Thus, the letter *i,* which had formerly been used only to represent the phonetically similar /iː/ and /i/, ended up representing the very dissimilar /aj/ (the descendant of /iː/) and /ɪ/ (the descendant of /i/). The end result can be seen in the spelling of *hide* and *hid, write* and *written, ride* and *ridden, wide* and *width,* and many other words.

Additional complications arose following the invasion of England by French-speaking Normans in the eleventh century. The use of English in official documents declined, and regional orthographies developed in the absence of a national standard. To make matters worse, scribes who were trained primarily to write French and Latin introduced a number of conventions from those languages into English spelling. Among those that have survived are the use of *ch* rather than *c* for /tʃ/ (*cheese, chin,* etc.); *th* rather than *þ* (thorn) and *ð* (eth) for /θ/ and /ð/ (*thin, this*); and *c* rather than *s* for /s/ (*grace, ice, mice*).

Toward the end of the fifteenth century, yet another trend developed—the practice of spelling words in a manner that reflected their etymological origin. Enduring examples of this influence are found in the spelling of the words *debt, doubt, receipt,* and *salmon* (formerly spelled *dette, doute, receite,* and *samon*), all of which were given a "silent" consonant to make them look more like the Latin words from which they descended.

By the 1500s, English orthography had become increasingly irregular and idiosyncratic, with many different spellings in use for the same word. The word *pity,* for example, could be spelled *pity, pyty, pitie, pytie, pittie,* and *pyttye.* As printing presses came into greater use and books became more widely available, the need to reform and regularize English orthography became apparent. In the late 1500s and early 1600s, a number of individuals (most notably Richard Mulcaster and Edmond Coote) formulated and published spelling rules, which were gradually adopted by printers and other literate speakers of English. While these rules retained many of the practices discussed above, they at least had the effect of stabilizing English spelling. By the 1700s, English orthography was more or less fixed.

The vast majority of the spelling conventions introduced during this period are still in use today. One of the most famous, proposed by Mulcaster in 1582, involves the use of "silent" *e* at the end of words to indicate a preceding long (tense) vowel, as in *name, same,* and *mate.* Even here, though, there are complications and exceptions. In an earlier period, word-final *e* had represented [ə]. Following the loss of this sound in this position in the fourteenth century, final *e* was used quite haphazardly and was often added to words that would otherwise end in a single consonant. The *e* in the modern spelling of *have, done,* and *gone,* which contain lax vowels, reflects this practice and has survived even though it does not comply with Mulcaster's rule.

5.2 Obstacles to Reform

Over the years, there have been numerous proposals for the reform of English orthography, including those put forward by Benjamin Franklin, George Bernard Shaw, and Noah Webster. However, far-reaching reforms are unlikely for a variety of reasons. For one thing, they would require a long and difficult period of transition. As the following letter to *The Economist* by M. J. Shields illustrates, reform would not be painless even if it took place over a period of many years.

> For example, in Year 1 that useless letter 'c' would be dropped to be replased either by 'k' or 's', and likewise 'x' would no longer be part of the alphabet. The only kase in which 'c' would be retained would be the 'ch' formation, which will be dealt with later. Year 2 might reform 'w' spelling, so that 'which' and 'one' would take the same konsonant, wile Year 3 might well abolish 'y' replasing it with 'i' and Iear 4 might fiks the 'g-j' anomali wonse and for all.
>
> Jenerally, then, the improvement would kontinue iear bai iear with Iear 5 doing awai with useless double konsonants, and Iears 6–12 or so modifaiing vowlz and the rimeining voist and unvoist konsonants. Bai Iear 15 or sou, it wud fainali be posibl tu meik ius ov thi ridandant leterz 'c,' 'y' and 'x'—bai now jast a memori in the maindz of ould doderers—tu replais 'ch,' 'sh' and 'th' rispektivli.
>
> Fainali, xen, after sam 20 iers ov orxogrephkl riform, we wud hev a lojikl, kohirnt speling in ius xrewawt xe Ingliy spiking werld . . .

People who knew only the reformed spelling system proposed in this letter would have difficulty reading books written in traditional orthography. Those who wished to read any of the millions of books or articles currently in print would therefore have to either learn the traditional spelling system or have the documents that interested them converted into the new orthography.

A second factor militating against serious orthographic reform has to do with the dialectal variation found within English. Because English is spoken in more parts of the world than any other language, it has many different dialects. Any attempt to establish an orthography based on a principle of one segment, one symbol, would result in serious regional differences in spelling. For instance, speakers of Boston English would write *far* as *fa* since they do not pronounce syllable-final /ɹ/. Speakers of some dialects of Newfoundland English would write both *tin* and *thin* as *tin,* and *day* and *they* as *day,* since they have no /t/-/θ/ or /d/-/ð/ distinction. Moreover, while many Americans would have identical spellings for *cot* and *caught* (since these words are homophonous in their speech), speakers of English in many other parts of the world would spell them differently because they pronounce them differently.

Morphological considerations also militate against reform. For information about these considerations, go to **bedfordstmartins.com/linguistics/writingandlanguage** and click on **other considerations**.

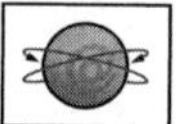

6 Writing and Reading

The three types of writing described earlier in this chapter each represent different types of linguistic units—morphemes and words in the case of logographic systems, syllables in the case of syllabaries, and consonants and vowels in the case of alphabets. Because of these differences, each orthography places different demands on readers. We know that different parts of the brain are used for reading logographic writing systems and phonographic orthographies such as syllabaries and alphabets. Because phonological structure is largely irrelevant to logographic writing, people suffering from Broca's aphasia (see Chapter 14) do not typically lose the ability to write and read logograms. However, the use of syllabaries and alphabets can be severely disrupted by this type of brain disorder. There are reports of Japanese patients suffering from Broca's aphasia who are unable to use hiragana or katakana (the Japanese syllabaries), but retain mastery of kanji (the logographic writing system).

Further information about the relationship between language and writing systems comes from the study of the congenitally deaf. Because they have never heard speech, congenitally deaf individuals have little or no understanding of the phonological units that alphabets represent. Significantly, they have a great deal of difficulty learning to read English.

The type of linguistic unit represented by an orthography also has an effect on how children with normal hearing learn to read. Each system has its own advantages and disadvantages. Children learning Chinese characters, for instance, have little difficulty understanding what each symbol represents, but it takes them many years to learn enough symbols to be able to write and read all the items in their vocabulary. (Knowledge of several thousand separate symbols is required just to read a newspaper.) Even educated people typically know only a few thousand characters and must use dictionaries for new or unfamiliar words.

This problem does not arise in syllabic and alphabetic orthographies. Because languages have far fewer syllables and phonemes than morphemes or words, the entire inventory of symbols can be learned in a year or two and then used productively to write and read new words. This is the major advantage of sound-based orthographies over word-based writing systems.

There is reason to believe that children find syllabaries easier to master than alphabets. Children learning syllabaries (such as Japanese hiragana) are reported to have fewer reading problems than children learning alphabetic orthographies. Although at least some difficulties encountered by children learning to read English may be due to the complexity of English spelling conventions, Italian and German children learning to use their relatively regular alphabetic orthographies also have reading problems.

The advantage of syllabaries over alphabets for young readers apparently stems from the fact that children have less difficulty identifying syllables than phonemes. One study revealed that 46 percent of four-year-olds and 90 percent of six-year-olds can segment words into syllables. In contrast, virtually no four-year-olds and only about two-thirds of all six-year-olds can segment words into phoneme-sized units. Since learning to read involves an understanding of the type of unit represented by written symbols, it is not surprising that syllabaries are generally easier for young children to learn.

Of course, it must be remembered that syllabaries may have disadvantages of other sorts. While syllabic writing is feasible for languages such as Japanese that have a relatively small number of syllable types, it would be quite impractical in English where there are dozens of different syllable structures. Ultimately, an orthography must be judged in terms of its success in representing language for the purpose of reading and writing. There is no doubt that an alphabetic orthography is superior to a syllabary for representing the phonological structure of English.

Summing Up

The development of **writing** has been one of humanity's greatest intellectual achievements, built on the relationship between graphic symbols and spoken language. The graphic representation of language has included **pictograms**, **logograms**, **syllabic writing**, and **alphabetic writing**.

Many of the large number of writing systems in use today owe their origin directly or indirectly to the Semitic writing systems of the eastern Mediterranean, where writing first emerged in Mesopotamia and Egypt. As the idea of writing spread, new forms of the signs were independently invented, and sound-symbol correspondences were altered to accommodate individual languages. Some two thousand years after the first ancient Near Eastern writing systems appeared, the Phoenician alphabet was invented, later to be adopted and adapted by the Greeks. The Greek alphabet in turn was adapted by the Romans.

In Asia, Chinese **characters**, which are logograms, are used in the writing systems of Japan and Korea. The Japanese system also uses a **syllabary**, while the Korean writing system is based on an alphabet.

Syllabaries are particularly suited to the phonological structure of languages such as Japanese and Cherokee, and are actually easier to learn to read than alphabetic writing. English **orthography** has a number of irregularities, some of which can be traced to historical developments. However, there are a number of reasons making reform undesirable.

Key Terms

Terms concerning types of writing

alphabetic writing
logograms
logographic (writing)
orthography
phonographic writing
syllabary
syllabic writing
writing

Terms related to the history of writing

acrophonic principle
boustrophedon
cuneiform
determinatives
hieroglyphs
pictograms
prewriting
rebus principle

Terms related to non-European writing systems

characters
hangul
hanja
hiragana
kanji
katakana
phonetic determinative
pinyin
radical
symbolic signs

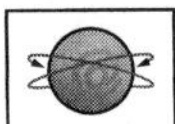

For more information on the sources used in this chapter, go to **bedfordstmartins .com/linguistics/writingandlanguage** and click on **Sources**.

Recommended Reading

Collier, Mark, and Bill Manley. 1998. *How to Read Egyptian Hieroglyphs.* Berkley: University of California Press.

Cummings, D.W. 1988. *American English Spelling.* Baltimore: Johns Hopkins University Press.

Daniels, Peter. 2001. "Writing Systems." In *The Handbook of Linguistics.* Edited by Mark Aronoff and Janie Rees-Miller, 43–80. Malden, MA: Blackwell.

DeFrancis, John. 1989. *Visible Speech: The Diverse Oneness of Writing Systems.* Honolulu: University of Hawaii Press.

Gelb, I. 1952. *A Study of Writing.* Chicago: University of Chicago Press.

Gibson, E., and H. Levin. 1975. *The Psychology of Reading.* Cambridge, MA: MIT Press.

Gleitman, L., and P. Rozin. 1977. "The Structure and Acquisition of Reading I: Relations Between Orthographies and the Structures of Language." In *Toward a Psychology of Reading.* Edited by A. Reber and D. Scarborough, 1–53. Hillsdale, NJ: Lawrence Erlbaum.

Jensen, H. 1970. *Sign, Symbol and Script.* G. Unwin, trans. London: George Allen and Unwin.

Sampson, G. 1985. *Writing Systems: A Linguistic Introduction.* Stanford, CA: Stanford University Press.

Schmandt-Besserat, Denise. 1989. "Two Precursors of Writing: Plain and Complex Tokens." In *The Origins of Writing.* Edited by W.M. Senner, 27–42. Lincoln: University of Nebraska Press.

Senner, W.M. (ed.). 1989. *The Origins of Writing.* Lincoln: University of Nebraska Press.

Wallace, Rex. 1989. "The Origins and Development of the Latin Alphabet." In *The Origins of Writing.* Edited by W.M. Senner, 121–36. Lincoln: University of Nebraska Press.

Exercises

1. Suppose you are the user of a pictographic writing system that can already represent concrete objects in a satisfactory way. Using the pictographic symbols of your system, propose ideographic extensions of these symbols to represent the following meanings.

a) hunt	f) cook
b) cold	g) tired
c) fast	h) wet
d) white	i) angry
e) strength	j) weakness

2. Construct a syllabary for English that can be used to spell the following words. What problems do you encounter?

foe	law	shoe
slaw	slow	slowly
lee	day	daily
sue	pull	shop
ship	loop	food
lock	shock	unlock
locked	shocked	pulled
shops	locker	shod
float	splint	schlock

3. Briefly outline the advantages and disadvantages of the three major types of writing that have evolved throughout history.

seventeen

Animal Communication

Michael Dobrovolsky

As I listened from a beach-chair in the shade
To all the noises that my garden made,
It seemed to me only proper that words
Should be withheld from vegetables and birds.

– W.H. Auden

Objectives

In this chapter, you will learn:

- how animals communicate nonvocally
- what types of signs are used in communication
- how bees, birds, and nonhuman primates communicate
- what arguments are made for and against linguistic ability in nonhuman primates
- how the communication systems of humans and animals may be compared

Communication—the passing on or exchange of information—distinguishes what is living from what is nonliving in nature. Communication is found even in the apparently passive world of plants; trees, for example, have been found to pass on information about advancing predators by means of chemical signals. Animals communicate among themselves and with humans so effectively that they are often said to use "language." But the words *communication* and (human) *language* do not mean the same thing. Human language is a specific way of representing the world and passing on information. From the linguist's point of view, not just any form of communication qualifies as language.

A question that therefore interests many linguists is whether animals make use of any system of communication that genuinely resembles or approximates human language. If animals communicate with a system that is structured like human language, then language as we know it is not the unique property of our species. This chapter investigates the ways in which animal communication is like human language and the ways in which it is different.

1 Nonvocal Communication

One of the most striking things about animal communication is the variety of means with which it is carried out. Animals communicate not only with sounds but with scent, light, ultrasound, visual signs (see Figure 17.1), gestures, color, and even electricity. From the slime mold to the Kalahari barking gecko to the giant blue whale, all living things communicate. Some nonvocal modes of communication are described in detail at **bedfordstmartins.com/linguistics/animalcommunication** (click on **nonvocal communication**).

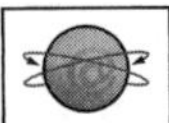

Figure 17.1 Some chimpanzee facial expressions: *a.* anger; *b.* fear-anger; *c.* affection; *d.* frustration-sadness; *e.* playfulness

2 Communication Structure: The Study of Signs

Certain common elements underlie the bewildering variety of communicative methods found in nature. An understanding of these is necessary for comparing the differences and similarities among systems of communication.

2.1 Signs

Communication relies on using something to stand for something else. Words are an obvious example of this: you do not have to have a car, a sandwich, or your cousin present in order to talk about them—the words *car, sandwich,* and *cousin* stand for them instead. This same phenomenon is found in animal communication as well. Instead of fighting over territory, for example, many animals produce sounds or make gestures that threaten and intimidate intruders—the message replaces the attack. Birds utter warning calls that represent the presence of a threat. A threatening animal or human need not be seen by other birds before they take flight—perception of the warning call replaces visual perception of the threat.

Each of these things that stand for other things is technically known as a **sign**. The sign is a unit of communication structure that consists of two parts: a **signifier**—be it a word, a scent, a gesture, or an electrical frequency—and the thing **signified**—something that exists in the real world and that is mentally represented by the sign's conceptual content. The real world can be thought of as external, mental, or emotional, and so what is signified by a sign can be as diverse as a tree, an abstract idea, a perception, or a feeling. Because their content is conceptual, all signs are associated with a **meaning**, such as 'danger' or 'item of furniture with legs and a flat top'. Individual instances of signs are called **tokens**. For example, in the sentence *The baby threw the rattle,* there are five word tokens but only four signs; *the* occurs twice as a token, but it is the same sign in both instances. Figure 17.2 illustrates these distinctions.

The study of signs is known as **semiotics**. Semiotics is a field of study that links many diverse disciplines, among them linguistics, anthropology, philosophy, zoology, genetics, literary study, and computer science. An understanding of signs is essential for understanding how messages are transmitted. So that we can understand signs better before proceeding to an analysis of animal communication, the next section examines their structure in more detail.

The Signifier

A signifier is that part of a sign that stimulates at least one sense organ of the receiver of a message. The phonological component of the word *tree,* represented as /tri/ and pronounced [tr̥i], is a typical linguistic signifier. A signifier can also be a picture, a photograph, a sign language gesture, or one of the many other words for *tree* in different languages.

The Signified

The signified component of the sign refers to both the real-world object it represents and its conceptual content.

The first of these is the real-world content of the sign—its extension or referent (Chapter 6, Section 1.3) within a system of signs such as English, avian communication, or sign language. In our example, the referent is represented by a drawing, since there is no room to include a real tree between the pages of this book. (Of course, the signifier /tri/ could also have a picture of a tree as its referent.) It is easiest to think of referents as concepts or persons or things, but they may be ideas or feelings as well.

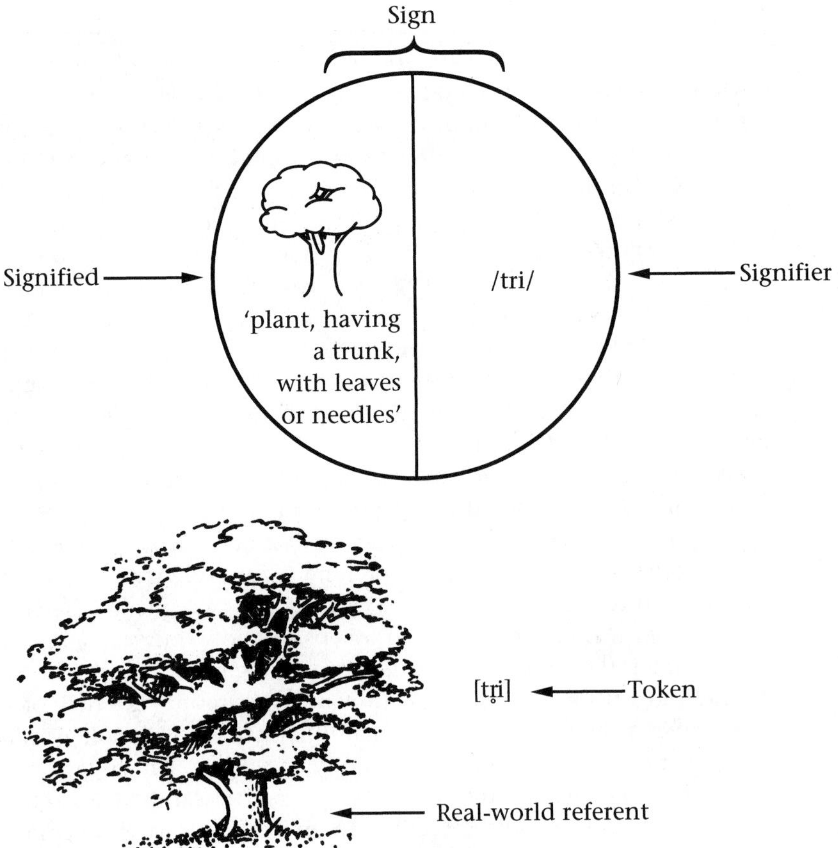

Figure 17.2 A sign

The signified component of a sign also evokes an intension (Chapter 6, Section 1.3) to users of the system in question. A word for 'tree' evokes concepts that probably include 'plant', 'having a trunk', and 'bearing leaves or needles' in the minds of speakers of any language who are familiar with trees. Some animals appear to conceptualize in terms of classes or categories as well. Certain monkeys, for example, distinguish among various types of predators on the basis of size, shape, and motion (see Section 5.3).

2.2 Types of Signs

Signs can be divided into three basic types, depending on (1) whether the signifier naturally resembles its referent, (2) whether the signifier is directly linked with the referent in a physical or mechanical sense, or (3) whether signifier and referent are arbitrarily associated. Table 17.1 summarizes the three types of signs. For more detailed information, go to **bedfordstmartins.com/linguistics/animalcommunication** and click on **types of signs**.

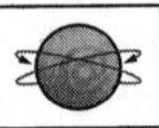

Table 17.1 Types of signs

Type of sign	Characteristics	Examples: Sign	Examples: Referent
Iconic sign	resembles its referent	photograph	things in the photo
		onomatopoeic words	actual sounds
Indexical sign	points out referent by partial representation	animal tracks	animal
Symptomatic sign	involuntarily shows inner state of sender	spontaneous cry of pain	pain
Symbolic sign	bears arbitrary relationship to referent	most words	things words refer to

2.3 Sign Structure

No matter what their type, signs show different kinds of structure. A basic distinction is made between **graded** and **discrete signs** (see Table 17.2). For more detailed information, go to **bedfordstmartins.com/linguistics/animalcommunication** and click on **sign structure**.

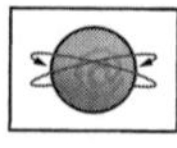

Table 17.2 Sign structure

Structure	Characteristics	Examples
Graded	signs can convey meaning by changes in degree	increasing voice volume
		movement of hands on an analog clock
Discrete	signs are clearly distinguished from each other with no gradual transition from one to another	discrete words (e.g., *stop* vs. *go*)
		digital time display

2.4 A View of Animal Communication

> They're like Swiss watches . . . they just react. Their genes and hormones and experience tell them what to do. They don't think about it.
>
> Zookeeper Ben Beck (on golden lion tamarin monkeys)

Most animal communication, it is claimed, shows little arbitrariness and is not deliberate or conscious in intent. Animal communication is also said to lack symbols in its sign repertory. For example, if a monkey gives a certain cry in the presence of danger, it is assumed that the monkey is spontaneously signaling its fear by vocalizing but is not deliberately warning other group members of the danger. The symptomatic vocalization, which is a nonarbitrary symptom of the animal's internal state, is interpreted and used by other members of a troop for their own benefit.

It follows from this view of animal communication that the acquisition of communicative systems by animals was once assumed to be largely devoid of learning and experience. Rather, it was claimed that the systems are rather strictly limited by genetic inheritance and, in this sense, are radically unlike human language—the acquisition of which requires exposure to a mature system. This limitation certainly appears to be true in some cases. When raised in isolation, animals as diverse as the fox, the elephant seal, the cat, and certain monkeys develop the full range of vocalizations typical of their species. However, as we will see in Sections 4–6 of this chapter, the situation can be more complex than this.

It is also claimed that animal communication is neither conscious nor deliberate. It is not widely believed, for example, that a monkey assesses a situation and then deliberately chooses to warn group members of danger by selecting a sign from a repertoire of meaningful sound symbols at its disposal. For this reason, the term **stimulus-bound** is also used to describe animal communication, since it is often claimed that animal communication only occurs when it is triggered by exposure to a certain stimulus or for certain specific ends. Animals do not communicate about anything but the here and now. As the philosopher Bertrand Russell once noted, "No matter how eloquently a dog may bark, it cannot tell you that its parents were poor but honest."

With respect to structure, animal communication is said to show few traces of discrete structuring beyond the obvious fact that one group of symptomatic, graded signals may sound very different from another. Whining in dogs, for example, is clearly different from barking, but both are assumed to be symptomatic, and the two may grade into each other. Combining and recombining of discrete units of structure such as phonemes, morphemes, and words is not characteristic of the way animals communicate. Dogs do not combine whines and barks to produce novel messages.

This does not mean that animal communication consists of random emotional outbursts. Nor does it mean that animal communication does not show structure. Animal communication is both complex and organized. Evolutionary pressure has guaranteed that animal communication is optimally in tune with the survival requirements of each species. The electrical communication of Amazonian eels is an excellent means of communication in muddy waters. The danger whistle of a small tree-dwelling primate like the galago is ideal for nocturnal communication in a dense forest. Small jungle frogs in South America communicate by sticking out their long and colorful legs, ideal for sending messages in the dim and noisy jungle. But jungle frogs do not try new combinations of leg movements in order to come up with an original message any more than the electric eel recombines frequencies in order to signal something it has never conveyed before. Animal communication appears to be limited in the messages it can convey.

But is animal communication so unlike human language in every respect? The next sections examine the communication systems of several kinds of animals and compare them with human language.

3 The Bees

I have no doubt that some will attempt to "explain" the performances of the bees as the results of reflexes and instincts . . . for my part, I find it difficult to assume that such perfection and flexibility in behavior can be reached without some kind of mental processes going on in the small heads of the bees.

August Krogh, *Scientific American*

3.1 The System

Forager bees display a remarkable system of communicating the location of a food source to other bees in their hive. When a food source has been discovered, the forager flies back to the hive and communicates information about it by performing special movements (which humans call *dancing*) before other members of the hive. The dancing conveys information about the location of the food source, its quality, and its distance from the hive.

Distance

Distance is conveyed by one of three different dances performed on the wall or floor of the hive (some species have only two different dances, and so may be said to have a different "dialect"). In doing the round dance, the bee circles repeatedly. This indicates a food source within five meters or so of the hive. The sickle dance indicates a food source from five to twenty meters from the hive. It is performed by the bee dancing a curved figure-eight shape. The tail-wagging dance indicates distances farther than twenty meters. In this dance, the bee wags its abdomen as it moves forward, circles to the right back to its starting point, repeats the wagging forward motion, and circles left. The cycle then begins again.

Direction

The round dance does not communicate direction, presumably since the food source is so close to the hive. The direction of more distant food sources is indicated in the other two types of dance.

As the bee performs the sickle and tail-wagging dances, it is simultaneously indicating the direction of the food source. Bees orient themselves in flight relative to the angle of the sun. When danced on the floor of the hive, the angle of the open side of the sickle dance's figure eight or the angle of the wagging path during the tail-wagging dance indicates the direction of flight. When the dancing is performed on the vertical wall of the hive, it is apparently understood that the top of the hive wall represents the current position of the sun in the sky. During the sickle dance, the angle of the open side of the figure eight relative to the hive's vertical alignment indicates the direction of flight toward the food source relative to the sun. When the bee performs the tail-wagging dance, the angle of its wagging path relative to the hive's vertical angle indicates the path of flight toward the food source relative to the sun. Figure 17.3 on page 562 illustrates the dances and their manner of indicating the direction of the food source.

Quality

Quality of the food source is indicated by the intensity of the dancing and the number of repetitions of the circling movements. As the food source is depleted, the dance is performed with less vivacity.

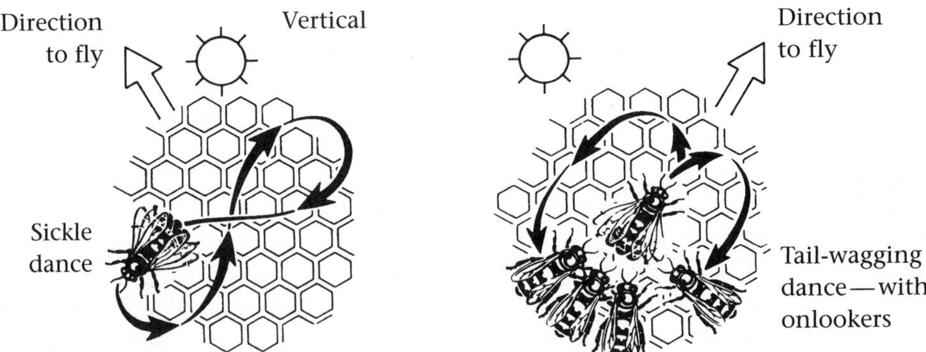

Figure 17.3 Bee dancing

Other Factors

These messages are not communicated with perfect accuracy, nor are they the only ones involved in bee communication. At the site of the food source, bees also leave a trace of a hive-specific **pheromone** (a chemical used for communication), thereby directing their fellow foragers to the precise location. The bees also carry back traces of the food-source odors, which further aid other bees in the search. A complex of communicative modes operating on different channels—a constellation—is thus employed in bee communication. This use of different modalities to communicate the same information is called **redundancy**. Redundancy helps guarantee that communication will succeed in the event that one or another modality fails or is imperfectly transmitted. All communication systems make use of redundancy. (Human language is no exception. For example, the presence of allophonic features such as voicelessness and aspiration on syllable-initial voiceless stops, or both length and quality differences on vowels, provides redundancy that assists in decoding the signals.)

3.2 Bees and Humans

How does bee communication compare with human language? The three patterns that the bees dance are not obviously connected with the messages they communicate and so are symbolic in nature (though it is possible to argue that relative distance is iconically represented in that a greater distance covered by the bee in each cycle of the dance corresponds to a greater distance of the nectar source from the hive). The total communicative constellation involves other, redundant sources of communication as well. The performance even involves audience participation. During its dance, the returning bee is expected to provide samples from the food source. If it fails to do so, it may be stung to death.

In its use of symbolic messages, redundancy, and interaction, bee communication resembles human language. However, there is a major difference between the two systems of communication: the topic of bee language is severely constrained. Bees communicate only about food sources. Furthermore, their potential for communication is very limited. Only certain locations of food sources can be conveyed. Bees cannot communicate the notion of up or down. They can be easily tricked into communicating the wrong direction of the food source if a strong light source is placed in an incorrect position with relation to the food source. They can also be tricked into giving the wrong information about distance to the food source if they are forced to walk or stop several times during their trip. This indicates that they gauge distance by time. The bees show no means of assessing varying information and communicating this fact. Their system of communication appears to be close-ended and limited to a specific number of facts about a specific type of information.

It also appears that bee language is largely innate—that is, there is very little need for a new forager bee to be exposed to the system in the presence of other bees. Foragers on their first flight perform the appropriate dances, although they refine their performance to some extent with time and exposure to other dancing. Their flight orientation to the sun is imperfect at first, but it develops within a few hours.

The innateness of bee dancing has been tested by cross-breeding Austrian bees, which do not perform the sickle dance to express intermediate distance of the food source from the hive, with Italian honeybees, which do. The results of such experiments further support a genetic interpretation of bee communication. In the cross-breeding experiment, the bees that bore a physical resemblance to their Italian parent performed the sickle dance to indicate intermediate distance 98 percent of the time. The bees that bore a physical resemblance to their Austrian parent performed the round dance to indicate intermediate distance 96 percent of the time; they did not perform the sickle dance at all. The dance pattern used in a specific situation appears to be inherited from a certain parent along with other more obvious genetic traits.

In 1948, when the Danish physiologist August Krogh made the statement quoted at the beginning of this section, he struck at the widely accepted notion that animal behavior was either the result of some kind of conditioning or, in some ill-defined way, instinctive. Much has been learned since then about the enormous quantity of information imparted by genetic transfer. It is now possible to state with a fair degree of certainty that the complex and sophisticated behavior of bees and other equally remarkable insects is in all probability largely genetically predetermined and, unlike human language, relies very little on exposure to the mature system in order to be acquired.

4 The Birds

> How intelligent is a creature that can amuse himself for 15 minutes by uttering, over and over, the following sounds: uhr, uhr, uhr, Uhr, URH, URH, Wah, Wah, wah, wah, wah.
>
> Jake Page (on his Amazon parrot)

4.1 Bird Vocalization

Birds, as Jake Page later discovered, can do a lot more than utter sounds over and over. It used to be thought that talking parrots were stimulus-bound mimics, merely "parroting" responses to external stimuli as a result of repetitive conditioning. This perception has been challenged by Dr. Irene Pepperberg's work with an African grey parrot named Alex and other African greys. Pepperberg's training regime differs from previous work in that two human trainers model the language interaction in the parrot's presence, finally inviting the parrot to take part. When the creature (human or parrot) being "trained" answers correctly, the reward is the object being named—such as a rock, key, or nut—thus associating meaning with object. Trainers also use the word for the object in sentences, thus contextualizing it (e.g., "Such a big piece of *paper*!"). Alex has been trained to produce over forty words for objects (e.g., *key, grape, nut*) and some stock phrases such as *I want a . . .* (*nut, grape, key*), *Wanna go . . . , Come here*. Using *I want a . . . ,* Alex is able to request rewards, and he indicates that he understands the words he utters by rejecting rewards he has not requested. He is able to identify colors, numbers up to six, and shapes based on the number of corners an object has. He has also demonstrated understanding of the concepts of 'same' and 'different'; for example, when presented with a blue triangle and a green triangle and asked "What's same?" Alex is able to respond "shape."

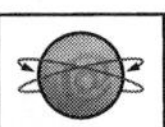

For information on Alex the parrot's ability, go to **bedfordstmartins.com/linguistics/animalcommunication** and click on **Alex the parrot**.

The behavior of a trained parrot is an indication of the bird's abilities but cannot be equated with behavior in the wild. In the wild, bird vocalization can be divided into two types, **call** and **song**. Calls are typically short bursts of sound or simple patterns of notes. Songs are lengthy, elaborate patterns of mostly pitched sounds.

Calls

Calls serve very specific functions in the bird community. They typically warn of predators, coordinate flocking and flight activity, express aggression, and accompany nesting or feeding behavior. The cawing of crows is a typical call. It appears to convey a generalized mobilization because of possible danger. When a crow hears cawing, it flies up to a tree if it is on the ground, or flies higher in a tree—or to another tree—if it is already in one. (If there are crows in your neighborhood, you can test this yourself, as cawing is easy to imitate.)

In some birds, individual calls are associated with specific activities; a danger call is quite different from a call given when birds are grouped in flight. The danger call given by small birds when larger avian predators threaten them is typically thin and high-pitched. This kind of sound is difficult to locate, and so can be given as a warning without revealing the position of the caller. A flight call is generally short, crisp, and easy to locate by other group members. The honking of geese in flight is a typical example of this sort of call. Because it is loud and easy to locate, it is well suited to enable the bird flock to stay together. Such functional utility is typical of bird calls, and in fact, calls that serve the same communicative purpose are often remarkably similar among different species of birds.

Song

Birdsong is different from calling. Although calls are produced year-round, singing is largely limited to spring, summer, and autumn. Furthermore, it is generally only male birds that sing.

The main purposes of song are, as far as we know, to announce and delimit the territory of the male and to attract a mate. Birds establish territory for breeding purposes and defend it vigorously. Across the country, it is a common sight in the spring to see a red-winged blackbird (*Agelaius phoeniceus*) and its mate team up to drive away a male of their species that has strayed into their territory. The use of song enables male birds to establish and maintain this territory without constant patrolling and fighting. Moreover, once a bird has established its territory, its song serves to attract and maintain contact with a mate. It follows that birdsong is unique from species to species, and even varies to some degree from bird to bird within the same species, since its purposes require species and individual recognition.

In some species, songs are nothing more than a successive repetition of calls. In others, songs consist of complex patterns of pitches—sometimes called syllables—that form longer repeated units or themes. The sometimes elaborate complexity of song structure reflects individual variation among the singers and, as pointed out previously, serves a specific purpose. Figure 17.4 shows a **spectrogram** (an acoustic recording that shows pitch and intensity of sound along a time axis) of the song of the European robin (*Erithacus rubecula*). Note how the different subsections of the song are distinct and recognizable. There is also some evidence that sections of a song are combined in different orders by certain birds, but there is no evidence that recombination is associated with different meanings.

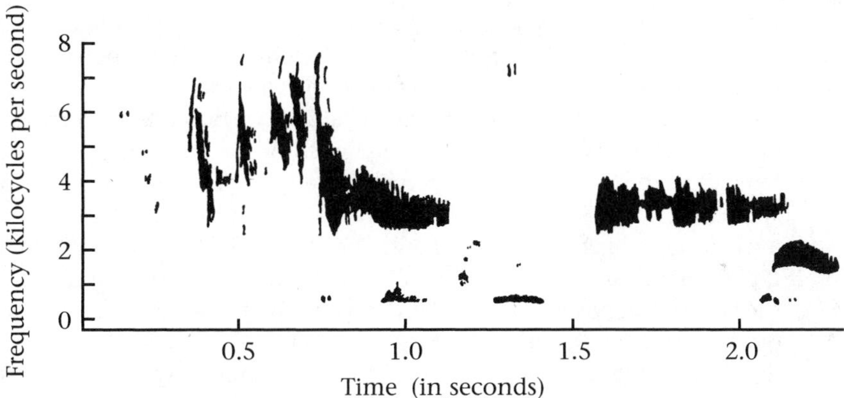

Figure 17.4 Spectrogram of a robin song; pitch is shown vertically along the L-R time axis, intensity by greater darkness

Avian Dialects

There is evidence for both song and call dialects among bird species. Researchers even speak of avian isoglosses (lines drawn on a map to indicate shared characteristics among dialects; see Chapter 15, Section 2.2) that are based on variations in the melody of song "syllables" or themes (see Figure 17.5 on page 566). The reason for the existence of dialects is still unclear; it may be no more than a reflection of individual avian variation in song and call learning. If it is, we are led to an intriguing issue in the relationship of bird vocalization to human language—the question of how bird vocalizations are acquired.

4.2 Birds and Humans

The acquisition of call and song by birds shows interesting parallels with recent hypotheses about the acquisition of language by human children (see Chapter 11).

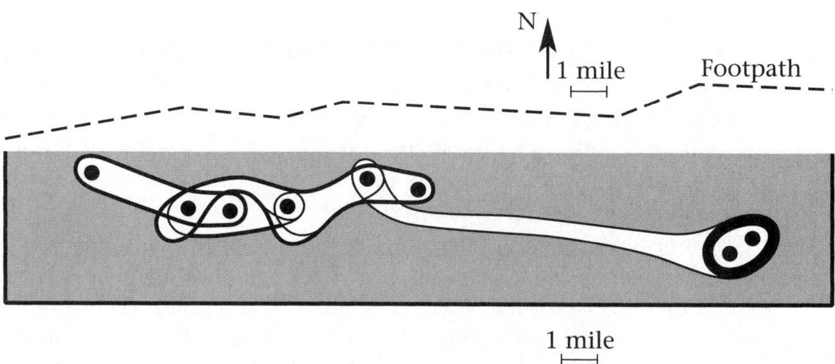

Figure 17.5 Avian isoglosses: call patterns of male hill mynahs (black dots show mynah groups; the shaded area shows forested hills and the unshaded, open plain; the heavier the black lines, the more song characteristics are shared by the group within its boundaries)

Though a great deal of bird vocalization—particularly calling—appears to be innate, there is much that appears to be acquired. Studies of avian dialects have shown that birds reared in the same nest acquire different song dialects when they live in different dialect areas. It also appears to be the case that singing ability is lateralized in the left brains of birds, as is linguistic ability in humans. Still more significant for linguistic study is the fact that some birds must acquire the species-specific characteristics of their song within a certain time span or critical period. A number of bird species do not develop fully characteristic songs if they are deprived of hearing them during the early stages of their lives. The chaffinch (*Fringilla coelebs*) is one such bird. If chaffinches are reared in isolation, they sing—but replicate only in a general way the typical song of the species. If young chaffinches are reared away from fully developed singers but with other young chaffinches, the entire experimental community develops an identical song. Finally, chaffinches that have been exposed to only some part of the fully developed song (those that are captured in the autumn of the first year of life) will, the following spring, develop a song that is partially typical but not completely well formed.

These experiments indicate that there are some songbirds that have both an innate and a learned component in their song. The innate component predisposes them to perform a general song that is extremely simplified. This has been called a **template** or a blueprint. Only exposure to the fully formed song of the species will enable them to produce the correct song. (Exposure to other songs causes some species to imitate in this direction; other species simply do not acquire anything they are exposed to unless it is their own species-characteristic song.) Finally, it is clear that certain birds do not acquire their characteristic song in a brief span of time, but require several seasons of exposure to do so. The evidence from songbird studies, while not directly transferable to humans, gives strong support to the idea that a combination of innate and acquired components is one way that the acquisition of complex behavior takes place in nature.

5 Nonhuman Primates

> Some animals share qualities of both man and the four-footed beasts, for example, the ape, the monkey, and the baboon.
>
> Aristotle, *On Animals*

Fascination with nonhuman primates goes far back in human history. Their social behavior has long been seen as an amusing (and sometimes instructive) parody of human behavior. Since the recent establishment of the fact that we are closely related genetically to these animals—some 99 percent of our genetic matter is shared with chimpanzees and gorillas—the resemblance of their behavioral, social, and communicative traits to ours has been seen as more than a droll counterpart to human activity. For some linguists, the question of our shared cognitive—and especially linguistic—ability has become more important; it is thought that a better understanding of nonhuman primates may shed light on the evolution of human social and cognitive abilities.

Primates form a large class of mammals, which range from the tiny tarsier to the imposing mountain gorilla. Among the nonhuman primates, some are nocturnal and some diurnal in their activity cycle. Some are solitary, and some form part of complex social groups. Many are tree-dwelling, and many are ground-dwelling. Some are quadrupeds, and some show periods of bipedal locomotion. Figure 17.6 shows one widely accepted classification of the primates.

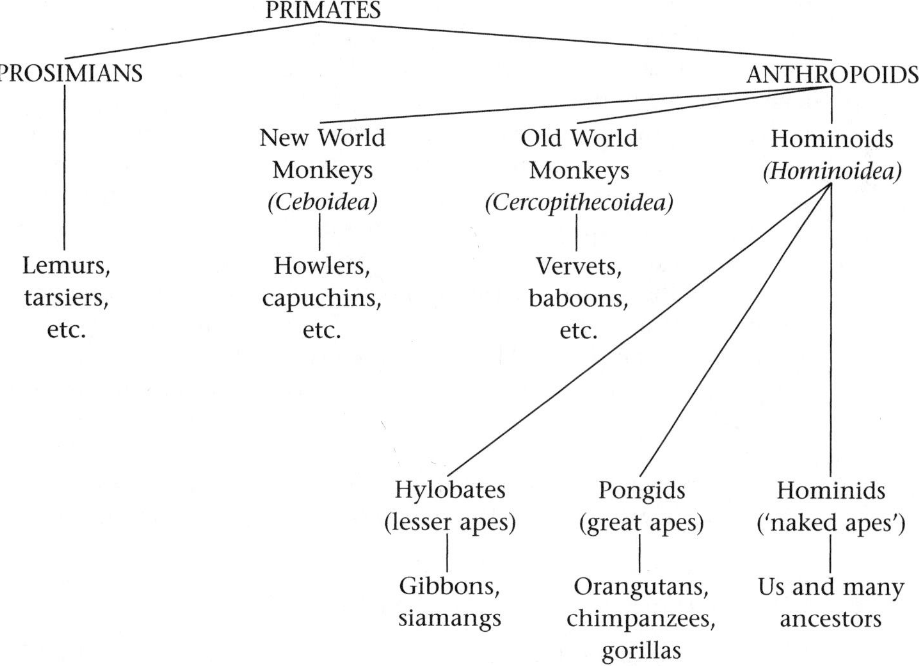

Figure 17.6 The primates

The prosimians are an evolutionarily early group found on the island of Madagascar, in sub-Saharan Africa, and in Southeast Asia. New World Monkeys range from Mexico through South America. Among them are the only primates with prehensile (grasping) tails. Old World Monkeys include the many tree- and ground-dwelling species of Africa and the Far East. The larger nonhuman primates—baboons, chimpanzees, and gorillas—are not native to North and South America. Baboons—large, mainly ground-dwelling primates—are found from central to northern Africa. They show a high degree of social organization, intelligence, and aggressiveness. The hominoids include the agile gibbons, solitary orangutans (both found only in Southeast Asia), the large but peaceful gorillas, the chimpanzees, and humans.

In Section 5.1, we first turn our attention to nonhuman primate communication in the wild. It is there that we can gain an initial understanding of how forms of nonhuman primate communication resemble or differ from our own in terms of function and structure.

5.1 Some Functions of Nonhuman Primate Communication

The validity of studies of communication among captive primates has been criticized because the animals' social existence is highly limited and compromised in zoos. Studies of nonhuman primate communication have largely left the zoo and laboratory and moved into the animals' natural habitat. While careful observation of nonhuman primate communication is still the basis of this work, the use of playback experiments—in which tape recordings of natural calls are played back over hidden loudspeakers—has led to a greater understanding of the communicative systems of these animals.

Although the social life of even the most gregarious nonhuman primate is relatively simple when compared to that of humans, primates, like humans, communicate for many different reasons. Typical nonhuman primate communication serves to mark and announce territory, to warn other group members of danger, to seek or maintain contact with a mate or other members of the species, and to interact with members of the troop or species in various ways we can call "socializing." Socializing vocalizations are particularly important in mother-child bonding and in primate groups with a complex and hierarchical social structure. In these groups, it is important to know which members have a higher or lower rank so that group members can behave accordingly in their presence. Vocalization is a key factor in maintaining this behavior.

As we briefly survey some aspects of the structure of nonhuman primate communication systems, we will also refer to the ways in which structure and function are linked.

5.2 Prosimian Communication

Prosimian communication shows a small repertoire of sounds that are patterned into discrete groups. The lemur (*Lemur catta*) of Madagascar is a typical prosimian with respect to its vocal communication system. It has been described as making essentially two types of vocalization—noises and calls—each of which shows some grading. The vocalizations appear to be **symptomatic signs**, in that they are spontaneous expressions of an inner state. They are classified in Table 17.3; quasi-phonetic descriptions like *spat* should be interpreted as onomatopoeic.

Table 17.3 Lemur vocalization

Noises		*Calls*	
Sound	*Context*	*Sound*	*Context*
Single click	In response to strange objects	Light spat (yip)	When driving off threatening inferiors
Clicks, grunts	During locomotion or for friendly greeting	Spat	When crowded or handled roughly
Purr	While grooming	Bark	When startled

Each graded set of sounds is used in a circumscribed range of situations. The calls in particular are limited to threat or fear encounters. They seem to form a graded series, ranging from the light spat to the bark in intensity. A small repertoire of distinct vocalizations is the norm among prosimians. The slow loris (*Nycticebus coucang*), an Asian prosimian, is reported to have no more than five calls.

5.3 Monkeys

The study of communication among the many varieties of New and Old World Monkeys is too vast for this chapter. An oversimplified picture reflects what most researchers agree is primarily a symptomatic system but one that shows a larger number of signs, with more gradation among them, than does the communication of prosimians.

One study of the Bonnet macaque (*Macaca radiata*), a South Asian monkey, presents a system of twenty-five different basic patterns that are used in various social interactions, including contact, agonistic encounters, foraging, greeting, sexual contact, and alarm giving. These vocalizations are determined by correlating observation with spectrographic analysis; descriptive labels are also given to the vocalizations, such as *whoo, rattle, growl, whistle,* and *bark*. These basic patterns are described as grading into each other. It is also claimed that they occur in combinations. There is no evidence, however, that these recombinations mean anything novel when they occur.

The communication systems of many monkeys appear to be genetically determined. This has been established by raising newborns in isolation. However, this statement cannot be made for all monkeys. For some monkeys, input from the adult system appears to be required.

The study of one small monkey has suggested that not all monkey vocalizations are symptomatic, and that experience and learning can play a role in the acquisition of the communicative system. The East African vervet monkey (*Cercopithecus aethiops*) is said to have three distinctive and arbitrary calls that announce the presence of

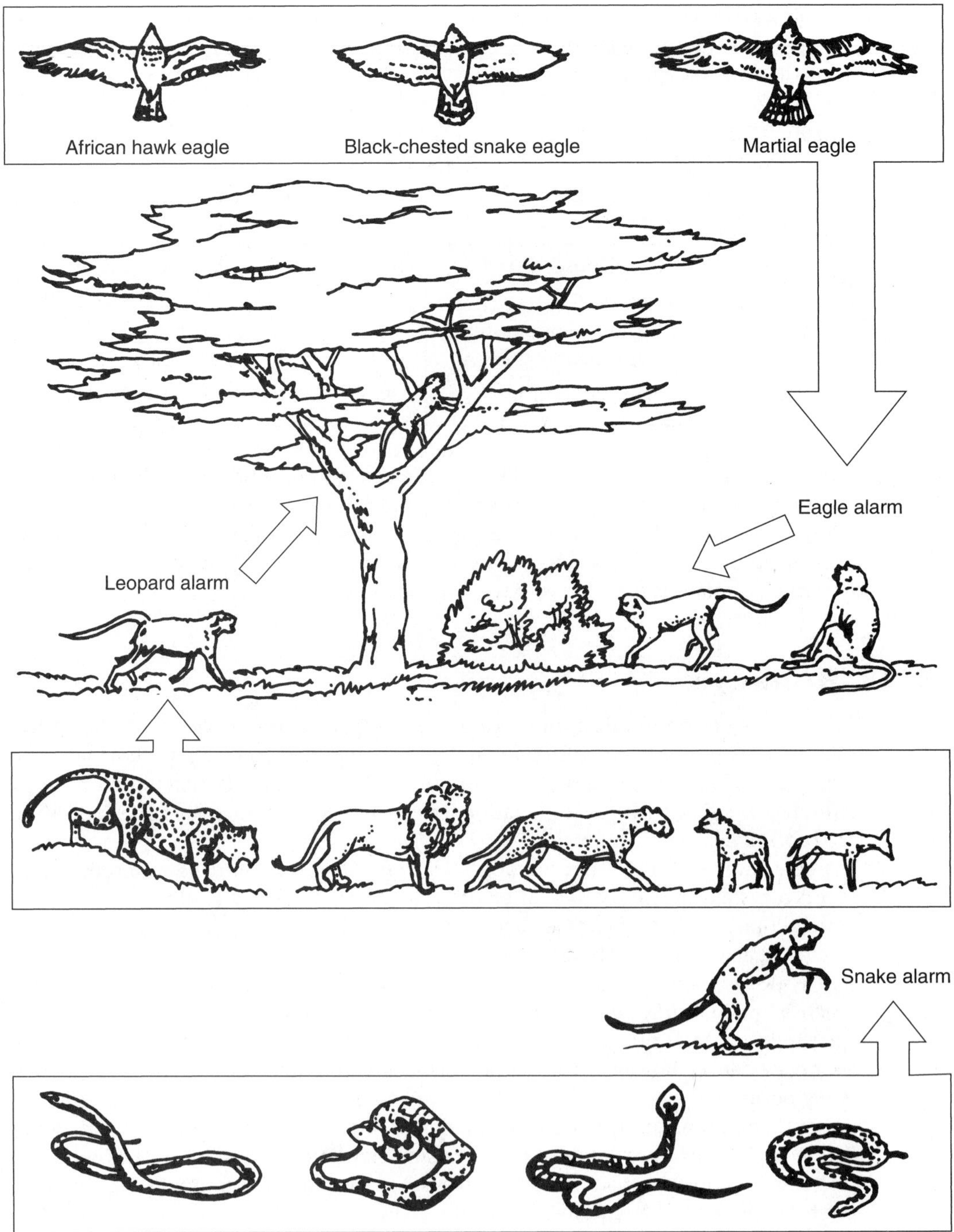

Figure 17.7 Response of vervet monkeys to specific predators

either eagles, snakes, or large terrestrial mammals posing a threat. These calls are associated with different responses by the monkeys. When they hear the eagle call, the monkeys look up or run into the bushes. The snake call causes them to look down at the ground near them. The mammal alarm sees them run up into the trees, or climb higher in a tree if they are already in one.

These findings, which appear to have been well established by playback experiments since they were first reported in 1967, suggest that not all nonhuman primates rely strictly on symptomatic signals to communicate or to trigger behavior in others. It is claimed rather that the vervets assess the potential danger situation and then choose a specific call with a clearly defined referent to announce the danger. Furthermore, each call is a vocalization signifier that is arbitrarily linked with its referent. Other monkeys respond appropriately to the calls without necessarily observing the danger themselves. All this taken together suggests a cognitive ability for classification of objects in the world, and an ability to link this classification system to arbitrary sounds for purposes of intentional communication (see Figure 17.7).

The vervet is not an isolated case. Goeldi's Monkey (*Callimico goeldii*), found in South America, is said to have five different alarm calls, three of which are used when terrestrial predators approach, and two of which have been heard in the presence of large birds. Similar types of calls have also been reported for macaques, meerkats, prairie dogs, and even chickens.

It appears that correct use of these calls among vervets requires learning. Infant vervets seem to distinguish innately among broad classes of mammals, snakes, and birds, but they also give the eagle call when other birds appear and the leopard call when other terrestrial mammals appear. Adults distinguish between leopards and less dangerous mammals, and between eagles and less dangerous birds (as well as between snakes and sticks), and it is claimed that this ability must be perfected through experience.

Like human language, the calls of vervet monkeys are arbitrary signs, and their appropriate use must be learned. However, in contrast with human language, there are only a small number of calls, the calls are restricted to present circumstances, and there is no evidence that the animals in question create new calls. Furthermore, evidence of intentionality is lacking; in other words, it does not seem that the animal making the call considers the responses of its hearers.

5.4 Gibbons, Orangutans, and Chimpanzees

Since the higher primates are close genetic relatives of humans, it is natural to expect their vocal communication to resemble that of humans. Perhaps surprisingly, communication among the higher primates does not show much indication of discrete vocal signs that could be interpreted as resembling human words. For the most part, the communication systems of these animals are made up of groups of graded vocal signs, some of which appear to display a certain level of sign-symbol correspondence.

Gibbons and Orangutans

Gibbons display an interesting form of vocal interaction known as **duetting**. This is the interchange of calls in a patterned manner between two members of a species, and is found among certain birds, bats, and even antelopes. Duetting is, however, atypical of primate communication—among the hominoids, only gibbons perform it. Recent playback experiments show that duetting among gibbons serves to maintain spacing among territories much as does birdsong (see Section 4.1). Playback of duetting within a gibbon's territory will cause it to approach the apparent source of the vocalizations, possibly with the intent of driving the intruders out. Playback of singing and duetting from outside a group's territory only infrequently evokes a response. Recognition of individuals does not appear to play a role in these vocalizations.

Unlike gibbons, which live in family groups, orangutans largely keep to themselves (except for mother-child pairs). Some sixteen distinct vocalizations have been identified, many of them straightforwardly symptomatic. Among the solitary forest males, loud calls up to three minutes long serve a territorial and spacing function. These calls also identify the individuals who produce them. High-ranking males approach calls, presumably to confront the intruder, while low-ranking males stay away from areas where they hear the calls of high-ranking males. These calls, in other words, stand in for the individual animals themselves, and orangutans must identify and assess each of these calls before acting on them.

Chimpanzees

Chimpanzees vocalize with a number of graded calls. As many as thirty-four distinct calls have been reported for one species (*Pan troglodytes*). Some of these appear to show rather specific referents. Chimps typically produce a vocalization called rough grunting in the presence of a favorite food source. A more powerful vocalization known as a pant-hoot (a sound that carries well in dense forest) often indicates location. Pant-hooting is also used in greeting or when chimps are excited about something. A third vocalization, pant-grunting, appears to be used by lower-ranking animals in the presence of higher-ranking ones, apparently acknowledging a subordinate status in a social hierarchy. Recent work suggests that the pant-hoots of a band of Ugandan chimpanzees in the wild may be composed of several discrete subtypes with no sharp boundaries between the different types of call. This study also suggested that there is some association of vocalization and particular behavioral and social contexts (travel, feeding, resting, etc.).

"Language" in the Wild?

Especially among highly socialized species, nonhuman primate vocalizations all show a great deal of variation. There is every indication that their vocalizations form part of a constellation of redundant communicative acts including gesture, posture, gaze (eye "pointing"), and the expression of affect, all of which must be interpreted by other troop members. The obvious complexity of communication systems among these animals suggests that the level of mental activity devoted to communicative behavior is sophisticated and well developed.

But despite the high degree of intelligence and social organization that these animals demonstrate, there is not a great deal of evidence for arbitrary relationships between sound and meaning among apes. Even more significantly, there is no evidence of recombining various sections of a message to form new messages. Nothing that parallels the phonemic or morphological recombination of human language has been discovered in the natural communication systems of nonhuman primates.

It is possible that the lack of parallels with human linguistic communication in species closely related to our own may be because of the nature of their social organization. The small groups or family units typical of chimpanzees and gorillas living in a food-rich environment may not have required the development of any other mode of communication. What has evolved is suited to their needs. This does not mean, however, that our near-relatives do not possess any of the cognitive abilities necessary for using a system of communication akin to human language. There is some evidence, for example, of left hemisphere development of the type associated with human linguistic ability. A number of recent experiments with nonhuman primates have attempted to determine the extent—if any—of their linguistic abilities.

6 Testing Nonhuman Primates for Linguistic Ability

Much attention has been paid in recent years to nonhuman primates that communicate with humans through the use of sign language.

Controlled testing of the possible shared linguistic abilities of nonhuman primates and humans goes back to 1948, when two psychologists attempted to train Viki, a young chimpanzee, to say meaningful words in English. With great effort, Viki learned to approximate the pronunciations of a few words like *cup* and *papa* over a period of fourteen months. Unfortunately, the experiment was doomed to failure from the start, since the vocal fold structure and supralaryngeal anatomy of the chimpanzee are unsuited for producing human sounds.

Chimpanzee vocal folds are fatty and less muscular than those of humans, and the neurological pathways between the brain and vocal folds are less developed than in humans. The chimpanzee's epiglottis extends well up into the throat cavity, which lessens the range of sounds it can produce. Finally, the whole larynx-tongue linkage rests higher in the chimpanzee throat than in humans, which results in limitations on its humanlike sound production as well. In short, chimpanzee anatomy is unsuited for human speech, and concentrating effort on teaching one to articulate words was distracting from the more provocative question, To what extent is the chimp mentally capable of linguistic behavior?

6.1 Some Experiments

An experiment conducted from 1965 to 1972 by Allen and Beatrice Gardner with a young female chimpanzee named Washoe created a new perspective on nonhuman primate linguistic abilities. The Gardners attempted to raise Washoe much as a human child would be raised, and to teach her American Sign Language (ASL), on the assumption that it was a genuinely linguistic form of communication (of which there is no doubt). Given the known manual dexterity of chimpanzees, it was felt that sign language might provide a window on chimpanzee linguistic abilities.

Washoe

The Gardners' reports claim that Washoe communicated intentionally with arbitrary signs in a creative manner, and thus showed the rudiments of human linguistic ability. Washoe learned to produce approximately 130 signs over a period of three years, and she recognized many more. Most significantly, it is claimed that Washoe spontaneously combined these signs to form novel utterances. She is reported to have signed WATER BIRD (in this chapter, signs are indicated by capital letters) on seeing a duck. Washoe also is said to have spontaneously produced BABY IN MY CUP when her toy doll was placed in her drinking cup and she was asked WHAT THAT?

Washoe was the first but not the only chimpanzee to be taught sign language. The results have suggested to some linguists that chimpanzees show greater ability to associate arbitrary tokens with referents than was believed earlier, and that they demonstrate rudimentary syntactic behavior. Other chimps, gorillas, and an orangutan that have been taught ASL since the pioneering Washoe experiment are reported to have performed even better. For information on Koko the gorilla, including a video clip of her interacting with humans, go to **bedfordstmartins.com/linguistics/animalcommunication** and click on **Koko**.

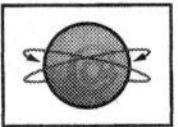

Nim

Still other experiments in teaching chimpanzees sign language have produced contradictory results. The achievements of a chimpanzee named Nim have been interpreted by his teachers as consisting of frequent repetitions of a small number of all-purpose signs (NIM, ME, YOU, EAT, DRINK, MORE, and GIVE) that were largely appropriate to any context. These signs are said to have made up almost 50 percent of Nim's production. Furthermore, there are no reports of his engaging in creative combining of signs.

6.2 Nonsigning Experiments

Criticism was leveled at Washoe's performance because of the relative informality of her training and the use of ASL. Other chimpanzees have been trained with computer-controlled apparatus and arbitrary plastic symbols. See examples of some of these symbols in Figure 17.8. To read more about these experiments, go to **bedfordstmartins.com/linguistics/animalcommunication** and click on **nonsigning experiments**.

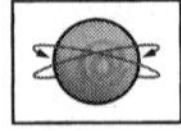

Figure 17.8 Arbitrary symbols used in experiments with the chimpanzee Sarah

Interest in human-animal communications is not new. Language-using dogs, cats, pigs, and even turtles have been reported for thousands of years. The basis of much of the current criticism of these ancient reports and contemporary experiments rests on the performance of a horse in Germany in the early twentieth century.

6.3 The Clever Hans Controversy

When I play with my cat, who is to say that my cat is not playing with me?
Michel de Montaigne, *Essays*

In 1904, a Berlin school teacher named Wilhelm von Osten claimed to possess a horse that showed evidence of a humanlike capacity to think. His horse, **Clever Hans** (*der kluge Hans*), could supposedly calculate and convey messages by tapping out numbers or numbered letters of the alphabet with a front hoof or by nodding its head.

Experimentation by a skeptical scientist, Oskar Pfungst, eventually showed that Clever Hans was not so much a creative thinker as a careful observer: the horse perceived cues that indicated that he had performed correctly. For example, von Osten involuntarily moved his head very slightly when a correct answer had been reached. This movement (less than five millimeters) was outside the normal perceptual range of human observers, but the horse had learned to associate it with the correct answer. When observers did not know the answer to a question, or when Clever Hans was blindfolded, he failed to perform his miracles.

Clever Hans's performance resulted from **dressage**, a type of interaction between trainer and animal that depends on the animal's interpreting subtle cues given by the trainer. The Clever Hans phenomenon is an excellent example of dressage, which need not involve conscious communication on the part of humans. The highly developed perceptual ability displayed by Clever Hans is common to many animals. Many scientists believe that chimpanzees and gorillas that use sign language and perform other language-like tasks are demonstrating nothing more than the Clever Hans phenomenon.

The position is explained as follows. Human trainers want very much for their animal charges to succeed. This desire is translated into involuntary actions, which can be seized on by the animal because of its keen perceptual abilities; it is these cues that determine the animal's performance. A typical example of this is pointed out in Washoe's signing of BABY IN MY CUP, which has been recorded on film (*First Signs of Washoe*). A careful examination of this interchange shows that the human repeatedly holds out the object to be signed and then points rapidly at the cup. Probably none of this cueing was intentional on the human's part.

Some so-called linguistic activity may be the result of factors other than the Clever Hans effect. Some reports of creative signing, such as Washoe's WATER BIRD, are dismissed as reflex signing that shows no intention of forming combinations on the part of the chimp. Reports of the gorilla Koko's displays of wit (she occasionally produces the opposite sign of the one requested, such as UP for DOWN) are also considered to be exaggerated or simply wishful thinking by researchers.

Some reports of linguistic behavior are attributed to nonsystematic or inaccurate observing. (For example, if Washoe answered WHAT THAT with any noun sign, the answer was considered correct.) Other reports are attributed to overoptimistic interpretation of signs. (Koko is reported to intentionally produce "rhyming" signs—those that are very similar to the ones asked for or expected.) In short, those who do not view chimpanzee signing and symbol manipulation as linguistically relevant claim that this behavior is more simply explained as arising from straightforward response-reward association and/or from dressage, and not a reflection of linguistic competence. As one researcher noted, training two pigeons to bat a ping-pong ball across a net does not mean that the birds know the rules of ping-pong.

6.4 The Great Ape Debate

> We believe that . . . there is no basis to conclude that signing apes acquired linguistic skills.
>
> Mark S. Seldenberg and Laura Petitto

> When these projects [Washoe, Nim, and others] are taken together, it can be seen that chimpanzees are within the range of language behavior of humans and therefore have the capacity for language.
>
> Roger Fouts

Researchers involved with the chimpanzees and gorillas who are being taught to sign attest to the emotional bonds they form with them and also emphasize that in using human language, such bonds are a prerequisite to normal communication. They strongly insist that apes communicate spontaneously and creatively with humans. Roger Fouts, who has spent many years in close contact with Washoe and other chimpanzees, puts the case this way.

> I reject the notion that there is some ultimate cut-and-dried criterion that distinguishes language from all other social and cognitive behaviors, or that distinguishes human communication and thought from that of all other species.

It is important to emphasize that most researchers sympathetic to the idea that apes show human linguistic abilities employ a broader definition of language than many of their critics. For these researchers, language use includes socialization and the use of communicative constellations.

For many linguists critical of these projects, a definition of language that rests on its social or functional aspects is unacceptable. In much current linguistic thinking, language is viewed as independent of the purposes it serves. This view, sometimes called the linguistic autonomy hypothesis, equates language with grammar—the "mental system that allows human beings to form and interpret the sounds, words, and sentences of their language," to quote from Chapter 1 of this text. It follows from this definition that linguistic ability in nonhuman primates can only be claimed to exist if the animals produce, at the very least, spontaneous and intentional symbolic signs that are manipulated in a rule-governed manner.

Symbol Use

All researchers who support the claim that nonhuman primates can employ intentional symbolic communication deny that cueing is a major factor in the apes' abilities, although most admit that it might be present on occasion. In order to refute charges of the Clever Hans effect, researchers employ a strict form of experimentation.

Primate sign-language researchers try to avoid cueing by using the **double-blind test**. In this test, a researcher shows the ape objects or pictures of objects that are invisible to a second human researcher. The ape's signing is then recorded by the second researcher, and the record is interpreted by a third researcher who has not seen the signing. In this way, unintentional cueing is said to be avoided.

Critics of this research claim that even double-blind tests can be affected by human-animal interaction. First, the apes must be taught to perform the task. During this process they may be conditioned to provide certain responses. Second, it is difficult to avoid any human-animal interaction during these tests, and this could lead to subliminal cueing. As we have also seen, many claims for symbolic behavior on any ape's part have been dismissed as stimulus-response conditioning—the mere "aping" of behavior in order to obtain a reward. We still have no way of knowing whether Washoe's use of a sign sequence like TIME EAT indicates that she has a concept of time.

Ongoing work with two chimpanzees named Sherman and Austin has led to their exchanging signed information about classes of objects, such as 'tool' and 'food'. These experiments are claimed to have circumvented any reliance on the Clever Hans effect and shown that signing apes can communicate about whole referential classes of items rather than be bound to simple stimulus-response association with individual items, such as a 'banana' and 'ice cream'.

Careful control of experiments has convinced some linguists that limited symbol use has been exhibited by some apes, perhaps even up to the level of a two-year-old human child. But some linguists who allow that a level of symbolic signing has been achieved have also denied that this is a critical feature for defining language. Rather, rule-governed, creative symbol combinations and syntactic behavior are said to be the critical features.

Creative Signing?

A feature of language that sets it apart from most animal communication is its creativity—the fact that humans can use language to create novel messages. Sign researchers claim that such creativity is present in the many instances of novel combinations signed by the animals.

An early and famous instance of alleged creative signing was Washoe's WATER BIRD (referred to in Section 6.1), which she signed when seeing a duck in the water for the first time. Such alleged compound signing behavior has been noted in various signing apes. Some of the gorilla Koko's novel combinations are provided in Table 17.4.

Table 17.4 Some sign combinations produced by the gorilla Koko

Compound	*Referent*
MILK CANDY	rich tapioca pudding
FRUIT LOLLIPOP	frozen banana
PICK FACE	tweezers
BLANKET WHITE COLD	rabbit-fur cape
NOSE FAKE	mask
POTATO APPLE FRUIT	pineapple

Critics say either that such combinations are accidental or that the ape produces the two signs independently of each other and thus does not display true compounding. There is no doubt that Washoe signed both WATER in the presence of water, and BIRD in the presence of the bird, but there is no consistent indication from her other output that she has a rule of compound formation.

It has been claimed that in more recent and carefully controlled experiments with a pygmy chimpanzee (*Pan paniscus*) named Kanzi, statistically significant differences in the spontaneous ordering of symbols have been observed. The conclusion drawn from this is that Kanzi has exhibited a form of grammatical rule. For example, Kanzi frequently used combinations of signs that link two actions, such as CHASE HIDE, TICKLE SLAP, and GRAB SLAP. In fifty-four out of eighty-four cases, the first sign corresponded to the invitation to play and the second to the type of play requested.

Is There Syntax?

Claims for syntactic behavior among signing apes have also been made. Even though it has been claimed that the general (though flexible) syntax of ASL is copied by the apes, reports on the signing chimp Nim (Section 6.1) showed that the animal had no consistent word-order patterning. In fact, Nim's syntactic output was structurally incoherent. His longest sentence is reported as GIVE ORANGE ME GIVE EAT ORANGE ME EAT ORANGE GIVE ME EAT ORANGE GIVE ME YOU.

Koko is said to have developed her own word order in noun phrases—the adjective consistently follows the noun it modifies. It is difficult to prove claims for syntactic behavior in animal signing because all signing forms constellations with facial expression and gestures, and so may be said to reduce the need for rigorous syntax. Koko, for example, can sign a meaning like 'I love Coca-Cola' by hugging herself (the sign for *love*) while signing *Coca-Cola* at the same time with her hands.

In spite of what is now widely considered to be the disappointment of the earlier studies (possibly because they expected too much), some controlled experimentation continues. Recently, the pygmy chimpanzee Kanzi is reported to have produced significant (though not wholly consistent) differences in the placement of animate agents in sign combinations. When another chimpanzee named Matata was grabbed, Kanzi produced GRAB MATATA, but when Matata performed an action such as biting, Kanzi produced MATATA BITE.

Lingering Doubts

As we have seen, supporters of language use among apes have not yet proved to the satisfaction of their critics that genuine symbolic behavior is occurring, much less anything resembling rule-governed creativity in compounding or syntactic patterning.

Researchers who see the results of ape studies as positive evidence for linguistic ability in these animals claim that their opponents keep raising the stakes every time a chimp or a gorilla accomplishes something that could be interpreted as linguistic behavior. Possible evidence of symbol use or creative signing to indicate linguistic ability is dismissed by these opponents as unsurprising or irrelevant. Supporters of ape studies note that their critics are motivated by a long tradition of viewing animals as "organic machines" that are locked into specific behavioral and communicative repertoires by their genetic inheritance, and that can therefore only respond automatically to a given situation with a narrow range of signs. Their own view, they claim, is at once more ancient and more modern in granting animals a certain as yet unknown degree of intentionality and cognitive ability in their behavior.

In general, recent experiments have established more convincingly than earlier ape studies that symbol use and referential behavior form part of the cognitive makeup of some nonhuman primates. Taken together with naturalistic studies, they help circumvent the claim that all evidence of symbol use among nonhuman primates is caused by the Clever Hans phenomenon.

Nonetheless, questions about creative sign combination and syntactic use still remain. Kanzi's alleged rules have been equated with those of a two-year-old child. But the major difference between a chimpanzee and a child at that point in their lives is that the elementary grammar of a two-year-old is the first hint of a full system that is rapidly developing and that will be in place in a matter of a few more years. While Kanzi's communicative behavior constitutes interesting evidence for a chimpanzee's awareness of the world, it does not unequivocally imply a system of grammar. It has been noted, for example, that Kanzi's "rules" are often bound up with a natural order of action or relationships (as when the sign GRAB precedes the sign SLAP).

To critics of these experiments, the apparent lack of rule-governed behavior among signing apes (especially in the realm of syntax) remains the linguistic hurdle that the animals have not overcome. It is certain that apes do not show syntactic behavior to any degree that humans do (for example, embedding is completely lacking), and many linguists claim that without such behavior, the apes cannot be said to be using language. Syntax, in the strict linguistic sense, provides a system of rules capable of producing a sentence of potentially infinite length (even though in practice this is never required). There is no evidence that primates have shown this ability.

Critics of the ape studies have at this time carried the day. Many funding sources for comparative ape-human research have dried up, and most of the subjects have lost their privileged relationships with humans and been returned to zoos. But the severe reaction to the apparent failure of ape-human linguistic communication research has had positive effects on the field as well. Recent trends—the number of experiments on animal cognition in the wild and the more carefully controlled experiments with apes like Kanzi—are slowly leading us closer to new evidence that bears on this age-old issue.

6.5 Implications

The real significance of these experiments in ape-human linguistic communication goes far beyond popular enthusiasm about what an ape might say to us if it could talk. It has often been pointed out that an animal's view of the world must be totally unlike our own. It is perhaps not surprising that apes appear to communicate largely about their fundamental emotions and such basic needs as food and play.

It is certain that animals have communication systems that are as rich, sophisticated, and subtle as anything found in human language, but are they equivalent to human language? A recent article in the journal *Science* (listed in the recommended reading at the end of the chapter) considers the distinction between animal communication and human language. Recent research has demonstrated that animals are capable of distinguishing human speech sounds and producing some symbolic signs. Macaques and birds, for example, have been shown to have **categorical perception**—that is, the ability to distinguish one human language phoneme from another—and some nonhuman primates have shown an ability to discriminate sentences from two different human languages. While most species do not have the physiology to produce oral phones similar to those in human languages, some nonhuman primates have shown the ability to learn some signs in ASL or to manipulate signs on a keyboard. However, nonhuman primates lack the ability humans have for vocal imitation.

There is evidence from work with mammals and birds that abstract concepts like color, geometric relationship, and number can be acquired and used. The performance of Alex the parrot and Kanzi the pygmy chimpanzee suggests that some animals can understand and use individual signs meaningfully; they seem to understand signs that are combined in sentences and may even be able to combine signs themselves in a limited fashion. However, unlike humans, even the most intelligent animals lack the possibility of creating an infinite number of sentences from a limited set of rules. This **computational system** allows humans to generate and comprehend novel sentences with a hierarchical phrase structure; in this regard, human language has unlimited power of expression, and no other species has shown the ability to combine smaller units into an infinite number of larger units.

7 Comparing Communication Systems: Design Features

Throughout this chapter, we have emphasized the distinction between communication and language. In this final section, we will compare human linguistic communication with what we have learned about systems of animal communication.

7.1 The Features

Differences and similarities between human language and natural animal communication systems can be highlighted by comparing essential characteristics of the systems. These characteristics are called **design features** and are set up (perhaps unfairly) with reference to human language. Since this book emphasizes the essentially mental nature of linguistic ability, the design features that follow do not include the traditional reference to vocal-auditory transmission. What is emphasized is the nature of the semantic and organizational structuring of each system. These design features represent an adaptation of those of Charles Hockett and W. H. Thorpe.

1. *Interchangeability* All members of the species can both send and receive messages.

   This is obviously true of human language. It is not the case with bee dancing (performed only by foragers) or birdsong (performed only by males). Nonhuman primate vocalizations appear to be largely interchangeable.

2. *Feedback* Users of the system are aware of what they are transmitting.

   Humans monitor their linguistic output and correct it. It is debatable whether bees do so when they dance, or whether birds monitor their calls. It is not known if birds monitor their song; it is likely that they do.

3. *Specialization* The communication system serves no other function but to communicate.

   Human language represents reality—both external (real world) and internal (states, beliefs)—symbolically in the mind. Manifested as speech, language serves uniquely as a communicative system. Bee dancing and birdsong also appear to be specialized communicative activity. Alarm calls of any species may be symptomatic but at the same time are specialized for different types of predators. Symptomatic tokens, on the other hand, are unspecialized. Crying is a symptomatic sign that may be interpreted by someone else and thus function communicatively, but its primary purpose is physiological (the clearing of foreign matter from the eye, the release of emotional tension). If animal communication is primarily symptomatic—a claim that is hotly disputed by specialists in animal communication—then it would not qualify as a specialized communicative system.

4. *Semanticity* The system conveys meaning through a set of fixed relationships among signifiers, referents, and meanings.

   Human language conveys meaning through arbitrary symbols. Bee dancing conveys meaning, but within a very limited range, as do bird calls and song. The range of meaning is broader and more subtle in nonhuman primate vocalizations. Although we cannot claim to know the minds of such near relatives as chimpanzees and gorillas, it appears that the range of meanings suggested by their behavior in the wild does not approach the vastness of human semanticity (see feature 8).

5. *Arbitrariness* There is no natural or inherent connection between a token and its referent.

   This is true of human language, with the possible exception of a few onomatopoeic terms. Bee dancing shows arbitrariness in that there may be no connection between the form of the dance and the distance from the hive. Expressions of food source quality and direction are not arbitrary, however. Many bird calls are highly suited for their purpose—such as danger calls, which are difficult to locate—and in this sense are not arbitrary. Most nonhuman primate vocalization appears to be equally adaptive, though arbitrariness has been claimed for vervet monkey alarm calls.

6. *Discreteness* The communication system consists of isolatable, repeatable units.

   Human language shows distinctive features, phonemes, syllables, morphemes, words, and still larger combinations. There are two (three, in some dialects) discrete types of bee dances, but these dances are not combined in various ways to produce novel messages. There is some evidence for subunits in birdsong. They are also present in primate call systems.

7. *Displacement* Users of the system are able to refer to events remote in space and time.

   Bee dancing shows displacement. No evidence for displacement is found in bird calls or songs. Baboons occasionally produce threat and fight vocalizations long after an aggressive encounter, but there is no evidence that this is reflecting displacement; it probably reflects a slow winding down of the animal's emotional state. Among apes, it is not yet clear whether some degree of displacement is a feature of either their communication in the wild or the systems they have learned from humans. Nonhuman primates do not appear to communicate about imaginary pasts or futures, which humans are able to do with language.

8. *Productivity* New messages on any topic can be produced at any time.

   This is obviously true of human language. Bees show limited productivity. Bird calls show none. Birdsong shows evidence of recombination (the songs of laughing gulls are well documented in this respect), but it is doubtful whether these recombinations transmit novel messages. This is also true of recombination in the calls of certain monkeys, such as macaques.

9. *Duality of patterning* Meaningless units (phonemes) are combined to form arbitrary signs. These signs in turn can be recombined to form new, meaningful larger units.

   In human language, phonemes can be combined in various ways to create different symbolic tokens: *spot*, *tops*, *opts*, and *pots*. These tokens in turn can be combined in meaningful ways: *Spot the tops of the pots*. There is no evidence of this type of patterning in any known animal communication system.

10. *Tradition* At least certain aspects of the system must be transmitted from an experienced user to a learner.

    This is obviously a factor in the acquisition of human language. It is possibly present in a very limited way in bee communication, and it is definitely present in the acquisition of birdsong for some species. There is some recent evidence for a degree of tradition among chimpanzees.

11. *Prevarication* The system enables the users to talk nonsense or to lie.

    Undoubtedly, this property is found in human language. There are specialized mimics among birds, fishes, and even insects. A few examples of animal deception have been noted among the arctic fox and among vervets, but it is not clear whether this is normal species-specific behavior or the acts of a few isolated individuals. The question of intentionality is crucial here. Current work with birds suggests that some species learn as many songs as possible and use this repertoire to maintain territorial advantage by "impersonating" other species. This may well be purely genetically determined behavior, but in any event, it is highly complex.

12. *Learnability* A user of the system can learn other variants.

    Humans can learn a number of different languages. Bees are limited to their own genetically specified dialect. Bird calls are apparently limited in this same way. As noted previously, some birds learn the songs of other species, but this may well be simply mimicry. Nonhuman primates seem restricted to their own systems in the wild.

13. *Reflexiveness* The ability to use the communication system to discuss the system itself.

    No evidence exists that any other species writes grammars or linguistics textbooks. Tables 17.5 and 17.6 summarize this survey of design features.

Table 17.5 Summary of design features for bees and birds

Design feature	*Bees*	*Birds*
1. Interchangeability	no; foragers only	no; only males sing
2. Feedback	?	?
3. Specialization	yes	yes
4. Semanticity	yes, very limited	yes, limited
5. Arbitrariness	yes, for expressing distance	yes, though highly adaptive
6. Discreteness	in a limited way	yes, in song
7. Displacement	yes	no
8. Productivity	yes, very limited	possibly
9. Duality of patterning	no	no
10. Tradition	possibly, but highly limited	yes, limited
11. Prevarication	no	possibly
12. Learnability	no	possibly
13. Reflexiveness	no	no

Table 17.6 Summary of design features for nonhuman primates and humans

Design feature	*Nonhuman primates*	*Humans*
1. Interchangeability	yes	yes
2. Feedback	probably	yes
3. Specialization	in part	yes
4. Semanticity	yes	yes
5. Arbitrariness	limited confirmation; selectively adaptive	yes
6. Discreteness	in call systems	yes
7. Displacement	no	yes
8. Productivity	possibly	yes
9. Duality of patterning	no	yes
10. Tradition	possibly	yes
11. Prevarication	possibly	yes
12. Learnability	no	yes
13. Reflexiveness	no current evidence	yes

Summing Up

This brief overview of animal communication systems emphasizes that human language is one communication system among the many that life forms on this planet employ. Communication can be described with reference to the **sign**, which is composed of two components—a **signifier** and that which is **signified**. Most animal communication has traditionally been viewed as **symptomatic**, though studies of communication among birds and bees suggest that **symbolic signs** are used. A significant innate component may interact with some exposure to the communication system, especially among birds. Nonhuman primate communication consists of graded series of vocalizations and appears to show little arbitrariness, though some has been reported for the alarm calls of several monkeys.

Experiments with nonhuman primates have created controversy over whether chimpanzees and gorillas have shown symbolic behavior and a capacity for linguistic behavior. Many researchers have dismissed the work as an example of **dressage** or the **Clever Hans** phenomenon.

Human language and systems of animal communication share certain **design features**. Humans, however, lack many communicative skills that animals possess. We are hopelessly inadequate at following scent trails, we cannot change color for communicative purposes with the facility of an octopus, and we are not as gifted as horses and many other mammals at assessing and interpreting subtle body gestures. Humans do possess an ability to symbolize, far exceeding that of chimpanzees and gorillas (our nearest genetic relatives)—even allowing for the most generous interpretation possible of recent experiments. Human language is also more flexible and productive in manipulating these symbols than any known animal communication system. Language is as natural a part of human life patterns as the communication systems of our fellow creatures are for their modes of existence.

Key Terms

Terms concerning nonvocal communication and signs used in communication

discrete signs
graded signs
iconic sign
indexical sign
meaning
semiotics
sign
signified
signifier
stimulus-bound
symbolic signs
symptomatic sign
tokens

Terms related to communication of birds and bees

(bird) call
(bird)song
pheromone
redundancy
spectrogram
template

Terms concerning communication of nonhuman primates

categorical perception
Clever Hans
computational system
design features
double-blind test
dressage
duetting

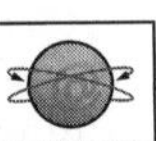

For more information on the sources used in this chapter, go to **bedfordstmartins.com/linguistics/animalcommunication** and click on **Sources**.

Recommended Reading

Bright, Michael. 1984. *Animal Language*. London: British Broadcasting Corporation.

Budiansky, Stephen. 1998. *If a Lion Could Talk*. New York: The Free Press.

Cheney, Dorothy L., and Robert M. Seyfarth. 1991. *How Monkeys See the World*. Chicago: University of Chicago Press.

de Luce, Judith, and Hugh T. Wilder, eds. 1983. *Language in Primates: Perspectives and Implications*. New York: Springer-Verlag.

Hauser, M. 1996. *The Evolution of Communication*. Cambridge, MA: MIT Press.

Hauser, Marc D., Noam Chomsky, and W. Tecumseh Fitch. 2002. "The Faculty of Language: What Is It, Who Has It, and How Did It Evolve?" *Science* 298(5598): 1569–1579.

Hockett, Charles. 1960. "The Origin of Speech." *Scientific American* 203(3): 88–96.

Lieberman, Philip. 1998. *Eve Spoke*. New York: W.W. Norton.

Parker, Sue Taylor, and Kathleen Rita Gibson. 1990. *"Language" and Intelligence in Monkeys and Apes: Comparative Developmental Perspectives*. Cambridge, UK: Cambridge University Press.

Pinker, Steven. 1994. *The Language Instinct*. New York: Harper Perennial.

Sebeok, Thomas A., and Jean Umiker-Sebeok. 1980. *Speaking of Apes*. New York: Plenum Press.

Sebeok, Thomas A., and Robert Rosenthal (eds.). 1981. *The Clever Hans Phenomenon: Communication with Horses, Whales, Apes, and People*. Annals of the New York Academy of Sciences, 364. New York: The New York Academy of Sciences.

Snowden, C.T., C.H. Brown, and M.R. Petersen (eds.). 1982. *Primate Communication*. London: Cambridge University Press.

Exercises

1. What do the following chimpanzee facial expressions convey? Using a mirror, try to imitate the facial expressions; does this make it easier for you to label them? What characteristics of the signs lead you to your conclusion in each case?

2. Observe an animal in a zoo or at home for at least thirty minutes. Try to discover at least three unambiguous signs the animal employs to communicate. Describe each one in terms of both *signifier* and *signified.* (A good way to do this is to note carefully the context in which the sign is given, to whom it is addressed, and the receiver's response to the communication.)

3. Add two columns to the list of design features presented in Tables 17.5 and 17.6. For one column, take the perspective of a researcher who believes that apes show true linguistic ability in their signing, and fill in the column from this point of view. Fill in the other column from the perspective of a researcher who does not believe such ability has been shown. Be sure to comment on each design feature.

4. Now that you have been exposed to both sides of the ape language issue, summarize your own conclusions about it. Do you believe that human language is different in degree or in kind from the communicative behavior of the great apes? Why?

eighteen

Computational Linguistics

Judith Klavans
Amanda Stent

How comes it that human beings, whose contacts with the world are brief and personal and limited, are nevertheless able to know so much as they do know?

– BERTRAND RUSSELL

OBJECTIVES

In this chapter, you will learn:

- what is involved in computer synthesis and recognition of human speech
- how computers can analyze morphology
- why analyzing and generating sentences is a complex task for a computer
- the kind of information that a computer needs in its dictionary
- how computers interpret discourse
- how computational linguistics can be applied to practical problems

Imagine a wireless computer you carry in your pocket that can read or hear communications—for example, e-mail or voice mail—and understand and respond to them as easily as you can. Such a device could organize your messages, search through them, read them out loud, and create replies based on a few ideas provided by you. The device could even translate your messages into other languages for you.

While the study of linguistics is centuries old, **computational linguistics** is a relatively new discipline that lies at the intersection of linguistics and computer science. In the 1990s, the field of computational linguistics made rapid strides as the Internet—formerly accessible only to select scientists and researchers and to the military—became available to the public. This single development has rapidly increased the impact of computational research and applications. Whenever you use a text editor, an Internet search engine, or a speech-driven automated customer-service center, you are using technology developed by computational linguists.

The central question in computational linguistics is this: What information and processes does a computer program have to know in order to process, understand, and produce human languages such as English? Humans use language almost effortlessly, without realizing its complexity. Consider the amount and type of information that a computer would have to know about language in order to understand a simple sentence such as the following famous example:

1)

This is the house that Jack built.

First, the computer would have to understand the usage of each of the words in sentence *1*. For example, the fact that *Jack* is capitalized means that it is a name, and the form of the verb *build* used here indicates that the action took place in the past. The computer would also have to understand the structure of this sentence. For example, in this sentence, *that Jack built* is a relative clause. The object of *built* is *that,* which has been moved to the front of the clause. In addition to morphological and grammatical knowledge, the computer needs semantic and world knowledge in order to understand sentence *1*. It must know, for example, that the sense of the noun *house* used here is 'a building in which to live' rather than any of the other eight senses for this word found in *Merriam Webster's Collegiate Dictionary.* It must also know that men are more likely than women to be named *Jack*. Ideally, it would recognize this sentence as the beginning of a children's rhyme.

What sort of knowledge would a computer need to know to utter this sentence? The rules of pronunciation, like the rules of grammar, are different for each language and even for dialects within the same language. Pronunciation is likely to vary within the same language, depending on many factors. For example, it would have to know that the noun *house* is pronounced differently from the verb *house.* It would also have to know that the vowel in *the* when preceding a consonant is pronounced as a schwa [ə] (see Chapter 2), whereas when preceding a vowel, it is pronounced as [i], as in *the apple.* English speakers know that the letter *e* in *the* is pronounced differently depending on the initial phoneme in the word that follows, but this is not true for every word ending in the sound /i/. For example, the words *we* and *flea* do not change pronunciation so drastically according to the word that follows, although there is always some adjustment in spoken language.

These examples are sufficient to illustrate the quantity and variety of information that humans know about language. We take this knowledge for granted; it is so obvious to us that even to write about it sometimes seems trivial. Until we try to write computer programs to understand or generate even the simplest sentence, there is no need to pick apart the knowledge about language that we possess. However, computers are only as capable as the humans who program them, so it is the task of the computational linguist to spell out this knowledge for the computer. This is a major undertaking, involving all aspects of knowledge of language.

Originally, linguistics had an impact on the development of computer science, primarily through the language theory of Noam Chomsky. Today, techniques developed by computer scientists are being used in the service of linguistics. The computer's ability to simulate processes is being used to test linguistic theories, and its ability to process large amounts of data is being used in corpus linguistics—a data-driven approach to the study of human languages. This in turn will lead to the refinement of linguistic knowledge, which can then be used to improve computer applications such as spoken dialogue interfaces, machine translation systems, and document indexing and retrieval. Thus, computer science and computational linguistics have become interdependent.

One of the changes in computational linguistics over the last fifteen years has been an increasing reliance on statistical analysis and other data-driven approaches rather than traditional approaches in which linguistic structure is explicitly represented. This introduction to computational linguistics will focus on describing the tasks that computational linguists face, the resources they use, and the general approaches they take. Places where statistical approaches are used will be pointed out but not described in depth.

The study of computational linguistics covers phonetics, phonology, morphology, syntax, semantics, and pragmatics—in other words, the many subfields of conventional linguistics. In addition, computational linguistics includes computational lexicography. The first part of this chapter shows how each linguistic subfield forms the basis for subfields in computational linguistics. The second part of the chapter shows some ways in which these various subsystems are combined to create computer systems that use language.

1 Computational Phonetics and Phonology

1.1 The Talking Machine: Speech Synthesis

At the 1939 World's Fair in New York, a device called a vocoder was displayed. The machine, developed by scientists at Bell Laboratories, reconstructed the human voice by producing a sound source that was then modified by a set of filters. The settings for the filters were derived from the analysis of human speech. The vocoder system consisted of a source of random noise for unvoiced sound, an oscillator to give voicing, a way to control resonance, and some switches to control the energy level. This was to simulate vowel sounds and fricatives (see Chapter 2). There were also controls for the consonants /p, b/, /t, d/, and /k, g/. An amplifier converted the modified source signal into sound resembling the human speech it was modeled after.

The vocoder was nicknamed the Talking Machine. It was a crude device, but it demonstrated that speech synthesis could be achieved. Current speech synthesis systems use different technology, but the principles remain the same. The goal is to replicate the waveforms that reflect those of human speech in order to produce speech that, at the very least, will be intelligible and aesthetically pleasing.

Speech recognition and speech synthesis rely on a detailed knowledge of **acoustic phonetics** as well as articulatory phonetics, although there are correlations between the acoustic and articulatory properties of sounds. Acoustic phonetics is the study of the structure of the waveforms that constitute speech. As was explained in Chapter 2, the lungs push a stream of air through the vocal tract. The airstream is modified first at the glottis and then by the tongue and lips.

Each sound can be broken down into its fundamental waveforms, as shown in Figure 18.1. The figure shows a spectrographic analysis, or **spectrogram**, of the words *heed, hid, head, had, hod, hawed, hood,* and *who'd* as spoken by a British speaker of English. The diagrams give a visual representation of the duration of the utterance on the horizontal axis, and the different frequencies in the waveform on the vertical axis. The main frequencies, or **formants**, show up because they have more intensity than other frequencies. Note the different locations of the formants along the frequency dimension for the different vowels. The sound /h/ is only slightly visible as fuzzy lines across the spectrum because /h/ is a voiceless fricative with little or no glottal constriction (see Chapter 2, Section 5). The acoustic effect is weak white noise resembling fuzz or static. The /d/ is a stop, so there is just a low-frequency voice bar resulting from the vibrations in the glottis, but there are no vowel for-

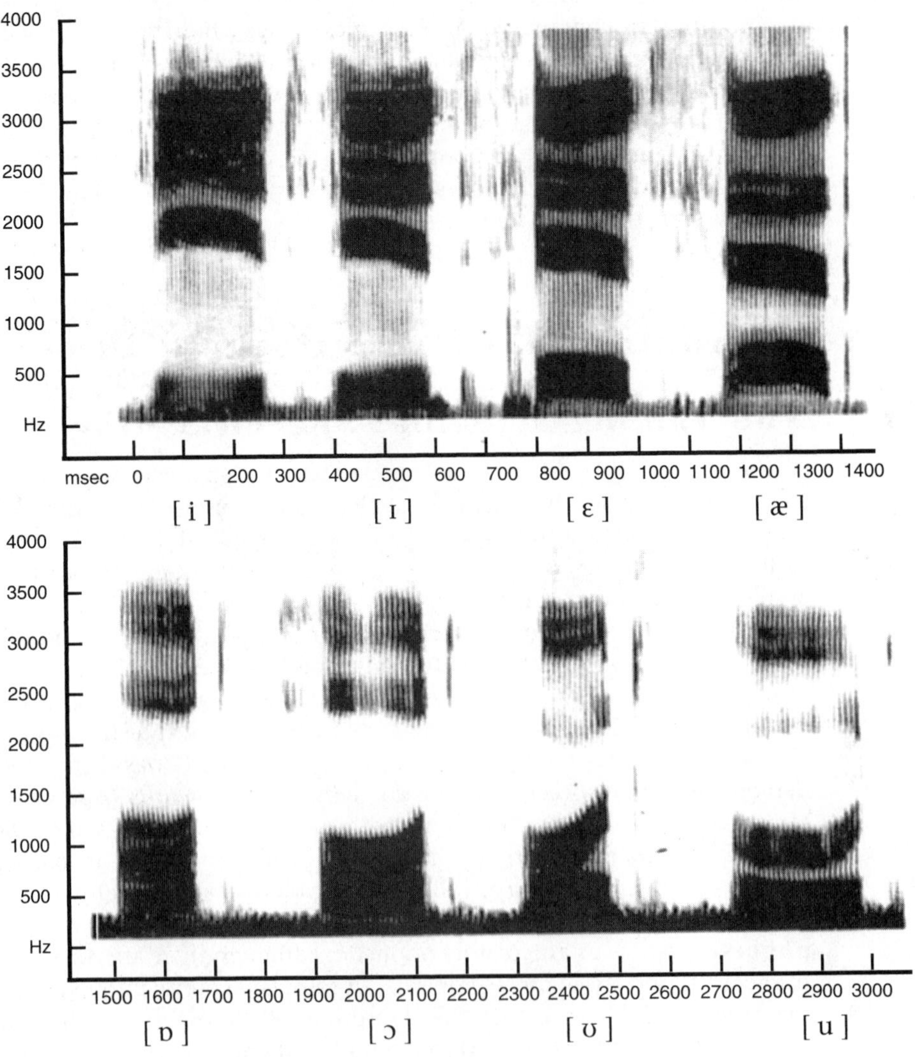

Figure 18.1 Spectrograms of vowels

mants for the period of closure since the airflow is blocked. This shows up as blank space on the spectrogram.

For speech synthesis, the first three formants are the most critical for identifying different vowels. The others add some refinement to the sound, but they do not determine intelligibility or naturalness with the same significance as the first three basic formants. Since different vowels are composed of different frequencies, theoretically the task of the speech synthesizer is simply to replicate those vowel sounds, put in a few consonants, and string them together to make words and sentences. Unfortunately, the matter is not so simple, since sounds are not fixed but vary according to the segments that surround them. Effects occur on adjacent segments and across groupings, sometimes as far as six phonemes away. For example, Figure 18.2 shows the same phonetic vowel [æ], but notice the rises and slumps in the formants. The figure shows how adjacent consonants can modify vowels. Similarly, vowels modify consonants, and nasal sounds modify larger chunks of surrounding speech. On top of these local changes, there are changes to entire phrases based on suprasegmental features such as stress and intonation (see Chapter 2, Section 8).

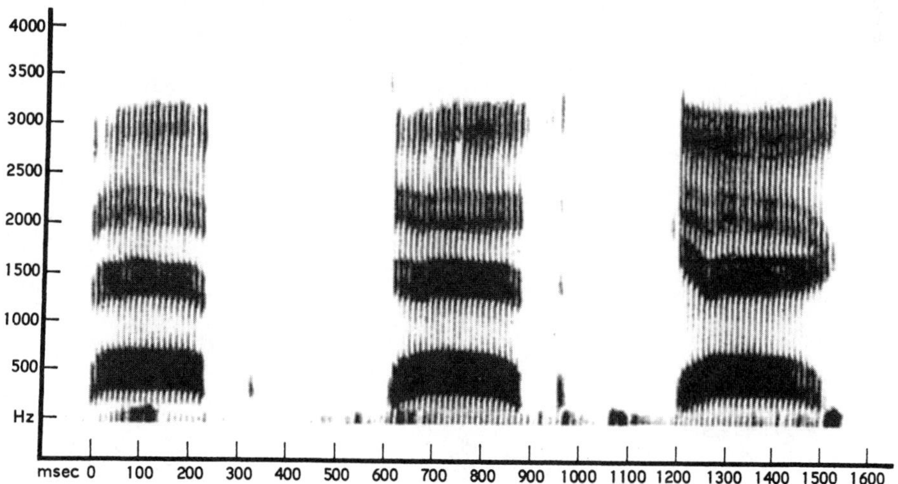

Figure 18.2 Spectrograms of the words *bab, dad, gag*

Speech synthesis involves several steps, as shown in Figure 18.3. The text to be spoken has to be analyzed to identify sentence boundaries; proper names; abbreviations or acronyms; and other syntactic, semantic, and orthographic features. Then pronunciations must be found for all words in the text. There are exceptional words such as *have* /hæv/ and *four* /fɔr/ that do not follow the predictable letter-sound correspondences of English: *have* does not rhyme with *nave* or *rave,* and *four* does not rhyme with *sour* or *glamour.* There are also heteronyms—words that are spelled the

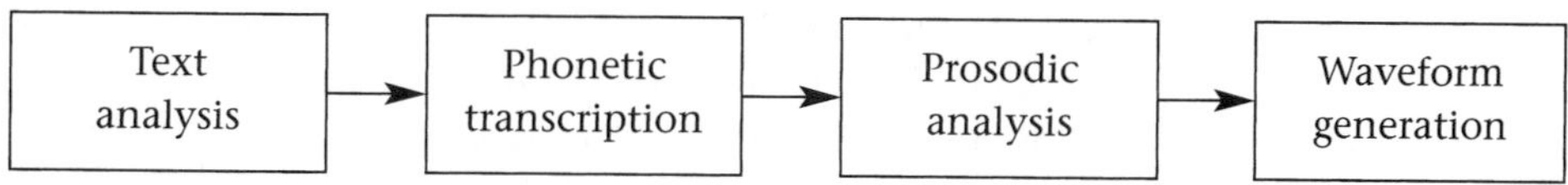

Figure 18.3 Stages of speech synthesis

same but pronounced differently, such as the verb *recórd* and the noun *récord*. After a system chooses the correct phoneme, it must look at the environment to see which allophone of the phoneme to choose. For example, to return to Figure 18.2, if the system were trying to pronounce *bab* /bæb/, the vowel /æ/ corresponding to the labial onset and labial offset would be chosen, since labials tend to lower adjacent formants.

The third stage—prosodic analysis—requires syntactic and semantic analyses of a sentence to identify possible phrasings and give an idea of the focus and stress of words that might go together. For example, prosody assignment is important for noun compounds in English. The pronunciation of the compound can change the listener's interpretation of the meaning. For example, the phrase *London museum guide* could have two interpretations, depending on its structure. One intrepretation, shown in Figure 18.4a, is that the guide is a guide for a museum called the London Museum. The other, shown in Figure 18.4b, is that the guide refers to all museums in London. Prosody assignment is also important for prepositional phrase disambiguation. Consider the sentence *Mary will take the statue from Kenya to the museum.* Does this sentence mean that the statue is Kenyan, or that the statue is currently in Kenya?

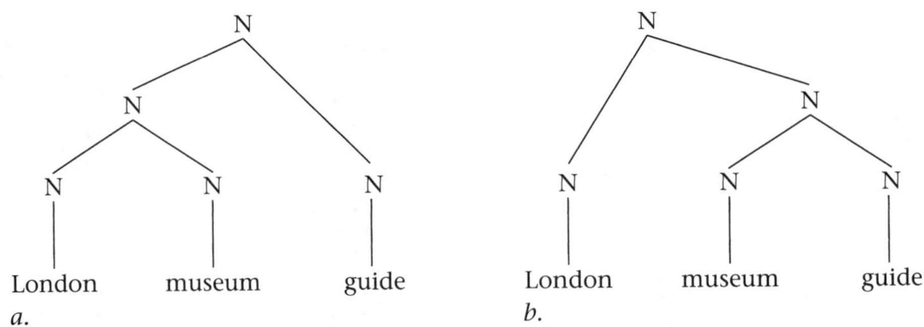

Figure 18.4

Finally, prosody assignment is important for parentheticals such as:

2)

Here are the apples, as you can see.

3)

He said, although I don't believe it, that he was a good driver.

Parentheticals are typically pronounced at a lower pitch and loudness. When pronounced with main phrase intonation, they are difficult to understand. These features must be translated into duration (length), pitch, and loudness in order for synthetic speech to sound completely natural.

Systems of intelligible speech synthesis have already been created and are widely and freely available. However, synthesized speech still sounds synthetic. A number of difficult problems remain, such as improving individual sounds and incorporating prosodic variety to eliminate the droning quality of synthesized speech.

1.2 Speech Recognition

As we have seen, speech consists of very complex waveforms changing rapidly across time and in subtle ways, which can affect the perception of a message. The task of **speech recognition** is to take these waveforms as input and decode them. This is exactly what humans do when listening to speech. The waveform that reaches the ear is a continuous stream of sound; we segment this sound into words, phrases, and meaningful units so that we can determine the meaning of an utterance.

Early speech-recognition research was conducted primarily at Bell Laboratories in the 1950s, and focused on recognizing individual numbers. It was not until the 1990s that speech-recognition systems became widely commercially viable. Currently, speech-recognition technology is widely used for tasks ranging from dictation to automated customer service.

There are two basic types of speech-recognition systems in existence today. **Speaker-independent speech recognizers** are used for customer-service applications and research on spoken dialogue. These devices will recognize speech from many speakers, but have a fairly small vocabulary (around one thousand words). **Speaker-dependent speech recognizers**, available for purchase in any computer store, are used for dictation and other tasks for which per-word accuracy is important. They recognize a larger vocabulary but need to be trained to recognize the user's speech, and perform well for only that user.

For both types of speech recognizers, the speech-recognition process involves the three basic steps shown in Figure 18.5. First, the incoming speech signal is converted into a form the computer can process. Second, the computer matches parts of the input signal to phonemes, considering features of the waveform itself as well as phonemes it has recently recognized. Third, the computer associates sequences of phonemes with words, using information about word pronunciations as well as information about words it has recently recognized.

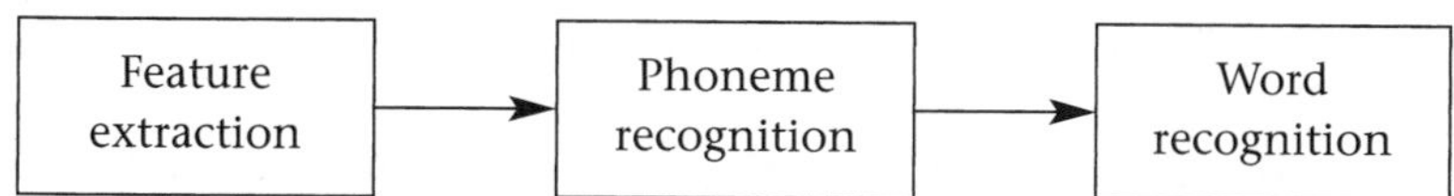

Figure 18.5 Stages of speech recognition

Even though human beings have no trouble decoding speech waveforms, speech recognizers often have trouble segmenting speech. As discussed in Chapter 2, Section 9, speech sounds are modified by adjacent sounds in natural speech. The faster and more informal the speech, the more sounds are merged and dropped. Consider the sentence *I'll have the steak.* For this sentence, a speech recognizer might output *All have these take* or *Olive the steak*. Knowledge of context, syntactic structure, and probabilities of occurrence is helpful, but it doesn't solve the problem.

Another very difficult problem for speech recognition is the **cocktail party effect**. Even though a hearer's environment may include noise from other people, from music, or from the street, humans manage to focus on a particular sound or conversation. Speech-recognition systems, by contrast, have difficulty distinguishing speech signals from background noise and therefore perform better in reasonably quiet environments.

The state of the art in speech recognition is similar to that in speech synthesis: usable systems exist, but sophisticated ones whose level of performace ranks with that of human performance are still in the future.

2 Computational Morphology

Morphology is the study of the internal structure of words and covers such topics as affixation, compounding, and infixation (see Chapter 4). Most research in computational morphology arose as a by-product of the development of **natural language processing systems**. Researchers found that looking up words in a computational dictionary was more complicated than they expected, precisely because of morphological processes that could conceal the base word. For example, if a dictionary had the word *book,* the word *books* would not necessarily be found through a simple search. Unless a system is explicitly told that *book* is related to *books* by a productive and regular rule of inflectional morphology, it will not be able to infer how the two words are related. Thus, a program needs to include the rule of pluralization in English (as well as other rules) in order to recognize or generate the morphological permutations of words.

2.1 Morphological Processes

Most morphologically conditioned changes in written English involve spelling, with some changes in stems. Examples are *stop/stopped, sing/sang,* and *tolerate/tolerant.* In general, morphological variations in English are not as opaque as in other languages. Some languages, such as German, have very productive compounding, whereas others have infixation and reduplication, or complex stem changes. Words altered by morphological processes cannot be easily recognized by a natural language processor unless they are properly related to their bases for lexical lookup.

Implementing Morphological Processes: Stemming

Broadly speaking, there are two approaches to computational morphology. The first is called **stemming**. In stemming, affixes are recursively stripped off the beginnings and ends of words, and base forms are proposed. If the base form is found in the base-form dictionary, then the word is analyzable. Successful analyses provide information about the internal structure of the word. They also provide information contributed by a given affix, such as part-of-speech change, inherent semantic changes (e.g., *-ess* is +feminine), or other information (e.g., abstract, Latinate, singular, plural). Most of these systems are sensitive to constraints on affix ordering, such as those described in Chapter 4. Inflectional affixes occur outside of derivational affixes, and there may be some derivational affixes that occur outside of other derivational affixes.

Two different types of dictionaries are possible with the stemming approach: **word-based** and **stem-based**. A word-based system has a dictionary with words only. For word generation, all input to morphological rules must be well-formed words in order for all output to be well-formed words. For word analysis, all proposed stems will be words. The word-based system has proven to be very useful for projects that use large computer-readable dictionaries, since dictionaries list words, not stems.

Table 18.1 Word-based system: Input word *conceptualize*

Analysis	*Part of speech*	*Features*
concept	N	num(sing)
-ual	A	
-ize	V	form(inf)

Table 18.1 presents an example of the type of analysis given by a word-based stemming system. To analyze the word *conceptualize* as an infinitive verb (V form(inf)), first the base word *conceptual* must be analyzed as an adjective (A). This would be done by a rule stating that the suffix *-ize* can attach to certain adjectives to create verbs. *Conceptual* can be analyzed as an adjective if the base word *concept* can first be analyzed as a singular noun (N num(sing)). This would be done by a rule stating that the suffix *-ual* can attach to certain nouns to create adjectives. *Concept* is stored in the dictionary as a singular noun, so the lexical lookup serves as the final step of the analysis. The analyses shown here actually result from successive applications of the morphological rules. Each rule has conditions that restrict its operation. The condition for the *-ize* rule is that the base must be an adjective (but compare *terrorize* and *hospitalize,* where in each case the base, namely *terror* and *hospital,* is a noun). Since each condition is met, an analysis is possible. The word *conceptualize* is deemed a well-formed infinitive verb.

Table 18.2 Word-based system: Input word *conceptualizations*

Analysis	*Part of speech*	*Features*
concept	N	num(sing)
-ual	A	
-ize	V	form(inf)
-ation	N	num(sing)
-s	N	num(plur)

How would the system analyze a more complex form? Consider the analysis in Table 18.2 of the word *conceptualizations*. In this example, the suffix *-ation* attaches to infinitive verbs. Notice that when *-ation* attaches to *conceptualize,* there is a spelling change. If no spelling rules were written, then the word **conceptualizeation* would be allowed by the system. Finally, the plural marker *-s* is attached at the outside of the noun. For the plural suffix *-s,* there is no change in the part of speech, only in the number feature of the word from singular to plural. These examples illustrate a word-based system. Both the dictionary entry, in this case *concept,* and the complex words *conceptualize* and *conceptualizations* are well-formed words of English.

Table 18.3 Stem-based system: Input word *conceptualizations*

Analysis	*Part of speech*	*Features*
con-		
-cept	N	num(sing)
-ual	A	
-ize	V	form(inf)
-ation	N	num(sing)
-s	N	num(plur)

How would this system differ if it were stem-based? For this example, the morpheme *-cept* might be listed in a stem dictionary, due to its presence in other words in English, such as *reception, conception, inception,* and *perception.* Since *-ceive* and *-cept* are related in a regular way, this relationship might also be given in the stem dictionary, or the words could be related by rule. Consider again *conceptualizations,* analyzed down to a stem in Table 18.3. In this example, the prefix *con-* attaches to *-cept.* Unlike a word-based morphology system, a stem-based system cannot use a regular dictionary as its lexicon. In order for stem-based morphology to get wide coverage, a large dictionary of stems is required. (More on this topic is found in Section 4 later in this chapter.)

Implementing Morphological Processes: Two-Level Morphology

Another way to look at computational morphology is with the two-level approach. Both stemming and the two-level approach use a lexicon, or dictionary, although **two-level morphology** requires a stem-based lexicon. Both approaches use rules, but the rules are very different. In two-level morphology, the rules define correspondences between lexical and surface representations; they specify whether a correspondence is restricted to, required by, or prohibited by a particular environment. *Lexical* roughly translates to 'underlying', whereas *surface* usually means 'orthographic' but sometimes 'phonemic'. In Figure 18.6, the lexical representation of *try* followed by the *+s* is matched with a surface representation *tries.*

Lexical and surface representations are matched using a special kind of rule system called a finite-state transducer. Simply put, the rules would decide whether the lexical *y* could correspond to the surface *i* based on information the rules have already seen. The rules that compare lexical and surface form move from left to right, so when a successful correspondence is made, the analysis moves along. This two-level system can also be used in reverse for morphology assignment. One of the strengths of this method is that since the procedure moves from left to right, it accurately reflects the way that people process words. Since people read English from left to right and hear the beginning of a word before the end, a system that incorporates left-to-right directionality might be an actual model of human processing. Furthermore, since the two-level system processes from left to right for morphological analysis, it can easily be reversed and function from right to left for morphological generation. The primary drawback of the two-level system is that it requires a specialized stem dictionary complete with rules that restrict the stems so that not all affixes attach to all stems.

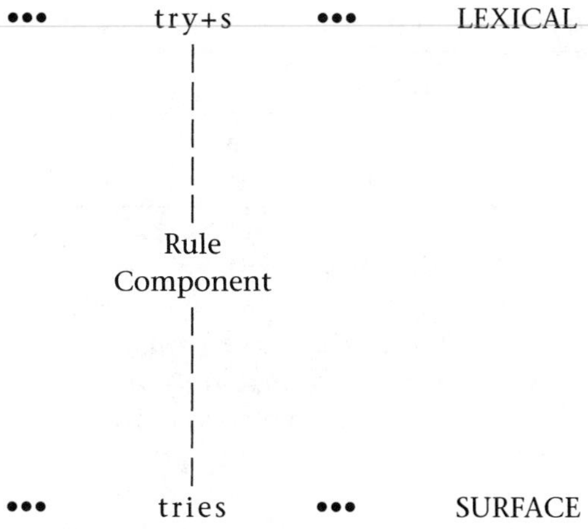

Figure 18.6

2.2 Some Problems in Computational Morphology

Compounding is a particularly thorny problem since it tends to be so productive that compounds are often not listed in a dictionary. Until recently the word *bookworm,* for example, did not appear in *Merriam Webster's Collegiate Dictionary.* A good morphological analyzer should be able to analyze *bookworm* as shown in Table 18.4.

Table 18.4 Input word: *bookworm*

Analysis	*Part of speech*	*Features*
book	N	num(sing)
worm	N	num(sing)

However, what about a word like *accordion*? The analysis in Table 18.5 shows that *accordion* could be composed of the noun *accord* plus the word *ion.* However, *accordion* is not a compound analogous to *bookworm.* Since *accordion* never has this analysis, it might be marked as an exception to this kind of morphological analysis.

Table 18.5 Input word: *accordion*

Analysis	*Part of speech*	*Features*
accord	N	num(sing)
ion	N	num(sing)

A related problem arises from overenthusiastic rule application. Table 18.6 presents an analysis of *really.* Here *really* is analyzed as [*re*- [*ally*$_{\text{verb}}$]$_{\text{verb}}$], meaning 'to ally oneself with someone again'. This analysis is correct although highly improbable. Cases like that of *re*- in *really* bring up a difficult issue. Should a word like *really* be specially marked in the dictionary as a nonanalyzable word, an exception to the rules

Table 18.6 Input word: *really*

Analysis	*Part of speech*	*Features*
re-		
ally	V	form(inf)

that would apply to regular formations like *reapply, redo,* and *reduplicate*? Or should the rules be allowed to apply freely? What about a word like *resent,* which could either be [*re*-[$sent_{\text{verb}}$]$_{\text{verb}}$], as in *She didn't get my letter, so I resent it,* or [$resent_{\text{verb}}$], as in *Did he resent that comment*? The spelling of this word is truly ambiguous, so a decision about its analyzability requires knowledge of syntactic and semantic features in the sentence and context. Usually the decision is driven by practical concerns. A system that is designed to implement a theory but that does not need to perform well on a task that uses the theory would probably allow the rules to apply freely. A system that needs to perform accurately on large texts would probably mark *really* and *resent* as nonanalyzable words, even though strictly speaking they are not.

3 Computational Syntax

Research in computational syntax arose from two sources. One was the practical motivation resulting from attempts to build working systems to analyze and generate language. Some of these systems, such as machine translation and spoken-dialogue systems, are discussed later in the chapter (see Section 7). The other motivation was a desire on the part of theoretical linguists to use the computer as a tool to demonstrate that a particular theory is internally consistent. Recently, builders of practical systems have taken greater advantage of theoretical insights, and linguistic theoreticians have paid more attention to practical problems. This has also been the case in research on syntactic parsing, although this is a fairly new development.

3.1 Natural Language Analysis

Parsers and Grammars

Chapter 5 showed how sentences can be analyzed into substructures such as noun phrases, verb phrases, prepositional phrases, and so on. Given a system of rules, an analyzer will be able to break up and organize a sentence into its substructures. A grammar can be viewed as the set of rules that define a language. These rules can be of different types, which accordingly give them different properties. A **parser** is a program that applies these rules, and it can have different strategies for applying them. The rules for sentence structure differ among languages (see Chapter 5), and the differences are reflected in the grammars of these languages. The parser, however, does not depend on individual languages. (Recall the discussion of the role of parsers in language processing in Chapter 13.) In fact, computational linguists frequently implement and refine grammar formalisms taken from traditional linguistics.

Determinism versus Nondeterminism

Often a syntactic parser can produce more than one analysis of an input sentence. For example, if the beginning of the sentence in Figure 18.7 is read word by word, there is more than one possible ending. In choice *a, I see you in the mirror,* the word *you* is the object of the main verb *see.* For *b, I see you have finished,* the word *that* has been left out, as is permitted in English, and the word *you* is the subject of the clause *you have finished.* If the parser follows path *a,* and that path turns out to be the wrong one, how can the situation be rectified to get the right analysis? Or can choices be controlled so that a parser never has to undergo the time-consuming task of going back and starting over? If a sentence leads to a false path, it is called a garden path sentence (see Chapter 13).

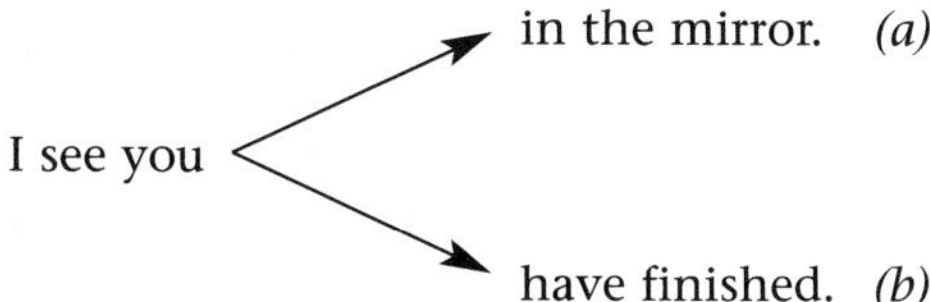

Figure 18.7

Nondeterministic parsers may go back or start over if an analysis turns out to be incorrect. Alternatively, they may build all possible analyses at once. By contrast, **deterministic parsers** always give their first analysis. The problem of choice in parsing is a serious one since the number of alternatives increases as the coverage of a system increases. The result is that as an analyzer improves, it becomes more and more cumbersome because it is presented with more and more options.

Top-Down versus Bottom-Up Parsing

Consider the following phrase structure rules for English:

4)

a.	IP	→	NP I'
b.	NP	→	(Det) N'
c.	N'	→	N (PP)
d.	I'	→	I VP
e.	VP	→	(Adv) V'
f.	V'	→	V (NP) (PP)
g.	PP	→	(Deg) P'
h.	P'	→	P (NP)

There are two ways to build an analysis of a sentence using just these rules. This section illustrates the principles of **top-down parsing** and **bottom-up parsing**. Working systems may not function exactly like this, but the principles are the same.

In addition to the rules in *4,* we also need to give some lexical items, or **terminals**, for each category of nonterminal. Generally speaking, a **nonterminal** is not a word in the language. Rather, it is a part of speech or a phrase type, such as N or

NP. A terminal can be thought of as a word (although sometimes a terminal is a part of a word or several words). In top-down parsing, the parser always starts with the topmost node—in this case IP—and expands it until there are no nonterminals left. The only rule in example *4* for IP is *a*. The next rules to apply are the NP expansion rule and the I' expansion rule. Both NP and I' are nonterminals. Although N' is a nonterminal, it has no expansions, so we move right along to the I' rule (results are shown in Figure 18.8).

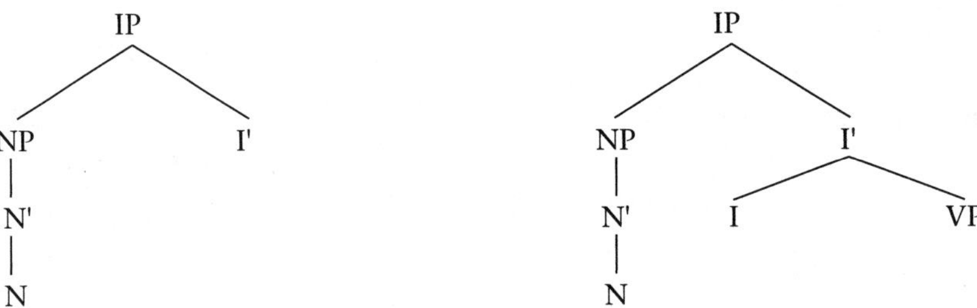

Figure 18.8

If the subject of the sentence had been *the batter,* then the NP would have been expanded to Det and N'. This process continues until no more expansions can be applied, and until all the lexical items or words along the bottom of the parse tree occur in the correct position to match the input sentence (in this case, using the terminal assignments in *5,* the two possible input sentences are *Larry sat on the grass* and *The grass sat on Larry*).

5)

N → Larry
I → past
V → sat
P → on
Det → the
N → grass

By contrast, bottom-up parsers take the terminals (words) of a sentence one by one, replace the terminals with proposed nonterminal labels, and then build the analysis up to the topmost node. For example, the word *Larry* would be assigned to the category N, then *sat* would be assigned to V, and so on. The partial analysis up to this point is shown in Figure 18.9. The only applicable rules here are *4b* and *c* (the structure resulting from applying these rules is shown in Figure 18.10). Rule application continues until the structure of a sentence is built.

N	V	P	Det	N
Larry	sat	on	the	grass

Figure 18.9

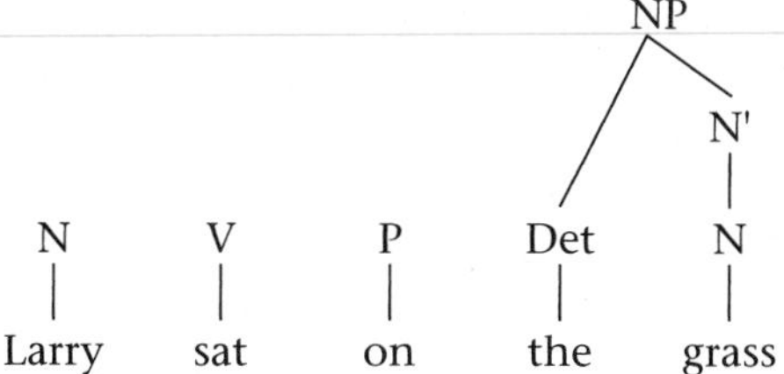

Figure 18.10

A third type of parser is a **chart parser**. A chart parser is a special type of parser that keeps track of all possible parses in parallel. It uses a special representation called a chart, which contains a column for each word in the input sentence. The sentence is parsed in one left-to-right pass. All rules that can be applied at each word position are applied, and a new entry is added to the column for that word for each rule. This entry contains information about how much of the input sentence the rule covers. When there is an entry that covers the whole input, at least one successful parse has been found. The chart permits efficient parsing without backtracking. Chart parsers can be bottom-up or top-down.

Generative Capacity

The term *generative* in this context refers to formal properties of grammars as mathematical systems. It does not refer to language generation, which is discussed in Section 3.2. Recall that a grammar consists of a set of rules that describe a language. Informally, we can say that a language consists of items from the vocabulary of the language, such as those shown in *6*.

6)

player, shoe, child, lost, a . . .

Of course, a sentence is more than just a string of words, as shown in Chapter 5. Furthermore, the set of strings is greater than the set of well-formed sentences, as examples *7* through *9* show. Even though the vocabulary may be finite, the language may be finite or infinite. This is because of **recursion**, a very powerful property of natural languages. Recursion allows the repeated application of the same rule to create a hierarchically organized sentence with one structure embedded in another. The application of a finite number of recursive rules results in languages that can contain an infinite number of well-formed strings. The following sentences consist of vocabulary from the set in *6*. While *7* is a well-formed sentence in English, *8* and *9* are not:

7)

A child lost a shoe.

8)

*Child shoe a.

9)

*Lost a shoe a child.

Although *9* is not an allowable string of words for English, it could be found in Spanish, given the same vocabulary.

10)

Perdió un zapato un niño.
Lost a shoe a child.

The grammar of English would give a correct description of *7,* but not *8* or *9.* On the other hand, the grammar of Spanish would allow both *7* and *9,* but not *8.* The goal of an implemented grammar that is programmed into a computer is exactly the same. An **implementation** is simply a practical system. The grammar rules are programmed into a computer, and the computer program then decides if the sentence is permitted in the language. If the sentence is permitted, the program then has the task of giving the sentence the correct description.

Natural languages (as opposed to computer languages) are highly complex, since there are many ambiguities and subtleties; therefore, discovering the correct grammar for a given language is an extremely difficult task. The complexity and subtlety of natural languages continue to present a challenge to linguists. There are many competing theories of what the "correct" grammar of natural languages will be like. Even the grammar for English, a very well-studied natural language, is not at all well understood. One issue that all theories agree on, however, is that a grammar should have certain properties. Grammars should give a correct description of the following:

A. The strings of a language

B. The structures corresponding to the strings in the language

Property A is called **weak generative capacity**. Property B is called **strong generative capacity**.

For example, Figure 18.11 shows an analysis in which the first two words—*the* and *player*—are joined into a noun phrase (NP). I is dominated by IP. The verb phrase (VP) is described by the grammar as consisting of a verb (V), followed by a noun phrase (NP), followed by a prepositional phrase (PP). These three constituents

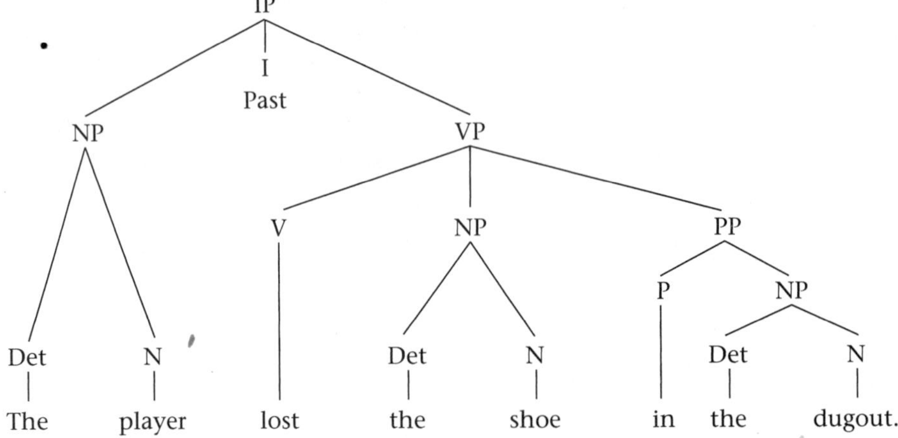

Figure 18.11 A syntactic analysis performed by a parser

are immediately dominated by the VP node. What if a different grammar were to claim a different structure for this sentence? Consider the structure in Figure 18.12. This analysis makes different claims about the structure of the sentence, but the actual string of words stays the same. The tree in Figure 18.12 has two levels in the verb phrase. One is VP, which dominates everything in the predicate of the sentence (everything in the sentence except the subject and I'). The other is V', which dominates only the main verb and the direct object. The grammar generating the structure in Figure 18.12 differs in strong generative capacity from the grammar for Figure 18.11. However, both grammars may have the same weak generative capacity since they both have the ability to describe the string *The player lost the shoe in the dugout.*

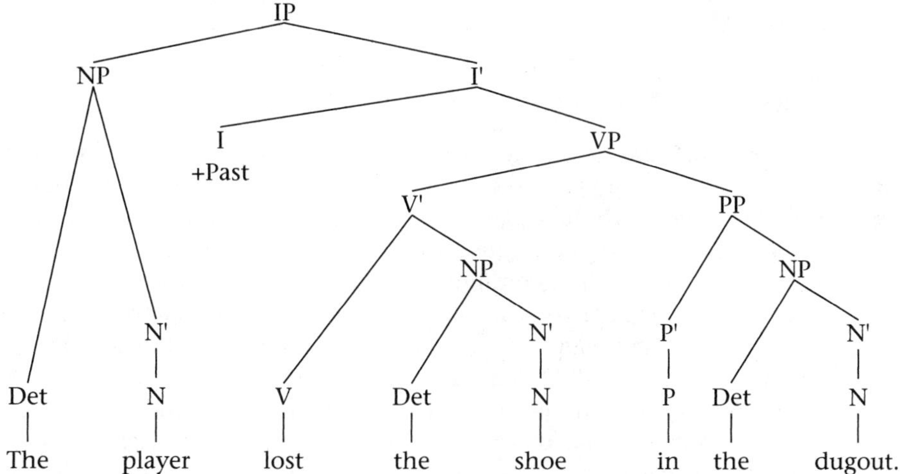

Figure 18.12

The Role of Syntax and Semantics

The division between what should be handled by the syntactic component of a system and what should be handled by the semantic component is a matter of great debate. Some systems might claim that selection of prepositions by verbs, often considered a syntactic property, is actually dependent on the semantic category of the verb. For example, not all verbs can take the instrumental, as in the reading of *11* in which the bone was used to reward the dog.

11)

He rewarded the dog with a bone.

If a different VP is substituted for *rewarded the dog,* would the sentence be semantically or syntactically ill-formed?

12)

*He told his story with a bone.

Some systems assume that a syntactic analysis precedes a semantic one, and that the semantics should be applied to the output of syntactic analyses. This is the position of the earliest transformational models, which were incorporated into many computational systems. Some systems perform syntactic and semantic analyses hand-in-hand. Other systems ignore the syntactic, viewing it as a second-step derivative from semantic analyses.

With access to an increasing amount of text in machine-readable form, computational linguists now have much more language data to study. Instead of using a grammar written by hand, the computer can learn a grammar automatically from a collection, or **corpus**, of text parsed by humans. When the computer constructs a grammar inductively from a corpus, the accuracy of the grammar is highly dependent on the data in the corpus. However, a computer can learn a grammar more quickly than a human can write a grammar, and because the grammar is learned from data, frequency information can be used to disambiguate between alternative parse trees.

3.2 Natural Language Generation

The term **natural language generation** refers to all the processes that transform an intention to communicate into an actual communication, written or spoken. These processes include content planning, text planning, sentence planning, and surface realization, as shown in Figure 18.13. Content planning involves selecting the information that will best communicate the speaker's and writer's intent while still obeying the Cooperative Principle (see Chapter 6). For example, if a sales representative wants to compare two computers, he or she will select information that distinguishes one from the other. The goal of text planning is to organize the selected content so as to communicate the speaker's intent clearly and effectively. In sentence planning, some aspects of sentence structure are selected (e.g., use of cues such as *therefore,* passive/active). Finally, in surface realization, words are selected and arranged to form coherent sentences. Although syntactic information may be used in sentence planning, syntactic processing in natural language generation is primarily performed during surface realization.

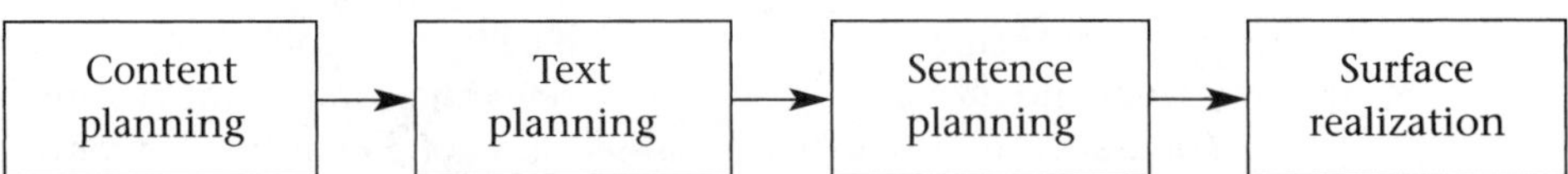

Figure 18.13 Stages of natural language generation

The language generation problem is often viewed as the reverse of the language analysis problem, but this is not entirely accurate. In the same way, the generation of speech (discussed in Section 1.1) is in no way simply the reverse of speech recognition. In language analysis, the computer is given an input sentence. The usual assumption is that there is one correct syntactic and semantic analysis for that sentence, and the goal is to find it. For language generation, in contrast, the computer is given a communicative goal and a set of content. The computer must then make choices about which content to include, how to structure it, and which words to use. There is frequently no one best solution; the computer's task is simply to communicate the selected content while respecting conversational maxims (see Chapter 6, Section 4.4). To illustrate this, consider the seemingly simple task of generating a noun phrase to describe a children's block. One possible noun phrase is *the block*. However, what if there are two blocks, one green and one blue? Then the description *the block* violates the Maxim of Quantity. Instead, the program might choose *the blue toy*. This will work unless there is another blue toy (for example a blue ball). On the other hand, if there is only one toy, the description *the large blue block* might violate the Maxim of Manner.

There are three general approaches to surface realization. If the range of possible sentence structures to be used is very limited, the most efficient approach may be **template generation**. Template generation uses a set of patterns, called templates, which can be thought of as sentences with gaps. For example, a template for an air travel reservation system might look like *"[Flight Number] leaves from [Destination] at [Time]."* Template generation produces high quality output but cannot achieve broad language coverage. It is often used for speech interfaces to databases, where the range of possible outputs is known in advance and there is a need for fast generation.

Two other approaches to surface realization, **grammar-based generation** and **forest-based generation**, both use grammars of the language to be produced. These grammars may be similar to those used for language analysis. In grammar-based generation, an extensive grammar is used. In forest-based generation, a very simple, underconstrained grammar is used, which causes the grammar to overgenerate. The resulting sentences—both syntactically valid sentences and syntactically invalid sentences—are then ranked, and the highest-ranked one is selected. Grammar-based and forest-based surface realizers are typically used for text generation because they provide greater language coverage and greater flexibility than template generation.

The Generation Lexicon

Access to a high-quality, highly specific lexicon is critical to natural language generation. An inappropriate word can lead to misunderstanding; missing information (such as a missing object to a verb) can result in syntactically incorrect or confusing sentences. Lexicons used for language analysis may not be specific enough to use for language generation.

Consider the sentence *Susan sent the letter.* The action of sending is a type of move action, involving two required **arguments**—the subject and the object (the term *argument* here refers to grammatical dependents of a verb). So a language analyzer might analyze this sentence as involving a type of move action (*send*) taking place in the past; a subject (*Susan*) who performed the action; and an object (*the letter*) that was moved. How might a surface realizer generate this same content? It will look for verbs that are move actions—for example, the verb *go*. However, *go* only takes one argument—a subject—so if it selects *go,* it will only be able to generate *Susan went* or *The letter went.* It might pick the transitive form of the verb *move.* Then it would generate *Susan moved the letter,* which does not communicate the same information as the original sentence. It might even pick the verb *send,* but then it would have to choose which part of the content becomes the subject and which becomes the object of the sentence. In the absence of information about semantic restrictions on the verb's arguments, it might generate *The letter sent Susan.* Even with semantic and syntactic information about the words in the lexicon, without morphological information it might generate *Susan sended the letter.*

The design and content of the generation lexicon is one of the most difficult areas in language generation. The lexicon needs to contain many different types of information, such as syntactic facts about verbs, facts about usage and focus, and facts about types of modifiers. Building lexicons for generation is one of the goals of computational lexicology, as discussed in the following section.

4 Computational Lexicography

Computational linguists are realizing that a natural language analyzer or generator is only as good as its dictionary or lexicon. The task of capturing and representing this information falls to **computational lexicography**.

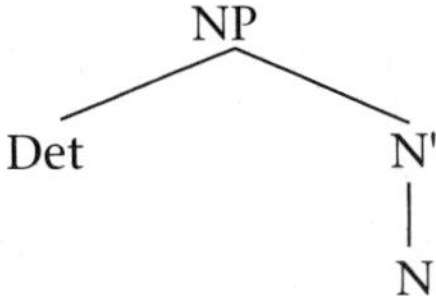

Figure 18.14

The lexicon is the repository of whatever information about words a particular system needs. The individual words in the lexicon are called lexical items. In order for a bare structure such as Figure 18.14 to be filled out with real words, a program would need to have a match between a word marked Det (determiner) in the lexicon and the slot in the tree requiring a Det. The same goes for any part of speech, such as a noun, verb, or adjective. Given the lexical items listed for terminals in 5 on page 600, a valid match for Figure 18.14 would be Figure 18.15 *a*. Figure 18.15 *b* would not be a valid match; the preposition *on* occurs under the determiner node, and the verb *sat* occurs under the noun node. At the very least, the condition of matching parts of speech has to be met.

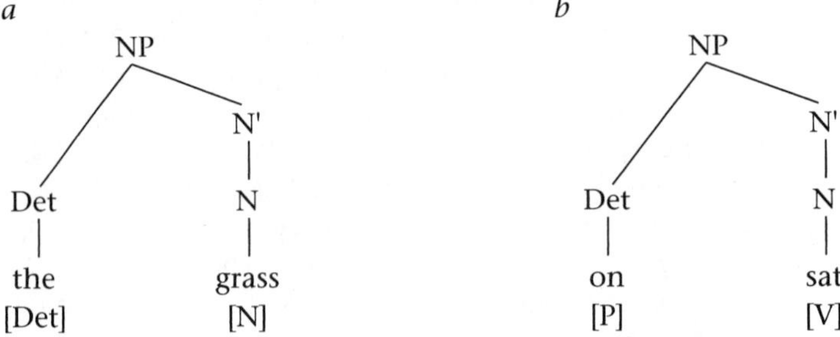

Figure 18.15

A computer program would need to know more than just the part of speech to analyze or generate a sentence correctly. Subcategorization—that is, the number of arguments a verb can take—must be considered (see Chapter 5, Section 2). Knowledge of thematic roles is also needed (see Chapter 6, Section 3.3). A syntactic analyzer would also need to know what kinds of complements a verb can take (see Chapter 5).

13)

I decided to go.

14)

*I decided him to go.

15)

*I persuaded to go.

16)

I persuaded him to go.

The verb *decide* can take the infinitive *to go* as in *13,* but it cannot take an *NP* object and then the infinitive, as in *14.* The verb *persuade* is the opposite.

The lexicon needs to know about the kinds of structures in which words can appear, about the semantics of surrounding words, and about the style of the text. For example, the sentence in *17* is strange in meaning, but the structure is fine.

17)

I broke the concept.

The verb *break* is transitive and so can take an object. The problem here is the type of the object. Only concrete objects are breakable unless the meaning is metaphorical, as in *The disease broke his will to live.* (See Chapter 6 for more discussion of semantics.)

What does a computational lexicon look like? So far the list of information includes:

18)

Lexical Entry

a. Part of speech
b. Sense number
c. Subcategorization
d. Semantic properties

Keeping in mind that a computational lexicon has to contain as much information as possible in order to correctly analyze and generate sentences, the following are also needed:

19)

(continued information for the lexical entry)

e. Pronunciation
f. Context and style
g. Etymology
h. Usage (e.g., taboos)
i. Spelling (including abbreviations)

The task of collecting all the important information for every existing word in the English language is overwhelming. Given that the kind of information needed cannot be found in conventional dictionaries, how are computational lexicons built? There are several approaches. One is to build the lexicon by hand, specifying only those features that a given system needs and using only the lexical items that are most likely to occur. For example, assume that an analyzer is reading the *Wall Street Journal,* and assume that the sentence to be analyzed is *His stock is high.* If the analyzer is to assign a meaning to this sentence, it has to know at least the information below.

Word: *stock*[1]

1. Part of speech: noun
2. Semantic properties: [+concrete], . . .
3. Context: financial

In just this usage, there is no reason to know about any other meanings of *stock,* as in *vegetable stock.* The lexical entry for this other sense would include the information below.

Word: *stock*[2]

1. Part of speech: noun
2. Semantic properties: [+concrete], . . .
3. Context: food

Most words have many different senses, and sometimes the different senses have very different grammatical behavior. If a new word with a new feature is added to the lexicon, the dictionary builder will have to go back through the lexicon and modify every word to match the new expanded word. When *stock*[2] was added to the dictionary, new features had to be added: *stock*[1] does not have a context "food," and *stock*[2] does not have a context "financial." One of the major problems in building dictionaries is how to add new information and modify old information without starting over each time.

Another option in building large lexicons is to use two resources: the power of the computer and the data of machine-readable dictionaries. A **machine-readable dictionary** (**MRD**) is a conventional dictionary in machine-readable form (i.e., on the computer rather than on the bookshelf). Many MRDs can be found on the Internet at Web sites where people often go for clarification or translation. MRDs are useful in building large lexicons because the computer can be used to analyze information that has already been organized by lexicographers (the writers of dictionaries). Unfortunately, the type of information that is needed for a computational dictionary is not always easy to find in a conventional dictionary. However, with some clever approaches many important facts can be pulled out of MRDs and put into a computational lexicon.

For example, the knowledge that a word has a sense that is [+human] is needed in a computational lexicon for both syntactic and semantic reasons. The tenth edition of *Merriam-Webster's Collegiate Dictionary,* which has about seventy thousand headwords, has just over a thousand nouns that are defined in terms of the word *person.* Some examples are given below:

accessory

a *person* not actually or constructively present but contributing as an assistant or instigator to the commission of an offense—called also accessory before the fact *acquaintance*

a *person* whom one knows but who is not a particularly close friend

intellectual

a very intelligent or intellectual *person*

scatterbrain

a giddy, heedless *person*: FLIBBERTIGIBBET

unbeliever

one that does not believe: an incredulous *person*: DOUBTER, SKEPTIC

Notice that each word can have other senses. *Accessory,* for example, can mean an object or device that is not essential but that enhances the main object. Programs can be written to extract these words. The headwords are then marked [+human], and synonyms such as *flibbertigibbet, doubter,* and *skeptic* can also be marked [+human] in one sense.

Although this approach is appealing, caution is in order. In the first place, lexicographers are people, which makes human error a possibility. Also, dictionaries are huge undertakings written by many different contributors, which means they have less internal consistency than computer programs need. Finally, and most seriously, most words have more than one sense. Keeping track of which senses have which features is not an easy task, and deciding what is a sense is also not clear-cut. Even with all these restrictions, however, machine-readable dictionaries have been widely used for constructing large lexicons.

One recent solution is WordNet. Developed at Princeton University by psycholinguist George Miller and his team, WordNet is an unusual machine-readable lexical resource. It is not in the form of a traditional dictionary, but is nonetheless widely used by computational linguists. In WordNet, each form of a word (noun, verb, adjective, or adverb) belongs to one or more **synsets** (sets of synonyms), which act as definitions for the word. For example, the noun *dog* belongs to seven synsets, and the verb *dog* to one synset. A synset may have other information associated with it, including hypernyms and hyponyms (represented as links to other synsets), usage examples collected from linguistic data, and glosses that resemble traditional dictionary definitions. Computational linguists use WordNet to perform word-sense disambiguation for applications such as information retrieval and automatic text summarization (see Section 7).

Another approach to building large lexicons for natural language analysis and generation is **corpus analysis**. The larger the corpus, or text, the more useful it is, since the chances of covering the language as it is actually used increase. In addition, a good corpus includes a variety of writing genres, such as journalism, instructional prose, popular writing, fiction, and technical material. As an example of the way large corpora (the plural of *corpus*) are useful, consider the verb of movement *flounce.* The definitions given for the verb in the tenth edition of *Merriam-Webster's Collegiate Dictionary* are:

flounce[1]

to move with exaggerated jerky or bouncy motions
to go with sudden determination

These definitions tell nothing about likely subjects, but corpus data will. From a large corpus, about twenty occurrences of the verb *flounce* were extracted. Thirteen had subjects that were female, as in examples *20* and *21.*

20)

Carol flounced out to the kitchen for an apron.

21)

She flounced off with a following of hens behind her.

Four had subjects that were clothing:

22)

The white cashmere dressing-gown flounced around her.

One had horses as the subject, and the others had pronouns as subjects. The point is that given a good parser, it would be possible to extract automatically all the subjects of a given verb, and then to look for properties of those subjects. For *flounce,* that information would appear in the lexicon as:

Word: *flounce*^{1}

1. Part of speech: Verb
2. Subcategorization: Intransitive
3. Semantic properties: Female human subject

Word: *flounce*^{2}

1. Part of speech: Verb
2. Subcategorization: Intransitive
3. Semantic properties: Clothing subject

It is becoming more common in computational linguistics to use computers to extract linguistically useful information from dictionaries and texts for the purpose of constructing large lexicons. Using statistical methods to build computational lexicons out of already existing resources shows promise. At this point, even as clever programs give large and comprehensive lists of words with a potential characteristic, human judgments are still necessary. If the computer is viewed as a tool for collecting lists of words, then the endeavor is successful. If the goal is to view the computer as the only tool, and to eliminate the human judge, then computational lexicon builders have a long way to go.

5 Computational Semantics

So far in this chapter we have focused on structure—the structure of sentences and words. However, in order to understand what a word, sentence, or text means, a computer program has to know the semantics of words, sentences, and texts. This section treats briefly some of the semantic representations and processes that have been proposed in computational linguistics.

Semantic issues were touched on in the preceding section. Unlike WordNet, which uses synonyms, in most other lexicons, the lexical item contains a field for semantic information, such as what kind of semantic features a verb requires for its subject or which thematic roles a verb requires or permits. The semantic fields for the two senses of *flounce* are:

Word: *flounce*^{1}

Semantic restrictions: Female human subject

Word: *flounce*^{2}

Semantic restrictions: Clothing subject

Although the semantics of words is an important component of any language system, analyzing or generating language also involves representing the semantics of sentences. Broadly speaking, two approaches to semantics and language analysis have been proposed: syntactically based systems and semantically based systems. In a syntactically based natural language analyzer, the sentence is first assigned a syntactic analysis, as outlined earlier in this chapter (also see Chapter 5). A semantic representation is built from the syntactic analysis (see Figure 18.16). The problems arise in getting from one representation to the other. This is sometimes called the mapping problem.

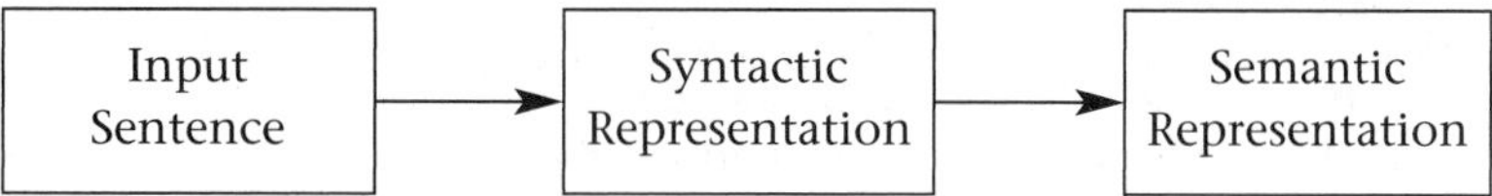

Figure 18.16 Syntactically based systems

In a semantically based natural language analyzer, either the semantic representation is built along with the syntactic analysis or there is no syntactic analysis at all (see Figure 18.17).

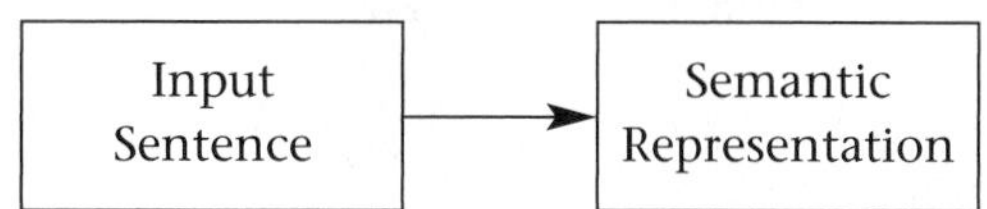

Figure 18.17 Semantically based systems

Consider a response to the question *Who got the coffee today?*

23)

The new student went.

A syntactic analysis of the sentence would show that *the new student* is the first NP directly dominated by IP (see Figure 18.18). From there, the parser might guess that the subject of the sentence is *the new student* because it precedes the verb. This is often true in English, although it is not always the case. Still, nothing is said about the fact that the subject is the actor (the one who performs the action) with a verb like *go.* Compare this to the intransitive version of the verb *open.*

24)

The door opened.

In this case, the subject *door* is not performing an action; something or someone opened the door. A syntactically based system obtains this knowledge about a sentence after a structure is built.

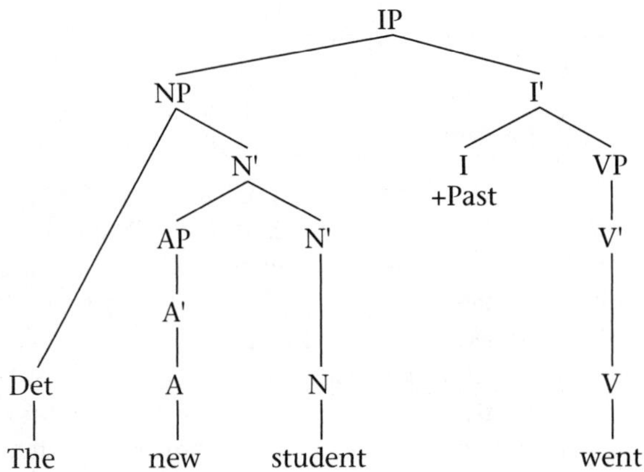

Figure 18.18

In contrast, a semantically based system builds a semantic representation first. For sentence *23*, it might look something like the one in Figure 18.19. The word order is not represented, but the underlying semantic information is expressed. The semantic representation of related sentences might be the same.

25)

It was the new student who went.

The mapping into the various syntactic forms of what is basically the same sentence occurs after the semantic representation is decided on.

Go — Actor
NP
went the new student

Figure 18.19

Both approaches still need to accomplish the same goal, namely that of assigning word meaning, sentence meaning, and text meaning. Because natural language can be used to communicate complex information, the task of semantic representation is not an easy one. In fact, it intersects with other areas of computer science, particularly the artificial intelligence area of knowledge representation and reasoning.

Some types of information are harder to represent than others. Much effort has been devoted to the problems of representing time, aspect, belief, and intentions. As a concrete example of one problem related to semantic representation, consider sentences *26* through *28:*

26)

Pregnant women and children get out first.

27)

Ripe apples and peaches make a good fruit salad.

28)

Every person speaks two languages.

In all these sentences, the problem is one of scope. For *26,* the scope of *pregnant* is probably *women,* not *women and children.* But in *27,* the syntactic twin of *26,* the likely interpretation is exactly the opposite: that is, that both the apples and the peaches are ripe. Finally, in *28,* does every person speak the same two languages or a different two languages?

The semantics of some natural language sentences is purely compositional—in other words, the whole sentence can be understood by understanding each word. This makes it possible to perform syntactically based semantic analysis. However, many sentences do not obey the principle of compositionality. Idioms pose a particular problem for semantic analysis. Consider:

29)

Computers are the best thing since sliced bread!

30)

The antique table was a real diamond in the rough.

31)

The stock market is going down; the bubble has burst.

Metaphors, similes, idioms, and related constructions pose unique problems for language analysis and generation. However, they are also a unique opportunity to bring to bear statistical corpus-based techniques for studying language.

6 Pragmatics

Pragmatics is the study of how language is used in communication. It is a rich and varied subject, and is the topic of considerable computational linguistics research. We will focus here on three examples: reference resolution, discourse markers, and spoken dialogue.

6.1 Reference Resolution

The task of **reference resolution** is to identify when two natural language expressions denote the same object or set of objects. Consider the following pair of sentences:

32)

John and Sally went to the movie. They hated it.

In this pair of sentences, *they* refers to the set of people consisting of John and Sally, and *it* refers to the movie they saw. *John, Sally, the movie, they,* and *it* are **referring expressions**, and the **referents** of these referring expressions are John, Sally, the movie, John and Sally, and the movie, respectively. Humans can generally figure this out fairly easily, using a combination of syntactic, semantic, and world knowledge. For example, because the pronoun *they* is plural, it must denote a set of objects rather than a single object. John and Sally form a set of objects (people who saw a movie). Furthermore, *they* is the subject of the second sentence in *32,* and *John and Sally* is the subject of the first sentence.

In order for a computer to identify that *they* refers to John and Sally, it must be told exactly which syntactic and semantic information and world knowledge to consider, and how to use that knowledge. The general task of reference resolution is therefore very complex and is usually subdivided. For example, computational linguists have identified several algorithms for resolving third person pronouns. We will describe one algorithm, attributed to Shalom Lappin and Herbert Leass. For each third person pronoun found in a text, the algorithm collects all referring expressions in the four preceding sentences. Those that do not agree in gender or number with the pronoun are eliminated; the rest are scored using several pieces of information, including grammatical role (subject, direct object, indirect object, complement); whether they are in an adverbial or existential role; whether they have the same grammatical role as the pronoun; and whether they are close to the pronoun in the text. The object or set with the highest score is selected as referent.

Reference resolution algorithms are useful in text analysis, information retrieval, and spoken dialogue systems. However, they are not perfect; the highest accuracy for any reference resolution algorithm is still well below human performance on the same task. Part of this is due to errors from syntactic and semantic analysis and to lack of world knowledge, but better algorithms are also needed. Reference resolution is an area of active research in computational linguistics.

6.2 Discourse Markers

Consider the following two short texts:

33)

I dislike papaya. I eat bananas all the time.

34)

I dislike papaya. On the other hand, I eat bananas all the time.

The text in example *34* is much easier to understand than the text in *33.* This is because *34* contains the discourse cue *on the other hand,* which clarifies the intent and structure of the text. One of the tasks of natural language generation is to insert discourse markers (e.g., *therefore, on the other hand*) at appropriate places in a text. This is a difficult task for several reasons. First, there is the matter of determining the functions performed by particular discourse markers. Second, the use of discourse markers depends somewhat on context. For example, *nevertheless* and *on the other hand* both indicate contrast, but *35* is not as clear as *34:*

35)

I dislike papaya. Nevertheless, I eat bananas all the time.

Finally, it is important not to use discourse markers too often because they can burden the text.

Characterizing the use of discourse markers is another task well-suited to corpus linguistics. However, most existing explanations are dependent on very specific underlying theories of discourse and this makes it more difficult for computational linguists to use each other's results.

6.3 Spoken Dialogue

Computer systems that analyze conversations between humans, or that interact with humans using natural language, must understand the conventions that govern the interaction (see Chapter 6, Section 4, and Chapter 15, Section 1.1). Consider the following conversation:

36)

A: It's a lovely day.
B: Mm-hm.
A: Would you like some coffee?
B: Sure.

As we saw in Chapters 6 and 15, understanding the roles of context and convention is crucial to effective communication. This conversation illustrates several of the conventions that make it possible for humans to communicate effectively and easily. First, A and B take turns speaking. If B were to interrupt A in the middle of A's question, that would contravene the conversational conventions of turn-taking. Second, B acknowledges A's statement to demonstrate that A has been heard and understood. This means that A can continue speaking without having to repeat an utterance. Also, B answers A's question; failure to do so would indicate either lack of understanding or rudeness.

These conventions are well understood by humans (although they may vary somewhat between cultures). However, a computer will not automatically understand how to obey conversational rules—it must be programmed to do so. Proper modeling of the conventions of spoken dialogue is important in spoken-dialogue systems and conversational analysis. However, interacting with a computer rather than with another human changes the conventions somewhat. For example, in human-computer interaction, the computer typically acknowledges the user's utterances more often than a human would, and the human rarely directly acknowledges the computer's utterances. Computational linguists are actively exploring the differences between human-human interaction and human-computer interaction, and analyzing the implications for language processing.

7 Applications of Computational Linguistics

The previous sections of this chapter have shown how the use of computers has forced linguists to formulate rigorous statements of theory and facts, because all of the implicit knowledge that humans have about language has to be made explicit. Theories become testable in a concrete way. Implementations of practical systems tend to force researchers (and students) to understand a particular language process in very detailed terms.

This section discusses some specific applications of computational linguistics. An **application** can be defined as the use to which a program or set of programs is put. Applications discussed in this section include indexing and concordances, information retrieval, automatic summarization, machine translation, and spoken dialogue systems.

7.1 Indexing and Concordances

Indexing means finding, identifying, and usually counting all occurrences of a certain word or phrase in a large corpus of texts. This application of computers to language study does exactly what computers are best at doing: locating a word, recording the location by line or sentence number, and counting how many times it appears. The examples of the use of the word *flounce* in Section 4 were extracted from text using an indexing program. The program searched text on the computer to find occurrences of the words *flounce, flouncing, flounced,* and *flounces.* When one of the words was found, the computer program stored the sentence in a separate file. A count was kept of each time each word was found.

A **concordance** tells which words occur near other words. Concordance and indexing programs are used widely in literary analysis, since some authors seem to favor using certain words in the context of other words. Concordance programs can find these relationships. A concordance program could tell, for example, how many times the word *she* occurred next to *flounce.*

Perhaps the most widely used word count was performed by Henry Kucera and Nelson Francis in 1962 on the Brown corpus of one million words. Kucera and Francis took fifteen different texts and wrote a program to count the number of times each word appeared. The ten most frequent words of English from this study are:

the	69,971
of	36,411
and	28,852
to	26,149
a	23,237
in	21,341
that	10,595
is	10,099
was	9,816
he	9,543

Word frequency lists have been useful to psycholinguists who need to pay attention to frequency when designing experiments.

These early applications are still very useful to linguists, but they are not linguistic in nature. They use the power of the computer to count and categorize words, but they do not rely on any linguistic knowledge. For example, to find *flounce,* the related words *flounced, flounces,* and *flouncing* also have to be looked for. Early systems were not endowed with morphological knowledge, so they could only look for the exact word given. Furthermore, all occurrences of the word were pulled out without regard to what part of speech it represented. If the goal is to look at subjects of verbs, it is necessary to distinguish between the verb *flounce* and the noun *flounce.* Notice the implications of this: two of the top ten most frequent words as found by Kucera and Francis are forms of the verb *be,* but the computer counts the two forms separately because it lacks the linguistic knowledge necessary to distinguish them. The inability of early systems to relate words had other problems. Consider the following example:

minute	53
min	5
min.	1
min,	1

The above are probably all variants of the word *minute,* although this would have to be verified by checking the original text. The count of *minute* is 53, but it should really be 60. Note, however, that there is a possible complication: some of the occurrences of *minute* may be examples of the noun *minute* meaning 'memorandum' rather than '60 seconds', or of the unrelated, differently pronounced adjective *minute* [majnút] meaning 'very small'; they could also be an abbreviation of *minister, ministry, minimum,* or *minim* (a fluid measure roughly equivalent to a drop). We cannot be sure.

Most current concordance and indexing programs have solved some of the easier problems such as abbreviations and acronyms. For example, the abbreviation *CIA* could stand for either Central Intelligence Agency or Culinary Institute of America. Without adequate context to tell which organization the abbreviation refers to, it would be difficult for a computer program to make a reliable guess. Much larger corpora are now being used to overcome some of the problems of sparse and limited data, and more sophisticated statistical techniques are being employed. Yet most of the harder problems still remain. First, morphological knowledge is needed to relate various forms of the same word to just one base word. Second, syntactic knowledge is needed to establish the part of speech of the word in a sentence and to determine the arguments of the verb, such as subject and object. Finally, semantic knowledge is needed to know the thematic roles of the arguments and to know which meaning of a word is intended.

7.2 Information Accessing and Retrieval

The development of Internet browsers has enabled the creation of bodies of text, image, sound, and video that can be searched easily. There are now dozens of freely available search engines for roaming through this data. However, anyone who has ever tried to search for information on a particular topic has had the frustrating experience of wading through masses of irrelevant material. For example, when the word *morphology* was searched for in a library index of book titles, the following titles were among the results:

Principles of Polymer Morphology

Image Analysis and Mathematical Morphology

Drainage Basin Morphology

French Morphology

If a linguistically sophisticated program had been used to retrieve these titles, it is likely that they would have been divided according to the semantic subject field. Thus, a chemist would not get titles on French, and a linguist would not get titles on chemistry.

As with indexing and concordances, the three critical subareas that text-retrieval systems use are computational morphology, syntax, and semantics. Someone wanting to know about the theory of light might want to find all references to the word *light* in an encyclopedia. Searching for the character sequence *light* anywhere in the text might yield *lightning, enlightenment,* and *lighthearted,* but also *delight* and *candlelight.* On the other hand, if the user searched only for *light* surrounded by blanks, then words like *lighting* or *lights* would be missed. The user might want to find synonyms or related words, such as *colorless* or *clear* for the adjective, or *illuminate* for the verb. Without a parser and semantics, an automatic search system has no clue about the real meaning of the word *light* when it is found in text.

Several creative solutions to this problem are currently being developed. These approaches build on computational linguistic knowledge rather than on more complex knowledge built into the system, and use simple parsing combined with some statistical analysis. First, very frequent words (such as those in the list given in Section 7.1) are filtered out, since they have low information value. This speeds up a computational linguistic system considerably, since it can remove nearly half of the possible words. Next, word frequency and co-occurrence are computed. Co-occurrence means determining whether words are likely to occur together. The phrase *bad weather* is more common than *clarified weather,* even though both *bad* and *clarified* are adjectives. Similarly, the phrase *clarified butter* is more frequent than *tart butter,* even though both *clarified* and *tart* are adjectives. This permits the application of statistical computational linguistic methods to determine whether an article refers to a topic that appears frequently in the collection or whether it refers to an unusual topic. For example, newspapers on a certain day tend to have a set of articles on breaking news; co-occurrences from these articles will rise to the top. Occurrences of a phrase such as *Madrid bombing* might peak on certain days, whereas occurrences of a phrase such as *hunger in Africa* will tend to be more constant.

Simple parsing can sometimes improve the performance of statistical computational linguistic techniques. For example, programs that find all the noun phrases can extract and list these NPs, both from within articles and across articles. Once the noun phrases are extracted, they can be sorted and organized according to the head of the phrase and according to modifiers. Given that the goal of information retrieval is to determine who did what to whom, it is a well-known fact that *who, what,* and *whom* are usually found in the noun phrases of a text. Highlighting just these noun phrases without the verbs tends to give a sensible overview of the essence of an article. Sorting, counting, and applying statistical manipulation to these phrases is another way to represent the true meaning of text, and thus gives a more principled and computationally smart way to retrieve and present text that truly answers a particular question.

7.3 Automatic Summarization

A relatively new application using computational linguistic techniques is **automatic summarization**. Summarization refers to the process of automatic analysis of either a single text (single-document summarization) or a set of texts (multidocument summarization); from the summarization, an abstract is created that reflects the key ideas in a concise and coherent way. With the recent development of information overload and the increasing use of information retrieval systems, the need for summarization systems has become urgent: many people just do not have the time to keep up with so much reading. At times, a summary will suffice as a way of screening a set of documents so that the user can decide which ones to read in depth and which ones to ignore.

Two approaches to summarization currently prevail. First is the purely statistical approach, a method based on techniques developed in the 1950s. The words in a document are listed by frequency (except the most frequent words, such as those listed in Section 7.1). Sentences that contain these commonly occurring words are extracted from the article one by one, and each new sentence is checked to make sure that it is different from those already selected. This technique is crude but somewhat effective. Its main drawbacks are that it allows limited analysis of the articles, and that the sentences, when strung together, can be choppy and difficult to read.

The second approach to automatic summarization extracts key concepts from articles by means of computational linguistic analysis. With the help of language generation, an entirely new abstract is created from the concepts. This approach creates a coherent and fluent summary that captures the key ideas in the source text, both for single- and multidocument summarization. However, it is not feasible to use this approach for all texts because of the difficulty of performing large-scale natural language analysis and generation.

7.4 Machine Translation

The purpose of a **machine translation** system is the same as that of any translation system: taking text written or spoken in one language and writing or speaking it in another (see Figure 18.20). Translation poses challenging problems both for the human translator and for the machine attempting to do what the human does. Projects in machine translation in the 1940s and 1950s spawned much of the early research in computational linguistics. Think of a single institution like the United Nations. Every day millions of words need to be translated from one language to another. Add to that other political and scientific institutions, plus businesses and publishers, and it becomes clear that there is an overwhelming need for translation. Translation is a time-consuming and mentally demanding task requiring a lot of linguistic knowledge, making it seem like an ideal application for computational linguistics.

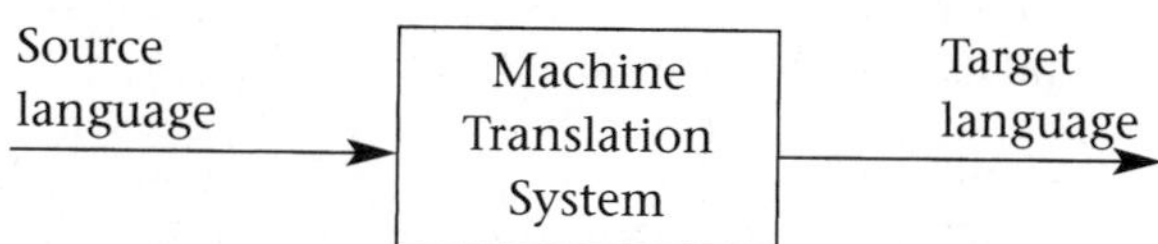

Figure 18.20

The problems of translation turned out to be far more difficult than computer scientists and linguists had imagined. Although money was poured into the machine translation task from the late 1940s to the early 1960s, results were slow to emerge. The subtlety of language—the nuances and lack of precision—caused problems because computers are suited to mathematical computation where subtleties do not prevail. Funding agencies became disillusioned, and although most researchers were still hopeful, they were humbled by the difficulties encountered in these early years.

Researchers are now more realistic about their goals. Rather than attempting to build full-fledged machine translation systems that automatically convert a text from one language to another, some projects are aiming toward machine-assisted translation. In these projects, the computer is viewed as a tool to aid the translator. The computer makes suggestions, but the human translator makes final decisions. Another simplification is to aim the translation at a specific subject area; this way, word ambiguities are reduced to a minimum. For example, in the financial domain, the word *vehicle* is probably a device for investment, but in the automobile domain, *vehicle* is most likely a device for driving.

Still other projects are developing ways to pass texts through a preprocessor—a system that looks at sentences and figures out which ones might present problems. Once the computer has identified the problem, it can ask the original writer to clarify. Take the following example:

37)

Many elephants smell.

This sentence could be confusing due to the ambiguousness of the verb *smell:* is the intended interpretation that many elephants stink or that many elephants are capable of perceiving odors? It might be sent back to the writer for clarification. Machine translation tools that adopt one or more of these simplifying assumptions are now widely available on the Internet.

Machine translation applications encompass many aspects of computational linguistics. In addition, a machine that is capable or nearly capable of mimicking a very complex and subtle human activity is intriguing. The source language needs to be analyzed syntactically and semantically. Lexical items need to be matched—a task that is particularly difficult, as not only do words in one language often not exist in another, but sometimes several words are used for one. One example involves the German words *essen* and *fressen*. Both words mean 'eat' in English, but the verb *essen* is used for humans, whereas *fressen* is used for animals. If the system made the mistake of using *fressen* for people, the usage would be insulting. Syntax can also be a problem. An example from Spanish concerns a missing word, as shown in *38* and *39*. Sentence *40* gives the word-by-word translation of the Spanish in *39*.

38)

The elephants slept but didn't snore.

39)

Los elefantes durmieron pero no roncaron.

40)

*The elephants slept but not snored.

The word-by-word translation in *40* is not English. What is wrong? In English, a negative sentence without an auxiliary verb needs the properly inflected form of the verb *do* to be inserted. Since *38* is in the past tense and since the subject is plural, the correct form is *did*. There is no word for *did* in the Spanish version of the same sentence. Just as the human translator has to know this fact, so does the machine translation system. If the input language were Spanish and the input sentence were *39*, then the English generation system would need to know to insert the verb *do*, properly inflected, and not to inflect the main verb. The difficulties increase with languages that are not in the same family, such as English and Japanese, or Spanish and Finnish (see Chapter 8). If the machine translation system is required to take spoken language as input and give spoken language as output, then the system becomes even more complex, as is shown in Figure 18.21.

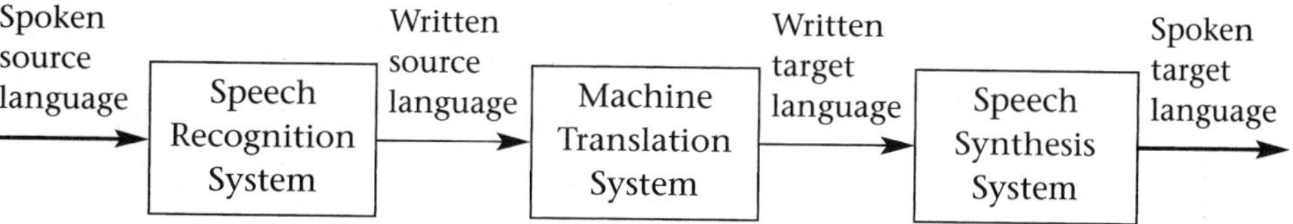

Figure 18.21

Recent research in machine translation has given new impetus to this field for two reasons. First, the global economy is creating a need for international cooperation that in turn requires communication across languages. Second, advances in statistical modeling for machine translation are making it faster and easier to experiment with different language pairs and different translation tasks. These two factors have not only spurred research but also resulted in new commercial text and speech machine translation systems, many available for use on the Internet.

7.5 Spoken-Dialogue Systems

Spoken-dialogue systems are used commercially and in research for tasks ranging from providing weather information or educational tutoring to planning travel. They provide users with an efficient, user-friendly audio interface in situations where other interfaces are not available (e.g., over the telephone), cannot be used (e.g., when the user is blind or is a child who cannot yet read), or are not preferred (e.g., when museum visitors are more attracted to an interactive audio tour guide than to a printed guidebook). Like machine translation, spoken-dialogue applications use many techniques of computational linguistics (see Figure 18.22). Speech recognizers convert spoken language to written language for analysis by language analyzers (which perform parsing and semantic analysis). Dialogue managers interpret utterances in context and use knowledge of conversational conventions to determine how to respond. Language generators produce text responses, which are then converted to speech using speech synthesizers.

Spoken-dialogue systems exist at the intersection of computational linguistics and computer-human interaction, a field that explores ways to make the high-tech environment we all live in more efficient, helpful, and safe. However, spoken-dialogue

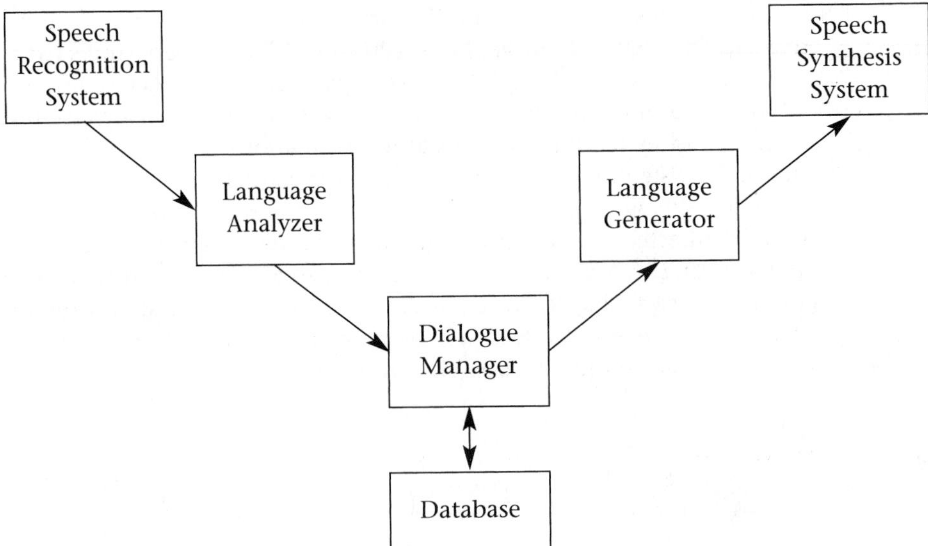

Figure 18.22 Structure of spoken-dialogue systems

systems use imperfect technology; speech recognizers, text-to-speech engines, natural language analyzers, and generation systems often fail or are based on incomplete databases or other knowledge sources. One important area of research in spoken-dialogue systems focuses on guiding the human-computer interaction in ways that minimize errors.

One spoken-dialogue system is the JUPITER system at MIT, which provides weather information over the telephone. Users ask questions such as, "What is the forecast in Boston?" JUPITER recognizes the user's speech, parses the user's utterance, and interprets it to a database query. The answer is generated using a template-based generator, and output using a speech synthesizer. JUPITER can recognize input in several languages and respond in the user's own language.

Another example of a spoken-dialogue system is NASA's Personal Satellite Assistant—a system contained in a small round robot and designed for use on the International Space Station. It can be directed by voice command to visit locations on the space station and report various measurements, including temperature, air pressure, and gas levels. It can also patrol the space station on its own, reporting any anomalous readings using speech or text.

Summing Up

Computational linguistics deals with what a computer program has to "know" in order to process, understand, and produce language. To program a computer to produce or recognize speech, the computational linguist must use knowledge of **acoustic phonetics**, the influence of surrounding segments, and prosody. In **speech recognition**, the computer must filter out background noise and extract features, phonemes, and words. Computational morphological analysis involves either **stemming**

(stripping successive affixes off a word until a base element is recognized) or using **two-level morphology** to derive surface forms from underlying forms. When it comes to sentences, a computer may parse a sentence **top-down** or **bottom-up**, or a **chart parser** may try various analyses until it finds a match. There are various ways in which a computer can construct a grammar for decoding or for **natural language generation**. In any case, it is crucial that the computer have information about the words in the language; the study of this is **computational lexicography**. In order to understand discourse, the computer has to know the semantics and **pragmatics** of how words and sentences are used to create meaning. As our technology improves, there are increasingly more sophisticated **applications** of computational linguistics, such as **indexing**, information retrieval, **automatic summarization**, **machine translation**, and spoken-dialogue systems.

Key Terms

General terms

computational linguistics

Terms concerning computational phonetics and phonology

acoustic phonetics
cocktail party effect
formants
speaker-dependent speech recognizers
speaker-independent speech recognizers
spectrogram
speech recognition

Terms concerning computational morphology

natural language processing systems
stem-based (dictionary)
stemming
two-level morphology
word-based (dictionary)

Terms concerning computational syntax

bottom-up parsing
chart parser
corpus
deterministic parsers
implementation
nondeterministic parsers
nonterminals
parser
recursion
strong generative capacity
terminals
top-down parsing
weak generative capacity

Terms concerning natural language generation

arguments
forest-based generation
grammar-based generation
natural language generation
template generation

Terms concerning computational lexicography

computational lexicography
corpus analysis
machine-readable dictionary (MRD)
synsets

Terms concerning computational semantics and pragmatics

pragmatics
reference resolution
referents
referring expressions

Terms concerning applications of computational linguistics

application
automatic summarization
concordance
indexing
machine translation

Recommended Web Sites

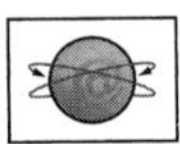

For links to Web sites and journals related to computational linguistics, go to **bedfordstmartins.com/linguistics/computational** and click on **recommended Web sites**.

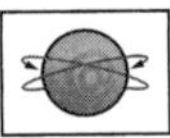

For more information on the sources used in this chapter, go to **bedfordstmartins.com/linguistics/computational** and click on **Sources**.

Recommended Reading

Allen, James. 1995. *Natural Language Understanding.* 2nd ed. Menlo Park, CA: Addison Wesley.

Biber, Douglas, Susan Conrad, and Randi Reppen. 1998. *Corpus Linguistics: Investigating Language Structure and Use.* Cambridge: Cambridge University Press.

Dale, Robert, Hermann Moisl, and Harold Somers, eds. 2000. *Handbook of Natural Language Processing.* New York: Marcel Dekker.

Dutoit, Thierry. 1997. *An Introduction to Text-to-Speech Synthesis.* Norwell, MA: Kluwer Academic Publishers.

Fellbaum, Christiane, ed. 1998. *WordNet: An Electronic Lexical Database.* Cambridge, MA: MIT Press.

Iwanska, Lucja M., and Stuart C. Shapiro, eds. 2000. *Natural Language Processing and Knowledge Representation.* Cambridge, MA: MIT Press.

Jelinek, Frederick. 1998. *Statistical Methods for Speech Recognition.* Cambridge, MA: MIT Press.

Jurafsky, Daniel, and James H. Martin. 2000. *Speech and Language Processing: An Introduction to Natural Language Processing, Computational Linguistics and Speech Recognition.* Upper Saddle River, NJ: Prentice Hall.

Klavans, Judith, and Philip Resnick. 1996. *The Balancing Act: Combining Symbolic and Statistical Approaches to Language.* Cambridge, MA: MIT Press.

Manning, Christopher D., and Hinrich Schutze. 1999. *Foundations of Statistical Natural Language Processing.* Cambridge, MA: MIT Press.

Mitkov, Ruslan, ed. 2003. *The Oxford Handbook of Computational Linguistics.* Oxford: Oxford University Press.

Reiter, Ehud, and Robert Dale. 2000. *Building Natural Language Generation Systems.* Cambridge: Cambridge University Press.

Smith, Ronnie W., and D. Richard Hipp. 1997. *Spoken Natural Language Dialog Systems: A Practical Approach.* Oxford: Oxford University Press.

Strzalkowski, Tomek, ed. 1999. *Natural Language Information Retrieval.* Norwell, MA: Kluwer Academic Publishers.

Exercises

1. What kinds of problems might a computer have with these sentences?
   a) Sue bought red apples and plums.
   b) It was a large animal house.
   c) Susan baked in the kitchen.
   d) Susan baked in the sun.
   e) Susan baked.

2. What information does the computer need to know in order to pronounce these sentences in informal style?
   a) What are you doing tonight?
   b) The woman was delighted.
   c) That article misled me.
   d) That's a new car, isn't it?
   e) It was a tough test, although I did well.
   f) Can't you sing better?

3. What rules are necessary for a computer program to analyze these words? (*Hint:* First figure out the prefixes and suffixes. Refer to Chapter 4 if necessary.)
   a) kindness
   b) kindly
   c) kindnesses
   d) nationalism
   e) countability
   f) nontransformational
   g) reusable

4. What different structures might a parser propose for the following ambiguous sentences?
   a) She saw the man with a telescope.
   b) Watch dogs bark.
   c) Broadcast programs like *60 Minutes.*

5. Think of a word that has many different meanings, such as *bank* or *interest.* Then give information about that word using the categories discussed in Section 4. Give at least two senses for each part of speech. The following example has one sense for the noun part of speech, and two senses for the verb part of speech.

   Word: *bank*
   a) Part of speech: Noun (Sense 1)
   b) Semantic properties: Of a river
   c) Pronunciation: [bæ̃ŋk]

d) Context and style: Normal
e) Example: The bank of the river was grassy.

Word: *bank*
a) Part of speech: Verb (Sense 1)
b) Subcategorization: Transitive, requires the preposition *on*
c) Semantic properties: Object of preposition is either a person or a thing
d) Pronunciation: [bæ̃ŋk]
e) Context and style: Informal
f) Example: I can't bank on him to do it.

Word: *bank*
a) Part of speech: Verb (Sense 2)
b) Subcategorization: Transitive
c) Semantic properties: Object is money
d) Pronunciation: [bæ̃ŋk]
e) Context and style: Normal
f) Example: She banks her money at the local branch.

6. List three applications of computational linguistics. How can these systems improve the quality of life for people with physical disabilities?

7. The use of the Internet and the World Wide Web has changed the way people access information. In the context of requesting information from an electronic source:
   i) List three cases in which linguistic information would help you find your way around the Internet. For example, if you are looking for information on *attorney*, it would help in your search to know that the British equivalents are *barrister* and *solicitor.*
   ii) List three cases in which linguistic ambiguity would hurt you in your search for information electronically. For example, in looking for articles on the word *bank,* you would find articles on rivers and financial institutions. What are some other words and phrases that would give you problems? For each example, explain what the problem is and how you could solve it.

GLOSSARY

Ablative The **case** form characteristically used to mark a noun indicating the point away from which there is movement.

Ablaut A vowel alternation that marks a grammatical contrast (e.g., *mouse/mice*).

Absolute universals Patterns or traits that occur in all languages.

Absolutive In some languages, the **case** associated with both the direct object of a transitive verb and the subject of an intransitive verb.

Abstract Hypothetical, not phonetically realized. *See* **Underlying**.

Abstract Case Case that need not be expressed as inflection.

Abstract clause A type of narrative utterance that sometimes appears at the beginning of a narrative to provide a general summary of the story to be told.

Abstract representation A phonological description that is to a greater or lesser degree distinct from its phonetic realization.

Accent Phonetic qualities of a language variety that identify it to speakers of other varieties as different from their own.

Accidental gaps Nonoccurring but possible forms of a language (e.g., in English, *blork*).

Accommodation The modification of speech patterns according to the speech of other participants in a discourse.

Accuracy Second language production in which the structures are nativelike.

Accusative The **case** form characteristically used to mark a direct object.

Acoustic phonetics An approach to phonetics that is concerned with measuring and analyzing the physical properties of sound waves produced when we speak.

Acquired dysgraphia The impairment of writing ability in patients who previously possessed normal writing ability (also called acquired agraphia).

Acquired dyslexia The impairment of reading ability in patients who previously possessed normal reading ability (also called acquired alexia).

Acrolect A **creole** variety that is relatively similar to the standard language from which it arose. (*See also* **Basilect** and **Mesolect**.)

Acronym A word that is formed by taking the initial letters of (some or all) of the words in a phrase or title and pronouncing them as a word (e.g., *NATO* for *North Atlantic Treaty Organization*).

Acrophonic principle The representation of sounds by pictures of objects whose pronunciation begins with the sound to be represented (e.g., the sound [b] might be represented by a picture of a bird).

Active (sentence) A sentence in which the NP in the subject position is the **agent** (the doer) of the action (e.g., *Helen painted the room*).

Address terms The various forms that are used to address people, indicating something of one's relationship to the individual addressed (e.g., in English, *Ms. Callaghan, Professor Van Haar, Jake*).

Adjacency pair An ordered pair of utterances spoken by two different participants in a conversation.

Adjective (A) A **lexical category** that designates a property that is applicable to the entities named by nouns, can often take comparative and superlative endings in English, and functions as the **head** of an adjective phrase (e.g., *red, obese, hearty*).

Adjunct *See* **Modifier**.

Adjunct Island Condition Prohibition against moving an element such as a *wh*-word out of a modifier.

Adstratum influence The mutual influence of two equally dominant languages on each other (e.g., the influence of English and French on each other in Montreal).

Adverb (Adv) A **lexical category** that typically names properties that can be applied to the actions designated by verbs (e.g., *quickly, fearfully*). May also occur in the **specifier** position for verbs (e.g., *never* surrender).

Affective factors Feelings or attitudes that can affect the success of second language acquisition (e.g., motivation).

Affix (Af) A bound morpheme that modifies the meaning and/or syntactic (sub)category of the stem in some way (e.g., *un-* and *-able* in *unreadable*).

Affixation The process that attaches an affix to a base.

Affricates Noncontinuant consonants that show a slow release of the closure (e.g., [tʃ, dʒ]).

Affrication A process in which stops become affricates.

African American Vernacular English (AAVE) A cover term describing distinctive varieties of English spoken by Americans of African descent.

Age-grading The correlation of a particular linguistic variant with social situations that are closely associated with a particular age group.

Agent The **thematic role** of the doer of an action (e.g., *Marilyn* in *Marilyn fed the dolphin*).

Agent-patient pattern Sentence pattern in which the **agent** role is assigned to the subject of an **intransitive verb** and the agent of a **transitive verb**; the **patient** role is assigned to the object of a transitive verb or the subject of a state.

Agglutinating languages Languages in which words typically contain several morphemes, of which usually only one is a lexical category. The others are clearly identifiable affixes, each of which typically encodes a single grammatical contrast.

Agrammatism An aphasic disturbance characterized by the omission of function words and inflectional affixes and by syntactic comprehension deficits.

Agraphia *See* **Acquired dysgraphia**.

Agreement The result of one category being inflected to mark properties of another (e.g., the verb marked for the person and/or the number of the subject).

Alexia *See* **Acquired dyslexia**.

Allomorphs Variants of a **morpheme** (e.g., [-s], [-z], and [-əz] are allomorphs of the English plural morpheme).

Allophones Variants of a **phoneme**, usually in **complementary distribution** and phonetically similar (e.g., voiced and voiceless *l* in English).

Allophonic distribution The set of distinct phonetic environments in which variants of a phoneme occur.

Alpha notation In stating phonological rules, the use of a conventional formula in which variables (α, β, etc.) are introduced to represent the value of distinctive features.

Alpha rules Phonological rules stated in a conventional formula in which variables (α, β, etc.) are introduced for the value of distinctive features.

Alphabetic writing A type of writing in which symbols represent consonant and/or vowel segments.

Alveolar ridge The small ridge just behind the upper front teeth.

Alveopalatal (area) The area just behind the alveolar ridge where the roof of the mouth rises sharply (also called **palatoalveolar**).

Ambisyllabicity The simultaneous presence of a segment in two adjoining syllables.

Amelioration The process in which the meaning of a word becomes more favorable (e.g., *pretty* used to mean "tricky, sly, cunning").

Amerind The group into which all the Native American languages (except for Na-Dené and Eskimo-Aleut **stocks**) have been placed, according to one controversial classification system.

Amerindian languages Languages spoken by the aboriginal peoples of North, South, and Central America.

Analogy A source of language change that involves the generalization of a regularity based on the inference that if elements are alike in some respects, they should be alike in others as well (e.g., *bring* becoming *brung* by analogy with *ring/rung*).

Analytic languages *See* **Isolating languages**.

Anaphoric reference The use of a pronoun that refers to an NP earlier in the discourse (e.g., *her* in *Hilary ate her dinner*).

Angular gyrus An area of the brain that plays an important role in reading.

Animacy *See* **Animate**.

Animate In some languages, a class consisting of nouns, most of which have living referents.

Antecedent The element that determines the interpretation of a pronoun (e.g., *Jeremy* in *Jeremy looked at himself in the mirror*).

Anterior A place feature that characterizes sounds articulated in front of the alveopalatal region.

Antonyms Words or phrases that are opposites with respect to some component of their meaning (e.g., *big* and *small*).

Aphasia A language deficit caused by damage to the brain.

Apocope The deletion of a word-final vowel (e.g., *name* used to be pronounced with a word-final schwa).

Application The use to which a computer program is put.

A-prefixing A **relic form** in Appalachian English in which *a-* may be attached to the front of verbs in the progressive aspect *(She's a-coming)* or the front of adverbial complements to the verb *(He sat there a-thinking)*.

Arbitrariness A property of communication whereby there is no natural or inherent connection between a sign and its referent.

Areal classification An approach to language classification that identifies characteristics shared by languages that are in the same geographical area.

Arguments Grammatical dependents required by a verb (e.g., the verb *hit* requires two arguments, namely a hitter as subject and a person or thing being hit as object).

Articulatory phonetics An approach to phonetics that studies the physiological mechanisms of speech production.

Articulatory processes Adjustments in articulation that can occur during the production of speech (e.g., **deletion**, **epenthesis**, **assimilation**).

Articulatory simplification A process that facilitates acquisition (e.g., by deleting a consonant in a complex cluster or inserting a vowel to break up a cluster).

Arytenoids Two small cartilages in the **larynx** that are attached to the **vocal folds**, enabling the vocal folds to be drawn together or apart.

Aspect In syntax and morphology, an inflectional category indicating the manner in which an action or event takes place, in particular its duration in time (punctual, repetitive, etc.).

Aspiration The lag in the onset of vocalic voicing—accompanied by the release of air—that is heard after the release of certain stops in English (e.g., the first sound of *top* is aspirated).

Assimilation The influence of one segment on another, resulting in a sound becoming more like a nearby sound in terms of one or more of its phonetic characteristics (e.g., in English, vowels become nasal if followed by a nasal consonant).

Association line A line linking a symbol that represents a sound segment with a symbol that represents a tone or feature.

Atlas survey A linguistic survey that samples speakers according to regional speech communities.

Automatic summarization An **application** of **computational linguistics** in which a computer uses key ideas to create an abstract of an article or set of articles.

Autopsy studies Studies based on a postmortem examination.

Autosegmental notation The type of notation in phonology that links segments with tones or individual features by **association lines**.

Autosegmental principles Rules that account for phonological processes, including rules that associate **features** to **segments** and segments to features, and rules that prohibit the crossing of **association lines**.

Autosegmental representation A means of illustrating how phonological **features** are organized and how they change as a result of phonological **processes**. (*See also* **Autosegmental (notation)** and **Autosegments**.)

Autosegments Phonological features (such as **manner features** and **place features**) that operate more or less autonomously.

Auxiliary verb (Aux) A verb that must occur with a main verb and that can undergo inversion (e.g., *was* in *was walking; will* in *will win*).

Babbling Speech-like sounds produced as babies acquire and exercise articulatory skills.

Back A feature of sounds articulated behind the palatal region in the oral cavity.

Back (of the tongue) The part of the tongue that is hindmost but still lies in the mouth.

Back vowel A vowel that is made with the tongue positioned in the back of the mouth (e.g., the vowel sounds in *h<u>oo</u>t* and *b<u>oa</u>rd*).

Backformation A word-formation process that creates a new word by removing a real or supposed affix from another word in the language (e.g., *edit* came from *editor* through the removal of *-or*).

Base The form to which an affix is added (e.g., *book* is the base for the affix *-s* in *books, modernize* is the base for the affix *-ed* in *modernized*).

Basilect A **creole** variety that shows the least influence from the standard language from which it arose. (*See also* **Acrolect** and **Mesolect**.)

Bilabial Involving both lips (e.g., *p, b,* and *m* are all bilabial consonants).

Bilingual education An educational program that involves the use of two languages in instruction in content areas such as math, science, reading.

Bilingualism The state of possessing knowledge of two languages; the discipline devoted to the study of the simultaneous acquisition of two languages by children.

Binary feature A phonetic or phonological feature that can have one of only two values (e.g., + or – voice).

(Bird) call *See* **Call**.

(Bird)song *See* **Song**.

Blade (of the tongue) The area of the tongue just behind the tip.

Blend A word that is created from parts of two already existing items (e.g., *brunch* from *breakfast* and *lunch*).

Blissymbolics A contemporary development of pictographic writing that uses a number of recombinable symbols representing basic units of meaning; primarily used for nonspeaking individuals.

Body (of the tongue) The main mass of the tongue.

Borrowing A source of language change that involves adopting aspects of one language into another.

Bottom-up parsing A method of speech analysis that starts with individual words and builds structures upward in successively larger units.

Bottom-up processing A type of mental processing in which more complex representations (e.g., words) are accessed through simpler constituent representations (e.g., phonemes).

Bound morpheme A morpheme that must be attached to another element (e.g., the past tense marker *-ed*).

Boustrophedon The practice of reversing the direction of writing at the end of each line, which was typical of many old writing systems.

Breathy voice *See* **murmur**.

Broad transcription Phonetic transcription that uses a relatively simple set of symbols to represent contrasting segments. (*Compare* **narrow transcription**.)

Broca's aphasia A **nonfluent aphasia** in which speech is very halting, there are numerous phonemic errors, and there is a lack of intonation.

Broca's area The area in the lower rear portion of the left **frontal lobe** of the brain that plays an important role in language production.

Bundles of isoglosses *See* **Isogloss bundle**.

Call In avian communication, a short burst of sound or simple patterns of notes, typically used as warnings or other group-related signals.

Canadian raising Allophonic variation in some dialects of English in which the [a] in the sounds [aj] and [aw] is raised to [ʌ] before a voiceless consonant (e.g., *house* [haws] becomes [hʌws] in this dialect).

Canonical Sentence Strategy A processing strategy that leads children to expect the first NP in a sentence to bear the **agent** role and the second NP to bear the **theme** role.

Caregiver speech *See* **Motherese**.

Case A morphological category that encodes information about an element's grammatical role (subject, direct object, and so on) (e.g., the contrast between *he* and *him*). *See also* **(Abstract) Case**.

Case Filter, The The requirement that every NP in a grammatical sentence be assigned a case feature.

Cataphoric reference The use of a pronoun that refers to an NP later in the discourse (e.g., *she* in *When she heard the news, Ann smiled*).

Categorical (rules) Rules that always apply.

Categorical perception Ability to perceive the distinctions between phonemes in human language and to ignore phonetic differences that are not phonemic.

Category change A change in the part of speech of a word as a result of **affixation** (e.g., adding *-ize* to *modern,* an adjective, makes it into a verb, *modernize*).

C-command A syntactic notion that is involved in pronoun interpretation and is formulated as: NP_a c-commands NP_b if the first category above NP_a contains NP_b.

Central sulcus The fold that extends from the top of the **cerebral cortex** to the lateral fissure (also called the fissure of Rolando).

Cerebral cortex The gray wrinkled mass that sits like a cap over the rest of the brain and is the seat of cognitive functioning.

Cerebral hemispheres The left and right halves of the brain, separated by the longitudinal fissure.

Cerebrovascular accident *See* **Stroke**.

Chain Connection between a moved *wh*-element and its trace that allows assignment of **case**.

Characters The units of the contemporary Chinese writing system, many of which consist of two parts—a **phonetic determinative** and a **radical**.

Chart parser A computer program that analyzes phrase structure by charting all possible parses of a sentence and choosing the analysis that best fits the whole sentence.

Class 1 affixes A group of affixes that (in English) often trigger changes in the consonant or vowel segments of the base and may affect the assignment of stress.

Class 2 affixes A group of affixes that tend to be phonologically neutral in English, having no effect on the segmental makeup of the base or on stress assignment.

Class node A label that represents each phonological feature grouping in the feature hierarchy (also called simply a **node**).

Class (sound) A group of sounds that shares certain phonetic properties (e.g., all voiced sounds).

Classificatory verbs In Athabaskan languages of North America, verb stems that are matched with noun classes on the basis of the type of movement or handling involved in the verb meaning.

Classifier constructions In sign languages, the combination of hand shapes for different types of nouns with different manners of movement and location in space. Similar to **classificatory verbs** in Athabaskan languages.

Clever Hans A horse that seemed to have a humanlike capacity to think.

Clipping A word-formation process that shortens a polysyllabic word by deleting one or more syllables (e.g., *prof* from *professor*).

Clitic A word that is unable to stand alone as an independent form for phonological reasons.

Cliticization The process by which a **clitic** is attached to a word.

Closed syllable A syllable with a coda (e.g., both syllables in *camping*).

Closing A discourse unit conventionally used to end a conversation.

Coarticulation An articulation in which phonemes overlap to a certain extent.

Cocktail party effect The ability to filter out background noise and pick out a particular sound.

Coda (Co) The elements that follow the nucleus in the same syllable (e.g., [ɹf] in *surf*).

Coda clause A type of narrative utterance sometimes found at the end of a narrative that shifts the time of the narrative into the present.

Code-switching The systematic alternation between language systems in discourse.

Cognates Words of different languages that have descended from a common source, as shown by systematic phonetic correspondences (e.g., English *father* and German *Vater*).

Cognitive development The emergence of the various mental abilities (such as language) that make up the human intellect.

Cognitive style The way in which we are predisposed to process information in our environment.

Cohesive device A device that establishes a connection among two or more elements in the discourse (e.g., anaphoric reference, cataphoric reference, lexical cohesion, and ellipsis).

Cohort In a psycholinguistic model of spoken-word recognition, a set of possible words. (*See also* **Cohort model**.)

Cohort model A model of spoken-word recognition according to which word recognition proceeds by isolating a target word from a set of words that share initial segments.

Coinage *See* **Word manufacture**.

Communication strategies Strategies used by L2 learners when they are lacking the necessary linguistic knowledge to say what they want to say (e.g., paraphrasing).

Communicative competence A speaker's underlying knowledge of the linguistic and social rules or principles for language production and comprehension in particular speech situations.

Comparative method In historical linguistics, the reconstruction of properties of a parent language through systematic comparison of its descendant languages.

Comparative reconstruction The reconstruction of properties of a parent language through comparison of its descendant languages.

Competence The mental system that underlies a person's ability to speak and understand a given language; distinguished from **performance**.

Complement A syntactic constituent that provides information about entities and locations implied by the meaning of the **head**.

Complement clause A sentence-like construction that is embedded within a larger structure (e.g., *that his car had been totaled* in *Jerry told Mary that his car had been totaled*).

Complementary distribution The distribution of allophones in their respective phonetic environments such that one never appears in the same phonetic context as the other (e.g., the distribution of long and short vowels in English).

Complementizer (C) A **functional category** that takes an IP complement, forming a CP (complementizer phrase) (e.g., *whether* in *I wonder whether Lorna has left*).

Complex NP Constraint Prohibition against moving an element out of a CP that is embedded inside an NP.

Complex word A word that contains two or more morphemes (e.g., *theorize, unemployment*).

Complicating action clause A type of narrative utterance that describes the events in a story.

Componential analysis The representation of a word's **intension** in terms of smaller semantic components called features.

Compound word A word made up of two or more words (e.g., *greenhouse, pickpocket*).

Compounding Creating a new word by combining two or more existing words (e.g., *fire + engine*).

Comprehensible input The linguistic input to which the L2 learner is exposed that is slightly beyond his or her competence in the target language (i+1).

Computational lexicography The subfield of **computational linguistics** that deals with words in the **lexicon** (e.g., their parts of speech, **subcategorization**, semantic properties).

Computational linguistics The area of common interest between linguistics and computer science.

Computational system The syntactic component of grammar that can combine and arrange words in particular ways.

Computerized axial tomography A technique for observing the living brain that uses a narrow beam of X-rays to create brain images that take the form of a series of brain slices (also called **CT scanning**).

Concatenative A term used for the morphological process that builds word structure by assembling morphemes in an additive, linear fashion.

Concord A kind of agreement in which determiners and adjectives agree with their noun (e.g., in number or case).

Concordance An index of words showing every occurrence of each word in its context.

Conflation pattern A class of meanings created by combining semantic elements such as manner and motion or direction and motion.

Conjugation The set of inflected forms associated with a verb (also called a verbal paradigm).

Conjunction (Con) A **functional category** that joins two or more categories of the same type, forming a coordinate structure (e.g., *and* in *a man and his dog*).

Connectionist model A psycholinguistic theory built around the claim that the mind can be best modeled by reference to complex associations of simple units that approximate neurons.

Connotation The set of associations that a word's use can evoke (e.g., in Wisconsin, *winter* evokes ice, snow, bare trees, etc.). (*See also* **Denotation**.)

Consonant deletion A phonetic process that deletes a consonant (e.g., the deletion of [θ] in *fifths*).

Consonant weakening A lessening in the time or degree of a consonant's closure.

Consonantal A major class feature that characterizes sounds produced with a major obstruction in the vocal tract.

Consonantal strength Increasing time or degree of a consonant's closure.

Consonants Sounds that are produced with a narrow or complete closure in the vocal tract.

Constituent One or more words that make up a syntactic unit (e.g., *the apple* in *the apple fell onto the floor*). (*See also* **Coordination test, Substitution test**, and **Movement test**.)

Constricted glottis (CG) A laryngeal feature that characterizes sounds made with the glottis closed (in English, only [ʔ]).

Constructional meaning The meaning associated with a structural pattern above and beyond the meaning of its component words.

Continuant A manner feature that characterizes sounds made with free or nearly free airflow through the oral cavity: vowels, fricatives, glides, and liquids.

Continuants Sounds that are produced with a continuous airflow through the mouth.

Contour tones Tones that change pitch on a single syllable.

Contradiction A relationship between sentences wherein the truth of one sentence requires the falsity of another sentence (e.g., *Raymond is married* contradicts *Raymond is a bachelor*).

Contralateral The control of the right side of the body by the left side of the brain and vice versa.

Contrast Segments are said to contrast when their presence alone may distinguish forms with different meanings from each other (e.g., [s] and [z] in the words *sip* and *zip*).

Converge *See* **Convergence**.

Convergence The modification of language so that it becomes more similar to that of another speaker or group of speakers.

Conversation analysis *See* **Ethnomethodology**.

Conversational implicature Information that is understood through inference but is not actually said.

Conversational maxims *See* **Maxims**.

Conversion A word-formation process that assigns an already existing word to a new syntactic category (also called **zero derivation**) (e.g., *nurse* [V] from *nurse* [N]).

Cooperative overlaps Overlapping of turns in a **high-involvement-style** conversation according to mutually held conventions of the participants.

Cooperative Principle, The The general overarching guideline thought to underlie conversational interactions: Make your contribution appropriate to the conversation.

Coordinate structure A phrase that is formed by joining two (or more) categories of the same type with a conjunction such as *and* or *or* (e.g., *those men and that woman*).

Coordinate Structure Constraint The prohibition against extracting material out of a structure joined with a conjunction such as *and* or *or* (e.g., *The exam will cover phonetics and phonology* → **What will the exam cover phonetics and?*).

Coordination The process of grouping together two or more categories of the same type with the help of a conjunction (e.g., *Mary and the white horse*).

Coordination schema A blueprint for conjoining two categories of the same type with a **conjunction** (e.g., $[\text{extremely poor}]_{AP}$ but $[\text{very honest}]_{AP}$).

Coordination test A test used to determine if a group of words is a **constituent** by joining it to another group of words with a conjunction such as *and* or *or*.

CORONAL A place feature that characterizes sounds made with the tongue tip or blade raised (e.g., [t, d, s, θ]).

Corpus A collection of texts that provides a database, e.g., for a computer grammar.

Corpus analysis A technique for building lexicons by means of automated analysis of a body of texts.

Corpus callosum The bundle of nerve fibers that serves as the main connection between the cerebral hemispheres, allowing the two hemispheres to communicate with one another.

Creativity The characteristic of human language that allows novelty and innovation in response to new thoughts, experiences, and situations.

Creole A language that originated as a **pidgin** and has become established as a first language in a speech community.

Cricoid cartilage The ring-shaped cartilage in the larynx on which the thyroid cartilage rests.

Critical period A particular time frame during which children have to be exposed to language if the acquisition process is to be successful.

Critical Period Hypothesis The hypothesis that achievement of nativelike proficiency in a second language depends on age of acquisition and is rarely attainable unless the learner begins second language acquisition during the **critical period**.

Cross-sectional (research) Research that investigates and compares subjects selected from different developmental stages.

CT scanning *See* **Computerized axial tomography**.

Cuneiform Writing invented in the fourth millennium B.C. in Mesopotamia and produced by pressing a wedge-shaped stylus into soft clay tablets.

Cyrillic alphabet An alphabet that combined adaptations of **Glagolitic script** with Greek and Hebrew characters, evolving into the alphabets that are currently used to represent some of the languages spoken in the former Soviet Union and in the Balkans.

Dative The **case** form characteristically used to mark a recipient.

Deaffrication A type of segmental simplification that turns affricates into fricatives by eliminating the stop portion of the affricate (e.g., [dʒ] becoming [ʒ]).

Declension *See* **Nominal paradigm**.

Deep dyslexia A type of **acquired dyslexia** in which the patient produces a word that is semantically related to the word he or she is asked to read (e.g., producing *father* when asked to read *mother*).

Deep structure The structure generated by the phrase structure rules in accordance with the subcategorization properties of the heads.

Degemination The weakening of a geminate consonant (double consonant) to a nongeminate consonant (e.g., [tt] becoming [t]).

Degree word (Deg) A **functional category** that serves as the specifier of a preposition or an adjective (e.g., *quite* in *quite tired, very* in *very near the house*).

Deictics Forms whose use and interpretation depend on the location of the speaker and/or addressee within a particular setting (e.g., *this/that, here/there*).

Delayed release (DR) A manner feature that refers to the release of the stop in affricate consonants.

Deletion A process that removes a segment from certain phonetic contexts (e.g., the pronunciation of *fifths* as [fɪfs]).

Denasalization A common substitution process in child language acquisition that involves the replacement of a nasal stop by a nonnasal counterpart (e.g., *come* is pronounced [kʌb]).

Denotation Entities that a word or expression refers to (also called its **referents** or **extension**).

Dense social networks Social networks in which almost everyone in the network knows everyone else in the network.

Dentals Sounds made with the tongue placed against or near the teeth.

Dependent variable In an experiment, the behavior or event that is measured.

Derivation (1) In morphology, a word-formation process by which a new word is built from a stem—usually through the addition of an affix—that changes the word class and/or basic meaning of the word. (2) The set of steps or rule applications that results in the formation of a sentence in syntax or of a phonetic representation from an underlying form in phonology.

Derived (phonology) Resulting from the application of phonological rules to underlying representations.

Descriptive (grammar) A grammar that seeks to describe human linguistic ability and knowledge, not to prescribe one system in preference to another. (*See also* **Prescriptive [grammar]**.)

Design features Essential characteristics of communication systems that have been established with reference to human language.

Determinative A symbol used in nonalphabetic writing systems to assist the reader in knowing the intended meaning or pronunciation of a word.

Determiner (Det) A **functional category** that serves as the specifier of a noun (e.g., *a, the, these*).

Deterministic parsers Sentence processors that pursue no more than one analysis at a time.

Devanagari script Writing system that developed in India and was used for Sanskrit.

Developmental bilingual education An educational program for language minority students usually lasting throughout elementary school in which language proficiency and literacy in both the minority language and the majority language are promoted.

Developmental sequences The stages of linguistic development that are relatively invariant across language learners.

Devoicing Voicing assimilation in which a sound becomes voiceless because of a nearby voiceless sound (e.g., the *l* in *place* is devoiced because of the voiceless stop preceding it).

Diacritics Marks added to a phonetic symbol to alter its value in some way (e.g., a circle under a symbol to indicate voicelessness).

Dialect A regional or social variety of a language characterized by its own phonological, syntactic, or lexical properties.

Dialectology A branch of linguistics concerned with the analysis and description of regional varieties of a language.

Diaphragm The large sheet of muscle that separates the chest cavity from the abdomen and helps to maintain the air pressure necessary for speech production.

Diary study A type of naturalistic investigation in which a researcher (often a parent) keeps daily notes on a child's linguistic progress.

Dichotic listening studies Research based on an experimental technique in which the subject listens to different sounds in each ear.

Diglossia The relationship between multiple varieties spoken by one speech community but with sharply distinct **domains of use**.

Diphthongization A process in which a monophthong becomes a diphthong (e.g., [i:] became [aj] during the Great English Vowel Shift).

Diphthongs Vowels that show a noticeable change in quality within a single syllable (e.g., the vowel sounds in h<u>ou</u>se and r<u>i</u>de).

Direct negative evidence Language instruction involving correction or focus on form.

Direct object The NP **complement** of a verb (e.g., *a fish* in *Judy caught a fish*).

Discourse A set of utterances that constitute a speech event.

Discourse analysis The field that deals with the organization of texts, including ways in which parts of texts are connected and the devices used for achieving textual structure.

Discourse markers Words or expressions that bracket utterances in discourse and organize the sequence and/or the relationship between them (e.g., *well, y'know*).

Discrete sign A sign that is distinguished from other signs by stepwise differences (e.g., voiced and voiceless sounds, the numbers of a digital clock).

Displacement A property by which the users of the communication system are able to refer to events that are remote in space and time.

Dissimilation A process whereby one segment becomes less like another segment in its environment (e.g., *anma* 'soul' in a form of Latin became *alma* in Spanish).

Distinctive feature A feature that serves to distinguish contrastive forms (e.g., the feature [voice] is distinctive in English because it underlies the contrast between /p/ and /b/, /t/ and /d/, etc.).

Distribution The set of elements with which an item can co-occur.

Diverge *See* **Divergence**.

Divergence The modification of language so that it becomes more different from that of another speaker or group of speakers.

***Do* insertion** The syntactic rule that places *do* into an empty I position, making **inversion** possible in English questions.

Domain The smallest IP or NP containing a reflexive pronoun and a separate NP specifier.

Domains of use Speech situations in which a particular variety is commonly used.

DORSAL A place feature that represents sounds produced when the body of the tongue is involved (e.g., vowels and [k, g]).

Dorsum (of the tongue) The body and back of the tongue.

Double-blind test A test in which a subject's responses are interpreted independently by someone other than the administrator of the test.

Downdrift The maintenance of a distinction among the pitch registers of an utterance even as the overall pitch of the utterance falls.

Dressage Interaction between trainer and animal in which the animal responds to subtle cues given by the trainer.

D-structure *See* **Deep structure**.

Dual-language programs *See* **Two-way immersion** (TWI) programs.

Dual-route model A psycholinguistic theory built around the claim that a particular type of language processing can be accomplished in more than one manner.

Duality of patterning A property of communication systems in which meaningless units are combined to form arbitrary signs that, in turn, are recombined to form new larger signs.

Duetting The interchange of calls in a patterned manner between two members of a species.

Dysprosody The lack of sentence intonation, a common characteristic of the speech of Broca's aphasics.

Ebonics *See* **African American Vernacular English (AAVE)**.

Economy constraint A grammatical constraint whose effect is to reduce the computational cost of derivations.

Ejectives Stops or affricates that are made with simultaneous closure of the glottis and constriction of the throat, producing a distinctive "popping" sound.

Enclitic A **clitic** that attaches to the end of a word.

Endocentric compound A compound word in which one member identifies the general class to which the meaning of the entire word belongs (e.g., *dog food* is a type of food in English). (*See also* **Exocentric compound**.)

English language learners (ELLs) Nonnative speakers of English, particularly used for those in U.S. schools (previously known as Limited English Proficient [LEP] students).

Entailment A relation between sentences in which the truth of one sentence necessarily implies the truth of another (e.g., *Gary is Bernice's husband* entails the sentence *Bernice is married*).

Environment The phonetic context in which a sound occurs.

Epenthesis A process that inserts a segment into a particular environment (e.g., the insertion of a schwa in the pronunciation of *athlete* as [æθəlit]).

Ergative The case associated with the subject of a **transitive verb** (but not that of an **intransitive verb**).

Ergative-absolutive pattern Sentence pattern in which **ergative** case is assigned to the **agent** of a **transitive verb**, but **absolutive** case is assigned to the subject of an **intransitive verb** or the object of a transitive verb.

Ethnic dialect A dialect spoken by a particular ethnic group.

Ethnography of communication A type of discourse analysis that concentrates on how language is used to achieve communicative goals in particular social situations.

Ethnolinguistic vitality The strength of an ethnic group identity and the variety of language associated with it as measured by the number of people in the group relative to the majority, the degree of institutional support they receive, and their relative pride in their identity.

Ethnomethodology A type of discourse analysis that focuses on the structural relationship between utterances in conversations.

Euphemism A word or phrase that is less direct than the taboo word it replaces and is considered to be more socially acceptable (e.g., *passed away* for *died*).

Evaluation clause A type of narrative utterance that gives comments or evaluations regarding the events being narrated.

Event-related potentials (ERPs) A measurement of electrical activity in the brain that is correlated with the presentation of particular stimulus events.

Evidentiality A system of morphological contrasts indicating the type of evidence for the truth of a statement.

Evidentials Morphological or syntactic elements (frequently **enclitic** morphemes) that indicate the speaker's source of information for the statement he or she is making.

Exclusive A type of first person plural pronoun whose referents do not include the addressee. (*See also* **Inclusive**.)

Exocentric compound A compound whose meaning does not follow from the meaning of its parts (e.g., *redneck*, since its referent is not a type of neck).

Experimental paradigm A method of investigation that involves a particular way of presenting stimuli and a particular way of measuring responses.

Experimental studies Studies in child language in which researchers make use of specially designed tasks to elicit linguistic activity relevant to a particular phenomenon.

Extension The set of entities to which a word or expression refers (also called its **denotation** or **referents**).

Face-threatening acts Speech acts such as requests, diagreement, or complaints that can disrupt social solidarity or impose on the freedom of action of participants.

Feature (phonological) The smallest unit of analysis of phonological structure, combinations of which make up segments (e.g., [nasal], [continuant]).

Feature hierarchy A hierarchical representation of how features are related to each other.

Features (semantic) The semantic components that make up a word's **intension**.

Field dependence A learning style in which the learner operates holistically, perceiving the "field" as a whole rather than in terms of its component parts.

Field independence A learning style in which the learner operates analytically, perceiving the "field" in terms of its component parts rather than as a whole.

Field technique A method of study that does not involve manipulation and control of factors in a laboratory, but rather involves observing phenomena as they occur.

Fissure A relatively deep **sulcus** of the cerebral cortex.

Fixed stress Stress whose position in a word is predictable.

Fixed stress languages Languages in which the position of stress in words is predictable. (*See also* **Fixed stress**.)

Flap A sound commonly identified with *r* and produced when the tongue tip strikes the alveolar ridge as it passes across it (e.g., in North American English, the medial consonant in *bi<u>tt</u>er* and *bi<u>dd</u>er*).

Flapping A phonetic process in which an alveolar stop is pronounced as a voiced flap between vowels, the first of which is generally stressed (e.g., [bʌ́tɹ̩] → [bʌ́ɾɹ̩]).

Fluency Second language speech that is produced automatically and without noticeable hesitation.

Fluent aphasia The **aphasia** that occurs due to damage to parts of the left cortex behind the central sulcus, resulting in fluent speech but great difficulty selecting, organizing, and monitoring language production (also called **sensory aphasia**).

Focus on form In second language teaching, the practice of giving explicit instruction about the second language and overtly correcting errors.

Folk etymology Reanalysis of a word that is based on an incorrect historical analysis (e.g., *hamburger* being reanalyzed into two morphemes, *ham* and *burger*).

Foreigner talk The type of speech that is typically addressed to second language learners, characterized by such properties as simple word order and more common vocabulary items (also called **teacher talk**).

Forest-based generation In computational linguistics, a method of creating text by programming a computer with a simple, underconstrained grammar and allowing the computer to select the best sentence that is generated.

Formants The main frequencies of a speech wave.

Fossilized Characteristic of an **interlanguage** grammar that has reached a plateau, i.e., ceased to improve.

Free form An element that can occur in isolation and/or whose position with respect to neighboring elements is not entirely fixed.

Free morpheme A **morpheme** that can be a word by itself (e.g., *fear*).

Free stress Stress whose position in a word is not predictable and must be learned on a case-by-case basis.

Free stress languages Languages in which the position of stress in words is not predictable. (*See also* **Free stress**.)

Free variation The free alternation of allophones and/or phonemes in a given environment (e.g., *sto*[pˀ], *sto*[p]; /ɛ/*conomics*, /i/*conomics*).

Frequency effect The common experimental finding that words that occur more frequently in a language are processed more quickly and more accurately.

Frication The weakening of a stop to a fricative (e.g., [d] becoming [ð]).

Fricatives Consonants produced with a continuous airflow through the mouth, accompanied by a continuous audible noise (e.g., [f], [ʃ]).

Front *See* **Front vowel**.

Front vowel A vowel that is made with the tongue positioned in the front of the oral cavity (e.g., the vowel sounds in *seal* and *bat*).

Frontal lobe The lobe of the brain that lies in front of the central sulcus and in which Broca's area is located.

Fronting A common substitution process in child language acquisition that involves the moving forward of a sound's place of articulation (e.g., *cheese* pronounced as [tsiz]).

Full reduplication A morphological process that duplicates the entire word (e.g., in Turkish, tʃabuk 'quickly'/tʃabuk tʃabuk 'very quickly').

Function words Words such as determiners and conjunctions that specify grammatical relations rather than carry semantic content.

Functional analysis An approach to syntactic analysis that attempts to understand syntactic phenomena in terms of their communicative function.

Functional category A word-level syntactic category whose members specify grammatical relations rather than carry semantic content (e.g., auxiliary verbs, conjunctions, determiners, and degree words) (also called **nonlexical category**).

Functional magnetic resonance imaging (fMRI) A brain imaging technique that yields information on areas of high brain activity during the performance of cognitive tasks.

Fusion A morphological change in which a word becomes an affix (e.g., English affixes such as *-hood, -dom,* and *-ly* used to be words).

Fusional languages Languages in which words typically consist of several morphemes, and the morphemes that are affixes often mark several grammatical categories simultaneously (e.g., Russian).

Fuzzy concepts Concepts that do not have clear-cut boundaries that distinguish them from other concepts (e.g., the concept POOR).

Garden path sentence A sentence that is difficult to process and interpret because its structure biases sentence parsing toward an incorrect analysis.

Gender *See* **Noun class**.

Gender-exclusive (differentiation) A type of social differentiation in which the use of some linguistic forms depends on the gender of the speakers.

Gender-variable (differentiation) The relative frequency with which men and women use certain features of language.

Genetic classification The categorization of languages according to the ancestor languages from which they developed.

Genetic relationships Relationships among languages that have descended from a common ancestor language. (*See also* **Genetic classification** and **Genetically related languages**.)

Genetically related languages Languages that have descended from a common parent (e.g., German and Italian have both descended from Indo-European).

Genitive The **case** form characteristically used to mark a possessor.

Given information Knowledge that the speaker assumes is available to the addressee at the time of the utterance, either because it is shared by both or because it has already been introduced into the discourse (also called **old information**).

Glagolitic script A script that was introduced in Slavic-speaking areas in the ninth century A.D. for the translation of the Bible.

Glide strengthening The strengthening of a glide to an affricate (e.g., [j] becoming [dʒ]).

Glides Sounds that are produced with an articulation like that of a vowel, but move quickly to another articulation (e.g., [j], [w]).

Gliding A common substitution process in child language acquisition that involves the replacement of a liquid by a glide (e.g., *play* is pronounced [pwej]).

Global aphasia The most severe form of **nonfluent aphasia**, in which the patient is completely mute.

Glottalization A consonant that is made with simultaneous closure of the glottis and constriction of the throat. Glottalized stops and affricates (**ejectives**) are the most common glottalized consonants.

Glottals Sounds produced by using the vocal folds as the primary articulators (e.g., [h], [ʔ]).

Glottis The space between the **vocal folds**.

Glyphs The symbols used in Mayan writing.

Goal A **thematic role** that describes the end point for a movement (e.g., *Mary* in *Terry gave the skis to Mary*).

Graded (concept) A concept whose members display varying degrees of the characteristics that are considered typical of the concept.

Graded sign A sign that conveys its meaning by changes in degree (e.g., voice volume, a blush).

Grammar The mental system of rules and categories that allows humans to form and interpret the words and sentences of their language.

Grammar-based generation In computational linguistics, a method of creating text by programming the computer with an extensive grammar.

Grammatical (sentence) A sentence that speakers judge to be a possible sentence in their language.

Grammatical competence Competence in the structural aspects at or below the sentence level.

Grammatical knowledge Knowledge of the meaning and use of words in sentences. (*Compare* **real-world knowledge**.)

Grammaticalization The change of a lexical form into a grammatical form (e.g., an **affix** or member of a **functional category**).

Grammaticalized *See* **grammaticalization**.

Grammaticized concepts Concepts that are expressed as affixes or nonlexical categories (e.g., the concept of 'obligation' as expressed by the auxiliary verb *must*).

Great English Vowel Shift A series of nonphonetically conditioned modifications to long vowels that occurred from the Middle English period to the eighteenth century.

Grimm's Law A set of consonant shifts that took place between Proto-Indo-European and Proto-Germanic.

Gyri Plural of **gyrus**.

Gyrus An area where the cerebral cortex is folded out.

Habitual (invariant) *be* Uninflected *be* used to indicate a habitual state or action in **African American Vernacular English** (e.g., *The coffee be cold* means 'the coffee is usually cold').

Hangul The alphabetic script used to represent Korean, the symbols of which are grouped to represent the syllables of individual morphemes.

Hanja The Korean word for the Chinese characters used in Korean writing.

Head (of a phrase) The category around which a phrase is built (e.g., V is head of VP, N is head of NP, A of AP, P of PP).

Head (of a word) The morpheme that determines the category of the entire word in a compound (e.g., *bird* in *blackbird*).

Head-final (language) Language in which the **head** of a phrase follows its **complement** (e.g., the verb comes after the direct object in the VP).

Head-initial (language) Language in which the **head** comes before its **complement** (e.g., the verb comes before the direct object in the VP).

Head position parameter A parameter that offers two versions of the **X' schema**—one in which the head precedes its complement and one in which the head follows its complement.

Heavy syllable Syllable that has either a **coda** or two elements in the **nucleus** (e.g., a diphthong or a long vowel).

Heritage language programs Educational programs designed to preserve, maintain, or revive the ancestral languages of indigenous peoples, immigrants, or refugees in the United States.

Hierarchies In the classification of languages, the degrees of **markedness** of particular structures in the world's languages, going from least marked (i.e., most common) to most marked (i.e., least common).

Hieroglyphs An ancient Egyptian writing system that used pictures as pictograms, logograms, and consonant phonemes.

High A DORSAL feature that characterizes sounds produced with the tongue body raised.

High involvement style A style of turn-taking in a conversation in which speaker turns overlap.

High vowel A vowel that is made with the tongue raised (e.g., the vowel sounds in *beat* and *lose*).

Hiragana The Japanese syllabary that is used in conjunction with **katakana** and **kanji** to write Japanese.

Historical linguistics The linguistic discipline that is concerned with the description and the explanation of language change over time.

Holophrases Utterances produced by children in which one word expresses the type of meaning that would be associated with an entire sentence in adult speech (e.g., *up* used to mean 'Pick me up').

Homophony The situation in which a single form has two or more entirely distinct meanings (e.g., *club* 'a social organization', *club* 'a blunt weapon').

Host The element to which a **clitic** is attached.

Hypercorrection Overgeneralization of particular rules in a language in an attempt to speak (or write) "correctly."

Iconic sign A sign that bears some resemblance to its referent (e.g., a picture of a woman on a washroom door).

Icon *See* **Iconic sign**.

Illocutionary competence The ability to understand a speaker's intent and to produce a variety of forms to convey intent.

Illocutionary force The intended meaning of an utterance.

Immersion A method of teaching a second language to children in which students are given most of their content courses and school activities in the target language.

Impaired Representation Hypothesis The hypothesis that states that second language learners who produce errors lack an underlying representation of the structure in which they have produced errors.

Implementation A practical application of a formal system.

Implicational universals A universal of language that specifies that the presence of one trait implies the presence of another (but not vice versa).

Inalienably possessed nouns Nouns that must always have a pronominal possessor indicated; usually parts of the body or kinship terms.

Inanimate A noun class category in some languages generally assigned to nonliving referents. (*See also* **Animate**.)

Inclusive A contrast in some languages that indicates that the addressee is to be included in the interpretation of the first person plural morpheme. (*See also* **Exclusive**.)

Incorporation The combination of a word (usually a noun) with a verb to form a compound verb.

Index *See* **Indexical sign**.

Indexical sign A sign that fulfills its function by pointing out its referent, typically by being a partial sample of it (e.g., the track of an animal).

Indexing Finding, identifying, and counting all occurrences of a word in large texts.

Indexing analysis A means of analyzing sociolinguistic variation by putting each instance of a variable on a continuum; used especially to evaluate degree and direction of vowel movement.

Indirect negative evidence The assumption that nonoccurring structures in the linguistic environment are ungrammatical.

Indo-European family The **language family** that includes most of the languages in a broad curve from northern India through western Asia (Iran and Armenia) to Europe.

Infix An **affix** that occurs within a base.

Inflection The modification of a word's form to indicate the grammatical subclass to which it belongs (e.g., the *-s* in *books* marks the plural subclass).

Inflectional language *See* **Fusional languages**.

Insertion rule An operation that adds an element to a tree structure.

Instrumental motivation The desire to achieve proficiency in a new language for utilitarian reasons, such as a job promotion.

Integrative motivation The desire to achieve proficiency in a new language in order to participate in the social life of the community that speaks the language.

Intension An expression's inherent sense; the concepts that it evokes.

Intercostals The muscles between the ribs that help to maintain the air pressure necessary for speech production.

Interdentals Sounds made with the tongue placed between the teeth (e.g., [θ], [ð]).

Interlanguage (IL) The changing grammatical system that an L2 learner is using at a particular period in his or her acquisition of a second language as he or she moves toward proficiency in the target language.

Interlocutors Participants in a conversation.

Internal change A process that substitutes one nonmorphemic segment for another to mark a grammatical contrast (e.g., *sing, sang, sung*).

Internal reconstruction The reconstruction of a **protolanguage** that relies on the analysis of morphophonemic variation within a single language.

International Phonetic Alphabet (IPA) A system for transcribing the sounds of speech that attempts to represent each sound of human speech with a single symbol.

Internet survey A linguistic survey completed by subjects who happen to access a given Web site, Internet bulletin board, or special interest list on the Internet.

Intonation Pitch movement in spoken utterances that is not related to differences in word meaning.

Intransitive verb A verb that does not take a direct object (e.g., *sleep*).

Inversion A **transformation** that moves the element in the I position to a position in front of the subject, formulated as: Move I to C.

Island A constituent that does not permit a component part to be moved from it (e.g., a coordinated phrase such as *Jerry and Gretchen*).

Island constraints Prohibitions against moving elements out of particular kinds of constituents such as subject NPs and complex NPs.

Isogloss bundle Convergence of several lines drawn on a dialect map to represent boundaries between dialects.

Isoglosses Lines drawn on a dialect map to represent boundaries between dialects.

Isolate A language that is not known to be related to any other living language (e.g., Basque, Kutenai).

Isolating languages Languages whose words typically consist of only one morpheme (e.g., Mandarin). (Also called **analytic languages**.)

Jargon (1) Vocabulary peculiar to a particular field; (2) a simple pidgin used in very limited circumstances.

Jargonaphasia A symptom of severe cases of **Wernicke's aphasia** in which speech contains very few real words of the language.

Kanji The Japanese word for the Chinese characters used to write Japanese.

Katakana The Japanese syllabary that is used in conjunction with **hiragana** and **kanji** to write Japanese.

LABIAL A place feature that characterizes sounds articulated with one or both lips.

Labials Sounds made with closure or near closure of the lips (e.g., the initial sounds of *win* and *forget*).

Labiodentals Sounds involving the lower lip and upper teeth (e.g., the initial sounds of *freedom* and *vintage*).

Labiovelars Sounds made with the tongue raised near the velum and the lips rounded at the same time (e.g., the initial sound of *wound*).

Language Bioprogram Hypothesis The hypothesis that similarities among creoles reflect linguistic universals both in terms of first language acquisition and with respect to processes and structures that are innate.

Language contact Interaction between speakers of one language and speakers of another language or dialect.

Language family In language classification, a group of languages with a historical origin in the same **protolanguage**.

Language nest An educational program for preschoolers in which a (usually endangered) minority language is used exclusively.

Language planning Official policy with the goal of increasing or limiting the domain of use of a particular language or languages.

Laryngeal features Phonological features that represent laryngeal states (e.g., [voice], [spread glottis], and [constricted glottis]).

Laryngeal node A node in the feature geometry in autosegmental phonology that dominates laryngeal features such as voicing, spread glottis, and constricted glottis.

Larynx The box-like structure located in the throat through which air passes during speech production; commonly known as the voice box.

Late closure A parsing principle that claims that in sentence comprehension, humans prefer to attach new words to the clause currently being processed.

Lateral (feature) A manner feature that characterizes a sound made with the sides of the tongue lowered (e.g., varieties of *l*).

Lateral (sound) A sound made with the sides of the tongue lowered (e.g., varieties of [l]).

Lateral fissure The fissure that separates the temporal lobe from the frontal and parietal lobes in the brain.

Lateral fricative A **lateral sound** made with a narrow enough closure to be classified as a fricative.

Lateralization The unilateral control of cognitive functions by either the left or the right side of the brain (e.g., language is lateralized to the left hemisphere in most people).

Lateralized *See* **Lateralization**.

Laterals Sounds made with the sides of the tongue lowered (e.g., varieties of *l*).

Lax vowels Vowels that are made with a placement of the tongue that results in relatively less vocal tract constriction (e.g., the vowel sounds in *hit* and *but*).

Learning strategies The activities in which language learners engage to help them develop linguistic knowledge.

Length The subjective impression of time occupied by the duration of a **phone**.

Lesion Severe damage to the brain.

Lexical ambiguity A situation in which a single form has two or more meanings (e.g., a *trunk* is a 'piece of luggage' or an 'elephant nose').

Lexical category The word-level syntactic categories noun (N), verb (V), adjective (A), and preposition (P).

Lexical decision An experimental paradigm in which a person sees or hears a stimulus and must judge as quickly as possible whether or not that stimulus is a word of his or her language.

Lexical diffusion Linguistic change that first manifests itself in a few words and then gradually spreads through the vocabulary of the language.

Lexical gaps Gaps in the lexicon that result from technological innovation or contact with another culture.

Lexicalization The process whereby concepts are encoded in the words of a language (e.g., the concepts of 'motion' and 'manner' are both encoded by the word *roll*).

Lexicon A speaker's mental dictionary, which contains information about the syntactic properties, meaning, and phonological representation of a language's words.

Lexifier language The language that provides most of the lexical items to a contact variety.

Lingua franca A language that is used when speakers of two or more different languages come into contact and do not know each other's languages.

Linguistic competence Speakers' knowledge of their language, which allows them to produce and understand an unlimited number of utterances, including many that are novel.

Linguistic insecurity The degree to which speakers believe that their own variety is not standard.

Linguistic typology An approach to language classification that classifies languages according to their common structural characteristics without regard for **genetic relationships**.

Linguistic universals Structural characteristics that occur across the languages of the world.

Linguistics The discipline that studies the nature and use of language.

Liquids A class of consonants containing *l* and *r* sounds and their variants.

Lobes Substructures of the hemispheres of the brain that appear to have distinct responsibilities (e.g., **frontal lobe**, **temporal lobe**).

Location A **thematic role** that specifies the place where an action occurs (e.g., *the SkyDome* in *The athletes practiced in the SkyDome*).

Locative The **case** form characteristically used for the noun that is *in, to,* or *at* a location.

Logogram A written symbol representing a morpheme or word.

Logographic writing A type of writing in which symbols represent morphemes or even entire words.

Longitudinal fissure The fissure that extends from the front of the brain to the back and separates the left and right cerebral hemispheres.

Longitudinal studies Studies that examine language development over an extended period of time.

Loudness The subjective impression of a speech sound's volume relative to the sounds around it.

Low (feature) A DORSAL feature that characterizes sounds made with the tongue body lowered.

Low (sound) A sound made with the tongue lowered (e.g., [a], [ɑ], [æ]).

Low vowel A vowel that is made with the tongue lowered (e.g., the vowel sounds made in the words c<u>a</u>t and t<u>o</u>p).

Machine-readable dictionary (MRD) A dictionary that can be read by a computer.

Machine translation The process by which a machine (e.g., a computer) takes text spoken or written in one language and translates it into another language.

Macrofamilies *See* **Phyla**.

Magnetoencephalography (MEG) A technique that provides detailed information on which parts of the brain are involved in language-processing activity by recording changes in magnetic fields generated within the brain.

Major class features Phonological features that represent the classes consonant, obstruent, nasal, liquid, glide, and vowel.

Majority rules strategy A secondary strategy used to reconstruct protoforms, which stipulates that the segment found in the majority of cognates should be assumed to be part of the **protoform**. (*See also* **Phonetic plausibility strategy**.)

Manner features Phonological features that represent manner of articulation.

Manners of articulation The various configurations produced by positioning the lips, tongue, velum, and glottis in different ways (e.g., nasal, fricative, liquid).

Marginal analysis Analysis of sociolinguistic data in which overall percentages of occurrences in relevant linguistic and social contexts are reported for each variant.

Marked Occurring less commonly in world languages. (*See also* **Marked traits** and **Markedness theory**.)

Marked traits Complex or less common features or characteristics of languages.

Markedness The quality of being relatively complex or rare in world languages. (*See also* **Marked traits** and **Markedness theory**.)

Markedness Differential Hypothesis The hypothesis that L2 elements that are different and more **marked** than the L1 elements will cause difficulty in learning L2.

Markedness theory A theory that classifies traits or patterns of languages as marked (those that are considered to be more complex and/or universally rarer) and unmarked (those that are considered to be less complex and/or universally more common).

Matched guise test A test of language attitudes that asks subjects to evaluate recordings of the same person speaking different language varieties.

Matrix A representation of sounds in which all the relevant distinctive features and their values are placed in an array.

Matrix clause The larger IP in which a **complement clause** occurs.

Maxim of Manner A principle that is thought to underlie the efficient use of language and is formulated as: Avoid ambiguity and obscurity; be brief and orderly.

Maxim of Quality A principle that is thought to underlie the efficient use of language and is formulated as: Try to make your contribution one that is true. (Do not say things that are false or for which you lack adequate evidence.)

Maxim of Quantity A principle that is thought to underlie the efficient use of language and is formulated as: Do not make your contribution more or less informative than required.

Maxim of Relevance A principle that is thought to underlie the efficient use of language and is formulated as: Be relevant.

Maxims The specific principles that ensure that conversational interactions satisfy **The Cooperative Principle.**

Meaning The message or content that a sign or utterance conveys.

Mental lexicon See **Lexicon**.

Merge A syntactic operation that combines elements to create phrases and sentences.

Merger A change in a phonological system in which two or more phonemes collapse into one, thereby reducing the number of phonemes in that language.

Mesolect A **creole** variety that falls between an **acrolect** and a **basilect** in terms of the amount of influence from the standard language.

Metaphor The understanding of one concept in terms of another, sometimes responsible for language change (e.g., 'argument' understood in terms of 'war': *She annihilated him in the debate*).

Metaphorical code-switching The use of code-switching to express solidarity with or distance from the speech communities associated with the languages being switched.

Metathesis A process that reorders a sequence of segments (e.g., in child language, pronouncing *spaghetti* as [pəskɛɾi]).

Mid vowels Vowels that are made with the tongue neither raised nor lowered (e.g., the vowel sounds in *set* and *Coke*).

Minimal attachment A proposed parsing principle that claims that in sentence comprehension, humans tend to attach incoming material into phrase structure using the fewest nodes possible.

Minimal pair Two forms with distinct meanings that differ by only one segment found in the same position in each form (e.g., [ʃɪp] and [ʃip]).

Missing Surface Inflection Hypothesis The hypothesis that states that second language learners who produce errors may actually have correct underlying representations for the structure in which they have made errors but have difficulty mapping these underlying representations to their surface forms.

Modal auxiliary An English **auxiliary verb** in the I position that is not inflected for agreement with the subject (e.g., *may, can, will, must, could*) but may show tense (e.g., *could, would* may be past).

Modifier An optional element that describes a property of a **head** (e.g., *blue* in *that blue car,* or *that Gloria likes* in *the car that Gloria likes*).

Module A unit of processing that is relatively autonomous from other processing units.

Morpheme The smallest unit of language that carries information about meaning or function (e.g., *books* consists of the two morphemes *book* + *s*).

Morphological parsing The computational process in the brain that analyzes constituent morphemes of a word.

Morphology The system of categories and rules involved in word formation and interpretation.

Morphophonemics Rules that account for alternations among **allomorphs**.

Morphophonology *See* **Morphophonemics**.

Motherese The type of speech that is typically addressed to young children (also called **caregiver speech**).

Motion verbs Words that can describe motion through space (e.g., *come, go,* and *move* in English).

Motor aphasia *See* **Nonfluent aphasia**.

Move A syntactic operation that transports an element to a new position within a particular sentence.

Movement test A test used to determine if a group of words is a **constituent** by moving it as a single unit to a different position within the sentence.

MRD *See* **Machine-readable dictionary**.

Multiplex networks Social networks in which the connections are based on several kinds of relationships.

Murmur The glottal state that produces voiced sounds with the vocal folds relaxed enough to allow enough air to escape to produce a simultaneous breathy effect (also called **breathy voice**).

Mutual intelligibility The criterion that is sometimes used to distinguish between a language and a dialect: Mutually intelligible varieties of a language can be understood by speakers of each variety and are therefore dialects of the same language.

Narrative A type of discourse unit that tells a story.

Narrow transcription Phonetic transcription that uses a fairly elaborate set of symbols and **diacritics** to show phonetic detail.

Nasal A manner feature that characterizes any sound made with the **velum** lowered.

Nasal phones Sounds produced by lowering the velum, allowing air to pass through the nasal passages.

Nasal vowels Vowels produced with a lowered **velum** so that air passes through the oral and nasal cavities at the same time.

Nasalization The nasalizing effect that a nasal consonant can have on an adjacent vowel.

Native speakers Those who have acquired a language as a child in a natural setting.

Nativism The view that certain grammatical knowledge is inborn.

Natural class A class of sounds that shares a **feature** or features (e.g., voiced stops).

Natural language generation All the processes that transform an intention to communicate into written or spoken communication.

Natural language processing systems Computer systems that can process human language.

Naturalistic approach An approach to investigating child language in which researchers observe and record children's spontaneous verbal behavior.

Naturalness A criterion that guides language reconstruction by determining whether or not changes are natural.

Near-minimal pair Two forms with distinct meanings that contrast segments in nearly identical environments.

Negative evidence Information as to the ungrammatical nature of utterances.

Negative face The need of every person to remain autonomous and free from imposition.

Negative politeness Strategies used by the speaker to lessen the imposition on the hearer (e.g., expressing tentativeness by phrasing a request in the form of a question).

Network density The degree to which speakers in a social network are interconnected to each other.

Neurolinguistics The study of how language is represented and processed in the brain.

Neurons The basic information-processing units of the nervous system, also called nerve cells.

Neuroscience The scientific study of the brain.

New information Knowledge that is introduced into the discourse for the first time.

Newcomer programs Programs designed to provide intensive language instruction, literacy development, and cultural orientation for English language learners who arrive in U.S. schools with very low-level skills in English and/or little previous experience in school.

Node (1) Large association of simple units in the mind; (2) *See* **class node**.

Nominal paradigm The set of related forms associated with a noun (also called a **declension**).

Nominative The **case** form characteristically used to mark a subject.

Nominative-accusative pattern Sentence pattern in which the subject of the sentence is identified by nominative **case**, and the direct object is marked by accusative **case**.

No-naming The practice of avoiding address terms when participants are unsure which term to use.

Nondeterministic parsers Sentence processors that can pursue more than one analysis at a time.

Nonfluent aphasia Aphasia that results from damage to parts of the brain in front of the central sulcus and that is characterized by slow, effortful speech production (also called **motor aphasia**).

Nonlexical category *See* **Functional category**.

Nonmanual grammatical markers In sign languages, facial expression or body posture used to indicate a particular grammatical structure, such as a subordinate clause.

Nonmodal auxiliaries Auxiliary verbs that show agreement with the subject, originate in VP, and raise to I when there is no **modal auxiliary**; in English, the auxiliary verbs *be* and *have* when they occur with a main verb (e.g., *was* writing; *have* seen).

Nonstandard (dialect) A variety of language that differs from the standard dialect in systematic ways.

Nonstridents Coronal fricatives and affricates that have less acoustic noise than **stridents** ([θ, ð] are nonstridents).

Nonsyllabic (sounds) Sounds that do not act as syllable peaks, as distinguished from **syllabic** sounds.

Nonterminal (intonation) contour Rising or level intonation at the end of an utterance, often signaling that the utterance is incomplete.

Nonterminals Parts of a structure that are not lexical items, for example VP, NP, Det, N'. Compare with **terminals**.

Northern Cities Shift The systematic change in vowel sounds taking place in cities around the Great Lakes. (*See also* **Shift**.)

Noun (N) A **lexical category** that typically names entities, can usually be inflected for number and possession (in English), and functions as the **head** of a noun phrase (e.g., *key, Bob, perception*).

Noun class A grammatical category dividing nouns into classes often based on shared semantic properties (also called **gender**).

Noun incorporation *See* **Incorporation**.

NP Movement A transformation that moves a noun phrase into the subject position.

Nucleus (N) A vocalic element that forms the core of a syllable (e.g., the vowel [æ] is the nucleus of the first syllable of *Patrick*).

Null Subject Parameter A cross-linguistic variation that allows some languages to drop subject pronouns, while other languages require an overt grammatical subject.

Number The morphological category that expresses contrasts involving countable quantities (e.g., in English, the two-way distinction between singular and plural).

Object permanence A developmental milestone characterized by the child's ability to recognize that objects have an existence independent of one's interaction with them.

Oblique NP A noun phrase that combines with a preposition.

Obstruent Any nonsonorant consonant: fricatives, affricates, oral stops.

Occipital lobe The area of the brain to the rear of the angular gyrus in which the visual cortex is located.

Official language A language that has been designated by political or other official authorities as the working language of a region, nation, or other group.

Old information *See* **Given information**.

One-way bilingual education An educational program in which language minority students are offered instruction in their first language and the majority language.

One-word stage A stage of first language acquisition at which children characteristically produce one-word utterances.

Onomatopoeic words Words that sound like the thing that they name (e.g., *plop, hiss*).

Onset The portion of a syllable that precedes the nucleus (e.g., /spl/ in *spleen*).

Open syllable A syllable that is not closed by a consonant.

Opening A discourse unit conventionally used to begin a conversation.

Oral phones Sounds produced with the velum raised and the airflow through the nasal passage cut off.

Ordered rule application In a phonological **derivation**, an application of rules in which the rules must be applied in a certain order to derive the surface form from the **underlying representation**.

Ordered rules Rules that must be applied in a particular order. *See* **ordered rule application**.

Orderly heterogeneity Variation in use of language among groups (e.g., social groups) such that members from one group can be distinguished from members of other groups on the basis of linguistic **variants**.

Orientation clause A type of narrative utterance that gives background information to the story; e.g., the time and place where it occurred.

Orthography A set of conventions for representing language in written form.

Overextension A developmental phenomenon in which the meaning of a child's word overlaps with that of the equivalent adult word but also extends beyond it (e.g., *dog* is used to refer to other animals as well as dogs).

Overgeneralization A developmental phenomenon that results from the overly broad application of a rule (e.g., *falled* instead of *fell*).

Overregularization *See* **Overgeneralization**.

Palatalization The effect that front vowels and the palatal guide [j] typically have on velar, alveolar, and dental stops, making their place of articulation more palatal (e.g., the first sound of *keep* is palatalized).

Palatals Sounds produced with the tongue on or near the palate (e.g., [j]).

Palate The highest part of the roof of the mouth.

Palatoalveolar *See* **Alveopalatal (area)**.

Paragraphia Writing errors made by Broca's aphasics that have characteristics corresponding to their speech.

Parallel processing model A psycholinguistic theory built around the claim that phonological, lexical, and syntactic processes are carried out simultaneously.

Parameter The set of alternatives for a particular phenomenon made available by **Universal Grammar** to individual languages.

Parameter setting The determination of which option permitted by a particular **parameter** is appropriate for the language being learned.

Paraphrases Two sentences that have the same basic meaning (e.g., *A Canadian wrote that book* is a paraphrase of *That book was written by a Canadian*).

Parietal lobe The lobe of the brain that lies behind the central sulcus and above the temporal lobe.

Parser A program or mental process for doing grammatical analysis.

Parsing The procedure through which speech or text is analyzed by assigning categories to words and assigning structure to strings of words.

Partial reduplication A morphological process in which part of a stem is repeated to form a new word (e.g., in Tagalog, *takbuh* 'run' and *tatakbuh* 'will run').

Partial suppletion A morphological process that marks a grammatical contrast by replacing part of a morpheme (e.g., *think/thought*).

Passive sentence A sentence whose grammatical subject is the **theme** (the entity affected by the action of the verb) (e.g., *The report was prepared by the committee members*).

Patient The recipient of an action (e.g., *dolphin* in *Marilyn fed the dolphin*).

Pejoration A semantic change in which the meaning of a word becomes more negative or unfavorable (e.g., the meaning of *wench* used to be 'girl').

Performance Actual language use in particular situations.

Person A morphological category that typically distinguishes among the first person (the speaker), the second person (the addressee), and the third person (anyone else) (e.g., in English, the difference between *I*, *you*, and *she/he/it*).

Pharyngeals Sounds made through the modification of airflow in the **pharynx** by retracting the tongue or constricting the pharynx.

Pharynx The area of the throat between the **uvula** and the **larynx**.

Pheromone Chemical used by an animal specifically for communicative purposes.

Phoenician script An early writing system that had twenty-two consonantal signs, devised by the Semitic peoples of ancient Phoenicia as early as 1000 B.C.

Phonemes Distinctive sounds in a language that contrast with other sounds in that language (e.g., the sounds [ɪ] and [i] as in *rich* and *reach* contrast with each other as separate phonemes in English but not in Spanish).

Phonemic level *See* **Phonemic representation**.

Phonemic paraphasias Speech errors that result from phonemic substitutions and omissions (e.g., *spoon* may be pronounced as *poon*).

Phonemic representation The representation that consists of the phonemes to which allophones belong; predictable phonetic information is not represented.

Phonemic transcription A type of transcription of sounds where phonetic details are ignored and only phonemic contrast is recorded.

Phones Any sounds used in human language (also called **speech sounds**).

Phonetic determinative The part of a Chinese character that provides information about the pronunciation of the corresponding morpheme.

Phonetic level *See* **Phonetic representation**.

Phonetic plausibility strategy The primary strategy used to reconstruct protoforms that requires any sound changes posited to be phonetically plausible. (*See also* **Majority rules strategy**.)

Phonetic representation What is actually produced in speech after rules have been applied to the **underlying representation** (i.e., predictable variants, or **allophones**).

Phonetic sound change A sound change that results in a new allophone of an already existing phoneme.

Phonetic transcription A type of transcription of sounds in which not only phonemic differences but also phonetic details are recorded.

Phonetically conditioned change Sound change that begins as subtle alterations in the sound pattern of a language in particular phonetic environments.

Phonetics The study of the inventory and structure of the sounds of language.

Phonographic writing A type of writing in which symbols represent syllables or segments.

Phonological dyslexia A type of acquired dyslexia in which the patient seems to have lost the ability to use spelling-to-sound rules and can only read words that they have seen before.

Phonological processes *See* **Processes**.

Phonological representation *See* **Phonemic representation**.

Phonological rules Rules that relate the underlying forms of words to their phonetic forms.

Phonological (sound) change A sound change that results in the addition, elimination, or rearrangement of phonemes (e.g., splits, mergers).

Phonology The component of a grammar made up of the elements and principles that determine how sounds pattern in a language.

Phonotactics The set of constraints on how sequences of segments pattern.

Phrase A unit of syntactic structure that is built by combining words together so that the phrase consists of a **head** and an optional **specifier** and/or **complement** (e.g., *the apple, Bob, hurried to class*).

Phrase structure rule A rule that specifies how a syntactic **constituent** is formed out of other smaller syntactic constituents (e.g., IP → NP I').

Phrase structure schema The blueprint for the internal structure of phrases (*see* also **X' schema**).

Phyla The groups into which purportedly related language **stocks** are placed (also called *superstocks*).

Pictograms Pictorial representations of objects or events.

Pidgin A **lingua franca** with a highly simplified grammatical structure that has emerged as a mixture of two or more languages and has no native speakers.

Pinyin The system of writing Mandarin with a modified Latin alphabet, used for such things as street signs and brand names.

Pitch The auditory property of a sound that enables us to place it on a scale that ranges from low to high.

Place features Phonological features that represent place of articulation.

Place node A node in the feature geometry in autosegmental phonology, which dominates major place features.

Place or manner assimilation The process by which one segment becomes more like another in either the place at which it is articulated or the manner by which it is articulated.

Places of articulation The points at which the airstream is modified in the vocal tract to produce **phones** (also called *points of articulation*).

Plural An inflectional category associated with nouns with more than one referent.

Points of articulation *See* **Places of articulation**.

Polysemy The situation in which a word has two or more related meanings (e.g., *bright* 'intelligent', *bright* 'shining').

Polysynthetic languages Languages in which single words can consist of long strings of lexical categories and affixes, often expressing the meaning of an entire sentence in English (e.g., Inuktitut).

Positive evidence Grammatical utterances in the learner's linguistic environment.

Positive face The need of every person to belong to a group and to maintain solidarity with a group.

Positive politeness The use of politeness conventions to express regard and solidarity with other participants in discourse.

Positron emission tomography (PET) A brain imaging technique that uses radioactive isotopes to measure changes in brain metabolism associated with particular cognitive and behavioral tasks.

Postal survey A linguistic survey given in the form of a written questionnaire and distributed by mailing batches of questionnaires to selected intermediaries in the community who then pass them on to subjects.

Postlexical decomposition The process by which the constituents of a multimorphemic word are activated in the brain through the representation of the whole lexical item.

Postposition A P that occurs after its complement. (*See* **Preposition**.)

Postvocalic *r* An *r* that occurs after a vowel in the same syllable (e.g., the *r* in *core* or *darling*).

Power The degree of control that one group or individual may hold over another.

Pragmatics Speakers' and addressees' background attitudes and beliefs, their understanding of the context of an utterance, and their knowledge of how language can be used for a variety of purposes.

Predicate A traditional term for the verb phrase in a sentence.

Prefix An **affix** that is attached to the front of its base (e.g., *re-* in *replay*).

Prelexical decomposition The computational process by which the individual morphemes of a multimorphemic word are scanned and isolated in the brain.

Preposition (P) A minor **lexical category** whose members typically designate relations in space or time (e.g., *in, before*); they come before the NP complement with which they combine to form a PP.

Prescriptive (grammar) A grammar that aims to state the linguistic facts in terms of how they should be. (*See also* **Descriptive [grammar]**.)

Presupposition The assumption or belief implied by the use of a particular word or structure.

Prewriting Possible forerunners of writing, such as incised bone or clay counters used to keep records.

Primary stress The most prominent stress of a word.

Prime In a priming experiment, this is the stimulus that is expected to affect a subject's **response accuracy** and **response latency** to the following stimulus.

Priming A situation in which the presentation of a stimulus makes it easier to process the following stimulus.

Priming effect In a priming experiment, this is the extent to which a priming stimulus facilitates the processing of the next stimulus.

Principal component A set of variables that when taken together, show patterns of variation that provide the best statistical fit for determining how test subjects should be grouped together.

Principal components analysis (PCA) An approach to studying social differentiation in which the statistical investigation of a large number of linguistic variants precedes determining what social similarities are shared among them.

Principle A The syntactic principle that constrains the interpretation of reflexive pronouns and is formulated as: A **reflexive pronoun** must have an antecedent (within the same clause) that c-commands it.

Principle B The syntactic principle that constrains the interpretation of pronominals and is formulated as: A **pronominal** must not have an antecedent (within the same clause) that c-commands it.

Principle of Compositionality, The A principle underlying sentence interpretation that is formulated as: The meaning of a sentence is determined by the meaning of its component parts and the manner in which they are arranged in syntactic structure.

Processes *See* **Articulatory processes**.

Proclitic A **clitic** that attaches to the beginning of a word.

Productivity In morphology, the relative freedom with which affixes can combine with bases of the appropriate category.

Progressive assimilation Assimilation in which a sound influences a following segment (e.g., liquid-glide devoicing).

Pronominal A pronoun whose interpretation may, but does not have to, be determined by an antecedent in the same sentence (e.g., *he, her*).

Pronoun (Pro) A minor **lexical category** whose members can replace a noun phrase and look to another element for their interpretation (e.g., *he, herself, it*).

Prosodic properties *See* **Suprasegmental properties**.

Prosody Rhythm, prominence, or intonation, often used to separate parts of a sentence, emphasize selected elements, or communicate other important information.

Protoform The form that is reconstructed as the source of cognate words in related languages.

Proto-Indo-European (PIE) The protolanguage from which evolved most of the languages of Europe, Persia (Iran), and the northern part of India.

Protolanguage The reconstructed language that is presumed to be the common source for two or more related languages (e.g., Proto-Indo-European).

Prototypical Characteristic of the best exemplars of a concept (e.g., robins or sparrows are prototypes of the concept BIRD).

Psycholinguistic model A schematic representation based on experimental results of how language is processed mentally.

Psycholinguistics The study of the mental processes and representations involved in language comprehension and production.

Q feature In syntax, a feature in the **complementizer** position that marks a sentence as a question and that may attract elements (such as an **auxiliary verb**) to the complementizer position.

Radical The part of a Chinese character that provides clues about the morpheme's meaning (also called a *key*).

Reading The interpretation for a particular utterance.

Real-world knowledge Knowledge of what is likely in real life.

Reanalysis A source of language change that involves an attempt to attribute an internal structure to a word that formerly was not broken down into component morphemes (e.g., *ham + burger*).

Rebus principle In writing, the use of a sign for any word that is pronounced like the word whose meaning the sign represented initially.

Recast A repetition of a child's utterance that includes adjustments to its form and/or content.

Recursion Repeated application of the same rule to create a more and more complex sentence, such as a series of embedded clauses (e.g., *This is the cat that killed the rat that ate the malt that lay in the house that Jack built*).

Reduced A phonological characteristic of schwa [ə], indicating a weakly articulated, unstressed variant of stressed vowels.

Reduced vowel *See* **Schwa**.

Redundancy The use of different modalities to convey the same information.

Reduplication A morphological process that repeats all or part of the base to which it is attached. (*See also* **Partial reduplication** and **Full reduplication**.)

Reference resolution Identifying who or what a **referring expression** is naming.

Referents The set of entities to which a word or expression refers (also called its **denotation** or **extension**).

Referring expressions Words or expressions (typically nouns or pronouns) that name entities (e.g., *Johanna, the class, they*).

Reflexive pronoun A pronoun that must have a c-commanding antecedent, usually in the same clause (e.g., *himself, herself*).

Regional dialect A speech variety spoken in a particular geographical area (e.g., Appalachian English).

Register A speech variety appropriate to a particular speech situation (e.g., formal versus casual).

Register tones Tones that have a stable pitch over a single syllable.

Regressive assimilation Assimilation in which a sound influences a preceding segment (e.g., **nasalization** in English).

Regressive saccades Eye movements in which the eyes dart backward to a section of text that has been previously read.

+ Rel feature In syntax, a feature in the complementizer position that attracts the WH- word of a **relative clause** to the **specifier** position of CP.

Relational analysis A syntactic analysis in which phenomena are described in terms of grammatical relations such as **subject** and

direct object rather than morphological patterns or the order of words.

Relative clause A sentence-like construction that follows a noun (in English) and gives information about the noun it follows (e.g., the linguistics class *that my favorite professor teaches*).

Relexification Hypothesis The hypothesis that **creoles** are formed by using words from one language and the grammatical system of another.

Relic forms Forms that used to be widespread in a language but have survived only in a particular dialect (e.g., **a-prefixing** is a relic form in Appalachian English).

Representations Models of one aspect of language (e.g., phonological representation, syntactic representation).

Response accuracy The correctness of a subject's responses to particular stimuli in an experiment.

Response latency The amount of time taken by a subject in an experiment to respond to a stimulus.

Retroflex Sounds produced by curling the tongue tip back into the mouth (e.g., American English [ɹ]).

Rhotacism A type of weakening that typically involves the change of /z/ to /r/.

Rhyme (R) The **nucleus** and the **coda** of a syllable (e.g., [uts] in the word *boots*).

Right ear advantage (REA) A phenomenon where speech is louder and clearer when it is heard in the right ear than in the left ear for right-handed people.

Root (of a word) In a complex word, the morpheme that remains after all affixes are removed (e.g., *mind* in *unmindfulness*).

Root (of the tongue) The part of the tongue that is contained in the upper part of the throat.

Root node The highest node of the feature hierarchy.

Round A place feature that characterizes sounds made by protruding the lips (e.g., [ɔ], [w]).

Rounded (sounds) Sounds made with the lips protruding (e.g., [ow], [ɔ]).

Rounding The act of protruding the lips to make **rounded sounds**.

Runic writing A writing system that was developed shortly after the beginning of the Christian era by Germanic tribes and that lasted until the sixteenth century.

Saccades The quick and uneven movements of the eyes during reading.

Schwa The mid lax unrounded vowel that is characterized by briefer duration than any of the other vowels (also called a **reduced vowel**) (e.g., the underlined vowels in *Can<u>a</u>d<u>a</u>, s<u>u</u>ppose*).

Second language acquisition (SLA) The acquisition of a language that is not one's native language.

Secondary stress The second most prominent stress in a word.

Segmental change A sound change that affects a segment.

Segments Individual speech sounds.

Semantic broadening The process in which the meaning of a word becomes more general or more inclusive than its historically earlier form (e.g., the word *aunt* used to mean only 'father's sister').

Semantic decomposition *See* **Componential analysis**.

Semantic features The components of meaning that make up a word's **intension** (e.g., *man* has the feature [+human]; *dog* has the feature [-human]).

Semantic narrowing The process in which the meaning of a word becomes less general or less inclusive than its historically earlier meaning (e.g., the word *meat* used to mean any type of food).

Semantic shift The process in which a word loses its former meaning, taking on a new, often related meaning (e.g., *immoral* used to mean 'not customary').

Semantics The study of meaning in human language.

Semiotics The study of signs.

Sensory aphasia *See* **Fluent aphasia**.

Sentence (IP) A syntactic unit consisting of a noun phrase and a verb phrase.

Sentence ambiguity The possibility that a sentence can be interpreted in more than one way.

Sequential change Sound change that involves sequences of segments (e.g., **assimilation**).

Serial processing model A psycholinguistic theory built around the claim that language processing proceeds in a step-by-step manner.

Seriation A child's ability to arrange objects in order of increasing or decreasing size.

Setting Contextual information having to do with the physical environment in which a sentence is uttered.

Sheltered instruction A type of English as a second language (ESL) program that combines English language instruction with instruction in academic content for English language learners in U.S. schools.

Shift A change in a phonological system in which a series of phonemes is systematically modified so that their organization with respect to each other is altered (e.g., the **Great English Vowel Shift**).

Shortest move The requirement in syntax that constituents should be moved the shortest possible distance from their original position.

Sibilants *See* **Stridents**.

Sign A unit of communication structure that consists of two parts: a **signifier** (such as a sequence of sounds [tri]) and something **signified** (such as a tree in the real world).

Signal A sign that triggers a specific action on the part of the receiver (e.g., traffic lights).

Signified The real-world object that a sign represents, as well as the sign's conceptual content.

Signifier That part of a sign that stimulates at least one sense organ of the receiver of a message.

Similarity Differential Rate Hypothesis The hypothesis that claims that the rates of acquisition for dissimilar phenomena in two languages are faster than for similar phenomena.

Simple vowels Vowels that do not show a noticeable change in quality during their production (also called *monophthongs*) (e.g., the vowel sounds of c*a*b and g*e*t).

Simple word A word that consists of a single **morpheme** (e.g., *horse*).

Single-route model A psycholinguistic theory built around the claim that a particular type of language processing is accomplished in one manner only.

Singular An inflectional category associated with nouns with a single referent.

Situational code-switching Switching between languages for clearly identifiable reasons, such as when reporting the speech of another or when the topic of conversation switches from personal to business affairs.

Size and shape classifiers (SASSes) In sign languages, hand shapes that represent the size or shape of an object and that can be combined with morphemes of motion, location, or manner of movement to form morphologically complex structures. (*See also* **classifier constructions**).

Slang An informal nonstandard speech variety characterized by newly coined and rapidly changing vocabulary.

Social network analysis An approach to sociolinguistic research in which the researcher is a participant-observer of a social group and interprets linguistic variation in terms of the kinds and densities of relationships experienced by speakers.

Sociolect A speech variety spoken by a group of people who share a particular social characteristic, such as socioeconomic class, ethnicity, or age.

Sociolinguistic competence The ability to understand and produce a variety of social dialects in appropriate circumstances.

Sociolinguistic norms Conventions for use of language structures in particular social situations.

Sociolinguistic variables Alternative ways of saying the same thing.

Sociolinguistics The study of the social aspects of language.

Sociolinguistics of language The study of how language structures are associated with particular social circumstances.

Sociolinguistics of society The study of how language structures are related to a speaker's social identity.

Solidarity The degree of intimacy or similarity that one group or individual may feel for another.

Song In bird communication, lengthy, elaborate patterns of mostly pitched sounds.

Sonorant (feature) A major class feature that characterizes all and only the "singables": vowels, glides, liquids, and nasals.

Sonorant (sound) A sound that is "singable," in contrast with an **obstruent**.

Sonorous Characterized by a relatively open vocal tract with relatively little obstruction of airflow as a sound is made (e.g., vowels are sonorous sounds).

Sound change A systematic change of sounds that took place over a long period.

Sound class *See* **Class (sound)**.

Sound shift The systematic modification of a series of phonemes (e.g., Grimm's Law).

Source A **thematic role** that describes the starting point for a movement (e.g., *Maine* in *The senator sent the lobster from Maine to Nebraska*).

Southern Shift The systematic change in pronunciation of vowels in the southern states of the United States. (*See also* **Shift**.)

Spatial metaphor Use of a word that is primarily associated with spatial orientation to talk about physical and psychological states.

Speaker-dependent speech recognizers Computer programs that decode the spoken language of a particular individual.

Speaker-independent speech recognizers Computer programs that are able to decode the spoken language of many individuals (e.g., for customer service telephone calls).

Specifier A word that helps to make more precise the meaning of the **head** of the phrase and that occurs immediately beneath XP (e.g., *the* in *the book*).

Spectrogram An acoustic recording that graphically shows the frequency, intensity, and time of sounds.

Speech act theory A theory explaining how speakers use language to accomplish intended actions and how hearers infer intended meaning from what is said.

Speech community A group whose members share both a particular language or variety of language and the norms for its appropriate use in social context.

Speech event An identifiable type of discourse associated with a particular speech situation.

Speech recognition The ability (e.g., of a computer) to decode the waveforms that constitute spoken language.

Speech situation The social situation in which language is used.

Speech sounds *See* **Phones**.

Speech synthesis system A computerized system (sometimes called text-to-speech synthesis) that converts written text to spoken language (e.g., reading aloud to the visually impaired).

Speech variety The language or form of language used by any group of speakers.

Spelling pronunciation One factor in sound change, where a new pronunciation reflects the spelling of the word (e.g., *often*).

Split brain experiments Studies that investigate the effects of surgically severing the **corpus callosum**.

Splits Phonological changes in which two allophones become separate phonemes due to the loss of the conditioning environment.

Spoonerisms A type of speech error, named after Reverend William A. Spooner, in which words or sounds are rearranged with often humorous results.

Spread Glottis (SG) A laryngeal feature that refers to the position of the **vocal folds** and that distinguishes unaspirated from aspirated sounds.

Spreading Association of a feature to neighboring segments in autosegmental phonology.

S-structure *See* **Surface structure**.

Standard language The prestige variety of a language that is employed by the government and media, is used and taught in educational institutions, and is the main or only written variety.

Stem The base to which an inflectional **affix** is added (e.g., *modification* is the stem for *-s* in the word *modifications*).

Stem-based dictionary In computational linguistics, a dictionary that lists stems rather than words (e.g., it would list *-cept* as a stem rather than the words *reception* or *perception*).

Stemming A computer program for doing automated morphological analysis by stripping affixes off words and matching base forms to forms stored in the database.

Stimulus-bound communication Communication that only occurs when it is triggered by exposure to a certain stimulus or for certain specific ends (e.g., the warning call of a bird).

Stocks In language classification, groups of related language families.

Stopping In child language acquisition, the replacement of a fricative by a corresponding stop (e.g., *zebra* is pronounced [dibrə]).

Stops Sounds made with a complete and momentary closure of airflow through the vocal tract (e.g., [p], [t], [k]).

Stress *See* **Stressed vowels**.

Stressed vowels Vowels that are perceived as relatively more prominent due to the combined effects of pitch, loudness, and length.

Strident A place feature of fricatives and affricates characterized by greater acoustic noise (in English, [s, z, ʃ, ʒ, tʃ, dʒ]).

Stridents The noisier coronal fricatives and affricates (in English, [s, z, ʃ, ʒ, tʃ, dʒ]) (also called **sibilants**).

Stroke A hemorrhage in the brain or the blockage or rupture of an artery, causing brain damage (also called a **cerebrovascular accident**).

Strong generative capacity Capacity to describe correctly the structures of the strings of a language.

Structurally ambiguous A property of phrases or sentences whose component words can be combined in more than one way (e.g., *fast cars and motorcycles*).

Style The level of formality associated with a linguistic structure or set of structures classified along a continuum from most informal to most formal.

Subcategorization The classification of words in terms of their complement options (e.g., the verb *devour* is subcategorized for a complement NP).

Subject The NP occurring immediately under IP (e.g., *Irene* in *Irene is a tailor)*.

Subject Constraint, The A constraint on transformations that prevents elements from being moved out of a subject phrase.

Subject-object agreement Agreement of verbs in person and number with their subjects and objects.

Subordinate clauses Sentence-like constructions that are embedded inside other sentences (e.g., the string of words beginning with *that* in *Jamie told me that Johanna is graduating soon*).

Subset Principle, The The initial or default setting of a parameter will correspond to the option that permits fewer patterns.

Substitution (of sounds) Replacement of one segment with another similar sounding segment.

Substitution test A test used to determine if a group of words is a syntactic **constituent** by replacing it with a single word.

Substrate language A language hypothesized to have supplied the basic grammatical structure for a contact variety.

Substratum influence The influence of a politically or culturally nondominant language on a dominant language in the area (e.g., the borrowing of words into English from Native American languages).

Suffix An **affix** that is attached to the end of its base (e.g., *-ly* in *quickly*).

Sulci Plural of **sulcus**.

Sulcus An area in the brain where the **cerebral cortex** is folded in.

Superstratum influence The influence of a politically or culturally dominant language on a less dominant language in the area (e.g., the effects of Norman French on English during the Middle English period).

Suppletion A morphological process that marks a grammatical contrast by replacing a morpheme with an entirely different morpheme (e.g., *be/was*).

Suprasegmental Above the individual speech sound. (Syllables are suprasegmental.)

Suprasegmental properties Those properties of sounds that form part of their makeup no matter what their place or manner of articulation: pitch, loudness, and length (also called **prosodic properties**).

Surface dyslexia A type of acquired dyslexia in which the patient seems unable to recognize words as wholes, but must process all words through a set of spelling-to-sound rules (e.g., *yacht* would be pronounced /jæʧt/).

Surface representation In phonology, the form that is actually produced by a speaker. Also called **phonetic representation**.

Surface structure The structure that results from the application of whatever transformations are appropriate for the sentence in question (also called **S-structure**).

Syllabary A set of signs used for writing the syllables of a language.

Syllabic A major phonological class feature assigned to segments that function as the nuclei of syllables (vowels and liquids).

Syllabic (sounds) Sounds that could be peaks of syllables (e.g., vowels in English).

Syllabic liquids Liquids that function as syllabic nuclei (e.g., the *l* in *bottle*).

Syllabic nasals Nasals that function as syllabic nuclei (e.g., the *n* in *button*).

Syllabic writing A type of writing in which each symbol represents a syllable.

Syllable A unit of linguistic structure that consists of a syllabic element and any segments that are associated with it. (*See also* **Onset**, **Nucleus**, **Coda**.)

Symbolic model A psycholinguistic theory built around the claim that models of linguistic knowledge make reference to rules and representations consisting of symbols such as phonemes, words, syntactic category labels, and so forth.

Symbolic sign A sign that bears an arbitrary relationship to its referent (e.g., nononomatopoeic words, a stop sign).

Symptomatic sign A sign that spontaneously and involuntarily conveys an internal state or an emotion (e.g., crying).

Syncope The deletion of a word-internal vowel (e.g., the deletion of the schwa in *po̲lice*).

Synonyms Words or expressions that have the same meanings in some or all contexts (e.g., *buy* and *purchase*).

Synsets Sets of synonyms that act as definitions for a word in the WordNet machine-readable lexical resource.

Syntactic category The category into which an element is placed depending on the type of meaning that it expresses, the type of affixes it takes, and the type of structure in which it occurs (includes both lexical and functional categories).

Syntactic parser The theoretical construct that accounts for the human ability to assign grammatical categories and hierarchical structure to elements in a stream of language input.

Syntax The system of rules and categories that underlies sentence formation in human language.

Synthetic language A language that makes extensive use of polymorphemic words (e.g., words containing a root and one or more affixes) (also called an **inflectional language**) (e.g., Spanish).

Systematic gaps Nonoccurring forms that would violate the phonotactic constraints of a language (e.g., in English **mtlow*).

Systematic phonetic correspondences Sound correspondences between two or more related languages that are consistent throughout the vocabularies of those languages.

Taboo Expressions that are seen as offensive and are therefore often euphemized.

Target (1) In second language acquisition, the language the learner is learning. (2) In a priming experiment, the stimulus to which a subject must respond and for which **response accuracy** and **response latency** are measured.

Teacher talk *See* **Foreigner talk**.

Telegraphic speech Speech lacking functional categories and bound morphemes.

Telegraphic stage The stage in child language acquisition in which children's utterances are generally longer than two words but lack bound morphemes and most functional categories.

Telephone survey A linguistic survey conducted over the telephone.

Template The innate blueprint of birdsong that predisposes birds to perform a general song that is extremely simplified.

Template generation In computational linguistics, the creation of sentences by using a set of basic patterns (e.g., for an air-travel reservation system).

Temporal lobe The lobe of the brain that lies beneath the lateral fissure and in which Wernicke's area is located.

Tense (feature) A DORSAL feature that expresses the distinction between a **tense** and a **lax vowel**.

Tense (verb) In syntax and morphology, an inflectional category indicating the time of an event or action relative to the moment of speaking.

Tense vowels Vowels that are made with a relatively tense tongue and greater vocal tract constriction than a **lax vowel** (e.g., the vowel sounds in *he̲a̲t* and *bo̲a̲t*).

Terminal (intonation) contour Falling intonation at the end of an utterance, signaling that the utterance is complete.

Terminals The lexical items or prefixes, suffixes, stems, or words of a language.

Text analysis A type of discourse analysis that studies how linguistic structures are used to perform particular discourse functions.

Textual competence Competence in the organization of language beyond the sentence.

***That*-trace filter** Constraint against having both *that* and a trace inside a CP.

Thematic grid The part of a word's lexical entry that carries information about the thematic roles that it assigns.

Thematic role The part played by a particular entity in an event (e.g., agent, theme, source, goal, location).

Theme The **thematic role** of the entity directly affected by the action of the verb (e.g., *the ball* in *Tom caught the ball*).

Thyroid cartilage The cartilage that forms the main portion of the larynx, spreading outward like the head of a plow.

Tiers Different levels of structure in which only certain elements are represented (e.g., in phonology, a syllabic tier and a tonal tier; in morphology, an affix tier and a root tier).

Tip (of the tongue) The narrow area at the front of the tongue.

Tip-of-the-tongue phenomena Instances of temporary inability to access a word in the mental lexicon.

Token An individual instance of a variable or sign.

Tone Pitch differences that signal differences in meaning.

Tone language A language in which differences in word meaning are signaled by differences in pitch.

(Tongue) back *See* **Back**.

(Tongue) blade *See* **Blade**.

(Tongue) body *See* **Body**.

(Tongue) dorsum *See* **Dorsum**.

(Tongue) root *See* **Root**.

(Tongue) tip *See* **Tip**.

Top-down parsing A method of sentence analysis in which the entire sentence is considered first, before its component parts.

Top-down processing A type of mental processing using a set of expectations to guide phonetic processing and word recognition.

Topic What a sentence or group of sentences is about.

Topicalization The process by which the topic of a sentence is moved to the front of the sentence (e.g., *Vanilla pudding I like*).

Total assimilation The **assimilation** of all the features of neighboring segments.

Trace The empty element, marked by the symbol *t*, that is left in syntactic structure after an element has been moved.

Trachea The tube below the larynx through which air travels when it leaves the lungs, commonly known as the windpipe.

Transfer The process by which the first language (L1) influences the **interlanguage** grammar of the learner of a second language.

Transformation A type of syntactic rule that can move an element from one position to another.

Transformational generative grammar A widely accepted approach to syntactic analysis in which syntactic phenomena are described in terms of building phrase structures and moving elements (transformations) as a result of **Merge** and **Move** operations.

Transitional bilingual education An educational program for language minority students in which initial instruction is provided in the minority language along with the majority language, but full literacy in the minority language is not a goal. (Compare with **developmental bilingual education**).

Transitive *See* **Transitive verb**.

Transitive verb A verb that takes a **direct object** (e.g., *hit*).

Tree A diagram that represents the internal organization of a word, phrase, or sentence.

Trill An *r*-like sound that is made by passing air over the raised tongue tip, allowing it to vibrate.

Truth conditions The circumstances under which a sentence is true.

Turn-taking The changeover between speakers' turns in a conversation.

Two-level morphology In computational linguistics, an approach to morphological analysis that uses a **stem-based dictionary** and rules to derive surface forms from the underlying stems.

Two-way immersion (TWI) programs Educational programs that provide instruction in two languages for language minority students and language majority students together (also known as **dual-language programs**).

Two-word stage A stage of first language acquisition in which children normally utter two succeeding words to make a sentence.

Typological plausibility A criterion that guides language reconstruction by referring to universals or existing properties of language.

Umlaut The effect that a vowel (or sometimes a glide) in one syllable can have on the vowel of another (usually preceding) syllable.

Underextension A developmental phenomenon in which a child uses a lexical item to denote only a subset of the items that it denotes in adult speech (e.g., *car* used to refer to only moving cars).

Underlying Unpredictable and basic (e.g., features of a phonemic segment before **derivation**).

Underlying form *See* **underlying representation**.

Underlying representation In phonology, a form from which phonetic forms are derived by rule.

Universal Grammar (UG) The system of categories, operations, and principles shared by all human languages and considered to be innate.

Universal tendencies Patterns or traits that occur in all or most languages.

Unmarked Tending to be relatively common in world languages and/or less complex. (*See also* **Unmarked traits**.)

Unmarked traits Those characteristics of language that are considered to be less complex and/or universally more common in languages.

Unordered rule application In a phonological **derivation**, an application of rules in which the outcome will be the same regardless of the order in which rules are applied.

Utterance Any bit of talk produced by a speaker that is distinct from other bits of talk in a speech situation.

Uvula The small fleshy flap of tissue that hangs down from the velum.

Uvulars Sounds made with the tongue near or touching the **uvula**.

Variable rule analysis Method of analyzing sociolinguistic data in which statistical procedures allow a variety of social and linguistic factors to be considered simultaneously.

Variant One of a set of several possible forms that can be used to express the same function or meaning.

Velars Sounds made with the tongue touching or near the **velum** (e.g., [ŋ], [k]).

Velum The soft area toward the rear of the roof of the mouth.

Verb (V) A **lexical category** that typically designates actions, sensations, and states; can usually be inflected for **tense**; and functions as the **head** of a verb phrase (e.g., *see, feel, remain*).

Verb Movement Parameter A cross-linguistic variation involving whether the verb does or does not raise to I.

Verb raising transformation A syntactic rule that moves the verb to the I position in **S-structure** in languages such as French.

Verbal hedges Words or phrases that make statements less assertive (e.g., *maybe, sort of*).

Verbal paradigm The set of inflected forms associated with a verb (also called a **conjugation**).

Verner's Law A generalization made by Karl Verner, which states that a word-internal voiceless fricative resulting from **Grimm's Law** underwent voicing if the original Proto-Indo-European accent did not immediately precede it.

Vocal cords *See* **Vocal folds**.

Vocal folds A set of muscles inside the larynx that may be positioned in various ways to produce different glottal states (also called **vocal cords**).

Vocal tract The oral cavity, nasal cavity, and pharynx.

Voice A laryngeal feature that distinguishes between **voiced** and **voiceless** sounds.

Voiced The glottal state in which the **vocal folds** are brought close together but not tightly closed, causing air passing through them to vibrate (e.g., [æ], [z], [m] are voiced).

Voiceless The glottal state in which the **vocal folds** are pulled apart, allowing air to pass directly through the glottis (e.g., [t], [s], [f] are voiceless).

Voicing A historical process of **consonant weakening** in which voiceless stops or fricatives become voiced.

Voicing assimilation Process in which one sound becomes more like another sound in terms of whether it is **voiced** or **voiceless**.

Vowel harmony Phonological phenomenon in which all vowels of a word share one or more features (e.g., all [+back, +round]).

Vowel qualities Vowel sounds.

Vowel reduction A process that converts a full vowel, typically unstressed, to the short, lax **schwa**.

Vowel shift *See* **Shift**.

Vowels Resonant, syllabic sounds produced with less obstruction in the vocal tract than that required for glides.

Weak generative capacity Capacity to describe properly all the strings of a language.

Weakening (phonetic) A type of **assimilation** in which a lessening in the time or degree of a consonant's closure occurs (also called lenition).

Weakening of meaning The process in which the meaning of a word has less force (e.g., *soon* used to mean 'immediately' but now means 'in the near future').

Wernicke's aphasia The **aphasia** that results in fluent but nonsensical speech, sometimes characterized by **jargonaphasia**.

Wernicke's area The area of the brain involved in the interpretation and the selection of lexical items.

***Wh* Movement** A **transformation** that moves a *wh* phrase to the beginning of the sentence, formulated as: Move a *wh* phrase to the specifier position under CP.

***Wh* question** A sentence that begins with a *wh*- word such as *who, what, where, when* (e.g., *Who did you see?*).

Whisper The glottal state in which the **vocal folds** are adjusted so that the front portions are pulled close together while the back portions are apart.

Word The smallest free form found in language.

Word manufacture The creation of a word from scratch, sometimes with the help of a computer (also called **coinage**) (e.g., *Kodak*).

Word-based dictionary In computational linguistics, a dictionary that lists words only and not stems that are not words (e.g., the word *reception* would be listed but not the stem *-cept*).

Word-based morphology Morphology that can form a new word from a base that is itself a word (e.g., *re-do* and *treat-ment* in English).

Writing The representation of language by graphic signs or symbols.

X' rule A phrase structure rule that deals with intermediate categories, which states that an intermediate category X' consists of a head, X, and any optional complements.

X' schema The template for phrase structure, indicating that a phrase is hierarchically organized with a head, complement, and specifier.

XP rule A phrase structure rule that deals with maximal categories, which states that a maximal category XP consists of an optional specifier and an X'.

***Yes-no* questions** Questions that require an answer of either *yes* or *no* (e.g., *Is linguistics interesting? Do you speak a second language?*).

Zero derivation *See* **Conversion**.

Acknowledgments

Chapter 1

Word creation discussion adapted from "When Nouns Surface as Verbs" by Eve Clark and Herb Clark in *Language* 55 (1979): 767–811. Reprinted by permission of the Linguistic Society of America.

Walbiri data adapted from "Person Marking in Walbiri" in *A Festschrift for Morris Halle* edited by Stephen R. Anderson and Paul Kiparsky. © 1973 Stephen R. Anderson and Paul Kiparsky. Reprinted by permission of Thomson Learning.

Word order preference data adapted from p. 46 in *Typology and Universals,* 1st edition, by William Croft. Copyright © 1990 by William Croft. Reprinted with the permission of Cambridge University Press.

Chapter 2

International Phonetic Alphabet data from the International Phonetic Association, University College, Gower Street, London, WC1E 6BT, England. www.arts.gla.ac.uk.

Figure 2.10. Sarcee data from "Vowels and Tones in Sarcee" by E.-.D. Cook in *Language* 47: 164–79. Reprinted by permission of the Linguistic Society of America.

Table 2.22. Scots Gaelic data courtesy of James Galbraith.

Chapter 3

Tables 3.12 and 3.16. "Nasalization in Malay," "Phonetic and phonemic transcription of Malay nasal vowels." Adapted data (phonetic and phonemic transcription of Malay nasal vowels) from *Generative Phonology* by M. Kenstowicz and C. Kissberth. Copyright © 1979 by M. Kenstowicz and C. Kissberth. Reprinted with permission from Elsevier. Additional examples provided by S.I. Lee.

Data sources for problems (Mokilese) are adapted from *Mokilese Reference Grammar* by S. Harrison. Copyright © 1976 by S. Harrison. Reprinted with permission from the University of Hawaii Press.

Chapter 4

Figure 4.4. "Tier-based analysis of Arabic word structure." Adapted from data in "A Prosodic Theory of Nonconcatenative Morphology" by John McCarthy from *Linguistic Inquiry* 12 (1981): 373–418. Reprinted by permission.

Nine Arabic examples from p. 17 in *Morphological Theory* by Andrew Spencer. © 1991 by Andrew Spencer. Reprinted with the permission of Blackwell Publishers.

Chapter 5

Leslea Newman. "Tiff and I" from *Sweet Dark Places* by Leslea Newman. © 1991 Leslea Newman. Reprinted by permission of the author.

Chapter 6

Table 6.7. Words for "snow" in Inuktitut. From *The Handbook of American Indian Languages* by F. Boas. Smithsonian Institution, 1911.

Chapter 7

Table 7.1. Data on word order in Old and Middle English from *Origins of the English Language: A Social and Linguistic History* by Joseph Williams. Copyright 1975 by Joseph Williams. Reprinted by permission.

Tables 7.2–7.6. All data adapted from catalogs proposed by Theo Vennemann, "Linguistic Typologies in Historical Linguistics" in *Società di linguistica italiana 23:* (1985): 87–91 and *Preference Laws for Syllable Structure and the Explanation of Sound Change* published by Mouton de Gruyter 1988. Reprinted by permission.

Table 7.7. Palatalization—front vowels/examples of Romance languages. *Proto-Romance Phonology* by Robert A. Hall, Jr. from Elsevier, 1976. Reprinted by permission.

Chapter 8

Table 8.1. "The geographical distribution of world's living languages." Adapted from *Ethnologue: Languages of the World* 14th edition by Barbara F. Grimes. © 2003 by Barbara F. Grimes. Reprinted by permission of SIL International. www.ethnologue.com.

Table 8.2. "The world's 20 most spoken languages." Adapted from *Ethnologue: Languages of the World* 14th edition by Barbara F. Grimes. Copyright © 2003 by Barbara F. Grimes. Reprinted by permission of SIL International. www.ethnologue.com.

"Data on OVS and OSV languages." Adapted from "Object-initial Languages" by D. Derbyshire and G. Pullum in *International Journal of American Linguistics* 47 (1981): 192–214. Copyright © 1981 by D. Derbyshire & G. Pullum. Reprinted by permission of the University of Chicago Press, Journals Division.

"Discussion of consonant systems." Based on "Phonetic Universals in Consonant Systems" by B. Lindblom and I. Maddieson in *Language, Speech and Mind: Studies in Honor of Victoria Fromkin* edited by L. Hyman and C. Li. Routledge & Kegan Paul, 1988: 62–78. © 1988 by L. Hyman and C. Li. Reprinted by permission.

Figures 8.8 and 8.9. Maps adapted from pp. 83–84 in *Problems in the Origin and Development of the English Language,* 3rd edition, by John Algeo. Copyright 1982. Reprinted with permission of Heinle, a division of Thomson Learning: www.thomsonrights.com. Fax: 800–730–2215.

Figure 8.10. "North and Central American language groups." Adapted from *A Guide to the World's Languages, Volume 1* by M. Ruhlen. Copyright © 1987 by Stanford University Press. Reprinted by permission.

Chapter 9

Table 9.1. "Standard classification of North American Languages." Adapted from the *Handbook of North American Indians,* vol. 17, *Languages,* ed. by Ives Goddard. Reprinted by permission of the Smithsonian Institution.

Table 9.3. "Glottalized (ejective) consonants." Adapted from the *Handbook of North American Indians,* vol. 17, *Languages,* ed. by Ives Goddard. Reprinted by permission of the Smithsonian Institution.

Nuuchahnulth data from *Nootka Texts* by Edward Sapir and Morris Swadesh (1939). Reprinted by permission of the Linguistic Society of America.

Lakota noun incorporation from "Sketch of Lakhota, a Siouan Language" by David S. Rood and Allan R. Taylor, pp. 440–482, in *Handbook of North American Indians* by Ives Goddard, ed. Reprinted by permission of the Smithsonian Institution.

Tables 9.7 and 9.8. P. 401, 403. Examples of Wishram Chinook tenses, Central Pomo evidentials, and Tuscarora and Central Pomo grammatical roles are taken from pp. 163, 164, 181, and 209–221 of *The Languages of Native North America* by Marianne Mithun. Copyright © 1999. Cambridge University Press. Reprinted with the permission of Cambridge University Press.

Table 9.9. "Possessed nouns in Yurok." Adapted from material outlined in *The Yurok Language,* volume 15 by R.H. Robins. © 1958 University of California Publication in Linguistics. Reprinted by permission of the University of California Press.

Table 9.10. "Animate/inanimate nouns in Cree." Derived from *Meet Cree: A Guide to the Cree Language* by H.C. Wolfart and J. Carroll. Copyright © 1981 by U. Alberta Press. Used with permission of The University of Alberta Press.

Table 9.11. "Classificatory categories in Navajo." Data from pp. 2–15 in *The Navajo Verb System: An Overview* by Robert W. Young. Copyright © 2000 by Robert W. Young. Reprinted by permission of the University of New Mexico Press.

Chapter 11

Table 11.1. "Cross-linguistic similarities in babbling." Adapted from data on pp. 9–11 in *Phonological Acquisition and Change* by J. Locke. Published by Academic Press, 1983. Reprinted by permission.

Figure 11.1. "Syntax and Semantics in the Acquisition of Locative Verbs." Adapted data from *Journal of Child Language,* Volume 18 (1991): 115–51, by Jess Gropen, Steven Pinker, Michelle Hollander and Richard Goldberg. Reprinted with the permission of Cambridge University Press.

Figure 11.3. "The Child's Learning of English Morphology," from *Word* 14 (1958): 150–77. Reprinted courtesy of Jean Berko Gleason.

"Brown and Hanion Revisited: Mothers' Sensitivity to Ungrammatical Forms." Excerpted data from the *Journal of Child Language,* Volume 11 (1984): 81–82, by K. Kirsh-Pask, R. Treiman, and M. Schnelderman. Reprinted with the permission of Cambridge University Press.

Figure 11.8. "Common items in the first 50 words." Excerpted data from p. 149 in *First Language Acquisition: Method, Description and Explanation* by David Ingram. © 1989 David Ingram. Reprinted with the permission of Cambridge University Press.

"Description of Genie and Rick" based on "Abnormal Language Acquisition and the Modularity of Language," by S. Curtiss in *Linguistics: The Cambridge Survey,* volume 2, edited by F. Newmeyer, (1988): 96–116. Reprinted with the permission of Cambridge University Press.

Table 11.19. "Sample utterances from a child's speech over a 12 month period." Adapted from data on pp. 269–70 in *The Language Instinct* by Steven Pinker. Copyright © 1994 by Steven Pinker. Reprinted by permission of HarperCollins Publishers, Inc.

Table 11.21. "Some Examples of Maternal Speech." Adapted from "Derivational Complexity and the Order of Acquisition in Child Speech," by R. Brown and C. Hanlon in *Cognition and the Development of Language* edited by J. Haynes. Copyright © 1970 by J. Haynes. Reprinted by permission of John Wiley & Sons, Inc.

"Children's use of *me* and *myself*" from "Children's Knowledge of Binding and Coreference: Evidence from Spontaneous Speech" by P. Bloom, A. Barss, J. Nicol, and L. Conway in *Language* 70 (1994): 53–71. Reprinted by permission of the Linguistic Society of America.

"*WH* questions" adapted from data documented (pp. 1084–92), "WH questions: Linguistic Factors That Can Contribute to the Sequence of Acquisition" in *Child Development* 53, 1982 by L. Bloom, S. Merkin, and J. Wooten. Reprinted by permission of Blackwell Publishing.

"Acquisition of passive structures." Adapted from a study by E. Turner and R. Rommetveit, reprinted in "The Acquisition of Sentence Voice and Reversibility" in *Child Development* 38, 1967 (pp. 650–60). Reprinted by permission of Blackwell Publishing.

Chapter 12

Ontogeny Model, adapted from "A Model for Interlanguage Phonology" by R. Major, in *Interlanguage Phonology,* edited by G. Loup and S. Weinberger. Published by Harper & Row, 1987: 101–24. Reprinted by permission of Thomson Learning.

Table 12.6. "Markedness Differential Hypothesis." Developed by F. Eckman's "Markedness and the Contrastive Analysis Hypothesis" featured in *Language Learning* 27 (1977): 315–330. Reprinted by permission of Blackwell Publishing Ltd.

Figure 12.2. Adapted data from *Fundamental Considerations in Language Testing* by L. Bachman. Copyright © 1990 by L. Bachman. Reprinted with permission from Oxford University Press.

Figure 12.4. Adapted data from Arabic syllabification, "Prosodic Phonology and the Acquisition of a Second Language," by E. Broselow in *Linguistic Theory in Second Language Acquisition* by S. Flynn and W. O'Neil, eds. Copyright © 1988 by S. Flynn and W. O'Neil, eds. Reprinted by permission of Kluwer Academic Publishers.

Stress data excerpted from *Language, Learnability and 1.2 Phonology* by J. Archibald. Copyright © 1993 by J. Archibald. Reprinted by permission of Kluwer Academic Publishers.

Null subject analysis drawn from *Universal Grammar and Second Language Acquisition* by L. White. Publisher, John Benjamins. Reprinted by permission.

Figure 12.5. Adapted data from "Adverb Placement in Second Language Acquisition: Some Effects of Positive and Negative Evidence in the Classroom" in *Second Language Research* 7 (1991). Copyright © 1991 by Arnold Publishers. Reprinted by permission of Hodder (UK).

Figure 12.6. "Null subject analysis." Adapted from *Universal Grammar and Second Language Acquisition* by L. White. Copyright © 1989 by L. White. Reprinted by permission.

"Markedness Differential Hypotheses" adapted from "Markedness and the Contrastive Analysis Hypotheses" in *Language Learning* 27 (1977): 315–30. Reprinted by permission of Blackwell Publishing.

L2 Morphology data: adapted from data on pp. 159–80, "Functional Categories and Acquisition Order," by H. Zobel and J. Liceras as published in *Language Learning* 44:1. Copyright © 1994. French gender data adapted from "Second-Language Acquisition and the Computational

Paradigm," by S. Carroll in *Language Learning* 39: 4 (1989): 535–94. Reprinted by permission of Blackwell Publishing Ltd.

Instrumental integrative distinction comes from R. Gardner, J.B. Day, and P.D. MacIntyre, in "Integrative Motivation, Induced Anxiety and Language Learning in a Controlled Environment," *Studies in Second Language Acquisition* 14: 2 (1992): 197–214. Cambridge University Press (UK). Reprinted by permission.

"Do Listeners Compute Linguistic Representations?" by M.K. Tannenhous, G.N. Calson, and M. S. Seidenberg. Sentence ambiguity adapted from *National Language Parsing,* edited by D.R. Dowty, L. Kartrunen, and A.M. Zwicky. © 1985 by M.K. Tannenhous. Reprinted with the permission of Cambridge University Press.

Chapter 13

Figure 13.4. Bar-pressing times in sentence reading. Adapted from "On-Line Processing of Written Text by Younger and Older Children" by E.A. Stine in *Psychology and Aging* 5: 68–78, fig. 1, p. 73. © 1990 by the American Psychological Association. Adapted with permission.

Figure 13.5. Adapted data from p. 103 in *Handbook of Psycholinguistics,* edited by Marta Kutas and Cyrus Van Petten. Copyright © 1994. Reprinted with permission from Elsevier.

Selected restrictions experiments/hierarchical structure adapted from "Are Morphological Structures Computed During Word Recognition?" by Libben in the *Journal of Psycholinguistic Research* 22 (1993): 535–44. © 1993 Kluwer Academic Publishers. Reprinted with permission. All rights reserved. Also adapted from "Computing Hierarchical Morphological Structure: A Case Study" by Libben in the *Journal of Neurolinguistics* 8 (1994): 49–55. © 1994 Elsevier. Reprinted with permission from Elsevier.

Section on processing of garden path sentences adapted from "Sentence Processing: A Tutorial Review," (559–96) in *Attention and Performance (XIII): The Psychology of Reading* edited by M. Coltheart. Copyright 1987 by Lawrence Erlbaum Associates, Inc. Reprinted by permission of the publisher.

Chapter 14

Figure 14.5. PET scans. Adapted from "Mind and Brain" by Gerald D. Fischbach in *Scientific American* (September 1992). Reprinted with permission by Professor Marcus E. Raichle.

Chapter 15

Table 15.2. Adapted data from *U.C.L.A. Slang: A Dictionary of Slang Words and Expressions Used at U.C.L.A. Occasional Paper in Linguistics* #8 (1989), edited by Pamela Munro. Reprinted by permission of the editor.

Table 15.4. Adapted data from "Accommodating Your Data: The Use and Misuse of Accommodation Theory in Sociolinguistics" by M. Meyerhoff, in *Language and Communication,* vol. 18, 1998, pp. 205–225. Copyright © 1998. Reprinted with permission from Elsevier.

Table 15.5. Adapted data from "Linguistic Etiquette" by C. Geertz, in *Socialinguistics* edited by J.B. Pride and Janet Holmes (1972): 167–69. Reprinted by permission of Penguin Group (UK).

Table 15.7. Adapted data from "Men's and Women's Speech in Koasati" by M. Haas, in *Language* 20: 147–49. Reprinted with the permission of the Linguistic Society of America.

Table 15.9. "Items on the linguistic insecurity text given to New Yorkers." Adapted data from *The Social Stratification of English in New York City* by William Labov. © 1966. Reprinted by permission.

Figure 15.1. Words for "fishhook" in French dialects of Atlantic Canada & western France. From "Linguistic Atlas of French Maritime Terminology" in *Journal of English Linguistics* 22 (1): 25–29 (1990), by L. Peronnet and P.A. Arsenault. Copyright © 1990. Reprinted by permission of Sage Publications.

Figure 15.2. Adapted from p. 12 in *American Regional Dialects: A Word Geography* by Craig M. Carver. © 1987 Craig M. Carver. Reprinted by permission of the University of Michigan Press.

Figure 15.3. Adapted data from *American Regional Dialects: A Word Geography* by C.M. Carver. © 1989 by C.M. Carver. Published by the University of Michigan Press; *American English: Dialects and Variation* by W. Wolfram and N. Schilling-Estes. © 1998 Published by Blackwell Ltd. (UK) and the Phonological Atlas of North America. 1999 www.ling.upenn.edu.

Tom Stoppard. Excerpt from *Rosencrantz and Guildenstern Are Dead* by Tom Stoppard. Copyright © 1967 by Tom Stoppard. Used by permission of Grove/Atlantic, Inc.

Chapter 16

Figure 16.1/a. Adapted from Andre Leroi-Gourhan, "Les animaux et les signes." In Arlette Leroi-Gourhan and J. Allain (eds.) Lascaux inconnu, 13th supplément à Gallia Préhistoire (Paris: CNRS 1979).

Figure 16.1/b. "Le Placard eagle bone." From *The Roots of Civilization: The Cognitive Beginnings of Man's First Art, Symbol, and Notation* by Alexander Marshack. © 1971, 1972 by Alexander Marshack. Reprinted by permission of McGraw-Hill.

Figure 16.2. Ancient Mesopotamian tokens. "Two Precursors of Writing: Plain and Complex Tokens" (pp. 27–42) by Denise Schmandt-Besserat. From *The Origins of Writing,* ed. by W.M. Senner. Copyright © 1989 by Musée du Louvre. Reprinted by permission.

Figure 16.3. "Aboriginal pictography." Adapted from p. 43 in *Sign, Symbol and Script: An Account of Man's Efforts to Write,* 3rd edition by Hans Jensen. Translated and revised by G. Unwin. Reprinted by permission.

Figure 16.4. Contemporary pictograms. Courtesy of the Olympic Trust of Canada. Official Mark © Canadian Olympic Association, 1972.

Figure 16.5. "Sumerian logograms." Adapted from *Sign, Symbol and Script: An Account of Man's Efforts to Write,* 3rd edition, revised and English translation by G. Unwin. George Allen and Unwin. Reprinted by permission.

Figure 16.6. The Sumerian logogram for "anger" from *Manuel d'Epigraphie Akkadienne,* 5th edition by Rene Labat, P. Geuthner, 1976.

Figure 16.7. "Sumerian rebus inscription." From "Über die protosumerische Schrift" in *Acta Antigua Academiae Scientiarum Hungaricae* 22 by A.A. Viaman. (1974): 18. As reproduced in *Visible Speech: The Diverse Oneness of Writing Systems* by John DeFrancis. University of Hawaii Press, 1989, p. 76. Reprinted by permission.

Figure 16.8. "Overlapped Sumerian syllabic signs." Adapted from p. 95 in *Sign, Symbol and Script: An Account of Man's Efforts to Write,* 3rd edition, by Hans Jensen. Revised and English translation by G. Unwin. George Allen and Unwin. Reprinted by permission.

Figure 16.9. "Changes in cuneiform writing" illustration. Reprinted from *The Origins of Writing* by Wayne M. Senner, by permission of the University of Nebraska Press. Copyright © 1989 by the University of Nebraska Press.

Figure 16.10. "Egyptian hieroglyph." Adapted from p. 66 in *Sign, Symbol, and Script: An Account of Man's Efforts to Write,* 3rd edition, by Hans Jensen. Translated by George Unwin. Allen & Unwin. Reprinted by permission.

Figure 16.11. "Pictorial and logographic origins of some signs in the Phoenician alphabet." From *Writing Systems: A Linguistic Introduction* by G. Sampson. Copyright © 1985 by G. Sampson. Stanford University Press. Reprinted by permission.

Figure 16.12. "Evolution of the Greek and Latin alphabets." From *The Encyclopedia Americana,* 1968 edition. S.v. "Alphabet" by David Diringer. Copyright 1968 by Grolier Incorporated. Reprinted with permission.

Figure 16.13. "Historical development of the Chinese symbol for 'dog.'" From p. 59 in *Chinese* by Jerry Norman. Copyright © 1988 by Jerry Norman. Cambridge University Press.

Table 16.1. "Some Chinese Characters." Adapted from p. 107 of *Visible Speech: The Diverse Oneness of Writing Systems* by John DeFrancis. University of Hawaii Press. Copyright © 1989 by John DeFrancis. Reprinted by permission.

Figure 16.15. "Hiragana and Katakana syllabaries and their phonetic values." Adapted from *Read Japanese Today* by Len Walsh. Copyright © 1971 by Charles E. Tuttle. Reprinted by permission.

Chapter 17

W.H. Auden quote. "Their Lonely Betters" (1st verse). From *W.H. Auden: Collected Poems* by W.H. Auden. Copyright © 1951 by W.H. Auden. Reprinted by permission of Random House, Inc.

Figure 17.1, 17.2 (a-c), and q3 w/figures: By S. Chevalier-Skolnikoff, from "Facial Expressions of Emotion in Nonhuman Primates" adapted from Fig. 21/a,c,f,I,k on page 73; Fig. 4/a,e,g on page 27, and Fig. 21/d,I,g on page 73 in *Darwin and Facial Expression: A Century of Research in*

Review, edited by Paul Ekman. Copyright © 1973 by Academic Press. Reprinted by permission of Elsevier.

Figure 17.3. "Bee dancing." From *The Dance Language and Orientation of Bees* by K. von Frisch, translated by L.E. Chadwick. The Belknap Press of Harvard University Press, 1967, p. 57. Copyright © 1967, 1993 by the President and Fellows of Harvard College. Reprinted by permission of the publisher.

Figure 17.4. "Spectrogram of a robin song." Adapted from *Bird-Song* by W.H. Thorpe. Cambridge University Press. © 1961 by W.H. Thorpe. Reprinted with the permission of Cambridge University Press.

Figure 17.5. Avian isoglosses. Adapted from "Microgenographic and Macrogenographic Variation in Acquired Vocalization of Birds." By Paul Mundiger in *Acoustic Communication in Birds* edited by D.E. Kroodsma, E.H. Miller, and H. Ouellet, vol. 2, 1982: 147–208. © 1982. Reprinted with permission of Elsevier.

LANGUAGE INDEX

INDEX